Predominant forms of religions in the world today

ALASKA

GREENLAND

ICELAND

CANADA

NORWAY

SWEDEN

UNITED
KINGDOM

EIRE

DENMARK
NETH

GER.

POLAND

BEL.

CZECH. REP.

SWIT.

AUST.

FRANCE

ITALY

CRO.

UNITED STATES OF AMERICA

PORTUGAL

SPAIN

Mediterranean Sea

NORTH ATLANTIC OCEAN

MOROCCO

ALGERIA

LIBYA

MEXICO

WESTERN
SAHARA

CUBA

HAITI

BELIZE

MAURITANIA

MALI

NIGER

CHAD

HONDURAS

GUATEMALA

SENEGAL

EL SALVADOR

GAMBIA

BURKINA
FASO

BENIN

NICARAGUA

VENEZUELA

GUYANA

GUINEA BISSAU

GUINEA

NIGERIA

SURINAM

COSTA RICA

SIERRA LEONE

GHANA

TOGO

CAMEROON

PANAMA

FRENCH GUIANA

LIBERIA

IVORY
COAST

C.A.R.

COLOMBIA

EQUATORIAL
GUINEA

GABON

CONGO

ECUADOR

PERU

BRAZIL

BOLIVIA

ANGOLA

PARAGUAY

NAMIBIA

CHILE

SOUTH ATLANTIC OCEAN

ARGENTINA

URUGUAY

Indigenous religions

Hinduism and Islam

Buddhism

China: Remnants of Confucianism, Buddhism, Daoism

Japan: Shinto, Buddhism, Sects

Christianity (Roman Catholicism, Protestantism, Eastern Orthodox)

Islam

Judaism

Sikhism

Varied religions

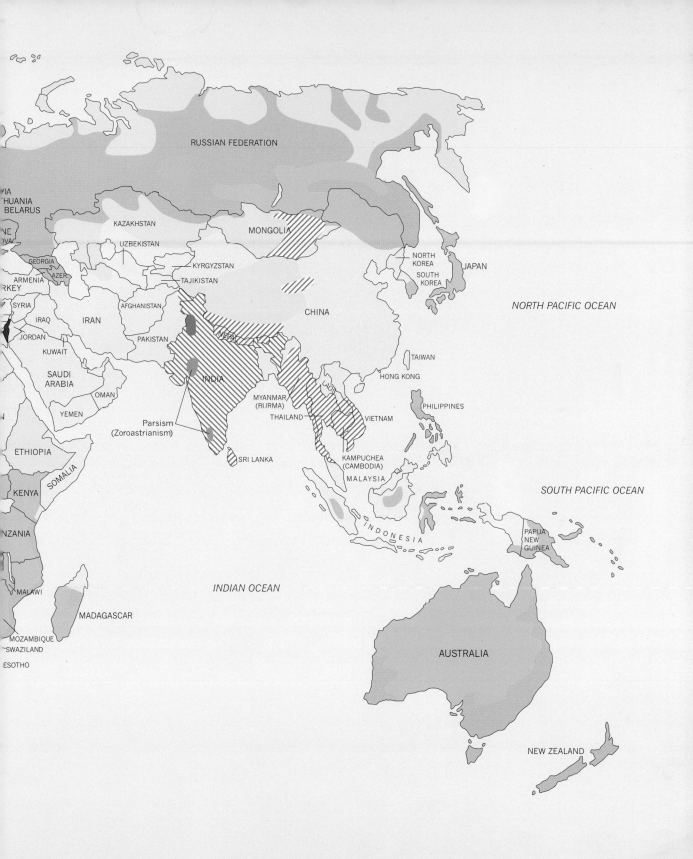

LIVING RELIGIONS

SIXTH EDITION

MARY PAT FISHER

SPECIALIST CONSULTANTS
John Kelsay, Florida State University
Suzanne J. Crawford, Pacific Lutheran University
Vijaya Ramaswamy, Jawaharlal Nehru University
Mark W. MacWilliams, St. Lawrence University
Randall Nadeau, Trinity University
Ruben L. F. Habito, Perkins School of Theology,
Southern Methodist University
Hillel Levine, Boston University
Lee Worth Bailey, Ithaca College
Akbar Ahmed, American University
G. S. Anand, Bhai Vir Singh Sahitya Sadan
Rebecca Moore, San Diego State University

PRENTICE-HALL
Upper Saddle River, N.J. 07458

Editorial Director: Charlyce Jones Owen
Assistant Editor: Wendy Yurash
Editorial Assistant: Carla Worner
Manufacturing Buyer: Christina Helder
Marketing Manager: Kara Kindstrom

Credits and acknowledgments borrowed from other sources and reproduced, with permission, in this textbook appear on page 527.

Pearson Education LTD.
Pearson Education Australia PTY, Limited
Pearson Education Singapore, Pte. Ltd
Pearson Education North Asia Ltd
Pearson Education, Canada, Ltd
Pearson Educación de Mexico, S.A. de C.V.
Pearson Education–Japan
Pearson Education Malaysia, Pte. Ltd

This book was designed and produced by
Laurence King Publishing Ltd, London
www.laurenceking.co.uk

Every effort has been made to contact the copyright holders, but should there be any errors or omissions, Laurence King Publishing Ltd would be pleased to insert the appropriate acknowledgment in any subsequent printing of this publication.

Editor: Rada Radojicic
Picture Researcher: Emma Brown
Maps: Andrea Fairbrass, Advanced Illustration Ltd., Cheshire
Typesetting: Fakenham Photosetting, Norfolk

Printed in Hong Kong

Front cover: *Sunrider* (acrylic on canvas) by Simon Cook (contemporary artist), Private Collection in copyright

1 0 9 8 7 6 5 4 3 2
ISBN 0-13-193315-9

CONTENTS

CHAPTER 5

BUDDHISM   129

CHAPTER 6

DAOSIM AND CONFUCIANISM   176

CHAPTER 7

SHINTO   207

ZOROASTRIANISM   222

CHAPTER 8

JUDAISM   226

CHAPTER 11

SIKHISM   417

CHAPTER 12

NEW RELIGIOUS MOVEMENTS   440

CHAPTER 13

RELIGION IN THE TWENTY-FIRST
CENTURY   476

PREFACE

Religion is not a museum piece. Religion is a vibrant force in the lives of many people around the world, and many religions are presently experiencing a renaissance.

Living Religions is a sympathetic approach to what is living and significant in the world's major religious traditions and in various new movements that are arising. This book provides a clear and straightforward account of the development, doctrines, and practices of the major faiths followed today. The emphasis throughout is on the personal consciousness of believers and their own accounts of their religion and its relevance in contemporary life.

Special features

This sixth edition of *Living Religions* preserves and improves upon the features that make *Living Religions* special.

Personal interviews with followers of each faith provide interesting and informative first-person accounts of each religion as perceived from within the tradition. I have presented these first-person quotations from many people, from a Siberian shamaness to a Holocaust survivor, in "Interview" feature boxes and also in excerpts woven throughout the text. A new interview box has been added in the Buddhism chapter as an example of the extraordinary pathways by which some Westerners have become Buddhist adepts.

Eight feature boxes on "Religion in Public Life" portray the spiritual roots of people who are making significant contributions to modern society, such as Jimmy Carter, the Dalai Lama, and Desmond Tutu.

Eight feature boxes on "Religion in Practice" portray the spiritual activities and beliefs of religious groups or individuals such as the Sun Dance, in which dancers in indigenous American societies practice self-sacrifice for the sake of their peoples, and Mother Teresa's example of Christian love in action.

Ten feature boxes containing "Teaching Stories" serve as take-off points for discussions about core values imbedded in each faith. New teaching stories have been added in the Religious Responses chapter, "Descendants of the Eagle" and in the Buddhism chapter, "The Great Ape Jataka Tale."

A four-page section on Zoroastrianism has been added to this edition in response to many requests, and emphasizes the ways in which this numerically shrinking faith has historically influenced both Western and Eastern religions.

Violence perpetrated in the name of religion is often in the news these days. This sixth edition includes probing discussions of this disturbing factor in many major religions and also in new religious movements. Distinctions are made between the basic teachings of religions, none of which condones wanton violence, and the ways in which religions have been politicized. Every religion is struggling with its responses to modernity, including fundamentalist and exclusivist responses, and these struggles are analyzed in every chapter. The roots of militancy in the name of religion are also carefully explored.

People of many faiths are also looking at ways in which their religious practices and beliefs affect the environment. This edition, therefore, includes new material on religious approaches to contemporary ecological concerns, such as the high dams that are threatening traditional cultures in India and strip-mining of sacred Navajo and Hopi lands.

Throughout the book, coverage of women's contributions and women's issues has been increased. Women's voices are woven into the discussions throughout, including female theologians who are bringing vital new perspectives to religious scholarship. African and African–American religious experiences are also of increasing interest, and these are extensively covered in this edition. There are poignant descriptions, for instance, of the lives of American Muslim converts who are trying to maintain traditional piety in the midst of modern materialistic society.

New religious movements are still proliferating in all directions. Some have turned to violent means of expressing their beliefs, so I have incorporated new scholarly perspectives on violence in new religious movements in Chapter 12. That chapter has been extensively revised, reorganized, and updated. Other chapters have also been reorganized for greater clarity, particularly the chapter on Hinduism.

The opening chapter, "Religious Responses," has been overhauled to bring more critical scholarship to bear on underlying issues in the study of religion, and particularly, approaches to studying and understanding scriptures. In all chapters, the latest scholarship has been applied. Valuable primary source material has also been updated and expanded in this sixth edition. The book incorporates extensive quotations from primary sources to give a direct perception of the thinking and flavor of each tradition. Particularly memorable brief quotations are set off in boxes.

One of the most engaging features of *Living Religions* is its illustrations. I have been glad to have the chance to add more color photographs to this sixth edition to help bring religions to life. Narrative captions accompanying the illustrations offer additional insights into the characteristics and orientation of each tradition and the people who practice it.

Learning aids

I have tried to present each tradition clearly and without the clutter of less important names and dates. **Key terms,** defined and highlighted in boldface when they first appear, are included in an extensive glossary and the most significant of these are also listed and defined at the end of each chapter. Because students are often unfamiliar with terms from other cultures, useful guides to pronunciation of words that may be unfamiliar are included in the glossary.

Maps are used throughout the text to give a sense of geographical reality to the historical discussions, as well as to illustrate the present distribution of the religions.

Timelines are used to recapitulate the historical development of the major religions. The simultaneous development of all religions can be compared in the overall timeline on the end pages.

New to this sixth edition are **Study questions** at the end of each chapter designed to enhance further thought and understanding.

There are **CD-Rom icons** in the margins throughout this new edition for cross-referring to the *Sacred World: Encounters with the World's Religions* CD-Rom and the *TIME Special Edition* magazine.

I assume that readers will want to delve further into the literature. At the end of each chapter, I offer a **Suggested reading** section, an annotated list of books that might be particularly interesting and useful in deeper study of that religion. Also at the end of every chapter is a list of relevant articles from the *TIME Special Edition* and *Research Navigator*™ activities that guide students through resources that will enrich their explorations of contemporary issues in world religion.

Acknowledgments

In order to try to understand each religion from the inside, I have traveled for many years to study and worship with devotees and teachers of all faiths, and to interview them about their experience of their tradition. People of all religions also come to the Gobind Sadan Institute for Advanced Studies in Comparative Religions, where it is my good fortune to meet and speak with them about their spiritual experiences and beliefs.

In preparing this book, I have worked directly with consultants who are authorities in specific traditions and who have offered detailed suggestions and resources. For breadth of scholarship, I have engaged the help of a new group of consultants for each edition. In this sixth edition, I have been blessed with extraordinarily capable and helpful consultants who delved deeply into the material to help me bring out the most current scholarly perspectives. They are John Kelsay of Florida State University; Suzanne Crawford of Pacific Lutheran University; Vijaya Ramaswamy of Jawaharlal Nehru University; Mark MacWilliams of St. Lawrence University; Randall Nadeau of Trinity University; Ruben Habito of Southern Methodist University; Hillel Levine of Boston University; Lee Bailey of Ithaca College who, as well as advising on the Christianity chapter, compiled the end of chapter Study questions; Akbar Ahmed of American University; G. S. Anand of Bhai Vir Singh Sahitya Sadan; Rebecca Moore of San Diego State University. I am extremely grateful for their generous and enthusiastic help, and for the assistance of the many scholars who have served as consultants to the previous editions and are specially acknowledged therein.

Living Religions has been extensively reviewed throughout all its editions by professors teaching courses in world religions. Reviewers of the fifth edition included Robert Imperato, Saint Leo University; Sallie King, James Madison University;

Jonathan Brumberg-Kraus, Wheaton College; George Mummert, Moberly Area Community College; Bob Badra, Kalamazoo Valley Community College; Hugh Urban, Ohio State University; John Gilman, San Diego State University; David Suter, St. Martin's College; Jeffrey Brodd, California State University, Sacramento; Mark MacWilliams, St Lawrence University; Mark Webb, Texas Technical University. Other people who have generously helped with source material for the fifth edition include Rev. Marcus Braybrooke, Shivaprakash, Dr M. A. Pradhani, Marianne Vandiver, Michelle Brand, Galina Ermolina, Edward Fisher, Vladimir Sova, William Beeman, Yale Partlow, Alexandra Engel, Jean Armour Polly, Wolfgang Hecker, G. Gispert-Sauch, S.J Mohammed Rafiq Shariq Warsi, and Swami Dharmanand.

Reviewers of this sixth edition were Maurine Stein, Prairie State College; James Hicks, Forsyth Technical Community College; David Carlson, Franklin College; Ross Aden, Rock Valley College; Athena DeGangi, New Hampshire Community Technical College, Nashua. In addition, Leskhe Tsomo read the chapter on Buddhism and made extensive suggestions. Margaret Krebs, Alan Nykamp, Ralph Singh, and Veena Sharma were very helpful in providing resource materials.

As always, Laurence King Publishing has provided me with excellent editorial help. Melanie White and Rada Radojicic have guided this edition through its development and production with brilliance, patience, and extraordinary helpfulness. Pamela Ellis has done an excellent job of proofreading and copy editing to make everything fit, and Emma Brown has worked hard to track down the new illustrations.

Finally, I cannot adequately express my gratitude to my own revered teacher, Baba Virsa Singh of Gobind Sadan. People of all faiths from all over the world come to him for his spiritual blessings and guidance. In the midst of sectarian conflicts, his place is an oasis of peace and harmony. Now more than ever, we are learning from Babaji to regard each other as members of one human family. May God bless us all to move in this direction.

Mary Pat Fisher
Gobind Sadan Institute for Advanced Studies
in Comparative Religion, New Delhi

TEACHING AND LEARNING RESOURCES

Whether you want to enhance your lectures, create tests, or assign outside material to reinforce content from the text, you and your students will find the most comprehensive set of instructional materials available with *Living Religions* to reinforce and enliven the study of world religions.

For instructors

Instructor's Resource Manual with Tests

This manual provides chapter summaries for use in organizing lectures and a complete test item file of multiple choice, true/false, and essay questions. The manual also includes references for assigning the special print and media supplements that accompany the text, including the videos from the *Sacred World* CD-Rom, the *TIME Special Edition: World Religions* magazine, and the *Prentice Hall Atlas of World Religions*.

Prentice Hall Test Generator

This computerized test bank contains the items from the test item file and allows flexibility in creating tests, editing questions, and adding instructor-generated items. *Test Generator* is available for Windows and Macintosh operating systems.

For students

TIME Special Edition: World Religions

In partnership with TIME magazine, Prentice Hall has created a special TIME edition on world religions that includes over twenty recent articles on major world religions and topics in religious studies. A list of articles relevant to the content of each chapter is included at the end of the chapter to guide students in their explorations of contemporary issues in world religion. This unique magazine is available free when packaged with *Living Religions*.

The Prentice Hall Atlas of World Religions

This collection of thirty maps created by Prentice Hall in partnership with Dorling Kindersley, innovative publisher of maps and atlases, provides students and instructors with extraordinarily designed, multi-dimensional maps that include global, thematic, regional, and chronological perspectives on world religion. Contact your local sales representative for details about obtaining copies of the atlas for use with *Living Religions*.

Penguin Bundle Program

Prentice Hall is pleased to offer significant discounts on titles relevant to the study of world religion from the acclaimed Penguin Classics series when purchased with *Living*

Religions. Contact your local Prentice Hall representative for more information about the titles and discounts available in this program.

OneSearch with Research Navigator™

This brief guide focuses on helping students develop critical thinking skills to effectively find and evaluate resources on the internet. In addition to a brief introduction to navigating the internet, it provides a comprehensive reference to websites specific to the study of world religions and an access code and instruction for using *Research Navigator*™, a powerful research tool also available from Prentice Hall. This supplementary guide is free when packaged with *Living Religions*.

Multimedia resources

The Sacred World: Encounters with the World's Religions CD-Rom

Included with each new copy of *Living Religions* is the *Sacred World: Encounters with the World's Religions* CD-Rom, a multimedia exploration of the rituals, beliefs, art, and key personalities in nine of the world's major religions. Religions included are: Judaism, Christianity, Islam, Hinduism, Buddhism, Confucianism and Taoism (Daoism), Sikhism, Jainism, and Shinto. Throughout the text, a CD-Rom icon connects the text to the video segments relevant to the content within the chapter.

 ### *Companion Website*™

www.prenhall.com/fisher

A powerful study tool, the Companion Website for *Living Religions* is organized by chapter and provides multiple-choice, true/false, and essay questions for review.

 ### *Research Navigator*™

Prentice Hall's *Research Navigator*™ helps students make the most of their research time. From finding the right articles and journals, to citing sources, drafting and writing effective papers, and completing research assignments, *Research Navigator*™ simplifies and streamlines the entire process.

Students receive an access code for *Research Navigator*™ with a copy of *OneSearch*, which is free when packaged with *Living Religions*. Contact your local sales representative for more details. To learn more about *Research Navigator*™ take a tour on the web at *http://www.researchnavigator.com*

Instructor's Resource CD-Rom

This new supplement includes the instructor's manual, test items, and other resource material available with the text to allow maximum flexibility as you prepare lectures and manage your class.

 ### *OneKey*

Everything you need to teach and your students need to learn is available on *OneKey*. This unique website includes chapter by chapter student and instructor resources, from lecture material to chapter review quizzes and tests. Contact your local Prentice Hall representative to see why *OneKey* may be all you need.

CHAPTER 1
RELIGIOUS RESPONSES

Before sunrise, members of a Muslim family rise in Malaysia, perform their purifying ablutions, spread their prayer rugs facing Mecca, and begin their prostrations and prayers to Allah. In a French cathedral, worshippers line up for their turn to have a priest place a wafer on their tongue, murmuring, "This is the body of Christ." In a South Indian village, a group of women reverently anoint a cylindrical stone with milk and fragrant sandalwood paste and place around it offerings of flowers. The monks of a Japanese Zen Buddhist monastery sit cross-legged and upright in utter silence, broken occasionally by the noise of the *kyosaku* bat falling on their shoulders. On a mountain in Mexico, men, women, and children who have been dancing without food or water for days greet an eagle flying overhead with a burst of whistling from the small wooden flutes they wear around their necks.

These and countless other moments in the lives of people around the world are threads of the tapestry we call "religion." The word is probably derived from the Latin, meaning "to tie back," "to tie again." All of religion shares the goal of tying people back to something behind the surface of life—a greater reality, which lies beyond, or invisibly infuses, the world that we can perceive with our five senses.

Attempts to connect with this greater reality have taken many forms. Many of them are organized institutions, such as Buddhism or Christianity. These institutions are complexes of such elements as leaders, beliefs, rituals, symbols, myths, scriptures, ethics, spiritual practices, cultural components, historical traditions, and management structures. Moreover, they are not fixed and distinct categories, as simple labels such as "Buddhism" and "Christianity" suggest. Each of these labels is an abstraction that is used in the attempt to bring some kind of order to the study of religious patterns that are in fact complex, diverse, ever-changing, and overlapping. In addition, not all religious behavior occurs within institutional confines. Some spiritual experience is that of individuals who belong to no institutionalized religion but nonetheless have an inner life of prayer, meditation, or direct experience of an inexplicable presence.

Religion is therefore such a complex and elusive topic that some contemporary scholars of religion are seriously questioning whether "religion" or "religions" can be studied at all. They have determined that no matter where they try to grab the thing, other parts will get away. Nonetheless, this difficult-to-grasp subject is so central to so many people's lives and has assumed such great political significance in today's world that we must make a sincere attempt to understand it.

In many cultures and times, religion has been the basic foundation of life, permeating all aspects of human existence. But from the time of the European

From candles and oil lamps to sacred fires, light is universally used to remind worshippers of an invisible reality. At Gobind Sadan, outside New Delhi, worship at a sacred fire continues twenty-four hours a day.

Enlightenment, religion has become in the West an object to be studied, rather than an unquestioned basic fact of life. Cultural anthropologists, sociologists, philosophers, psychologists, and even biologists have peered at religion through their own particular lenses, trying to explain what religion is and why it exists, to those who no longer take it for granted.

In this introductory chapter, we will make some general observations about what is called "religion" before trying in the later chapters to understand the major traditions known as "religions" practiced around the world today.

Modes of encountering Unseen Reality

How have people of all times and places come to the conclusion that there is some Unseen Reality, even though they may be unable to perceive it with their ordinary senses? In general, we have two basic ways of apprehending reality: rational thought and non-rational modes of knowing. To reason is to establish abstract general categories from the data we have gathered with our senses, and then to organize these abstractions to formulate seemingly logical ideas about reality. However, one person may use reason to determine that there is no Unseen Reality; another may use reason to determine that it does exist. For instance, the seventeenth-century English rationalist philosopher Thomas Hobbes (1588–1679) reasoned that God is simply an idea constructed by the human imagination from ideas of the visible world. His contemporary, the rationalist French philosopher René Descartes (1596–1650), asserted that his awareness of his own existence and his internal reasoning indicated the existence of God.

Some people come to religious convictions indirectly, through the words of great religious teachers or the teachings of religious tradition. Other people develop faith only through questioning. Martin Luther (1483–1546), father of the Protestant branches of Christianity, recounted how he searched for faith in God through storms of doubt, "raged with a fierce and agitated conscience."[1]

The human mind does not function in the rational mode alone; there are other modes of consciousness. In his classic study, *The Varieties of Religious Experience*, the philosopher William James (1842–1910) concluded:

> *Our normal waking consciousness, rational consciousness as we call it, is but one special type of consciousness, whilst all about it, parted from it by the flimsiest of screens, there lie potential forms of consciousness entirely different …*
>
> *No account of the universe in its totality can be final which leaves these other forms of consciousness quite disregarded.*[2]

In some religions, people are encouraged to develop their own intuitive abilities to perceive spiritual truths directly, beyond the senses, beyond the limits of human reason, beyond blind belief. This way is often called **mysticism**. George William Russell (1867–1935), an Irish writer who described his mystical experiences under the pen name "AE," was lying on a hillside:

> *not then thinking of anything but the sunlight, and how sweet it was to drowse there, when, suddenly, I felt a fiery heart throb, and knew it was personal and intimate, and started with every sense dilated and intent, and turned inwards, and I heard first a music as of bells going away … and then the heart of the hills was opened to me, and I knew there was no hill for those who were there, and they were unconscious of the ponderous mountain piled above the palaces of light, and*

Some religions try to transcend the mundane, glimpsing what lies beyond. Others, such as the Zen Buddhism that influenced this 18th-century drawing of The Meditating Frog, find unseen reality in the here and now, intensely experienced.

the winds were sparkling and diamond clear, yet full of colour as an opal, as they glittered through the valley, and I knew the Golden Age was all about me, and it was we who had been blind to it but that it had never passed away from the world.[3]

Encounters with Unseen Reality are given various names in spiritual traditions: enlightenment, God-realization, illumination, **kensho**, awakening, self-knowledge, **gnosis**, ecstatic communion, coming home. They may arise spontaneously, as in near-death experiences in which people seem to find themselves in a world of unearthly radiance, or may be induced by meditation, fasting, prayer, chanting, drugs, or dancing.

Many religions have developed meditation techniques that encourage intuitive wisdom to come forth. Whether this wisdom is perceived as a natural faculty within or an external voice, the process is similar. The consciousness is initially turned away from the world and even from one's own feelings and thoughts, letting them all go. Often a concentration practice, such as watching the breath or staring at a candle flame, is used to collect the awareness into a single, unfragmented focus. Once the mind is quiet, distinctions between inside and outside drop away. The seer becomes one with the seen, in a fusion of subject and object through which the inner nature of things often seems to reveal itself. To the frustration of many who try these techniques in search of enlightenment without seeing immediate results, it seems that we cannot grasp the Unseen Reality solely by our own efforts. Rather, it grasps us.

> *[The "flash of illumination" brings] a state of glorious inspiration, exaltation, intense joy, a piercingly sweet realization that the whole of life is fundamentally right and that it knows what it's doing.*
>
> *Nona Coxhead*[4]

Our ordinary experience of the world is that our self is separate from the world of objects that we perceive. But this dualistic understanding may be transcended in a moment of enlightenment in which the Real and our awareness of it become one. The *Mundaka Upanishad* says, "Lose thyself in the Eternal, even as the arrow is lost in the target." For the Hindu, this is the prized attainment of liberation, in which one enters into awareness of the eternal reality. This reality is then known with the same direct apprehension with which one knows oneself. The Sufi Muslim mystic Abu Yazid in the ninth century CE said, "I sloughed off my self as a snake sloughs off its skin, and I looked into my essence and saw that 'I am He.' "[5]

This spontaneous experience of being grasped by Reality is the essential basis of religion, according to the influential German professor of theology, Rudolf Otto (1869–1937). The experience is ineffable, "*sui generis* and irreducible to any other; and therefore, like every absolutely primary and elementary dictum, while it admits of being discussed, it cannot be strictly defined."[6] This experience of the Holy, asserts Otto, brings forth two general responses in a person: a feeling of great awe or even dread, and a feeling of great attraction. These responses, in turn, have given rise to the whole gamut of religious beliefs and behaviors.

A sense of the presence of the Great Unnamable may burst through the seeming ordinariness of life. (Samuel Palmer, The Waterfalls, Pistyll Mawddach, North Wales, 1835–36.)

Though ineffable, the nature of genuine religious experience is not unpredictable, according to the research of Joachim Wach (1898–1955), a German scholar of comparative religion. In every religion, it seems to follow a certain pattern: (1) It is an experience of what is considered Unseen Reality; (2) It involves the person's whole being; (3) It is the most shattering and intense of all human experiences; and (4) It motivates the person to action, through worship, ethical behavior, service, and sharing with others in a religious grouping.

Understandings of Sacred Reality

In the struggle to understand what the mind cannot readily grasp, individuals and cultures have come to rather different conclusions. Mircea Eliade (1907–1986) was a very influential scholar who helped to develop the field of **comparative religion**. This discipline attempts to understand and compare religious patterns found around the world. He used the terms "sacred" and "profane": the **profane** is the everyday world of seemingly random, ordinary, and unimportant occurrences. The **sacred** is the realm of extraordinary, apparently purposeful, but generally imperceptible forces. In the realm of the sacred lie the source of the universe and its values, and it is charged with great significance. However relevant this dichotomy may be in describing some religions, there are some cultures that do not make a clear distinction between the sacred and the profane. Many tribal cultures who have an intimate connection with their local landscape

Buddhism is sometimes referred to as a nontheistic religion, for its beliefs do not refer to a personal deity. Practitioners try to perceive an unchanging unseen reality.

feel that spiritual power is everywhere; there is nothing that is not sacred. Trees, mountains, animals—everything is alive with sacred presence.

Another distinction made in the study of comparative religion is that between "immanent" and "transcendent" views of sacred reality. To understand that reality as **immanent** is to experience it as present in the world. To understand it as **transcendent** is to believe that it exists outside of the material universe. In general, the Judeo-Christian-Islamic traditions tend to believe in the sacred as transcendent ("God is out there"), whereas many Eastern and indigenous traditions find that sacred Being or beings are present with them in the world.

The concept of sacred Being is another area in which we find great differences among religious traditions. Many people perceive the sacred as a personal being, as Father, Mother, Teacher, Friend, Beloved, or as a specific deity. Religions based on one's relationship to the Divine Being are called **theistic**. If the being is worshipped as a singular form, the religion is called **monotheistic**. If many attributes and forms of the divine are emphasized, the religion may be labeled **polytheistic**. Religions that hold that beneath the multiplicity of apparent forms there is one underlying substance are called **monistic**. Unseen Reality may also be conceived in **nontheistic** terms, as a "changeless Unity," as "Suchness," or simply as "the Way." There may be no sense of a personal Creator God in such understandings.

Some people believe that the sacred reality is usually invisible but occasionally appears visibly in human **incarnations**, such as Christ or Krishna, or in special manifestations, such as the flame Moses reportedly saw coming from the center of a bush but not consuming it. Or the deity that cannot be seen is described in human terms. Theologian Sallie McFague thus writes of God as "lover" by imputing human feelings to God:

> God as lover is the one who loves the world not with the fingertips but totally and passionately, taking pleasure in its variety and richness, finding it attractive and valuable, delighting in its fulfilment. God as lover is the moving power of love in the universe, the desire for unity with all the beloved.[7]

Throughout history, there have been religious authorities who have claimed that they worship the only true deity and label all others as "pagans" or "nonbelievers." For their part, the others apply similar negative epithets to them. When these rigid positions are taken, often to the point of violent conflicts or forced conversions, there is no room to consider the possibility that all may be talking about the same indescribable thing in different languages or referring to different aspects of the same unknowable Whole.

Atheism is the belief that there is no deity. Following the nineteenth-century socialist philosopher Karl Marx (1818–1883), many communist countries in the twentieth century discouraged or suppressed religious beliefs, attempting to replace them with secular faith in supposedly altruistic government. The distinguished Protestant theologian Reinhold Niebuhr (1892–1971) described atheistic communism as "an irreligion transmuted into a new political religion, canonized precisely in the writings of Marx (and the later Lenin) as sacred scripture" with Marx cast as "the revered prophet of a new world religion."[8] It was not uncommon for people of all faiths in all continents of the world to embrace as a new religion of sorts Marx's message of collectivism in contrast to the dehumanizing effects of modern industry and capitalism, and with it, his stinging criticism of oppression of the people in the name of religion.

Atheism may also arise from within, in those whose experiences give them no reason to believe that there is anything more to life than the mundane. One American college student articulates a common modern form of unwilling atheism:

> To be a citizen of the modern, industrialized world with its scientific worldview is to be, to a certain extent, an atheist. I myself do not want to be an atheist; the cold mechanical worldview is repugnant to my need for the warmth and meaning that comes from God. But as I have been educated in the secular, scientistic educational system—where God is absent but atoms and molecules and genes and cells and presidents and kings are the factors to be reckoned with, the powers of this world, not a divine plan or a divine force as my ancestors must have believed—I cannot wholly believe in God.[9]

Agnosticism is not the denial of the divine but the feeling, "I don't know whether it exists or not," or the belief that if it exists it is impossible for humans to know it. Religious scepticism has been a current in Western thought since classical times; it was given the name "agnosticism" in the nineteenth century by T. H. Huxley, who stated its basic principles as a denial of metaphysical beliefs and of most (in his case) Christian beliefs since they are unproven or unprovable, and their replacement with scientific method for examining facts and experiences.

These categories are not mutually exclusive, so attempts to apply the labels can sometimes confuse us rather than help us understand religions. In some

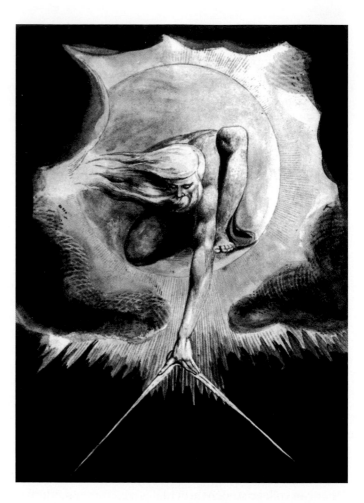

The concept of God as an old man with a beard who rules the world from the sky has been supported by the art of patriarchal monotheistic traditions, such as William Blake's frontispiece to "Europe," The Act of Creation, *1794.*

polytheistic traditions there is a hierarchy of gods and goddesses with one highest being at the top. In Hinduism, each individual deity is understood as an embodiment of all aspects of the divine. In the paradoxes that occur when we try to apply human logic and language to that which transcends rational thought, a person may believe that God is both a highly personal being and also present in all things. An agnostic may be deeply committed to moral principles. Or mystics may have personal encounters with the divine and yet find it so unspeakable that they say it is beyond human knowing. The Jewish scholar Maimonides (1135–1204) asserted that:

> *the human mind cannot comprehend God. Only God can know Himself. The only form of comprehension of God we can have is to realize how futile it is to try to comprehend Him.*[10]

Jaap Sahib, the great hymn of praises of God by the Tenth Sikh Guru, Guru Gobind Singh, consists largely of the negative attributes of God, such as these:

> *Salutations to the One without colour or hue,*
> *Salutations to the One who hath no beginning.*

Salutations to the Impenetrable,
Salutations to the Unfathomable . . .
O Lord, Thou art Formless and Peerless
Beyond birth and physical elements. . . .
Salutations to the One beyond confines of religion. . . .
Beyond description and Garbless
Thou art Nameless and Desireless.
Thou art beyond thought and ever Mysterious.[11]

Some people believe that the aspect of the divine that they perceive is the only one. Others feel that there is one being with many faces, that all religions come from one source. Bede Griffiths (1906–1993), a Catholic monk who lived in a community in India, attempting to unite Eastern and Western traditions, was one who felt that if we engage in a deep study of all religions we will find their common ground:

In each tradition the one divine Reality, the one eternal Truth, is present, but it is hidden under symbols. . . . Always the divine Mystery is hidden under a veil, but each revelation (or "unveiling") unveils some aspect of the one Truth, or, if you like, the veil becomes thinner at a certain point. The Semitic religions, Judaism and Islam, reveal the transcendent aspect of the divine Mystery with incomparable power. The oriental religions reveal the divine Immanence with immeasurable depth. Yet in each the opposite aspect is contained, though in a more hidden way.[12]

Given the centrality in religions of religious experiences, in this book we will keep delving into them in order to try to understand the various religions that are practiced today. To use Mircea Eliade's term, we will be exploring the **phenomenology** of religion—its specifically sacred aspects—rather than explaining religions only in terms of other disciplines such as history, politics, economics, sociology, or psychology. This involves an appreciative investigation of religious phenomena in order to comprehend their spiritual intention and meaning. We will also strive for "thick description," a term used by the cultural anthropologist Clifford Geertz, not only reporting outward behaviors but also attempting to explain their meaning for believers.

Worship, symbol, and myth

Many of the phenomena of religion are ways of worship, symbols, and myths. Worship of the sacred consists in large part of attempts to express reverence and perhaps to enter into communion with that which is worshipped or to request its help in ill health, disharmony, poverty, or infertility. Around the world, rituals, sacraments, prayers, and spiritual practices are used to create a sacred atmosphere or state of consciousness necessary to convey the requests for help, to bring some human control over things which are not ordinarily controllable (such as rainfall), to sanctify and explain the meaning of major life stages such as birth, puberty, marriage, and death, or to provide spiritual instruction for the people.

When such worshipful actions are predictable and repeated rather than spontaneous, they are known as **rituals**. Religious rituals usually involve repetition, specific intentions, patterned performance, traditional meanings, and purposeful-

Many religions use ritual cleansing with water to help remove inner filth that obscures awareness of Ultimate Reality.

ness. Group rituals may be conducted by priests or other ritual specialists or by the people themselves. Either way, there may be actions such as recitation of prayers, chants, scriptures or stories, singing, dancing, sharing of food, spiritual purification by water, lighting of candles or oil lamps, and offerings of flowers, fragrances, and food to the divine. Professor Antony Fernando of Sri Lanka explains that when food offerings are made to the deities:

Even the most illiterate person knows that in actual fact no god really picks up those offerings or is actually in need of them. What people offer is what they own. Whatever is owned becomes so close to the heart of the owner as to become an almost integral part of his or her life. Therefore, when people offer something, it is, as it were, themselves they offer. ... Sacrifices and offerings are a dramatic way of proclaiming that they are not the ultimate possessors of their life and also of articulating their determination to live duty-oriented lives and not desire-oriented lives.[13]

What religions attempt to approach is beyond human utterance. Believers build statues and buildings through which to worship the divine, but these forms are not the divine itself. Because people are addressing the invisible, it can be suggested only through metaphor. Deepest consciousness cannot speak the language of everyday life; what it knows can be suggested only in **symbols**—images borrowed from the material world that are similar to ineffable spiritual experiences. For example, attempts to allude to spiritual merger with Unseen Reality may borrow the language of human love. The great thirteenth-century Hindu saint Akka Mahadevi sang of her longing for union with the Beloved by using powerful symbolic language of self-surrender:

Like a silkworm weaving her house with love
From her marrow and dying in her body's threads
Winding tight, round and round, I burn
Desiring what the heart desires.[15]

Our religious ceremonies are but the shadows of that great universal worship celebrated in the heavens by the legions of heavenly beings on all planes, and our prayers drill a channel across this mist separating our earthbound plane from the celestial ones through which a communication may be established with the powers that be.

Pir Vilayat Inayat Khan[14]

Tracing symbols throughout the world, researchers find many similarities in their use in different cultures. Unseen Reality is often symbolized as a Father or Mother, because it is thought to be the source of life, sustenance, and protection. It is frequently associated with heights, with its invisible power perceived as coming from a "place" that is spiritually "higher" than the material world. The sky thus becomes heaven, the abode of the god or gods and perhaps also the pleasant realm to which good people go when they die. A vertical symbol—such as a tree, a pillar, or a mountain—is understood as the center of the world in many cultures, for it gives physical imagery to a connection between earth and the unseen "heavenly" plane. The area beneath the surface of the earth is often perceived as an "underworld," a rather dangerous place where life goes on in a different way than it does on the surface.

Some theorists assert that in some cases these common symbols are not just logical associations with the natural world. Most notably, the psychologist Carl Jung (1875–1961) proposed that humanity as a whole has a collective unconscious, a global psychic inheritance of archetypal symbols from which geographically separate cultures have drawn. These archetypes include such symbolic characters as the wise old man, the great mother, the dual mothers, the original man and woman, the hero, the shadow, and the trickster.

Extended metaphors may be understood as **allegories**—narratives that use concrete symbols to convey abstract ideas. The biblical book attributed to the Hebrew prophet Ezekiel, for instance, is full of such allegorical passages. In one he

This symbolic representation of a World Tree comes from 18th-century Iran. It is conceived as a tree in Paradise, about which the Prophet Muhammad reportedly said, "God planted it with His own hand and breathed His spirit into it."

says that God's spirit led him to a valley full of dry bones. As he watched and spoke as God told him, the bones developed flesh and muscles, became joined together into bodies, and rose to their feet. The voice of God explains the allegorical meaning: the bones represent the people of Israel, who have been abandoned by their self-serving leaders and become scattered and preyed upon by wild beasts, like the sheep of uncaring shepherds. God promises to dismiss the shepherds, raise the fallen people and restore them to the land of Israel, where they will live peacefully under God's protection (Ezekiel 34–37). Such passages, even though allegorical, may assume great significance in a people's self-understanding.

TEACHING STORY

Descendants of the Eagle

A long time ago, a really long time when the world was still freshly made, Unktehi the water monster fought the people and caused a great flood. Perhaps the Great Spirit, Wakan Tanka, was angry with us for some reason. Maybe he let Unktehi win out because he wanted to make a better kind of human being.

The waters got higher and higher. Finally everything was flooded except the hill next to the place where the sacred red pipestone quarry lies today. The people climbed up there to save themselves, but it was no use. The water swept over that hill. Waves tumbled the rocks and pinnacles, smashing them down on the people. Everyone was killed, and all the blood jelled, making one big pool. The blood turned to pipestone and created the pipestone quarry, the grave of those ancient ones. That's why the pipe, made of that red rock, is so sacred to us. Its red bowl is the flesh and blood of our ancestors, its stem is the backbone of those people long dead, the smoke rising from it is their breath. I tell you, that pipe comes alive when used in a ceremony; you can feel the power flowing from it.

Unktehi, the big water monster, was also turned to stone. Maybe Tunkashila, the Grandfather Spirit, punished her for making the flood. Her bones are in the Badlands now. Her back forms a long, high ridge, and you can see her vertebrae sticking out in a great row of red and yellow rocks. I have seen them. It scared me when I was on that ridge, for I felt Unktehi. She was moving beneath me, wanting to topple me.

When all the people were killed so many generations ago, one girl survived, a beautiful girl. It happened this way: When the water swept over the hill where they tried to seek refuge, a big spotted eagle, Wanblee Galeshka, swept down and let her grab hold of his feet. With her hanging on, he flew to the top of a tall tree which stood on the highest stone pinnacles in the Black Hills. That was the eagle's home. It became the only spot not covered with water. If the people had gotten up there, they would have survived, but it was a needle-like rock.

Wanblee kept that beautiful girl with him and made her his wife. There was a closer connection then between people and animals, so he could do it. The eagle's wife became pregnant and bore him twins, a boy and a girl. She was happy, and said, "Now we will have people again. *Washtay*, it is good." The children were born right there, on top of that cliff. When the waters finally subsided, Wanblee helped the children and their mother down from his rock and put them on the earth, telling them: "Be a nation, become a great Nation—the Lakota Oyate." The boy and girl grew up. He was the only man on earth, she was the only woman of child-bearing age. They married; they had children. A nation was born.

So we are descended from the eagle. We are an eagle nation. That is good, something to be proud of, because the eagle is the wisest of birds. He is the Great Spirit's messenger; he is a great warrior. That is why we always wore the eagle plume and still wear it.

As told by Lame Deer to Richard Erdoes[16]

Symbols are also woven together into **myths**—the symbolic stories that communities use to explain the universe and their place within it. Like many cultures, Polynesians tell a myth of the world's creation in which the world was initially covered with water and shrouded in darkness. When the Supreme Being, Io, wanted to rise from rest, he uttered words that immediately brought light into the darkness. Then at his word, the waters and the heavens were separated, the land was shaped, and all beings were created.

Joseph Campbell (1904–1987), who carried out extensive analysis of myths around the world, found that myths have four primary functions: mystical (evoking our awe, love, wonder, gratitude); cosmological (presenting explanations of the universe based on the existence and actions of spiritual powers or beings); sociological (adapting people to orderly social life, teaching ethical codes); and psychological (opening doors to inner exploration, development of one's full potential, and adjustment to life cycle changes). Understood in these senses, myths are not falsehoods or the work of primitive imagination; they can be deeply meaningful and transformational, forming a sacred belief structure that supports the laws and institutions of the religion and the ways of the community, as well as explaining the people's place within the cosmos. Campbell paid particular attention to myths of the hero's journey, in which the main character is separated from the group, undergoes hardships and initiation, and returns bearing truth to the people. Such stories, he felt, prepare and inspire the listener for the difficult inward journey that leads to spiritual transformation:

> It is the business of mythology to reveal the specific dangers and techniques of the dark interior way from tragedy to comedy. Hence the incidents are fantastic and "unreal": they represent psychological, not physical, triumphs. The passage of the mythological hero may be overground, [but] fundamentally it is inward—into depths where obscure resistances are overcome, and long lost, forgotten powers are revivified, to be made available for the transfiguration of the world.[17]

Absolutist and liberal interpretations

Within each faith people often have different ways of interpreting their traditions. The **orthodox** stand by an historical form of their religion, strictly following its established practices, laws, and creeds. Those who resist contemporary influences and affirm what they perceive as the historical core of their religion could be called **absolutists**. In our times, many people feel that their identity as individuals or as members of an established group is threatened by the sweeping changes brought by modern industrial culture. The breakup of family relationships, loss of geographic rootedness, decay of clear behavioral codes, and loss of local control may be very unsettling. To find stable footing, some people may try to stand on selected religious doctrines or practices from the past. Religious leaders may encourage this trend toward rigidity by declaring themselves absolute authorities or by telling the people that their scriptures are literally and exclusively true. They may encourage antipathy or even violence against people of other religious traditions.

The term **fundamentalism** is often applied to this selective insistence on parts of a religious tradition and to violence against people of other religions. This use of the term is misleading, for no religion is based on hatred of other people and because those who are labeled "fundamentalists" may not be engaged in a return to the true basics of their religion. A Muslim "fundamentalist" who insists on the veiling of women, for instance, does not draw this doctrine from the foundation of Islam, the Holy Qur'an, but rather from historical cultural practice in some Muslim countries. A Sikh "fundamentalist" who concentrates on externals, such as wearing a turban, sword, and steel bracelet, overlooks the central insistence of the Sikh Gurus on the inner rather than outer practice of religion. A Hindu "fundamentalist" who objects to the presence of Christian missionaries working among the poor ignores one of the basic principles of ancient Indian religion, which is the tolerant assertion that there are many paths to the same universal truth. Rev. Valson Thampu, editor of the Indian journal *Traci*, writes that this selective type of religious extremism "absolutises what is spiritually or ethically superfluous in a religious tradition. True spiritual enthusiasm or zeal, on the other hand, stakes everything on being faithful to the spiritual essence."[18]

A further problem with the use of the term "fundamentalism" is that it has a specifically Protestant Christian connotation. The Christian fundamentalist movement originated in the late nineteenth century as a reaction to liberal trends, such as historical-critical study of the Bible, which will be explained below. Other labels may, therefore, be more cross-culturally appropriate, such as "absolutist," "extremist," or "reactionary," depending on the particular situation.

Those who are called religious **liberals** take a more flexible approach to religious tradition. They may see scriptures as products of a specific culture and time rather than the eternal voice of truth, and may interpret passages metaphorically rather than literally. If activists, they may advocate reforms in the ways their religion is officially understood and practiced. Those who are labeled **heretics** publicly assert controversial positions that are unacceptable to the orthodox establishment. **Mystics** are guided by their own spiritual experiences, which may coincide with any of the above positions.

Historical–critical study of scriptures

While conservatives tend to take their scriptures and received religious traditions as literally and absolutely true, liberals have for several centuries been engaged in a different approach to understanding their own religions and those of others. Non-faith-based research methods reveal that scriptures seem to be a mixture of polemics against opponents of the religion, myths, cultural influences, ethical instruction, later interpolations, mistakes by copyists, literary devices, actual history, and genuine spiritual inspiration.

To sort out these elements, the Bible—and more recently, scriptures of other religions—has been analyzed objectively as a literary collection written within certain historical and cultural contexts, rather than as the absolute word of God. This process began at the end of the eighteenth century and continues today. One area of research is to try to determine the original or most reliable form of a particular text. Another focus is ferreting out the historical aspects of the text, with help from external sources such as archaeological findings, to determine the historical setting in which it was probably composed, its actual author or authors, and possible sources of its material, such as oral or written traditions. Such research may conclude that material about a certain period may have been written later and include perspectives from that later period, or that a text with one person's name as author may actually be a collection of writings by different people. A third area of research asks, "What was the intended audience?" A fourth examines the language and meanings of the words. A fifth looks at whether a scripture or passage follows a particular literary form, such as poetry, legal code, miracle story, allegory, parable, hymn, narrative, or sayings. A sixth focuses on the **redaction**, or editing and organizing of the scripture and development of an authorized canon designed to speak not only to the local community but also to a wider audience. Yet another approach is to look at the scripture in terms of its universal and contemporary relevance, rather than its historicity.

Although such research attempts to be objective, it is not necessarily undertaken with sceptical intentions. To the contrary, these forms of research are taught in many seminaries as ways of reconciling faith with reason.

The encounter between science and religion

Divisions among absolutist, liberal, and sceptical interpretations of religion are related to the development of modern science. Like religion, science is also engaged in searching for universal principles that explain the facts of nature. The two approaches have influenced each other since ancient times, when they were not seen as separate endeavors. In both East and West, there were continual attempts to understand reality as a whole.

In ancient Greece, source of many "Western" ideas, a group of thinkers who are sometimes called "nature philosophers" tried to understand the world through their own perceptions of it. By contrast, Plato (c. 427–347 BCE) distrusted the testimony of the human senses. He thus made a series of distinctions: between what is perceived by the senses and what is accessible through reason, between body and soul, appearance and reality, objects and ideas. In Plato's thought, the soul was superior to the body, and the activity of reason preferable to the distraction of the senses. This value judgment dominated Western thought through the Middle Ages, with its underlying belief that all of nature had been created by God for the sake of humanity.

In the seventeenth century, knowledge of nature became more secularized (that is, divorced from the sacred) as scientists developed models of the universe as a giant machine. Its ways could be discovered by human reason, by studying its component parts and mathematically quantifying its characteristics. However, even in discovering such features, many scientists regarded them as the work of a divine Creator or Ruler. Isaac Newton (1642–1727), whose gravitational theory shaped modern physics, speculated that space is eternal because it is the emanation of "eternal and immutable being." Drawing on biblical quotations, Newton argued that God exists everywhere, containing, discerning, and ruling all things.

During the eighteenth-century Enlightenment, rational ways of knowing were increasingly respected, with a concurrent growing scepticism toward

The Hubble space telescope reveals an unimaginably vast cosmos, with billions of galaxies in continual flux. The Eagle Nebula shown here is giving birth to new stars in "pillars of creation" which are 6 trillion miles high.

claims of knowledge derived from such sources as divine revelation or illuminated inner wisdom. The sciences were viewed as progressive; some thinkers attacked institutionalized religions and dogma as superstitions. According to **scientific materialism**, which developed during the nineteenth and twentieth centuries, the supernatural is imaginary; only the material world exists.

An influential example of this perspective can be found in the work of the nineteenth-century philosopher Ludwig Feuerbach (1804–1872). He reasoned that deities are simply projections, objectifications of human qualities such as power, wisdom, and love onto an imagined cosmic deity outside ourselves. Then we worship it as Supreme and do not recognize that those same qualities lie within ourselves; instead, we see ourselves as weak and sinful. Feuerbach developed this theory with particular reference to Christianity as he had seen it.

Following this theory of the divine as a projection of human qualities and emotions, psychoanalyst Sigmund Freud (1856–1938) described religion as a collective fantasy, a "universal obsessional neurosis"—a replaying of our loving and fearful relationships with our parents. Religious belief gives us a God powerful enough to protect us from the terrors of life, and will reward or punish us for obedience or nonobedience to social norms. From Freud's extremely sceptical point of view, religious belief is an illusion springing from people's infantile insecurity and neurotic guilt; as such it closely resembles mental illness.

Other scientific materialists believe that religions have been created or at least used to manipulate people. Historically, religions have often supported and served secular power. Karl Marx argued that a culture's religion—as well as all other aspects of its social structure—springs from its economic framework. In Marx's view, religion's origins lie in the longings of the oppressed. It may have developed from the desire to revolutionize society and combat exploitation, but in failing to do so, it became otherworldly, an expression of unfilled desires for a better, more satisfying life:

> *Man makes religion: religion does not make man. . . . The religious world is but the reflex of the real world. . . . Religion is the sigh of the oppressed creature, the sentiment of a heartless world, and the soul of soulless conditions. It is the opium of the people. . . .*[19]

According to Marx, not only do religions pacify people falsely; they may themselves become tools of oppression. For instance, he charged Christian authorities of his times with supporting "vile acts of the oppressors" by explaining them as due punishment of sinners by God. Other critics have made similar complaints against Eastern religions that blame the sufferings of the poor on their own misdeeds in previous lives. Such interpretations and uses of religious teachings lessen the perceived need for society to help those who are oppressed and suffering. Marx's ideas thus led toward atheistic communism, for he had asserted, "The abolition of religion as the *illusory* happiness of the people is required for their real happiness."[20]

While scientific materialism ultimately led toward the political system of communism in which atheism was taught as the only rational view of religion, the old unitary concepts of science and religion received another serious challenge in 1859, when the naturalist Charles Darwin (1809–1882) published *The Origin of Species*, a work that propounded the theory of evolution by natural selection. Darwin demonstrated that certain genetic mutations give an organism a competitive advantage over others of its species, and thus its lineage is naturally more likely to survive. According to Darwin's theory, over great lengths of time this process has directed the development of all forms of life. The theory of natural selection directly contradicted a literal understanding of the biblical Book of Genesis, in which God is said to have created all life in only six days. By the end of the nineteenth century, all such beliefs of the Judeo-Christian tradition were being questioned. The German philosopher Nietzsche (1844–1900) proclaimed, "God is dead!"

However, as science has progressed during the twentieth and twenty-first centuries, it has in some senses moved back toward a more nuanced understanding of religious belief. Science itself is now being questioned. Scientists have given up trying to find absolute certainties. From contemporary scientific research, it is clear that the cosmos is mind-boggling in its complexity and that what we perceive with our five senses is not Ultimate Reality. For instance, the inertness and solidity of matter are only illusions. Each atom consists mostly of empty space with tiny particles whirling around in it. These subatomic particles—such as neutrons, protons, and electrons—cannot even be described as "things." Twentieth-century theories of quantum mechanics, trying to account for the tiniest particles of matter, uncovered the Uncertainty Principle: that the position and velocity of a subatomic particle cannot be simultaneously determined. These particles behave like energy as well as like matter, like waves as well as like particles. Their position can be determined only statistically. Their behaviors can best be described in terms of a dynamic, interdependent system which includes the observer. Human consciousness is inextricably involved in what it thinks it is "objectively" studying. As physicist David Bohm puts it, "Everything interpenetrates everything."[21]

Our own bodies appear relatively solid, but they are in a constant state of flux and interchange with the environment. Our eyes, ears, noses, tongues, and skin do not reveal absolute truths. Rather, our sensory organs may operate as filters, selecting from a multi-dimensional universe only those characteristics that we need to perceive in order to survive. Imagine how difficult it would be simply to walk across a street if we could see all the electromagnetic energy in the atmosphere, such as x-rays, radio waves, gamma rays, and infrared and ultraviolet light, rather than only the small band of colors we see as the visible spectrum. Though the sky of a starry night appears vast to the naked eye, the giant Hubble telescope placed in space has revealed an incomprehensibly immense cosmos whose limits have not been found. It contains matter-gobbling black holes, vast starmaking clusters, inter-galactic collisions, and cosmic events that happened billions of years ago, so far away that their light is just now being captured by our most powerful instruments for examining what lies far beyond our small place in this galaxy. We know that more lies beyond what we have yet been able to measure. And even our ability to conceive of what we cannot sense may perhaps be limited by the way our brain is organized.

As science continues to question its own assumptions, various new hypotheses are being suggested about the nature of the universe. "Superstring theory" proposes that the universe may not be made of particles at all, but rather of tiny vibrating strings and loops of strings. According to Superstring theory, whereas we think we are living in four dimensions of space and time, there may be at least ten dimensions, with the unperceived dimensions "curled up" or "compactified" within the four dimensions that we can perceive. According to another current theory, the cosmos is like a soccer ball, a finite closed system with many facets.

New branches of science are finding that the universe is not always predictable, nor does it always operate according to human notions of cause and effect. And whereas scientific models of the universe were until recently based on the assumption of stability and equilibrium, physicist Ilya Prigogine observes that "today we see instability, fluctuations, irreversibility at every level."[22]

Science cannot accurately predict even the future orbits of planets within this solar system, for all the relevant factors will never be known to human researchers. Physicist Murray Gell-Mann says that we are "a small speck of creation believing it is capable of comprehending the whole."[23]

Contemporary physics approaches metaphysics in the work of physicists such as David Bohm. He describes the dimensions we see and think of as "real" as the *explicate* order. Behind it lies the *implicate* order, in which separateness resolves into unbroken wholeness. Beyond may lie other subtle dimensions, all merging into an infinite ground that unfolds itself as light. This scientific theory is very similar to descriptions by mystics from all cultures about their intuitive experiences of the cosmos. Indeed, Eastern religious traditions long ago recognized the value of perception and reason for the acquisition of ordinary, utilitarian knowledge, but discounted their use for the acquisition of transcendent knowledge of the mystery of being, which they hold, can be apprehended only through spiritual experience.

> *The most beautiful and profound emotion that we can experience is the sensation of the mystical. It is the sower of all true science. He to whom this emotion is a stranger, who can no longer wonder and stand rapt in awe, is as good as dead. To know that what is impenetrable to us really exists, manifesting itself as the highest wisdom and the most radiant beauty which our dull faculties can comprehend only in their most primitive forms—this knowledge, this feeling is at the center of true religiousness. . . . A human being is part of the whole. . . . He experiences himself, his thoughts and feelings as something separated from the rest—a kind of optical delusion of his consciousness. . . . Our task must be to free ourselves from this prison by widening our circle of compassion to embrace all living creatures, and the whole [of] nature in its beauty.*
>
> *Albert Einstein*[24]

One of the major conflicts between science and religion is that between religious concepts of intentional divine creation and the scientific concept of a universe evolving mechanistically by processes such as genetic mutations and random combinations of elements. Scientists are continually revealing a universe whose perfections are suggestive of purposefulness. They have found, for instance, that stars could never have formed if the force of gravity were ever so slightly stronger or weaker. Biologists find that the natural world is an intricate harmony of beautifully elaborated, interrelated parts. Even to produce the miniature propeller that allows a tiny bacterium to swim, some forty different proteins are required. The huge multinational Human Genome Project has discovered that the basic genetic units that are found in all life forms are repeated 3.1 billion times in complex combinations to create human beings.

The question arises: Can the complex maps that produce life be the consequences of chance arrangements of atoms, or are they the result of deliberate design by some First Cause? Current research has demonstrated that the development of certain complex biochemical systems, such as the Krebs citric acid cycle, which unleashes the chemical energy stored in food and makes it available

Some contemporary scientists feel that the perfect details of the natural world cannot have arisen without some kind of guiding intelligence in the cosmos.

to support life, can be explained by Darwinian mechanics. Some feel that evolution theory presupposes blind, uncaring mechanics, since so many species that have arisen have become extinct. The feeling is that if there were a Creator God, how could that God be so wasteful or cruel? However, the theory of evolution does not necessarily conflict with religious beliefs, if both are examined carefully. Biology professor Kenneth Miller proposes that:

> Evolution is certainly not so "cruel" that it cannot be compatible with the notion of a loving God. All that evolution points out is that every organism that has ever lived will eventually die. This is not a special feature of Darwinian theory, but an observable, verifiable fact. The driving force behind evolutionary charge is differential reproductive success, the fact that some organisms leave more offspring than others. Yes, the struggle for existence sometimes involves competition and predation, but just as often it involves cooperation, care, and extraordinary beauty.[25]

Geneticist Francis Collins, Director of the United States' National Human Genome Research Institute at the National Institutes of Health, is both a serious scientist and a "serious" Christian. He does not find the two facets to his life incompatible. Rather, he says:

> When something new is revealed about the human genome, I experience a feeling of awe at the realization that humanity now knows something only God knew before. It is a deeply moving sensation that helps me appreciate the spiritual side of life, and also makes the practice of science more rewarding.[26]

According to contemporary "Big Bang" theory, the entire cosmos originated from one point in an explosion whose force is still expanding. Astronomer Fred Hoyle (1915–2001), who originated the term "Big Bang," cautioned that it may not have been a chance happening:

> The universe has to know in advance what it is going to be before it knows how to start itself. For in accordance with the Big Bang Theory, for instance, at a time of 10 [to the minus 43] seconds the universe has to know how many types of neutrino there are going to be at a time of 1 second. This is so in order that it starts off expanding at the right rate to fit the eventual number of neutrino types. . . . An explosion in a junkyard does not lead to sundry bits of metal being assembled into a working machine.[27]

Religious beliefs that, if interpreted literally, seem to be contradicted by scientific fact can instead be interpreted as belonging to the realm of myth. Myths give us symbolic answers to ultimate questions that cannot be answered by empirical experience or rational thought, such as "What are we here for?"

At the cutting edge of research, scientists themselves find they have no ultimate answers that can be expressed in scientific terms. The renowned theoretical physicist Stephen Hawking asks, "What is it that breathes fire into the equations and makes a universe for them to describe?"[28]

Women and the feminine in religions

Another long-standing issue in the sphere of religion is the exclusion of women and the feminine in favor of male-dominated systems. According to some current though controversial theories, many of the myths surviving in today's religions may be related to the suppression of early female-oriented religions by later male-oriented religious systems. Archaeological evidence from many cultures was re-interpreted during the twentieth century as suggesting that worship of a female high goddess was originally widespread. Although there were, and are now, cultures that did not ascribe gender or hierarchy or personality to the divine, some that did may have seen the highest deity as a female.

Just as today's male high deity goes by different names in different religions (God, Allah), the Great Goddess had many names. Among her many identities, she was Danu or Diti in ancient India, the Great Mother Nu Kwa of China, the Egyptian cobra goddess Ua Zit, the Greek earth goddess Gaia, the sun goddess Arinna of Turkey, Coatlique the Mother of Aztec deities, Queen Mother Freyja of the Scandinavians, Great Spider Woman of the Pueblo peoples of North America, and Mawu, omnipotent creator of the Dahomey. A reverent address to Ishtar, an important Mesopotamian goddess, dating from some time between the eighteenth and seventh centuries BCE suggests some of the powers ascribed to her:

> *Unto Her who renders decision, Goddess of all things. Unto the Lady of Heaven and Earth who receives supplication; Unto Her who hears petition, who entertains prayer; Unto the compassionate Goddess who loves righteousness; Ishtar the Queen, who suppresses all that is confused. To the Queen of Heaven, the Goddess of the Universe, the One who walked in terrible Chaos and brought life by the Law of Love; And out of Chaos brought us harmony.*[29]

Temples and images that seem to have been devoted to worship of the goddess have been found in almost every Neolithic and early historic archaeological site in Europe and West Asia. She was often symbolically linked with water, serpents, birds, eggs, spirals, the moon, the womb, the vulva, the magnetic currents of the earth, psychic powers, and the eternal creation and renewal of life. In these agricultural cultures women frequently held strong social positions. Hereditary lineages were often traced through the mother, and women were honored as priestesses, healers, agricultural inventors, counselors, prophetesses, and sometimes warriors.

What happened to these apparently goddess-oriented religions? Scholars are now trying to piece together not only the reality, extent, and characteristics of goddess worship, but also the circumstances of its demise. A cross-cultural survey by Eli Sagan (*The Dawn of Tyranny*) indicates that male-dominant social and religious structures accompanied the often violent shift from communal kinship groups and tribal confederations to centralized monarchies. In these kingdoms, social order was based on loyalty to and fear of the king. In Europe and West Asia, worship of the goddess was suppressed throughout the third and second millennia BCE by invading Indo-European groups (probably from the steppes of southern Russia) in which dominant males worshiped a supreme male deity, often described as a storm god residing on a mountain and bringing light (seen as the good) into the darkness (portrayed as bad and associated with the female).

In some cases, goddess worship co-existed with or resurfaced within male deity worship. In India, the new gods often had powerful female consorts or counterparts or were androgynous (that is, both male and female). The Hindu Durga, represented as a beautiful woman riding a lion, is worshipped as the blazing splendor and power of the Godhead. In Christianity, some scholars feel that devotion to Mary, Mother of Jesus, may substitute for earlier worship of the goddess.

An early image of what appears to be the Great Mother, creator and sustainer of the universe. (Tel Halaf, 5th millennium BCE.)

In Hindu tradition, the great goddess Durga (left) is understood as the active principle that can vanquish the demonic forces. (Durga slaying the Buffalo Demon, India, c. 1760.)

Nevertheless, as worship of the goddess was suppressed, so was ritual participation of women. In patriarchal societies, women often became property and were expected to be obedient to the rule of men. Although Christ had honored and worked with women, his later male followers limited the position of women within the Christian Church. Not only was women's spiritual contribution cast aside; in replacing the goddess, patriarchal groups may also have devalued the "feminine" aspect of religion—the receptive, intuitive, ecstatic mystical communion that was perhaps allowed freer expression in the goddess traditions. Women have been the major victims of this devaluation of the feminine, but there has also been distrust of mystics of both sexes.

Although women are still barred from equal spiritual footing with men in many religions, this situation is now being widely challenged. The contemporary feminist movement includes strong efforts to make women's voices heard in the sphere of religion. Women are trying to discover their own identity, rather than having their identities defined by others. They are challenging patriarchal religious institutions that have excluded women from active participation. They are also challenging gender-exclusive language in holy texts and authoritarian masculine images of the divine. Their protests also go beyond gender issues to question the narrow and confining ways in which religious inspiration has been institutionalized. At prestigious Christian seminaries in the United States, women preparing for the ministry now outnumber men and are radically transforming views of religion and religious practice. Many feminists are deeply concerned about social ills of our times—violence, poverty, ecological disaster—and are insisting that religions be actively engaged in insuring human survival, and that they be life-affirming rather than punitive in approach. Feminist Christian theologian Rosemary Ruether feels that the movement toward greater religious participation by women may help to heal other fragmentations in our spiritual lives:

The feminist religious revolution ... reaches forward to an alternative that can heal the splits between "masculine" and "feminine," between mind and body, between males and females as gender groups, between society and nature, and between races and classes.[30]

The usefulness of religions

Religions are potentially quite valuable for society and for individuals. Pioneering work in this area was done by French sociologist Emile Durkheim (1858–1917). He proposed that humans cannot live without organized social structures, and that religion is a glue that holds a society together. Surely religions have the potential for creating harmony in society, for they all teach social virtues such as love, compassion, altruism, justice, and discipline over our desires and emotions.

John Bowker, author of the 1995 book *Is God a Virus?*, asserts that religions are organized systems that serve the essential biological purpose of bringing people together for their common survival, as well as giving their lives a sense of meaning. To Bowker, religion is found universally because it protects gene replication and the nurturing of children. He proposes that because of its survival value, the potential for religiosity may even be genetically inherent in human brains.

Statistically, research indicates that religious faith is also beneficial for our physical health. Research conducted by the Center for the Study of Religion/Spirituality and Health at Duke University found that those who attend religious services or read scriptures frequently are significantly longer lived, less likely to be depressed, less likely to have high blood pressure, and nearly ninety percent less likely to smoke. Many other studies have indicated that patients with strong faith recover faster from illness and operations.

Research also reveals that prayer likewise has powerful positive effects. In a double-blind experiment in San Francisco in which some heart patients were prayed for but others were not, patients for whom no one was praying were five times more likely to require antibiotics, three times more likely to develop pulmonary edema, and twelve times more likely to require a mechanical ventilator.[31]

Meditation can not only help reduce mental stress but also help to develop positive emotions, even in the face of great difficulties. Citing laboratory tests of the mental calmness of Buddhists who practice "mindfulness" meditation, the 14th Dalai Lama points out that:

Over the millenniums, many practitioners have carried out what we might call "experiments" in how to overcome our tendencies toward destructive emotions. The world today needs citizens and leaders who can work toward ensuring stability and engage in dialogue with the "enemy"—no matter what kind of aggression or assault they may have endured. If humanity is to survive, happiness and inner balance are crucial. We would do well to remember that the war against hatred and terror can be waged on this, the internal front, too.[32]

The twentieth-century psychoanalyst Erich Fromm (1900–1980) looked at the psychological usefulness of religion for individuals. He concluded that humans have a need for a stable frame of reference, and that religion fulfills this need. As Mata Amritanandamayi, a contemporary Indian spiritual teacher, explains:

Faith in God gives one the mental strength needed to confront the problems of life. Faith in the existence of God is a protective force. It makes one feel safe and protected from all the evil influences of the world. To have faith in the existence of a Supreme Power and to live accordingly is a religion. When we become religious, morality arises, which, in turn, will help to keep us away from malevolent influences. We won't drink, we won't smoke, and we will stop wasting our energy through unnecessary gossip and talk. . . . We will also develop qualities like love, compassion, patience, mental equipoise, and other positive traits. These will help us to love and serve everyone equally. . . . Where there is faith, there is harmony, unity and love. A nonbeliever always doubts. . . . He cannot be at peace; he's restless. . . . The foundation of his entire life is unstable and scattered due to his lack of faith in a higher principle.[33]

Many of our psychological needs are not met by the material aspects of our life on earth. For example, we have difficulty accepting the commonsense notion that this life is all there is. We are born, we struggle to support ourselves, we age, and we die. If we believe that there is nothing more, fear of death may inhibit enjoyment of life and make all human actions seem pointless. Confronting mortality is so basic to the spiritual life that, as the Christian monk Brother David Steindl-Rast observes, whenever monks from any spiritual tradition meet, within five minutes they are talking about death.

> *It appears that throughout the world man has always been seeking something beyond his own death, beyond his own problems, something that will be enduring, true and timeless. He has called it God, he has given it many names; and most of us believe in something of that kind, without ever actually experiencing it.*
>
> *Jiddu Krishnamurti*[34]

Many of us seek an assurance that life continues in some form beyond the grave. But we may also want this present life to have some meaning. For many, the desire for material achievement offers a temporary sense of purposefulness. But once achieved, these material goals may seem hollow. The Buddha said:

Look!
The world is a royal chariot, glittering with paint.
No better.
   Fools are deceived, but the wise know better.[35]

Religions propose ideals that can radically transform people. Mahatma Gandhi (1869–1948) was an extremely shy, fearful child. His transformation into one of the great political figures of the twentieth century occurred as he meditated single-mindedly on the great Hindu scripture, the **Bhagavad-Gita**, particularly the second chapter, which he says was "inscribed on the tablet of my heart."[36] It reads, in part:

He is forever free who has broken
Out of the ego-cage of I and mine
To be united with the Lord of Love.
This is the supreme state. Attain thou this
And pass from death to immortality.[37]

The Golden Temple in Amritsar, India. Religious edifices attempt to reflect the sacred realm.

People long to gain strength for dealing with personal problems. Those who are suffering severe physical illness, privation, terror, or grief often turn to the divine for help. Agnes Collard, a Christian woman, reported that her impending death after four painful years of cancer, was bringing her closer to God:

> *I don't know what or who He is, but I am almost sure He is there. I feel His presence, feel that He is close to me during the awful moments. And I feel love. I sometimes feel wrapped, cocooned in love.*[38]

Religious literature is full of stories of miraculous aid that has come to those who have cried out in their need. Rather than what is construed as divine intervention, sometimes help comes as the strength and philosophy to accept burdens. The eighteenth-century Hasidic Jewish master known as the Baal Shem Tov (c. 1700–1760) taught that the vicissitudes of life are ways of climbing toward the divine. Islam teaches patience, faithful waiting for the unfailing grace of Allah. Despite his own trials, the Christian apostle Paul wrote of "the peace of God, which passeth all understanding."[39] Gandhi was blissful in prison, for no human could bar his relationship with the Lord of Love.

Rather than seeking help from without, an alternative approach is to gain freedom from problems by changing our ways of thinking. According to some Eastern religions, the concept that we are distinct, autonomous individuals is an illusion; what we think of as "our" consciousnesses and "our" bodies are in perpetual flux. Thus, freedom from problems lies in accepting temporal change and devaluing the "small self" in favor of the eternal self. The ancient sages of India called it "This eternal being that can never be proved, . . . spotless, beyond the ether, the unborn Self, great and eternal, . . . the creator, the maker of everything."[40]

Many contemplative spiritual traditions teach methods of turning within to discover and eradicate all attachments, desires, and resentments associated with the small earthly self, revealing the purity of the eternal self. Once we have found it within, we begin to see it wherever we look. This realization brings a sense of acceptance in which, as philosopher William James observed:

> *Dull submission is left far behind, and a mood of welcome, which may fill any place on the scale between cheerful serenity and enthusiastic gladness, has taken its place.*[41]

Kabir, a fifteenth-century Indian weaver who was inspired alike by Islam and Hinduism and whose words are included in Sikh scripture, described this state of spiritual bliss:

> *The blue sky opens out farther and farther,*
> *the daily sense of failure goes away,*
> *the damage I have done to myself fades,*
> *a million suns come forward with light,*
> *when I sit firmly in that world.*[42]

Some people feel that their true selves are part of that world of light, dimly remembered, and long to return to it. The nineteenth-century Romantic poet William Wordsworth wrote:

> *Our birth is but a sleep and a forgetting;*
> *The Soul that rises with us, our life's Star*
> *Hath had elsewhere its setting*
> *And cometh from afar;*
> *Not in entire forgetfulness,*
> *And not in utter nakedness,*
> *But trailing clouds of glory do we come*
> *From God, who is our home.*[43]

We look to religions for understanding, for answers to our many questions about life. Who are we? Why are we here? What happens after we die? Why is there suffering? Why is there evil? Is anybody up there listening? For those who find security in specific answers, some religions offer **dogma**—systems of doctrines proclaimed as absolutely true and accepted as such, even if they lie beyond the domain of one's personal experiences. Absolute faith provides some people with a secure feeling of rootedness, meaning, and orderliness in the midst of rapid social change. Religions may also provide rules for living, governing everything from diet to personal relationships. Such prescriptions are seen as earthly reflections of the order that prevails in the cosmos. Some religions, however, encourage people to explore the perennial questions by themselves, and to live in the uncertainties of not knowing intellectually, breaking through old concepts until nothing remains but truth itself.

A final need that draws some people to religion is the discomforting sense of being alone in the universe. This isolation can be painful, even terrifying. The divine may be sought as a loving father or mother, or as a friend. Alternatively, some paths offer the way of self-transcendence. Through them, the sense of isolation is lost in mystical merger with the One Being, with Reality itself.

The negative side of organized religion

Tragically, religions have often split rather than unified humanity, have oppressed rather than freed, have terrified rather than inspired. Institutionalization of religion is part of the problem. As institutionalized religions spread the teachings of their founders, there is the danger that more energy will go into preserving the outer form of the tradition than into maintaining its inner spirit. Max Weber (1864–1920), an influential early twentieth-century scholar of the sociology of religion, referred to this process as the "routinization of charisma." **Charisma** is the rare quality of personal magnetism often ascribed to founders of religion. Their followers feel that these teachers have extraordinary or supernatural powers. When the founder dies, the center of the movement may shift to those who turn the original inspirations into routine rituals and dogma.

There is also the danger that power may devolve to those who have charisma but no genuine connection with divine wisdom. Since the human needs that religions answer are so strong, those who hold religious power are in a position to dominate and control their followers. In fact, in many religions leaders are given this authority to guide people's spiritual lives, for their wisdom and special access to the sacred is valued. Because religions involve the unseen, the mysterious, these leaders' teachings may not be verifiable by everyday physical experience. They must more often be accepted on faith and it is possible to surrender to leaders who are misguided or unethical. Religious leaders, like secular leaders, may not be honest with themselves and others about their inner motives. They may mistake their own thoughts and desires for the voice and will of God. Some people believe, however, that the most important thing for the disciple is to surrender the ego; even an unworthy leader can help in this goal simply by playing the role of one to whom one must surrender personal control.

Religions try to help us make ethical choices in our lives, to develop a moral conscience. But in people who already have perfectionist or paranoid tendencies, the fear of sinning and being punished can be exaggerated to the point of neurosis or even psychosis by blaming, punishment-oriented religious teachings. If people try to leave their religion for the sake of their mental health, they may be haunted with guilt that they have done a terribly wrong thing. Religions thus have the potential for wreaking psychological havoc on their followers.

Another potentially negative use of religion is escapism. Because some religions, particularly those that developed in the East, offer a state of blissful contemplation as the reward for spiritual practice, the faithful may use religion to escape from their everyday problems. Psychologist John Welwood observes that Westerners sometimes embrace Eastern religions with the unconscious motive of avoiding their unsatisfactory lives. He calls this attempt "spiritual bypassing":

The existential loneliness some feel is hauntingly depicted by the sculptures of Alberto Giacometti, such as his Walking Man, *c. 1947–48.*

Spiritual bypassing may be particularly tempting for individuals who are having difficulty making their way through life's basic developmental stages, especially at a time when what were once ordinary developmental landmarks—earning a livelihood through dignified work, raising a family, keeping a marriage together— have become increasingly difficult and elusive for large segments of the population. While struggling with becoming autonomous individuals, many people are introduced to spiritual teachings and practices which come from cultures that assume a person having already passed through the basic developmental stages.[44]

Because religions may have such a strong hold on their followers—by their fears, their desires, their deep beliefs—they are potential centers for political power. When church and state are one, the belief that the dominant national religion is the only true religion may be used to oppress those of other beliefs within the country. Religion may also be used as a rallying point for wars against other nations, casting the desire for control as a holy motive. Throughout history, huge numbers of people have been killed in the name of eradicating "false" religions and replacing them with the "true" religion. Rather than uniting us all in bonds of love, harmony, and mutual respect, it has often divided us with barriers of hatred and intolerance.

In our times, dangerous politicized polarizations between religions are increasing in some areas, albeit cooling off in others. Some of the most worrisome conflicts are pitting Christians and Jews against Muslims to such an extent that some have predicted a catastrophic "clash of civilizations." No religion has ever sanctioned violence against innocent people, but such political clashes have given a holy aura to doing just that, posing a grave threat to life and peace.

This is not the time to think of the world in terms of superficial, rigid distinctions between "us" and "them." It is the time when we must try to understand each other's beliefs and feelings clearly, carefully, and compassionately, and bring truly religious responses into play. To take such a journey does not mean forsaking our own religious beliefs or our scepticism. But the journey is likely to broaden our perspective and thus bring us closer to understanding other members of our human family. Perhaps it will bring us closer to Unseen Reality itself.

Angels Weep

Wherever there is slaughter of innocent men, women, and children for the mere reason that they belong to another race, color, or nationality, or were born into a faith which the majority of them could never quite comprehend and hardly ever practice in its true spirit; wherever the fair name of religion is used as a veneer to hide overweening political ambition and bottomless greed, wherever the glory of Allah is sought to be proclaimed through the barrel of a gun; wherever piety becomes synonymous with rapacity, and morality cowers under the blight of expediency and compromise, wherever it be—in Yugoslavia or Algeria, in Liberia, Chad, or the beautiful land of the Sudan, in Los Angeles or Abuija, in Kashmir or Conakry, in Colombo or Cotabato—there God is banished and Satan is triumphant, there the angels weep and the soul of man cringes; there in the name of God humans are dehumanized; and there the grace and beauty of life lie ravished and undone.

Dr. Syed Z. Abedin, Director of the Institute for Muslim Minority Affairs[45]

Suggested reading

Campbell, Joseph, *The Hero with a Thousand Faces,* second edition, Princeton, New Jersey: Princeton University Press, 1968. Brilliant leaps across time and space to trace the hero's journey—seen as a spiritual quest—in all the world's mythologics and religions.

Campbell, Joseph with Bill Moyers, *The Power of Myth*, New York: Doubleday, 1988. More brilliant comparisons of the world's mythologies, with deep insights into their common psychological and spiritual truths.

Capra, Fritjof, *The Tao of Physics*, third edition, Boston: Shambhala, 1991. A fascinating comparison of the insights of Eastern religions and contemporary physics.

Carter, Robert E., ed., *God, The Self, and Nothingness—Reflections: Eastern and Western*, New York: Paragon House, 1990. Essays from major Eastern and Western scholars of religion on variant ways of experiencing and describing Ultimate Reality.

Eliade, Mircea, *Patterns in Comparative Religion*, trans. Rosemary Sheed, Lincoln, Nebraska: University of Nebraska Press, 1958, 1996. A classic study in beliefs, rituals, symbols, and myths from around the world.

Ferguson, Kitty, *The Fire in the Equations: Science, Religion and the Search for God*, New York/London: Bantam Books, 1994. A wide-ranging, perceptive analysis of the implications of scientific research for religious beliefs.

Hick, John, *An Interpretation of Religion*, New Haven: Yale University Press, 1992. A leading philosopher of religion offers a rational justification for seeing the major world religions as culturally conditioned forms of response to the great mystery of Being.

King, Ursula, *Women and Spirituality: Voices of Protest and Promise*, second edition, University Park, Pennsylvania: Pennsylvania State University Press, 1993. Excellent cross-cultural survey of feminist theology and spiritual activism.

Lincoln, Bruce, *Holy Terrors: Thinking about Religion after September 11*, Chicago and London; University of Chicago Press, 2003. Thought-provoking examination of the rhetoric of religious extremists and the interactions of politics, culture, and religion.

Marty, Martin E. and R. Scott Appleby, *The Fundamentalism Project*, 5 volumes, Chicago: University of Chicago Press, 1991–2000. Scholarly analyses of fundamentalist phenomena in all religions and around the globe.

McCutcheon, Russell T., *Manufacturing Religion: The Discourse on Sui Generis Religion and the Politics of Nostalgia*, New York and Oxford: Oxford University Press, 1997. Critique of the comparative study of religions as isolated phenomena without social and historical contexts.

Otto, Rudolf, *The Idea of the Holy*, second edition, London: Oxford University Press, 1950. An important exploration of "nonrational" experiences of the divine.

Paden, William E., *Interpreting the Sacred: Ways of Viewing Religion*, Boston: Beacon Press, 1992. A gentle, readable introduction to the complexities of theoretical perspectives on religion.

Sharma, Arvind, ed., *Women in World Religions*, Albany, New York: State University of New York Press, 1987. Analyses of the historic and contemporary place of women in each of the major religions.

Shinn, Larry D., ed., *In Search of the Divine: Some Unexpected Consequences of Interfaith Dialogue*, New York: Paragon House Publishers, 1987. Scholars from various religions present a tapestry of understandings of the Sacred Reality.

Stone, Merlin, *When God was a Woman*, San Diego, California: Harcourt Brace Jovanovich, 1976. Pioneering survey of archaeological evidence of the early religion of the Goddess.

Ward, Keith, *God, Chance and Necessity*, Oxford: Oneworld Publications, 1997. A leading Christian theologian critiques scientific theories that deny the existence of God.

Ward, Keith, *The Case for Religion*, Oxford: Oneworld Publications, 2004. An attempt to justify and define religion in historical contexts and also contemporary understandings.

Key terms

myth   A symbolic story expressing ideas about reality or spiritual history.

mysticism   The intuitive perception of spiritual truths beyond the limits of reason.

gnosis   Intuitive knowledge of spiritual realities.

profane   Worldly, secular, as opposed to sacred.

sacred   The realm of the extraordinary, beyond everyday perceptions, the supernatural, holy.

atheism   Belief that there is no deity.

agnosticism   Belief that if there is anything beyond this life, it is impossible for humans to know it.

ritual   Repeated, patterned religious act.

symbol   Visible representation of an invisible reality or concept.

Study questions

1 List ten and describe two modes of encountering Unseen Reality.
2 Describe major positive and negative ways of understanding Unseen Reality. Discuss sacred/profane, immanent/transcendent, theism/monotheism/polytheism/monism/nontheism, incarnations, atheism, agnosticism, and phenomenology.
3 Analyze how the "Descendants of the Eagle" story can be seen to be meaningful as symbol, myth, allegory, and ritual. Refer to the ideas of Jung and Campbell.
4 What new views of religious texts have been brought to light by the historical–critical method? What are its problems and benefits?
5 Contrast older scientific materialism with recent views of science and religion. Discuss Feuerbach, Freud, Marx, Darwin, Nietzsche, absolute certainty, Hubble, Bohm, Einstein, and chance in creation.
6 How has understanding the ancient goddess traditions affected modern views of women in religion?

Refer to Pearson/Prentice Hall's **TIME Special Edition: World Religions** magazine for these and other current articles on topics related to many of the world's religions:

- *The Religious Experience: Birth and Childhood; The Legacy of Abraham; Mohandas Gandhi*
- *The Impact of Religion: Cult Shock; Relaxing in a Labyrinth; Will Politicians Matter?; Essay—God Is Not On My Side. Or Yours.*

Chapter 1 describes the history of, and elements common to, the earliest forms of religious expression in human history, and asks the reader to consider why we have religions. For further research in this area, use the tools available to you in Research Navigator:

As you investigate basic religions, consider this question: "What are the origins of religious belief?"

- **Ebsco's ContentSelect:** Search in the Religion and Anthropology databases using terms such as "animism," "magic," "taboos."
- **Link Library:** Search in the Religion database under the categories: "Religious Theories and Thought" and "Expressions and Characteristics of Religion."
- **The *New York Times* on the Web:** Search in the Religious Studies and Anthropology/ Archaeology databases for current articles on related topics.

CHAPTER 2

INDIGENOUS SACRED WAYS

"Everything is alive"

Here and there around the globe, pockets of people still follow local sacred ways handed down from their remote ancestors and adapted to contemporary circumstances. These are the traditional **indigenous** people—descendants of the original inhabitants of lands now controlled by larger political systems in which they may have little influence.

Indigenous people comprise at least four percent of the world population. Some who follow the ancient spiritual traditions still live close to the earth in non-industrial, small-scale cultures; many do not. But despite the disruption of their traditional lifestyles, many indigenous people maintain a sacred way of life that is distinctively different from all other religions. These enduring ways, which indigenous people may refer to as their "original instructions" on how to live, were almost lost under the onslaught of genocidal colonization, conversion pressures from global religions, mechanistic materialism, and the destruction of their natural environments by the global economy of limitless consumption.

Much of the ancient visionary wisdom has disappeared. There are few traditionally trained elders left and few young people willing to undergo the lengthy and rigorous training necessary for spiritual leadership in these sacred ways. Nevertheless, in our time there is a renewal of interest in these traditions, fanning hope that what they offer will not be lost.

> *To what extent can [indigenous groups] reinstitute traditional religious values in a world gone mad with development, electronics, almost instantaneous transportation facilities, and intellectually grounded in a rejection of spiritual and mysterious events?*
>
> *Vine Deloria, Jr.*[1]

Understanding indigenous sacred ways

Outsiders have known or understood little of the indigenous sacred ways, many of which have long been practiced only in secret. In Mesoamerica, the ancient teachings have remained hidden for five hundred years since the coming of the conquistadores, passed down within families as a secret oral tradition. The

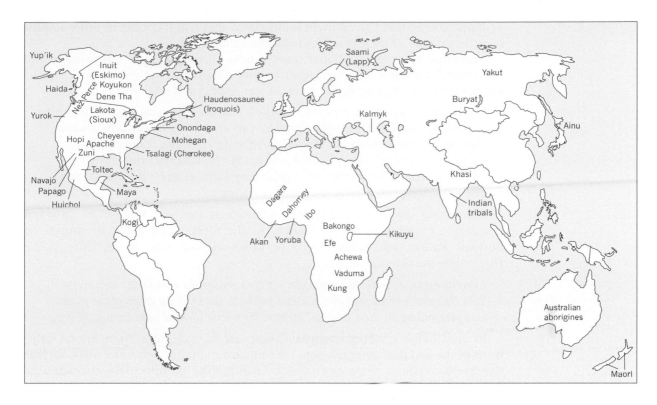

Buryats living near Lake Baikal in Russia were thought to have been converted to Buddhism and Christianity centuries ago; however, few attended the opening of a Buddhist temple after the fall of communism in 1989, whereas almost the entire population of the area gathered for indigenous ceremonies on Olkhon Island in 1992 and 1993.

The approximate distribution of indigenous groups mentioned in this chapter.

In parts of aboriginal Australia, the real teachings have been underground for two hundred years since white colonialists and Christian missionaries appeared. As aborigine Lorraine Mafi Williams explains:

> *We have stacked away our religious, spiritual, cultural beliefs. When the missionaries came, we were told by our old people to be respectful, listen and be obedient, go to church, go to Sunday school, but do not adopt the Christian doctrine because it takes away our cultural, spiritual beliefs. So we've always stayed within God's laws in what we know.*[2]

Not uncommonly, the newer global traditions have been blended with the older ways. For instance, Buddhism as it spread often adopted existing customs, such as the recognition of local deities. Now many indigenous people sincerely practice one of the global religions while still retaining many of their traditional ways.

Until recently, those who attempted to ferret out the native sacred ways had little basis for understanding them. Many were anthropologists who approached spiritual behaviors from the nonspiritual perspective of Western science or else the Christian understanding of religion as a means of salvation from sinful earthly existence—a belief not found among most indigenous people. Knowing that researchers from other cultures did not grasp the truth of their beliefs, the native peoples have at times given them information that was incorrect in order to protect the sanctity of their practices from the uninitiated.

Academic study of traditional ways is now becoming more sympathetic and self-critical, however, as is apparent in this statement by Gerhardus Cornelius Oosthuizen, a European researching African traditional religions:

> [The] Western worldview is closed, essentially complete and unchangeable, basically substantive and fundamentally non-mysterious; i.e. it is like a rigid programmed machine. . . . This closed worldview is foreign to Africa, which is still deeply religious. . . . This world is not closed, and not merely basically substantive, but it has great depth, it is unlimited in its qualitative varieties and is truly mysterious; this world is restless, a living and growing organism.[3]

Indigenous spirituality is a lifeway, a particular approach to all of life. It is not a separate experience, like meditating in the morning or going to church on Sunday. Rather, spirituality ideally pervades all moments. As an elder of the Huichol in Mexico puts it:

> Everything we do in life is for the glory of God. We praise him in the well-swept floor, the well-weeded field, the polished machete, the brilliant colors of the picture and embroidery. In these ways we prepare for a long life and pray for a good one.[4]

In most native cultures, spiritual lifeways are shared orally. There are no scriptures of the sort that other religions are built around (although some texts, such as the Mayan codices, were destroyed by conquering groups). This characteristic helps to keep the indigenous sacred ways dynamic and flexible rather than fossilized. It also keeps the sacred experience fresh in the present. These oral accounts are often rich in symbols, metaphors, and humor which are not easily understood by outsiders but which are central to a people's understanding of how life works. To the Maori of New Zealand, life is a continual dynamic process of becoming in which all things arise from a burst of cosmic energy. According to their creation

In the Kikuyu indigenous tradition of Kenya, it is very important to know intimately the land on which one lives, including its orientation to the sun and to Mount Kenya, the sacred "mountain of brightness."

story, all beings emerged from a spatially confined liminal state of darkness in which the Sky Father and Earth Mother were locked in eternal embrace, continually conceiving but crowding their offspring until their children broke that embrace. Their separation created a great burst of light, like wind sweeping through the cosmos. That tremendously freeing, rejuvenating power is still present and can be called upon through rituals in which all beings—plants, trees, fish, birds, animals, people—are intimately and primordially related. Oral narratives also may contain clues to the historical experiences of individuals or groups, but these are often carried from generation to generation in symbolic language.

The lifeways of many small-scale cultures are tied to the land on which they live and their entire way of life; they are meaningful only within this context. The people generally respect the rights of others to their own ways and make no attempt to convert outsiders to theirs. Traditional worldviews are not inevitably linked to materially simple ways of life. The Dene Tha of northwestern Alberta, Canada, now live in houses built by the government and ride snowmobiles instead of dog sleds, but they still seek spiritual help from "animal helpers" and find important meaning and guidance in their visionary experiences.

Despite the hindrances to understanding of indigenous forms of spirituality, the doors to understanding are opening somewhat in our times. Firstly, the traditional elders are very concerned about the growing potential for planetary disaster. Some are beginning to share their basic values, if not their esoteric practices, in hopes of preventing industrial societies from destroying the earth. Secondly, those of other faiths are beginning to recognize the value of indigenous ways, which were in the past suppressed by organized religions. Thirdly, many people who have not grown up in native cultures are attempting to embrace indigenous spiritual ways, finding their own traditions lacking in certain qualities for which they long, such as love for the earth. However, even outsiders who value the sacred teachings may disrupt or alter the indigenous practices. Osage theologian George Tinker describes what often happens in North America:

> The first Indian casualty today in any such New Age spiritual–cultural encounter is most often the strong deep structure cultural value of community and group cohesion that is important to virtually every indigenous people. . . . Well-meaning New Agers drive in from New York and Chicago or fly in from Austria and Denmark to participate in annual ceremonies originally intended to secure the well-being of the local, spatially configured community. These visitors see little or nothing at all of the reservation community, pay little attention to the poverty and suffering of the people there and finally leave having achieved only a personal, individual spiritual high.[5]

Indigenous traveling teachers are swamped with eager students. But many native peoples are wary of this trend. They feel that their sacred ways are all they have left and worry that even these may be sold, stolen, and ruined. Elders of the Lakota tribes have urged all indigenous nations to use every means possible to prevent the exploitation of their spiritual traditions, declaring in part:

> Whereas individuals and groups involved in "the New Age Movement," in "the men's movement," in "neo-paganism" cults and in "shamanism" workshops all have exploited the spiritual traditions of our Lakota people by imitating our ceremonial ways and by mixing such imitation rituals with non-Indian **occult**

practices in an offensive and harmful pseudo-religious hodgepodge, and whereas the absurd public posturing of this scandalous assortment of pseudo-Indian charlatans, "wannabes," commercial profiteers, cultists and "New Age shamans" comprises a momentous obstacle in the struggle of traditional Lakota people for an adequate public appraisal of the legitimate political, legal and spiritual needs of real Lakota people. . . .

Therefore we urge all our Indian brothers and sisters to act decisively and boldly in our present compaign to end the destruction of our sacred traditions, keeping in mind our highest duty as Indian people: to preserve the purity of our precious traditions for our future generations, so that our children and our children's children will survive and prosper in the sacred manner intended for each of our respective peoples by our Creator.[6]

Cultural diversity

In this chapter we are considering the faith-ways of indigenous peoples as a whole. However, behind these generalizations lie many differences in social contexts, as well as in religious beliefs and practices. There are hundreds of different tribal traditions in North America alone. Indigenous traditions have evolved within materially as well as religiously diverse cultures. Some are descendants of civilizations with advanced urban technologies that supported concentrated populations. When the Spanish conqueror Cortés took over Tenochtitlán (which now lies beneath Mexico City) in 1519, he found it a beautiful clean city with elaborate architecture, indoor plumbing, an accurate calendar, and advanced systems of mathematics and astronomy. Former African kingdoms were highly culturally advanced with elaborate arts, such as intricate bronze and copper casting, ivory carving, goldworking, and ceramics. In recent times, some Native American tribes have become quite materially successful via economic enterprises, such as gambling complexes. And some indigenous groups are using modern technologies such as the Internet to promote their concerns.

At the other extreme are those few cultures that still maintain a survival strategy of hunting and gathering. For example, some Australian aborigines continue to live as mobile foragers, though restricted to government-owned stations. A nomadic survival strategy necessitates simplicity in material goods; whatever can be gathered or built rather easily at the next camp need not be dragged along. But material simplicity is not a sign of spiritual poverty. The Australian aborigines have a complex **cosmogony**, or model of the origins of the universe and their purpose within it, as well as a working knowledge of their own bioregion.

Some traditional people live in their ancestral enclaves, somewhat sheltered from the pressures of modern industrial life, though not untouched by the outer world. Tribal peoples have lived deep in the forests and hills of India for thousands of years, utilizing the trees and plants for their food and medicines, although within the twentieth century their ancestral lands were taken over for "development" projects and encroached upon by more politically and economically powerful groups, rendering many of the 75 million Indian tribal people landless laborers. The Hopi people have continuously occupied a high plateau area of the southwestern United States for between eight hundred and one thousand years; their sacred ritual calendar is tied to the yearly farming cycle.

The indigenous community of Acoma Pueblo—built on a high plateau in New Mexico—may be the oldest continuously occupied city in the United States.

Other indigenous people visit their sacred sites and ancestral shrines but live in more urban settings because of job opportunities. The people who participate in ceremonies in the Mexican countryside include subway personnel, journalists, and artists of native blood who live in Mexico City.

In addition to variations in lifestyles, indigenous traditions vary in their adaptations to dominant religions. Often native practices have become interwoven with those of global religions, such as Buddhism, Islam, and Christianity. In Southeast Asia, household Buddhist shrines are almost identical to the spirit houses in which the people still make offerings to honor the local spirits. The Dahomey tradition from West Africa was carried to Haiti by African slaves and called **Vodou**, from *vodu*, one of the names for the chief non-human spirits. Forced by the European colonialists to adopt Christianity, worshippers of Vodou secretly fused their old gods with their images of Catholic saints. In Cuba, Yoruba slaves did the same, resulting in the practices known as **Santeria** (see Chapter 12).

While interaction with larger state societies or colonial powers has been extremely detrimental to indigenous peoples around the world, adaptation of the dominant religions has at times allowed the traditional people to survive. Indigenous people sometimes earnestly try to practice the dominant religion, and in doing so they bring new life into it, as in the lively practice of Christianity in rural Africa. In other places, forced converts may practice the new religion only indifferently. A third outcome is the mixing of traditions to produce a new hybrid.

Despite their different histories and economic patterns, indigenous sacred ways do have some characteristics in common. Perhaps from ancient contact across land-bridges that no longer exist, there are similarities between the languages of the Tsalagi in the Americas, Tibetans, and the aboriginal Ainu of Japan. Similarities found among the myths of geographically separate peoples can be accounted for by global diffusion by trade, travel, and other kinds of contact, and by parallel origin because of basic similarities in human experience, such as birth and death, pleasure and pain, and wonderment about the cosmos and our place in it.

Certain symbols and metaphors are repeated in the inspirational art and stories of many traditional cultures around the world, but the people's relationships to, and the concepts surrounding, these symbols are not inevitably the same. Nevertheless, the following sections look at some recurring themes in the spiritual ways of diverse small-scale cultures.

The circle of right relationships

For many indigenous peoples, everything in the cosmos is intimately interrelated. A symbol of unity among the parts of this sacred reality is a circle. This symbol is not used by all indigenous people; the Navajo, for instance, regard a completed circle as stifling and restrictive. However, many other indigenous people hold the circle sacred because it is infinite—it has no beginning, no end. Time is circular rather than linear, for it keeps coming back to the same place. Life revolves around the generational cycles of birth, youth, maturity, and physical death, the return of the seasons, the cyclical movements of the moon, sun, stars, and planets.

This understanding of life as a complex of circles is thought to be the perfect framework for harmony. As Lame Deer, a Lakota Sioux holy man, explained:

Nature wants things to be round. The bodies of human beings and animals have no corners. With us the circle stands for the togetherness of people who sit with one another around the campfire, relatives and friends united in peace while the pipe passes from hand to hand. The camp in which every tipi *had its place was also a ring. The* tipi *was a ring in which people sat in a circle and all the families in the*

Among the gentle Efe Pygmies of the Ituri Forest in the Democratic Republic of Congo (formerly Zaire), children learn to value the circle by playing the "circle game." With feet making a circle, each names a circular object and then an expression of roundness (the family circle, togetherness, "a complete rainbow").

Deity may be conceived as either male or female in indigenous religions. In Navajo belief, divinity is personified as both Father Sky and Mother Earth. In this traditional sand-painting, Father Sky is on the left, with constellations and the Milky Way forming his "body." Mother Earth is on the right, with her body bearing the four sacred plants: squash, beans, tobacco, and corn.

village were in turn circles within a larger circle, part of the larger hoop which was the seven campfires of the Sioux, representing one nation. The nation was only a part of the universe, in itself circular and made of the earth, which is round, of the sun, which is round, of the stars, which are round. The moon, the horizon, the rainbow—circles within circles within circles, with no beginning and no end.[7]

To maintain the natural balance of the circles of existence, most indigenous peoples have traditionally been taught that they must develop right relationships with everything that is. Their relatives include the unseen world of spirits, the land and weather, the people and creatures, and the power within.

Relationships with spirit

Many indigenous traditions worship a Supreme Being who they believe created the cosmos. This being is known by the Lakota as "Wakan Tanka" or "Great Mysterious" or "Great Spirit." African names for this being are attributes, such as "All-powerful," "Creator," "the one who is met everywhere," "the one who exists by himself," or "the one who began the forest." The Supreme Being is often referred to by male pronouns, but in some groups the Supreme Being is a female. Some tribes of the southwestern United States call her "Changing Woman"—sometimes young, sometimes old, the mother of the earth, associated with women's reproductive cycles and the mystery of birth, the creatrix. Many traditional languages make no distinction between male and female pronouns, and some see the divine as androgynous, a force arising from the interaction of male and female aspects of the universe.

Awareness of one's relationship to the Great Power is thought to be essential, but the power itself remains unseen and mysterious. An Inuit spiritual adept described his people's experience of:

a power that we call Sila, which is not to be explained in simple words. A great spirit, supporting the world and the weather and all life on earth, a spirit so mighty that [what it says] to mankind is not through common words, but by storm and snow and rain and the fury of the sea; all the forces of nature that men fear. But Sila has also another way of [communicating]; by sunlight and calm of the sea, and little children innocently at play, themselves understanding nothing. . . . When all is well, Sila sends no message to mankind, but withdraws into endless nothingness, apart.[8]

To traditional Buryats of Russia, the chief power in the world is the eternally blue sky, Tengry. African myths suggest that the High God was originally so close to humans that they became disrespectful. The All-powerful was like the sky, they say, which was once so close that children wiped their dirty hands on it, and women (blamed by men for the withdrawal) broke off pieces for soup and

Australian aborigines understand their environment as concentric fields of subtle energies. Snakes and Emus *by Nym Bunduk (1907–74).*

bumped it with their sticks when pounding grain. Although southern and central Africans believe in a high being who presides over the universe, including less powerful spirits, they consider this being either too distant, too powerful, or too dangerous to worship or call on for help.

It cannot therefore be said that indigenous concepts of, and attitudes toward, a Supreme Being are necessarily the same as that which Western monotheistic religions refer to as God or Allah. In African traditional religions, much more emphasis tends to be placed on the transcendent dimensions of everyday life and doing what is spiritually necessary to keep life going normally. Many unseen powers are perceived to be at work in the material world. In various traditions, some of these are perceived without form, as mysterious and sacred presences. Others are perceived as having more definite, albeit invisible, forms and personalities. These may include deities with human-like personalities, the nature spirits of special local places, such as venerable trees and mountains, animal spirit helpers, personified elemental forces, ancestors who still take an interest in their living relatives, or the **nagas**, known to the traditional people of Nepal as invisible serpentine spirits who control the circulation of water in the world and also within our bodies.

Ancestors may be extremely important. Traditional Africans understand that even the person is not an individual, but a composite of many souls—the spirits of one's parents and ancestors—resonating to their feelings. As Rev. William Kingsley Opoku, International Coordinator of the African Council for Spiritual Churches, explains:

> *Our ancestors are our saints. Christian missionaries who came here wanted us to pray to their saints, their dead people. But what about our saints? ... If you are grateful to your ancestors, then you have blessings from your grandmother, your grandfather, who brought you forth. ... Non-Africans came in and said we should not obey our ancestors, should not call upon them at all, because they are evil people. This has been a mental bondage, a terrible thing.*[9]

Continued communication with the "living dead" is extremely important to traditional Africans. These are ancestors who have died within living memory. Food and drink are set out for them, acknowledging that they are still in a sense living and engaged with the people's lives. Failure to keep in touch with the ancestors is a dangerous oversight, which may bring misfortunes to the family.

The Dagara of Burkina Faso in West Africa are familiar with the *kontombili*, who look like humans but are only about one foot tall, because of the humble way they express their spiritual power. Other West African groups, descendants of hierarchical ancient civilizations, recognize a great pantheon of deities, the **orisa** or *vodu*, each the object of special cult worship. The *orisa* are embodiments of the dynamic forces in life, such as Oya, goddess of death and change, experienced in tornadoes, lightning, winds, and fire; Olokun, ruler of the mysterious depths of consciousness; Shango, a former king who is now honored as the stormy god of electricity and genius; Ifa, god of wisdom; and Obatala, the source of creativity, warmth, and enlightenment. At the beginning of time, in Yoruba cosmology, there was only one godhead, described by Clyde Ford as "a beingless being, a dimensionless point, an infinite container of everything, including itself."[10] According to the mythology, this being was smashed by a boulder pushed down by a rebellious slave, and broke into hundreds of fragments, each of which became an *orisa*. According to some analysts, these can also be seen as archetypes of traits existing within the human

YORUBA TEACHING STORY

Osun and the Power of Woman

Olodumare, the Supreme Creator, who is both female and male, wanted to prepare the earth for human habitation. To organize things, Olodumare sent the seventeen major deities. Osun was the only woman; all the rest were men. Each of the deities was given specific abilities and specific assignments. But when the male deities held their planning meetings, they did not invite Osun. "She is a woman," they said.

However, Olodumare had given great powers to Osun. Her womb is the matrix of all life in the universe. In her lie tremendous power, unlimited potential, infinities of existence. She wears a perfectly carved, beaded crown, and with her beaded comb she parts the pathway of both human and divine life. She is the leader of the *aje*, the powerful beings and forces in the world.

When the male deities ignored Osun, she made their plans fail. The male deities returned to Olodumare for help. After listening, Olodumare asked, "What about Osun?" "She is only a woman," they replied, "so we left her out." Olodumare spoke in strong words, "You must go back to her, beg her for forgiveness, make a sacrifice to her, and give her whatever she asks."

The male deities did as they were told, and Osun forgave them. What did she ask for in return? The secret initiation that the men used to keep women in the background. She wanted it for herself and for all women who are as powerful as she is. The men agreed and initiated her into the secret knowledge. From that time onward, their plans were successful.[11]

psyche. The ultimate purpose of the *orisa*—and that of those who pay attention to them as inner forces—is to return to that original state of wholeness.

The spirits are available to reverent seekers as helpers, as intermediaries between the people and the power, and as teachers. A right relationship with these spirit beings can be a sacred partnership. Seekers respect and learn from them; they also purify themselves in order to engage their services for the good of the people. As we will later see, those who are best able to call on the spirits for help are the shamans who have dedicated their lives to this service.

Teachings about the spirits also help the people to understand how they should live together in society. Professor Deidre Badejo observes that in Yoruba tradition there is an ideal of balance between the creativity of women who give and sustain life, and the power of men who protect life. Under various internal and external pressures, this balance has swung toward male dominance, but the stories of feminine power and the necessity for men to recognize it remain in the culture, teaching an ideal symmetry between female and male roles.

Kinship with all creation

In addition to the unseen powers, all aspects of the tangible world are imbued with spirit. Josiah Young III explains that in African traditional religion, both the visible and invisible realms are filled with spiritual forces:

> The visible is the natural and cultural environment, of which humans, always in
> the process of transformation, are at the center. The invisible connotes the numinous

field of ancestors, spirits, divinities, and the Supreme Being, all of whom, in varying
degrees, permeate the visible. Visible things, however, are not always what they
seem. Pools, rocks, flora, and fauna may dissimulate invisible forces of which only
the initiated are conscious.[12]

Within the spiritually charged, visible world, all things may be understood as spiritually interconnected. Everything is therefore experienced as family. The community is paramount, and it may extend beyond the living humans in the area. Many traditional peoples know the earth as their mother. The land one lives on is part of her body, loved, respected, and well known. Oren Lyons, an elder of the Onondaga Nation Wolf Clan, speaks of this intimate relationship:

[The indigenous people's] knowledge is profound and comes from living in one
place for untold generations. It comes from watching the sun rise in the east and set
in the west from the same place over great sections of time. We are as familiar with
the lands, rivers and great seas that surround us as we are with the faces of our
mothers. Indeed we call the earth Etenoha, our mother, from whence all life
springs. . . . We do not perceive our habitat as wild but as a place of great security
and peace, full of life.[13]

Some striking feature of the natural environment of the area—such as a great mountain or canyon—may be perceived as the center from which the whole world was created. Such myths heighten the perceived sacredness of the land. Western Tibet's Mount Kailas, high in the Himalayas, is seen by the indigenous people of that area as the center of the earth, a sacred space where the earthly and the supernatural meet. Spiritual specialists therefore climb the mountain seeking visions.

The Western Apache remember vivid symbolic narratives about the exploits of people in specific places in their environment and contemplate them as aids to the spiritual goal of making their minds smooth, steady, and resilient. Dudley Patterson's grandmother taught him:

Wisdom sits in places. It's like water that never dries up. You need to drink water to
stay alive, don't you? Well, you also need to drink from places. You must remember
everything about them. You must learn their names. You must remember what
happened at them long ago. You must think about it and keep on thinking about it.
Then your mind will become smoother and smoother. Then you will see danger
before it happens. You will walk a long way and live a long time. You will be wise.
People will respect you.[14]

According to Audrey Shenandoah, elder of the Haudenosaunee (Iroquois) Nation, even the language of native people is tied to the land. This feature makes it hard to explain indigenous spiritual beliefs in other languages. She asserts, "In the English language, you have to use a whole bunch of cold words to try to describe what in any native language, because it's a land language, can be said completely, rounded out and whole."[15]

In contrast to the industrial world's attempts to dominate the earth, native people consider themselves caretakers of their mother, the earth. They are now raising their voices against the destruction of the environment, warning of the potential for global disaster. Nepali shamans who have recently undertaken the difficult pilgrimage to Lake Mansarovar at the base of revered Mount Kailas report that the lake level is low and the spirits are unhappy. Their prophecies indicate difficult times ahead unless we humans take better care of our planetary home. Some indigenous visionaries say they hear the earth crying. Contemporary Australian aboriginal elder Bill Neidjie speaks of feeling the earth's pain:

I feel it with my body,
with my blood.
Feeling all these trees,
all this country ...
If you feel sore ...
headache, sore body
that mean somebody killing tree or grass.
You feel because your body in that tree or earth. ...
You might feel it for two or three years.
You get weak ...
little bit, little bit ...
because tree going bit by bit ...
dying.[16]

The earth abounds with living presences, in traditional worldviews. Rocks, bodies of water, and mountains—considered inanimate by other peoples—are personified as living beings. Before one can successfully climb a mountain, one must ask its permission. Visionaries can see the spirits of a body of water, and many traditional cultures have recognized certain groves of trees as places where spirits live, and where

An indigenous earthwork in Ohio, representing a snake and an egg, symbols of fertility and transformation. The spiral in the snake's tail may be an appreciative symbol of the life force and wisdom inherent in the earth.

spiritual specialists can communicate with them. As a Pit River Indian explained, "Everything is alive. That's what we Indians believe."[17] Australian aboriginal people see their local landscape in terms of the "everywhen" of the **Dreaming**, the primordial time when the ancestors appeared from beneath the surface of the earth, investing the environment with their own presence and establishing the law.

All creatures may be perceived as kin, endowed with consciousness and the power of the Great Spirit. Many native peoples have been raised with an "ecological" perspective: they know that all things depend on each other. They are taught that they have a reciprocal, rather than dominating, relationship with all beings. Hawaiian *kahuna* (shaman-priest) Kahu Kawai'i explains:

> *How you might feel toward a human being that you love is how you might feel toward a dry leaf on the ground and how you might feel toward the rain in the forest and the wind. There is such intimacy that goes on that everything speaks to you and everything responds to how you are in being— almost like a mirror reflecting your feelings.*[18]

Even the dreams of indigenous peoples are often related to their particular environment and are understood as providing guidelines for proper ways to act.

Trees, animals, insects, and plants are all to be approached with caution and consideration. If one must cut down a tree or kill an animal, one must first explain one's intentions and ask forgiveness. Those who harm nature may themselves be harmed in return. Tribal peoples of Madhya Pradesh in central India will avoid killing a snake, for they feel that its partner would come after them to seek revenge. When a Buryat cuts a tree to build a house, he must first offer milk, butter, rice, and alcohol to the spirits of the forest and ask their forgiveness. In 1994, a half-French, half-Buryat businessman returned to Buryatia and started to build a guesthouse in a picturesque place that had long been considered sacred to the god Huushan-baabay. When the businessman began cutting trees, he was warned by the traditional people that he would not be successful. Nonetheless, he proceeded and finished the guesthouse. Three months later, it burned down.

Respect is always due to all creatures, in the indigenous worldview. The Yup'ik of southwestern Alaska know animals as thinking, feeling fellow beings. In fact, they may be even more sensitive and aware than humans. No one should handle the geese's eggs or goslings, lest the human smell should frighten the adults and they abandon the babies, to be eaten by predators. If humans treat animal populations carefully as guests, they will come back in plentiful numbers the following year to intentionally offer themselves to the hunters.

Many traditional peoples learn a sense of reverence for, and kinship with, the natural world, as suggested in this image from Botswana created by Elisabeth Sunday.

In the challenging environment of the Koyukon people of northern Canada, all interactions between humans and animals are conducted carefully according to a respectful moral code so that the animals will allow themselves to be caught. The animal spirits are very easily offended, not by animals' being killed but by disrespect shown to the animals or their remains. Killing must be done prayerfully and in a way that does not cause suffering to the animal; wounded animals must be found and put out of their misery. If displeased, the spirits can bring bad luck in the hunt for that species or perhaps illness or even death for the hunters. But if humans maintain good relationships with the animals, they will give themselves freely to the hunters and keep coming back year after year. It is the natural world that is dominant, not humans.

There are many stories of indigenous people's relationships with non-human creatures. Certain trees tell the healing specialists which herbs to use in curing the people. Australian aboriginal women are adept at forming hunting partnerships with dogs. Birds are thought to bring messages from the spirit world. A crow, a wild yak, and a pack of silver wolves revealed the sacred path to Mount Kailas in Tibet, revered as the center of the outer world and also of our inner world, the doorway through which other realms can most easily be reached. A Hopi elder said he spent three days and nights praying with a rattle-snake. "Of course he was nervous at first, but when I sang to him he recognized the warmth of my body and calmed down. We made good prayer together."[19]

Relationships with power

Another common theme is developing an appropriate relationship with spiritual energy.

> *All animals have power, because the Great Spirit dwells in all of them, even a tiny ant, a butterfly, a tree, a flower, a rock. The modern, white man's way keeps that power from us, dilutes it. To come to nature, feel its power, let it help you, one needs time and patience for that. . . . You have so little time for contemplation. . . . It lessens a person's life, all that grind, that hurrying and scurrying about.*
>
> *Lame Deer, Lakota nation[20]*

In certain places and beings, the power of spirit is believed to be highly concentrated. It is referred to as *mana* by the people of the Pacific islands. This is the vital force that makes it possible to act with unusual strength, insight, and effectiveness.

Tlakaelel, a contemporary spiritual leader of the descendants of the Toltecs of Mexico, describes how a person might experience this power when looking into an obsidian mirror traditionally made to concentrate power:

> *When you reach the point that you can concentrate with all your will, inside there, you reach a point where you feel ecstasy. It's a very beautiful thing, and everything is light. Everything is vibrating with very small signals, like waves of music, very smooth. Everything shines with a blue light. And you feel a sweetness. Everything is covered with the sweetness, and there is peace. It's a sensation like an orgasm, but it can last a long time.[21]*

Sacred sites may be recognized by the power that believers feel there. Some sacred sites have been used again and again by successive religions, either to capitalize on the energy or to co-opt the preceding religion. Chartres Cathedral in France, for instance, was built on an ancient ritual site. In New Zealand, the traditional Maori people know of the revivifying power of running water, such as waterfalls (now understood by scientists as places of negative ionization, which do indeed have an energizing effect). The Maori elders have told the public of the healing power of a certain waterfall on North Island; the area is dedicated to anyone who needs healing.

Because power can be built up through sacred practices, the ritual objects of spiritually developed persons may have concentrated power. Special stones and animal artifacts may also carry power. A person might be strengthened by the spiritual energy of the bear or the wolf by wearing sacred clothing made from its fur. Power can also come to one through visions or by being given a sacred pipe or the privilege of collecting objects into a personal sacred bundle.

In some cultures women are thought to have a certain natural power; men have to work harder for it. Women's power is considered mysterious, dangerous, uncontrolled. It is said to be strongest during their menstrual period. Women are secluded during their menstrual periods in many cultures, not necessarily because they are considered polluting; among the Yurok of northern California, houses have a separate back room for women who are menstruating so that they can concentrate on their inner selves, becoming inwardly stronger and purified by the flow of blood. In certain rituals in which both men and women participate,

At a remote shrine used by indigenous people in New Mexico, a ring of stones protects the sacred area where sun-bleached antlers and offerings have been placed around two stones naturally shaped like mountain lions.

women's menstrual blood is often thought to diminish or weaken the ritual or the men's spiritual power. In most Native American nations that have sweat lodge ceremonies for ritual purification, menstruating women are not allowed to enter the lodge. A few cultures, such as the Ainu of Japan, have prized menstrual blood as a potent offering returned to the earth.

Gaining power is both desirable and dangerous. If misused for personal ends, it becomes destructive and may turn against the person. To channel spiritual power properly, native people are taught that they must live within certain strict limits. Those who seek power or receive it unbidden are supposed to continually purify themselves of any selfish motives and dedicate their actions to the good of the whole.

Spiritual specialists

In a few of the remaining hunting and gathering tribes, religion is a relatively private matter. Each individual has direct access to the unseen. Although spirit is invisible, it is considered a part of the natural world. Anyone can interact with it spontaneously, without complex ceremony and without anyone else's aid.

More commonly, however, the world of spirit is thought to be dangerous. Although everyone is expected to observe certain personal ways of worship, such as offering prayers before taking plant or animal life, many ways of interacting with spirit are thought to be best left to those who are specially trained for the roles. These specialists are gradually initiated into the secret knowledge that allows them to act as intermediaries between the seen and the unseen. They sacrifice themselves through ritual purification, struggle, hardship, and protocol in order to remain in proper relationship with the spirits.

Storytellers and other sacred roles

Specialists' roles vary from one group to another, and the same person may play several of these roles. One common role is that of storyteller. Because the traditions are oral rather than written, these people must memorize long and complex stories and songs so that the group's sacred traditions can be remembered and taught, generation after generation. The orally transmitted epics of the indigenous Ainu of Japan are up to 10,000 "lines" long. Chants of the Yoruba *orisa* comprise 256 "volumes" of 800 long verses each.

These Yoruban chants about the *orisa* include an explanation of the genesis of the earth, with its center in what is now the Nigerian city of Ife. When time began, where the earth now exists there was only a vast watery area, with a dim and misty atmosphere, the domain of Olokun. The other *orisa* lived in an upper world of light until Obatala decided to go down to see if some solid land could be created so that the *orisa* could inhabit the earth. He had a sacred chain of gold made for his descent, and carried a shell of sand, a white hen, a palm nut, and a black cat. He climbed down to the watery world by means of the chain, but it was too short. Thus he poured the sand downward and then released the hen, who by scratching in the sand created the contours of the earth. Obatala settled on the land and planted his palm nut, which flourished and sent its seed far and wide,

A storyteller of the Kung people of Botswana, Africa, entertains an audience while passing on the oral teachings of the distant past.

developing the plant life of the earth At first he was alone, with only the black cat as his companion, but as the story continues, many things happen, accounting for the features of the earth and its inhabitants as we know them today. The golden chain is a common mythological symbol of a World Axis connecting heaven and earth; the palm tree also commonly appears in myths of the World Tree, giver and protector of the first forms of life on earth.

Such stories are important clues to understanding the universe and one's place in it. What is held only in memory cannot be physically destroyed, but if a tribe is small and all its storytellers die, the knowledge is lost. This happened on a large scale during contacts with colonial powers, as native people were killed by war and imported diseases. Professor Wande Abimbola, who is trying to preserve the oral tradition of the Yoruba, has made thousands of tapes of the chants, but there must also be people who can understand and interpret their meaning.

There are also bards who carry the energy of ancient traditions into new forms. Rather than memory, they cultivate the muse. In Africa, poets are considered "technicians of the sacred," conversing with a dangerous world of spirits. Players of the "talking drums" are highly valued as communicators with the spirits, ancestors, and Supreme Being. As the Akan of Ghana say:

The thumb, finger with mouth, wake up and speak!
The thumb armed with sticks for drumming

Is more loquacious and more eloquent
Than a human being sleeping;
Wake up and come![22]

Drumming creates a rhythmic environment in which the people can draw close to the unseen powers. By counterposing basic and complex cross-rhythmic patterns with a "return beat," Yoruba drummers create a tension that draws listeners into the unfilled spaces between the beats.

"Tricksters" such as foxes often appear in the stories of indigenous traditions. They are paradoxical, transformative beings. Similarly, sacred clowns may endure the shame of behaving as fools during public rituals in order to teach the people through humor. Often they poke fun at the most sacred of rituals, keeping the people from taking themselves too seriously. A sacred fool, called **heyoka** by the Lakota, must be both innocent and very wise about human nature, and must have a visionary relationship with spirit as well.

> *Life is holiness and everyday humdrum, sadness and laughter, the mind and the belly all mixed together. The Great Spirit doesn't want us to sort them out neatly.*
> Leonard Crow Dog, Lakota medicine man[23]

Another coveted role is that of being a member of a secret society in which one can participate by initiation or invitation only, whether to enhance one's prestige or to draw closer to the spirit world. When serving in ceremonial capacities, members often wear special costumes to hide their human identities and help them take on the personas of spirits they are representing. In African religions, members of secret societies periodically appear as impersonators of animal spirits or of dead ancestors, demonstrating that the dead are still watching the living and protecting the village. The all-male Oro secret society in some Yoruba tribes uses this authority to enforce male domination; when Oro appears, "roaring" by swinging a piece of wood on a cord, women stay inside their huts.

Women also have their secret societies, whose activities are yet little known by outsiders. Among aboriginal peoples of Australia, the men's and women's groups initiate members into separate but interrelated roles for males and females. For instance, when boys are separated from the tribe for circumcision by the men's secret society, the women's secret society has its own separation rituals and may stage mock ritual fights with the men's society. Men's and women's rituals ultimately refer to the eternal **Dream Time**, in which there is no male–female differentiation.

Sacred dancers likewise make the unseen powers visible. Body movements are a language in themselves expressing the nature of the cosmos, a language that is understood through the stories and experiences of the community. Such actions keep the world of the ancestors alive for succeeding generations.

In some socially stratified societies there are also priests and priestesses. These are specially trained and dedicated people who carry out the rituals that ensure proper functioning of the natural world, and perhaps also communicate with particular spirits or deities. Though West African priests or priestesses may have part-time earthly occupations, they are expected to stay in a state of ritual purity and spend much of their time in communication with the spirit being, paying homage and asking for guidance. In West Africa, there are also mediums associated with the temples; they enter a state of trance or allow themselves to be possessed by gods or spirits in order to bring messages to the people.

Mystical intermediaries

There is another distinctive type of spiritual specialist found among many indigenous peoples. They are called by many names, but the Siberian and Saami word **"shaman"** is used as a generic term by scholars for those who offer themselves as mystical intermediaries between the physical and the non-physical world for specific purposes, such as healing. Archaeological research has confirmed that shamanic methods are extremely ancient—at least 20,000 to 30,000 years old. Shamanic ways are remarkably similar around the globe.

These mystical intermediaries may be helpers to society, using their skills to benefit others. They are not to be confused with sorcerers, who practice black magic to harm others or promote their own selfish ends, interfering with the cosmic order. Spiritual power is neutral; its use depends on the practitioner. What Native Americans call **"medicine** power" does not originate in the medicine person. Black Elk explains:

Of course it was not I who cured. It was the power from the outer world, and the visions and ceremonies had only made me like a hole through which the power could come to the two-leggeds. If I thought that I was doing it myself, the hole would close up and no power could come through.[24]

There are many kinds of medicine. One is the ability to heal physical, psychological, and spiritual problems. Techniques used include physical approaches to illness, such as therapeutic herbs, sweatbathing, massage, cauterization, and sucking out of toxins. But the treatments are given to the whole person—body, mind, and spirit, with emphasis on healing relationships within the group—so there may also be divination, prayer, chanting, and ceremonies in which group power is built up and spirit helpers are called in. If an intrusion of harmful power, such as the angry energy of another person, seems to be causing the problem, the medicine person may attempt to suck it out with the aid of spirit helpers and then dry vomit the invisible intrusion into a receptacle.

These healing methods, once dismissed, are now beginning to earn respect from the scientific medical establishment. Medicine people are permitted to attend indigenous patients in some hospitals, and in the United States, the National Institute of Mental Health has paid Navajo medicine men to teach young Indians the ceremonies that have often been more effective in curing the mental health problems of Navajos than has Western psychiatry.

In addition to healing, certain mystical intermediaries are thought to have gifts such as being able to talk with plants and animals, control the weather, see and communicate with the spirit world, and prophesy. A gift highly developed in Africa is that of divination, using techniques such as reading patterns revealed by a casting of cowrie shells. According to Mado Somé of the Dagara:

Divination is a way of accessing information that is happening now, but not right where you live. ... The cowrie shells work like an intermediary between us and the other world. Divination is actually the inscription of information on those physical

Black Elk, visionary and healer.

Above left *Traditional diviners of Mali rake sand and leave it overnight. The tracks of animals which run over it are interpreted the next day for information the client seeks.*

Above right *Mexican* curandera *(healer) Maria Sabina has eaten hallucinogenic mushrooms to enter an ecstatic state. She chants, "I am a doctor woman ... I am the morning star woman ... I am the moon woman ... I am the heaven woman ... they say it is like softness there."*

things, allowing the shaman—whose eyes have been modified through the course of her various medicine journeys—to be able to read and interpret them.[25]

Mystical intermediaries are contemplatives, Lame Deer explains:

> *The* wicasa wakan *[holy man] wants to be by himself. He wants to be away from the crowd, from everyday matters. He likes to meditate, leaning against a tree or rock, feeling the earth move beneath him, feeling the weight of that big flaming sky upon him. That way he can figure things out. Closing his eyes, he sees many things clearly. What you see with your eyes shut is what counts. . . . He listens to the voices of the* wama kaskan—*all those who move upon the earth, the animals. He is as one with them. From all living beings something flows into him all the time, and something flows from him.*[26]

The role of shaman may be hereditary or it may be recognized as a special gift. Either way, training is rigorous. In order to work in a mystical state of ecstasy, moving between ordinary and non-ordinary realities, shamans must experience physical death and rebirth. Some have spontaneous near-death experiences. Uvavnuk, an Inuit shaman, was spiritually initiated when she was struck by a lightning ball. After she revived, she had great power, which she dedicated to serving her people.

Other potential mystical intermediaries undergo rituals of purification, isolation, and bodily torment until they make contact with the spirit world. Igjugarjuk from northern Hudson Bay chose to suffer from cold, starvation, and thirst for a month in a tiny snow hut in order to draw the attention of Pinga, a helping female spirit:

> *My novitiate took place in the middle of the coldest winter, and I, who never got anything to warm me, and must not move, was very cold, and it was so tiring having to sit without daring to lie down, that sometimes it was as if I died a little.*

Living Indigenous Sacred Ways

One of the remaining traditional shamans of Buryatia, Nadezhda Ananyevna Stepanova comes from a family of very powerful shamans. Her mother tried to prevent her from becoming a shaman. Buddhist **lamas** had spread the impression that shamans were to be avoided, saying that they were ignorant, primitive servants of dark, lower spirits. The reputation of shamans has also been recently damaged by pseudo-shamans—some of whom have certain extrasensory powers and others of whom are simply cheats. But when a shaman receives a true spiritual call, to deny that pull is dangerous. Nadezhda explains:

"As a child I knew when I would fall ill, and I could repeat by heart anything the teacher said or anything I read in a book, but I thought that was normal. When I was twenty-six, I was told I would be a shaman, a great shaman. When I told Mother, she said, 'No, you won't.' She took a bottle, went to her native town, and then came back. 'Everything will be taken away; you won't become a shaman,' she said. I didn't understand. The year I was said to become a shaman, I became seriously ill, and Mother was paralyzed. Usually paralyzed people have high blood pressure, but hers was normal. The doctors were surprised, but I understood then: We were both badly ill because she went against the gods.

"Nobody could heal me. Then one seer said, 'You must cure.' I replied, 'I don't know anything about curing.' But a voice inside me said, 'If you don't become a shaman, you will die. You will be overrun by a lorry with a blue number.' I began to collect materials about medicine, about old rites. Then I could do a lot, for all we need is seeing and feeling. I was initiated by the men shaman of all the families, each praying to his god in a definite direction, for every god has his direction. I sat in the middle. Every shaman asked his gods to help me, to protect me, to give me power. The ritual was in early March. It was very frosty and windy, and I was only lightly dressed, but I wasn't cold at all. The wind didn't touch me. I sat motionless for about four hours, but I was not cold.

"I began to cure. It is very difficult. You go through pain, through the tears of children and adults. I am able to see whether I will be able to cure a specific person. The main thing to me is to help a person if I can. I pray to my gods, ask them for mercy, I ask them to pay attention, to help. I feel the pain of those who come to me, and I want to relieve it. I have *yodo*—bark from a fir tree scratched by a bear; its smoke purifies. I perform rituals of bringing back the soul; often they work. My ancestors are very close to me; I see them as well as I see you.

"Last year in the island Olkhon in Lake Baikal, there was a great gathering of shamans from Tchita, Irkutsk, Ulan-Ude, Yakutiya, and Buryatia to pray to the great spirits of Baikal about the well-being and prosperity of the Buryat land. For a long time these spirits were not turned to. They were forgotten by the people, and they fell asleep. They could not take an active part in the life of people; they could not help them any more. *Teylagan*, the prayer of the shamans for the whole Buryatia, was to awaken the great spirits.

"It was a clear, clear sunny day, without a cloud. When the prayer began, it started to rain. It was a very good sign. There had been a long drought before. The Olkhon shamans had tried to call rain, but they couldn't. But when everyone gathered and three sheep were sacrificed, then they could, and the shamans of that district were grateful.

"We had always prayed to thirteen northern *nainkhats*, the great spirits of this area. But when the Buddhists came, persecution began, and people prayed secretly, only for their families. They could not pray for the whole Buryat nation, and they did not. They forgot. Shamans were killed. Then the atheistic Soviet regime tried to make us forget the faith, and we forgot. The most terrible thing about them was that they wanted to make people forget everything, to live by the moment and forget their roots. And what is man without roots? Nothing. It is a loss of everything. That is why now nobody has compassion for anybody. Now we are reaping the fruit: robbery, drinking, drugs. This is our disaster. That is why we must pray to our own gods.

"When we had the *teylagan*, on the first day three blue pillars rose from earth to the sky—it was a prayer to Ehon-Bahve, the head spirit of Baikal, and to all three gods. The second day we prayed to the bird-god, and there were very many birds flying and a rainbow in the sky."[27]

Only towards the end of the thirty days did a helping spirit come to me, a lovely and beautiful helping spirit, whom I had never thought of; it was a white woman; she came to me whilst I had collapsed, exhausted, and was sleeping. But still I saw her lifelike, hovering over me, and from that day I could not close my eyes or dream without seeing her. . . . She came to me from Pinga and was a sign that Pinga had now noticed me and would give me powers that would make me a shaman.[28]

For many mystical intermediaries, initiation into the role is not a matter of their own choice. The spirit enters whom it will. Tsering, an aged Nepali *dhami* (shaman), relates,

We never wanted to become dhamis. *In fact, we tried hard to get the gods to leave us. We pleaded, performed worship ceremonies, even carried manure around with us to offend them, but nothing seemed to work. When calamities began to hit my family—when my brother died falling off the roof and our best horse drowned in the river—I realized I had no choice and had to make the initiatory journey to Kailas.[29]*

Ichurek is a famous shaman from Tuva Republic, Russia. She has been a healer and visionary since childhood, but people originally thought she was mad.

Once there, the new *dhamis* had to plunge naked with unbound hair into the freezing Lake Mansarovar in order to commune with the spirits. Then, on returning to their village, the deities who had possessed them insisted that they prove their spiritual connection by terrible feats, such as drinking boiling oil. Thereafter, those *dhamis* were respected as authorities.

In addition to becoming familiar with death, a potential mystical intermediary must undergo lengthy training in spiritual techniques, the names and roles of the spirits, and secrets and myths of the tribe. Novices are taught both by older shamans and reportedly by the spirits themselves. If the spirits do not accept and teach the shaman, he or she is unable to carry the role.

The helping spirits that contact would-be mystical intermediaries during the death-and-rebirth crisis become essential partners in their sacred work. Often it is a spirit animal who becomes the shaman's guardian spirit, giving him or her special powers. The shaman may even take on the persona of the animal while working. Many tribes feel that healing specialists need the powers of the bear; Lapp shamans metamorphosed into wolves, reindeer, bears, or fish.

Not only do mystical intermediaries possess a power animal as an alter-ego, they also have the ability to enter parallel, spiritual realities at will in order to bring back knowledge, power, or help for those who need it. An altered state of consciousness is needed. Techniques for entering this state are the same around the world: drumming, rattling, singing, dancing, and in some cases hallucinogenic drugs. The effect of these influences is to open what the Huichol shamans of Mexico call the *narieka*—the doorway of the heart, the channel for divine power, the point where human and spirit worlds meet. It is often experienced and represented artistically as a pattern of concentric circles.

The "journey" then experienced by mystical intermediaries is typically into the Upperworld or the Lowerworld. To enter the latter, they descend mentally through an actual hole in the ground, such as a spring, hollow tree, cave, animal burrow, or special ceremonial hole regarded as a navel of the earth. These entrances typically lead into tunnels that, if followed, open into bright landscapes. Reports of such experiences include not only what the journeyer saw but also realistic physical sensations, such as how the walls of the tunnel felt during the descent.

The shaman enters into the Lowerworld landscape, encounters beings there, and may bring something back if it is needed by the client. This may be a lost guardian spirit or a lost soul, brought back to revive a person in a coma. The mystical intermediary may be temporarily possessed by the spirit of departed relatives so that an afflicted patient may finally clear up unresolved tensions with them that are seen as causing illness. Often a river must be crossed as the boundary between the world of the living and the world of the dead. A kindly old man or women may appear to assist this passage through the underworld. In cultures that have subdued the indigenous ways, this mystical process is retained only in myths, such as the Orpheus story.

Group observances

Indigenous ways are community-centered. Through group rituals, traditional people not only honor the sacred but also affirm their bonds with each other and all of creation. Humans can help to maintain the harmony of the universe by their ritual observances.

In order to maintain the natural balance and to ensure success in the hunt or harvest, ceremonies must be performed with exactitude. For instance, there is a specific time for the telling of specific stories. Chona, a Tohono O'odham (Papago) medicine woman, told anthropologist Ruth Underhill:

> I should not have told you this [the origin of Coyote, who helped to put the world in order, with a few mistakes]. These things about the Beginning are holy. They should not be told in the hot time when the snakes are out. The snakes guard our secrets. If we tell what is forbidden, they bite.[30]

Rituals often take people out of everyday consciousness and into awareness of the presence of the sacred. According to the Tsalagi (Cherokee) priestess Dhyani Ywahoo, paying attention to the proper forms brings clarity of attention and creates a sacred space in which many things can happen:

> What's important about ritual is that it has a beginning. And before that beginning there has been a preparation, so that people's bodies and minds are brought to a certain level of vibrancy.[31]

In such altered states, participants may experience a heightened group consciousness that powerfully binds individuals together as a community.

Each group has its own ways of ritual dedication to the spirits of life, but they tend to follow certain patterns everywhere. Some honor major points in the human life cycle, such as birth, naming, puberty, marriage, and death. These rites of passage assist people in the transition from one state to another and help them become aware of their meaningful contribution to life. When a Hopi baby is twenty days old, it is presented at dawn to the rays of Father Sun for the first time and officially given a name. Its face is ritually cleansed with sacred cornmeal, a ceremony that will be repeated at death for the journey to the Underworld.

Girls commonly go through a special ceremony marking their first menstruation, which signals the end of childhood and preparation for becoming wives and mothers. For both boys and girls, the rituals of reaching puberty typically involve separation from the community, a transition phase in which they are secluded with no clear identity and prepared for adulthood, and then a third phase in which they are re-incorporated into the community with a new adult identity. Girls in traditional Lakota households spend the transition time in practicing such useful skills as stitching and cooking. Madonna Swan reports that she was secluded in part of her grandmother's cabin for her first moon ceremony, and that each day her grandmother would coach her in domestic skills and ethical principles. Her grandmother and mother daily bathed her in water with purifying sage and green cedar, and prayed for her in this fashion:

> *Grandfathers above and in the four directions, make Madonna a good woman. Help her to treat guests with hospitality. Grandfathers, help her to be a good worker. Grandfathers, and Maka Ina (Mother Earth), help Madonna to be a good mother. I pray that the food she cooks in her life will be good for those that eat it. Grandfathers, help her to be a good wife and live with the same man all her life. Grandfathers, bless her with healthy children.*[32]

There are also collective rituals to support the group's survival strategies. In farming communities these include ways of asking for rain, of insuring the growth of crops, and of giving thanks for the harvest. In the Great Drought of 1988, Sioux holy man Leonard Crow Dog was asked by three non-native Midwestern communities to perform rainmaking ceremonies for them, thus honoring the power of the traditional medicine ways. Cherokee Dhyani Ywahoo explains, "When Native American people sing for the rain, the rain comes—because those singers have made a decision that they and the water and the air and the Earth are one."[33]

Ritual dramas about the beginnings and sacred history of the people engage performers and spectators on an emotional level through the use of special costumes, body paint, music, masks, and perhaps sacred locations. These dramas provide a sense of orderly interface among humans, the land, and the spiritual world. They also dramatize mysticism, drawing the people toward direct contact with the spirit world. Those who have sacred visions and dreams are supposed to share them with others, and often this is done through dramatization.

According to legend, the Plains Indians were given the sacred pipe by White Buffalo Calf Woman as a tool for communicating with the mysteries and understanding the ways of life. The bowl of the pipe represents the female aspect of the Great Spirit, the stem the male aspect. When they are ritually joined, the power of the spirit is thought to be present as the pipe is passed around the circle for collective communion with each other and with the divine.

Groups also gather for ritual purification and spiritual renewal of individuals. Indigenous peoples of the Americas "smudge" sites and possessions, cleansing them with smoke from special herbs, such as sage and sweetgrass. Many groups make an igloo-shaped "sweat lodge" into which hot stones are carried. People huddle together in the dark around the stone pit. When water is poured on the stones, intensely hot steam sears bodies and lungs. Everyone prays earnestly. Leonard Crow Dog says of the *inipi* (sweat lodge):

> The inipi *is probably our oldest ceremony because it is built around the simplest, basic, life-giving things: the fire that comes from the sun, warmth without which there can be no life;* inyan wakan, *or* tunka, *the rock that was there when the earth began, that will still be there at the end of time; the earth, the mother womb; the water that all creatures need; our green brother, the sage; and encircled by all these, man, basic man, naked as he was born, feeling the weight, the spirit of endless generations before him, feeling himself part of the earth, nature's child, not her master.*[34]

Pilgrimages to sacred sites are often communal. Buryats gather on top of Erde, the mountain where the spirit of the earth lives, and all join hands to encircle it; a great energy is said to appear in the huge circle. The Huichol Indians of the mountains of western Mexico make a yearly journey to a desert they call Wirikuta, the Sacred Land of the Sun. They feel that creation began in this place. And like their ancestors, they gather their yearly supply of peyote cactus at this sacred site. Peyote has the power to alter consciousness: it is their "little deer," a spirit who helps them to communicate with the spirit world.

When indigenous groups are broken up by external forces, they lose the cohesive power of these group rituals. Africans taken to the New World as slaves lost not only their own individual identity but also their membership in tight-knit

Below left To the Efe Pygmies of the Ituri rainforest, the Great Spirit is embodied in the forest itself, a benevolent presence that is both Mother and Father. Pygmy men perform a dance of gratitude to the forest for the animal food it provides.
Below right In West Africa, the gods and the spirits of the dead appear to the living in masquerade. The mysteries of spirit are made semi-visible by costumed initiates.

This altar in the home of a Mexican healer illustrates the blending of indigenous ways with those of later religions. The serpent, masks, vegetables, eggs, and "bird's nest" derive from indigenous sacred ways, but are juxtaposed with Christian symbols.

groups. In an attempt to re-establish a communal sense of shared spiritual traditions among African-Americans, Professor Maulana Ron Karenga created a contemporary celebration, Kwanzaa, based on indigenous African "first fruits" harvest festivals. Using symbolic objects to help create a special atmosphere (such as candles, corn, fruits and vegetables, and a "unity cup," all called by their Swahili names), families and groups of families meet from December 26 to January 1 to explore their growth over the past year. They look at their own experiences of the "seven principles"—unity, self-determination, collective work, family-centeredness, purpose, creativity with limited resources, and confidence—and reward each other for progress by giving gifts.

Individual observances

In indigenous sacred ways, it is considered important for each person to experience a personal connection with the spirits. The people acknowledge and work with the spirits in many everyday ways. For instance, when searching for herbs, a person is not to take the first plant found; an offering is made to it, with the prayer that its relatives will understand one's needs. Guardian spirits and visions are sought by all the people, not just mystical specialists. The shaman may have more spirit helpers and more power, but visionary experiences and opportunities for worship are available to all. Indigenous traditions have therefore been called "democratized shamanism."

Temples to the spirits may exist, but one can also worship them anywhere. Wande Abimbola observes:

Big temples aren't necessary to worship the orisa, *even though there are temples for most* orisa *in Africa. If you are a devotee of Ifa, you can carry the objects of Ifa in your pocket. If you want to make an offering to Ogun, put any piece of iron on the floor and make an offering to it. It's just like a Christian would carry a Bible or maybe a cross.*[35]

To open themselves for contact with the spirit world, individuals in many indigenous cultures undergo a **vision quest**. After ritual purification, they are sent alone to a sacred spot to cry to the spirits to help them in their journey.

Pre-puberty or the onset of puberty is commonly thought to be the best time for vision quests, for children are closest to the spirit world. Among the Dene Tha, children are informally encouraged to go out to the bush before the age of puberty and spend time alone, seeking a spirit helper. Intimate knowledge of the animal spirit is considered essential for a Dene Tha who helps others:

When you are young, you go alone in the bush and you stay there and an animal comes to you. He talks to you just like we do now [sitting next to each other], and he tells you about him and with his power he gives you his power to heal other people. With it you heal people. If it tells you all how he is from beginning to end, you help someone, you cure him. If he does not tell everything, and you do not know all about him, then, when you help someone, you cure him, but you get the sickness.[36]

Adults may also make vision quests before undertaking a sacred mission, such as the sun dance. Indigenous Mexican leader Tlakaelel describes the vision quest as he observes it:

You stay on a mountain, desert, or in a cave, isolated, naked, with only your sacred things, the things that you have gained, in the years of preparation—your eagle feathers, your pipe, your copal *[tree bark used as incense]. You are left alone four days and four nights without food and water. During this time when you are looking for your vision, many things happen. You see things move. You see animals that come close to you. Sometimes you might see someone that you care about a lot, and they're bringing water. You feel like you're dying of thirst, but there are limits around you, protection with hundreds of tobacco ties. You do not leave this circle, and this vision will disappear when they come to offer the water or sometimes they will just drop it on the ground. Or someone comes and helps you with their strength and gives you messages.*[37]

One is not supposed to ask for a vision for selfish personal reasons. The point of this individual ordeal, which is designed to be physically and emotionally stressful, is to ask how one can help the people and the planet.

Contemporary issues

Sadly, traditional spiritual wisdom has been largely obliterated in many parts of the world by those who wanted to take the people's lands or save their souls with some other path to the divine. Under the slogan "Kill the Indian and save the man," the American founder of the boarding school system for native children took them away from their families at a young age and transformed their cultural identity, presenting the native ways as inferior and distancing them from normal participation in the traditional sacred life. They were exposed to the "modern" worldview,

The Sun Dance Way of Self-Sacrifice

Sacrificing oneself for the sake of the whole is highly valued in most indigenous traditions. Through purification ceremonies, the people attempt to break through their small selves in order to serve as clear vehicles for the energy of the Great Spirit. In the Americas a powerful ceremony for these purposes is the sun dance. Among the Oglala Lakota, participants may dance for four days without food or water, looking at the sun and praying for blessings for the people. They say the ceremony as they practice it was first given to them through a vision received by a man named Kablaya.

In diverse forms, sun dances are now performed at many sites each spring and summer, most of them on the midwestern and northern plains of North America. In theory, only those who have had visions that they should perform the dance should do so. Some come in penance, for purification; others offer themselves as vehicles to request blessings for all people or for specific people who need help. It is not considered proper to dance for one's own needs.

Dancers make a commitment to do the dance for a certain number of times. Some sun dances include women dancers; some who dance are children. Non-indigenous people are generally barred from dancing.

The power of the sun dance requires that everything be handled in a sacred way. Dancers must do vision quests and purify themselves in sweat lodges before the ceremony begins. In spite of thirst and exhaustion, those in some sun dances continue to participate in sweat lodges each day of the dance. A tree is chosen to be placed at the center of the circle (among the Lakota, it is always a cottonwood, which when cut crosswise reveals a multi-pointed star pattern representing the sun). The tree's sacrifice is attended with ritual prayers. Participants may string prayer flags onto its branches before it is hoisted in the center of the dancing circle.

Sun Dance Tree at the center of an area prepared for the sun dance in Mexico. Cloth strips tied to it carry prayers for the people.

During the dance itself, the participants are guided through patterns with symbolic meanings. The choreography varies from one group to another. The Sioux sun dancers do not move around the circle except to shift slightly during the day so that they are always facing the sun. In Mexico the patterns continually honor the powers of the four directions by facing each one in turn.

As they dance, the dancers blow whistles traditionally made from the wing bones of the spotted eagle, but now often whittled from hollow sticks. When giving instructions for the dance, Kablaya reportedly explained, "When you blow the whistle always remember that it is the voice of the Spotted Eagle; our Grandfather, Wakan Tanka, always hears this, for you see it is really His own voice."[38]

A group of people support the dancers by singing special sacred songs and beating a large drum. If their energy flags, so does that of the dancers. A woman sun dancer* says that after a while, "The drum is no longer outside of you. It is as if in you and you don't even know that you're dancing." The dancers also support each other in ways such as using the feathers they carry to fan those whose energy seems low. There may also be communal vision ceremonies.

Each dancer is the carrier of a sacred pipe. Between rounds, these may be shared with group onlookers who are led into the circle and who pass the pipes around among the dancers to strengthen them with the power of the smoke.

Non-dancers may also be led into the circle for a special healing round on the third or fourth day. By that time, the dancers have been so purified and empowered that they can all act as healers, using their eagle feathers as instruments to convey the divine power.

The suffering that each dancer willingly undergoes is heightened during piercing. For those whose visions suggest it—and whose tribes use piercing, for some do not—at some point during the dance incisions are made in the skin of their chest, back, or arms and sharpened sticks are inserted. There are then various ways of tearing through the skin. One reserved for chiefs is to drag buffalo skulls from ropes attached to the piercing sticks, symbolizing their carrying of the burdens of the people. More often, ropes are thrown over the trees and attached to the piercing sticks. Each person who pierces is then pulled upward, "flying" by flapping eagle wings, until the sticks break through the skin. It is thought that the more one asks when making the sacrifice the more difficult it will be to break free. One Lakota dancer was instructed in a vision that he should be hung from the tree for a whole night. They had to pierce him in many places in order to distribute his weight, and then pull him down in the morning.

Why must the dance involve so much suffering? A Lakota sun dancer explains, "Nobody knows why, but suffering makes our prayers more sincere. The sun dance tests your sincerity, pushes your spirit beyond its limits." And as the dance goes on, many of the dancers transcend their physical agony and experience an increasing sense of euphoria. A Mexican dancer explains:

> It's not pain. It's ecstasy. We get the energy from the sun and from the contact with Mother Earth. You also feel the energy of the eagles [who often fly overhead], all the animals, all the plants that surround you, all the vegetation. That energy comes to sustain you for the lack of food and water. Also when you smoke the pipe it serves as food or energy; the smoke feeds you energy so that you can continue. And every so often we put our palms to the sun to receive the energy from the sun. You can feel it in your whole body, a complete bath of energy.

*Names of individual dancers interviewed are not given here, to preserve their privacy and the sacredness of the dance.

which does not believe in miracles, supernatural healings, or divine intervention—thus contradicting thousands of years of received wisdom in their own tradition.

Native Americans who converted to Christianity have sometimes been missionaries themselves, helping to spread Christian devotion among indigenous peoples. Sometimes Natives converted to try to appease the dominant non-Natives, but sometimes it was the personal example of these missionaries that caused Native Americans to embrace the "White Man's Faith," even though it was the religion of those who were oppressing them. A young nineteenth-century Choctaw Christian named Kanchi, for example, drowned while trying to save teenagers whose raft swamped as the Choctaw tribe crossed the swollen and turbulent Mississippi River under forcible removal from their ancestral lands. So touched were they by his sacrifice that the tribe members began reading his Bible in his memory and eventually formed a new Christian community in what is now Oklahoma. Indigenous spirituality has become so mixed with Christianity, often in the service of racism and colonialism, that many Native American Christians are now trying to re-examine their religious lives and identities honestly. Marie Therese Archambault asserts:

> When we read the Gospel, we must read it as Native people, for this is who we are. We can no longer try to be what we think the dominant society wants us to be. … We just learn to subtract the chauvinism and cultural superiority with which this Gospel was often presented to our people. We have to go beyond the white gospel in order to perceive its truth.[39]

A similar policy of attempted acculturation was conducted between the 1880s and 1960s with Australian aboriginal children. Taken away from their parents by force, the "stolen generation" were often abused or used as slaves. Five children of Eliza Saunders were taken away by social workers while she and her husband were looking for employment. She recalls, "You walk miles and miles and find they're not there. It's like your child has been killed." One of her children, the Green Party politician Charmaine Clarke, managed to run away from foster care after eleven years and rejoin her mother, but she says of her missing family history, "When myself and my brothers and sisters go home, we five have to sit there quite mute and just listen, observe. Because we were never there."[40] In 1998, Australian citizens attempted to apologize for this "attempted genocide," with some 300,000 signatures in Sorry Books and hundreds of emotional multi-racial ceremonies in churches, schools, and cities across Australia.

In Mexico, decades of rebellion of indigenous people against central rule and cultural suppression seemed to be turning a corner in 2001, when a caravan of rebel leaders from the south was welcomed by tens of thousands as they entered Mexico City to request political autonomy for the 10 million indigenous people of Mexico. Chiapas rebel leader Subcommander Marcos declared, "It is the hour of the Indian people, of the people of the color of the earth. What they fear is that there is no more 'you' and 'us,' because we are all the color of the earth."[41] However, a proposed indigenous rights bill which would have brought considerable autonomy for indigenous people in Mexico was altered to the extent that they may now have even fewer legal rights than before.

In Africa, despite changing social contexts, traditional religion is still strong among some groups, such as the Yoruba, whose priest-diviners are still respected, and to whom the *orisa* contacted in trance still reveal the nearness and importance of the invisible forces. However, in contemporary urban African areas, the traditional interest in the flow of the past into the present, with value placed on the intensity of present experience, has been rapidly replaced by a Westernized view of time, in which one is perpetually anxious about the future. This shift has led to severe psychological disorientation and social and political instability. Those whose spiritual cultures have been merged with world religions such as Islam, Buddhism, or Christianity are now examining the relationship of their earlier tradition to the intercultural missionary traditions. African scholars have noted, for instance, that to put God in the forefront, as Christians do, does violence to the greater social importance of ancestor spirits in African traditional religions.

Indigenous peoples have also been recent victims of disastrous development projects. In Zimbabwe, thousands of traditional self-sufficient Vaduma people were displaced when their ancestral lands were flooded to create a huge artificial lake for irrigating an area hundreds of kilometers away. Jameson Kurasha of the University of Zimbabwe describes the effects on the Vaduma:

> When the "idea" of development was imposed on them, families were separated by a massive stretch of water. Now the Murinye Mugabe families are alienated from each other. They are now peoples without a tangible past to guide and unite them because their past (i.e. ancestors) are either buried or washed away by the lake. They are basically a people without a home to point to. The separation has left a cultural damage that will never be restored.[42]

In the United States, reservations on which thousands of Navajos and Hopis were living were found to be sitting on the largest coal deposit in the country—the 4000-square-mile "Black Mesa." In 1966, the Navajo and Hopi tribal councils signed agreements allowing Black Mesa to be strip-mined by utility companies to provide electricity for southwestern cities, and presumably, economic development for the tribes. Since then, the sacred land has been devastated, ancient archaeological sites have been destroyed, thousands of Navajos have been displaced, and aquifers are drying up as 1.3 billion gallons of pure water per year have been used to pump the coal slurry to a power plant hundreds of miles away. It is now apparent that the government-established tribal councils—themselves not considered genuine representatives of the tribal peoples—were being advised by an attorney who was secretly employed by the coal company. The Black Mesa Trust is pressing for legal action that would pose limits on future damage to the area and curb pressure tactics being used against the indigenous people. Cherokee attorney Jace Weaver points out that there are difficulties in protecting the rights of indigenous people on religious grounds because the legal definition of "religion" is limited. He writes, "Lacking a concept of the holy, our legal system finally is incapable of comprehending Native religious freedom and land claims."[43]

Modern development schemes—as well as outright plunder of natural resources for profit—are being called into question by land-based traditional peoples around the world, and attempts have begun to revive the ancient wisdom by acknowledging its validity. In India, officials in the Ministry of Environment and Forests are now acknowledging that the remaining sacred groves of the indigenous people are treasure-houses of biodiversity and should not be destroyed. In such areas, it is often the shamans who teach the tribal people the importance of protecting the trees and vegetation.

Winona LaDuke

As the narrator of Winona LaDuke's semi-fictional novel, *Last Standing Woman*, puts it, her clanspeople have a special destiny:

In times past, they were warriors, the ogichidaa, *those who defended the people. Sometimes we still are. We are what we are intended to be when we have those three things that guide our direction—our name, our clan, and our religion.*[44]

Winona herself is a prime example. She is continually in the news as a fighter on behalf of the future of the earth and its disadvantaged peoples. When in 1996 she ran as the Green Party candidate for Vice-President of the United States, she campaigned for reforms oriented toward long-term survival:

I am interested in reframing the debate on the issues of this society, the distribution of power and wealth, abuse of power, the rights of the natural world, the environment, and the need to consider an amendment to the U.S. Constitution in which all decisions made today would be considered in light of the impact on the seventh generation from now.[45]

Winona now lives on her father's traditional tribal lands in northern Minnesota in the White Earth Reservation. Her father, like many, had left the reservation in search of economic opportunity and as a consequence of internal political oppression, but now Winona is trying to re-establish an economic base that will allow her Anishinaabe people to return to their land and to have the legal right to control its use. The land is of spiritual as well as economic importance to her people.

Part of the land on which Winona's Mississippi band of the Anishinaabe had long lived was formally granted to them by an 1867 treaty establishing a reservation of 837,000 acres, in exchange for their giving up their rights to most of Minnesota and Wisconsin. But over time, land slipped away through foreclosures, illegal land transfers, and a 1986 settlement in which Anishinaabe were forced to accept, under pressure from large government agencies and timber companies, sale of remaining lands for only pennies an acre. Now the White Earth Reservation occupies only about one-sixth of the original area. Using part of a $20,000 Reebok company award for her human rights work, Winona established the White Earth Land Recovery Project to begin to repurchase the land. She says, "We are going to recover our land acre by acre, inch by inch. Our burial grounds must be ours forever, even if we have to buy them back."[46]

The project she initiated has already repurchased over 1,300 acres of former tribal lands, and is trying to add more through further purchases, bequests, and legislation. The lands include burial grounds with undisturbed birch and sugar maple forests, and a 715-acre area encompassing two lakes, nesting sites for waterfowl, wild rice, and many medicinal plants. The latter area is earmarked to teach Anishinaabe children their own traditional cultural practices, and also to demonstrate to the world their value for planetary survival.

Winona, a Harvard-educated journalist, lives in a lakeside log cabin on the reservation with her two children, Ajuawak and Wasey, trying to teach them traditional beliefs. She has no fear of fighting against large-scale vested interests. In 1994, for instance, she chained herself to a paper company's gates to protest their clearance of forests including thousand-year-old trees to make phone books. As a result, she was put in jail for five hours but the publicity led other companies to cancel their contracts with that paper company.

She is now trying to help develop long-range plans for sustainable management of White Earth lands as ecosystems that, if restored, can provide medicines and materials for Anishinaabe traditional culture. The goal is to make it possible for people to return to the land. A tribal prophecy indicates that the people of the seventh fire—the current period—will look around and discover the things they had lost. With loss of the land had come loss of traditional spiritual principles. At the end of *Last Standing Woman*, the narrator speaks in the year 2018, describing her culture, which has rediscovered its spiritual traditions:

To understand our relationship to the whole and our role on the path of life. We also understand our responsibility. We only take what we need, and we leave the rest. We always give thanks for what we are given. What carries us through is the relationship we have to the Creation and the courage we are able to gather from the experience of our aanikoobijigan, *our ancestors, and our* oshkaabewisag, *our helpers.*[47]

In northern Thailand, damage from rainy season floods and sedimentation was so severe in 1995 that villagers whose houses and fields had been destroyed revived an ancient indigenous ritual to apologize to the Mae Chaem River. Respectful relationships with the river had lapsed with the introduction of modern water control technologies, such as dams and irrigation projects. At dawn, in the rain, villagers made altars in the river, filling them with sweets, nuts, bananas, sugar cane, foods, and cigarettes as offerings to the spirits of the forest, the earth deities, and the guardian spirits of the river. In their prayers, the people asked forgiveness of the river for misuse of the water and requested that the water level be lowered.

Some indigenous people feel that their traditional sacred ways are not only valid, but actually essential for the future of the world. They see these understandings as antidotes to mechanistic, dehumanizing, environmentally destructive ways of life. Rather than regarding their ancient way as inferior, intact groups such as the Kogi of the high Colombian rainforest feel they are the elder brothers of all humanity, responsible for keeping the balance of the universe and re-educating their younger brothers who have become distracted by desire for material gain.

One way of communicating with unseen spirits is to make material offerings to them. This woman is making offerings to the spirits involved in the rice crop in Bali, Indonesia.

Differences of opinion and lifestyle between native people who live traditionally and those who are embracing industrial materialistic culture have led to rifts within the communities. There are people for and against selling mineral rights to community land for economic gain; some indigenous people question the ethics of developing gambling casinos as a base for economic self-sufficiency. But gameplaying has interesting precedents in many world religions and was traditionally part of sacred rites in many indigenous cultures. Ceremonial throwing of dice has been symbolically associated with the cycles of death and rebirth, and the movement of the sun, moon, and stars. The chance turn of the dice or wheel of fortune often appears in myths as a metaphor for balance in the continual shifts between happiness and sorrow. Gaming rituals were used by some tribes to help the movement of the seasons and the shifts between night and day, to influence the weather, to assist in hunting, and to restore health. Addictive gambling is a different matter, for it can be disastrous for individuals and their families.

In the 2000 United States census, over 4 million people said they were at least partly Native American, over twice as many as made that claim during the 1990 census. Why this striking movement toward adopting a previously stigmatized indigenous identity? Possible reasons include the potential for a share in the gambling revenues, scholarships for minority students, the new-found popularity of native spiritual traditions, and the search for roots. There is thus considerable tension over the issue of native credentials, complicated by centuries of intermarriages. Those who consider themselves authentically "Indian" call the newcomers "wannabes" or "pretendians." Richard Allen, a Cherokee tribal policy analyst, says, "They may have Cherokee blood, I don't dispute it. But culturally, they're not Cherokee. They have no understanding of the traditions, of the ceremonies, of what it's like to be Cherokee."[48]

While there is a longing for exclusiveness on the part of some elders, others are adopting modern technologies to bring international attention and support for their causes. Personal visions and ancient prophecies about the dangers of a lifestyle that ignores the earth and the spiritual dimensions of life are leading native elders around the world to gather internationally and raise their voices together. They assert indigenous spiritual insights and observations about the state of the planet, political matters, and contemporary lifestyle issues.

Indigenous elders who are now speaking out seek converts not to their path but to a respect for all of life, which they feel is essential for the harmony of the planet. A respected elder of the Hopi nation, the late Thomas Banyacya, made a stirring appeal to the United Nations in 1992, in which he explained Hopi prophecies about our times. According to the prophecies, the creator made a perfectly balanced world but when humans turned away from spiritual principles for selfish reasons, the world was destroyed by earthquakes. The few survivors developed the second world, but repeated their mistakes, and the world was destroyed by the Ice Age. The few people who survived spoke one language and developed high technologies but when they turned away from natural laws and spiritual principles, the third world was destroyed by a great flood which is remembered in the ancient stories of many peoples. Now we are living in the fourth world. According to Hopi time lines, we are in the final stages of decay. Showing a rock drawing of part of the Hopi prophecy, Thomas Banyacya explained:

> There are two paths. The first with high technology but separate from natural and spiritual law leads to these jagged lines representing chaos. The lower path is one that remains in harmony with natural law. Here we see a line that represents a choice like a bridge joining the paths. If we turn to spiritual harmony and live from our hearts we can experience a paradise in this world. If we continue only on this upper path, we will come to destruction.[49]

> Many people have said that indigenous peoples are myths of the past, ruins that have died. But the indigenous community is not a vestige of the past, nor is it a myth. It is full of vitality and has a course and a future. It has much wisdom and richness to contribute. They have not killed us and they will not kill us now. We are stepping forth to say, "No, we are here. We live."
>
> Rigoberta Menchú of the K'iché Maya[50]

Suggested reading

Basso, Keith H., *Wisdom Sites in Places: Landscape and Language among the Western Apache*, Albuquerque: University of New Mexico Press, 1996. Interesting first-person ethnographic study of the meanings that Apache people attach to their environment.

Beck, Peggy V. and Walters, Anna L., *The Sacred: Ways of Knowledge, Sources of Life*, Tsaile (Navajo Nation), Arizona: Navajo Community College Press, 1977. A fine and genuine survey of indigenous sacred ways, particularly those of North America.

Bell, Diane, *Daughters of the Dreaming*, 2nd ed., Minneapolis: University of Minnesota Press, 1993. A pioneering study of Australian aboriginal women, by an anthropologist who lived among them.

Berger, Julian, *The Gaia Atlas of First Peoples: A Future for the Indigenous World*, New York: Anchor Books, 1990. An illustrated survey of contemporary survival issues facing the original inhabitants of many lands, with particular reference to threats to their environment from invading cultures.

Brown, Joseph Epes, *The Sacred Pipe*, 1953, New York: Penguin Books, 1971. Detailed accounts of the sacred rites of the Oglala Sioux by Black Elk, a respected holy man.

Eliade, Mircea, *Shamanism: Archaic Techniques of Ecstasy*, translated from the French by Willard Trask, London: Routledge & Kegan Paul, 1964. The first scholarly book to examine shamanism as an authentic religious form rather than as an anthropological oddity.

Erdoes, Richard and Alfonso, Ortiz, *American Indian Myths and Legends*, 1984, New York: Pantheon Books. A classic collection of stories from 80 North American tribes that offer a wealth of insights into traditional perceptions and lifeways.

Ewen, Alexander, *Voice of Indigenous Peoples*, Santa Fe, New Mexico: Clear Light Publishers, 1994. Speeches and writings from indigenous speakers at the 1992 United Nations Human Rights Day, analyzing the political conditions facing indigenous peoples.

Gill, Sam D., *Native American Religions*, Belmont, California: Wadsworth, 1982. A sensitive academic survey of indigenous sacred ways in the United States.

Goulet, Jean-Guy A., *Ways of Knowing: Experience, Knowledge, and Power among the Dene Tha*, Lincoln: University of Nebraska Press, 1998. Honest attempt by an anthropologist to directly experience and then explain to others the contemporary lifeways of these traditional people in northern Canada.

Grim, John, ed., *Indigenous Traditions and Ecology: The Interbeing of Cosmology and Community*, Cambridge: Harvard University Press, 2001. One of the excellent volumes of the series "Religions of the World and Ecology," this volume traces environmental themes across many different indigenous cultures.

Halifax, Joan, *Shamanic Voices: A Survey of Visionary Narratives*, New York: E. P. Dutton, 1979, and Harmondsworth, London: Penguin, 1980. First-hand accounts of shamanistic visionary experiences.

Harvey, Graham, *Indigenous Religions: A Companion*, London and New York: 2000. Scholarly articles about specific cultures, attempting to transcend the tendency to understand indigenous religions in terms of concepts taken from other religions.

Lame Deer, John and Richard Erdoes, *Lame Deer: Seeker of Visions*, New York: Pocket Books, 1976. Fascinating first-hand accounts of the life of a rebel visionary who tried to maintain the old ways.

Nelson, Richard K., *Make Prayers to the Raven: A Koyukon View of the Northern Forest*, Chicago: University of Chicago Press, 1986. Careful explanations of the close interrelationships between people and the rest of the natural world among these people of the western Canadian forest and tundra.

St. Pierre, Mark and Tilda Long Soldier, *Walking in the Sacred Manner*, New York: Simon and Schuster, 1995. First-person accounts of Plains Indian women's spiritual roles.

Weaver, Jace, ed., *Native American Religious Identity: Unforgotten Gods*, Maryknoll, New York: Orbis Books, 1998. A varied collection of essays examining facets of contemporary religious identities among Native Americans.

Zuesse, Evan M., *Ritual Cosmos: The Sanctification of Life in African Religions*, Athens, Ohio: Ohio University Press, 1979. A perceptive attempt to explain the essential differences between African traditional religions and Western monotheistic traditions, with detailed examples of African efforts to sanctify and find meaning in everyday life.

Key terms

indigenous	Native to an area.
cosmogony	A model of the evolution of the universe.
orisa	The Yoruba term for a deity, often used in speaking of West African religions in general.
shaman	A "medicine person," a man or woman who has undergone spiritual ordeals and can communicate with the spirit world to help the people.
Dreaming (Dream Time)	The timeless time of Creation, according to Australian aboriginal belief.
medicine power	Spiritual power, in some indigenous traditions.
vision quest	In indigenous traditions, a solitary ordeal undertaken to seek spiritual guidance about one's mission in life.

Study questions

1 Describe the worldviews of ancient indigenous peoples' sacred ways. Discuss ancestors, Supreme Being, integration, circles, land, and harmony.
2 Explain the relationships between indigenous sacred ways and modern industrial societies. Discuss examples of secrecy, blending, isolation, and contemporary conflicts.
3 Describe the indigenous peoples' sacred ways of understanding the environment. Discuss ecology, sun, water, language, animals, blood, sacred sites, and world axis.
4 Explain indigenous sacred ways' spiritual specialists. Discuss ritual, purity, secret societies, initiation, mystical intermediaries, shamans, medicine, divination, ordeals, spirit animals, altered states, and journeying.
5 Why is ritual important in indigenous sacred ways? Discuss life stage transitions, drums, the presence of the sacred, pipes, purification, vision quests, and the Sundance.

Refer to Pearson/Prentice Hall's **TIME Special Edition: World Religions** magazine for these and other current articles on topics related to many of the world's religions:

• *The Religious Experience: Birth and Childhood*

Chapter 2 explores the fundamental religious beliefs and rituals of Native Americans. For further research in this area, use the tools available to you in Research Navigator.

As you investigate Native American religions, consider this question: "What is the significance of the natural world in Native American religions?"

• **Ebsco's ContentSelect:** Search in the Anthropology, Religion, and Sociology databases using terms such as "animism," "Ecospirituality/Ecotheology," "Medicine Man."
• **Link Library:** Search in the Anthropology, Religion, and Sociology databases under the categories: "Religion," "Native American," and "Native American Religion."
• **The *New York Times* on the Web:** Search in the Religious Studies, Anthropology/Archaeology, and Sociology databases for current articles on related topics.

CHAPTER 3
HINDUISM

"With mind absorbed and heart melted in love"

In the Indian subcontinent there has developed a complex variety of religious paths. Some of these are relatively unified religious systems, such as Buddhism, Jainism, and Sikhism. Most of the other Indian religious ways have been categorized together as if they were a single tradition named "Hinduism." This term is derived from a name applied by foreigners to the people living in the region of the Indus River, and was introduced in the nineteenth century under colonial British rule as a category for census-taking.

An alternative label preferred today is **Sanatana Dharma**. *Sanatana*, "eternal" or "ageless," reflects the belief that these ways have always existed. ***Dharma***, often translated as "religion," encompasses duty, natural law, social welfare, ethics, health, and transcendental realization. *Dharma* is thus a holistic approach to social coherence and the good of all, corresponding to order in the cosmos.

The spiritual expressions of Sanatana Dharma range from extreme asceticism to extreme sensuality, from the heights of personal devotion to a deity to the heights of abstract philosophy, from metaphysical proclamations of the oneness behind the material world to worship of images representing a multiplicity of deities. According to tradition, there are actually 330 million deities in India. The feeling is that the divine has countless faces.

The extreme variations within Sanatana Dharma are reflections of its great age. Few of the myriad religious paths that have arisen over the millennia have been lost. They continue to co-exist in present-day India. Some scholars of religion argue that these ways are so varied that there is no central tradition that can be called Hinduism proper.

Truth is one; sages call it by various names.   Rig Veda

In villages, where the majority of Indians live, worship of deities is quite diverse and does not necessarily follow the more reified and philosophical Brahmanic tradition that is typically referred to as "Hinduism." Since it is not possible here to trace all these strands in their historical development, we will instead explore the main facets of Sanatana Dharma thematically: its philosophical and

The Indian subcontinent includes areas that are now politically separate from India. The Indus Valley, for instance, lies in what is now the Muslim state of Pakistan. Another Muslim state was carved out of the eastern portion of India in 1947, becoming the independent state of Bangladesh in 1972.

metaphysical elements, then its devotional and ritual aspects, and finally, its features as a way of life. These are not in fact totally separate categories, but we will separate them somewhat for clarity. Afterward, we will look at global and political aspects of the contemporary practice of Hinduism.

Philosophical and metaphysical elements

The Brahmanic tradition can be traced back to the Vedic age, thousands of years ago. The metaphysical beliefs in the Vedas were elaborated into various schools of thought by philosophers and sages. These beliefs were brought forth experientially by various methods of spiritual discipline.

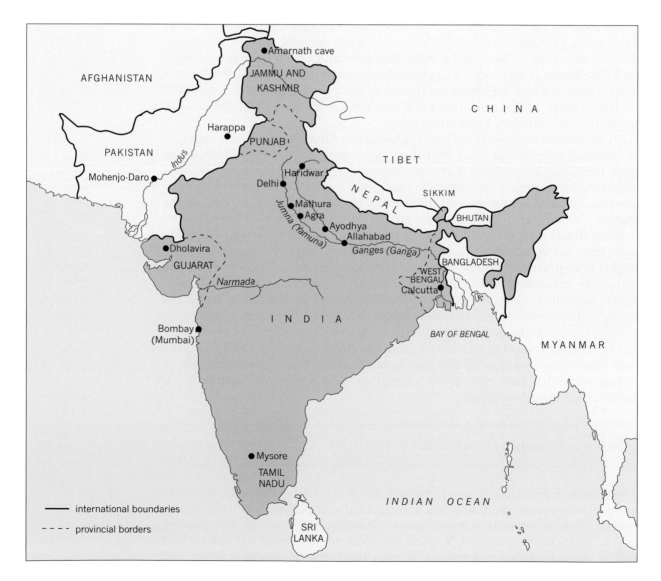

The Vedas include hymns praising the cow, which is still beloved and treated as sacred by Hindus: "The cow is our Mother, for she gives us her milk." Bali has its own unique ways of carrying on the beliefs, including this veneration of the cow in a cremation ceremony.

Vedic age

Many of the threads of Sanatana Dharma may have existed in the religions practiced by the aboriginal Dravidian peoples of India. There were also advanced urban centers in the Indus Valley from about 2500 BCE or even earlier until 1500 BCE. Major fortified cities with elaborate plumbing and irrigation systems have been found by archaeologists at Harappa, Mohenjo-Daro, and Dholavira; the culture they represent is labeled "Harappan."

In the **Aryan Invasion Theory** of Western historians, the highly organized cultures of the Indus Valley and the villages in other parts of the subcontinent were overrun by nomadic invaders from outside India. The theory argues that the **Vedas**, the religious texts often referred to as the foundations of Sanatana Dharma, were the product of the invaders, and not of indigenous Indians. These invaders were identified as **Aryans**, who were among the Indo-European tribes thought to have migrated outward from the steppes of southern Russia during the second millennium BCE. The material culture of these patriarchal tribes was relatively simple—although they had powerful means of making war, such as horse-drawn chariots, composite bows, and a warrior class—and they were probably illiterate. The Vedas sing the praises of the Indian subcontinent, and do not refer to any other homeland. The Harappan urban centers do seem to have declined, but there is no clear evidence why they should have done so.

Today the Aryan Invasion Theory is contested by some scholars and by Hindu nationalists who refuse to believe that their religion is foreign-born. There may have been considerable mixing between indigenous Dravidian people and those who composed the Vedas in **Sanskrit**, the ancient language whose origins are also not definitely established. If the Aryan Invasion Theory is not true, many ideas about the origins and evolution of Sanatana Dharma that have been prevalent among historians of religion for the last 150 years must be re-examined. The relationship between the Harappan civilization and the religion of the Vedas is still unclear. And the Vedas themselves are the foundation of upper-caste Brahmanic Hinduism, but not necessarily of all forms of Sanatana Dharma.

Although their origins and antiquity are still unknown, the Vedas themselves can be examined. They are a revered collection of ancient sacred hymns comprising four parts. The earliest are the *Samhitas*, hymns of praise in worship of deities. Then appeared the **Brahmanas**, directions about performances of the ritual sacrifices to the deities. The *Brahmanas* explain the symbolic correspondences between the microcosm of the ritual process and the "real world" in which rituals are performed. Some people went to the forests to meditate as recluses; their writings form the third part of the Vedas—the *Aranyakas*, or "forest treatises." Last came the **Upanishads**, consisting of teaching from highly realized spiritual masters. They explain the personal transformation that results from psychic participation in the ritual process.

These sacred teachings seem to have been written down by the middle of the first millennium BCE, though we know that they are much older than their earliest written forms. After being revealed to sages, they were transmitted orally from teacher to student and may then have been written down over a period of eight or nine hundred years. According to orthodox Hindus, the Vedas are not the work of any humans. They are the breath of the eternal, as "heard" by the ancient sages, or **rishis**, and later compiled by Vyasa. The name "Vyasa" means "Collector." He was traditionally considered to be one person, but scholars think it likely that many people were acting as compilers.

The Vedas are thought to transcend human time and are thus as relevant today as they were thousands of years ago. The *Gayatrimantra*, a verse in a Vedic hymn, is still chanted daily by the devout as the most sacred of prayers:

> *Aum [the primordial creative sound],*
> *Bhu Bhuvah Svah [the three worlds: earth, atmosphere, and heaven],*
> *Tat Savitur Varenyum,*
> *Bhargo Devasya Dheemahe [adoration of the glory, splendor, and grace that radiate*
>   *from the Divine Light that illuminates the three worlds],*
> *Dhiyo Yo Nah Prachodayat [a prayer for liberation through awakening of the light*
>   *of the universal intelligence].*[1]

The oldest of the known Vedic scriptures—and among the oldest of the world's existing scriptures—is the **Rig Veda**. This praises and implores the blessings of the **devas**—the controlling forces in the cosmos, deities who consecrate every part of life. The major *devas* included Indra (god of thunder and bringer of welcome rains), Agni (god of fire), Soma (associated with a sacred drink), and Ushas (goddess of dawn). The devas included both opaque earth gods and transparent deities of the sky and celestial realms. But behind all the myriad aspects of divinity, the sages perceived one unseen reality. This reality, beyond human understanding, ceaselessly creates and sustains everything that exists, encompassing all time, space, and causation.

HINDUISM

BCE	
8000	c.8000–6000 According to Indian tradition, Vedas heard by rishis, carried orally
3000	c.3102 According to Indian tradition, beginning of Kali Yuga; Vishnu incarnates as Vyasa, who writes down the Vedas c.2500–1500 Harappan civilization
2000	c.2000–900 Aryan invasions of northern India c.1500 Early Vedas first written down
1000	c.900–700 *Brahmanas* written down c.600–400 *Upanishads* recorded
500	c.400 BCE–200 CE *Ramayana* (present form) c.400 BCE–400 CE *Mahabharata* (present form) by 200 Patanjali systematizes Yoga Sutras [Indian tradition, yoga practices are ancient, indigenous]
CE	
	before 100 Code of Manu compiled c.300 Tantras written down [Indian tradition, Tantras are as old as the *Upanishads*]
500	c.600–1800 Bhakti movement flourishes 711 Muslim invasions begin c.788–820 or earlier, Shankara reorganizes Vedanta c.800–900 *Bhagavata Purana* written down
1000	
1500	
	1556–1707 Mogul Empire
1800	
	1828 Brahmo Samaj revitalization 1836–1886 Life of Ramakrishna 1857–1947 British rule of India 1869–1948 Life of Mahatma Gandhi 1875 Arya Samaj reform
1900	
	1947 Independence, partition of India and Pakistan 1992 Demolition of Babri mosque 2002 Violence erupts again over attempts to build Ram Temple at Ayodhya
2000	

The *Upanishads* are thought to have developed last, around 600 to 400 BCE. They represent the mystical insights of *rishis* who sought ultimate reality through their meditations in the forest. Many people consider these philosophical and metaphysical reflections on Vedic religion the cream of Indian thought, among the highest spiritual literature ever written. They were not taught to the masses but rather were reserved for advanced seekers of spiritual truth. The word *Upanishad* embraces the idea of the devoted disciple sitting down by the teacher to receive private spiritual instruction about the highest reality, loosening all doubts and destroying all ignorance. Emphasis is placed not on outward ritual performances, as in the earlier Vedic religion, but on inner experience as the path to realization and immortality.

The *rishis* explain that the bodily senses are made for looking outward; the eyes, ears, nose, tongue, and skin are enticed by sensory pleasures. But ultimately these are fleeting, impermanent. They pass away and then one dies, never having experienced what is of greater value because it is infinite, everlasting. What is real and lasting, they found, can be discovered only by turning away from transient worldly things. They taught their pupils to turn their attention inward and thus discover a transcendent reality from within. This unseen but all-pervading reality they called Brahman, the Unknowable: "Him the eye does not see, nor the tongue express, nor the mind grasp."[2]

From Brahman spring the multiplicity of forms, including humans. The joyous discovery of the *rishis* was that they could find Brahman as the subtle self or soul (**atman**) within themselves. One of the *rishis* explained this relationship thus:

Vedic worship with fire is still significant in contemporary rituals. Fire ceremonies may be conducted by Hindu pundits to invoke the blessings of the Unseen.

In the beginning there was Existence alone—One only, without a second. He, the One, thought to himself: Let me be many, let me grow forth. Thus out of himself he projected the universe, and having projected out of himself the universe, he entered into every being. All that is has its self in him alone. Of all things he is the subtle essence. He is the truth. He is the Self. And that, ... THAT ART THOU.
Chandogya Upanishad³

A Hindu statue conveys the compassion of the divine.

When one discovers the inner self, *atman*, and thus also its source, Brahman, the self merges into its transcendent source, and one experiences unspeakable peace and bliss.

The Upanishads express several doctrines central to all forms of Sanatana Dharma. One is **reincarnation**. In answer to the universal question, "What happens after we die?" the *rishis* taught that the soul leaves the dead body and enters a new one. One takes birth again and again in countless bodies—perhaps as an animal or some other life form—but the self remains the same. Birth as a human being is a precious and rare opportunity for the soul to advance toward its ultimate goal of liberation from rebirth and merging with the Absolute Reality.

An important related concept is that of **karma**. It means action, and also the consequences of action. Every act we make, and even every thought and every desire we have, shape our future experiences. Our life is what we have made it. And we ourselves are shaped by what we have done: "As a man acts, so does he become. ... A man becomes pure through pure deeds, impure through impure deeds."[4] Not only do we reap in this life the good or evil we have sown; they also follow us after physical death, affecting our next incarnation. Ethically, this is a strong teaching, for our every move has far-reaching consequences.

The ultimate goal, however, is not creation of good lives by good deeds, but a clean escape from the *karma*-run wheel of birth, death, and rebirth, or **samsara**. To escape from *samsara* is to achieve **moksha**, or liberation from the limitations of space, time, and matter through realization of the immortal Absolute. Many lifetimes of upward-striving incarnations are required to reach this transcendence of earthly miseries. This desire for liberation from earthly existence is one of the underpinnings of classical Hinduism, and of Buddhism as well.

Hinduism: Benares and Reincarnation

Major philosophical systems

In addition to the Vedas, elaborate philosophical systems were developed long ago in India. They all have certain features in common:

1 All have deep roots in the Vedas and other scriptures but also in direct personal experiences of the truth through meditation;

2 All hold ethics to be central to orderly social life. They attribute suffering to the law of *karma*, thereby suggesting incentives to more ethical behavior;

3 All hold that the ultimate cause of suffering is people's ignorance of the Self, whch is omniscient, omnipotent, omnipresent, perfect, and eternal.

Two other major philosophical systems born in India—Jainism and Buddhism—do not acknowledge the authority of the Vedas but nevertheless draw on many of the same currents as Sanatana Dharma. Prominent among the philosophical systems that are related to the Vedas are **Samkhya**, **Advaita Vedanta**, and **yoga**.

Samkhya

The Samkhya system, though undatable, is thought to be the oldest in India. Its founder is said to be the semi-mythical sage Kapila. Its principles appear in Jainism and Buddhism from the sixth century BCE, so the system probably preceded them and may be of pre-Vedic origin.

Samkhya philosophy holds that there are two states of reality. One is the Purusha, the Self, which is eternally wise, pure, and free, beyond change, beyond cause. The other is **Prakriti**, the cause of the material universe. All our suffering stems from our false confusion of Prakriti with Purusha, the eternal Self. A **dualistic** understanding of life is essential, according to this system, if we are to distinguish the ultimate transcendent reality of Purusha from the temporal appearances of Prakriti, which bring us happiness but also misery and delusion.

An illuminating story is told about Indra, who was once king of the gods. He was forced by the other *devas* to descend to earth in the body of a boar. Once there, he began to enjoy the life, wallowing in the mud, mating, and siring baby pigs. The *devas* were aghast; they came down to try to convince him to return, but Indra had forgotten his kingly state and insisted on remaining as a boar. The *devas* tried killing his babies; he was distraught but simply mated to have more piglets. Then the *devas* killed his mate. Indra grieved his loss but stayed in the mud. They finally had to kill him as well to bring him back to his senses. His soul could then see the body of the boar it had been inhabiting and was glad to return to heaven. The moral is that we, too, are like gods who forget the heights from which we came, so intent are we on the joys and sorrows of earthly life.

Advaita Vedanta

Whereas Samkhya is a dualistic system, Advaita ("non-dualist") Vedanta is generally **monistic**, positing a single reality. It is based on the *Upanishads*: its founder is said to be Vyasa, systematizer of the *Upanishads*. The eminent philosopher Shankara reorganized the teachings many centuries later, probably between the eighth and ninth centuries CE.

Whereas one view of the *Upanishads* is that the human self (*atman*) is an emanation of Brahman, Shankara insisted that the *atman* and Brahman are actually one. According to Shankara, our material life is an illusion. It is like a momentary wave arising from the ocean, which is the only reality. Ignorance consists in thinking that the waves are different from the ocean. The absolute spirit,

Brahman, is the essence of everything, and it has no beginning and no end. It is the eternal ocean of bliss within which forms are born and die, giving the false appearance of being real.

That which makes us think the physical universe has its own reality is **maya**, the power by which the Absolute veils itself. *Maya* is the illusion that the world as we perceive it is real. Shankara uses the metaphor of a coil of rope that, at dusk, is mistaken for a snake. The physical world, like the rope, does actually exist but we superimpose our memories and subjective thoughts upon it. Moreover, he says, only that which never changes is truly real. Everything else is changing, impermanent. In ignorance we think that we exist as individuals, superimposing the notion of a separate ego-self on the underlying absolute reality of pure being, pure consciousness, pure bliss. It is a mistake to identify with the body or the mind, which exist but have no unchanging reality. When a person reaches transcendent consciousness, superimposition stops and the oneness of reality is experienced.

Yoga

From ancient times, people of the Indian subcontinent have practiced spiritual disciplines designed to clear the mind and support a state of serene, detached awareness. This desired state of balance, purity, wisdom, and peacefulness of mind is described as *sattvic*. It is distinctly different from two other general states of mind: active and restless, or lethargic and dull. The practices for increasing *sattvic* qualities are known collectively as **yoga**. It means "yoke" or "union"—referring to union with the true Self, the goal described in the *Upanishads*.

The sages distinguished four basic types of people and developed yogic practices that are particularly suitable for each type, in order that each can attain the desired union with the Self. For meditative people, there is **raja yoga**, the path of mental concentration. For rational people, there is **jnana yoga**, the path of rational inquiry. For naturally active people, there is **karma yoga**, the path of right action. For emotional people, there is **bhakti yoga**, the path of devotion.

Raja yoga   Some believe that the **sadhanas**, or practices of raja yoga, were known as long ago as the Neolithic Age and were practiced in the Indus Valley culture. By 200 BCE, a yogi named Patanjali (or perhaps a series of people taking the same name) had described a system for attaining the highest consciousness through raja yoga—the path of mental concentration. Patanjali's *Yoga Sutras* is a book of 196 terse sayings called **sutras**. These include such observations as:

"From contentment comes the attainment of the highest happiness."
"From penance comes destruction of impurities, thence the perfection of the body and the senses."
"From study, comes communion with the desired deity."
"From the profound meditation upon Isvara [God], comes success in spiritual absorption."[5]

Yogis say that it is easier to calm a wild tiger than it is to quiet the mind, which is like a drunken monkey that has been bitten by a scorpion. The problem is that the mind is our vehicle for knowing the Self. If the mirror of the mind is disturbed, it reflects the disturbance rather than the pure light within. The goal of yogic practices is to make the mind absolutely calm and clear.

Yogic adepts have developed extreme control of their bodies to amplify meditation efforts.

In kundalini yoga, the body is thought to exist within a field of energy, which is most concentrated at the major chakras—subtle centers along the vertical axis of the body.

Patanjali distinguishes eight "limbs" of the yogic path: moral codes (*yama-niyama*), physical conditioning (*asana*), breath control (*pranayama*), sense control (*pratyahara*), concentration (*dharana*), meditation (*dhyana*), and the state of peaceful spiritual absorption (*samadhi*).

The moral and ethical principles that form the first limb of yogic practice are truth, non-violence, non-stealing, continence, and non-covetousness, plus cleanliness, contentment, burning zeal, self-study, and devotion to God. The **asanas** are physical postures used to cleanse the body and develop the mind's ability to concentrate. Regulated breathing exercises are also used to calm the nerves and increase the body's supply of **prana**, or invisible life energy. Breath is thought to be the key to controlling the flow of this energy within the subtle energy field surrounding and permeating the physical body. Its major pathway is through a series of **chakras**, or subtle energy centers along the spine. To raise the energy from the lowest, least subtle chakra at the base of the spine to the highest, most subtle energy center at the crown of the head is the goal of *kundalini* yoga practices, with **kundalini** referring to the latent energy at the base of the spine. Ideally, the opening of the highest chakra leads to the bliss of union with the Sublime. In its fully open state, the crown chakra is depicted as a thousand-petaled lotus, effulgent with light.

In addition to these practices using the body and breath, Indian thought has long embraced the idea that repetition of certain sounds has sacred effects. It is said that some ancient yogic adepts could discern subtle sounds and that **mantras** (sacred formulas) express an aspect of the divine in the form of sound vibration. The sound of the mantras was believed to evoke the reality they named. The language used for these verbal formulas since ancient times was Sanskrit. It was considered a re-creation of the actual sound-forms of objects, actions, and qualities, as heard by ancient sages in deep meditation. The most cherished sound vibrations are the "unheard, unstruck" divine sounds inaudible to our outer ears.

Chanting sacred syllables is thought to still the mind and attune the devotee to the Divine Ground of Existence. Indians liken the mind to the trunk of an elephant, always straying restlessly here and there. If an elephant is given a small stick to hold in its trunk, it will hold it steadily, losing interest in other objects. In the same way, the mantra gives the restless mind something to hold, quieting it by focusing awareness in one place. If chanted with devoted concentration, the mantra may also invoke the presence and blessings of the deity.

Many forms of music have also been developed in India to elevate a person's attunement and may go on for hours if the musicians are spiritually absorbed.

Another way of steadying and elevating the mind is concentration on some visual form—a candle flame, the picture of a saint or guru, the **OM** symbol, or **yantras**. A *yantra* is a linear image with complex cosmic symbolism. Large *yantras* are also created as designs of colorful seeds for ritual invocations of specific deities.

One-pointed concentration ideally leads to a state of meditation. In meditation, all worldly thoughts have dissipated. Instead of ordinary thinking, the clear light of awareness allows insights to arise spontaneously as flashes of illumination. There may also be phenomena, such as colored lights, visions, waves of ecstasy, or visits from supernatural beings. The mind, heart, and body may gradually be transformed.

The ultimate goal of yogic meditation is **samadhi**: a super-conscious state of union with the Absolute. Swami Sivananda attempts to describe it:

The OM *symbol, representing the original sound of creation, is topped by the sun and the moon, harmonized opposites. To chant* OM *is to commune with this cosmic sound vibration.*

Many forms of music and dance have evolved within Sanatana Dharma as ways of communicating with and about the divine.

> *Words and language are imperfect to describe this exalted state. . . . Mind, intellect and the senses cease functioning. . . . It is a state of eternal Bliss and eternal Wisdom. All dualities vanish in toto. . . . All visible merge in the invisible or the Unseen. The individual soul becomes that which he contemplates.*[6]

Hinduism:
OM

Jnana yoga   The path of rational inquiry—*jnana yoga*—employs the rational mind rather than trying to transcend it by concentration practices. In this path, ignorance is considered the root of all problems. Our basic ignorance is our idea of our selves as being separate from the Absolute. One method is continually to ask, "Who am I?" The seeker discovers that the one who asks the question is not the body, not the senses, not the pranic body, not the mind, but something eternal beyond all these. The guru Ramana Maharshi explains:

> *After negating all of the above-mentioned as "not this," "not this," that Awareness which alone remains—that I am. . . . The thought "Who am I?" will destroy all other thoughts, and, like the stick used for stirring the burning pyre, it will itself in the end get destroyed. Then, there will arise Self-realization.*[7]

In the *jnana* path, the seeker must also develop spiritual virtues (calmness, restraint, renunciation, resignation, concentration, and faith) and have an intense longing for liberation. The ultimate wisdom is spiritual rather than intellectual knowledge of the self.

> *Spiritual knowledge is the only thing that can destroy our miseries for ever; any other knowledge removes wants only for a time.*
>
> Swami Vivekananda[8]

Karma yoga   In contrast to these ascetic and contemplative practices, another way is that of helpful action in the world. *Karma yoga* is service rendered without any interest in its fruits and without any personal sense of giving. The yogi knows that the Absolute performs all actions, and all actions are gifts to the Absolute. This consciousness leads to liberation from the self in the very midst of work. Krishna, speaking as the Absolute, explains these principles in the *Bhagavad-Gita*:

> *The steadily devoted soul attains unadulterated peace because he offers the results of all activities to Me; whereas a person who is not in harmony with the divine, who is greedy for the fruits of his labor, becomes entangled.*[9]

Bhakti yoga   The final type of spiritual path is the one embraced by most Indian followers of Sanatana Dharma. It is the path of devotion to a personal deity, **bhakti yoga**. *Bhakti* means "to share," to share a relationship with the Supreme. For the **bhakta** (devotee), the relationship is that of intense love. Bhakta Nam Dev described this deep love in sweet metaphors:

> *Thy Name is beautiful, Thy form is beautiful, and very beautiful is Thy love, Oh my Omnipresent Lord.*
> *As rain is dear to the earth, as the fragrance of flowers is dear to the black bee, and as the mango is dear to the cuckoo, so is the Lord to my soul.*
> *As the sun is dear to the sheldrake, and the lake of Man Sarowar to the swan, and as the husband is dear to the wife, so is God to my soul.*
> *As milk is dear to the baby and as the torrent of rain to the mouth of the sparrow-*

The love between Radha and Krishna is a model for bhaktas' *devotion to the supreme person.*

hawk who drinks nothing but raindrops, and as water is dear to the fish, so is the Lord to my soul.[10]

Bhaktas' devotion is thought to be more dear to the Supreme than ritualistic piety. The story is told that a pious brahmin came daily to offer ritual worship to a stone statue of the deity Siva. One day he was horrified to see wild flowers and partly eaten pork decorating the shrine. These had been left by a hunter who stopped to worship Siva in his own fashion. Hoping to teach the brahmin a lesson, Siva appeared to him in a dream commanding that he watch from hiding while the hunter expressed his devotion. When the hunter then came to worship, he saw blood oozing from the eye of the statue. Without hesitation, he plucked out his own eye to place it on that of the idol. The bleeding stopped, but then the statue's other eye started bleeding. The hunter prepared to pull out his other eye when Siva manifested himself, healed the hunter, and took him as one of his chosen devotees, thenceforth called "the beloved of the eye."

A vision of a deity like that in the story is what the *bhakta* hopes for. Bhakta Ravi Das, a shoemaker who became a highly regarded spiritual teacher because of his intense devotion, implored his beloved: "I am a sacrifice unto You, my Omnipresent Lord. Why are you silent? For many births I have been separated from you. This life I dedicate to You. I live only with the hope of you. It is so long since I have seen You."[11]

Mirabai, a fifteenth-century Rajput princess, was married to a ruler at a young age, but from her childhood she had been utterly devoted to the deity Krishna. Her poetry expresses her single-minded love for her beloved:

Everything perishes,
sun, moon, earth, sky, water, wind,
everything.
Only the One Indestructible remains.
Others get drunk on distilled wine,
in love's still I distil mine;
day and night I'm drunk on it
in my Lover's love, ever sunk ...
I'll not remain in my mother's home,
I'll stay with Krishna alone;
  He's my Husband
  and my Lover,
  and my mind is
  at his feet forever.[12]

When Mirabai continued to spend all her time in devotions to Krishna, an infuriated in-law tried to poison her. It is said that Mirabai drank the poison while laughingly dancing in ecstasy before Krishna; in Krishna's presence the poison seemed like nectar to her and did her no harm. The Beloved One is said to respond and to be a real presence in the fully devoted *bhakta's* life.

In the *bhakti* path, even though the devotee may not transcend the ego in *samadhi*, the devotee's whole being is surrendered to the deity in love. Ramakrishna explains why the *bhakti* way is more appropriate for most people:

As long as the I-sense lasts, so long are true knowledge and Liberation impossible.
... [But] how very few can obtain this Union [Samadhi] and free themselves from

AN INTERVIEW WITH SARALA CHAKRABARTY

Living Hinduism

Sarala Chakrabarty, a Calcutta grandmother, has undertaken spiritual studies with a guru in the Ramakrishna tradition. Her love for the Supreme, in many forms, is highly personal.

"In our Hindu religion, we worship God in some form. God is infinite, but we cannot imagine the infinite. We must have some finite person—whom I love like friend, like father, like son, like lover. We make a relation with God like this. When I think he is my lover, I can always think of him. When I think he is my father, when I am in trouble, I pray to him, ask him to save me.

"And I always pray to the Holy Mother [Ramakrishna's spiritual bride and successor, Sarada Devi]. When I have a problem, Mother will save me. She has given word when she was leaving her body (you say 'dying')—she said, 'I am blessing all who have come, who are coming, who have not come yet but are coming, blessings for all.' Only Mother can say this—so big heart, so much affection for us.

"I feel something. Somebody is standing behind me. I feel always the hands on my shoulders, guarding me. Everybody is protected by God, everyone. I am not his only child. But I think God is only mine.

"I want everything from God. God does not want anything from me. He wants *bhakti*—devotion. A mother wants nothing from a child but love. She says only, 'Pray to me, call me, and I will do everything for you.' When I am traveling I say to Her, 'I am talking to you,' and this is done.

"As we love God, God loves us. Our Lord Krishna says Love is the rope. It ties God and pulls him down to you.

"I have a very powerful guru, a swami of the Ramakrishna Mission, who has passed on. He gave me a mantra, and it gives me very much peace. When I chant, I cannot leave it. Time is over, somebody is calling, I have to cook, I have to work—then I get up and still I am chanting in my mind. After bedding, I worship and chant. After that I realize I am pleased, I am quiet. There is no trouble in body and mind. I am very happy, very blissful. Whatever that problem is, all goes away."

this "I"? It is very rarely possible. Talk as much as you want, isolate yourself continuously, still this "I" will always return to you. Cut down the poplar tree today, and you will find tomorrow it forms new shoots. When you ultimately find that this "I" cannot be destroyed, let it remain as "I" the servant.[13]

Religious and ritual foundations

In ancient Vedic times, elaborate fire sacrifice rituals were created, controlled by **brahmins** (priests). Specified verbal formulas, sacred chants, and sacred actions were to be used by the priests to invoke the breath behind all of existence. This universal breath was later called **Brahman**, the Absolute, the Supreme Reality.

After a period when Brahmanic ritual and philosophy dominated Sanatana Dharma, the *bhakti* approach came to prominence around 600 CE. It opened spiritual expression to both *shudras* (a caste of manual laborers and artisans) and women, and has been the primary path of the masses ever since. It may also have been the initial way of the people, for it is difficult to pray to the impersonal Absolute referred to in the *Upanishads*, for it is formless and is not totally distinct from oneself. More personal worship of a Divine Being can be inferred from the

Hinduism:
Brahman and
Tolerance

goddess and Siva-like low reliefs found in the archaelogical sites of ancient India. Worship of major deities probably persisted during the Vedic period and was later given written expression. Eventually *bhakti*—intense devotion to a personal manifestation of Brahman—became the heart of Hinduism as the majority of people now experience it.

Of all the deities worshipped by Hindus, there are three major groupings: **Saktas** who worship a Mother Goddess, **Saivites** who worship the god Siva, and **Vaishnavites** who worship the god Vishnu. Each devotee has his or her own "chosen deity," but will honor others as well.

Ultimately, many Hindus rest their faith in one genderless deity with three basic aspects: creating, preserving, and destroying. The latter activity is seen as a merciful act that allows the continuation of the cosmic cycles.

Saktas

An estimated 50 million Hindus worship some form of the goddess. Some of these Saktas follow a Vedic path; some are more independent of Vedic tradition. As we have seen, worship of the feminine aspect of the divine probably dates back to the pre-Vedic ancient peoples of the Indian subcontinent. Her power is called *sakti* and is often linked with the *kundalini* energy. Lushly erotic, sensual imagery is frequently used to symbolize her abundant creativity.

Folk representation of the goddess Kali. It is said that when Kali threatened to destroy the whole world in her battle against evil, Lord Siva placed himself in her path to calm and stop her.

The feminine principle is worshipped in many forms. At the village level, especially in southern India, local deities are most typically worshipped as goddesses. They may not be perceived as taking human-like forms; rather, their presence may be represented by round stones, trees, *yantras*, or small shrines without images. These local goddesses are intimately concerned with village affairs, unlike the more distant great goddesses of the upper class, access to whose temples was traditionally forbidden to those of low caste.

The great goddesses have been worshipped both in the plural and in the singular, in which case one goddess is seen as representing the totality of deity—eternal creator, preserver, and destroyer. The great goddess **Durga** is often represented as a beautiful woman with a gentle face but ten arms holding weapons with which she vanquishes the demons who threaten the *dharma*; she rides a lion (see pages 21–22). She is the blazing splendor of God incarnate, in benevolent female form.

Kali, by contrast, is the divine in its fierce form. She may be portrayed dripping with blood, carrying a sword and a severed head, and wearing a girdle of severed hands and a necklace of skulls symbolizing her aspect as the destroyer of evil. What appears as

destruction is actually a means of transformation. With her merciful sword she cuts away all personal impediments to realization of truth, for those who sincerely desire to serve the Supreme. At the same time, she opens her arms to those who love her. Some of them worship her with blood offerings.

Fearsome to evil-doers, but loving and compassionate as a mother to devotees, Kali wears a mask of ugliness. The divine reality is a wholeness encompassing both creation and destruction. In Hindu thought, death and birth are linked, each giving way to the other in eternal cycles. All beings, all phenomena, are inter-related parts of the same divine essence. Sanskrit scholar Leela Arjunwadkar observes that there is a deeply sensed unity among all beings in classical Indian literature:

> That is why we find all types of characters in Sanskrit literature—human beings, gods and goddesses, rivers, demons, trees, serpents, celestial nymphs, etc., and their share in the same emotional life is the umbilical cord that binds all to Mother Nature.[14]

From ancient times, worship of the divine female has been associated with worship of nature, particularly great trees and rivers. The Ganges River is considered an especially sacred female presence, and her waters, flowing down from the Himalayas, are thought to be extraordinarily purifying. Pilgrims bathe in Mother Ganga's waters, facing the sun at sunrise, and corpses or the cremated ashes of the dead are placed in the river so that their sins will be washed away.

Hinduism:
Sacred Texts

Sacred texts called **Tantras** instruct worshippers how to honor the feminine divine. Ways of worship include concentration on *yantras*, meditation with the hands in *mudras* (positions that reflect and invoke a particular spiritual reality), *kundalini* practices, and use of mantras. One such text gives a thousand different "names" or attributes of the Divine Mother as mantras for recitation, such as these: "*Sri mata* (She who is the auspicious Mother), *Sri maha rajni* (She who is the Empress of the Universe) … *Raga svarupa pasadhya* (She who is holding the rope of love in Her hand) … *Nirmada* (She who is without pride), *Mada nasini* (She who destroys pride), *Niscinta* (She who has no anxiety about anything), *Nir ahankara* (She who is without egoism) … *Mahaisvarya* (She who has supreme sovereignty), *Maha virya* (She who is supreme in valor), *Maha bala* (She who is supreme in might), *Maha buddhih* (She who is supreme in intelligence).[15] Praising and invoking one deity by many divine names is also a common way of worshipping deities other than the goddess.

Sakti worship has also been incorporated into worship of the gods. Each is thought to have a female consort, often portrayed in close physical embrace signifying the eternal unity of male and female principles in the oneness of the divine. Here the female is often conceived as the life-animating force; the transcendent male aspect is inactive until joined with the productive female energy.

Siva as Lord of the Dance, trampling the demon of evil and bearing both the flame of destruction and the drum of creation. One of his two free hands gestures "Fear not"; the other points to his upraised foot, denoting bliss.

The female is highly venerated in Hinduism, compared to many other religions. Women are thought to make major contributions to the good earthly life, consisting of *dharma* (order in society), marital wealth (by bearing sons in a patriarchal society), and the aesthetics of sensual pleasure. Women are auspicious beings, mythologically associated with wealth, beauty, splendor, and grace. As sexual partners to men, they help to activate the spiritualizing life-force. No ceremonial sacrifice is complete unless the wife participates as well as the husband.

In the ideal marriage, husband and wife are spiritual partners. Marriage is a vehicle for spiritual discipline, service, and advancement toward a spiritual goal. Men and women are thought to complement each other, although the ideal of liberation has traditionally been intended largely for the male.

Women were not traditionally encouraged to seek liberation through their own spiritual practices. A woman's role is usually linked to that of her husband, who takes the position of her god and teacher. For many centuries, there was even the hope that a widow would choose to be cremated alive with her dead husband in order to remain united with him after death.

In early Vedic times, women were relatively free and honored members of Indian society, participating equally in important spiritual rituals. But because of social changes, by the nineteenth century wives had become like servants of the husband's family. With expectations that the girl will take a large dowry to the boy's family in a marriage arrangement, having girls is such an economic burden that many female babies are intentionally aborted or killed at birth. There are also cases today of women being beaten or killed by the husband's family after their dowry has been handed over. Nevertheless many women in contemporary India have been well educated, and many have attained high political positions.

Shaivite sadhu meditating in the Himalayas at the source of the holy Ganges River.

Saivites

Siva is a personal, many-faceted manifestation of the attributeless supreme deity. In older systems he is one of the three major aspects of deity: Brahma (Creator), Vishnu (Preserver), and Siva (Destroyer). Saivites nevertheless worship him as the totality, with many aspects. As Swami Sivasiva Palani, Saivite editor of *Hinduism Today*, explains: "Siva is the unmanifest; he is creator, preserver, destroyer, personal Lord, friend, primal Soul"; and he is the "all-pervasive underlying energy, the more or less impersonal love and light that flows through all things."[16] Siva is sometimes depicted dancing above the body of the demon he has killed, reconciling darkness and light, good and evil, creation and destruction, rest and activity in the eternal dance of life.

Siva is also the god of yogis, for he symbolizes asceticism. He is often shown in austere meditation on Mount Kailas, clad only in a tiger skin, with a snake around his neck. The latter signifies his conquest of the ego. In one prominent story, it is Siva who swallows the poison that threatens the whole world with darkness, neutralizing the poison by the power of his meditation.

Siva has various saktis or feminine consorts, including Durga. He is often shown with his devoted spouse **Parvati**. Through their union,

A large lingam from the 6th century CE honors Siva as the unmanifest creative force beyond time and space.

cosmic energy flows freely, seeding and liberating the universe. Nevertheless, they are seen mystically as eternally chaste. Siva and his sakti are also expressed as two aspects of a single being. Some sculptors portray Siva as androgynous, with both masculine and feminine physical traits. Tantric belief incorporates an ideal of balance of male and female qualities within a person, hopefully leading to enlightenment, bliss, and worldly success as well. This unity of male and female is often expressed abstractly, as a **lingam** within a **yoni**, a symbol of the female vulva.

The *lingams* used in worship of Siva are naturally occurring or sculpted cylindrical forms honored since antiquity in India (and apparently in other cultures as well, as far away as Hawaii). Those shaped by nature, such as stones polished by certain rivers, are most highly valued, with rare natural crystal lingams considered especially precious. Tens of thousands of devotees each year undergo dangerous pilgrimages to certain high mountain caves to venerate large lingams naturally formed of ice. While the lingam sometimes resembles an erect phallus, most Siva-worshippers focus on its symbolic meaning, which is abstract and asexual. They see the lingam as a nearly amorphous, "formless" symbol for the unmanifest, transcendent nature of Siva—that which is beyond time, space, cause, and form—whereas the yoni represents the manifest aspect of Sivaness.

Saivism encompasses traditions that have developed outside Vedic-based Brahmanism. These include sects such as the Lingayats, who wear a stone lingam in remembrance of Siva as the One Undivided Being. Their ancient ways of Siva worship underwent a strong reform movement in the twelfth century, refusing caste divisions, brahminical authority, and consideration of menstruating women as polluted. They practice strict vegetarianism and regard men and women as equals.

Another branch is represented by the sixty-three great Saivite saints of Tamil Nadu in southern India, who from the seventh century onward expressed great love for Siva. They experienced him as the Luminous One, present everywhere in subtle form but apparent only to those who love him. For this realization, knowledge of the scriptures and ascetic practices are useless. Only direct personal devotion will do. The Tamil saint Appar sang,

Why chant the Vedas, hear the shastras' lore? . . .
Release is theirs, and theirs alone,
Whose heart from thinking of its Lord shall never depart.[17]

The auspicious blessings of Ganesh are invoked for all occasions. Here his image has been painted on a wall before a marriage celebration.

Siva's son Ganesh, a deity with the head of an elephant, guards the threshold of space and time and is, therefore, invoked for his blessings at the beginning of any new venture. Ganesh was the subject of an extraordinary event that happened in temples in many parts of India, as well as in Hindu temples in other parts of the world. On September 21, 1995, statues devoted to Ganesh began drinking milk from spoons, cups, and even buckets offered by devotees. Scientists suggested explanations such as mass hysteria or capillary action in the stone, but the phenomenon lasted only one day.

Vaishnavites

In contrast to Sakti and Siva, Vishnu is beloved as the tender, merciful deity. In one myth, a sage was sent to determine who was the greatest of

Lakshmi is often pictured standing gloriously upon a lotus flower, bestowing coins of prosperity and flanked by elephants signifying her royal power.

the gods by trying their tempers. The first two, Brahma and Siva, he insulted and was soundly abused in return. When he found Vishnu, the god was sleeping. Knowing of Vishnu's good-naturedness, the sage increased the insult by kicking him awake. Instead of reacting angrily, Vishnu tenderly massaged the sage's foot, concerned that he might have hurt it. The sage exclaimed, "This god is the mightiest, since he overpowers all by goodness and generosity!"

Vishnu has been worshipped since Vedic times and came to be regarded as the Supreme as a person. According to ideas appearing by the fourth century CE, Vishnu is considered to have appeared in many earthly incarnations, some of them animal forms. Many deities have been drawn into this complex, in which

Hinduism:
Gods and Goddesses

they are interpreted as incarnations of Vishnu. Most beloved of his purported incarnations have been Rama, subject of the *Ramayana* (see page 89), and Krishna (see page 92). However, many people still revere Krishna without reference to Vishnu.

Popular devotion to Krishna takes many forms. If Krishna is regarded as the transcendent Supreme Lord, the worshipper humbly lowers himself or herself. If Krishna is seen as master, the devotee is his servant. If Krishna is loved as a child, the devotee takes the role of loving parent. If Krishna is the divine friend, the devotee is his friend. And if Krishna is the beloved, the devotee is his lover. The latter relationship was popularized by the ecstatic sixteenth-century Bengali saint and sage Sri Caitanya, who adored Krishna as the flute-playing lover. Following Sri Caitanya, the devotee makes himself (if a male) like a loving female in order to experience the bliss of Lord Krishna's presence. It is this form of Hindu devotion that was carried to America in 1965, organized as the International Society for Krishna Consciousness, and then spread to other countries. Its followers are known as Hare Krishnas.

Vishnu is often associated with his consort, **Lakshmi**, who is also an ancient goddess worshipped in her own right. Associated with prosperity and regal power, Lakshmi is often depicted as a radiant woman sitting on a water-borne lotus flower. The lotus floats pristine on the water but has its roots in the mud, thus representing the refined spiritual energy that rises above worldly contamination. The lotus also symbolizes the fertile growth of organic life, as the world is continually reborn on a lotus growing out of Vishnu's navel.

The epics and Puranas

Hinduism:
Sacred Texts

Personal love for a deity flowered in the spiritual literature that followed the Vedas. Two major classes of scriptures that arose after 500 BCE (according to Western scholarship) were the **epics** and the **Puranas**. These long heroic narratives and poems popularized spiritual knowledge and devotion through national myths and legends. They were particularly useful in spreading Hindu teachings to the masses at times when Buddhism and Jainism—movements born in India but not recognizing the authority of the Vedas—were winning converts.

In contrast to the rather abstract depictions of the Divine Principle in the *Upanishads*, the epics and Puranas represent the Supreme as a person, or rather as various human-like deities. As T. M. P. Mahadevan explains:

> *The Hindu mind is averse to assigning an unalterable or rigidly fixed form or name to the deity. Hence it is that in Hinduism we have innumerable god-forms and countless divine names. And, it is a truth that is recognized by all Hindus that obeisance offered to any of these forms and names reaches the one supreme God.*[18]

Two great epics, the **Ramayana** and the **Mahabharata**, present the Supreme usually as **Vishnu**, who intervenes on earth during critical periods in the cosmic cycles. In the inconceivable vastness of time as reckoned by Hindu thought, each world cycle lasts 4,320,000 years. Two thousand of these world cycles are the equivalent of one day and night in the life of Brahma, the Creator god. Each world cycle is divided into four ages, or *yugas*.

Dharma—moral order in the world—is natural in the first age. The second age is like a cow standing on three legs; people must be taught their proper roles in society. During the darker third age, revealed values are no longer recognized, people lose their altruism and willingness for self-denial, and there are no more saints. The final age, **Kali Yuga**, is as imbalanced as a cow trying to stand on one leg. The world is at its worst, with egotism, ignorance, recklessness, and war rampant. According to Hindu time reckoning, we are now living in a Kali Yuga period that began in 3102 BCE. Such an age is described thus:

> When society reaches a stage where property confers rank, wealth becomes the only source of virtue, passion the sole bond of union between husband and wife, falsehood the source of success in life, sex the only means of enjoyment, and when outer trappings are confused with inner religion . . .[19]

Each of these lengthy cycles witnesses the same turns of events. The balance inexorably shifts from the true *dharma* to dissolution and then back to the *dharma* as the gods are again victorious over the anti-gods. The Puranas list the many ways that Vishnu has incarnated in the world when *dharma* is decaying, to help restore virtue and defeat evil. For instance, Vishnu is said to have incarnated great **avatars** such as Krishna and Rama to help uplift humanity. It is considered inevitable that Vishnu will continually return in answer to the pleas of suffering humans. It is equally inevitable that he will meet with resistance from "demonic forces," which are also part of the cosmic cycles.

During the northern Indian festival Ram-lila, giant effigies of Ravana and the demons from the epic Ramayana *are dramatically burned to the delight of the crowds.*

Ramayana   The epics deal with the eternal play of good and evil, symbolized by battles involving the human incarnations of Vishnu. Along the way, they teach examples of the virtuous life—responsibilities to others as defined by one's social roles. One is first a daughter, son, sister, brother, wife, husband, mother, father, or friend in relationship to others, and only secondarily an individual.

The *Ramayana*, a long poetic narrative in the Sanskrit language thought to have been compiled between approximately 400 BCE and 200 CE, is attributed to the bard Valmiki. Probably based on old ballads, it is much beloved and is acted out with great pageantry throughout India every year. It depicts the duties of relationships, portraying ideal characters, such as the ideal servant, the ideal brother, the ideal wife, the ideal king. In the story, Vishnu incarnates as the virtuous prince Rama in order to kill Ravana, the ten-headed demon king of Sri Lanka. Rama is heir to his father's throne, but the mother of his stepbrother compels the king to banish Rama into the forest for fourteen years. Rama, a model of morality, goes willingly, observing that a son's duty is always to obey his parents implicitly, even when their commands seem wrong. He is accompanied into the ascetic life by his wife Sita, the model of wifely devotion in a patriarchal society, who refuses his offer to remain behind in comfort.

TEACHING STORY

Hanuman, the Monkey Chief

Hanuman was of divine origin and legendary powers, but he was embodied as a monkey, serving as a chief in the monkey army. When Rama needed to find his wife Sita after Ravana abducted her, he turned to the monkey king for help. The monkey king dispatched Hanuman to search to the south.

When the monkeys reached the sea dividing India from Sri Lanka, they were dismayed because monkeys do not swim. A vulture brought word that Sita was indeed on the other side of the water, a captive of Ravana. What to do? An old monkey reminded Hanuman of the powers he had displayed as an infant and told him that he could easily jump to Lanka and back if only he remembered his power and his divine origin.

Hanuman sat in meditation until he became strong and confident. Then he climbed a mountain, shook himself, and began to grow in size and strength. When at last he felt ready, he set off with a roar, hurling himself through the sky with eyes blazing like forest fires.

When Hanuman landed in Lanka, he shrunk himself to the size of a cat so that he could explore Ravana's forts. After many dangerous adventures, he gave Sita the message that Rama was preparing to do battle to win her back, and then he jumped back over the sea to the Indian mainland.

During the subsequent battle of Lanka, Rama and his half-brother Lakshman were mortally wounded. Nothing would save them except a certain herb that grew only in the Himalayas. In his devotion to Rama, Hanuman flew to the mountains, again skirting danger all the way. But once he got there, he could not tell precisely which herb to pick, so he uprooted the whole mountain and carried it back to Lanka. The herb would be effective only before the moon rose. From the air, Hanuman saw the moon about to clear the horizon so he swallowed the moon and reached Lanka in time to heal Rama and Lakshman.

After the victory, Rama rewarded Hanuman with a bracelet of pearls and gold. Hanuman chewed it up and threw it away. When a bear asked why he had rejected the gift from God, Hanuman explained that it was useless to him since it did not have Rama's name on it. The bear said, "Well, if you feel that way, why do you keep your body?" At that, Hanuman ripped open his chest, and there were Rama and Sita seated in his heart, and all of his bones and muscles had "Ram, Ram, Ram" written all over them.

Eventually Sita is kidnapped by Ravana, who woos her unsuccessfully in his island kingdom and guards her with all manner of terrible demons. Although Rama is powerful, he and his half-brother Lakshman need the help of the monkeys and bears in the battle to get Sita back. Hanuman the monkey becomes the hero of the story. He symbolizes the power of faith and devotion to overcome our human frailties. In his love for the Lord he can do anything. The bloody battle ends in single-handed combat between Ravana and Rama. Rama blesses a sacred arrow with Vedic mantras and sends it straight into Ravana's heart. In what may be a later addition to the poem, when Rama and Sita are reunited, he accuses her of infidelity, so, to prove her innocence, she undergoes an ordeal by fire in which Agni protects her.

Another version of the *Ramayana*, perhaps as elaborated by later ballad-singers, has Rama ordering Sita into the forest because his subjects are suspicious of what may have happened while she was in Ravana's captivity. She is abandoned near the **ashram** of Valmiki. There she takes shelter and gives birth to twin boys. Years later, Valmiki and the sons attend a great ritual conducted by King Rama, and the boys sing the *Ramayana*.

There is an emotional reunion of the children with their father. Thereupon, Sita, a daughter of the earth, begs the earth to receive her if she has been faithful to Rama. With these words, she becomes a field of radiance and disappears into the ground:

> *O Lord of my being, I realize you in me and me in you. Our relationship is eternal. Through this body assumed by me, my service to you and your progeny is complete now. I dissolve this body to its original state.*
>
> *Mother Earth, you gave form to me. I have made use of it as I ought to. In recognition of its purity may you kindly absorb it into your womb.[20]*

Mahabharata   The other famous Hindu epic is the *Mahabharata*, a Sanskrit poem of more than 100,000 verses. Perhaps partly historical, it may have been composed between 400 BCE and 400 CE. The plot concerns the struggle between the sons of a royal family for control of a kingdom near what is now Delhi. The story teaches the importance of sons, the duties of kingship, the benefits of ascetic practice and righteous action, and the qualities of the gods. In contrast to the idealized characters in the *Ramayana*, the *Mahabharata* shows all sides of human nature, including greed, lust, intrigue, and the desire for power. It is thought to be relevant for all times and all peoples. A serial dramatization of the *Mahabharata* has drawn huge television audiences in contemporary India. The *Mahabharata* teaches one primary ethic: that the happiness of others is essential to one's own happiness. This consideration of others before oneself is a central dharmic virtue.

The eighteenth book of the *Mahabharata*, which may have originally been an independent mystical poem, is the **Bhagavad-Gita** ("Song of the Supreme

Rama and Lakshman shoot arrows into the breast of the demon Ravana, with Hanuman and the monkeys in the background. Sita waits within Ravana's compound, guarded by his demons. (North India, c. 19th century.)

Lord Krishna and Arjuna discuss profound philosophical questions in a battle chariot, as represented in this archway above the sacred Ganges River in Rishikesh.

Exalted One"). Krishna, revered as a manifestation of the Supreme, appears as the charioteer of Arjuna, who is preparing to fight on the virtuous side of a battle that will pit brothers against brothers, thus occasioning a treatise about the conflict that may arise between our earthly duties and our spiritual aspirations.

Before they plunge into battle, Krishna instructs Arjuna in the arts of self-transcendence and realization of the eternal. The eternal instructions are still central to Hindu spiritual practice. Arjuna is enjoined to withdraw his attention from the impetuous demands of the senses, ignoring all feelings of attraction or aversion. This will give him a steady, peaceful mind. He is instructed to offer devotional service and to perform the prescribed Vedic sacrifices, but for the sake of discipline, duty, and example alone rather than reward—to "abandon all attachment to success or failure . . . renouncing the fruits of action in the material world."[21]

Actually, Lord Krishna says those who do everything for love of the Supreme transcend the notion of duty. Everything they do is offered to the Supreme, "without desire for gain and free from egoism and lethargy."[22] Thus they feel peace, freedom from earthly entanglements, and unassailable happiness.

This yogic science of transcending the "lower self" by the "higher self" is so ancient that Krishna says it was originally given to the sun god and, through his agents, to humans. But in time it was lost, and Krishna is now renewing his instructions pertaining to "that very ancient science of the relationship with the Supreme."[23] He has taken human form again and again to teach the true religion:

Whenever and wherever there is a decline in religious practice . . .
and a predominant rise of irreligion—at that time I descend Myself.
    To deliver the pious and to annihilate the miscreants, as well as to re-establish
the principles of religion, I advent Myself millennium after millennium.[24]

Krishna says that everything springs from his Being:

> *There is no truth superior to Me. Everything rests upon Me, as pearls are strung*
> *on a thread. . . .*
> *I am the taste of water, the light of the sun and the moon, the syllable* om
> *in Vedic mantras; I am the sound in ether and ability in man. . . .*
> *All states of being—goodness, passion or ignorance—are manifested by My*
> *energy. I am, in one sense, everything—but I am independent. I am not under*
> *the modes of this material nature.*[25]

This supreme Godhead is not apparent to most mortals. The deity can be known only by those who love him, and for them it is easy, for they remember him at all times: "Whatever you do, whatever you eat, whatever you offer or give away, and whatever austerities you perform—do that . . . as an offering to Me." Any small act of devotion offered in love becomes a way to him: "If one offers Me with love and devotion a leaf, a flower, fruit, or water, I will accept it."[26]

The Puranas   The Puranas, poetic Sanskrit texts that narrate the myths of ancient times, were probably compiled between 500 and 1500 CE. There are a total of eighteen Puranas—six about Vishnu, six about Brahma, and six about Siva. These narratives popularize the more abstract philosophical teachings found in the Vedas and *Upanishads* by giving them concrete form. Of the Puranas, the most well known and loved is the *Bhagavata Purana*, which includes the life story of Krishna. Most Western Indologists think it was written about the ninth or tenth century CE, but according to Indian tradition it was one of the works written down at the beginning of Kali Yuga by Vyasa.

In the *Bhagavata Purana*, the supreme personality of Godhead is portrayed first in its vast dimensions: the Being whose body animates the material universe:

> *His eyes are the generating centers of all kinds of forms, and they glitter and*
> *illuminate. His eyeballs are like the sun and the heavenly planets. His ears hear*
> *from all sides and are receptacles for all the Vedas, and His sense of hearing is the*
> *generating center of the sky and of all kinds of sound.*[27]

This material universe we know is only one of millions of material universes. Each is like a bubble in the eternal spiritual sky, arising from the pores of the body of Vishnu, and these bubbles are created and destroyed as Vishnu breathes out and in. This cosmic conception is so vast that it is impossible for the mind to grasp it. It is much easier to comprehend and adore Vishnu in his incarnation as Krishna. Whereas he was a wise teacher in the *Bhagavad-Gita*, Krishna of the *Bhagavata Purana* is a much-loved child, raised by cowherds in an area called Vrindavan near Mathura on the Jumna River.

The mythology is rich in earthly pleasures. The boy Krishna mischievously steals balls of butter from the neighbors and wanders garlanded with flowers through the forest, happily playing his flute. Between episodes of carefree bravery in vanquishing demons that threaten the people, he playfully steals the hearts of the *gopis*, the cowherd girls. His favorite is the lovely Radha, but through his magical ways, he multiplies himself so that each thinks that he dances with her alone. Each is so much in love with Krishna that she feels she is one with him and desires only to serve him. Swami Vivekananda explains the spiritual meaning of the *gopis'* divine love for Krishna, which is:

Particular family relationships are extremely meaningful in Sanatana Dharma. For this first food ceremony, it is the paternal grandfather (otherwise the mother's sister) who offers the child its first solid food.

too holy to be attempted without giving up everything, too sacred to be understood until the soul has become perfectly pure. Even the Gita, the great philosophy itself, does not compare with that madness, for in the Gita the disciple is taught slowly how to walk towards the goal, but here is the madness of enjoyment, the drunkenness of love, where disciples and teachers and teachings and books … everything has been thrown away. What remains is the madness of love. It is forgetfulness of everything, and the lover sees nothing in the world except that Krishna, and Krishna alone.[28]

Eventually Krishna is called away on a heroic mission, never returning to the *gopis*. Their grief at his leaving and their intense longing for him serve as models for the *bhakti* path—the way of extreme devotion. In Hindu thought, the emotional longing of the lover for the beloved is one of the most powerful vehicles for concentration on the Supreme Lord.

The Hindu way of life

Although there is no single founder, devotional tradition, or philosophy which can be said to define Sanatana Dharma, everyday life is so imbued with spiritually meaningful aspects that spirituality is never far from one's mind. Those we will examine here include rituals, castes and social duties, life stages, home *puja*, homage to the guru, fasting, prayer, auspicious designs, reverence paid to trees and rivers, pilgrimages, and religious festivals.

Rituals

From the cradle to the cremation ground, the Hindu's life is wrapped up in rituals. There are sixteen rites prescribed in the ancient scriptures to purify and sanctify the person in his or her journey through life, including rites at the time of conception, the braiding of the pregnant mother's hair, birth, name-giving, beginning of solid foods, starting education, investing boys with a sacred thread, first leaving the family house, starting studies of Vedas, marriage, and death. The goal is to continually elevate the person above his or her basically animal nature.

Public worship—**puja**—is usually performed by *pujaris*, or brahmin priests, who are trained in Vedic practices and in proper recitation of Sanskrit texts. They conduct worship ceremonies in which the sacred presence is made tangible through devotions employing all the senses. Siva-lingams may be anointed with precious substances, such as ghee (clarified butter), honey, or sandalwood paste, with offerings of rose water and flowers. In a temple, devotees may have the great blessing of receiving **darsan** (visual contact with the divine) through the eyes of the images. One hears the sounds of mantras and ringing bells. Incense and flowers fill the area with uplifting fragrances. **Prasad**, food that has been sanctified by being offered to the deities and/or one's guru, is passed around to be eaten by devotees, who experience it as sacred and spiritually charged.

In temples, the deity image is treated as if it were a living king or queen. Fine-haired whisks may be waved before it, purifying the area for its presence. Aesthetically pleasing meals are presented on the deity's own dishes at appropriate intervals; fruits must be perfect, without any blemishes. During visiting hours, the deity holds court, giving audience to devotees. In the morning, the image is ritually bathed and dressed in sumptuous clothes for the day; at night, it may be put to rest in bedclothes. If it is hot, the deity takes a nap in the afternoon, so arrangements are made for its privacy. For festivals, the deity is carefully paraded through the streets. The great Jagganath festival, held only once every twelve years in Puri, was attended by some one and a half million devotees in 1996, all clambering for *darsan* of the deity, pulled in a massive sixteen-wheeled chariot (misspelled long ago as "juggernaut" in English).

A family visit a temple together, seeking spiritual blessings via a ceremony conducted by a pujari for the family members.

Loving service to the divine makes it real and present. The statue is not just a symbol of the deity; the deity may be experienced through the statue, reciprocating the devotee's attentions. According to Swami Sivasiva Palani:

> *It is thought that the subtle essences of these things given in devotion are actually absorbed by the divine, in an invisible and rather mystical process. It's as though we are feeding our God in an inner kind of way. It's thought that if this is done properly, with the right spirit, the right heartfulness, the right mantras, that we capture the attention of the personal Lord and that he actually communes with us through that process, and we with him. Of course, when I say "us" and "him" I connote a dualism that is meant to be transcended in this process.[29]*

Ritual fire ceremonies around a **havan**, or sacred fire place, are also conducted by Brahmin pandits, following ancient Vedic traditions. The Vedic principle of sacrifice was based on the idea that generous offerings to a deity will be rewarded. Fruits, fragrances, mixtures of herbs and grains, and ghee are placed in the fire as offerings to the deities, as invoked and praised by chants, with offerings conveyed by Agni, the god of fire. Sitting before the fire, devotees are also reminded of the brightness of the divine and the power of truth which illuminates the darkness. Such havans may be conducted in celebration of a particular deity, or at the behest of a patron for the sake of his health or good fortune.

Death ceremonies are also carried out by fire, as the body is cremated soon after death. Carefully washed, rubbed with fragrant sandalwood paste, and dressed in fresh clothes, the body is wrapped in white sheets and carried on a wooden stretcher to a burning ground. Relatives and wellwishers place flowers on the shrouded body and then logs are stacked around it to make a hot fire. Pandits may chant Vedic verses designed to cleanse the body and assist the soul's release from the body and its passage to the spiritual realm. The senior mourner—usually the eldest surviving son—carries a clay pot of water around the body three times, gradually pouring out the water, and then dashes the pot to the floor, a dramatic and emotional moment signifying the end of this earthly body. It is also he who then lights the pyre. Alternatively, the shrouded body may be placed in an electric crematorium. Once the burning of the body is complete, survivors take the remaining bits of bone and ash for ritual immersion in the waters of a holy river. Participating in such a ceremony, the mourners are visually assured that the soul has been set free and the body is no more. Cremation is psychologically satisfying in the context of Sanatana Dharma, in which the body is regarded as merely a disposable vehicle for the immortal soul.

Castes and social duties

Hinduism: Caste

The caste system which still shapes lives in modern India to a considerable extent goes back to the Vedic age. Because the Vedic sacrifices were a reciprocal communion with the gods, priests who performed the public sacrifices had to be carefully trained and maintain high standards of ritual purity. Those so trained—the brahmins—comprised a special occupational group. The orderly working of society included a clear division of labor among four major occupational groups, which later became entrenched as **castes**. The brahmins were the priests and philosophers, specialists in the life of the spirit. The next group, later called *kshatriyas*, were the nobility of feudal India: kings, warriors, and vassals. Their general function was to guard and preserve the society; they were expected to be courageous and majestic. **Vaishyas** were the economic specialists: farmers and merchants. The *shudra* caste were the manual laborers and artisans. Even lower than these original four castes were those "outcastes" who came to be considered **untouchables**. They carried on work such as removing human wastes and corpses, sweeping streets, and working with leather from the skins of dead cows—occupations that made their bodies and clothing abhorrent to others.

Over time, Vedic religion was increasingly controlled by the brahmins, and contact between castes was limited. Caste membership became hereditary. The caste system became as important as the Vedas in defining Hinduism until its social injustices were attacked in the nineteenth century. One of its opponents was Mahatma Gandhi, who renamed the lowest caste *harijans*, "the children of God." In 1948 the stigma of "untouchability" was legally abolished, though many caste distinctions still linger in modern India. Marriage across caste lines, for instance, is still often disapproved in India. If a boy and girl—one of whom is from the lowest caste—fall in love, sometimes the families from both sides will kill them rather than allow their marriage, to prevent disgrace or retribution.

Hinduism: Gandhi, Women, and Untouchability

Despite its abuses, the division of labor represented by the caste system is part of Sanatana Dharma's strong emphasis on social duties and sacrifice of individual desires for the sake of social order. Its purpose is to uplift people from worldly concerns and to encourage them to behave according to higher laws. The Vedas, other scriptures, and historical customs have all conditioned the Indian people to accept their social roles. These were set out in a major document known as the Code of Manu, compiled by 100 CE. In it are laws governing all aspects of life, including the proper conduct of rulers, dietary restrictions, marriage laws, daily rituals, purification rites, social laws, and ethical guidance. It prescribes hospitality to guests and the cultivation of such virtues as contemplation, truthfulness, compassion, non-attachment, generosity, pleasant dealings with people, and self-control. It condemns untouchables to living outside villages, eating only from broken dishes, and wearing only clothes removed from corpses. On the other hand, the code proposed charitable giving as the sacred duty of the upper castes, and thus provided a safety net for those at the bottom of this hierarchical system: "A householder must give as he is able and to those who do not cook for themselves, and to all beings one must distribute without detriment."[30]

Hospitality to human guests is also a duty for people of all castes. To turn someone away from your door without feeding him or at least offering him a drink of water is a great sin, for every person is the deity incarnate. Ceremonies are often held for making offerings to a deity and feeding the public. The head of the household may, toward the end of his life, engage the services of a number of brahmins to help complete the requisite 24,000,000 repetitions of the *Gayatrimantra* during his lifetime. Beggars take advantage of belief in sacrifice by saying that those who give to them will be blessed. But the most important sacrifices are considered to be inner sacrifices—giving one's entire self over to the Supreme Reality.

Life stages

The process of attaining spiritual realization or liberation is thought to take at least a lifetime, and probably many lifetimes. Birth as a human being is prized as a chance to advance toward spiritual perfection. In the past, spiritual training was usually available to upper-caste males only; women and *shudras* were excluded. It was preceded by an initiation ceremony in which the boy received the sacred thread, a cord of three threads to be worn across the chest from the left shoulder.

A Brahmin male's lifespan was traditionally divided into four periods of approximately twenty-five years each. For the first twenty-five years he is a chaste student at the feet of a teacher. Next comes the householder stage, in which he is expected to marry, raise a family, and contribute productively to society. After this period, he starts to detach himself from worldly pursuits and to turn to meditation and scriptural study. By the age of seventy-five, he is able to withdraw totally from society and become a **sannyasin**.

Living as a renunciate, the *sannyasin* is a contemplative who cuts himself off from wife and family, declaring, "No one belongs to me and I belong to no one." Some *sannyasins* take up residence in comfortable temples; others wander alone with only a water jar, a walking staff, and a begging bowl as possessions. Some wandering *sannyasins* wear no clothes. In silence, the *sannyasin* is supposed to concentrate on practices that will finally release him from *samsara* into cosmic consciousness.

The majority of contemporary Hindu males do not follow this path to its *sannyasin* conclusion in old age, but many Hindus still become *sannyasins*. Some of them have renounced the world at a younger age and joined a monastic order, living in an **ashram**, a retreat community that has developed around a teacher.

Hinduism: Women

Home puja

As householders, both women and men carry on *puja* (worship) in their homes. Nearly every home in India has a shrine with pictures or small statues of various deities, and many have a prayer room set aside for worship. For *puja*, ritual purity is emphasized; the time for prayer and offerings to the deities is after the morning bath or after one has washed in the evening. *Puja* is an everyday observance, although among orthodox families, menstruating women are considered unclean and are not allowed to approach the shrines. Typically, a small oil lamp and a smoldering stick of incense are waved in a circle before the deities' images. If the devotee or family has a guru, a picture of him or her is usually part of the shrine.

The guru

Nearly every practicing Hindu seeks to place himself or herself at the feet of a spiritual teacher, or **guru**. The title "guru" is applied to venerable spiritual guides. Gurus do not declare themselves as teachers; people are drawn to them because they have achieved spiritual status to which the seekers aspire. Gurus are often regarded as enlightened or "fully realized" individuals. A guru does not provide academic instruction. Rather, he or she gives advice, example, and encouragement to those seeking enlightenment or realization.

Many gurus migrated to the West to spread Sanatana Dharma there. Paramahansa Yogananda's book Autobiography of a Yogi *continues to attract Western followers to Indian religious traditions.*

> *Anyone and everyone cannot be a guru. A huge timber floats on the water and can carry animals as well. But a piece of worthless wood sinks, if a man sits on it, and drowns him.*
>
> *Ramakrishna*[31]

Even the poorest Hindu families have a special room or place for puja *to their favorite deities.*

The Siddha tradition of southern India specializes in "teaching" by **shaktipat**—the power of a glance, word, touch, or thought. A disciple of the late Swami Muktananda describes the effect, referring to him as "Baba" (Father):

> *When a seeker receives* shaktipat, *he experiences an overflowing of bliss within and becomes ecstatic. In Baba's presence, all doubts and misgivings vanish, and one experiences inner contentment and a sense of fulfillment.*[32]

When seekers find their guru, they love and honor him or her as their spiritual parent. The guru does not always behave as a loving parent; often disciples are treated harshly, to test their faith and devotion or to strip away the ego. True devotees are nevertheless grateful for opportunities to serve their guru, out of love. They often bend to touch the feet or hem of the robe of the guru, partly out of humility and partly because great power is thought to emanate from the guru's feet. Humbling oneself before the guru is considered necessary in order to receive the teaching. A metaphor commonly used is that of a cup and a pitcher of water. If the cup (the disciple, or *chela*) is already full, no water (spiritual wisdom) can be poured into it from the pitcher (the guru). Likewise, if the cup is on the same level as the pitcher, there can be no pouring. What is necessary is for the cup to be empty and below the pitcher; then the water can be freely poured into the cup.

An Indian woman prepares a protective rice flour pattern on the earth outside her home, honoring the ancient tradition by which her female ancestors created intuitive designs to bring spiritual protection for their families.

Fasts, prayers, and auspicious designs

Orthodox brahmins observe many days of fasting and prayer, corresponding to auspicious points in the lunar and solar cycles or times of danger, such as the four months of the monsoon season. The ancient practice of astrology is so highly regarded that many couples are now choosing birth by Caesarean section for the purpose of selecting the most auspicious moment for their children's birth.

Many expressions of Indian spirituality, particularly in rural areas, are not encapsulated within Brahmanic traditions but rather have a timeless existence of their own. Such, for instance, are the homemade designs daily laid out before homes at dawn. They are created by women to protect their household by inviting a deity such as the goddess Lakshmi. Typically made of edible substances, such as rice flour, the designs are soon dismantled by insects and birds, but this is of no concern, for they help to fulfill the dharmic requirement that one should feed a thousand souls every day.

Reverence of trees and rivers

Practices such as worship under large trees stretches back into pre-history and is apparent in archaeological evidence from the Harappan civilization. Such worship continues at countless small shrines today. There is a strong taboo against cutting certain sacred tree species, such as the peepul tree, which sprouts wherever it can gain the slightest foothold, often in stone or brick walls, even on the sides of buildings. Whole tracts of virgin forest are kept intact by villagers in some parts of India. There they reverently protect both animal and plant life with the understanding that the area is the home of a deity. These sacred groves are now viewed by environmentalists as important islands of biological diversity.

Not only forests but also hilltops, mountains, and river sources are often viewed as sacred and their natural environment thus protected to a certain extent. The Narmada River, one of India's most sacred, is regarded by millions of people as a goddess (as are most Indian rivers). Its banks are lined with thousands of temples devoted to Mother Narmada and Lord Shiva. Pilgrims reverently circumambulate the entire 815-mile (1,312-km) length of the river, from its source in central India to its mouth in the Gulf of Khambhat, and back again. However, the river and its huge watershed are the subjects of the world's largest water development scheme. The highest of the dams is under construction, creating a reservoir with a final proposed height of 448 feet (136.5 m). When the reservoir is filled, some 245 villages will be submerged, temples and all. The idea is to capture the water and divert it to drought-ridden areas to benefit people there. However, the inhabitants of the watershed that will be inundated are closely linked to their local sacred landscape. One of them explains, "Our gods cannot move from this place. How can we move without them?"[33] Fierce conflicts have been raging since 1990 between environmentalists and social activists who are fighting the high dams, claiming they will adversely affect at least one million people in the watershed for the sake of vested interests elsewhere, and modernists who regard such high dams, as Nehru said, as "the secular temples of modern India."[34]

High dams are not the only threat to sacred rivers. Religious practices themselves may lead to high levels of water pollution. Mass bathing on auspicious occasions is accompanied by wastes, such as butter oil, flowers, and human excreta (contrary to scriptural injunctions about proper behavior in sacred rivers). The remains of dead bodies reverently immersed in the sacred rivers may be incompletely cremated. Immersion of idols of Ganesh or Durga on holy days as a symbol of purification (as explained in the next section) has become a major source of water pollution. In one year alone, ritual immersion of idols in Calcutta added to the Hoogli River an estimated 17 tons of varnish and 32 tons of paints, including manganese, lead, mercury, and chromium.[35]

Pilgrimages

Pilgrimages to holy places and sacred rivers are thought to be special opportunities for personal purification and spiritual elevation. Millions of pilgrims yearly undertake strenuous climbs to remote mountain sites that are thought to be blessed by the divine. One of the major pilgrimage sites is Amarnath cave. At an altitude of 11,090 feet (3,380 m) in the Himalayas of Kashmir, ice has formed a giant stalagmite, which is highly revered as a Siva lingam. Pilgrims may have been trekking to this holy place in the high Himalayas for up to three thousand years. The 14,800-feet (45-km) footpath over a glacier is so dangerous that 250 people were killed by freak storms and landslides in 1996, but in subsequent years, tens of

Millions of Hindus undertake difficult pilgrimages to worship at mountain shrines each year.

Pilgrims to Benares take a purifying bath and offer prayers at sunrise in the sacred Ganges River.

thousands of devotees continue to undertake the pilgrimage. Similarly, Saktas trek up to Saktipithas, fifty-one pilgrimage spots in the Indian subcontinent that are thought to mark abodes of the goddess or places where parts of Her body now rest.

The places where great saints and teachers have lived also automatically become places of pilgrimage during their lives and after they pass on. Their powerful vibrations are felt to still permeate and bless these sites. One such place is the holy mountain of Arunachala in southern India. The great saint Ramana Maharshi (1879–1951) lived there so absorbed in Ultimate Consciousness that he neither talked nor ate and had to be force-fed by another holy man. But the needs of those who gathered around him drew out his compassion and wisdom, and he spontaneously counseled them in their spiritual needs.

Festivals

Hinduism: Festivals

Sanatana Dharma honors the divine in so many forms that almost every day a religious celebration is being held in some part of India. Sixteen religious holidays are honored by the central government so that everyone can leave work to join in the throngs of worshippers. These are calculated partially on a lunar calendar, so dates vary from year to year. Most Hindu festivals express spirituality in its happiest aspects. Group energy attracts the gods to overcome evils, and humorous abandon helps merry-makers transform their fears.

On a midwinter night in northern India, people happily celebrate Lohari by building a bonfire and throwing popcorn, peanuts, and sesame candies into it. The feeling is that one is symbolically throwing away one's evils, and at the same time invoking blessings for the year to come. In particular, families who have given birth to a male child during the past year perform this ceremony for his auspicious future.

Holi is the riotously joyful celebration of the death of winter and the return of colorful spring. In northern Indian areas where Vaishnavism is strong, the holiday is associated with Krishna, for as an infant he is said to have killed a demon employed by the king of winter. Pilgrims flock to Mathura, purported birthplace of Krishna, for re-enactments of Krishna's exploits with the *gopis*. The festivities are probably of ancient indigenous origin, and in some areas, the two-day craziness is dedicated to Kama, the god of sexual love. Whatever the excuse, bands of people take to the streets throwing brightly colored powder or paint on

Youths fling paint upon each other with gay abandon at Holi.

Legends about Krishna as a child are often re-enacted by children as part of a holiday honoring Krishna's birthday, Janmashtami.

anyone they meet. At the end of this uninhibited gaiety, everyone hugs and old grudges are dropped as the new year begins.

In July or August a special day, Naga Panchami, is devoted to the *nagas*, or snakes. Snakes were considered powerful gods by the indigenous peoples, and the tradition persists. In southern Indian villages, where they are especially honored, thousands of live snakes are caught and exhibited by brave handlers. Worshippers sprinkle vermilion and rice on the hoods of cobras, considered especially sacred. On Naga Panchami, farmers abstain from ploughing to avoid disrupting any snake-holes.

In August or September, Vaishnavites celebrate Krishna's birthday (Janmashtami). Devotees fast and keep a vigil until midnight, retelling stories of Krishna's life or reading his enlightened wisdom from the *Bhagavad-Gita*. In some places Krishna's image is placed in a cradle and lovingly rocked by devotees. Elsewhere, pots of milk, curds, and butter are strung high above the ground to be seized by young men who form human pyramids to get to their prize. They romp about with the pots, drinking and spilling their contents like Krishna, playful stealer of these milk products he loved.

At the end of the summer, it is Ganesh who is honored, especially in western and southern India, during Ganesh Chaturti. Special potters make elaborate clay images of the jovial elephant-headed remover of obstacles, son of Parvati who formed him

On Janmashtami, devotees lovingly rock an image of the child Krishna in a cradle.

from her own body's dirt and sweat, and set him to stand guard while she bathed. Since he wouldn't let Siva in, her angry spouse smashed the boy's head into a thousand pieces. Parvati demanded that the boy be restored to life with a new head, but the first one found was that of a baby elephant. To soothe Parvati's distress at the peculiarity of the transplant, Siva granted Ganesh the power of removing obstacles. The elephant-headed god is now the first to be invoked in all rituals. After days of being sung to and offered sweets, the Ganesh images are carried to a body of water and bidden farewell with prayers for an easy year until Ganesh Chaturti comes around again.

In different parts of India, the first nine or ten days of Asvina, the lunar month corresponding to September or October, are dedicated either to the Durga Puja (in which elaborate images of the many-armed goddess celebrate her powers to vanquish the demonic forces) or to Dussehra (which marks Rama's nine nights of worshipping Durga before killing Ravana on the tenth day). The theme of both Durga Puja and Dussehra is the triumph of good over evil.

At the end of the Durga Puja, images of the ten-armed vanquisher of evil are carried to the river and consigned to the deep, so that she may return to her mate Siva, who awaits her in the Himalayas.

Twenty days later, on the night of the new moon, is Divali, the happy four-day festival of lights. Variously explained as the return of Rama after his exile, the *puja* of Lakshmi (goddess of wealth, who visits only clean homes), and the New Year of those following one of the Indian calendars, it is a time for tidying business establishments and financial records, cleaning and illuminating houses with oil lamps, wearing new clothes, gambling, feasting, honoring clay images of Lakshmi and Ganesh, and setting off fireworks.

Initially more solemn is Mahashivaratri, a day of fasting and a night of keeping vigil to earn merit with Siva. During the ascetic part of the observance, many pilgrims go to sacred rivers or special tanks of water for ritual bathing. Siva lingams and statues are venerated, and the faithful stay awake throughout the night, chanting and telling stories of their Lord. In one of the stories, a discussion among Brahma, Vishnu, and Siva leads to Siva's manifesting as a pillar of fire and challenging the others to touch the ends, which they will not. A reformist group, Arya Samaj, decries what it considers superstition and idolatry and honors the day as the end of a week-long celebration of their reform. They carry out Vedic fire sacrifices and hold spiritual talks, throwing personal offerings into the fire on the last day.

Every few years, millions of Hindus of all persuasions gather for the immense Kumbha Mela. It is held alternately at four sacred spots where drops of the holy nectar of immortality are said to have fallen. On one day in 2001, in what has been recorded as the largest ever gathering of human beings for a single purpose, over twenty-five million people amassed at the point near Allahabad where the Jumna River meets the sacred Ganges and the invisible Saraswati. There they took a purifying bath in the frigid waters on the most auspicious date, as determined by astrologers. Among the Kumbha Mela pilgrims are huge processions of ascetic *sadhus* from various orders, many of whom leave their retreats only for this festival. They gather to discuss religious matters and also social problems, sometimes leading to revisions of Hindu codes of conduct. Many of the lay pilgrims are poor people who undergo great hardships to reach the site. A typical pilgrim, an illiterate woman from West Bengal, traveled to Haridwar with her family in a crowded bus, slept in the open in the cold, and was fed free meals at immense tents set up by philanthropical groups and families. She explained, "We are poor, but we have enough. I asked God not for money but for peace and salvation."[36]

Hinduism in the modern world

Hinduism did not develop in India in isolation. Muslims began taking over certain areas beginning in the eighth century CE; during the sixteenth and seventeenth centuries a large area was ruled by the Muslim Mogul emperors. Islam and Hinduism generally co-existed, despite periods of intolerance, along with Buddhism and Jainism, which had also grown up within India. Indian traders carried some aspects of Sanatana Dharma to Java and Bali, where Hinduism survives today with a unique Balinese flavor.

When the Mogul Empire collapsed, European colonialists moved in. Ultimately the British dominated, and in 1857 India was placed under direct British rule. Christian missionaries set about to correct abuses they perceived in certain Hindu practices, such as widow-burning and the caste system. But they also taught those who were being educated in their schools that Hinduism was

Haridwar is one of the four sites where huge Kumbha Mela celebrations are held on the banks of the Ganges.

"intellectually incoherent and ethically unsound."[37] Some Indians believed them and drifted away from their ancient tradition.

To counteract Western influences, Mahatma ("Great Soul") Gandhi (1869–1948) encouraged grassroots nationalism, emphasizing that the people's strength lay in awareness of spiritual truth and in nonviolent resistance to military-industrial oppression. He claimed that these qualities were the essence of all religions, including Hinduism, which he considered the universal religion.

In addition to being made a focus for political unity, Hinduism itself was revitalized by a number of spiritual leaders. One of these was Ramakrishna (1836–1886) who was a devotee of the Divine Mother in the form of Kali. Eschewing ritual, he communicated with her through intense love. He practiced Tantric disciplines and the *bhavanas* (types of loving relationships). These brought him spiritual powers, spiritual insight, and reportedly a visible brilliance, but he longed only to be a vehicle for pure devotion:

> I seek not, good Mother, the pleasures of the senses! I seek not fame! Nor do I long for those powers which enable one to do miracles! What I pray for, O good Mother, is pure love for Thee—love for Thee untainted by desires, love without alloy, love that seeketh not the things of the world, love for Thee that welleth up unbidden out of the depths of the immortal soul![38]

Ramakrishna worshipped the divine through many Hindu paths, as well as Islam and Christianity, and found the same One in them all. Intoxicated with the One, he had continual visions of the Divine Mother and ecstatically worshipped her in unorthodox, uninhibited ways. For instance, once he fed a cat some food that was supposed to be a temple offering for the Divine Mother, for she revealed herself to him in everything, including the cat. He also placed his spiritual bride, Sarada Devi, in the chair reserved for the deity, honoring her as the Great Goddess.

The pure devotion and universal spiritual wisdom Ramakrishna embodied inspired what is now known as the Ramakrishna Movement, or the Vedanta Society. A famous disciple, named Vivekananda (1863–1902), carried the eternal message of Sanatana Dharma to the world beyond India and excited so much interest in the West that Hinduism became a global religion. He also reintroduced Indians to the profundities of their great traditions.

Within India Hinduism was also influenced by reform movements such as Brahmo Samaj and Arya Samaj. The former defended Hindu mysticism and *bhakti* devotion to an immanent deity. The latter advocated a return to what it saw as the purity of the Vedas, rejecting image worship, devotion to a multiplicity of deities, priestly privileges, and popular rituals. Though different, both movements were designed to convince intellectuals of the validity of "true" Hinduism.

Ramakrishna, the great nineteenth-century mystic, recognized the divine as being both formless and manifested in many forms, and also as transcending both form and formlessness.

> Do not care for doctrines, do not care for dogmas, or sects, or churches, or temples; they count for little compared with the essence of existence in each [person], which is spirituality. . . . Earn that first, acquire that, and criticise no one, for all doctrines and creeds have some good in them.
>
> Ramakrishna[39]

Global Hinduism

Hinduism is also experiencing vibrant growth beyond the Indian subcontinent, partly among expatriates and partly among converts from other faiths. For the past hundred years, many self-proclaimed gurus have left India to develop followings in other countries. Some were discovered to be fraudulent, with scandalous private behavior or motives of wealth and power. Despite increased Western wariness of gurus, some of the exported movements have continued to grow.

Many non-Indians discovered Sanatana Dharma by reading *Autobiography of a Yogi*, by Paramahansa Yogananda (1893–1952). The book describes his intriguing spiritual experiences with Indian gurus and also explains principles of Sanatana Dharma in loving fashion. Yogananda travelled to the United States and began a movement, the California-based Self-Realization Fellowship, which has survived his death and is still growing under the supervision of Western disciples, with centers, temples, and living communities in forty-six countries.

Another still-flourishing example is the Netherlands-based Transcendental Meditation (TM) movement, which was begun by Maharishi Mahesh Yogi in the 1960s. For a fee, he and his disciples teach people secret mantras and assert that repeating the mantra for twenty minutes twice each day will bring great personal benefits. These range from enhanced athletic prowess to increased satisfaction with life. By paying more money, advanced practitioners can also learn how to "fly." That is, they take short hops into the air while sitting cross-legged. The organization claims a success rate of sixty-five percent in ending drug and alcohol addiction. TM has now entered politics as well, with its Natural Law Party promoting its own candidates in fifty countries. It is a vast global organization, complete with luxurious health spas in Europe, a Vedic "theme park" near Niagara Falls in Canada, Vedic-based development projects in Africa, colleges, universities, and Maharishi Schools of Management in many countries, and an ashram for 10,000 people in India.

Another rather unlikely success story is found in ISKCON, the International Society for Krishna Consciousness. In 1965, the Indian guru A. C. Bhaktivedanta Swami Prabhupada arrived in the United States, carrying the asceticism and *bhakti* devotion of Sri Caitanya's tradition of Krishna worship from India to the heart of Western materialistic culture. Adopting the dress and diet of Hindu monks and nuns, his initiates lived in temple communities. Their days began at 4 a.m. with meditation, worship, chanting of the names of Krishna and Ram, and scriptural study, with the aim of turning from a material life of sense gratification to one of transcendent spiritual happiness. During the day, they chanted and danced in the streets to introduce others to the bliss of Krishna, distributed literature (especially Swami Prabhupada's illustrated and esteemed translation of the *Bhagavad-Gita*), attracted new devotees, and raised funds. Despite schisms and scandals, the movement has continued since Swami Prabhupada's death in 1977, and is growing in strength in various countries, particularly in India and eastern Europe. In England, followers have turned a great mansion into a huge ISKCON temple, which also serves Indian immigrants as a place to celebrate major festivals. Exposure of scandals, such as the physical, emotional, and sexual abuse of children in ISKCON schools, has prompted new reform efforts within the movement. At present there are approximately one million ISKCON followers worldwide.

Dharmic Principles: The Swadhyaya Movement

Today there are said to be 20 million people in 100,000 villages in India who are beneficiaries of a silent social revolution based on the principles of the ancient Hindu scriptures, especially the *Bhagavad-Gita*. The movement is called Swadhyaya. The term means self-study, using traditional scriptural teachings as a means for critically analyzing oneself in order to improve. On this basis, villagers and village life have profoundly improved.

The work began in the 1950s, as scriptural scholar Pandurang Shastri Athavale, known by his followers as "Dada" (elder brother), determined that the Gita was "capable of resolving the dilemmas of modern man and solving the problems of material life, individual and social."[40] He founded a school near Bombay, refusing until today to accept any financial help from the government or outside funding agency, insisting that "those institutions which depend upon others' favors are never able to achieve anything worthwhile or carry out divine work."[41] He named the buildings for the ancient sages who have inspired people to live according to Vedic principles. It was they who recognized that within each person is a divine spark whose realization gives them the energy and guidance with which to uplift themselves. As Dada once observed, the sage who wrote the *Ramayana* is

> *virtually urging us to take Ram—the awareness that the Lord is with us and within us all the time—to every home and every heart, as this alone will provide the confidence and the strength to the weakest of the weak and will bring joy and fragrance into the life of every human being.*[42]

Realization of the divine within themselves also leads to realization of the divine within others, which is the beginning of social harmony and cooperation.

The principle upon which Dada's social development work is centered is *bhakti*, or selfless devotion. He inspired his students to pay devotional visits to towns and villages in Gujarat state. They carried their own food and asked for nothing from the people. They simply met the inhabitants one to one and spoke of the divine love which made them reach out to distant places. After years of regular visits and assurance that gratefulness to God and brotherly love was developing among the villagers, they allowed the villagers to build simple hut temples of local materials, devotional places for villagers of all castes and creeds.

In gratitude toward the in-dwelling God for being present when they go to their farms, giving them energy to work, *swadhyayees* feel that God is entitled to a share in the produce. They therefore bring a portion of their income to the hut temples to be distributed among the most needy, as the benevolence of God.

Believing in work as worship, the villagers were also inspired to set aside a portion of land to be farmed in common, as "God's farm." All give a certain number of days of volunteer service on the farm, in grateful service to God. The harvests are treated as "impersonal wealth." One-third of the money is distributed directly to the needy; two-thirds are put into a community trust for long-term needs to help people stand on their own feet.

The movement spreads from village to village, as missionaries who have seen the positive results of the program voluntarily go to other areas to tell the people there about it. When Swadhyaya volunteers first appeared in fishing villages on India's west coast, they found the people were spending what income they had on gambling and liquor. Now, the same people place a portion of their earnings from fishing and navigation at the feet of God, as it were. Since they no longer waste money on gambling and liquor, they have created such a surplus that they have been able to purchase community fishing boats. These are manned by volunteers on a rotation basis, with everyone eager to take a turn, and the income is distributed impersonally as God's graceful beneficence to those in need.

In addition, *swadhyayees* have also created "tree temples," in which trees are planted in formerly barren lands and cared for in a spirit of devotion to God. *Swadhyayees* have also developed cultural programs, sports clubs, family stores, dairy produce centers, children's centers, centers for domestic skills, and discussion centers for intellectuals and professionals. Through waterharvesting by recharging of over ninety thousand wells and construction of over five hundred percolation tanks, *swadhyayees* by their own skill and labor are generating additional annual farm produce worth some 300 million US dollars for small and medium-sized farmers. They have also introduced soakpit systems for disposal of household drainwater and refuse, thus improving village hygiene and health.

Throughout the growing network of *swadhyayees*, there is no hierarchy and no paid staff. Those whose lives have been improved by inner study and devotional service become enthusiastic volunteers and living demonstrations that people are happiest when dharmic principles are placed ahead of self-interest.

Some contemporary gurus are also enjoying great global popularity. One of the most famous at present is Mata Amritanandamayi, a seemingly tireless, motherly saint from South India who takes people from all walks of life into her arms. She encourages her "children" to find personal solace and compassion for others through worship of the divine in any form. Many of her followers regard "Amma" herself as the personification of the Divine Mother.

Hindu identity

At the same time that Hinduism is reaching around the world, some Hindu groups within India are giving Hinduism a strongly nationalistic thrust. In particular, the RSS—Rashtriya Svayamsevak Sangh—arose early in the twentieth century, espousing Hindu cultural renewal in order to combat the ills of modernity and return to an idealized past referred to as "Ram Rajya," the legendary kingdom of Lord Ram, when Hindu virtues were maintained by a perfect ruler. This movement gave organized expression to the ideals of V. D. Savarkar, who wrote of an ancient Hindu nation and *Hindutva* ("Hindu-ness"), excluding Muslims and Christians as aliens in India, in contrast to the historical evidence that Sanatana Dharma is a noncentralized, evolving composite of variegated ways of worship.

The RSS continues to be a powerful force shaping politics in India today. Its activities run counter to the **secularism** established by India's constitution, which recognizes the multi-cultural, multi-religious fabric of the country and does not confer favored political status on any religion. But in the eyes of what could be called Hindu "fundamentalists," secularism is a cover which the political elite have used to hide their own corruption. Under the guise of secularism, they feel, people are being robbed of their religious values and identity, which the RSS, the religious organization Vishva Hindu Parishad (VHP), and political parties such as the Bharatiya Janata Party (BJP) say they are trying to restore, claiming the moral high ground even while engaging in illegal activities themselves.

Mata Amrityanandamayi comforts a man after his operation for a brain tumor and also embraces his father with her left arm.

A major focus of these activities is the small town of Ayodhya, which according to Hindu mythology is the birthplace of Lord Ram. According to Hindutva belief, Babur, the Muslim Mughal ruler, had the main temple commemorating Ram's birthplace torn down and the Babri Mosque built on its ruins. Archaeological research is presently being undertaken to determine whether this is historically accurate. However, firm believers had long attempted to take matters into their own hands and redress this perceived insult to their holy place. In 1992, some 200,000 Hindu extremists managed to enter Ayodhya and tear down the Babri Mosque. This act was followed by a spate of Hindu-Muslim violence throughout India. The site is still under dispute, with extremists demanding to build a new temple to Lord Ram there as a symbol of Ram Rajya.

The RSS maintains tens of thousands of branches in Indian villages and cities where Hindu men and boys meet for group games, martial arts training, songs, lectures, and prayers to the Hindu nation, conceived as the Divine Mother. The leader of the RSS has publicly urged throwing all Christian missionaries out of India and has asserted that all Indians are actually Hindus. There are estimated to be 12,000 RSS schools in India in which children are, according to the National Steering Committee for Textbook Evaluation, being taught from texts "designed to promote bigotry and religious fanaticism in the name of inculcating knowledge of culture in the young generation."[43]

Political affiliates of the RSS with a "Hindu agenda"—particularly the BJP (Bharatiya Janata Party)—have become very powerful in Indian politics. During recent years, the BJP was the leading party in the central government. It was in power in 2002 when one coach of a train carrying volunteers who were seeking to illegally construct the new temple in Ayodhya caught fire in the state of Gujarat and was surrounded by a presumably Muslim mob. Inside the coach, 59 Hindus burned to death, a horror that was followed by terrible inter-religious violence. Perhaps two thousand people, most of them Muslims, were killed by mobs while local officials did little to stop them. Muslim mosques and shrines were also destroyed. Terrified, many Muslims in the area abandoned their homes and became refugees.

Extremist Hindu groups are also trying to woo Christian converts back to Hinduism and are actively opposing Christianity in India. In recent years, Christian nuns in India have been raped, priests killed, Bibles burned, and churches and Christian schools destroyed, apparently by Hindu extremists. Some "untouchable" Hindus have converted to Christianity, Buddhism, or Islam because those religions do not make caste distinctions. Christians have instead offered social services for the poor such as schools and hospitals. An estimated fifty percent of all Christians in India were formerly of scheduled caste origin. Statements by certain Christians from outside India have exacerbated Hindu complaints against conversions to Christianity. Pope John Paul II, for instance, in his 1999 tour of India, said, "Just as in the first millennium the Cross was planted in the soil of Europe, and in the second one that of the Americas and Africa, we can pray that in the third Christian millennium a great harvest of faith will be reaped in this vast and vital continent."[44] And a Southern Baptist book published in the United States angered Hindus with a reference to "more than 900 million people lost in the hopeless darkness of Hinduism."[45]

Tensions also continue to run high between Hindus and Muslims in Kashmir, where efforts to bring Kashmiri independence from India often pits Hindus and Muslims against each other. Serious political concerns are often obscured by

Dr. Karan Singh

Globally active in an extraordinary number of public posts and projects, Dr. Karan Singh is also one of the world's most respected spokesmen for Hinduism. He was born wealthy, as heir to the Maharaja of Jammu and Kashmir, but has never retired from a life of intense public service. In fact, he turned over his entire princely inheritance to the service of the people of India and converted his palace into a museum and library, which houses his priceless collection of artworks and his personal library of over twenty thousand books.

Dr. Karan Singh's political life began in 1949 when he was only eighteen years old, for his father appointed him Regent of Jammu and Kashmir, as requested by Prime Minister Jawaharlal Nehru. Eventually he was elected to the Governorship of the area, thus becoming both the last representative of the old hereditary lineage and the first of the new democratic era. In 1967, he became the youngest person ever to become a Central Cabinet Minister in India, in the Cabinet of Prime Minister Indira Gandhi. Over the years, he has held three ministerial posts, as well as many other posts, including being the Chancellor of Jammu and Kashmir University, Founder of the International Centre of Science, Culture and Consciousness, President of the People's Commission on Environment and Development, Chairman of the Temple of Understanding, and a member of the international steering committee of the Global Forum of Parliamentarians and Spiritual Leaders on Human Survival.

A brilliant orator, Dr. Karan Singh quotes extensively and effectively from the Vedas in his talks and says he has been deeply influenced by them—in particular, the *Upanishads*. He states:

The Upanishads *are the high-water mark of Hindu philosophy. They are texts of tremendous wisdom and power. They represent some of the deepest truths with regard to the all-pervasiveness of the divine. One is the concept that every individual encapsulates a spark of the divine, the atman. There is also the concept of the human race as an extended family. Then there is the concept that "The truth is one; the wise call it by many names." That is the ultimate unity of all religions. We also have the concept of the welfare of the many, the happiness of the many. Thus, there are universal concepts in the Vedanta which have been of tremendous inspiration to me in all the work that I do in interfaith.*

Busy though he is, Dr. Karan Singh always takes time daily to perform his private *puja* (worship ceremonies). He is a worshipper of Lord Siva. Before Lord Siva, he also worships the goddess, as is common in Hindu tradition. He feels that acknowledging the feminine aspect of the divine is a very important part of Hindu worship, as is the freedom of choice of one's favorite deity.

My personal devotion is to Lord Siva; my philosophical background is the Vedanta. As part of my daily routine, I have my own puja. *I do it in the morning, again at night before going to bed, and in the course of the day. Ours is not a religion where you go once a week to a church and that's it. Hinduism is supposed to be something which permeates your entire consciousness. Therefore these* puja *sessions are supposed to be ways of reminding yourself of the Divinity.*

Despite his personal devotion to Lord Siva, Dr. Karan Singh emphasizes that Hinduism supports acceptance of all manifestations of the divine, and therefore all religions. He asserts,

The exclusivism or monopolistic tendencies in religions who claim that they have the sole agency in the sphere of the divine is not acceptable in this day and age. We have got to accept the fact that there are multiple paths to the divine. We have to not only accept them—we have to respect whoever is traveling on his or her path. That has come to me particularly from the Vedanta tradition.

Although Dr. Karan Singh has often been deeply involved in government, he is free from the taint of corruption and scandal that mars so many political careers. He attributes his clear reputation partly to the fact that the was born into "favourable financial circumstances," and also to his religious upbringing:

Not being corrupt is part of the basic religious teachings around the world. We are brought up on the stories of Raja Harish Chandra, who gave up everything for the sake of truth, and Sri Rama, who gave up everything for the sake of his father's word, and so on. Those sort of mythological stories based on truth and the quest for truth are very strong in wisdom. And if you are pursuing the path of truth, then I presume that automatically rules out your being corrupt.[46]

divisions along religious lines, and peace continues to elude the people of the beautiful Kashmir valley.

Such conflicts are not in keeping with Sanatana Dharma's ideal of tolerance for many ways to the divine. Although tensions between religions exist in many regions of India, what predominates is the spirit of accommodation with which the various communities have lived side by side for hundreds of years. Thus, in 2002 the Indian Supreme Court passed a landmark ruling supporting equal education about all religions in Indian schools. The ruling cites Mahatma Gandhi, father of independent India, who wrote:

Let no one even for a moment entertain the fear that a reverent study of other religions is likely to weaken or shake one's faith in one's own. The Hindu system of philosophy regards all religions as containing the elements of truth in them and enjoins an attitude of respect and reverence towards them all.[47]

The Indian Supreme Court has formally defined Hindu beliefs in a way that affirms universality rather than exclusiveness. According to the Court's definition, to be a Hindu means:

1 Acceptance and reverence for the Vedas as the foundation of Hindu philosophy;
2 A spirit of tolerance, and willingness to understand and appreciate others' points of view, recognizing that truth has many sides;
3 Acceptance of the belief that vast cosmic periods of creation, maintenance, and dissolution continuously recur;
4 Acceptance of belief in reincarnation;
5 Recognition that paths to truth and salvation are many;
6 Recognition that there may be numerous gods and goddesses to worship, without necessarily believing in worship through idols;
7 Unlike other religions, absence of belief in a specific set of philosophic concepts.[48]

Finally, Hindu scholar and statesman Karan Singh observes that the vast understandings of the ancient Vedas will always make them relevant to the human condition:

We, who are children of the past and the future, of earth and heaven, of light and darkness, of the human and the divine, at once evanescent and eternal, of the world and beyond it, within time and in eternity, yet have the capacity to comprehend our condition, to rise above our terrestrial limitations, and, finally, to transcend the throbbing abyss of space and time itself. This, in essence, is the message of Hinduism.[49]

Suggested reading

The Bhagavad-Gita, available in numerous translations. Central teachings about how to realize the immortal soul.

Chapple, Christopher Key and Tucker, Mary Evelyn, eds., *Hinduism and Ecology*, Cambridge, Massachusetts: Harvard University Press, 2000. Perceptive contemporary essays about the relationship between various Hindu paths and environmental protection.

Eck, Diana, *Darsan: Seeing the Divine Image in India*, second edition, Chambersburg, Pennsylvania: Anima Books, 1985. A lively explanation of deity images and how the people of India respond to them.

Jayakar, Pupul, *The Earth Mother*, New Delhi: Penguin Books, 1989. Explorations of ways of worshipping the goddess in rural India.

Lopez, Donald S., Jr., ed., *Religions of India in Practice*, Princeton, New Jersey: Princeton University Press, 1995. An interesting anthology of popular texts with contemporary rather than stereotypical understandings, primarily from Hinduism but also including Buddhist, Jain, and Sikh material.

Prabhavananda, Swami, *Spiritual Heritage of India*, Madras: Sri Ramakrishna Math, undated. Classic explanation of Indian spirituality and philosophy since the Vedic age by a disciple of Ramakrishna.

Sahi, Jyoti, *The Child and the Serpent*, London: Routledge & Kegan Paul, 1980. An artist's attempt to rediscover the inner meanings of traditional visual symbols by living in the villages of southern India.

Sastri, *The Cultural Heritage of India*, Calcutta, 1962. A classic survey of the social aspects of Sanatana Dharma.

Sharma, Veena, Kailash Mansarovar, *A Sacred Journey*, New Delhi: Rol: Books, 2004. Fascinating and informative first-person account of Hinduism's most difficult and sacred pilgrimage.

Singh, Karan, *Essays on Hinduism*, New Delhi: Ratna Sagar, 1987 and 1990. An excellent and concise introduction of the many facets of Hinduism, interpreted in modern terms.

Sondhi, Madhuri Santanam, *Modernity, Morality and the Mahatma*, New Delhi: Haranand Publications, 1997. A brilliant analysis of Indian responses to the challenges of modernity, including the contribution of many religious figures.

Sontheimer, Gunther-Dietz, and Hermann Kulke, *Hinduism Reconsidered*, New Delhi: Manohar, 1997. Provocative articles by Indian and Western scholars on controversial new ways of interpreting many facets of Sanatana Dharma.

Key terms

dharma	Moral order, righteousness, religion.
Vedas	Ancient scriptures revered by Hindus.
brahmin	A priest or member of the priestly caste.
karma	Our actions and their effects on this life and lives to come.
puja	Ritual worship.
sadhu	An ascetic holy man.
ashram	A usually ascetic spiritual community of those who have gathered around a guru.
Vishnu	The preserving aspect of the Supreme or the Supreme itself, incarnating again and again to save the world.
Siva	The Supreme as lord of yogis, absolute consciousness, creator, preserver, and destroyer of the world; or the destroying aspect of the Supreme.
sakti	The creative, active female aspect of Deity.

Study questions

1 Describe the major components of the historical background and the sacred texts of the Vedic Sanatana Dharma. Discuss Harappan culture, Aryans, Tamil Nandu, Sanscrit, Brahmanas, Upanishads, Ramayana, Mahabharata, Bhagavad Gita, Yoga sutras, Code of Manu (and castes), and the Tantras.

2 What are the major philosophical themes of Sanatana Dharma? Explain Brahman / Atman, reincarnation, karma, samsara, moksha, Samkyha, Advaita Vedanta, and Yoga's four types.

3 Describe some major Sanatana Dharma ritual practices. Discuss Brahmins, Vishnu, Silva, the Mother Goddess, Tantras, women's roles, lingams, Rama, Krishna, puja, darsan, prasad.

4 What are some major Sanatana Dharma spiritual practices? Explain sacred thread, ashram, sannyasins, gurus, sacred trees and rivers, pilgrimages, festivals, and *sadhus*.

5 Describe some important contemporary Hindu issues and leaders. Discuss Muslims, Britain, Gandhi, Ramakrishna, Vivekananada, the Swadhyaya movement, international Hinduism (Yogananda, Transcendental Meditation, ISKCON, Mata Amritanandamayi), Hindu nationalism, Ayodhdya, and Christians.

Refer to Pearson/Prentice Hall's **TIME Special Edition: World Religions** magazine for these and other current articles on topics related to many of the world's religions:

- *The Religious Experience: Mohandas Gandhi*
- *Islam: As American As …*
- *The Impact of Religion: In the Heart of Hate*

Chapter 3 begins the study of religions originating in India and focuses on Hinduism. For further research in this area, use the tools available to you in Research Navigator.

As you investigate Hinduism, consider this question: "What impact has Hinduism had on the world today?'

- **Ebsco's ContentSelect:** Search in the Religion and Sociology databases using terms such as "Hinduism," "Spirituality," "Ghandi."
- **Link Library:** Search in the Religion, and Sociology databases under the categories: "Religion," and "Hinduism."
- The *New York Times* **on the Web:** Search in the Religious Studies and Sociology databases for current articles on related topics.

CHAPTER 4
JAINISM

"Be careful all the while!"

Jainism:
Soul in the World,
Mahavira

Although the majority of Indians who are religious continue to follow the Hindu paths, Mother India has given birth to several other religions which are not based on the Vedas. One of them is Jainism, which has approximately six million adherents. Until recently, it has been little known outside India. Even within India it is practiced by only a small minority. Yet its ascetic teachings offer valuable clues to our global survival. It is becoming recognized as a complete and fruitful path with the potential for uplifting human awareness and inculcating high standards of personal ethics. For example, it has never condoned war or the killing of animals for any reason. Jain teachings recognize that we humans are imperfect, but hold out the promise that through strict control of our senses and thoughts we can attain perfection, freedom, and happiness.

The Tirthankaras and ascetic orders

Mahavira is said to have become so detached from worldly concerns that he shed his clothes as well as his royal status.

Jainism's major teacher for this age is Mahavira ("The Great Hero"). He was a contemporary of the Buddha and died approximately 527 BCE. Like the Buddha, he was the prince of a **kshatriya** clan and renounced his position and his wealth at the age of thirty to wander as a spiritual seeker. The austerities he tolerated while meditating without clothes in the intense summer heat and winter cold are legendary. Villagers are said to have treated him miserably to make him leave:

Once when he [sat in meditation], his body unmoving, they cut his flesh, tore his hair, and covered him with dirt. They picked him up and then dropped him, disturbing his meditational postures. Abandoning concern for his body, free from desire, the Venerable One humbled himself and bore the pain.[1]

Finally after twelve years of meditation, silence, and extreme fasting, Mahavira achieved liberation and perfection. For thirty years until his death at Pava, he spread his teachings. His community is said to have consisted of 14,100 monks, 36,000 nuns, and 310,000 female and 150,000 male lay followers. They came from all castes, as Jainism does not officially acknowledge the caste system.

The Jain teachings are not thought to have originated with Mahavira, however. He is considered the last of twenty-four **Tirthankaras** ("Fordmakers") of the current cosmic cycle. In Jain cosmology, the universe is without beginning or end. Eternally, it passes through long cycles of progress and decline. At the beginning of each downward cycle, humans are happy, long-lived, and virtuous; they have no need for religion. As these qualities decline, Tirthankaras must create religion in order to steer people away from the growing evil in the world.

The first Tirthankara introduced civilizing social institutions, such as marriage, family, law, justice, and government, taught the arts of agriculture, crafts, reading, writing, and mathematics, and built villages, towns, and cities. Twenty-three more Tirthankaras followed over a vast expanse of time. The twenty-second is generally acknowledged by scholars as an historic figure, Lord Krishna's cousin, renowned for his compassion toward animals. The twenty-third Tirthankara, a prince who became an extreme ascetic and a great preacher, lived from 877 to 777 BCE.

The extreme antiquity of Jainism as a non-Vedic, indigenous Indian religion is well documented. Ancient Hindu and Buddhist scriptures refer to Jainism as an existing tradition that began long before Mahavira.

After Mahavira's death, his teachings were not written down because the monks lived without possessions; they were initially carried orally. In the third century BCE, the great Jain saint Bhadrabahu predicted that there would be a prolonged famine where Mahavira had lived, in what is now Bihar in northeast India. He led some 12,000 monks to southern India to avoid the famine, which lasted for twelve years. When they returned, they discovered that two major changes had been introduced by the monks who had remained. One was relaxation of the requirement of nudity for monks; the other was the convening of a council to edit the existing Jain texts into a canon of forty-five books.

Eventually the two groups split into the **Digambaras**, who had left and did not accept the changes, and the **Svetambaras**, who had stayed near Mahavira's original location. Digambara ("sky clad") monks wear nothing at all, symbolizing innocence and non-attachment. They do not consider themselves "nude"; rather, they have taken the environment as their clothing. They have only two possessions: a broom of feathers dropped by peacocks and a gourd for drinking water. The Svetambara ("white-clad") monks feel that wearing a piece of white cloth does not prevent them from attaining liberation.

Rishabhadeva, the first Tirthankara of the present cosmic cycle. The Tirthankaras are always depicted either in cross-legged lotus position or standing up, a form of deep meditation for enlightened beings who are said never to sleep. (Northeast India, 12th–13th century.)

Jain nuns wearing mouth-cloths to prevent injury to inhaled minute beings; they are carrying all their worldly possessions.

The two orders also differ over the subject of women's abilities. Digambaras believe that women cannot become so pure that they could rise to the highest heaven or so impure that they would be reborn in the lowest hell; they cannot renounce clothes and be naked; they cannot be such skillful debaters as men; they are of inferior status in society and in the monastic order. They can be liberated only if they are reborn in a man's body. Svetambaras feel that women are capable of the same spiritual achievements as men, and that the nineteenth Tirthankara was a woman. In truth, even Svetambara nuns are of lower status than monks, but they still comprise the great majority of Jain nuns. Of today's approximately 6,000 Jain nuns, fewer than one hundred are Digambaras. The existence of this thriving order of female ascetics—which includes many skillful teachers and counselors and outnumbers the approximately 2,500 Jain monks—is unique in India, where no other native religion provides a monastic option for women; in Brahmanic Hindu tradition, women were never allowed to be mendicants and marriage was obligatory.

Freeing the soul: the ethical pillars

Jainism:
Soul in the World,
Mahavira

In the midst of a world of decline, as they see it, Jains are given great room for hope. The *jiva*—the individual's higher consciousness, or soul—can save itself by discovering its own perfect, unchanging nature and thus transcend the miseries of earthly life. Jains, like Hindus and Buddhists, believe that we are reborn again and again until we finally free ourselves from *samsara*, the wheel of birth and death.

The gradual process by which the soul learns to extricate itself from the lower self and its attachments to the material world involves purifying one's ethical life until nothing remains but the purity of the *jiva*. In its true state, it is fully omniscient, shining, potent, peaceful, self-contained, and blissful. One who has thus brought forth the highest in his or her being is called a **Jina** (a "winner" over the passions), from which the term Jain is derived. The Tirthankaras were Jinas who helped others find their way, by teaching inspiring spiritual principles.

Karma

Like Hindus and Buddhists, Jains believe that our actions influence the future course of our current life, and of our lives to come. But in Jain belief, **karma** is actually subtle matter—minute particles that we accumulate as we act and think. According to Jain belief, there are destructive and non-destructive types of *karma*. The destructive types obscure knowledge and intuition, cause delusion, and obstruct one's innate energy and action. The non-destructive *karmas* produce pleasure and pain, determine the length of a person's life, form the body characteristics, and determine one's family, caste, and nationality. Because both *karmas* limit the potential of the soul for infinite perception, wisdom, bliss, and power, Jains are taught to try to totally eliminate *karma* from their lives. To stop the accretion of new *karmas*, they try to develop pure thoughts and actions. To eradicate existing *karma*, they practice austerities such as fasting and renunciation of material comforts. Purification of the soul from *karma* depends entirely on one's own efforts; no supernatural being or deity can help. The three basic principles that Jains adopt to avoid accumulating karma are **ahimsa** (non-violence), **aparigraha** (non-attachment), and **anekantwad** (non-absolutism).

Ahimsa

The principle of non-violence—*ahimsa*—is very strong in Jain teachings, and through Jainism it also influenced Mahatma Gandhi. Jains believe that every centimeter of the universe is filled with living beings, some of them minute. A single drop of water contains 3,000 living beings. All of them want to live. Humans have no special right to supremacy; all things deserve to live and evolve as they can. To kill any living being has negative karmic effects.

It is difficult not to do violence to other creatures. Even in breathing, Jains feel, we inhale tiny organisms and kill them. Jains avoid eating after sunset, so as not to eat unseen insects that might have landed on the food, and some Jain ascetics wear a cloth over their mouth to avoid inhaling any living organisms.

The higher the life-form, the heavier the karmic burden of its destruction. The highest group of beings are those with many senses, such as humans, gods, and higher animals. Lower forms have fewer senses. The "one-sensed" beings have only the sense of touch. They include plants and the earth-bodies in soil, minerals, and stones, the water-bodies in rivers and lakes, fire-bodies in fires and lightning, and wind-bodies in winds and gases. The Jain *sutras* describe the suffering of even these one-sensed beings: it is like that of a blind and mute person who cannot see who is hurting him or express the pain.

The new Jain symbol: ahimsa *is inscribed on the open palm. The swastika is an ancient Indian symbol representing the wheel of* samsara *The three dots symbolize insight, knowledge, and conduct. The crescent and dot above symbolize the liberated soul in the highest region of the universe.*

> *All breathing, existing, living, sentient creatures should not be slain, nor treated with violence, nor abused, nor tormented, nor driven away. This is the pure, unchangeable, eternal law ... Correctly understanding the law, one should arrive at indifference for the impressions of the senses, and not act on the motives of the world.*
>
> *Akaranga Sutra, IV: Lesson 1*[2]

Jains are therefore strict vegetarians, and they treat everything with great care. In Delhi, Jain benefactors have established a unique charitable hospital for sick and wounded birds. Great attention is paid to their every need, and their living quarters are air-cooled in the summer. Jains also go to markets where live animals are usually bound with wire, packed into hot trucks, and driven long distances without water, to be killed for meat. Jains buy the animals at any price and raise them in comfort. Even to kick a stone while walking is to injure a living being. Jains are keenly aware that we may cause violence even through the clothes we buy. Many Jains thus eschew both leather and silk. Layman R. P. Jain tells a story of how he felt when he learned how silk is made:

> *I used to wear silk. On my eighteenth birthday I was telling one of my distant relatives not to eat chocolate because it had egg powder in it. He said, "Turn around—you're wearing silk. What are you preaching? Do you know that to make one yard of silk, nearly fifty thousand to one hundred thousand silkworms are boiled alive? To wear silk is a sin!" When I learned that is the way natural silk is made, I said, "R. P. Jain, what are you doing to your own soul? Shame on you!" From that day, I took a vow never in my life to wear natural silk.*[3]

Ahimsa also extends to care in speaking and thinking, for abusive words and negative thoughts can injure another. The revered ascetic Acharya Tulsi (1914–1997) explained,

A non-violent man is he who does not in the least discriminate between rich and poor or between friend and foe. . . . Non-violence is the best guarantee of humanity's survival and progress. A truly non-violent man is ever awake and is incapable of harbouring any ill will.[4]

One's profession must also not injure beings, so most Jains work at jobs considered harmless, such as banking, education, law, and publishing. Agriculture is considered harmful, for in digging one harms minute organisms in the earth; in harnessing bullocks to plows one harms not only the bullock but also the tiny life-forms on its body. Monks and nuns must move slowly with eyes downward, to avoid stepping on any being. In general, they will do the least harm if they devote their time to sitting or standing in meditation rather than moving around.

Global violence is of increasing concern, and here, too, Jains have great wisdom to offer. The late Acharya Tulsi taught that self-restraint is essential for the sake of world peace. He said:

Individual desire and ego are perennial human traits. Whenever they have been conjoined with power, there has been a general increase in war hysteria leading to the repetition of bloody and violent events in history. The reason why moral values have been held in the highest esteem is that they transform this evil combination of desire, ego and power into courteous humility. The history of the human race has been far more honorable and full of freedom during periods of such transformation. . . .

The fact cannot be ignored that the fate of the politicians is finally in the hands of the people. Even though it is generally true that it is the former who ultimately decide war and peace, the awakened conscience of the people is bound to ensure one day that a handful of over-ambitious people are not allowed to play with the future of mankind by imposing wars on them. The way to universal peace lies in our adherence to the precept of self-restraint.[5]

Aparigraha

Another central Jain ideal is non-attachment to things and people. One should cut one's living requirements to a bare minimum. Possessions possess us; their acquisition and loss drive our emotions. Some Jain monks wear no clothes; the Tirthankaras are always depicted as naked, and therefore free. Even attachments to our friends and relatives bind us to *samsara*. We are to live helpfully and consciously within the world but not be drawn into its snares.

Aparigraha, or non-acquisitiveness, is considered the way to inner peace. If we can let go of things and situations, moment by moment, we can be free. A Jain nun of the Rajasthan desert, Samani Sanmati Pragya, belongs to an order in which the nuns' clothing and bedding is limited to four white saris, one white shawl, and one woolen cloth. She explains:

In the winter we do not have a quilt for warmth at night, for it would be too bulky to carry. In the summer we use no fan. It is so hot that we cannot sleep at night. We bear any kind of circumstances. In fact, we remain very happy. Our happiness comes from inside.[6]

Aparigraha is of value to the world community as well. Contemporary Jains point out that their principle of limiting consumption offers a way out of the global poverty, hunger, and environmental degradation that result from unequal grasping of resources by the wealthy. As His Holiness Acharya Sushil Kumar explained:

RELIGION IN PRACTICE

Jain Purification

A central Jain practice undertaken both by laypeople and by ascetics has for thousands of years been used for freeing the soul from internal impurities. Anger, pride, deceit, and greed are lasting stains that must be completely eradicated if the soul is to realize its true nature: pure consciousness, infinite knowledge, and bliss. Even a momentary realization of this state brings a feeling of great inner purity and calmness and a longing to return to it permanently. The ritual for achieving this inner purification is known as *samayika*.

Jain laypeople usually undertake this practice in the evening, after work and meal. They sit in a quiet and solitary place, remove excess clothing, sit cross-legged on a mat, and chant formulas to cleanse and pacify their mind. These begin with a pledge to renounce all harmful activities, followed by requesting forgiveness:

I ask forgiveness of all beings
may all beings forgive me.
I have friendship with all beings,
and I have hostility with none.[7]

They reach out mentally to all life forms, saying

Friendship toward all beings,
Delight in the qualities of virtuous ones,
Utmost compassion for affected beings,
Equanimity towards those who are not well-
disposed towards me,
May my soul have such dispositions forever![8]

Then follow verses that commit the person to renouncing food, bodily desires, and passions for the period of the meditation, persisting in equanimity, come what may. The meditation ends with the universal Jain prayer:

Cessation of sorrow
Cessation of karmas
Death while in meditation,
Attainment of enlightenment.
O holy Jina! friend of the entire universe, let these
be mine, for
I have taken refuge at your feet.

If we live simply, limit our needs and do not try to fulfill every desire, collecting more and more, automatically we will protect the environment. Because we will not need so many things, we will not need big industries to produce unnecessary things. ... If we live simply, automatically the environment will stay clean.[9]

Anekantwad

The third central principle is *anekantwad*, roughly translated as "relativity." Jains try to avoid anger and judgmentalism, remaining open-minded by remembering that any issue can be seen from many angles, all partially true. They tell the story of the blind people who are asked to describe an elephant. The one who feels the trunk says an elephant is like a tree branch. The one grasping a leg argues that an elephant is like a pillar. The one feeling the ear asserts that an elephant is like a fan. The one grasping the tail insists that an elephant is like a rope. And the one who encounters the side of the elephant argues that the others are wrong; an elephant is like a wall. Each has a partial grasp of the truth.

In the Jain way of thinking, the fullness of truth has many facets. Shree Chitrabhanu describes the results of eliminating false impressions and allowing the pure consciousness to flow in:

Once you have closed the open gates, dried up the polluted water, and cleaned out all the debris, then you can open them again to receive the fresh, clean rainfall.

What is that rainfall? It is the flow of maitri—*pure love, compassion, and communication. You feel free. . . . See how easily you meet people when there is no feeling of greater or lesser, no scar or bitterness, no faultfinding or criticism.*[10]

Spiritual practices

Jainism is an ascetic path and thus is practiced in its fullest by monks and nuns. In addition to practicing meditation, monks and nuns adopt a life of celibacy, physical penance and fasting, and material simplicity. They may sleep on the bare ground or wooden slabs, and are expected to endure any kind of weather with indifference. At initiation, they may pull their hair out by the roots rather than be shaved. They must learn to accept social disapproval, to depend on others for their food, and to feel no pride at being more spiritually advanced than others.

Jain monks and nuns carry *ahimsa* to great extremes in their wariness of injuring one-sensed beings. Among the many activities they must avoid are digging in the ground (because of the earth-bodies there), bathing, swimming, or walking in the rain (because of the water-bodies they might injure), extinguishing or lighting fires (because even to light a fire means that a fire-body will eventually be destroyed), fanning themselves (to avoid sudden changes in air temperature that would injure air-bodies), and walking on vegetation or touching living plants.

In New Delhi, a wealthy sixty-year-old Jain businessman, head of a large construction company, astounded the populace in 1992 by advancing from lay austerities, such as eating and drinking only once in twenty-four hours, to the utterly renunciate life of a naked Digambara monk. Before a huge celebration in which he shed his clothes and his possessions, Lala Sulekh Chand announced:

I have no interest in life. I have found that life just means one remains agitated for twenty-four hours and there is no peace of mind. I have fulfilled all my responsibilities and obligations in life and handed over my business to my son and family. I am not taking this path due to some problem.[11]

Jain monks and nuns are celibate ascetics. This 15th-century illustrated text of Mahavira's last teachings shows a monk resisting the attractions of women.

He then sat unflinching as his mentor, Muni Amit Sagar, pulled all the hairs from his head, a process that took an hour and a half. Afterward, Muni Amit Sagar admonished the crowd that the way to spiritual liberation lies in non-attachment and patient, indifferent forbearance of all difficulties. "We cannot change anything, but we can change our attitude of expectation," he said. "The peace one gets from renunciation cannot be gained by reading a lot of religious books."[12]

> *Difficult to conquer is oneself; but when that is conquered, everything is conquered.*
> *Uttaradhyayana Sutra 9.34–36*

Most householders cannot carry renunciation as far as monks and nuns, but they can nonetheless purify and perfect themselves. Jain homes and temples are typically scrupulously clean, their diets carefully vegetarian, and the medicines they use are prepared without cruel testing on animals. The mind and passions are also to be held under strict control. Jains believe that the universe is without beginning and that it has no creator or destroyer. Our lives are therefore the results of our own deeds; only by our own efforts can we be saved. Padma Agrawal explains:

In Jainism, unlike Christianity and many Hindu cults, there is no such thing as a heavenly father watching over us. To the contrary, love for a personal God would be an attachment that could only bind Jainas more securely to the cycle of rebirth. It is a thing that must be rooted out.[13]

The world operates by the power of nature, according to natural principles. Jains do believe in gods and demons, but the former are subject to the same ignoble passions as humans. In fact, one can only achieve liberation if one is in the human state, because only humans can clear away karmic accumulations on the soul. Until it frees itself from *karmas*, the mundane soul wanders about through the universe in an endless cycle of deaths and rebirths, instantly transmigrating into another kind of being upon death of its previous body. Acharya Shri Kund Kund asserts, "Nowhere throughout the space in the entire universe is there any place in its course where the mundane soul has not taken birth in many forms, big and small."[14]

Birth as a human is the highest stage of life short of liberation. One should therefore lose no time in this precious, brief period in human incarnation, for within it lies the potential for perfection. Householders can journey toward the final state by passing through fourteen stages of ascent of the soul, or *gunasthana*. The first four are efforts to remove false mental impressions. Moral effort to purify oneself of negative tendencies begins with the fifth stage. Then, as spiritual inertia is overcome, self-control and relinquishing of the passions follow. Throughout this process, the veils of karma are lifting and the soul experiences more and more of its natural luminosity. In the highest state of perfection, known as **kevala**, the liberated being has "boundless vision, infinite righteousness, strength, perfect bliss, existence without form, and a body that is neither light nor heavy."[15]

Although severe vows of renunciation can be taken by householders, lay spiritual life is more likely to consist of six duties: the practice of equanimity through meditation, praise of the Tirthankaras, veneration of teachers (who live as mendicants), making amends for moral transgressions, indifference to the body (often by holding a particular position for a length of time), and renunciation of certain foods or activities for specific periods. Laypeople as well as ascetics often undertake total fasts lasting for days—or for the ascetics, weeks or even months. This is done to help weaken the bonds of karma. To eat anything has karmic repercussions since no food can be consumed without harming some life-form. If one can uproot the craving for food, the most primary of instincts, one can eliminate all passions. Ideally, any money saved by fasting and other acts of renunciation is to be given in charity to help those in need, thus increasing the merit of the fast or other form of penance.

Practicing strict ethics and self-control, Jains are often quite successful and trusted in their professions. Many Jains have thus become wealthy. Because of the religion's emphasis on non-possessiveness, wealthy Jains are often philanthropists. Willingness to give is considered the best of the good emotions.

Jains' charitable works include the construction of very ornate Jain temples, which are kept immaculately clean. Within the temples, the Tirthankaras are honored through images. They all look alike, for the perfect soul is non-particularized; symbols such as the bull, always shown with the first Tirthankara, are used to help worshippers identify each of the twenty-four. The worshipper's feeling is one of reverence rather than supplication; the Tirthankaras are elevated beyond the human plane and are not available as helpers. They are instead models for one's own life,

TEACHING STORY

The Story of Bahubali

Rishabha, the first Tirthankara of the current cosmic cycle, had one hundred sons from one wife and one son, Bahubali, from the other. He gave his eldest son, Bharat, the lion's share. Bharat was eager to be the supreme king, and he wanted his other brothers, who had been given smaller portions of land, to come under his subjugation. All the people surrendered to his sovereignty, except for Bahubali, who refused to surrender his kingdom. He said to Bharat, "You are independent, I am independent. Why should I come under your rule?"

The armies of the two sides were drawn up on the battleground. The wise men from the two sides came forth and said, "In the clash of two brothers, millions of people will be killed. Millions of innocent people will be killed to satisfy the egos of two brothers. Why should this happen?" So it was decided that the two would fight it out between themselves. They would fight in three ways to see who was defeated.

First, they looked into each other's eyes, concentrating until one looked away. Bahubali knocked out Bharat in this combat. Then they fought underwater, and again Bahubali was victorious. Thirdly, Bahubali picked up Bharat

physically and held him overhead, ready to dash him to the ground. That is how he got the name Bahubali—"He whose arms are very powerful."

As Bahubali was holding Bharat aloft, a thought crossed his mind: "Whom am I throwing? My own brother. For what? For this parcel of land? For this kingdom? Only for that, I would kill my brother?" He put Bharat down.

At that point, Bahubali felt like renouncing the world. He ceased to make war, and he went standing into meditation. For twelve years he meditated, standing. Vines grew on his legs. Snakes made their homes around his body. Many people tried to convince him to come out of his meditation, but he was unmoved. Nevertheless, he could not attain ultimate liberation.

Rishabha, his father, was asked why Bahubali was not attaining liberation. From his omniscient knowledge, Rishabha said that just before Bahubali started his meditation, he had a thought left in his mind: "I am standing on my brother's soil." So Bharat went and prayed to him: "This soil is universal, not yours or mine." The moment that thought entered Bahubali's mind, he was liberated.

and since there can be no divine intervention, there is not a great emphasis on priesthood. Laypeople can carry out worship services themselves, either alone or in groups. People pay their respects before images of the Tirthankaras with offerings and waved lamps, but do not expect any reciprocation from them. Liberation from *samsara* is a result of personal effort, often portrayed by a symbolic diagram laid out with rice grains. Acharya Tulsi expressed the Jain point of view: "The primary aim of *dharma* is to purify character. Its ritualistic practices are secondary."[16]

Just as a fire quickly reduces decayed wood to ashes, so does an aspirant who is totally absorbed in the inner self and completely unattached to all external objects shake to the roots, attenuate, and wither away his karma-body.

Samantabhadra, Aptamimamsa 24–7

World Jainism

Through the centuries, Jainism managed to survive as a small heterodox (non-orthodox) minority within largely Hindu India. Today there are approximately 6 million Jains. Since the twentieth century, Jainism has been carried to the outside world by several teachers. One of them, Shree Chitrabhanu, was for twenty-nine years a monk who walked barefoot over 30,000 miles (48,279 km) of Indian soil to teach Jain principles to the populace. When he was invited to address the Temple of Spiritual Understanding Summit Conferences in Switzerland and the United States in 1970 and 1971, his controversial decision to attend in person marked the first time in Jain history that a Jain monk had traveled outside India. He then established Jain meditation centers in the United States, Brazil, Canada, Kenya, the United Kingdom, and India.

Acharya Shri Sushil Kumar likewise established Jain centers in the United Kingdom and the United States as well as in India. He pointed out that the Jain scriptures consider as "Jains" all those who practice Jain principles:

If somebody is a real symbol of non-violence, love, compassion, peace, harmony, oneness, then he is the perfect Jain. We can't convert any Jains, but you can convert your habits, your mind.[17]

The revered Acharya Tulsi initiated new orders of *samans* (semi-monks) and *samanis* (semi-nuns) who are allowed to travel abroad in order to spread Jain teachings. He also began the Anuvrat Movement in 1949, to enlist people of all faiths and nationalities to commit themselves to *anuvrats* (small vows). He developed these to help people rejuvenate strong moral standards of self-restraint in the midst of an ethically unhealthy society. The small vows include these: to avoid willful killing of any innocent creature, to refrain from attacks and aggression and to work instead for world peace and disarmament, to avoid discrimination on the basis of caste or race, to eschew religious intolerance, to avoid false business and political practices, to limit acquisition of possessions, to eschew addictive substances, and to avoid wasting water or cutting down trees.

In 1995, Acharya Tulsi renounced even his own position as the leader of his order by installing Acharya Mahapragya as his successor. The latter's self-description is an indication of the internal qualities which keep Jain faith alive:

Jainism:
Temple of One
Thousand Pillars

Living Jainism

In addition to monastic orders of monks and nuns, there is now another order of "semi-monks" and "semi-nuns" developed by Acharya Tulsi in 1980. The main difference between them and traditional monks and nuns is that they are allowed to travel and thus teach their religion in other countries. The women who have taken vows in this order are called *samanis*. Samani Charitra Prajna took initiation into this order ten years ago, and has traveled to the United States with groups from her organization to teach meditation and Jain principles there. She explains her lifestyle:

"Basically, our lifestyle is very similar to the monks and nuns. The rules are the same. We have given up our family. We don't keep money or property or anything in our name. We have dedicated our whole life for this institution, for our Acharya, for our organization. The main purpose for us is to learn ourselves and teach others, too, what we have got.

"Basically, the main restrictions are that we have to follow the principles of non-violence, truth, celibacy, non-acquisition, and non-stealing. Just like monks and nuns, every morning and evening we repeat the vows we have taken and ask forgiveness for whatever mistakes we have made. It means, 'I am a monk now, so I have to follow these principles and lead a very peaceful life.'

"We sleep on the floor on a piece of cardboard, over which we spread our blanket. No pillow, nothing. We do not switch on lights or fans with our own hands. If some other people come and sit with us, for their convenience they may turn on the light. Instead of fans, we just open the windows and take the fresh air.

"We have three pairs of clothes. We use only two pairs a day—one for the morning, one for the night. And then two or three handkerchiefs and one or two small napkins. We keep our wooden bowls in which we eat our food. These are made by our own hands, and we polish them every year.

"Normally we get up at 3 or 4 a.m. Then we repeat the scriptures which we have learned, without looking at the books. And then before sunrise we do meditation, prayer, and our repetition of vows and asking forgiveness for any mistakes. And after sunrise, we do our yoga exercise. Then we go to collect our alms, because we don't cook food ourselves. We go to different houses and take a little portion from each house. I go to ten to fifteen houses every day, in the morning, in the lunchtime, and in the dinnertime. It is not like we are begging from them. They give us full respect, appreciating that someone has come into their home so that they can give them food."

After receiving the breakfast offerings in their wooden bowls, the *samanis* listen to a lecture for an hour and a half, followed by a short interval, and then again going from house to house to receive their lunch offerings. After a rest of half an hour, they learn scriptures, sometimes accompanied by lay followers. After the evening round of food collection, there is another lecture, followed at 10 o'clock by sleeping on the floor. Having followed this life for ten years, Samani Charitra Prajna says:

"I am really enjoying it. I feel myself more happy and tension-free, because I need not worry for myself. Our Acharya looks after each and everybody with full care and attention—what she has to do next, what is the planning for her. Before taking this initiation, I took training for six years in an institution for people who come from all over India, because ultimately they are dedicating their whole life. For monks and nuns, and *samans* and *samanis*, it is not that 'I am taking vows for one month or six months or two years and then I can go back.' It is for the whole life long. After doing graduation, post-graduation, master's degree, and PhD research work, we can be initiated only when Acharya Ji has given permission that we are capable of doing this practice. Ultimately it depends on our willpower. If I am not fully completed and dedicated, maybe my mind can wander and I can go back. But when my mind is steady and I have dedicated myself, then Acharya gives us permission and we start this life.

"Families usually object because they do not want their daughters and sons to lead such a hard life. They think we should live a normal life like they are living. In the beginning, they don't give us permission. But afterwards when they see that he or she is very committed and that they are going in their right path, ultimately they give their permission.

"My family belongs to the Jain religion. My father and mother are very religious, and I had a good environment from them. And especially I can say that some of my previous imprints—which we call *sanskars*, a kind of memories from previous births—taught me a lesson. Then such feelings can arise in your mind: 'I have to do this lifestyle.'

"Religion says that our life should be self-disciplined, having some restraint. If you have no discipline, no vows in your life, ultimately this materialistic stuff can give you more pressure instead of peace of mind. But if you are limiting your desire, if you are satisfied with what you have, it means that you get the ultimate peace of mind, tranquillity of mind, and you can think, 'I have gained something in my life.'

"We have seen persons who are very rich, but even at the time of dying, they feel that their mind is empty. They have not gained in their life. But for those who have practiced religion, in a true sense, in life as well as at the time of death they are more satisfied and happy, having bliss and actually enjoying their life. So we think that religion is the basic part of our life. We have to practice according to our faculty, according to our extent of time, according to our interest. At least we have to do it every day."

In Jain worship, images of the Tirthankara are ideally to be venerated without expectation of a personal response to their prayers or help for the worshippers.

I am an ascetic. My asceticism is not bound by inert rituals. ... I follow a tradition, but do not treat its dynamic elements as static. I derive benefit from the scriptures, but do not believe in carrying them as a burden. ... In my consciousness there is no bondage of "yours and mine." It is free from it. My spiritual practice is not to "worship" truth, but to subject it to minute surgery. The only mission of my life is boundless curiosity to discover truth. ... It is not an external accoutrement. Like a seed it is sprouting out of my being.[18]

Suggested reading

Chitrabhanu, Gurudev Shree, *Twelve Facets of Reality: The Jain Path to Freedom*, New York: Jain Meditation International Center/Dodd, Mead & Company, 1980. Classic Jain reflections on the realities of life, with many teaching tales.

Fischer, Eberhard, and Jain, Jyotindra, *Jaina Iconography*, parts 1 and 2, Leiden: E. J. Brill, 1978. An inside look at Jainism through the visual representations of its beliefs.

Jaini, Padmanabh S., *The Jaina Path of Purification*, Berkeley: University of California Press, 1979. An appreciative, scholarly analysis of the Jaina path.

Jaini, Padmanabh S., ed., *Collected Papers on Jaina Studies*, Delhi: Motilal Banarsidass Publishers, 2000. In-depth examination of many contemporary issues in Jain scholarship and practice.

Kumar, Acharya Sushil, *Song of the Soul*, Blairstown, New Jersey: Siddhachalam Publishers, 1987. Insights into Jain mantra practice, as taught by a twentieth-century monk.

Muller, F. Max, ed., *Jaina Sutras*, vols. XLV and XXII of *Sacred Books of the East*, Oxford: Clarendon Press, 1884 and 1895. Engaging translations of various sorts of *sutras*, including both philosophical treatises and rules of conduct for Jain ascetics.

Nyayavijayaji, Munisri, trans. by Nagin J. Shah, *Jaina Philosophy and Religion*, Delhi: Motilal Banarsidass Publishers, 1998. A renowned twentieth-century monk's comprehensive tome describing the major aspects of Jain philosophy, liberation practices, logics, metaphysics, and ethics in contemporary terms.

Sangave, Vilas A., *Aspects of Jaina Religion*, New Delhi: Bharatiya Jnanpith, 1990. Concise, accurate discussions of Jain antiquity, principles, practice, relationships to other religions, and cultural contributions.

Tobias, Michael, *Life Force: The World of Jainism*, Berkeley, California: Asian Humanities Press, 1991. A highly appreciative and readable account of Jain practices and philosophy by a Western observer.

Key terms

Tirthankaras	The great enlightened teachers in Jainism, of whom Mahariva was the last in the present cosmic cycle.
Digambara	A highly ascetic order of Jain monks who wear no clothes.
Svetambara	Jain order of monks who are less ascetic than the Digambara.
jiva	The soul.
samsara	The continual round of birth, death, and rebirth.
ahimsa	Non-violence, a central Jain principle.
anekantwad	The Jain principle of relativity or open-mindedness.
aparigraha	Non-acquisitiveness, a major Jain principle.
muni	Jain monk.

Study questions

1 What are the goals of the Jain quest for purity? Discuss *samsara*, caste, *karma*, *kevala*, *jiva*, *jina*.
2 What are the major practices of Jainism? Discuss *ahimsa*, *aparigraha*, *anekatwad*, meditation, consumption, caste, food, hair, asceticism, clothing, the elephant story, tolerance, and Bahubali.
3 Who are the Tirthankaras and what did they teach?
4 Discuss the role of women in Jainism. Explain the Digambara–Svetambara differences. Why are there more nuns than monks among Jains?
5 What is the Jain belief about gods and their role in spiritual liberation?

Refer to Pearson/Prentice Hall's **TIME Special Edition: World Religions** magazine for current articles on topics related to many of the world's religions.

Chapter 4 continues the study of religions originating in India and focuses on Jainism. For further research in this area, use the tools available to you in Research Navigator:

As you investigate Jainism, consider this question: "What is the importance of non-violence in religions such as Jainism?"

- **Ebsco's ContentSelect:** Search in the Philosophy, Religion, and Sociology databases using terms such as "Jainism," "non-violence," "ahimsa."
- **Link Library:** Search in the Philosophy and Religion databases under the categories: "Religion and Environment" and "Jainism."
- **The *New York Times* on the Web:** Search in the Religious Studies and all other databases for current articles on related topics.

CHAPTER 5
BUDDHISM

*"He will deliver by the boat of knowledge
the distressed world"*

At approximately the same time that Mahavira was teaching the way of Jainism, the man who came to be known as the Buddha preached another alternative to the ritual-bound Brahmanism of India. The Buddha taught about earthly suffering and its cure. Many religions offer comforting supernatural solutions to the difficulties of earthly life. Early Buddhism was quite different: it held that our salvation from suffering lies only in our own efforts. The Buddha taught that in understanding how we create suffering for ourselves we can become free.

We might imagine that the discomfort of having to face ourselves and take responsibility for our own liberation would be an unappealing path that would attract few followers. But the way of the Buddha spread from his native India throughout East Asia, becoming the dominant religion in many Eastern countries. In the process, it took on devotional and mystical qualities from earlier local traditions, with various buddhas to whom one could appeal for help. And now, more than two and a half thousand years after the Buddha's death, the religion that he founded is also attracting considerable interest in the West.

The life and legend of the Buddha

Although the Buddha was apparently an historical figure, what we know about him is sketchy. His prolific teachings were probably not collected in written form until at least four hundred years after his death. In the meantime they were apparently held, and added to, as an oral tradition, chanted from memory by monks, groups of whom were responsible for remembering specific parts of the teachings. Only a few factual details of the Buddha's own life have been retained. While stories from the life of the Buddha are abundant in authorized Buddhist texts, these stories were never organized into a single canonical biography. Extant complete biographies of the Buddha date from four centuries after his passing on. These texts venerate the Buddha as a legendary hero, and were written by storyteller poets rather than historians. One example of such a sacred biography is Asvaghosa's famous epic, the *Buddhacarita* (Acts of the Buddha), which was composed in the first century CE.

The one who became the Buddha (a generic term meaning "Enlightened One") probably lived for eighty years during the fifth century BCE, though his life may have extended either into the late sixth or early fourth centuries. His father was apparently a wealthy landowner serving as one of the chiefs of a *kshatriya*

Buddhism:
Beginnings

clan, the Shakyas who lived in the foothills of the Himalayas. The family name, Gautama, honoured an ancient Hindu sage whom the family claimed as ancestor or spiritual guide. His mother Maya is said to have given birth to him in the garden of Lumbini near Kapilavastu. The epics embellish his birth story as an immaculate conception in which a white elephant carrying a lotus flower entered his mother's womb in her dream. He is portrayed as the reincarnation of a great being who had been born many times before and was drawn to earth once again by his compassion for all suffering beings.

The child—referred to in later texts as Siddhartha, meaning "wish-fulfiller" or "he who has reached his goal"—was reportedly raised in the lap of luxury. In early texts he is quoted as describing a life of fine clothes, white umbrellas for shade, perfumes, cosmetics, a mansion for each season, the company of female musicians, and a harem of dancing girls. According to the texts, he was also trained in martial arts and married to at least one wife, who bore a son. In the midst of this life of ease, Siddhartha was reportedly unconvinced of its value. According to the "Four Sights" legend, the gods arranged for him to see the "four sights" that his father had tried to hide from him: a bent old man, a sick person, a dead person, and a monk seeking eternal rather than temporal pleasure. Seeing the first three sights, he was dismayed by the impermanence of life and the existence of suffering, old age, and death; the sight of the monk suggested the possibility of a life of renunciation. At the age of twenty-nine Siddhartha renounced his wealth, left his wife and newborn son (whom he named "Rahul," or "fetter"), shaved his head, and donned the coarse robe of a wandering ascetic. He was later said to have adopted a very difficult goal: finding the way of total liberation from suffering.

Many Indian *sannyasins* were already leading the homeless life of poverty considered appropriate for seekers of spiritual truth. Although the future Buddha would later develop a new spiritual path that departed significantly from

The region where Siddhartha grew up is in full view of the high peaks of the Himalayas.

Brahmanic Hindu beliefs, he initially tried the traditional methods. He headed southeast to study with a famous brahmin teacher who had many followers.

Still searching, Siddhartha then reportedly underwent six years of extreme self-denial techniques: nakedness, exposure to great heat and cold, breath retention, a bed of brambles, severe fasting. Finally he acknowledged that this extreme ascetic path had not led to enlightenment. He described his appearance after his long and strenuous fasting:

> Because I ate so little, all my limbs became like the knotted joints of withered creepers; because I ate so little, my protruding backbone became like a string of balls; because I ate so little, my buttocks became like a bullock's hoof; because I ate so little, my gaunt ribs became like the crazy rafters of a tumbledown shed; because I ate so little, the pupils of my eyes appeared lying low and deep in their sockets as sparkles of water in a deep well appear lying low and deep.[1]

Siddhartha then shifted his practice to a Middle Way of neither self-indulgence nor self-denial. He revived his failing health by accepting food once more and began a period of reflection. In an event now celebrated as having occurred on the night of the full moon in the sixth lunar month, as he sat in deep meditation beneath a tree at Gaya (now famous as Bodh Gaya), he finally experienced Supreme Enlightenment.

After passing through four states of serene contemplation, he reportedly recalled all his previous lives. Then he had a realization of the wheel of deaths and rebirths, in which past good or bad deeds are reflected in the next life. Finally, he realized the cause of suffering and the means for ending it. After this supreme experience, it is said that he radiated light. According to legend, he was tempted by Mara, the personification of evil, to keep his insights to himself, for they were too complex and profound for ordinary people to understand. But the Buddha compassionately determined to set the wheel of teaching in motion. He then spent decades walking and teaching a growing group of followers. This pattern was a familiar one in northern India, but this Enlightened One's teachings and personality were apparently so compelling that many people were transformed by meeting him. The addition of his clan name and *muni*, or sage, led to his being referred to as "Shakyamuni Buddha."

Out of the abundance and variety of scriptures later attributed to the sayings of Shakyamuni Buddha, historians agree on the validity and centrality of what became the essence of the *dharma* (Pali: *dhamma*)* that he taught: the Four Noble Truths about suffering and the Eightfold Path for liberation from suffering.

The Buddha gives his first sermon, using the mudra *(sacred gesture) representing the karmic wheel of birth, death, and rebirth.*

Buddhism:
The Bodhi Tree

---

* Buddhist terms have come to us both in **Pali**, an Indian dialect first used for preserving the Buddha's teachings (the Buddha himself probably spoke a different ancient dialect), and in Sanskrit, the language of Indian sacred literature. For instance, the Pali *sutta* (aphorism) is equivalent to the Sanskrit **sutra**. In this chapter Sanskrit will be used, as it is more familiar to Westerners, except in the section on Theravada, which uses Pali.

BUDDHISM

BCE	
600	c.*5thC* Life of Gautama Buddha
300	
	c.258 King Asoka begins spreading Buddhism outward from India
200	c.200 BCE–200 CE Development of Theravada Buddhism
100	c.100 BCE–300 CE Perfection of Wisdom scriptures originally developed
	c.80 Pali Canon written down in Sri Lanka
CE	
	c.50 Buddhism transmitted to China and then East Asia
	1st century Development of Mahayana Buddhism
100	
	c.150–250 Life of Nagarjuna
500	
	c.550 Buddhism enters Japan
	589–845 Peak of Chinese Buddhism
600	c.609–650 Life of Songtsan, who declares Buddhism the national religion of Tibet
	845 Persecution of Buddhism begins in China
1000	1079–1153 Life of Milarepa
1200	1200–1253 Life of Dogen, who spread Zen Buddhism in Japan
	1222–1282 Life of Nichiren
	c.1200–1500 Buddhism declines in northern India, then southern India
1500	
1900	1905 Zen Buddhism carried to the USA
	1958 Sarvodaya movement begins in Sri Lanka
	1959 Communist Chinese repress Buddhism in Tibet, Dalai Lama escapes to India
2000	1998 Full ordination of 135 nuns from 23 countries

As he walked through the northern Indian countryside for forty-five years as a voluntarily poor teacher with a begging bowl, he gave sermons to people of all sects and classes. His son Rahul was one of those who became a **bhikshu** (Pali: *bhikkhu*), a monk emulating his life of poverty and spiritual dedication; others adopted his teachings but continued as householders.

The **sangha**—the order of Buddha's disciples—was free from the caste system; people from all levels of society became Buddhists. His stepmother Mahaprajapati, who had raised him after the death of his mother, and his wife, Yashodara, became **bhikshunis** (Pali: *bhikkhunis*), members of the order of nuns that the Buddha founded. After the death of his father King Shuddhodana, the Buddha's stepmother asked permission to enter the *sangha*, but the Buddha hesitated to admit her. Then she and five hundred women from the court reportedly shaved their heads, put on yellow robes, and walked a great distance to where he was, making the same request. At last he agreed, reportedly on the condition that nuns should observe Eight Special Rules which would make them forever subordinate to the monks, no matter how senior the nun or how junior the monk. His alleged reluctance is today a matter of much speculation. Some think that later monks may have added the rules or else that the rules were laid down with the monks' weaknesses in mind. Be this as it may, in the context of patriarchal Indian society, for women to leave their homes and become itinerant mendicants would likely have been perceived as socially disruptive, as well as being difficult for women of the court. According to Hindu social codes, a woman could not lead a religious life and could achieve spiritual salvation only through devotion to her husband. By contrast, the Buddha asserted that women were as capable as men of achieving enlightenment. Also in contrast to some Hindu traditions, the Buddha forbade animal sacrifice, admonishing his followers to be kind to all living beings.

The traditionally accepted account of the Buddha's death at the age of eighty bespeaks his selfless desire to spare humankind from suffering. His last meal, served by a blacksmith, inadvertently included some poisonous mushrooms or perhaps spoiled pork. Severely ill and recognizing his impending death, the Buddha pushed on to his next teaching stop at Kusinara, teaching a young man along the way. He sent word to the blacksmith that he must not feel remorse or blame himself for the meal, for his offering of food brought him great merit. When he reached his destination, he lay down on a stone couch. As his monks came to pay their last respects, he urged them to tend to their own spiritual development:

> You must be your own lamps, be your own refuges. . . . A monk becomes his own lamp and refuge by continually looking on his body, feelings, perceptions, moods, and ideas in such a manner that he conquers the cravings and depressions of ordinary men and is always strenuous, self-possessed, and collected in mind.[2]

He designated no successor, no one to lead the order. But it survived and spread because, as his closest helper, Ananda, explained, before his passing away, the Buddha had made it clear that his followers should take the *dharma* and discipline as their support. They should study the *dharma*, put it into practice, and if outsiders criticized it, they should be able to defend it.

Another way in which the Buddha's mission was spread was through dissemination of the bone relics from his cremated body. These were reportedly given to messengers from seven clans, who built memorial domes, or *stupas*, over them in ten locations throughout India. These became great centers of devotion to the Buddha. Inscriptions dated back to the third century BCE or even earlier show that priests as well as laypeople made pilgrimages to these sacred sites, feeling that the Buddha was in some sense present there.

The dharma

The Buddha's final liberation into nirvana when he physically died is symbolized by this enormous Sri Lankan statue in which he is serenely lying down with eyes closed to the world.

Buddhism is often described as a nontheistic religion. There is no personal God who creates everything and to whom prayers can be directed. The Buddhists at the 1993 Chicago Parliament of the World's Religions found it necessary to explain to people of other religions that they do not worship the Buddha:

Shakyamuni Buddha, the founder of Buddhism, was not God or a god. He was a human being who attained full Enlightenment through meditation and showed us the path of spiritual awakening and freedom. Therefore, Buddhism is not a religion of God. Buddhism is a religion of wisdom, enlightenment and compassion. Like the worshippers of God who believe that salvation is available to all through confession of sin and a life of prayer, we Buddhists believe that salvation and enlightenment

are available to all through removal of defilements and delusion and a life of
meditation. However, unlike those who believe in God who is separate from us,
Buddhists believe that Buddha which means "one who is awake and enlightened"
is inherent in us all as Buddhanature or Buddhamind.[3]

Unlike other Indian sages, the Buddha did not focus on descriptions of unseen reality, the nature of the soul, life after death, or the origin of the universe. He said that curiosity about such matters was like a man who, upon being wounded by a poisoned arrow, refused to have it pulled out until he was told the caste and origin of his assailant, his name, his height, the color of his skin, and all details about the bow and arrow. In the meantime, he died.

Buddhism:
Middle Way

Being religious and following dhamma *has nothing to do with the dogma that the*
world is eternal; and it has nothing to do with the other dogma that the world is not
eternal. For whether the world is eternal or otherwise, birth, old age, death, sorrow,
pain, misery, grief, and despair exist. I am concerned with the extinction of these.[4]

The Buddha spoke of his teachings as a raft to take us to the farther shore, rather than a description of the shore or something to be carried around once we get there. The basic planks of this raft are insights into the truths of existence and the path to liberation; **nirvana** (Pali: *nibbana*) is the farther shore, the goal of spiritual effort, about which more will be said later.

The basic facts of existence

In what is considered his very first sermon, the Deer Park sermon, the Buddha set forth the "Four Noble Truths" around which all his later teachings revolved. These were:

Buddhism:
Basic Principles—The
Four Noble Truths

1 Life inevitably involves suffering, is imperfect and unsatisfactory.
2 Suffering originates in our desires.
3 Suffering will cease if all desires cease.
4 There is a way to realize this state: the Noble Eightfold Path.

The Buddha is therefore neither pessimistic nor optimistic about our human condition. Sri Lankan monk and scholar Walpola Rahula speaks of the Buddha as "the wise and scientific doctor for the ills of the world."[5] To look at the diagnosis and treatment of our human condition one step at a time, the Buddha's First Noble Truth is the existence of **dukha**, which means suffering or frustration. We all experience grief, unfulfilled desires, sickness, old age, physical pain, mental anguish, and death. We may be happy for a while, but happiness is not permanent. Even our identity is impermanent. There is no continual "I." What we regard as our self is simply an ever-changing bundle of fleeting feelings, sense impressions, ideas, and evanescent physical matter. One moment's identity leads to the next like one candle being lit from another.

The Second Noble Truth is that *dukha* has its origin in desire—for sensory pleasures, for fame and fortune, for things to stay as they are or become different—and in attachment to ideas. The reason that desire leads us to suffering, the Buddha taught, is that we do not understand the nature of things, of that which we desire. Everything is actually impermanent, changing all the time. We seek to grasp and hold life as we want it to be, but we cannot, since everything is in constant flux.

The Buddha taught skillful means of freeing oneself from the delusions and desires of worldly life.

In Buddhism, unhappiness is understood as the inevitable companion of happiness. The sun will give way to rain; a flower will decay; friends will die; our bodies will surely age. As the contemporary monk Ajahn Sumedho points out, "trying to arrange, control and manipulate conditions so as to always get what we want, always hear what we want to hear, always see what we want to see, so that we never have to experience unhappiness or despair, is a hopeless task."[6]

What a Buddhist strives for instead is the recognition of *dukha*, *anaitya* (Pali: *anicca*, impermanence), and *anatman* (Pali: *anatta*), the revolutionary and unique doctrine that there is no separate, permanent, or immortal self; rather, a human being is an interdependent, impermanent, composite of physical, emotional, and cognitive components. This realization of *anatman* is spiritually valuable because it reduces attachment to one's mind, body, and selfish desires. Suffering is also useful because it helps us to see things as they really are. When we realize that everything changes and passes away, moment by moment, we can become aware that nothing in this world has an independent, solid character. There are only momentary configurations within a continual process of change. Once we have grasped these basic facts of life, we can be free in this life, and free from another rebirth. Ajahn Sumedho explains:

> When you open the mind to the truth, then you realize there is nothing to fear. What arises passes away, what is born dies, and is not self—so that our sense of being caught in an identity with this human body fades out. We don't see ourselves as some isolated, alienated entity lost in a mysterious and frightening universe. We don't feel overwhelmed by it, trying to find a little piece of it that we can grasp and feel safe with, because we feel at peace with it. Then we have merged with the Truth.[7]

The Third Noble Truth is that *dukha* can cease if desire ceases. Thus illusion ends, and ultimate reality, or nirvana, is revealed. One lives happily and fully in the present moment, free from self-centeredness and full of compassion for others. One can serve them purely, for in this state there is no thought of oneself.

The Fourth Noble Truth is that only through a life of morality, concentration, and wisdom which the Buddha set forth as the Noble Eightfold Path—can desire and therefore suffering be extinguished.

The Eightfold Path of liberation

The Buddha set forth a systematic approach by which dedicated humans could pull themselves out of suffering and achieve the final goal of liberation. The Eightfold Path offers ways to burn up all past demerits, avoid accumulating new demerits, and build up merit for a favorable rebirth. Perfection of the path means final escape from the cycle of death and rebirth, into the peace of nirvana.

One factor is right understanding—comprehending reality correctly through deep realization of the Four Noble Truths. Initially, this means seeing through illusions, such as the idea that a little more wealth could bring happiness. Gradually one learns to question old assumptions in the light of the Four Noble Truths. Everything we do and say is governed by the mind. The Buddha said that if our mind is defiled and untrained, suffering will follow us just as a chariot follows the horse. If we think and act from a purified, trained mind, happiness will always follow us.

A second aspect of the Eightfold Path is right thought or motives. The Buddha encourages us to uncover any "unwholesome" emotional roots behind our thinking, such as a desire to hide our imperfections or avoid contact with others. As we discover and weed out such emotional blocks, our thought becomes free from the limitations of self-centeredness—relaxed, clear, and open.

A third factor is right speech. The Buddha cautions us to relinquish our propensity to vain talk, gossip, divisive speech, harsh words, and lying, and to use communication instead in the service of truth and harmony. He also advises us to speak in a positive manner to our own minds—to say to ourselves, "May you be well and happy today."

A fourth factor, right action, begins for the layperson with observing the five basic precepts for moral conduct: avoid destroying life, stealing, sexual misconduct, lying, and intoxicants. Beyond these, we are to base our actions on clear understanding. "Evil deeds," said the Buddha, are those "done from motives of partiality, enmity, stupidity, and fear."[8]

Fifth is right livelihood—being sure that one's way of making a living does not violate the five precepts. One's trade should not harm others or disrupt social harmony.

Right effort, the sixth factor, bespeaks continual striving to cut off "unwholesome states," past, present, and future. This is not a way for the lazy.

A seventh factor, right mindfulness, is particularly characteristic of Buddhism, for the way to liberation is said to be through the mind. We are urged to be aware in every moment. In the **Dhammapada** (Sayings of the Dharma, a very early text) there appears this pithy injunction:

Check your mind.
Be on your guard.
Pull yourself out
as an elephant from mud.[9]

The eighth factor, right meditation, applies mental discipline to the quieting of the mind itself. "It is subtle, invisible, treacherous,"[10] explains the Buddha. Skillful means are therefore needed to see and transcend its restless nature. When the mind is fully stilled, it becomes a quiet pool in which the true nature of everything is clearly reflected. The various schools of Buddhism that have developed over the centuries have taught different techniques of meditation, but this basic principle remains the same.

Try to be mindful, and let things take their natural course. Then your mind will become still in any surroundings, like a clear forest pool. All kinds of wonderful, rare animals will come to drink at the pool, and you will clearly see the nature of all things. You will see many strange and wonderful things come and go, but you will be still. This is the happiness of the Buddha.
Achaan Chah, meditation master, Wat Pa Pong, Thailand[11]

The wheel of birth and death

Buddhist teachings about rebirth are slightly different from those of Hindu orthodoxy, for there is no eternal soul to be reborn. In Buddhism, one changing state of being sets another into motion: every event depends on a cause. The central cause in this process is **karma** (Pali: *kamma*)—our actions of body, speech, and mind. These influence the level at which that personality-developing process we think of as "me" is reborn. The impressions of our good and bad actions help to create our personality moment-by-moment. When we die, this process continues, passing on the flame to a new life on a plane that reflects our past *karma*.

This wheel of birth and death is spun primarily by the negative intentions known as the Three Root Evils: greed, hate, and delusion. But to the extent that our actions are motivated by the opposites of these intentions—non-greed (such as generosity, renunciation for others' sake), non-hate (such as friendliness, compassion, and patience), and non-delusion (such as mental clarity and insight)—we can ultimately leave the circle of birth and death.

In Buddhist thought, not only do life-forms take birth many times; they also incarnate in many forms, creating an interconnected web of life. This has important implications for one's relationships with all life. One text explains:

The Wheel of Life: in the center are animals representing the Three Root afflictions; lust, hatred, and delusion. The next circle shows the fate of those with good karma (left) and bad karma (right). The third circle represents the six spheres of existence from the gods to the infernal regions. The outer rim shows the chain of cause and effect. Grasping the wheel is a monster representing death, impermanence.

*In the long course of **samsara** [reincarnation], there is not one among living beings with form who has not been mother, father, brother, sister, son, or daughter, or some other relative. Being connected with the process of taking birth, one is kin to all wild and domestic animals, birds, and beings born from the womb.*[12]

It is thought that the Buddha remembered all his past lives and told stories about them to illustrate moral lessons. Hundreds of these stories have been collected as

TEACHING STORY

The Great Ape Jataka Tale

When Brahmadatta was king of Benares, the Buddha took birth among the apes and became the powerful king of the eighty thousand monkeys living near the Ganges. Overhanging the river there was a great mango tree, with huge and delicious fruits. When ripe, some fell on the ground and some fell into the river. Eating these mangos with his monkeys, the Great Being foresaw that those that fell into the water would some day bring danger to the herd. He ordered that all the mangos growing on branches over the river should be plucked when very small and discarded. However, one fruit was hidden by an ant's nest. When it was ripe, it fell into the nets which the king's fishermen had placed into the river. When they pulled out the ambrosial fruit, they took it to the king in Benares. When he tasted it, he developed a great craving for more and insisted to be taken to the tree from which it came.

A flotilla of boats brought the king to the great mango tree. Camping beneath it, he ate mangos to his heart's delight. At midnight, the Great Being and his monkeys came and leapt from branch to branch above, eating the mangos. The king woke up and saw them. He ordered his men to surround the tree and prepare to shoot arrows at the monkeys so that they could feast on mangos and monkey-flesh the following day.

Terrified, the monkeys appealed to the Great Being for help. He told them not to be afraid, for he would save their lives. So saying, he at once climbed to one of the branches over the river and then made a tremendous leap across the wide river to the opposite bank. There he cut a long bamboo shoot which he calculated would be long enough to reach across the river. Lashing it to a bush on the farther shore, he lashed the opposite end to his waist and then made a terrific leap back toward the mango tree where the monkeys were cowering in fear for their lives. The shoot being slightly short, he grabbed an overhanging branch so that his own body's length filled the remaining distance. He signalled to the monkeys that they were to run across his body and then the bamboo shoot in order to escape to the other shore. Paying their obeisances to the Great Being and asking his forgiveness, the eighty thousand monkeys ran across him to safety. In the process, Devadatta [cousin of the Buddha, who reportedly once tried to poison him], who was one of the monkeys, took the opportunity to leap from an upper branch onto the great ape's back, breaking his heart.

After all the monkeys had crossed to safety, the wounded Great Being was left alone, hanging from the tree. The king, who had watched the whole thing, was struck by the greatness of his self-sacrifice for the sake of his monkeys. At daybreak, he ordered his people to gently bring the great ape down from the tree, bathe him, rub his body with fine oil, dress him in yellow, and lay him to rest. Sitting beside the great ape, the king questioned him about his action. The Great Being explained to him that no worry nor death could trouble him, and that he had acted for the welfare of all those whom he governed, as an example for the king to emulate. After thus advising the king, the Great Being died. King Brahmadatta ordered funeral ceremonies due to a king for him, and then had a shrine built at the place of his cremation and had his skull inlaid with gold, which he then enshrined at Benares. According to the instructions of the Great Being, Brahmadatta then became a very righteous ruler and a traveler to the Bright World.

When the Buddha told this Jataka Tale, he revealed that the human king was Ananda, and that the ape-king was himself.

the Jataka Tales, or birth stories of the Buddha's past lives as a bodhisattva. The one recounted here, "The Great Ape Jataka Tale" (see box), illustrates not only Buddhism's role as a way of personal development but also its importance in guiding rulers and establishing moral precepts for monastics and laity alike.

There are thirty-one planes of existence. Whether interpreted as psychological metaphors or metaphysical realities, these include realms of hells, "hungry ghosts" (beings tormented with unsatisfied desires), animals, humans, and gods. Like the lower levels, the gods are imperfect and impermanent. Round and round we go, life after life, caught in this cycle of *samsara's* worldly phenomena, repeatedly experiencing aging, decay, suffering, death, and painful rebirth, unless we achieve nirvana, which is beyond all the cause-and-effect-run planes of existence.

Nirvana

About the goal of Buddhist practice, nirvana, the Buddha had relatively little to say. The only way to end the cycle in which desire feeds the wheel of suffering is to end all cravings and lead a passion-free existence that has no karmic consequences. Thence one enters a condition of what the Buddha called "quietude of heart."[13] "Where there is nothing," he said, "where naught is grasped, there is the Isle of No-beyond. Nirvana do I call it—the utter extinction of aging and dying,"[14] "the unborn, ...undying, ...unsorrowing, ... stainless, the uttermost security from bonds."[15] For the **arhant** (Pali: *arhat, arahat*), worthy one, who has found nirvana in this life:

No suffering for him
who is free from sorrow
free from the fetters of life
free in everything he does.
He has reached the end of his road. ...

Like a bird invisibly flying in the sky,
he lives without possessions,
knowledge his food, freedom his world,
while others wonder. ...

A nun leaves the meditation hall in Dharamsala, India, after sunrise practices.

He has found freedom—
peaceful his thinking, peaceful his speech,
peaceful his deed, tranquil his mind.[16]

When such a being dies individuality disappears and one enters the ultimate state of nirvana, about which the Buddha was silent. Why? At one point he picked up a handful of leaves from the forest floor and asked his disciples which were more numerous, the leaves in his hand or those in the forest. When they replied, "Very few in your hand, lord; many more in the grove," he said:

Exactly. So you see, friends, the things that I know and have not revealed are more than the truths I know and have revealed. And why have I not revealed them? Because, friends, there is no profit in them; because they are not helpful to holiness; because they do not lead from disgust to cessation and peace, because they do not lead from knowledge to wisdom and nirvana.[17]

Buddhism south and north

As soon as he had attracted a small group of disciples, the Buddha sent them out to help teach the *dharma*. This teaching mission spread in all directions. Two hundred years after the Buddha died, a powerful Indian king, Asoka, led a huge military campaign to extend his empire, and then after seeing the tremendous loss of life on both sides, reportedly felt great remorse. He became a Buddhist and espoused non-violence. He had inscriptions written on rocks and pillars through-out his empire teaching the *dharma*, with an emphasis on developing an attitude of social responsibility. Under Asoka's leadership Buddhism was disseminated throughout the kingdom and outward to other countries as well, beginning its development as a global religion. After Asoka's death, brahmins reasserted their political influence and Buddhists were persecuted in parts of India. By the time of the twelfth-century Muslim invasions of India, Buddhism had nearly died out and never became the dominant religion in the Buddha's homeland.

As the Buddha's teachings have been expanded upon and adapted to local cultures, two primary divisions have developed. The form that tries to adhere closely to what it considers the original teachings is called **Theravada**, or "Way of the Elders." It is prevalent in Southeast Asian countries such as Sri Lanka, Myanmar (formerly Burma), Thailand, Cambodia, and Laos. The other major grouping is dominant in Nepal, Tibet, China, Korea, Mongolia, Vietnam, and Japan. Those of this group call it **Mahayana**, the "Greater Vehicle," because they feel that theirs is a bigger raft that can carry more people across the sea of samsara than the stark teachings of the Theravadins. Both groups are in general agreement about the Four Noble Truths, the Eightfold Path, and the teachings about *karma* and nirvana.

Theravada: the path of mindfulness

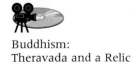

Buddhism:
Theravada and a Relic

Theravada is a conservative and traditional Buddhist way. Theravadin Buddhists study the early scriptures in Pali, honor the life of renunciation, and follow mindfulness meditation teachings. These characteristics are more obvious among intellectuals and monastics; the common people are more devotional in their practices.

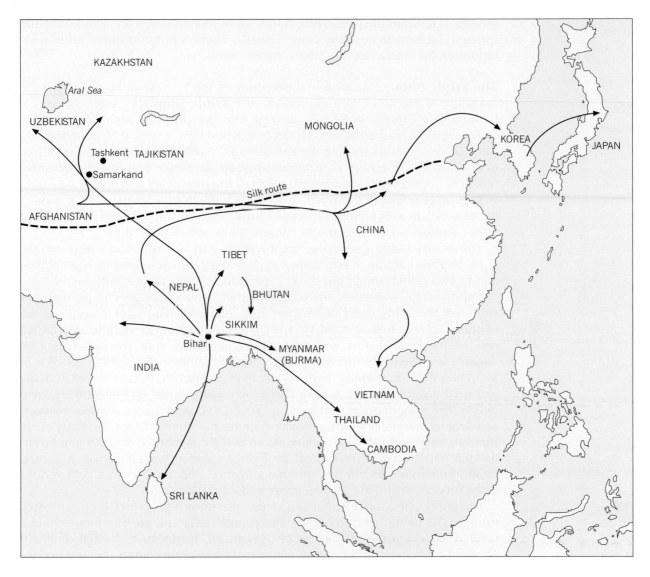

KAZAKHSTAN

(Aral Sea)

UZBEKISTAN

Tashkent TAJIKISTAN

Samarkand

MONGOLIA

KOREA

JAPAN

Silk route

AFGHANISTAN

CHINA

TIBET

NEPAL BHUTAN

SIKKIM

Bihar MYANMAR (BURMA)

INDIA

VIETNAM

THAILAND

CAMBODIA

SRI LANKA

The Pali Canon Buddhists who follow the Theravada tradition study a large collection of ancient scriptures preserved in the Pali language of ancient India. This ancient **canon**, or authoritative collection of writings, is called the Pali Canon. It is also referred to as the **Tipitaka** (Sanskrit: *Tripitaka*), the "Three Baskets." This label derives from the old practice of storing palm-leaf manuscripts in wicker baskets; thus, the "Three Baskets" are three collections of sacred writings: rules, teachings, and scholastic treatises. After the Buddha's death, leading members of the community of monks started compiling an authoritative canon of teachings and monastic discipline. According to Buddhist lore, this was done by a council of five hundred elders who had studied directly with the Buddha, in which the Venerable Ananda reportedly recited his discourses from memory, and another close disciple rehearsed the discipline of the order. Then the elders agreed on a definitive body of the Buddha's teachings, which were carried orally until the first

Buddhism spread in all directions from India but nearly disappeared in India itself by the 13th century CE.

century BCE, when the *sutras* (Pali: suttas) were written down on palm leaves and stored in baskets. In addition to the Tipitaka, Theravadins also honor other non-canonical Pali works, such as later commentaries.

The Triple Gem   Like all Buddhists, those of the Theravada School soften the discipline of the mind with devotion to the **Triple Gem (**or "Three Refuges"): Buddha (the Enlightened One), *dharma* (the doctrine he taught), and *sangha* (community of realized beings). To become a Buddhist, a person "takes refuge" in these three jewels by reciting the Pali formula, *Buddham saranam gacchami* ("I go to the Buddha for refuge"), *dhammam saranam gacchami* ("I go to the *dharma* for refuge"), *sangham saranam gacchami* ("I go to the *sangha* for refuge").

One takes refuge in the Buddha not by praying to him for help but by paying homage to him as supreme teacher and inspiring model. In a sense, taking refuge in the Buddha is honoring the Buddha-wisdom within each of us.

The *dharma* is like a medicine, but it will not cure our suffering unless we take it. In the Pali chanting, it is described as immediate, timeless, leading to calmness, and known only through our direct experience and personal effort.

The *sangha* is ultimately the community of realized beings, and on the conventional level, the order of *bhikshus* and *bhikshunis* who have renounced the world in order to follow, preserve, and share the *dharma*. The Buddha established one of the world's first monastic orders, and this core remains strong in Theravada. There are presently about half a million Theravadin monks in Southeast Asia. To simplify their worldly lives and devote themselves to studying and teaching the *dharma*, monks shave their heads, dress in simple robes, own only a few basic material items, eat no solid foods after noon, practice celibacy, and depend on the laity for their food, clothing, and medical supplies. Early every morning they set forth with an alms bowl, and the laypeople regard it as a merit-making opportunity to offer food to them. In this interdependent system, the monks reciprocate by offering spiritual guidance, chanted blessings, and various social services, including secular advice and education.

Buddhism:
Monastic Life

Buddhist monasteries are at the center of village life, rather than separated from it. The monasteries are open, and people come and go. The monks hold a revered social position as models of self-control, kindness, and intelligence. In Thailand it is common for young men to take temporary vows of monkhood—often for the duration of the rainy season when little farmwork can be done. They wear the saffron robes, set forth with shaven heads and alms bowls, and receive religious instruction while they practice a life of simplicity.

By contrast, there has traditionally been little social support for *bhikshunis*, or Buddhist nuns, in Southeast Asia. Provisions were made during the time of the Buddha for women monastics to live in their own monasteries, with the same lifestyle as monks, but the order of fully ordained nuns disappeared completely in Theravadin countries about a thousand years ago. Many of the early Buddhist scriptures take an egalitarian position toward women's capacity for wisdom and attainment of nirvana, but spiritual power was kept in the hands of monks and there was little opportunity for nuns to grow into positions of teaching and leadership.

Over time, some of the monks and the texts they edited apparently became somewhat sexist. Even today a Thai Buddhist monk is not allowed to come into direct contact with a woman, with the idea that women are hindrances to monks'

A twenty-year-old Buddhist nun in Dharamsala, north India.

spiritual development. Feminist scholars object to this interpretation. Thai Buddhist Dr. Chatsumarn Kabilsingh, for instance, asserts:

> *Newly ordained monks who have not had much experience with practice and are very weak in their mental resolve may be easily swayed by sensual impulses, of which women are the major attraction. Even if no women are present, some monks still create problems for themselves by images of women they have in their minds. Women are not responsible for the sexual behavior or imaginings of men; the monks themselves must cope with their own sensual desires. Enlightened ones are*

well-fortified against such mental states and are able to transcend gender differences. The Buddha himself found no need to avoid women, because women no longer appeared to him as sexual objects. He was well-balanced and in control of his mental processes.[18]

There are now attempts to revive fully ordained orders of nuns in Theravadin countries. In 1998 a landmark occurred: the full ordination at Bodh Gaya of 135 nuns from many countries. According to the code of discipline, ordination of nuns is possible only if both ordained monks and nuns are present. The lack of ordained nuns had been used by conservative senior monks as a way of blocking women's ordinations. But in China, Taiwan, Japan, and Korea, women's orders had continued, and therefore it was possible to assemble the requisite number of ten *bhikshus* and ten *bhikshunis* in Bodh Gaya to preside over the full ordination of *bhikshunis* from Sri Lanka, where the order had become extinct, for the first time in almost a thousand years.

Vipassana meditation In addition to trying to preserve what are thought to be the Buddha's original teachings, Theravada is the purveyor of mindfulness meditation techniques. ***Vipassana*** literally means "insight," but the meditation methods used to develop insight begin by increasing one's attentiveness to every detail as a way of calming, focusing, and watching the mind. As taught by the Burmese meditation master Mahasi Sayadaw, the way to begin *vipassana* practice is simply to watch oneself breathing in and out, with the attention focused on the rise and fall of the abdomen. To keep the mind concentrated on this movement, rather than dragged this way and that by unconscious, conditioned responses,

Some 135 women from 23 countries received full ordination as Buddhist nuns at Bodh Gaya in 1998, helping to revive orders of bhikshunis.

one continually makes concise mental notes of what is happening: "rising," "falling." Inevitably other mental functions will arise in the restless mind. As they do, one simply notes what they are—"imagining," "wandering," "remembering"—and then returns the attention to the rising and falling of the breath. Body sensations will appear, too, and one handles them the same way, noting "itching," "tight," "tired." Periods of sitting meditation are alternated with periods of walking meditation, in which one notes the exact movements of the body in great detail: "lifting," "moving," "placing."

This same mindfulness is carried over into every activity of the day. If ecstatic states or visions arise, the meditator is told simply to note them and let them pass away without attachment. In the same way, emotions that arise are simply observed, accepted, and allowed to pass away, rather than labeled "good" or "bad." By contrast, says *dharma* teacher Joko Beck, we usually get stuck in our emotions:

> *Everyone's fascinated by their emotions because we think that's who we are. We're afraid that if we let our attachment to them go, we'll be nobody. Which of course we are! When you wander into your ideas, your hopes, your dreams, turn back— not just once but ten thousand times if need be, a million times if need be.*[19]

The truths of existence as set forth by the Buddha—*dukha* (suffering), *anicca* (impermanence), *anatta* (no eternal self)—will become apparent during this process, and the mind becomes calm, clear, attentive, and flexible, detached from likes and dislikes. Thus it is free.

Devotional practices

The actual practice of Theravada Buddhism in Southeast Asia is considerably different from the contemplative and philosophical traditions described above. Lay Buddhists and also many monastics are more likely to turn to the Buddha in devotion, taking refuge in the sense of his protective presence and power. Thus temples, halls, and roadside shrines have been built with images of the Buddha before which the people bow, light candles, wave incense, offer flowers, press bits of gold leaf onto the images, and pray for help. Some monastics and intellectuals—including Protestant Christians who became interested in Buddhist studies in the late nineteenth century—have labelled such practices antithetic to the spirit of Buddhism, which they consider rationalistic, philosophical, nonritualistic, noniconic, and nontheistic. Despite increasing commercialization of the veneration of objects, some commentators are now trying to trace the history of image-oriented worship. Popular devotional practices are so widespread and so influential in popular Buddhist practice that scholars have begun to examine them as perhaps being part of the mainstream of Buddhism after all.

A key text in this regard is the Pali scripture *Mahaparinibbana Sutta*, which describes the Buddha's cremation and the dispersal of his body relics, and deals with the issue of devotionalism. According to this text, before his death the Buddha recommended devotion to relics in his memory alongside dedication to practice of the *dharma*, saying, "Whoever lays wreaths or puts sweet perfumes and colors [at a stupa honouring the Buddha] ... with a devout heart, will reap benefit and happiness for a long time,"[20] and simultaneously advocated devotion to the *dharma* as a way of respecting, revering, and paying homage to the Buddha. When lay Buddhists recite the Three Refuges, taking refuge in the Buddha, the *dharma*, and the *sangha*, they may experience this refuge not merely as a philosophical idea but as a metaphysical link with the timeless presence of the Buddha.

Consider one popular ritual: In northern Thailand, a network of threads attached to a large statue of the Buddha is used in special ceremonies to conduct his spiritual power to the *sangha*, to holy water or amulets, or to new images to be consecrated. The 108 squares formed overhead by the strings are believed to form a magical cosmos whose sacred energy touches the earth through cords hanging downward. People may wrap these cords around their heads during chanting of *sutras* by monks, and thus receive spiritual blessings. To consecrate new images of the Buddha, monks initially seal them by closing the eyes with beeswax and covering the heads with cloth. They chant, meditate, and preach about the Buddha and the *dharma* throughout the night to train and sacralize the images. In the process, the *sangha* is also drawn into a strong sense of unity with each other, with the *dharma*, and with the Buddha. At sunrise the coverings are removed from the images, and they are offered milk and sweet rice, for they are now in a sense living presences.

Similarly, followers consider the Buddha's power to be present mystically in relics from his cremated body. These images of the Buddha are placed in **stupas**, reliquary mounds reaching toward the sky, perhaps derived from indigenous spiritual traditions. A tiny bone chip believed to be a relic from the Buddha, for instance, is enshrined at Doi Suthep temple in Chiang Mai in Thailand. To share this sacred relic with the people, the ruler was said to have placed it on the back

A relic purported to be a tooth of the Buddha is so revered that it is carried on an elephant palanquin in a huge yearly procession in Sri Lanka.

of a white elephant—legendary symbol of the Buddha—so that it would choose the best place for the temple. The elephant climbed a nearby hill until it reached the auspicious spot and went down on its knees. Today, flocks of pilgrims climb the 290 steps to the temple, praying for blessings by acts such as pressing squares of gold leaf onto an image of the Buddha, lighting three sticks of incense to honor the Triple Gem, lighting candles, and offering flowers. So great are the powers associated with relics that huge processions carrying what are thought to be the Buddha's tooth relics have been used by the governments in Sri Lanka and Myanmar to legitimize their claims to temporal power.

Loving images of the Buddha proliferate in the temples and roadside shrines (which are almost identical to the indigenous spirit shrines, which are still quite common in Thailand, where Buddhism is a combination of indigenous spirituality, Buddhism, and Brahmanism). These physical images of the Buddha give a sense of his protective, guiding presence.

In Southeast Asia, aspects of Theravada Buddhism have often been adopted by shamans for greater efficacy in healing rituals. In Sri Lanka, the *yakeduras* invoke the power of the Buddha and the *dharma* to ward off evil spirits and thus help cure supernaturally afflicted people. In the cosmic hierarchy, the Buddha and *dharma* are considered the ultimate powers, and therefore useful in subduing lesser forces. During healing rituals, patients listen to Buddhist stories to help free and protect themselves by the power of the mind. Even monks are regarded as magical protectors of sorts, and the faithful can request chantings of blessings for protection.

Stupas, such as these bell-shaped monuments in Borobudur, Java, may house relics or statues of the Buddha and are sacred places for pilgrimage. The Buddha's long ears symbolize long life; elders are valued because of their experience and wisdom. The raised upper part of his head represents higher consciousness developed through years of meditation practice. The flame at the top signifies extinction of the flames of anger, hatred, and delusion.

The golden feet of a 105 ft (32 m) tall Buddha at Wat Indra Viharn, Bangkok.

In all Buddhist cultures, Buddhist temples are important centers for community identity and integration. There the monks not only teach the *dharma* but also conduct agricultural festivals to improve the harvest, ceremonies to assist the dead to better rebirth, and ceremonies to please the deities in order to receive their blessings and to generate festive atmospheres for community joy.

Mahayana: the path of compassion and wisdom

Further Buddhist practices and teachings appeared in a wide range of scriptures from the early centuries CE. These innovations in thought and practice beyond the Pali scriptures gradually developed into what is called Mahayana, the Greater Vehicle. The Mahayana scriptures emphasize the practice of monastics and laypeople equally, toward the goal of liberating all sentient beings from suffering. The Mahayana traditions honor all the teachings set forth in the Pali canon and, in addition, accept the extensive Mahayana literature originally found in Sanskrit and later translated into Chinese, Tibetan, and other languages. This literature praises the deeds and qualities of innumerable Buddhas and bodhisattvas, and inspires practitioners to develop the compassion and wisdom needed to become Buddhas and bodhisattvas themselves.

The Mahayana scriptures emphasize the importance of religious experience. The *dharma* is not embodied only in scriptures; for the Mahayanist it is the source of a conversion experience that awakens the quest for enlightenment as the greatest value in life. Each school, and there are many branches within Mahayana, offers a special set of methods, or "skillful means," for awakening. They are quite varied, in contrast to the relative uniformity of Theravada, but most Mahayana traditions have many characteristics in common.

Buddhism: Mahayana and Zen

Bodhisattvas An early Mahayana scripture, the Lotus Sutra, defended its innovations beyond the Pali Canon by claiming that the earlier teachings were merely skillful means for those with lower capacities. The idea is that the Buddha geared his teaching to his audience, and that his teachings were at different levels of completeness depending on the readiness of his audience to hear the full truth. This is explained by some researchers as a way to give credit to earlier teachings while going beyond them. Like other Mahayana texts, the Lotus Sutra claimed that a higher goal was to aspire to become **bodhisattvas** (being dedicated to attaining enlightenment) and work to achieve perfect enlightenment for the sake of saving others. The Lotus Sutra says that all beings have the capacity for Buddhahood and are destined to attain it eventually. Both monastics and laity took the bodhisattva vow to become enlightened.

Today Mahayana Buddhists often express this commitment in the Four Great Bodhisattva Vows compiled in China in the sixth century CE by Tien-t'ai Chih-i (founder of the Tendai School of Mahayana Buddhism):

Beings are infinite in number, I vow to save them all;
The obstructive passions are endless in number, I vow to end them all;
The teachings for saving others are countless, I vow to learn them all;
Buddhahood is the supreme achievement, I vow to attain it.

As His Holiness the fourteenth Dalai Lama says:

The motivation to achieve Buddhahood in order to save all sentient beings is really a marvelous determination. That person becomes very courageous, warm-hearted, and useful in society.[21]

You are not just here for yourself alone, but for the sake of all sentient beings. Keep your mind pure, and warm.

Soen Nakagawa-roshi[22]

Bodhisattvahood is not just an ideal for earthly conduct; numerous celestial bodhisattvas are available to hear the pleas of those who are suffering. On the path to Buddhahood, the bodhisattvas practice generosity, ethical conduct, patience, diligence, concentration, wisdom, and so on. As emanations of wisdom and compassion, they are sources of inspiration and blessing.

The most popular bodhisattva in East Asia is Kuan-yin (Japanese: *Kannon*), who symbolizes compassion and refuses help to no one. Although this being is depicted as a male (Avalokitesvara) in Indian images, the Lotus Sutra says that Kuan-yin will take any form that is needed to help others, and it lists thirty-three examples. In East Asia, Kuan-yin is typically represented as female, often as the giver or protector of babies. An image with a baby has become especially popular in East Asia as a source of inspiration and blessing for women and children.

The Three Bodies of Buddha   In Theravada, Buddha is an historical figure who no longer exists but who left his *dharma* as a guide. By contrast, Mahayana regards the Buddha as a universal principle. Metaphysically, Buddha is said to be an immanent presence in the universe with three aspects, or "bodies": first, the enlightened wisdom of a Buddha, which is formless; second, the body of bliss, celestial aspect of Buddhahood that communicates the *dharma* to bodhisattvas; and the third body of transformation, by which the Buddha principle becomes human to help liberate humanity. It was in this third body that the Buddha appeared for a time on the earth as the historical figure Shakyamuni Buddha.

Both Theravada and Mahayana are nontheistic, in that the existence or non-existence of gods is not a primary concern, yet ordinary people are inclined to seek

Many Buddhists anticipate the coming of Maitreya, the Buddha of the future, to re-establish the purity of the dharma.

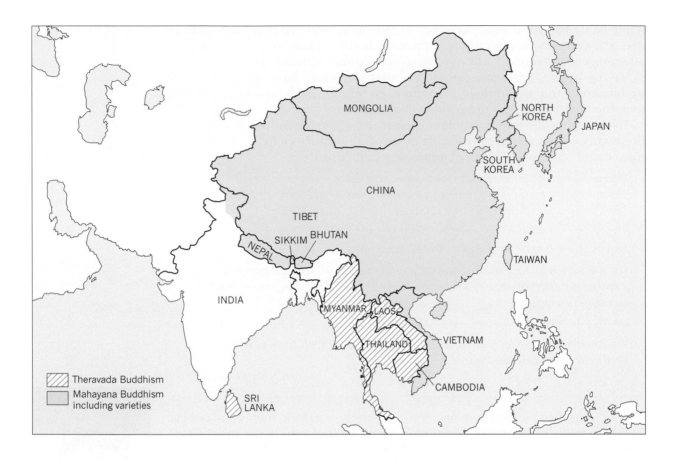

Map showing the approximate distribution of Theravada and Mahayana Buddhism in the world today.

help in times of need. In Mahayana, the Buddhas are seen to embody perfect purity, boundless compassion, omniscient wisdom, and many other enlightened qualities. Although some may interpret the Buddhas and bodhisattvas as metaphors for various aspects of enlightened awareness, others regard them as living presences ready to impart blessings and guidance to those who call on them.

Emptiness   Mahayana scriptures portray Buddhas moving swiftly through intergalactic space and time, cloning and appearing at different places simultaneously, dematerializing and materializing at will. However, practitioners are not to be attached to these appearances. Many schools within Mahayana also affirm, along with Theravadins, that there is an ultimate reality, which is the true nature of things, but this "suchness" is simply the lack of any essence or permanent, independent reality. In accordance with the universal law of cause and effect, all conditioned phenomena arise and perish continuously. Nirvana is in a different category since it is a non-regressive state of liberation from mental afflictions, suffering, and rebirth. In the Udana scripture from the Pali Canon, the Buddha stated, "O monks, there is an unborn, undying, unchanging, uncreated. If it were not so, there would be no point to life, or to training."

Some of the most complex and paradoxical of Mahayana teachings concern the concept of **sunyata**, meaning voidness or emptiness. They were elaborated by the Indian philosopher Nagarjuna around the second and third century CE on the basis of the earlier Perfection of Wisdom scriptures. According to Nagarjuna, all earthly things arise and pass away, as a process of events dependent on other events, and having no independent origin and no eternal reality. The world of phenomena—*samsara*—is therefore empty of inherent existence. Nirvana is also empty in the sense that it is a thought construct, even though it is not dependent on conditions. In the Perfection of Wisdom scriptures, the student to whom the lengthy teachings on *sunyata* are given is at last asked if he has understood them. The student declares, "In truth, nothing has been taught."

Everything being empty, there is nothing to cling to, so one who realizes Emptiness is freed to experience reality directly and to be compassionate without attachment. The concepts of selflessness and emptiness help practitioners understand things "as they are" and also help them overcome attachment to things, including attachment to concepts. As Professor Ruben Habito explains:

> One is able to celebrate every moment, every act, every thought, every sensation, as expressive of a dynamic, unobjectifiable, unfathomable, indescribable realm that, for lack of words, we call Emptiness. To experience each moment in this world of form as a manifestation of Emptiness is likewise to experience the world in the light of compassion. Having been freed of the notion of "self" as a "subject in here" grasping "objects out there," one is also freed of this notion of "self" as separate from "other selves."[23]

Kuan-yin, "hearer of cries," bodhisattva of mercy.

The Perfection of Wisdom scriptures that celebrate the liberating experience of emptiness are foundational texts for most of Mahayana. What is distinctive and startling about Mahayana is the application of the idea of emptiness to all things, even including the teachings of the Buddha. In the popular Heart Sutra that is used liturgically throughout East Asia, the core doctrines of traditional Buddhism are systematically shattered: bodhisattva Kuan-yin sees that the five aggregates of a person (form, sensation, perception, reaction, and consciousness) are each empty of absolute self-nature; they exist only relative to other aggregates. With this realization, the bodhisattva becomes free of delusion. Next, birth and death, purity and defilement, increase and decrease are seen as empty; the six sense objects, the six sense organs, and the six sense awarenesses are seen as empty; the Wheel of Life is seen as empty; the Four Noble Truths and Eightfold Path are seen as empty. Even knowledge and attainment are proclaimed to be empty. With this "perfection of wisdom," there are no obstacles, and no fear, and going beyond delusions one attains nirvana, having emptied Buddhism of its central objects. The Heart Sutra replaces the doctrines with a mantra: *Gate, Gate, paragate, parasamgate, bodhi, svaha!* ("Gone, gone, gone beyond, gone to the other shore. O enlightenment, all hail!"). As Professor David Chappell observes,

> The systematic emptying of the central doctrines of the tradition is unparalleled in religious history. (Imagine a Christian saying that the Ten Commandments and Lord's Prayer and Apostles' Creed are empty!) And yet, insight into the impermanence of all things, and their connectedness, gives Mahayana a self-critical profundity and an inclusive acceptance of diversity, which provides balance in the midst of movement, and peace in the midst of compassion.[24]

Vajrayana: indestructible way to unity

Of the many branches of Mahayana Buddhism, perhaps the most elaborate is **Vajrayana**. It developed in India, was transmitted to Tibet, and has also historically been practiced in Nepal, Bhutan, Sikkim, and Mongolia. Currently it is practiced throughout the Tibetan diaspora and increasingly in North America and Europe.

Prior to the introduction of Buddhism from India, the mountainous Tibetan region was home to a shamanistic religion called Bon (pronounced "pern"). In the seventh century CE a particularly powerful king of Tibet, Songtsan, became interested in the religion that surrounded his isolated kingdom. He sent a group of students to study Buddhism in India, but they all died in the searing heat of the plains. Only one member of a second group survived the arduous trip across the Himalayas, returning with many Sanskrit texts. After some of these works were translated into Tibetan, Songtsan declared Buddhism the national religion and encouraged Buddhist virtues in his subjects.

The Bon shamans are said to have kept trying to sabotage this threat to their power until a tantric adept, Padmasambhava, was invited to the country from Kashmir in the eighth century CE. On the way, it is said, he subdued and converted the local Bon deities. Along with his consort Yeshe Tsogyal, Guru Padmasambhava firmly established the tantric Buddhist teachings in Tibet. Although the Tibetans' understanding of Buddhism was no doubt influenced by their earlier beliefs, and the use of prayer flags and an emphasis on practices for the dying may reflect Bon concerns, the Tibetans spent many centuries attempting to understand the Indian Buddhist teachings as purely as possible. After a period of decline in the tenth century, when some misinterpreted the tantric teachings, a teacher named Atisha was invited from the great center of Buddhist learning at Nalanda, India, to set things right.

Under Atisha, Tibetan Buddhism became a complex path with three stages, said to have been prescribed by the Lord Buddha. While the Buddha did not develop them to their current state, he is said to have supported the idea of different levels of teachings for the less and more evolved. The first of these is called Hinayana by the Tibetans: quieting of the mind and relinquishing of attachments through meditation practices. The second is Mahayana: training in compassion and loving-kindness. The third is the advanced esoteric path called Vajrayana ("the diamond vehicle") or Tantrayana, said to be the speeded-up path that allows enlightenment within a single lifetime. It includes extremely rigorous practices derived from the tantric yoga of India. Adepts in this path attempt to construct an indestructible "diamond-body" for themselves that will allow them physically to sustain entries into the intense energies of higher levels of consciousness.

Buddhism:
Vajrayana and Tibet

Tibetan Buddhist monks and nuns have set up a community in exile in the mountains of north India, Dharamsala, with the fourteenth Dalai Lama, but always remember their homeland in Tibet.

Buddhist nuns from Tibet, where a distinct version of Mahayana developed. Behind them, prayer flags flutter in the wind.

Vajrayana aspirants are guided through a series of tantric practices by teachers, the highest of whom are **lamas**. Some are considered as incarnate bodhisattvas and carefully trained from a young age for their role as those who have realized the Supreme Truth and can help others advance toward it.

> *The masses have their heads on backwards. If you want to get things right, first look at how they think and behave, and consider going the opposite way.* [25]
> *Lama Drom Tonpa, 11th century*

Vajrayana initiates practice **deity yoga**: meditating on one of the many deities who embody various qualities that the practitioner wishes to manifest. These radiant forms are themselves illusory. But meditating on them is considered a way of reflecting on and thus bringing forth one's own true nature. Some of the deities are wrathful, such as Mahakala, defender of *dharma*. Buddhists understand that wrathful acts without hatred are sometimes necessary to protect truth and justice.

The highest form of Vajrayana is the use of the subtle vital energies of the body to transform the mind. A very high state of consciousness is produced after lengthy practice in which the "gross mind" is neutralized and the "subtle mind" manifests powerfully, as "the clear light of bliss." This innermost subtle mind of clear light is the true empty quality of one's own mind. Once it is realized, one is said to be capable of attaining Buddhahood in a single lifetime. The beloved seventh Dalai Lama of Tibet (1708–1757) gave this encouraging perspective:

> *Even the most seemingly evil person has the primordial clear light mind at the heart of his or her existence. Eventually the clouds of distortion and delusion will be cleared away as the being grows in wisdom, and the evil behavior that emanates*

from these negative mindsets will naturally evaporate. That being will realize the essential nature of his or her own mind, and achieve spiritual liberation and enlightenment.[26]

The practices used to transform the mind also enable levitation, clairvoyance, meditating continuously without sleep, and warming the body from within while sitting naked in the snow. Milarepa, the famous Tibetan poet-saint, whose enlightenment was won through great austerities, once sang this song:

*Blissful within, I don't entertain
The notion "I'm suffering,"
When incessant rain is pouring outside.*

*Even on peaks of white snow mountains
Amidst swirling snow and sleet
Driven by new year's wintry winds
This cotton robe burns like fire.[27]*

Tibetans have suffered persecution by the communist Chinese, who overran the country in 1951, destroying ancient monasteries and scriptures and killing an estimated one-sixth of the people over decades of occupation. Since 1951, hundreds of thousands of Tibetans have escaped into exile. Among them is the highest of the lamas—the beloved fourteenth Dalai Lama, spiritual and political leader

Right *The Chinese communists dismantled the system whereby one quarter of the men in Tibet were monks, supported by the laity and holding considerable secular power. But spirituality persists among the people, who include full-length prostrations in their prayers.*

Far right *One of the most beloved of Tibetan Buddhist deities is Tara. She is savior and mother of the world; she protects us and helps us to achieve our spiritual longings. (Detail of Tibetan thangka, 18th/19th century, tempera on cotton.)*

His Holiness the Dalai Lama

Surely one of the best-known and most-loved spiritual leaders in the world, His Holiness the fourteenth Dalai Lama is a striking example of Buddhist peace and compassion. Wherever he goes, he greets everyone with evident delight. Even when addressing an audience of thousands, he looks around the hall with a broad, childlike grin, which seems directed to each person individually. His example is all the more powerful because he is the leader in exile of Tibet, a small nation that knew extreme oppression and suffering during the twentieth century.

The simplicity of His Holiness's words and bearing belie his intellectual power. His Holiness was only a peasant child of two in 1937 when he was located and carefully identified as the reincarnation of the thirteenth Dalai Lama. He was formally installed as the fourteenth Dalai Lama when he was only four and a half years old, thus becoming the spiritual and temporal ruler of Tibet. He was raised and rigorously educated in Lhasa in the Potala. One of the world's largest buildings, it then contained huge ceremonial halls, thirty-five chapels, meditation cells, the government storehouses, national treasures, all records of Tibetan history and culture in 7,000 huge volumes, plus 2,000 illuminated volumes of the Buddhist scriptures. He was educated according to the traditional system of Tibet, which stressed broadening and developing the mind to acquire many kinds of knowledge and also to study and practice advanced Buddhist teachings.

Such a rigorous grounding in religion, maintains the Dalai Lama, brings steadiness of mind in the face of any misfortunes. He says,

Humanitarianism and true love for all beings can only stem from an awareness of the content of religion. By whatever name religion may be known, its understanding and practice are the essence of a peaceful mind and therefore of a peaceful world. If there is no peace in one's mind, there can be no peace in one's approach to others, and thus no peaceful relations between individuals or between nations.[28]

The Dalai Lama's equanimity of mind must have been sorely challenged by the Chinese invasion and oppression of his small country. In 1959, when he escaped from Tibet to lessen the potential for bloodshed during a widespread popular revolt against the Chinese, Tibet was home to more than 6,000 monasteries. Only twelve of them were still intact by 1980. It is said that at least one million Tibetans have died as a direct result of the Chinese occupation, and the violence against the religion, the culture, and the people of Tibet continues today as Chinese settlers fill the country.

In the face of the overwhelming military power of the Chinese, and in any case armed with Buddhist precepts, the Dalai Lama has persistently tried to steer his people away from violent response to violence. Asserting that "Nonviolence is the only way. . . . It's a slower process sometimes, but a very effective one," he explains:

Practically speaking, through violence we may achieve something, but at the expense of someone else's welfare. That way, although we may solve one problem, we simultaneously seed a new problem. The best way to solve problems is through human understanding, mutual respect. On one side make some concessions; on the other side take serious consideration about the problem. There may not be complete satisfaction, but something happens. At least future danger is avoided. Non-violence is very safe.[29]

While slowly, patiently trying to influence world opinion so that the voice of Tibet will not be extinguished by Chinese might, the Dalai Lama has established an entire government in exile in Dharamsala, India, in the Himalayas. There he and Tibetan refugees have built schools, orphanages, hospitals, craft cooperatives, farming communities, monasteries, and groups preserving traditional music and drama. From this base, he travels tirelessly, and with a punishing schedule. In his effort to keep the voice of Tibet alive, he has also emerged as a great moral leader in the world. His quintessentially Buddhist message to people of all religions is that only through kindness and compassion toward each other and the cultivation of inner peace shall we all survive as a species.

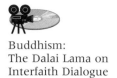

of the people. His speaking appearances around the world have been a major factor in the contemporary revival of interest in Buddhism. He has established his headquarters, Dharamsala, in the mountains of northern India. A repository of traditional Tibetan culture, it has become a magnet for spiritual seekers.

Despite persecution, religious fervor and ceremony still pervade every aspect of Tibetan life, from house-raising to ardent pilgrimages. Monks and laypeople alike meditate on *thangkas* and **mandalas**, visual aids to concentration and illumination, which portray a Buddha or bodhisattva surrounded by deities in a diagram symbolically representing the universe. Both also chant mantras. A favorite one is the phrase associated with the beloved Tibetan bodhisattva of mercy, Avalokitesvara: *Om mani padme hum*. It evokes awareness of the "jewel in the lotus of the heart," that beautiful treasure lying hidden within each of us. Because some emphasis is placed on the number of repetitions, mantras are written out thousands of times and spun in prayer wheels or placed on prayer flags which continue the repetition of the mantra as they blow in the wind.

Zen: the great way of enlightenment

Buddhism was transmitted from India to China around 50 CE and thence to Korea, Japan, and Vietnam, absorbing elements of Daoism along the way. Then, according to tradition, in the fifth century, Bodhidharma, a successor to the Buddha, traveled from southern China to a monastery in northern China. There he reportedly spent nine years in silent meditation, "facing the wall." On this experiential foundation, he became the first patriarch of the radical path that came to be called Ch'an Buddhism, from the Sanskrit *dhyana*, the yogic stage of meditation. Although this traditional account of its origins and founder is not fully accepted by scholars as absolute fact, it is known that this way was transmitted to Japan, where its name became **Zen**.

Zen claims to preserve the essence of the Buddha's teachings through direct experience, triggered by mind-to-mind transmission of the *dharma*. It dismisses scriptures, Buddhas, and bodhisattvas in favor of training for direct insight into the true nature of one's own mind, known as **Buddha-nature**.

A central way of directly experiencing the underlying unity is *zazen* (sitting meditation). "To sit," said the Sixth Zen Patriarch, "means to obtain absolute freedom and not to allow any thought to be caused by external objects. To meditate means to realize the imperturbability of one's original nature."[30]

> *The Great Way is not difficult*
> *for those who have no preferences.*
> *When love and hate are both absent*
> *everything becomes clear and undisguised.*
> *Make the smallest distinction, however,*
> *and heaven and earth are set infinitely apart.*
>
> *Sengtsan*[31]

Prescriptions for the manner of sitting are quite rigorous: one must take a specific upright posture and then not move during the meditation period, to avoid distracting the mind. Skillful means are then applied to make the mind

Zen Oxherding Pictures

The ten Zen Oxherding Pictures metaphorically illustrate the stages along the spiritual path, with the meaning of each picture to be found through meditation. We are the herdsman (worldly self) who is searching for the elusive ox (our true nature) in the wilderness. In the second picture, the herdsman notices the footprints of the ox. In the third, he catches sight of the ox. In the fourth, he struggles mightily to grasp the ox. In the fifth, he tames the ox with tether and whip, until "well tended and domesticated, the ox grows pure and gentle."

In the sixth stage (illustrated upper right), the seeker has found and tamed the ox and leisurely returns home riding high upon it, playing tunes "full of profound meaning." In the seventh, he reaches his home but the ox disappears.

In the eighth stage (below left), both ox and herdsman have disappeared—"Whip, tether, person, ox: ALL IS EMPTY! Blue sky, all and all around." In the ninth stage, Returning to the Source, "Inside his hut, he does not see any object outside." The final, tenth stage (below right), the enlightened one returns to the marketplace with helping hands and a wide grin on his face.[32]

Brush and ink drawings by Gyokusei Jikihara

Ceremonial tea in Japan, a ritual way of inculcating direct awareness, simplicity, and self-restraint.

one-pointed and clear. One beginning practice is simply to watch and count each inhalation and exhalation from one to ten, starting over from one if anything other than awareness of the breath enters the mind. Although this explanation sounds simple, the mind is so restless that many people must work for months before finally getting to ten without having to start over. Getting to ten is not really the goal; the goal is the process itself, the process of recognizing what comes up in the mind and gently letting it go without attachment or preferences.

As one sits in *zazen*, undisturbed by phenomena, as soon as one becomes inwardly calm, the natural mind is revealed in its original purity. This "original mind" is spacious and free, like an open sky. Thoughts and sensations may float through it like clouds, but they arise and then disappear, leaving no trace. What remains is insight into "thusness," the true nature of things. In some Zen schools, this perception of thusness comes in a sudden burst of insight, or **kensho**.

When the mind is calmed, action becomes spontaneous and natural. Zen practitioners are taught to rest in the natural simplicity of their own Buddha-nature. It is said that two Zen monks, on gaining a glimpse of enlightenment, ran naked through the woods scribbling on rocks.

On the other hand, the Zen tradition links spontaneity with intense, disciplined concentration. In the art of calligraphy, the perfect spontaneous brushstroke—executed with the whole body, in a single breath—is the outcome of years of attentive practice. Giving ourselves fully to the moment, to be aware only of pouring tea when pouring tea, is a simplicity of being that most of us have yet to realize. Then whatever we give ourself to fully, be it painting, or serving tea, or simply breathing, reveals the "thusness of life," its unconditioned reality.

Another tool used in one Zen tradition is the **koan**. Here the attention is focused ardently on a question that boggles the mind, such as "What was your original face before your parents were born?" As Roshi (venerable teacher) Philip Kapleau observes, "*Koans* deliberately throw sand into the eyes of the intellect to force us to open our Mind's eye and see the world and everything in it undistorted by our concepts and judgments." To concentrate on a *koan*, one must look closely at it without thinking about it, experiencing it directly. Beyond abstractions, Roshi Kapleau explains, "The import of every *koan* is the same: that the world is one interdependent Whole and that each separate one of us is that Whole."[33]

The aim of Zen practice is enlightenment, or **satori**. One directly experiences the unity of all existence, often in a sudden recognition that nothing is separate from oneself. As one Zen master put it:

> *The moon's the same old moon,*
> *The flowers exactly as they were,*
> *Yet I've become the thingness*
> *Of all the things I see!*[34]

All aspects of life become at the same time utterly precious, and utterly empty, "nothing special." This paradox can be sensed only with the mystically expanded consciousness; it cannot be grasped intellectually.

Pure Land: calling on Amida Buddha

Zen is essentially an inner awareness in which great attention is given to every action, but this requires years of disciplined meditation practice. Other forms of Buddhist practice that developed in India and East Asia have much greater popular appeal. The most widespread Buddhist school in East Asia is known as **Pure Land** Buddhism. At times of great social upheaval (for instance, when the old Japanese feudal aristocracy was falling apart), it was widely thought that people had become so degenerate that it was nearly impossible for them to attain enlightenment through their own efforts. Instead, many turned to the saving power of **Amida** Buddha, the Buddha of Boundless Light. Amida (who first appeared in India under the Sanskrit name Amitabha) was believed to have been an ancient prince who vowed to attain enlightenment. After he did, he used his pure virtue to prepare a special place of bliss, the Pure Land, for all those who called his name.

Japan had an ancient tradition of worshipping mountains as the realm to which the dead ascend and from which deities descend to earth. The originally abstract Indian Buddhists' concept of a "Pure Land" far to the west to which devotees return after death was transformed in Japan into concrete images. They depicted Amida Buddha riding on clouds billowing over the mountains, coming to welcome his dying devotees.

Buddhism:
Thich Nhat Hanh on
Mindfulness

Amida Buddha descends to welcome the faithful to the Western Paradise. Welcoming Descent of Amida Buddha, *Anon., 18th century.*

Many people contributed to the growth of Pure Land Buddhism into a mass movement. The thirteenth-century religious leader Shinran, who broke with monastic tradition by marrying, emphasized the principle that salvation comes through repeating the name of Amida Buddha with sincere trust, not by separating oneself from society. The Shin Buddhist path developed by Shinran's followers has become one of the major Buddhist movements throughout the world.

The monk Genshin described the ineffable pleasures of being reborn into the Pure Land upon death:

> *Rings, bracelets, a crown of jewels, and other ornaments in countless profusion adorn his body. And when he looks upon the light radiating from the Buddha, he obtains pure vision, and because of his experiences in former lives, he hears the sounds of all things. And no matter what color he may see or what sound he may hear, it is a thing of marvel.*[35]

Many believers interpret these passages literally, anticipating that if they have sufficient faith in the saving power of Amida they will enjoy a beautiful life after death. But some understand the Pure Land as a state that can be achieved in this life—a metaphor for the mystical experience of enlightenment, in which one's former identity "dies" and one is reborn into an expanded state of consciousness. Some modern thinkers have placed their emphasis on "Building the Pure Land in the Human Realm," making their goal transformation of this world by purifying it of social evils such as oppression, pollution, and sexism.

Nichiren: salvation through the Lotus Sutra

While some Pure Land Buddhists despair of purifying themselves by their own efforts and therefore humbly submit to the grace of Amida Buddha, a thirteenth-century Japanese fisherman's son, who named himself Nichiren, stressed the importance of striving to reform not only ourselves but also society. For Nichiren, the highest truths of Buddhism were embodied in the Lotus Sutra, a large compilation of parables, verses, and descriptions of innumerable forms of beings who support the teachings of the Buddha. Nichiren gave particular attention to two of these beings: the Bodhisattva of Superb Action, who staunchly devotes himself to spreading the Perfect Truth, even in evil times, and the Bodhisattva Ever-Abused, who is persecuted because of his insistence on revering everyone with unshaken conviction that each person is potentially a Buddha. Nichiren himself was repeatedly abused by authorities but persisted in his efforts to reform Buddhism in Japan and then spread its purified essence, the Bodhisattva ideal, to the world.

The phrase chanted by Nichiren and his followers, *"Namu myoho rengekyo,"* refers to faith in the entire Lotus Sutra. Today it is chanted by Nichiren monks and nuns by the hour, slowly revealing its depths as it works inwardly, beyond thought. In our time, some in the Nichiren tradition undertake long peace walks, such as one sponsored by Nipponzan Myohoji in 1995, in which people walked from Auschwitz in Poland to Hiroshima and Nagasaki in Japan, to commemorate the fiftieth anniversary of the end of World War II with a plea for nonviolence and respect for all of life. They beat small hand drums while chanting *"Namu myoho rengekyo,"* and hope to contribute to world peace by truly bowing to the Buddha in each person, even if they encounter abuse. As the Most Venerable

Nichidatsu Fujii, who passed away in 1985 at the age of one hundred and who influenced Gandhi's doctrine of non-violence, explained:

> We do not believe that people are good because we see that they are good, but by believing that people are good we eliminate our own fear and thus we can intimately associate with them. To believe in the compassionate power of the Supreme Being which we cannot see is a discipline in order to believe in the invisible good in others.[36]
>
> Civilization has nothing to do with having electric lights, airplanes, or manufacturing atomic bombs. It has nothing to do with killing human beings, destroying things or waging war. Civilization is to hold one another in mutual affection and respect.[37]

The chanting of "*Namu myoho rengekyo*" has also caused seventy Peace Pagodas to arise thus far in many countries, built with donated materials and labor by people of all faiths in hopes of world peace and the elimination of all weapons.

Another new offshoot of Nichiren's movement is Soka Gakkai, based in Japan but having millions of members around the world. Its twentieth-century founders called for a peaceful world revolution through transformation of individual consciousness. The central practice is the chanting of Nichiren's phrase (which they transliterate as "*Nam myoho renge kyo*") combined with modern social activism in areas such as humanitarian relief, environmental awareness, human rights, literacy, and cultural and interfaith exchanges. Members are encouraged to develop their "unlimited potential" for hope, courage, and altruism.

Yet another new branch of Buddhism inspired by the Lotus Sutra is Rissho Kosei-kai, founded in the 1930s by Rev. Nikkyo Niwano and Myoko Naganuma to bring the message of the Lotus Sutra to the world in practical ways in order to encourage happiness and peace. Members meet to discuss ways of applying the Buddha's teachings to specific problems in their own lives. The organization, which is active in international inter-religious activities, asserts that "The Eternal Buddha, invisible but present everywhere, is the great life-force of the universe, which sustains each of us."[38]

> *The Bodhisattva loves all living beings as if each were his only child.*
>
> *Vimalakirtinirdesha Sutra 5*

Buddhism in the West

Images of the Buddha are now enshrined around the world, for what began in India has gradually spread to the West as well as the East. Much of this transmission occurred in the twentieth century, when the United States became a vibrant center of Buddhism. Scholars are studying Buddhist traditions at many universities, and many people are trying to learn Buddhist meditation practices.

The exodus of over 100,000 people from Tibet, including most of its highest lamas, has led to the establishment of Tibetan Buddhist centers in many Western countries as well as in India, the Dalai Lama's home in exile. Several hundred thousand Westerners now have some spiritual involvement with Tibetan

Living Buddhism

Karma Lekshe Tsomo is an American from Hawaii who has become a very active Tibetan Buddhist nun. Her story illustrates the unusual pathways by which Westerners have come to adopt Buddhism. Karma explains, "I was very much attracted to the teachings of Jesus as a child but there were a lot of unanswered questions for me, especially about the meaning of life and what happens to us after we die. When I asked the ministers they would say, 'If you are good you go to heaven, and if you are bad then you go to hell.' It seemed a little bit too simplistic for me. I really wanted to know more. So I kept searching.

"I think I was about twelve when I read some books on Buddhism—*The Way of Zen* by Alan Watts and G.T. Suzuki on Zen Buddhism. At once I thought, 'Wow, home free!' At about nineteen I went to Japan for surfing, but I was studying Zen and reading Haiku. Still searching, I went on to Thailand, India, and Nepal. On the way I had a really clear and beautiful dream that I was a nun. I knew I wanted to be a nun, but where? It took me a long time (thirteen years!) from then until I actually became one.

"It wasn't until I wound up in the Tibetan library in Dharamsala that I got a real systematic education. As I burst into the classroom for the first time, there on a cushion at the other end of the room was a little lama with a yellow pointed hat, and he was explaining, "At the second stage after death you will see a faint smoke." He was explaining in great detail exactly what happens to us after we die. I thought, 'Bingo! This is it!' So I sat at his feet for five years. I never missed a day of class. I just loved it.

"The more I studied Buddhism and the more I practiced, the more I liked it. I wanted to dedicate my whole life to it. It was in 1977 that I met the Karmapa and six months later I told him I was ready to be ordained. He said, 'What will you do after you are ordained?' I said, 'I will go to India and study.' He said, 'Perfect. I am giving the ordination tomorrow. You will be the fifth.' Five is an auspicious number, because the Buddha first ordained five monks. Then two monks cut my long strawberry blonde curls. I can't describe the sense of joy I felt when I saw all that hair in my lap. The ordination ceremony is carried out by five monks. After prayers they give you a set of questions to make sure that you are without debts and that you have the agreement of your parents, spouse, or whoever might be responsible, and they endeavour to make sure that you are healthy and able to withstand the hardships of monastic life. They want to make sure that your motivation is pure in taking precepts. In the Tibetan tradition it is a lifetime commitment.

"Life in India at the center where I stayed was tremendously difficult. The Himalayas were icy cold in the winter. No indoor plumbing. I was living in a mud hut at seven to eight thousand feet. We are supposed to keep a certain dress standard, which does not include a sweater or jacket. Plus I was so poor. I had no support as a nun. The Tibetans take care of their own ethnic peoples, but they don't feel any responsibilities for other kinds of people, and they don't have a tradition of seeking alms. The Americans who have become Buddhists don't have a tradition of supporting renunciates. They think, 'What is different about your practice from mine? So why should I support you? Get a job.' It's a complete contradiction to the original idea, which is that you live like the birds of the air and the beasts of the field, depending on the goodwill of your followers. Things got really difficult, so I would go to the devotional ceremonies and get the *prasad*, and eat that. The fourth year an American women invited me to take lunch with her family for two rupees a day so I got some sort of a balanced meal once a day, otherwise it was very tough.

"I got skinny and really sick—hepatitis a few times—but somehow I survived. I was really determined to survive. Not only the climate, the difficulty of getting food, but also the visa to stay in India a long time was very difficult to get. And then there was living in that mud hut. There were rats living in the walls and scorpions under my pillow. Rats fell down on my head as I meditated. There were fleas and in the monsoon there were three or four months of torrential rains when it was never dry. One time we had an earthquake at the center where I stayed, and I immediately dived under the bed. Four rooms fell down in that earthquake. I had to rebuild them.

"Despite such many challenges, I knew without question that the best place to study Buddhism was right there. Not only because these were some of the greatest scholars the Tibetan tradition has ever produced, but also because study was combined with practice—meditation practices. The tenor of the teachings was to transform the mind. I thought, 'I may not know the inner workings of Buddhist philosophy, but I think I am becoming a better person.'

"We began to notice that conditions for Buddhist practice for women were not the same as for men. Conditions and facilities for education for nuns have been lagging way behind. It was assumed that men would be the teachers, so they get given the education. Fortunately, since Buddhism is a rather logical and sensible path, once you question people if women have equal capacity for enlightenment and liberation, they have to admit that they do, because the Buddha himself said so. Sometimes, however, social reality doesn't match theory. I work with Sakyadhita International Association of Buddhist Women trying to gain equal opportunities for women to study, equal facilities for meditation practice, and also opportunities for them to become ordained if they so wish. It seems that once women get an opportunity for education they express a deep concern for the needs of others in their communities—the children, the old folks, the sick. I strongly feel that Buddhist women can contribute a great deal to society even on a very local level. There are 300 million Buddhist women out there. That is a tremendous source for peace, goodwill, and energy to work for the benefit of humanity."

Buddhism. Zen meditation centers are also flourishing, with over 400 in North America alone, as well as Zen monasteries giving training in *zazen* and offering a monastic lifestyle as a permanent or temporary alternative to life in the world.

Intensive *vipassana* retreats of up to three months are carried out in Theravadin centers such as the Insight Meditation Society in rural Barre, Massachusetts. Theravadin teachers from Southeast Asia and Europe make frequent appearances to conduct retreats, and American teachers undertake rigorous training in Southeast Asia under traditional meditation masters.

The American monk Venerable Sumedho, classically trained in Theravada Buddhism in Thailand, has established monastic forest communities and meditation centers in England, Switzerland, Italy, and the United States. Many Buddhist centers in the West are led by women, in contrast to the cultural suppression of females in the East. They are explaining traditional Buddhist teachings to Westerners in fresh, contemporary ways. Some are also setting examples of dedicated spiritual practice, such as Tenzin Palmo, a British woman turned Tibetan Buddhist nun who lived alone for twelve years in a cave 13,200 feet high in the Himalayas, undergoing tremendous austerities in the quest for enlightenment.

The Vietnamese monk Venerable Master Thich Nhat Hanh now lives in exile in France, where he conducts retreats for both women and men in his Plum Village community. When he travels internationally, large audiences gather to be inspired by his teachings. He speaks simply, using homely examples, and

A meditation teacher at the Buddhist Dharma School in Brighton, England, with her young students.

RELIGION IN PRACTICE

Life in a Western Zen Monastery

Side-by-side in still rows, with birdsong and sunlight streaming in through the tall windows, sit the monks and laypeople of Zen Mountain Monastery. For thirty-five minute blocks, separated by periods of attentive walking, they support each other by practicing *zazen* together in silence. With this group structure, many find it easier to carry on the rigorous discipline of serious Zen training than they would by themselves.

This particular monastery, located in the Catskill Mountains near Mount Tremper, New York, reflects the changing face of religion in the United States. A hundred years ago the main building was handcrafted of stone as a Benedictine monastery; later it became a Lutheran summer camp. Now back-to-back with the Christ on the cross on the outside of the building is a statue of Buddha on the altar in the *zendo*. The monastery houses eleven fully ordained monastics (six of them women) who have taken lifetime vows of service, several novices and postulants in training (an aspect adopted from Western monasticism), lay residents who stay for up to a year, and groups of people who come for special retreats and classes. Increasingly these are professionals and family people from the mainstream culture, rather than the hippies who embraced Buddhism in the 1960s and 1970s. They do not come for a comfortable vacation, for *zazen* is hard work and the teachers are dedicated to creating snags that help people discover the places where they are not free. They are expected to practice intensely and then leave, carrying what they have learned back into the world. As the monk Shugen observes, "If Zen doesn't work in the world, it's not working."

In addition to long sessions of silent sitting and walking, *dharma* talks by the resident Zen master John Daido Loori Sensei (an American ordained in both authentic Zen lineages), and private coaching by the monks, monastery residents participate in structured nontheistic liturgical services designed to foster attentiveness and appreciation. They chant in Japanese and English, with frequent bowing to each other, to their meditation cushions, and to the Buddha on the altar in identification

John Daido Loori Sensei, abbot of Zen Mountain Monastery.

The stillness of the zendo *at Zen Mountain Monastery.*

Oriyoki, *a ceremonial meal, at Zen Mountain Monastery.*

with all beings and gratitude for the teachings. Zen master Daido notes that liturgy reflects the innards of a religion: "In Catholicism, cathedrals are awe-inspiring, the chants expansive; in Zen the form is simple and the chanting is grounded, not other-worldly."

The rest of the day is devoted to caretaking of the buildings and 200-acre (81-hectare) nature sanctuary, mindful practice done in silence, and work practice. Those with office jobs combine ancient and modern arts: they sit cross-legged on low cushions before their computers and use calligraphic skills to hand-letter signs. Meals are simple and include coarse breads donated by a nearby whole-grain bakery. Every action—even brushing one's teeth—is treated as liturgy, in the sense of bringing total attentiveness to the sacredness of even the most "mundane" activity as a teaching that enlightenment takes place in one's everyday experience.

Following the lead of their teacher Daido, who is at once highly disciplined in the pure mind-to-mind *dharma* transmission and very down-to-earth, approachable, compassionate, and married, monastery residents are human, playful, and loving. The women monks shave their hair when ordained and keep it very short thereafter, but for them near-baldness feels like freedom rather than self-sacrificing asceticism. The monk Myotai observes:

I could feel every breeze, and being bald definitely altered the way I saw the habit patterns I brought to my interactions with other people, clarifying how much "extra" was still there, to a degree that surprised me. There is a several-year entry period before ordination, to get clear on what it means, but one aspect of actually having no hair was that it really opened up the male–female dynamic. I no longer felt myself relating to men as a woman. That was very freeing. It was also wonderful to have this daily reminder of what I was doing with my life.

emphasizes bringing the awareness fostered by meditation into everyday life, rather than making spirituality a separate compartment of one's life. He says:

When we walk in the meditation hall, we make careful steps, very slowly. But when we go to the airport, we are quite another person. We walk very differently, less mindfully. How can we practice at the airport and in the market?[39]

Buddhism:
A Zen Rock Garden

Buddhism has often been embraced by Westerners because of their longing for the peace of meditation in the midst of a chaotic materialistic life. Many psychotherapists are studying Buddhism for its insights into the mind and human suffering. Richard Clarke, who is both a Zen teacher and a psychotherapist, feels that a discipline such as Zen should be part of the training of therapists:

Emptiness is ... the source of infinite compassion in working with people: to really feel a person without any agenda, to be spacious to that person, to will that they be the way they are. When a person experiences that in someone's presence, then they can drop away those things that they've invented to present themselves with. Those faces, those armors, those forms of the self become unnecessary.[40]

But are Westerners able to achieve enlightenment by taking Buddhist workshops here and there? Particularly in the case of Tibetan Buddhist practices, Westerners often want to be initiated into the highly advanced teachings without years of patiently practicing and being inwardly transformed by the step-by-step foundational teachings. A further question is whether teachings developed within a specific cultural context can be directly transplanted into the soil of an entirely different culture. Most Westerners who are adopting Buddhist practices are living in highly materialistic rather than monastic settings. And in their impatience to get results, many keep shopping around from one teacher to the next rather than persisting over a long time in one path. As Alan Wallace remarks,

In Tibetan society, fickleness is considered to be one of the worst of vices, while reliability, integrity, trustworthiness, and perseverance are held in high regard. So a few of the finest lamas are now refusing even to come to the West. Some are feeling—given the brevity and preciousness of human life—that devoting time to people with such fickleness and so little faith is time not very well spent.[41]

Another issue that has arisen is training of teachers for the West. Two large Tibetan Buddhist organizations from the Gelukpa order, for instance, have opened nearly six hundred centers for study and meditation around the world but do not have enough fully trained lamas to staff them all. Traditional training takes up to twenty-five years of rigorous study and debate of the finer points of Buddhist philosophy, logic, meditation, cosmology, psychology, and monastic life. Close guidance by an advanced teacher has traditionally been considered essential, but this is not possible for all the Western aspirants, given the shortage of qualified teachers and the language problems.

Given the differences in culture, background, and motivation, are Western students and their teachers in the process of creating new forms of Buddhism adapted to Western ways? Some observers feel that Western Buddhism is actually closer to what they construe as the earliest practice of Buddhism than are its later developments in the East, in that there is an emphasis on inner practice rather than outer forms, and that people have to make a conscious choice of taking up the religion since they have not been born into it. Contemporary Western

Buddhists also tend to be oriented to the goal of achieving enlightenment by their own efforts, which is reportedly what the Buddha prescribed for his followers. Whether or not Western Buddhism conforms to early patterns, it seems to be evolving in different directions from contemporary Asian versions, with some Westerners remaking Buddhism in their own image. For instance, the American Buddhist Stephen Batchelor argues in his book *Buddhism Without Beliefs* that what the West needs is Buddhism stripped of belief in reincarnation and *karma*, emphasizing instead a secularized version, an "existential, therapeutic and liberating agnosticism."[42] Another difference between Western Buddhism and the historical developments in Eastern Buddhism is the Western tendency to support equal participation of women, as renunciates and teachers as well as practitioners.

As Asia entered the modern world, many of its peoples lost interest in their traditional religions, which became superficial re-enactments of ceremonial practices. But as Westerners themselves are taking strong interest in Buddhism, those who have grown up as Buddhists are reassessing their religion and finding new depths in it. There are now many Eastern laypeople interested in studying meditation, and their teachers include women.

Buddhist women from West and East have joined hands to hold international gatherings to enhance the role of women in Buddhism. The international Association of Buddhist Women, Sakyadhita or "Daughters of the Buddha," is working to improve conditions for women's Buddhist practice and education, full ordination of women, and training of women as teachers of Buddhism.

Socially engaged Buddhism

An emerging focus in contemporary Buddhist practice is the relevance of Buddhism to social problems. Contrary to popular assumptions, the Buddha did not advise people to permanently leave society to seek their own enlightenment. Sri Lankan Buddhist monk Walpola Rahula explains:

> *It may perhaps be useful in some cases for a person to live in retirement for a time in order to improve his or her mind and character, as preliminary moral, spiritual, and intellectual training, to be strong enough to come out later and help others. But if someone lives an entire life in solitude, thinking only of their own happiness and salvation, without caring for their fellow beings, this surely is not in keeping with the Buddha's teaching which is based on love, compassion, and service to others.[43]*

Buddhism, like other world religions, has always been engaged with the wider society and political life. In Thailand, for instance, the king is the bearer of the Buddhist heritage, and thus has sacred legitimization. But Thailand also has a tradition of socially-conscious lay practice of Buddhism. The renowned Thai monk Buddhadasa Bhikkhu (1906–1993) was a great critic of capitalism, teaching that it increases egoism and selfishness, thus causing distress both to the individual and to society.

In Vietnam, Thich Nhat Hanh and other socially active Buddhists refused to take sides with the governments and military movements of either North Vietnam or South Vietnam during the Vietnam War, for they felt that both were oppressing the common people and also American soldiers. All were victims of an ideological conflict between communism and anti-communism. Buddhists worked hard to bring a negotiated end to the war, and helped the suffering people as best they could by evacuating villagers caught in the midst of battles, helping to rebuild damaged buildings, taking care of orphans, and providing medical care to people from all sides. They believed that all life is interdependent—violence and suffering affect everyone. Thus they meditated to generate selfless compassion, according to the teachings of the Buddha, who said:

> *Hatred is never appeased by hatred. It is appeased by love. This is an eternal law. Just as a mother would protect her only child, even at the risk of her own life, even so let one cultivate a boundless heart towards all beings. Let one's thoughts of boundless love pervade the whole world.*[44]

However, Buddhism's link with politics has not always been primarily altruistic. In Sri Lanka, a selective interpretation of Theravada Buddhist tradition was used to bolster nationalistic sentiments among the Sinhalese Buddhist majority against the Tamil (mostly Hindu and Muslim) minority. As in many contemporary fundamentalist movements elsewhere, a chauvinistic, rigid version of the religion developed in response to rapid modernization and Westernization by colonial powers. The reaffirmation of Buddhist identity became a tool of ethnic oppression of the minority, leading to a violent separatist movement among the Tamils and ultimately civil strife which has disrupted life on the lovely island for decades.

Nipponzan Myohoji monks in the Peace Park, Hiroshima, Japan.

In general, however, the Buddha's emphasis on compassion has prevailed, and even when Buddhists have been social activists, they have tended to be non-violence activists. In this posture, some contemporary Buddhists have tried to correct injustice, oppression, famine, cruelty to animals, nuclear testing, warfare, and environmental devastation. E. F. Schumacher preached what he called "Buddhist economics," to affirm human beings' willingness to live simply, generously, and humanely with each other. Ajahn Pongsak, a Thai Buddhist monk, was so troubled by the devastation of the northern Thai forests that he rallied 5,000 villagers to reforest an area by building a tree nursery, terracing the eroded hillsides, planting nearly 200,000 seedlings, laying irrigation pipes, and fencing the area to protect the new trees. He taught them the importance of a respectful relationship with the forest as their own home, their own parent. He says:

> A mind that feels no gratitude to the forest is a coarse mind indeed—without this basic siladhamma [dharma], how can a mind attain enlightenment? ... The times are dark and siladhamma is asleep, so it is now the duty of monks to reawaken and bring back siladhamma. Only in this way can society be saved.

Venerable Maha Ghosananda of Cambodia has led numerous long marches to promote peace in his country. Even though the country is now beginning to heal after decades of war, the walks continue, carrying a message about the necessity of developing inward peace through meditation and "learning and listening with mind and heart." Monks, nuns, and laypeople walk through still-dangerous areas that are heavily landmined, facing issues such as domestic violence, AIDS, deforestation, and dire poverty. Maha Ghosananda explains,

> We must find the courage to leave our temples and enter the temples of human experience, temples that are filled with suffering. If we listen to the Buddha, Christ, or Gandhi, we can do nothing else. The refugee camps, the prisons, the ghettos and the battlefields will then become our temples.[45]

Buddhism was returned to its native India after some one thousand years' absence by the bold action of a converted Buddhist activist, Dr. B. R. Ambedkar (1891–1956). Born an untouchable Hindu, he was the chief architect of India's new democratic constitution, and built into it many provisions designed to end the oppression of the traditional Hindu caste system. In his personal search for a religion offering freedom and dignity to all human beings, he chose Buddhism. And when he publicly converted shortly before his death, he was the inspiration for almost half a million untouchables to do likewise. Despite this, he openly questioned and changed certain Buddhist teachings. Among them, he reinterpreted the Second Noble Truth that suffering results from desires and ignorance. He felt that such a concept may prevent recognition that some people are victims of oppression rather than their own faults, and thus may prevent action to end social injustices. Another traditional Buddhist ideal he challenged was the emphasis on renunciation and meditation rather than active social engagement, helping the people. His slogan was "Educate, Agitate, and Organize."

In the midst of the civil strife between the Sinhalese Buddhist majority and the Hindu and Muslim Tamil minority in Sri Lanka, the Buddhist monks of the Sarvodaya Shramadana Sangamaya movement have tried to promote harmony and rural development. The founder, a Buddhist schoolteacher named Dr. A. T.

Ariyaratne, asserts that renunciation is not the best path for most people. Rather, they can best realize their spiritual potential in the midst of society, working for its betterment. He and the monks of the Sarvodaya movement have engaged people of all religions in thousands of villages in work camps where they come together to eliminate social decadence and poverty by developing schools, nutrition programs, roads, and irrigation canals and to learn to live by the Four Noble Truths and the Eightfold Path. Dr. Ariyaratne encourages people to look at their own egotism, distrust, greed, and competitiveness and to recognize that these are the cause of their suffering and inability to work together for progress.

Sulak Sivaraksa, founder of the International Network of Engaged Buddhists, explains that socially engaged Buddhism does not mean promoting Buddhism per se:

> *The presence of Buddhism in society does not mean having a lot of schools, hospitals, cultural institutions, or political parties run by Buddhists. It means that the schools, hospitals, cultural institutions, and political parties are permeated with and administered with humanism, love, tolerance, and enlightenment, characteristics which Buddhism attributes to an opening up, development, and formation of human nature. This is the true spirit of nonviolence.*[46]

Even when one intends to be nonviolent in one's approach to life, difficult ethical questions may still arise. For example, contemporary scholars of Buddhist medical ethics are trying to determine how best to apply Buddhist principles to issues such as abortion, reproductive technologies, genetic engineering, organ transplants, suicide, coma patients, and euthanasia. Although the issues seem modern, some of them were actually addressed during the time of the Buddha, according to the scriptures. Euthanasia, for instance, is the subject of a number of stories in the texts. The general principle which seems to be applied is to avoid taking human life, even when the person requests help in dying. However, careful reading of the texts seems to allow a dying person to refuse life-extending technology, for death is ultimately one of the realities of life that must be faced.

Buddhism is thus as relevant today, and its insights as necessary, as in the sixth century, when the one who became Shakyamuni Buddha renounced a life of ease to save all sentient beings from suffering.

Suggested reading

Batchelor, Martine and Kerry Brown, eds., *Buddhism and Ecology*, World Wide Fund for Nature, 1992. Buddhist teachings, stories, and activities from various countries, illustrating the sympathetic relationship between Buddhism and nature.

Carter, John Ross and Mahinda Palihawadana (trans.), *The Dhammapada: The Sayings of the Buddha*, Oxford: Oxford University Press, 2000. A basic book of sayings attributed to the Buddha that covers the essentials of *dharma* in memorable, pithy verses.

Conze, Edward, Horner, I. B., Snellgrove, David, and Waley, Arthur, ed. and trans., *Buddhist Texts through the Ages*, Oxford, England: Oneworld Publications, 1995. A fine collection of Buddhist scriptures translated from the Pali, Sanskrit, Chinese, Tibetan, and Japanese.

Eppsteiner, Fred, ed., *The Path of Compassion: Writings on Socially Engaged Buddhism*, Berkeley, California: Parallax Press, 1988. A highly readable and relevant collection of essays by leading contemporary Buddhist teachers about the ways in which Buddhism can be applied to social problems.

Fremantle, Francesca, and Trungpa, Chogyam, trans., *The Tibetan Book of the Dead*, Boston and London: Shambhala Publications, 1975. The classic Tibetan Buddhist scripture on the projections of the mind and the practices of deity yoga to attain enlightenment.

Friedman, Lenore, *Meetings with Remarkable Women: Buddhist Teachers in America*, Boston and London: Shambhala Publications, 1987. Wisdom from Buddhist traditions shared in very personal, perceptive interviews.

Gross, Rita M., *Buddhism after Patriarchy*, Albany, New York: State University of New York Press, 1993. A feminist reconstruction of Buddhist history, revealing its core of gender equality but later overlays of sexism, plus analysis of key Buddhist concepts from a feminist point of view.

Habito, Ruben, *Experiencing Buddhism: Ways of Wisdom and Compassion*, Maryknoll, New York: Orbis Books, 2005. Clear and sensitive exploration of various ways that Buddhists are attempting to practice the Buddha's teachings, especially in the contemporary world.

Hanh, Thich Nhat, *The Heart of the Buddha's Teaching: Transforming Suffering into Peace, Joy, and Liberation*, New York: Broadway Books, 1998. In simple, compassionate language, the famous Vietnamese monk explains the efficacy of Buddhist teachings for dealing with today's problems.

Heine, Steven and Charles S. Prebish, *Buddhism in the Modern World: Adaptations of an Ancient Tradition*, New York: Oxford University Press, 2003. Essays examining how specific schools of Buddhism have adapted to contemporary challenges and yet maintained their links with tradition.

Levine, Stephen, *A Gradual Awakening*, Garden City, New York: Doubleday, 1979 and London: Rider & Company, 1980. Gentle, poetic presentation of *vipassana* techniques in their relevance to contemporary life.

Lopez, Donald S., Jr., ed., *Buddhism in Practice*, Princeton: Princeton University Press, 1995. Annotated translation of original sources dealing with Buddhist practice around the world, organized around the Triple Jewels of Buddha, *dharma*, and *sangha*.

Lopez, Donald S., Jr. *The Story of Buddhism: A Concise Guide to its History and Teachings*, San Francisco: HarperSanFrancisco, 2001. An introduction incorporating the latest scholarship.

Mackenzie, Vicki, *Cave in the Snow*, London: Bloomsbury Publishing, 1999. Fascinating story of a Western woman's twelve years alone in a Himalayan cave in order to concentrate on intense meditation practices and achieve enlightenment in a woman's body.

Queen, Christopher S. and King, Sallie B., eds., *Engaged Buddhism: Buddhist Liberation Movements in Asia*, Albany: State University of New York Press, 1996. A thorough survey of contemporary Buddhist activism in Asian countries.

Rahula, Walpola Sri, *What the Buddha Taught*, New York: Grove Press, 1974. The classic introduction to Buddhist teachings—an accurate and clear guide through the complexities of Buddhist thought and practice, with representative texts.

Reynolds, Frank E. and Jason A. Carbine, eds., *The Life of Buddhism*, Berkeley: University of California Press, 2000. Attempts to analyze Buddhist ways in their cultural and historical contexts.

Sivaraksa, Sulak, *Seeds of Peace: A Buddhist Vision for Renewing Society*, Berkeley, California: Parallax Press, 1992. A renowned Thai social activist examines the "politics of greed" and issues involved in transformation of society, from the point of view of Buddhist ideals.

Suzuki, Shunryu, *Zen Mind, Beginner's Mind*, New York and Tokyo: Weatherhill, 1970. A beautiful book, leading one gracefully and seemingly simply through the paradoxes of Zen.

Key terms

Theravada	The remaining orthodox school of Buddhism, which adheres closely to the earliest scriptures and emphasizes individual efforts to liberate the mind from suffering.
Mahayana	The "greater vehicle" in Buddhism, the more liberal and mystical Northern School, which stressed the virtue of altruistic compassion rather than intellectual efforts at individual salvation.
Zen	A Chinese and Japanese school emphasizing that all things have buddha-nature, which can only be grasped when one escapes from the intellectual mind.
bhikshu (Pali: *bhikkhu;* feminine: *bhikshuni or bhikkuni)*	A monk or nun who renounces worldliness for the sake of following the path of liberation and whose simple physical needs are met by lay supporters.
nirvana (Pali: *nibbana*)	The ultimate egoless state of bliss.
dukkha	According to the Buddha, a central fact of human life, variously translated as discomfort, suffering, frustration, or lack of harmony with the environment.
karma	Our actions and their effects on this life and lives to come.
samsara	The continual round of birth, death, and rebirth.

Study questions

1 Describe the historical origins and subsequent geographic expansion of Buddhism. Discuss Shakya, Maya, Middle Way, Mara, Buddha, caste, Rahul, Pali, Sanskrit, *sangha*, monks and nuns, animal sacrifice, stupas, and Asoka.
2 Explain the basic Buddhist *dharma*. Discuss gods, salvation, Enlightenment, meditation, life after death, nirvana, the Four Noble Truths, rebirth, *karma*, the Three Root Evils, and *samsara*.
3 Explain the history, geography, and main beliefs of Theravada. Discuss *vipassana*, devotions, *sangha*.
4 Explain the history, geography, and main beliefs of Mahayana. Discuss bodhisattvas, sutras, Kuan-yin, Avalokitesvara, three bodies, Emptiness.
5 Explain the history, geography, and main beliefs of Vajrayana. Discuss Bon, Padmasambhava, Atisha, lamas, deity yoga, Milarepa, 1951, Dalai Lama, mandalas, mantras, Tara.
6 Explain the history, geography, and main beliefs of Zen. Discuss Bodhidharma, zazen, original mind, kensho, oxherding, koans, satori, Pure Land, Amida, Nichiren, Sokka Gakkai, Thich Nhat Hanh, John Daido Loori Sensei, Buddhist Social Engagement.

Refer to Pearson/Prentice Hall's **TIME Special Edition: World Religions** magazine for these and other current articles on topics related to many of the world's religions.

* *Buddhism: Buddhism in America; The Dalai Lama – "It's Time to Prepare New Leaders"; Essay – Lost Without a Faith*

Chapter 5 continues the study of religions originating in India and focuses on Buddhism and its variations. For further research in this area, use the tools available to you in Research Navigator:

As you investigate Buddhism, consider this question: "What is the role and value of meditation in the varieties of Buddhism?"

* **Ebsco's ContentSelect:** Search in the Religion and Sociology databases using terms such as "Buddhism," "Zen Buddhism," "Meditation," "guru."
* **Link Library:** Search in the Religion and Sociology databases under the categories: "Religions from India: Buddhism" and "Buddhism."
* **The *New York Times* on the Web:** Search in the Religious Studies and all other databases for current articles on related topics.

CHAPTER 6

DAOISM AND CONFUCIANISM

The unity of opposites

While India was giving birth to Hinduism, Jainism, and Buddhism, three other major religions were developing in East Asia. Daoism and Confucianism grew largely in China, and later spread to Japan and Korea; Shinto was distinctively Japanese. These religions have remained associated primarily with their homelands. In this chapter we will explore the two that developed in China from similar roots but with different emphases: Daoism and Confucianism. Shinto will be the subject of Chapter 7. Buddhism also spread to East Asia, and its practice has often been mixed with the native traditions.

In East Asia, religions that will be treated as separate entities in this chapter and the next are, in fact, more subtly blended and practiced. Daoism and Confucianism, though they may seem quite opposite to each other, co-exist as complementary value systems in East Asian societies, and a person's thought and actions may encompass both streams.

In this chapter we will be transliterating Chinese words according to the contemporary Pinyin system, which has replaced the older Wade-Giles system. Thus "Daoism" is the Pinyin transliteration; "Taoism" was the earlier Wade-Giles transcription of the same word. When terms are first introduced in this chapter, the Wade-Giles equivalent—which is still found in many English books—will be given in parenthesis.

Ancient traditions

Chinese civilization is very old and continuous. By 2000 BCE, people were living in settled agrarian villages in the Yellow River Valley, with a written language, musical instruments, and skillful work in bronze, silk, ceramics, and ivory. The spiritual ways of this early civilization permeate all later religious developments in China, Korea, and Japan. One major feature is the veneration of ancestors. The spirits of deceased ancestors remain very closely bonded to their living descendants for some time. Respect must be paid to them—especially the family's founding ancestor and those recently deceased—through funerals, mourning rites, and then continuing sacrifices. The sacred rituals are called *li*. They are essential because the ancestors will help their descendants, if treated with proper respect, or cause trouble if ignored.

DAOISM AND CONFUCIANISM

	BCE	
	Legendary Yellow Emperor	
Ancient Traditions	Shang Dynasty (c.1751–1123)	Ancient Traditions
DAOISM		**CONFUCIANISM**
between c.600–300 Life of Laozi c.365–290 Life of Zhuangzi	Chou Dynasty (c.1122–221)	c.551–479 Life of Confucius c.390–305 Life of Meng Tzu c.340–245 Life of Xunzi
Immortality movements Queen Mother of the West cult	Chin Dynasty (221–206)	Confucian scholars suppressed, books burned
Early religious Daoist sects Heavenly Master tradition begins	Han Dynasty (206 BCE– 220 CE)	Confucian Classics used as basis of civil service exams
	CE	
Mutual influences between Daoism and Buddhism. 748 Daoist Canon first compiled	T'ang Dynasty (618–907)	Buddhism reaches peak, then is persecuted. Confucianism makes comeback
Taiji quan appears Northen Daoist sects flourish	Sung Dynasty (960–1280)	Neo-Confucianism 1130–1200 Life of Zhu Xi
1911 Imperial dynasty overthrown	1900	1911 Last imperial dynasty overthrown. Confucianism de-established as state religion
National Association of Daoism (White Clouds Temple, Beijing)	1950	1949 onward Mao Zedong red book replaces Confucian Classics
Temples and books destroyed	Cultural Revolution (1966–1976)	Temples and books destroyed
	1980	1989 Scholars' requests refused at Tiananmen Square
Daoist sects, temples re-established. First Daoist Grand Ritual. Popular faith and practices Chinese government attempts to suppress Falun Gong/Falun Dafa	1990–2000	Confucian Classics reintroduced in schools. Confucius's birthday celebrated. International Association of Confucians established

Kings, even those of the earliest Chinese dynasty, sought their ancestors' help through the medium of oracle bones. These were shells or bones onto which the divining specialist scratched questions the king wanted the ancestors to answer. Touching the bones with a hot poker made them crack, forming patterns, which the diviner interpreted as useful answers from the ancestors. Later, demons and ghosts who had been ignored or ill-treated during their lifetime, were seen as causing so much mischief that many efforts were made to thwart them, including evil-deflecting charms, gongs, and firecrackers, appeals through mediums, spirit-walls to keep them from entering doorways, exorcisms, prayers, incense, and fasts. These activities continue today.

To the early Chinese and in continuing popular belief, the world is full of invisible spirits. In addition to ancestors, there are charismatic humans who have died but are still available to help the people.

As is understood in indigenous religions everywhere, the world is also full of nature spirits. Plants, animals, rivers, stones, mountains, stars—all parts of the natural world are vitalized by cosmic energy and often personified and honored as deities. From early times, Chinese people made offerings to these beings and sought their aid with personal problems, sometimes through the mediumship of a shaman who can communicate with the spirit world.

According to Chinese belief, which can be traced back at least to the earliest historical dynasty, the Shang (c. 1751–1123 BCE), there also exists a great spiritual being referred to as *Shangdi* (**Shang Ti**), the Lord-on-High, ruler of the universe, the supreme ancestor of the Chinese. Deities governing aspects of the cosmos and the local environment are subordinate to him. This deity is conceived of as being masculine and closely involved in human affairs, though not as a Creator God.

During the Zhou (Chou) dynasty (c. 1122–221 BCE), which overthrew the Shang, the focus shifted to Heaven as an impersonal power controlling the universe. Rulers then developed the idea of the "Mandate of Heaven" to justify their rule. The Mandate is the self-existing moral law of virtue, the supreme reality. According to the Zhou rulers, human destiny is determined by virtuous deeds. Rulers have a moral duty to maintain the welfare of the people and a spiritual duty to conduct respectful ceremonies for the highest heavenly beings.

In addition to ancestors, spirits, and Heaven, there has long existed in China a belief that the cosmos is a manifestation of an impersonal self-generating energy called *qi* (*ch'i*). This force has two aspects whose interplay causes the ever-changing phenomena of the universe. **Yin** is the dark, receptive, "female" aspect; **yang** is the bright, assertive, "male" aspect. Wisdom lies in recognizing their ever-shifting, but regular and balanced, patterns and moving with them. This creative rhythm of the universe is called the **Dao** (**Tao**), or "way." As traditionally diagrammed, yin and yang interpenetrate each other (represented by the small circles). As soon as one aspect reaches its fullest point, it begins to diminish, while its polar opposite increases. Nothing is outside of this process. As Neo-Confucian scholar Tu Weiming explains:

In ancient Chinese tradition, the universe arises from the interplay of yin and yang. They are modes of energy commonly represented as interlocking shapes, with dominance continually shifting between the dark, receptive yin mode and the bright, assertive yang mode.

All modalities of being, from a rock to Heaven, are integral parts of a continuum which is often referred to as the "great transformation." Since nothing is outside of this continuum, the chain of being is never broken. ... The continuous presence of qi *in all modalities of being makes everything flow together as the unfolding of a single process. Nothing, not even an almighty creator, is external to this process.[1]*

To harmonize with the cosmic process, the ancients devised many forms of divination. One system developed during the Zhou dynasty was eventually written down as the *Yijing* (*I Ching*), or *Book of Changes*. It is a common source for both Daoism and Confucianism and is regarded as a classic text in both traditions. The *Yijing* was highly elaborated with commentaries by scholars beginning in the Han dynasty (206 BCE–220 CE). To use this subtle system, one respectfully purifies the divining objects—such as yarrow stalks or coins, which symbolize yin and yang—asks a question, casts the objects six times, and then consults the *Yijing* for symbolic interpretation of the yin–yang combinations.

The pattern of throws is diagrammed in the *Yijing* as a hexagram, with yin represented as a broken line and yang by a straight line. For example, hexagram number 46, called Sheng or "Pushing Upward," has been likened to a tree emerging from the earth, growing slowly and invisibly:

> Thus the superior person of devoted character
> Heaps up small things
> In order to achieve something high and great.[2]

Another set of commentaries is based on the two trigrams within the hexagram. In the case of hexagram 46, the upper pattern of three yin lines can be interpreted as devotion and yielding, and the lower pattern of two yang lines above one yin line suggests gentleness. According to the commentaries, these non-aggressive qualities will ultimately lead to supreme success.

By studying and systematizing the ways of humans and of nature, the ancient Chinese tried to order their actions so that they might steer a coherent course within the changing cosmos. They recognized that any extreme action will produce its opposite as a balancing reaction and thus they strived for a middle way of discretion and moderation. From these roots gradually developed two contrasting ways of harmonizing with the cosmos—the more mystically religious ways, which are collectively called Daoism, and the more political and moral ways, which are known as Confucianism. Like yin and yang, they interpenetrate and complement each other, and are themselves evolving dynamically.

Pilgrimage to holy Mount Huashan. Certain mountains have been revered in China from ancient times to today.

Daoism—the way of nature and immortality

Daoism is as full of paradoxes as the Buddhist tradition it influenced: Ch'an or Zen Buddhism. It has been adored by Westerners who seek a carefree, natural way of life as an escape from the industrial rat race. Yet beneath its words of the simple life in harmony with nature is a tradition of great mental and physical

The hexagram Sheng is a visual symbol of the various meanings attached to "Pushing Upward."

Daoism and
Confucianism:
Daoist Immortality

discipline. As it has developed over time, Daoism includes efforts to align oneself with the unnamable original force (the Dao), ceremonial worship of deities from the Jade Emperor to the kitchen god, and cultivation of physical and spiritual strength. Some Daoist scriptures counsel indifference about birth and death; others teach ways of attaining physical immortality. These variations developed within an ancient tradition that had no name until it had to distinguish itself from Confucianism. "Daoism" is actually a label invented by scholars and awkwardly stretched to cover a philosophical or "literati" tradition, a multitude of longevity techniques, and an assortment of religious sects whose relationship to the literati tradition is complex, but which probably developed at least in part from the early philosophical texts and practices. Religious Daoism itself is often an amalgam, with the Daoist way of natural life and meditation as its base, plus Confucian virtues, health disciplines, Buddhist-like rituals, and immortality as its final goal.

Teachings of Daoist sages

Aside from its general basis in ancient Chinese ways, the specific origin of Daoist philosophy and practices is unclear. In China, tradition attributes the publicizing of these ways to the Yellow Emperor, who supposedly ruled from 2697 to 2597 BCE. He was said to have studied with an ancient sage and to have developed meditation, health, and military practices based on what he learned. After ruling for one hundred years, he ascended to heaven on a dragon's back and became one of the Immortals.

The philosophical or literati form of Daoism has been pursued by intellectuals and artists over the millennia. Its foundation is expounded in the famous scripture, the *Daode jing* (*Tao-te Ching*, "The Classic of the Way and the Power"). It is second only to the Bible in the number of Western translations, for its ideas are not only fascinating but also elusive for translators working from the terse ancient Chinese characters and variations in existing copies of the Chinese text.

Even the supposed author of the *Daode jing* is obscure. According to tradition, the book was written by Laozi (Lao-tzu), a curator of the royal library of the Zhou dynasty, for a border guard as he left society for the mountains at the reported age of 160. The guard recognized Laozi as a sage and begged him to leave behind a record of his wisdom. Laozi reportedly complied by inscribing the 5,000 words now known as the *Daode jing*. This is traditionally said to have happened during the sixth century BCE, with Laozi purportedly fifty-three years older than Confucius. But recent archaeological finds date the existent version of the *Daode jing* to 350 BCE and suggest it was an alternative to Confucianism. Some think the *Daode jing* was an oral tradition, derived from the teachings of several sages, and question whether Laozi ever existed.

The book's central philosophy is a practical concern with improving harmony in life. It says that one can best harmonize with the natural flow of life by being receptive and quiet. These teachings were elaborated more emphatically and humorously by a sage named Zhuangzi (Chuang-tzu), (c. 365–290 BCE). He, too, was a minor government official for a while but left political involvement for a hermit's life of freedom and solitude. Unlike Laozi, whose philosophy was addressed to those in leadership positions, Zhuangzi asserted that the best way to live in a chaotic, absurd civilization is to become detached from it.

Flowing with Dao   At the heart of Daoist teachings is the idea of Dao, the "unnamable," the "eternally real."[3] Contemporary Master Da Liu asserts that Dao is so ingrained in Chinese understanding that it is a basic concept that cannot be defined, like "goodness." Moreover, Dao is a mystical reality that cannot be grasped by the mind. The *Daode jing* says:

> *The Dao that can be told of*
>   *Is not the Absolute Dao,*
> *The Names that can be given*
>   *Are not Absolute Names.*
> *The Nameless is the origin of Heaven and Earth;*
> *The Named is the Mother of All Things . . .*
> *These two (the Secret and its manifestations)*
>   *Are (in their nature) the same; . . .*
> *They may both be called the Cosmic Mystery:*
> *Reaching from the Mystery into the Deeper Mystery*
> *Is the Gate to the Secret of All Life.[4]*

Chapter 25 of the *Daode jing* is more explicit about the mysterious Unnamable:

> *There is a thing confusedly formed,*
> *Born before heaven and earth.*
> *Silent and void*
> *It stands alone and does not change,*
> *Goes round and does not weary.*
> *It is capable of being the mother of the world.*

Laozi, one of the major conveyers of the Daoist tradition, is often depicted as a humorous old man riding off into the mountains after reportedly drawing the 5,000 characters of the Daode jing.

I know not its name
So I style it "the way."
I give it the makeshift name of "the great."[5]

Although we cannot describe the Dao, we can live in harmony with it. Ideally, says Laozi:

Humans model themselves on earth,
Earth on heaven,
Heaven on the way,
And the way on that which is naturally so.[6]

There are several basic principles for the life in harmony with Dao. One is to experience the transcendent unity of all things, rather than separation. Professor Chang Chung-yuan observes that "the value of Dao lies in its power to reconcile opposites on a higher level of consciousness."[7] This higher level can only be attained when one ceases to feel any personal preferences. Daoism is concerned with direct experience of the universe, accepting and cooperating with things as they are, not with setting standards of morality, not with labeling things as "good" or "bad." Zhuangzi asserts that herein lies true spirituality:

Such a man can ride the clouds and mist, mount the sun and moon, and wander
beyond the four seas. Life and death do not affect him. How much less will he be
concerned with good and evil![8]

The Daoist sage takes a low profile in the world. He or she is like a valley, allowing everything needed to flow into his or her life, or like a stream. Flowing water is a Daoist model for being. It bypasses and gently wears away obstacles

TEACHING STORY

Three in the Morning

Whether you point to a little stalk or a great pillar, a leper or the beautiful Hsi-shih, things ribald and shady or things grotesque and strange, the Way makes them all into one. . . . Only the man of far-reaching vision knows how to make them into one. So he has no use [for categories], but relegates all to the constant. The constant is the useful; the useful is the passable; the passable is the successful; and with success, all is accomplished. He relies upon this alone, relies upon it and does not know he is doing so. This is called the Way.

But to wear out your brain trying to make things into one without realizing that they are all the same—this is called "three in the morning." What do I mean by "three in the morning"? When the monkey trainer was handing out acorns, he said, "You get three in the morning and four at night." This made all the monkeys furious. "Well, then," he said, "you get four in the morning and three at night." The monkeys were all delighted. There was no change in the reality behind the words, yet the monkeys responded with joy and anger. Let them, if they want to. So the sage harmonizes with both right and wrong and rests in Heaven the Equalizer.

Zhuangzi[9]

rather than fruitlessly attacking them, effortlessly nourishes the "ten thousand things" of material life, works without struggling, leaves all accomplishments behind without possessing them. Laozi observes:

> Water is the softest thing on earth,
> Yet its silken gentleness
> Will easily wear away the hardest stone.
>
> Everyone knows this;
> Few use it in their daily lives.
> Those of Tao yield and overcome.[10]

This is the uniquely Daoist paradox of *wu wei*—"actionless action," or taking no intentional or invasive action contrary to the natural flow of things. *Wu wei* is spontaneous, creative activity proceeding from the Dao, action without ego-assertion, letting the Dao take its course. Zhuangzi uses the analogy of a butcher whose knife always stays sharp because he lets his hand be guided by the makeup of the carcass, finding the spaces between the bones where a slight movement of the blade will glide through without resistance. Even when difficulties arise, the sage does not panic and take unnecessary action.

> Sweet music and highly seasoned food
> Entertain for a while,
> But the clear, tasteless water from the well
> Gives life and energy without exhaustion.   *Laozi*[11]

The result of *wu wei* is non-interference. Much of Laozi's teaching is directed at rulers, that they might guide society without interfering with its natural course. Nothing is evil, but things may be out of balance. The world is naturally in harmony; Dao is our original nature. But according to tradition, the Golden Age of Dao declined as humans departed from the "Way." "Civilization," with its intellectual attempts to improve on things and its rigid views of morality, actually leads to world chaos, the Daoists warn. How much better, Laozi advises, to accept not-knowing, moving freely in the moment with the changing universe.

Then again, Daoism places great value on withdrawal from the madding crowd to a contemplative life and love of nature. The latter is greatly aided by **feng shui** (geomancy), an increasingly popular practice in China and other countries today. By observing the contours of the land and the flows of wind and water, specialists in *feng shui* could reportedly determine the best places for the harmonious placement of a temple, dwelling place, or grave. By examining the flow of *qi* within a dwelling, they decide on the optimal placement of furniture and wall decorations.

The literati Daoist seeks to find the still center, save energy for those times when action is needed, and take a humble, quiet approach to life. As asserted in a fourth-century BCE essay on inner training:

> The vitality of all people inevitably comes from their peace of mind.
> When anxious, one loses this guiding thread; when angry, one loses this basic point.
> When one is anxious or sad, pleased or angry, the Way has no place to settle. . . .

Sites for Daoist and Buddhist temples in China were traditionally chosen according to the ancient art of feng shui, *or geomancy, the awareness of the presence and movement of natural energies. The energies of waterfalls and mountains were considered conducive to spiritual practices.* (Buddhist Temple Amid Clearing Mountain Peaks, Northern Song, c.940–67 CE.)

That mysterious vital energy within the mind, one moment it arrives, the next it departs.
So fine nothing can be contained within it, so vast nothing can be outside it.
The reason we lose it is because of the harm caused by agitation. [12]

Organized Daoism

Beginning in the second century CE, Daoist-organized groups or sects developed, employing practices such as alchemy, faith-healing, sorcery, and the use of power objects, which seem to have existed from ancient times in China, converting them into institutionalized and distinctive social movements with detailed rituals, clergy, and revealed texts. This institutionalization of ancient practices developed as the Han dynasty (206 BCE–220 CE) was declining amidst famine and war. An array of revelations and prophecies predicted the end of the age and finally led to the rise of religious/political organizations. For example, Kan Ji received a visionary revelation that yin and yang were no longer in balance in heaven or on earth, for the rulers had forgotten to follow the ways of nature, and that in 184 CE the blue heaven of the Han would be replaced by the yellow heaven. In that year, inspired by this vision of Great Peace, hundreds of thousands of followers of a leader who was known as a faith healer and advocate of egalitarian ideas rebelled in eight of China's twelve provinces; their rebellion took several years to suppress and presaged the fall of the Han dynasty. Simultaneously, in western China, Zhang Daoling (Chang Tao-ling) had a vision of Laozi as the heavenly Lord Lao in which he was appointed representative of the Dao on earth and given the title Celestial Master. He advocated similar practices of healing by faith and developed a quasi-military organization of religious officials, attracting numerous followers. The older Han religion had involved demons and exorcism, belief in an afterlife, and a god of destinies, who granted fortune or misfortune based on heavenly records of good and bad deeds. These roles were now ascribed to a pantheon of celestial deities, who in turn were controlled by the new Celestial Master priesthood led by Zhang's family. This hereditary clergy performed imperial investitures as well as village festivals, with both men and women serving as libationers in local dioceses.

After the sack of the northern capitals early in the fourth century, the Celestial Masters and other aristocrats fled south and established themselves on Dragon-Tiger Mountain in southeast China. Today the sixty-fourth patriarch in the lineage lives in Taiwan, although practices are being revived on Dragon-Tiger Mountain.

In approximately 365 CE another aristocratic family in exile in southern China began receiving revelations from a deceased member, Lady Wei. These revelations of the names and powers of newly discovered deities, meditation methods, alchemy, and rituals were recorded in exquisite calligraphy and transmitted to a few advanced disciples. This elite group of celibates, who resided on Mount Mao, called their practices "Highest Purity Daoism." They looked down on the Celestial Master tradition and its sexual rituals as crude, and they avoided village rituals and commoners. Instead, they focused on meditations for purifying the body with divine energies so as "to rise up to heaven in broad daylight." Although the Highest Purity Daoism did not reach the mass of the people, its texts and influence continue to be revered today as the elite tradition of Daoism.

In the late fourth century, another group arose in the wake of Highest Purity: the Numinous Treasure school. It assimilated many elements of Buddhism, creating a medley of new meditation practices, divine beings, rituals, scriptures, heavens, rebirth, and hells. This tradition was in turn succeeded in the twelfth century by Complete Perfection, which has been the dominant monastic school ever since. It unites Daoist inner alchemy with Ch'an Buddhist meditation and Confucian social morality, harmonizing the three religions. Actively monastic, it focuses on meditation and non-attachment to the world. Today its major center is the White Cloud Monastery in Beijing, the headquarters of the government-approved Chinese Daoism Association. Complete Perfection is also the foundation for most Hong Kong Daoist temples and martial arts groups.

The many revealed scriptures of Daoist movements were occasionally compiled and canonized by the court. The present Daoist canon was compiled in 1445 CE. Containing about 1,500 sophisticated scriptures, it has only recently begun to be studied by non-Daoist scholars. It includes a wealth of firsthand accounts by mystical practitioners—poems of their visionary shamanistic journeys, encounters with deities, advanced meditation practices, descriptions of the perfected human being, methods and elixirs for ascending to heavenly realms and achieving immortality, and descriptions of the Immortals and the heavenly bureaucracies. The rituals and inner cultivation practices of the canon are in use today. For example, in Fujian Province in the mountains of Southeast China, festivals are periodically organized to honor a local god named Guo Chongfu, who was originally a mortal who took birth in 963 CE, died mysteriously when he was only thirteen, and then appeared in visions and dreams to people of the area. In these rituals, the celebrants include Daoist priests in embroidered robes, puppeteers, theatre troupes, and representatives of the community. The Daoist priests read a scripture in classical Chinese which describes the god's virtues and heavenly mission, which was demonstrated in his audience with the entire Daoist pantheon of gods.

At death either Daoist or Buddhist priests may be hired by families to perform rituals to help the deceased appear before the Ten Hell Judges, as well as to join in communal rituals of grave-cleaning in April and of liberation and feeding of hungry ghosts in August. Every temple has a side shrine to Tudi gong (T'u-ti Kung), Lord of the Earth, who can transport offerings to deceased loved ones.

Longevity Daoism Flowing with Dao is easy and natural, while controlling the spirits is ritually formalized. But both require masterful discipline, which forms the third major aspect of Daoism. Laozi describes what mastery entailed:

The ancient Masters were profound and subtle.
Their wisdom was unfathomable. . . .
They were careful
as someone crossing an iced-over stream.
Alert as a warrior in enemy territory.
Courteous as a guest.
Fluid as melting ice.
Shapable as a block of wood.
Receptive as a valley.
Clear as a glass of water.[13]

The mastery to which Daoist writers refer may be the result of powerful unknown ascetic practices traditionally passed down secretly from teacher to pupil. These teachers lived in the mountains; great Daoist teachers are said to be still hidden in the remote mountains of China and Korea.

One of the goals of esoteric Daoist practice is to separate the spirit from the body so that the former can operate independently, both before and after death.

The aim of the longevity practices is to use the energy available to the body in order to become strong and healthy and also to intuitively perceive the order of the universe. Within our body is the spiritual micro-universe of the "three treasures" necessary for the preservation of life: generative force (*jing*), vital life-force (*qi*), and spirit (*shen*). These three are activated with the help of various methods: breathing techniques, vocalizations, diets, gymnastics, absorption of solar and lunar energies, sexual techniques, visualizations, and meditations.

Inner alchemy began with the practitioner's building a reservoir of *jing* energy in the "cauldron" several inches below the navel, whence it rises up the spine as a vapor, transmuted into *qi* energy. *Qi* is in turn transmuted into *shen* in an upper cauldron in the head (an area similar to the Third Eye of Indian yogic practice), drops down to illuminate the heart center, and then descends to an inner area of the lower cauldron. There it forms what is called the Immortal Fetus, which adepts can reportedly raise through the Heavenly Gate at the top of the head and thus leave their physical body for various purposes, including preparation for life after death. In addition, the adept learns to draw the *qi* of the macro-universe of heaven and earth into the micro-universe of the body, unifying and harmonizing inner and outer, heaven and earth.

> *The secret of the magic of life consists in using action in order to attain non-action.*
> *The Secret of the Golden Flower*[14]

The lure of immortality   Daoist texts on immortality specify a twofold process: physically regaining and expanding health and vitality, and spiritually merging into the greater oneness of the Dao through total harmony. Immortality is both a refinement of the body and an overcoming of the limits of worldly existence. Already Zhuangzi counseled indifference to birth and death: "The Master came because it was time. He left because he followed the natural flow. Be content with the moment, and be willing to follow the flow."[15] Laozi referred enigmatically to immortality or long life realized through spiritual death of the individual self, the body and mind transmuted into selfless vehicles for the eternal. Still, for many the first step is good enough. As Professor Huai-Chin Han puts it, people who are interested in Daoist practices:

> *usually forget the highest principles, or the basis of philosophical theory behind the cultivation of Tao and the opening of the* ch'i *routes for longevity. . . . Longevity consists of maintaining one's health, slowing down the ageing process, living without illness and pain, and dying peacefully without bothering other people. Immortality does not mean indefinite physical longevity; it indicates the eternal spiritual life.*[16]

A quiet contemplative life in natural surroundings, with sexual abstinence, peaceful mind, health-maintaining herbs, healthy diet, practices to strengthen the inner organs and open the meridians (subtle energy pathways known to Chinese doctors), and meditations to transmute vital into spiritual energy bring a marked tendency to longevity. Chinese literature and folk knowledge contain many references to venerable sages thought to be centuries old. They live hidden in the mountains, away from society, and are said to be somewhat translucent. The most famous of the legendary long-lived are the Eight Immortals, humans who were said to have gained immortality, each with his or her own special magical power.

Since ancient times, one of the most revered celestial beings has been the Queen Mother of the West. She guards the elixir of life and is the most wondrous incarnation of yin energy. The Daoist canon also includes the writings of some female Daoist sages who undertook the great rigors of Daoist meditation practices and reportedly mastered its processes of inner transformation. In her mystical poetry, the twelfth-century female sage Sun Bu-er describes the ultimate realization:

> *All things finished.*
> *You sit still in a little niche.*
> *The light body rides on violet energy,*
> *The tranquil nature washes in a pure pond.*
> *Original energy is unified, yin and yang are one;*
> *The spirit is the same as the universe.*[17]

Daoism today

All forms of Daoist practice are still actively undertaken today, in communist mainland China, Taiwan, Hong Kong, and Chinese communities overseas as well as in Western cultures. Daoist rituals have blended with popular religion, so that robed Daoist priests conduct elaborate liturgies to honor and interact with gods, spirits, and ancestors. Chinese temples combine Confucian, Buddhist, and Daoist elements, but the liturgies tend to be Daoist. For instance, there is a commonly-used Daoist service for the dead that originated during the Song (Sung) dynasty. Lasting two days, it begins with a mandate to the major gods to attend the event. With music and acrobatics, Daoist priests then carry on a ritual drama of descending to the underworld to deliver a writ of pardon forgiving the person of sins and delivering him or her from punishment. Talismans are also used to rescue the soul and invoke the protection of dragons, and a file is produced verifying the soul's rebirth in heaven and deliverance from death.

Both Daoist and Buddhist groups continue to be recipients of new revelations and scriptures. These texts, known as "precious scrolls," emanate from deities such as the Golden Mother of the Celestial Pool. It is believed that in the past the Divine Mother sent Buddha and Laozi as her messengers but that now the crisis of the present world requires her direct intervention.

Contemporary religion also follows the ancient practice of worshipping certain people as divine, appointed to heavenly office after they died. There are many examples, such as the valiant and loyal late Han dynasty general Guan-gong (Kuan-kung), who is honored everywhere in China as the righter of wrongs and supporter of justice. A virtuous daughter of the Lin family saved members of her own family and others in distress during the Sung dynasty, and now she is worshipped as Tian hou (Tien-hou), the Holy Mother in Heaven, especially in coastal regions. Recently in mainland China, worship has revived for the Great Emperor Who Protects Life, who is traced back to an inspired eleventh-century doctor.

Historically, whenever the central Chinese government has been strong, it has tended to demand total allegiance to itself as a divine authority and to challenge or suppress competing religious groups. The emperors of ancient China either claimed divine origin or referred to themselves as the Sons of Heaven appointed from on high. Confucian scholars were suppressed and their books were burned by the Qin (Ch'in) dynasty (221–206 BCE), shamans were forbidden during the Han dynasty, Buddhists were persecuted during the Tang dynasty, the Taiping rebellion of the nineteenth century attempted to purge China of Daoism and Buddhism, and during the Cultural Revolution of 1966 to 1976, zealous young Red Guards destroyed Daoist, Buddhist, and Confucian temples and books. However, during the economic liberalization of the late twentieth century in mainland China, in spite of an atheistic communist ideology, temples were maintained as historic sites, pilgrimages to temples in natural sites and religious tourism were encouraged, and an explosion of temple building occurred.

Since the 1980s, a few ancient Daoist practitioners in China have tried to teach groups of young students so that the disciplines can be continually transmitted. They meet with many bureaucratic obstacles within China but receive considerable support from Chinese communities and scholars abroad. Academic study of Daoism is intensifying on the mainland with the help of Daoist religious organizations such as the Chinese Daoist Association, university scholars, social science research institutes, and cultural and artistic institutions. Despite the restrictions of party politics, the Chinese government's Center for Religious Studies carries on activities such as a major project to republish the entire Daoist canon with vast amounts of explanatory material from current research.

Interest in Daoist practices and philosophy has boomed in the West from the middle of the twentieth century, and by now there are many masters and centers in the United States. They typically fall into the same three categories that have

Daoist religion is still practiced in non-communist Chinese areas. At the Matsu Yen Tao Temple in Anping, Taiwan, Daoist elements are incorporated into worship of the goddess Matsu.

long characterized Daoism in the East: organized religious institutions, societies for self-cultivation, and practitioners of techniques for spiritual development, health, and longevity. The latter have become very popular. Many people outside China are now benefiting from acupuncture therapy, which uses traditional spiritual knowledge of the subtle energy meridians that run through the organs and spine for medicinal purposes. Needle stimulation or burning of herbs above specific points along the meridians is successfully used to cure or alleviate many ailments. Traditional Chinese herbal medicine is also of increasing interest, as are energy training practices. Of these, **Taiji quan** (T'ai chi ch'uan) was developed in the eighteenth century as a training for martial arts. It is still practiced today by many Chinese at dawn and dusk for their health. It looks like slow swimming in the air, with continual circular movement through a series of dance-like postures. They are ideally manifestations of the unobstructed flow of *qi* through the body. According to the *Taiji Quan Classics*, "In any action the entire body should be light and agile and all of its parts connected like pearls on a thread."[18] *Qi* is cultivated internally but not expressed externally as power. In combat, the practitioner of Taiji is advised to "yield at your opponent's slightest pressure and adhere to him at his slightest retreat,"[19] using mental alertness to subtle changes rather than muscular strength in order to gain the advantage. Taiji is also a physical way of becoming one with the eternal interlocking of yin and yang, and of movement and stillness. Taiji master Al Chung-liang Huang says:

Think of the contrasting energies moving together and in union, in harmony, interlocking, like a white fish and a black fish mating. If you identify with only one side of the duality, then you become unbalanced. . . . Movement and stillness become one. One is not a static point. One is a moving one, one is a changing one, one is everything. One is also that stillness suspended, flowing, settling, in motion.[20]

Taiji quan is also often physically beneficial in controlling blood pressure, muscular coordination, and balance, and thus is useful to elderly people.

Al Huang embodies the fluidity of Taiji quan, practiced both for physical health and for teaching the mind to flow with change so that action is effortless.

In the early twentieth century, a weakly tuberculosis patient cured himself by practicing the energy training disciplines from an old Daoist inner alchemical text describing traditional meditation and longevity techniques. He learned to detect the inner movements of *qi* within himself and then wrote about them clearly in contemporary biomedical terms. Others also thence became interested in the traditional health exercises. The self-cultivation systems they popularized are now generally known as **Qigong** (Ch'i-kung) and are widely used not only in China but also in the West to cure diseases, increase physical vitality, and improve concentration. Some people today claim that the combination of meditation methods, breath control, martial arts, and diet are even helpful in thwarting the ravages of AIDS. During the 1990s, Chinese masters made the techniques even more popular by advertising that one could attain supernatural powers by means of the practices.

The most famous of these claims have been made by Li Hongzhi, who in 1992 developed a form of Qigong that mixed Buddhism with Daoist energy practices, producing a hybrid known as **Falun Gong** or **Falun Dafa**. He proposed that he would spiritually install a "falun" or Dharma Wheel in followers' abdomens so that they could perform advanced energy practices. His system also differs from other forms of Qigong in that it emphasizes ethics—the development of three cardinal virtues: truthfulness, benevolence, and forbearance. Li, who moved to the United States, claims that practitioners of Falun Dafa can attain excellent health, supernatural power, and cosmic enlightenment if they develop the cardinal virtues as well as carrying on the daily exercises. These are taught for free by volunteers at thousands of locations around the world. Falun Dafa now claims millions of followers. But in China, the movement has been severely repressed since 1999 because the government fears that it may gain political power. Practitioners of Falun Dafa have been imprisoned and tortured to discourage others from joining the movement, which the government portrays as an evil cult using the pretence of religion to practice political and criminal activities. The government has even cracked down on other forms of Qigong which it once supported and legislation has been passed that may be used to suppress any mystical Chinese group and any other religious group that has not been sanctioned by the Chinese Communist party.

Nonetheless, interest in all forms of Daoism is running high in other countries, replete with numerous websites, international Daoist organizations, and international scholarly conferences. In the Western popularization of Daoism, classic Daoist texts are even being used by businesses to teach management practices.

Confucianism—the practice of virtue

To trace a different strand of Eastern religion, we return to the sixth century BCE, which was a period of great spiritual and intellectual flourishing in many cultures. It roughly coincided with the life of the Buddha and perhaps of Laozi, the Persian Empire, the Golden Age of Athens, the great Hebrew prophets, and in China with the life of another outstanding figure. Westerners call him Confucius and his teaching Confucianism. His family name was Kong; the Chinese honored him as Kong fuzi (Master Kong) and called his teaching **Juchiao** (the teaching of the scholars). It did not begin with Confucius. Rather, it is based on the ancient Chinese beliefs in the Lord on High, the Mandate of Heaven, ancestor worship, spirits, and the efficacy of rituals. Confucius developed from these roots a school of thought that emphasizes the cultivation of moral virtues and the interaction between human rulers and Heaven, with political involvement as the way to transforming the world. This philosophy became highly influential in China and still permeates the society, despite great political changes. It exists not only as a school of thought but also as the practice of religious ethics, as a political ideology, and as the link between the state and the Mandate of Heaven.

For two thousand years, Daoism, Buddhism, and Confucianism have co-existed in China, contributing mutually to the culture. Both Daoism and Buddhism emphasize the ever-changing nature of things in the cosmos, whereas Confucianism focuses on ways of developing a just and orderly society.

Individuals often harmonize the apparently opposite characteristics of Daoism and Confucianism in their own lives. For example, elderly Daoist Master An speaks on one hand of the fact that he and his fellows sweep the temple when they feel like it—"We're not caught up in routines"—and on the other of the ways that his father's teaching of Confucian maxims shaped his life:

> My father was very cultured and adamant about teaching us the true Tao. He mastered the classics, and would write out quotations all the time. Over on the wall there is a quotation by Confucius he wrote:
>
> If I'm not generous with those below me,
> If I'm disrespectful toward the proprieties,
> Or if I do not properly mourn at a funeral,
> How can I have self-esteem?
>
> He'd paste these quotations on our wall above the bed. I'd turn my head and there it was, sinking in my brain. . . . Confucius also said, "One who seeks the Tao cannot be deficient in manners."[21]

Professor Yu Yingshi explains that Daoism and Confucianism can co-exist because in Chinese tradition there are no major divisions between mind and matter, utopian ideals and everyday life:

> For Chinese, the transcendental world, the world of the spirit, interpenetrates with the everyday world though it is not considered identical to it. If we use the tao to represent the transcendental world and the Confucian ideal of human relationships to represent the human world, we can see how they interface. The tao creates the character of these human relations. For these relations to exist as such, they must follow the tao, they cannot depart from the tao for a moment. These two worlds operate on the cusp of interpenetration, neither dependent on or independent of the other. So mundane human relationships are, from the very beginning, endowed with a transcendental character.[22]

Master Kong's life

Confucius was born in approximately 551 BCE, during the Zhou dynasty, into a family whose ancestors had been prominent in the previous dynasty. They had lost their position through political struggles, and his father, a soldier, died when the boy was only three years old. Although the young boy was determined to be a scholar, the family's financial straits necessitated his taking such humble work as overseeing granaries and livestock. He married at the age of nineteen and had at least two children. His mother died when he was twenty-three, and during three years of mourning he lived ascetically and studied ancient ceremonial rites (*li*) and imperial institutions. When he returned to social interaction, he gained some renown as a teacher of *li* and of the arts of governing.

It was a period of political chaos, with the stability of the early Zhou dynasty giving way to disorder. As central power weakened, feudal lords held more power

Confucianism idealized gentlemen-scholars, who became the highest class in China until the 20th-century revolution.

than kings of the central court, ministers assassinated their rulers, and sons killed their fathers. Confucius felt that a return to classical rites and standards of virtue was the only way out of the chaos, and he unsuccessfully sought rulers who would adopt his ideas. He then turned to a different approach: training young men to be wise and altruistic public servants. He proposed that the rulers should perform classical rites and music properly so that they would remain of visibly high moral character and thus inspire the common people to be virtuous. He thus instructed his students in the "Six Classics" of China's cultural heritage: the *Yijing*, poetry, history, rituals, music and dance, and the Spring and Autumn Annals of events in his state, Lu. According to tradition, it was Confucius who edited older documents pertaining to these six areas and put them into the form now known as the Confucian Classics. There are now only five; the treatises on music were either destroyed or never existed. Of his role, Confucius claimed only: "I am a transmitter and not a creator. I believe in and have a passion for the ancients."[23]

Confucius's work and teachings were considered relatively insignificant during his lifetime. After his death in 479 BCE, interstate warfare increased, ancient family loyalties were replaced by large and impersonal armies, and personal virtues were replaced by laws and state control. After the brutal reunification of China by the Qin and Han dynasties, however, rulership required a more cultured class of bureaucrats who could embody the virtues advocated by Confucius. In the second century BCE the Confucian Classics thus became the basis of the civil service examinations for the scholar-officials who were to serve in the government. The life of the gentleman-scholar devoted to proper government became the highest professed ideal. Eventually temples were devoted to the worship of Confucius himself as the model for unselfish public service, human kindness, and scholarship. However, the official state use of the Confucian Classics can be seen as a political device to give the government a veneer of civility.

The Confucian virtues

Foremost among the virtues that Confucius felt could save society was **jen**. Translations of this central term include innate goodness, love, benevolence, perfect virtue, humaneness, and human-heartedness. In Chapter IV of *The Analects*, Confucius describes the rare person who is utterly devoted to *jen* as one who is not motivated by personal profit but by what is moral, is concerned with self-improvement rather than public recognition, is ever mindful of parents, speaks cautiously but acts quickly, and regards human nature as basically good.

The prime example of *jen* should be the ruler. Rulers were required to rule not by physical force but by the example of personal virtue:

> *Confucius said: If a ruler himself is upright, all will go well without orders. But if he himself is not upright, even though he gives orders they will not be obeyed. . . . One who governs by virtue is comparable to the polar star, which remains in its place while all the stars turn towards it."*[24]

Daoism and
Confucianism:
Confucian Virtues

Asked to define the essentials of strong government, Confucius listed adequate troops, adequate food, and the people's trust. But of these, the only true necessity is that the people have faith in their rulers. To earn this faith, the ruling class should "cultivate themselves," leading lives of virtue and decorum. They should continually adhere to *jen*, always reaching upward, cherishing what is right, rather than reaching downward for material gain.

The modern Chinese character for *jen* is a combination of "two" and "person," conveying the idea of relationship. Those relationships emphasized by Confucians are the interactions between father and son, older and younger siblings, husband and wife, older and younger friend, ruler and subject. In these relationships, the first is considered superior to the second. Each relationship is nonetheless based on distinct but mutual obligations and responsibilities. This web of human relationships supports the individual like a series of concentric circles.

At the top, the ruler models himself on Heaven, serving as a parent to the people and linking them to the larger cosmic order through ritual ceremonies. Confucius says that this was the source of the greatness of Yao—a sage king of c. 2357 BCE: "It is Heaven that is great and Yao who modelled himself upon it."[25]

In Confucius's ideal world, there is a reciprocal hierarchy in which each knows his place and respects those above him. As the *Great Learning* states it, peace begins with the moral cultivation of the individual and order in the family. This peace extends outward to society, government, and the universe itself like circular ripples in a pond.

The heart of moral rectification is filial piety to one's parents. According to Confucian doctrine, there are three grades of filial piety: the lowest is to support one's parents, the second is not to bring humiliation to one's parents and ancestors, and the highest is to glorify them. In the ancient *Book of Rites*, as revived by Confucius, deference to one's parents is scrupulously defined. For instance, a husband and wife should go to visit their parents and parents-in-law, whereupon:

On getting to where they are, with bated breath and gentle voice, they should ask if their clothes are (too) warm or (too) cold, whether they are ill or pained, or uncomfortable in any part; and if they be so, they should proceed reverently to stroke and scratch the place. They should in the same way, going before or following after, help and support their parents in quitting or entering (the apartment). In bringing in the basin for them to wash, the younger will carry the stand and the elder the water; they will beg to be allowed to pour out the water, and when the washing is concluded, they will hand the towel. They will ask whether they want anything, and then respectfully bring it. All this they will do with an appearance of pleasure to make their parents feel at ease.[26]

Confucius also supported the ancient Chinese custom of ancestor veneration, as an extension of filial piety—indeed, as the highest achievement of filial piety.

Confucius said relatively little about the supernatural, preferring to focus on the here-and-now: "While you are not able to serve men, how can you serve the ghosts and spirits?"[27] He made a virtue of *li* (the rites honoring ancestors and deities), suggesting that one make the sacrifices with the feeling that the spirits were present. According to some interpreters, he encouraged the rites as a way of establishing earthly harmony through reverent, ethical behavior. The rites should not be empty gestures; he recommended that they be outwardly simple and inwardly grounded in *jen*.

Although Confucius did not speak much about an unseen Reality, he asserted that *li* are the earthly expressions of the natural cosmic order. *Li* involves right conduct in terms of the five basic relationships essential for a stable society:

kindness in the father and filial piety in the son; gentility in the older brother and respect in the younger; righteous behavior in the husband and obedience in the wife; humane consideration in the older friend and deference in the younger friend; and benevolence in rulers and loyalty in subjects.

Everything should be done with a sense of propriety. Continually eulogizing the typical gentleman of China's ancient high civilization as the model, Confucius used examples such as the way of passing someone in mourning. Even if the mourner were a close friend, the gentleman would assume a solemn expression and "lean forward with his hands on the crossbar of his carriage to show respect; he would act in a similar manner towards a person carrying official documents."[28] Even in humble surroundings, the proprieties should be observed: "Even when a meal consisted only of coarse rice and vegetable broth, [the gentleman] invariably made an offering from them and invariably did so solemnly."[29]

Divergent followers of Confucius

The Confucian tradition has been added to by many later commentators. Two of the most significant were Meng Tzu (Mencius) and Xunzi (Hsun Tzu), who differed in their approach.

A little over a hundred years after Confucius died, the "Second Sage" Meng Tzu (commonly latinized as Mencius) was born. During his lifetime (c. 390–305 BCE) Chinese society became even more chaotic. Like his predecessor, the Second Sage tried to share his wisdom with embattled rulers, but to no avail. He, too, took up teaching, based on stabilizing aspects of the earlier feudal system.

Meng Tzu's major additions to the Confucian tradition were his belief in the goodness of human nature and his focus on the virtue of *yi*, or righteous conduct. Meng Tzu emphasized the moral duty of rulers to govern by the principle of humanity and the good of the people. If rulers are guided by profit motives, this self-centered motivation will be reflected in all subordinates and social chaos will ensue. On the other hand, "When a commiserating government is conducted from a commiserating heart, one can rule the whole empire as if one were turning it in one's palm."[30] This is a natural way, says Meng Tzu, for people are naturally good: "The tendency of human nature to do good is like that of water to flow downward."[31] Heaven could be counted on to empower the righteous.

Another follower quite disagreed with this assessment. This was Xunzi, who seems to have been born when Meng Tzu was an old man. Xunzi argued that human nature is naturally self-centered and that Heaven is impersonal, operating according to natural laws rather than intervening on the side of good government or responding to human wishes ("Heaven does not suspend the winter because men dislike cold"[32]). Humans must hold up their own end. Their natural tendency, however, is to envy, to compete, and to desire personal gain and sensual pleasure. The only way to constrain these tendencies is to teach and legally enforce the rules of *li* and *yi*. Though naturally flawed, humans can gradually attain sagehood by persistent study, patience, and good works and thereby form a cooperative triad with Heaven and earth.

Xunzi's careful reasoning provided a basis for the new legalistic structure of government. The idealism of Meng Tzu was revived much later as a Chinese response to Buddhism and became required for the civil service examinations from the thirteenth to the twentieth centuries. However, their points of agreement are basic to Confucianism: the appropriate practice of virtue is of great value; humans can attain this through self-cultivation; and study and emulation of the ancient sages are the path to harmony in the individual, family, state, and world.

The state cult

Since ancient times, as we have seen, rulers have been regarded as the link between earth and Heaven. This understanding persisted in Chinese society, but Confucius and his followers had elaborated the idea that the ruler must be virtuous for this relationship to work. During the Han dynasty, Confucius's teachings were at last honored by the state. The Han scholar Dong Zhongshu (Tung Chung-shu, c. 179–c. 104 BCE) set up an educational system based on the Confucian Classics that lasted until the twentieth century. He used Confucian ideals to unite the people behind the ruler, who himself was required to be subject to Heaven.

During this period, civil service examinations based on the Confucian Classics were first established as a means of attaining government positions. The

The Temple of Heaven in Beijing. Since ancient times in China, there has been an open-air altar used by the emperor himself once or twice a year to make sacrifices to Heaven, the main governing and guiding force of the Confucian universe.

Confucian Classics were established as the Five Classics and the Four Books as the standard textbooks during the Song dynasty by the **Neo-Confucian** scholar, Zhu Xi (Chu Hsi, 1130–1200 CE). *His Reflections on Things at Hand* gave a metaphysical basis for Confucianism: the individual is intimately linked with all of the cosmos, "forming one body with all things." According to Zhang Zai's *Western Inscription*:

> *Heaven is my father and earth is my mother and even such a small creature as I finds an intimate place in their midst. Therefore, that which extends throughout the universe I regard as my body and that which directs the universe I regard as my nature. All people are my brothers and sisters and all things are my companions. The great ruler [the emperor] is the eldest son of my parents [Heaven and Earth], and the great ministers are his stewards. . . . To rejoice in Heaven and to have no anxiety—this is filial piety at its purest.*[33]

By becoming more humane one can help to transform not only oneself but also society and even the cosmos. The Neo-Confucianists thus stressed the importance of meditation and dedication to becoming a "noble person."

Women were encouraged to offer themselves in total sacrifice to others. Confucian women had previously been expected to take a subordinate role in the family and in society, but at the same time to be strong, disciplined, wise, and capable in their relationships with their husbands and sons. In Neo-Confucianism, such virtues were subsumed under an extreme ideal of self-sacrifice.

Although Confucius had counseled restrained use of *li*, Neo-Confucianism also included an increased emphasis on offerings, as practiced since ancient times and set forth in the traditional *Book of Rites* and *Etiquette and Ritual*, which had been reconstructed during the Han dynasty. These rites were thought to preserve harmony between humans, Heaven, and earth. At the family level, offerings were made to propitiate the family ancestors. Government officials were responsible for ritual sacrifices to beings such as the gods of fire, literature, cities, mountains, waters, the polar star, sun, moon, and former rulers. The most important ceremonies were performed by the emperor, to give thanks and ask blessings from Heaven, earth, gods of the land and agriculture, and the dynastic ancestors. Traditionally these were performed at the tops of five holy mountains in the four cardinal directions and the center of the kingdom, each associated with a particular season and symbolic meaning, such as rites for spring and new growth that were held in the east. Of these, the highest ritual was the elaborate annual sacrifice to Shangdi at the white marble Altar of Heaven by the emperor. He was considered Son of Heaven, the "high priest of the world." Both he and his large retinue prepared themselves by three days of fasting and keeping vigil. In a highly reverent atmosphere, he then sacrificed a bull, offered precious jade, and sang prayers of gratitude to the Supreme, such as this one:

> *With reverence we spread out these precious stones and silk, and, as swallows rejoicing in the spring, praise Thy abundant love. . . . Men and creatures are emparadised, O Ti, in Thy love. All living things are indebted to Thy goodness, but who knows whence his blessings come to him? It is Thou alone, O Lord, who art the true parent of all things.*[34]

Some Confucian rites are still observed today in South Korea. These people making offerings in Chungdak-dong village have maintained a traditional Confucian lifestyle for hundreds of years.

Confucianism under communism

The performance of rituals was a time-consuming and major part of government jobs, carried out on behalf of the people. But as China gradually opened to the West in recent centuries, a reaction set in against these older ways, and the last of the imperial dynasties was overthrown in 1911. In the 1920s Republic, science and social progress were glorified by radical intellectuals of the New Culture movement who were opposed to all the old systems. Under the communist regime established in 1949, communism took the place of religion, attempting to transform the society by secular means. Party Chairman Mao Zedong was venerated almost as a god, with the "Little Red Book" of quotations from Chairman Mao replacing the Confucian Classics.

During the Cultural Revolution (1966–76), Confucianism was attacked as one of the "Four Olds"—old ideas, culture, customs, and habits. The Cultural Revolution attempted to destroy the hierarchical structure that Confucianism had idealized and to prevent the intellectual elite from ruling over the masses. Contrary to the Confucian virtue of filial piety, young people even denounced their parents at public trials, and scholars were made objects of derision. An estimated one million people were attacked. Some were killed, some committed suicide, and millions suffered.

Mao said that he had hated Confucianism from his childhood. What he so disliked was the intellectual emphasis on the study of the Classics, the "superstitious" rituals, and the oppression of the lowest members of hierarchical Chinese

During the years of Mao Zedong's ascendency, the Chairman was treated as a larger-than-life hero of a grand drama that replaced but also resembled religion.

society—women and peasants. He had urged peasants to overthrow all authoritarian traditions, including religion:

> *A man in China is usually subjected to the domination of three systems of authority: (1) the state system (political authority) . . . ; (2) the clan system (clan authority), ranging from the central ancestral temple and its branch temples down to the head of the household; and (3) the supernatural system (religious authority), ranging from the King of Hell down to the town and village gods belonging to the nether world, and from the Emperor of Heaven down to all the various gods and spirits belonging to the celestial world. As for women, in addition to being dominated by these three systems of authority, they are also dominated by the men (the authority of the husband). These four authorities—political, clan, religious and masculine—are the embodiment of the whole feudal-patriarchal system and ideology, and are the four thick ropes binding the Chinese people, particularly the peasants.[35]*

Nevertheless, in some respects, Confucian morality continued to form the basis of Chinese ethics. Mao particularly emphasized the (Confucian) virtues of selfless service to the people and of self-improvement for the public good:

> *All our cadres, whatever their rank, are servants of the people, and whatever we do is to serve the people. How then can we be reluctant to discard any of our bad traits?[36]*

For decades, communist China prided itself on being the most law-abiding country in the world. The streets were safe, and tourists found that if they could not understand the currency, they could trust taxi drivers to take the exact amount, and no more, from their open wallets. But recently there has been a rise in crime and official corruption. The society has changed abruptly since China opened its doors to the West in 1978, undermining what remained of traditional Confucian virtues. The government blames the influx of materialistic values, resulting from the indiscriminating embrace of the underside of Western culture and the rapid shift toward a free market economy. In 1989, Chao Tzu-yang, then Communist Party leader, urged officials to maintain Confucian discipline (without naming it that) in the midst of the changes: "The Party can by no means allow its members to barter away their principles for money and power."[37] But when the people picked up this cry, aging leaders chose brutally to suppress popular calls for greater democracy and an end to official corruption; they did so in the name of another Confucian value: order in society.

For their part, the intellectuals of the democracy movement had tried to do things in the proper way but were caught on the horns of the poignant Chinese dilemma. Under Confucian ethics, it has been the continuing responsibility of scholars to play the role of upright censors. On the other hand, scholars had to remain loyal to the ruler, for they were subjects and observing one's subservient position as a subject preserved the security of the state. The leaders of the democracy movement tried to deal with this potential conflict by ritualized, respectful action: they formally walked up the steps of the Great Hall of the People in Tiananmen Square to present their written requests to those in power. But they were ignored and brutally suppressed.

Again, in 1995, forty-five of China's most distinguished scholars and scientists delivered a petition to the government urging freedom of thought and accountability of the government to the public, in order to end socially corrosive corruption. Some observers speculate that slow transformations will bring a new form of Confucian tradition. Already, interest in Confucian thought is increasing among intellectuals. Conferences have recently been held on the mainland in China and also in Taiwan and Singapore to discuss Confucianism. Today it is being analyzed not as an historical artifact but as a tradition that is relevant to modern life. Even though it may not be practiced in the same ways as before, it may nonetheless contribute significantly to cultural identity, economic progress, social harmony, and a personal sense of the meaning of human life.

Confucianism may inform capitalistic behavior as well as Marxist communism. There is now talk of "Capitalist Confucianism"—business conducted according to Confucian ethics such as humanity, trustworthiness, sincerity, and altruism. The Confucian value system has significant potential for informing capitalist freedom of choice. As Professor Xinzhong Yao explains,

Free choice is the foundation of modern society, and the pre-condition of market economy. However, freedom without responsibility would result in the collapse of the social network and in the conflict between individuals and between individuals and society, and would lead to the sacrifice of the future in order to satisfy short-term needs. This has become a serious challenge to human wisdom and to human integrity. In this respect, Confucianism can make a contribution to a new moral sense, a new ecological view and a new code for the global village.[38]

Living Confucianism

Ann-ping Chin grew up in Taiwan, the daughter of parents from the northern part of mainland China. She teaches Confucianism and Daoism at Wesleyan University and has visited China five times to do research on the continuing changes in that society. Of the contemporary situation there with regard to traditional values she says:

"Lots of things are changing in China. First of all, the economic boom is changing women's perceptions of themselves and of their family. For instance, if a woman is determined to have a profession of her own, in this huge marketplace of China this implies that she would become involved in a private enterprise or begin one herself. If she does that, this means that she would have to consider child-rearing as secondary. Usually these women depend on their parents or in-laws to bring up their children, in their own homes.

"Divorce is very common. Family units are breaking up and children have less security—there are all the problems that we associate with divorce in the West. The woman simply says, 'Look—I'm going to leave or you leave.'

"Making money is now the most important thing for the Chinese. It's finally a free market. Even though it's economic freedom, it's some kind of freedom. 'So,' they feel, 'why not make the most of that sort of freedom? Political freedom can wait. Let's make the most of this that we have, and not ask too much.'

"From an initial impression, perhaps you can say that the fundamental Confucian values are disappearing. Through more than two thousand years of Chinese history, both in traditional Confucian teachings and in Daoist teachings as well, you find a tremendous deprecation of the idea of making money—of taking advantage or making a profit, be it in money or in human relationships. Now unless you have the determination to make money, you are not considered a true man in Chinese society.

"On the other hand, if you really delve into their private lives, and try to understand what is really important to the Chinese, I would say that the very basic relationships of parents and children, and of friends to friends are still very strong. The Chinese have given up their relationship with the ruler; that's really a joke. The relationship between husband and wife is much more complicated. Men love the idea of having a very devoted wife. They know that is perhaps impossible, but they still yearn for it. And they still value the traditional qualities that you find in the biographies of virtuous women. If they can find that in their mothers, they still appreciate those values.

"Other values have been abandoned. I'm very disturbed and saddened, pained, by what is happening to the Chinese scholars. They cannot go out and do private enterprise, for they are scholars. They get paid a very pathetic amount of money each month, not enough to make ends meet. Scholars have always been really respected even though people didn't understand them. But now there isn't even that respect since the society is placing so much emphasis on making money.

"My parents both came from very scholarly backgrounds. They passed down to us the traditions without the formalities, without the rigidities, so we were extremely fortunate. I think my father passed down to us his love of students, his love of teaching, and of the very special relationship between teachers and disciples. That relationship is a very special one in Chinese tradition. If you are lucky, you can still see that between an elderly teacher and his disciples. It's not obedience—rather, it's a concern that the disciple expresses toward the teacher.

"In looking at what I've absorbed from my parents, there's also the matter of character. My father's character had a profound effect on me. I just intuitively know that he always tried to do the right thing. And to do the right thing sometimes can be so difficult. This was the only way that he could live—to always try to do the right thing, whether it was for a friend, or for us, for my mom, for his own parents, or for strangers. He would never compromise that."

Confucian values are also being reappraised as a significant addition to holistic education. In them is imbedded the motivation to improve oneself and become a responsible and ethical member of one's family and society. Self-perception, according to Confucian ideals, is a lifelong process. Thus the Neo-Confucians developed multi-stage learning programs that extend beyond the years of formal schooling. Confucianism has always promoted education as the only means to social reform, and further encourages a sense of voluntary service to the community.

In the moral and spiritual vacuum left after the demise of fervent Maoism, Confucianism may also help restore a sense of holy purpose to people's lives. The traditional feeling was that the Mandate of Heaven gives transcendent meaning to human life. Professor Tu Wei-ming, a modern Neo-Confucian, explains:

> *We are the guardians of the good earth, the trustees of the Mandate of Heaven that enjoins us to make our bodies healthy, our hearts sensitive, our minds alert, our souls refined, and our spirits brilliant. ... We serve Heaven with common sense, the lack of which nowadays has brought us to the brink of self-destruction. Since we help Heaven to realize itself though our self-discovery and self-understanding in day-to-day living, the ultimate meaning of life is found in our ordinary, human existence.[39]*

Chinese authorities have recently reintroduced the teaching of Confucius in elementary schools as a vehicle for encouraging social morality. After a gap of more than half a century, the Confucian-based civil service examinations are being partially reintroduced in the selection of public servants. Earlier castigated as "feudal institutions," Confucian academies are being described as fine centers for learning. Chinese authorities are also reviving aspects of the religious cult, such as observance of the birthday of Confucius, perhaps mostly for the sake of tourism. But believers such as members of the Confucian Academy in Hong Kong take such observances seriously. In rural areas, observance of Confucian virtues has remained rather steady through time.

Confucianism in East Asia

Countries near China, which have historically been influenced by China politically and culturally, also show signs of having been influenced by Confucian values. The city-state of Singapore has since 1978 sponsored an annual courtesy campaign to inspire virtuous behavior in the midst of fast-paced modern life. In 1997, the focus of the campaign was courteous use of mobile phones and pagers. It was politely suggested that one should turn them off in theaters, places of worship, and public functions to avoid disturbing others.

In Korea, where few people now consider themselves adherents of Confucianism as a religion, lectures and special events are being sponsored by hundreds of local Confucian institutes to promote Confucian teachings. In some cases, Confucianism is associated with particular clans in East Asia, and thus with political favoritism. Some of the Korean institutes are politically conservative, opposing women's efforts to revise family laws. The Korean Overseas Information Service advocates a flexible, liberal version of the tradition, open to other cultures and to all religions but still providing a firm foundation for social order:

> *Confucianism can present contemporary Koreans with a set of practical standards of conduct in the form of rituals and etiquette. Extensive introduction of Western*

modes of behavior led to the confusion and adulteration of Korea's native behavior pattern. Civility and propriety in speech and deportment enhance the dignity of man. Rites and conduct befitting to a civilized people should be refined and adjusted to the conditions of the time. . . . Korea should, through its Confucian heritage, sustain the tradition of propriety and modesty and defend the intrinsically moral nature of man from submergence in economic and materialistic considerations.[40]

Confucian organizations in Hong Kong, Taiwan, and other parts of East Asia are attempting to restore religious versions of Confucianism, such as the worship of Confucius himself or study of the Confucian Classics.

Confucian thought has also played a significant role in Japan. It entered Japan during the seventh century when Chinese political thought and religious ideas first began to have significant influence there. It left its mark on the first constitution of Japan, on the arrangement of government bureaucracy, and in the educational system. From the twelfth to the sixteenth century, Confucianism was studied in Zen Buddhist monasteries. Then from the seventeenth to nineteenth century, Confucianism began to spread more widely among the people of Japan because of its adoption as an educational philosophy in public and private schools. Confucian moral teachings became the basis for establishing proper human relationships in the family and in Japanese society.

Both Confucianism and Shinto were manipulated by the military during the pre-war period to inculcate a nationalist expansionist ideology. More in keeping with the original motives of Confucianism, some scholars have observed that Japan's notably effective modernization in the last one hundred years is partly due to values derived from Confucianism. These values include a high regard for diligence, consensus, education, moral self-cultivation, frugality, and loyalty.

Dr. Mary Evelyn Tucker, noted scholar of East Asian Studies and the relationships between religions and environment, concludes that Confucianism is not outdated. Rather, it can be seen as quite relevant now and for the future as well, for "It aims to promote flourishing social relations, effective educational systems, sustainable agricultural patterns, and humane political governance within the context of the dynamic, life-giving processes of the universe."[41]

Suggested reading

Chang, Wing-Tsit, *A Sourcebook in Chinese Philosophy*, Princeton: Princeton University Press, 1963. A large and helpful anthology of Confucian, Daoist, and Buddhist texts.

de Bary, William Theodore, *East Civilizations: A Dialogue in Five Stages*, Cambridge: Harvard University Press, 1988. A masterful overview of 3,000 years of East Asian civilization, including the classical legacy, the Buddhist age, the Neo-Confucian stage, and East Asia's modern transformation.

de Bary, William Theodore, Chan, Wing-tsit, and Watson, Burton, eds., *Sources of Chinese Tradition*, New York: Columbia University Press, 1960. Useful commentaries and extensive texts from Confucian and Daoist schools.

The I Ching, translated into German by Richard Wilhelm and thence into English by Cary Baynes, third edition, Princeton, New Jersey: Princeton University Press, 1967. Insights into the multiple possibilities of the interplay of yin and yang in our lives.

Kohn, Livia, *The Taoist Experience*, Albany, New York: State University of New York Press, 1993. Interesting translations of ancient and more recent texts covering the various aspects of Daoism.

Kohn, Livia, *Daoism and Chinese Culture*, Cambridge, Massachusetts: Three Pines Press, 2001. Concise survey of different forms of Daoism in chronological order, considering comparative aspects and providing additional bibliography.

Lopez, Donald S., ed., *Religions of China in Practice*, Princeton, New Jersey: Princeton University Press, 1996. Excellent articles illustrating the overlap between Confucianism, Daoism, and Buddhism in traditional and contemporary practice, with translations of original texts.

Mencius, trans. by D. C. Lau, New York: Viking Penguin, 1970.

Robinet, Isabelle, *Taoist Meditation: The Mao-shan Tradition of Great Purity*, trans. Julian Pas and Norman Girardot, Albany, New York: State University of New York Press, 1993. A careful analysis of the central scriptures and practices used by elite Daoists to become Immortals.

Schipper, Kristofer M., *The Taoist Body*, trans. Karen Duvall, Berkeley: University of California Press, 1992. Explores integration of religious and philosophical Daoism within the Celestial Masters movement, from the Han dynasty to contemporary Taiwan.

Sommer, Deborah, ed., *Chinese Religions: An Anthology of Sources*, New York/Oxford: Oxford University Press, 1995. Interesting primary source material from Daoist, Confucian, Buddhist, and communist writings about religious topics.

Tao-te Ching, attributed to Laozi, available in numerous translations, including the English translation by D. C. Lau, London: Penguin Books, 1963.

Taylor, Rodney, *The Religious Dimensions of Confucianism*, Albany: State University of New York Press, 1990. A collection of essays dealing with the central question of whether Confucianism is a religion.

Tucker, Mary Evelyn and John Berthrong, *Confucianism and Ecology: the Interrelation of Heaven, Earth, and Humans*, Cambridge, Massachusetts; Harvard University Press, 1998. Interesting articles from a major series of conferences probing the relationships between particular religious teachings and the environment.

Watson, Burton, *Chuang Tzu: Basic Writings*, New York: Columbia University Press, 1964. An engaging translation of major writings by Zhuangzi, with an introduction that is particularly helpful in dealing with this paradoxical material.

Weiming, Tu and Mary Evelyn Tucker, *Confucian Spirituality*, New York: Crossroad Publishing Company, 2003. Eastern and Western scholars analyze Confucianism as a spiritual path.

Wong, Eva, *The Shambhala Guide to Taoism*, Boston: Shambhala Press, 1996. Introduction to the synthesis of Daoism, Buddhism, and Confucianism in China, Daoist history, techniques, and rites.

Yao, Xingzhong, *Introduction to Confucianism*, Cambridge: Cambridge University Press, 2000. A noted specialist blends traditional and contemporary scholarship to explore the many facets of Confucianism and their relevance today.

Key terms

li — Ceremonies, rituals, and rules of proper conduct, in the Confucian tradition.

qi (ch'i) — The vital energy in the universe and in our bodies according to Far Eastern esoteric traditions.

yin	In Chinese philosophy, the dark, receptive, "female" energy in the universe.
yang	In Chinese philosphy, the bright, assertive, "male" energy in the universe.
Dao (Tao)	The way or path, the Nameless.
wu-wei	In Daoism, "not doing", in the sense of taking no action contrary to the natural flow.
jen	Humanity, benevolence—the central Confucian virtue.
yi	Righteous conduct, the Confucian virtue stressed by Mencius
Neo-Confucianism	Confucianism stressing the importance of meditation and dedication to becoming a "noble person" established during the Chinese Han and Sung dynasties.

Study questions

1 Describe the Chinese relationship between humans, ancestors, nature, and heaven. Discuss *li*, firecrackers, rivers, Shanghai, Yijing, Mandate of Heaven, *qi*, Dao, yin–yang. Draw and explain the yin–yang circle.
2 Explain the main themes of historical Daoism. Discuss the Daode jing, *yi*, paradox, opposites, *wu-wei*, *feng shui*, highest purity, flow, meditation, death, Divine Mother, Taiji quan, Falun gong.
3 In what ways are the teachings of Kong fuzi and other Confucians religious, and in what ways are they not religious? Discuss jen, spirits, ritual, ancestors, parents, faith, and cosmic order. Do you think that in general, ethics require a transcendent motive or not? Why?
4 Why is it said that Daoism and Confucianism complement each other? Give specific, convincing examples.
5 What were the motives of the communists who overthrew Confucian China? Discuss the date, text, major leader, and reasons for the revival of Confucianism later.

Refer to Pearson/Prentice Hall's **TIME Special Edition: World Religions** magazine for current articles on topics related to many of the world's religions.

Chapter 6 begins the study of religions originating in China and Japan and focuses on Chinese religions. For further research in this area, use the tools available to you in Research Navigator:

As you investigate Chinese religions, consider this question: "Can or should Daoism or Taoism and Confucianism be better understood as philosophies or as religions?"

- **Ebsco's ContentSelect:** Search in the Philosophy and Religion databases using terms such as "Confucianism," "Taoism or Daoism," "Falun gong or Falun dafa."
- **Link Library:** Search in the Religion database under the category: "Religions of the Far East: Confucianism and Daoism/Taoism" and "Falun dafa/Falun gong."
- **The *New York Times* on the Web:** Search in the Religious Studies and all other databases for current articles on related topics.

CHAPTER 7
SHINTO
The way of the kami

Japan has embraced and adapted many religions that originated in other countries, but it also developed its own unique path, closely tied to nature and the unseen world: Shinto. According to current scholarship, Shinto is not a single self-conscious religious tradition but rather an overarching label applied to ways of honoring the spirits in nature. These ways have at times been combined with imperial myths supporting the worldly rulers.

Many modern Japanese combine practices from several religions, for each offers something different. Confucianism informs organizations and ethics, Buddhism and Christianity offer ways of understanding suffering and the after life, traditional veneration of ancestors links the living to their family history, and the way called "Shinto" harmonizes people with the natural world.

The essence of Shinto

The spiritual heart of Shinto has no founder, no orthodox canon of sacred literature, and no explicit code of ethical requirements. It is so deep-seated and ancient that the symbolic meanings of many of its elaborate rituals have been forgotten by those who practice them. It had no name until Buddhism was imported in the sixth century CE. To distinguish the indigenous Japanese way from the foreign one, the former was labeled *shin* (divine being) *do* (way). During one period it was used by the central government to inspire nationalism, but since the forced separation of church and state after World War II Shinto has quietly returned to its roots. They can be described through three central aspects of the path: affinity with natural beauty, harmony with the spirits, and purification rituals.

Kinship with nature

Despite industrial pollution and urbanization, Japan still is a country of exquisite natural beauty. The islands marry mountains to sea, and the interiors are laced with streams, waterfalls, and lush forests. Even the agriculture is beautiful, with flowering fruit trees and terraced fields. The people lived so harmoniously with this environment that they had no separate word for "nature" until they began importing modern Western ideas late in the nineteenth century. Living close to nature, the people organized their lives around the turn of the seasons, honoring the roles of the sun, moon, and lightning in their rice farming. Mount Fuji, greatest of the

The Japanese people have traditionally honored the natural beauty of their land and have considered Mount Fuji to be its most sacred peak. Pilgrims have long made the arduous climb up Fuji seeking purification and good fortune.

volcanic peaks that formed the islands, was honored as the sacred embodiment of the divine creativity that had thrust the land up from the sea. The sparkling ocean and rising sun, so visible along the extensive coastlines, were loved as earthly expressions of the sacred purity, brightness, and awesome power at the heart of life.

> *To be fully alive is to have an aesthetic perception of life because a major part of the world's goodness lies in its often unspeakable beauty.*
>
> *Rev. Yukitaka Yamamoto, Shinto priest* [1]

Although industrialization and urbanization have blighted some of the natural landscape, the sensitivity to natural beauty survives in small-scale arts. In rock gardening, flower arranging, the tea ceremony, and poetry, Japanese artists honor the simple and natural. If a rock is placed "just right" in a garden, it seems alive, radiating its natural essence. In a tea ceremony, great attention is paid to each natural sensual delight, from the purity of water poured from a wooden ladle to the genuineness of the clay vessels. These arts are often linked with Zen Buddhism, but the sensitivities seem to derive from the ancient Japanese ways.

Honoring the kami

Shinto:
Nature and Ancestor
Spirits

Surrounded by nature's beauty and power, the Japanese people found the divine all around them. In Shinto, the sacred is both immanent and transcendent. In Japanese mythology, the divine originated as one essence:

> *In primeval ages, before the earth was formed, amorphous matter floated freely about like oil upon water. In time there arose in its midst a thing like a sprouting reedshoot, and from this a deity came forth of its own.* [2]

This deity gave birth to many **kami**, or spirits, two of which—the Amatsu ("heavenly") *Kami*—were told to organize the material world. Standing on the Floating Bridge of Heaven, they stirred the ocean with a jeweled spear. When they pulled it out of the water, it dripped brine back into the ocean, where it coagulated into eight islands (interpreted either as Japan or the whole world). To rule this earthly kingdom they created the Kami Amaterasu, literally "the one who illuminates the sky," or Goddess of the Sun. The Amatsu Kami also gave birth to the ancestors of the Japanese. All of the natural world—land, trees, mountains, waters, animals, people—is thus joined in kinship as the spiritual creation of the *kami*.

Although the word *kami* (a way of pronouncing the character *shin*) is usually translated as "god" or "spirit," these translations are not exact. *Kami* can be either singular or plural, for the word refers to a single essence manifesting in many places. Rather than evoking an image, like the Hindu or Mahayana Buddhist deities, *kami* refers to a quality. It means, literally, "that which is above," and also refers to that which evokes wonder and awe in us. The *kami* harmonize heaven and earth and also guide the solar system and the cosmos. It/they tend to reside in beautiful or powerful places, such as mountains, certain trees, unusual rocks, waterfalls, whirlpools, and animals. In addition, it/they manifest as wind, rain, thunder, or lightning. *Kami* also appear in abstract forms, such as the creativity of growth and reproduction. Since the seventh century CE, using the imported Chinese idea of the Mandate of Heaven, the emperor himself came to be revered as a *kami*—a living god, the divinely descended ruler upon whom the well-being of the country depends. In general, explains Sakamiki Shunzo, *kami* include:

Shinto shrines are set apart by a torii, *an ever-open sacred gateway at the entrance to all shrine precincts. This floating* torii *is the symbolic gate to Itsukushima Jjinja shrine, Miyajima.*

all things whatsoever which deserve to be dreaded and revered for the extraordinary and preeminent powers which they possess. . . . [Kami] need not be eminent for surpassing nobleness, goodness, or serviceableness alone. Malignant and uncanny beings are also called kami, *if only they are the objects of general dread.[3]*

Shrines

Recognizing the presence of *kami*, humans have built shrines to honor it/them. There are even now more than 100,000 Shinto shrines in Japan. Shrines may be as small as bee-hives or elaborate temple complexes covering thousands of acres. Some honor *kami* protecting the area; some honor *kami* with special responsibilities, such as healing or protecting crops from insects. The shrines are situated on sites thought to have been chosen by the *kami* for their sacred atmosphere. At one time, every community had its own guardian *kami*.

It is thought that the earliest Shinto places of worship were sacred trees or groves, perhaps with some enclosure to demarcate the sacred area. Shrine complexes that developed later also have some way of indicating where sacred space begins: tall gate-frames, known as *torii*, walls, or streams with bridges, which must be crossed to enter the holy precinct of the *kami*. Water is a purifying influence, and basins of water are also provided for washing one's mouth and hands before passing through the *torii*. Statues of guardian lions further protect the *kami* from evil intrusions, as do ropes with pendants hanging down.

In temple compounds, one first comes to a public hall of worship, behind which is an offering hall where priests conduct rites. Beyond that is the sacred sanctuary, which is entered only by the high priest. Here the spirit of the *kami* is invited to dwell within a special natural object or perhaps a mirror, which reflects the revered light of brightness and purity, considered the natural order of the universe. If there is a spiritually powerful site already present—a waterfall, a crevice in a rock, a hot spring, a sacred tree—the spirit of the *kami* may dwell there. Some shrines are completely empty at the center. In any case, the worshippers do not see the holy of holies; their worship is imageless. As Kishimoto Hideo explains:

A faithful believer would come to the simple hall of a Shinto sanctuary, which is located in a grove with a quiet and holy atmosphere. He may stand quite a while in front of the sanctuary, clap his hands, bow deeply, and try to feel the deity in his heart. . . . Shinto being a polytheistic religion, each sanctuary has its own particular deity. But seldom do the believers know the individual name of the deity whom they are worshipping. They do not care about that. . . . The more important point for them is whether or not they feel the existence of the deity directly in their hearts.[4]

The *kami* of a place may be experienced as energies rather than pictured as forms. At times Shinto has been strongly iconoclastic (opposed to images of the divine). In the eighteenth century, for instance, a famous Shinto scholar wrote:

Never make an image in order to represent the Deity. To worship a deity is directly to establish a felt relation of our heart to the living Divinity through sincerity or truthfulness on our part. If we, however, try to establish a relation between Deity and man indirectly by means of an image, the image will itself stand in the way and prevent us from realizing our religious purpose to accomplish direct communion with the Deity. So an image made by mortal hands is of no use in Shinto worship.[5]

Modern Japanese visit Shinto shrines for many purposes, asking the blessing of kami *on the patterns of their lives. Most Shinto shrines are built with an appreciation for simple natural materials, and the larger ones are periodically rebuilt with great ceremony.*

Ceremonies

To properly encourage the spirit of the *kami* to dwell in the holy sanctuary, long and complex ceremonies are needed. In some temples, it takes ten years for the priests to learn them. The priesthood was traditionally hereditary. One temple has drawn its priests from the same four families for over a hundred generations. Not uncommonly, the clergy are women priestesses. Neither priests nor priestesses live as ascetics; it is common for them to be married, and they are not tradition-ally expected to meditate. Rather, they are specialists in the arts of maintaining the connection between the *kami* and the people.

Everything has symbolic importance, so rites are conducted with great care. The correct materials in temple furnishings, the nine articles held by priests during ceremonies (such as branch, gourd, sword, and bow), the bowing, the sharp clapping of hands, beating of drums, the waving of a stick with paper strips—everything is established by tradition and performed with precision. Traditionally, there are no personal prayers to the *kami* for specific kinds of help, but rather a reverent recognition of the close relationship between the *kami*, the ancestors, the people, and nature. When people have made a pilgrimage to a special shrine, they often take back spiritual mementos of their communion with the *kami*, such as a paper symbol of the temple encased within a brocade bag.

Followers of the way of the *kami* may also make daily offerings to the *kami* in their home. Their place of worship usually consists of a high shelf on which rests a miniature shrine, with only a mirror inside. The daily home ritual may begin with greeting the sun in the east with clapping and a prayer for protection for the household. Then offerings are placed before the shrine: rice for health, water for cleansing and preservation of life, and salt for the harmonious seasoning of life. When a new house is to be built, the blessings of the *kami* are ceremonially requested.

To follow the *kami* is to bring our life into harmony with nature, Shinto adherents feel. The word used for this concept is **kannagara**, same as the word used for the movements of the sun, moon, stars, and planets. *Kannagara*, "the way or nature of the Kami," can be understood as "Natural Religion," according to Yukitaka Yamamoto, ninety-sixth Chief Priest of the Tsubaki Grand Shrine:

> *Natural Religion is the spontaneous awareness of the Divine that can be found in any culture. . . . The Spirit of Great Nature may be a flower, may be the beauty of the mountains, the pure snow, the soft rains or the gentle breeze. Kannagara means being in communion with these forms of beauty and so with the highest level of experiences of life. When people respond to the silent and provocative beauty of the natural order, they are aware of* kannagara. *When they respond in life in a similar way, by following ways "according to the* kami,*" they are expressing* kannagara *in their lives. They are living according to the natural flow of the universe and will benefit and develop by so doing.*[6]

Purification

In the ancient traditions now referred to as Shinto, the world is beautiful and full of helpful spirits. Sexuality *per se* is not evil; the world was created by mating deities, and people have traditionally bathed together communally in Japan. However, ritual impurity is a serious problem that obscures our originally pristine nature; it may offend the *kami* and bring about calamities, such as drought, famine, or war.

The quality of impurity or misfortune is called *tsumi*. It can arise through defilement by corpses or menstruation, by hostility towards others or the environment, or through natural catastrophes. In contrast to repentance required by religions that emphasize the idea of human sinfulness, *tsumi* requires purification. One way of removing *tsumi* is paying attention to problems as they arise:

> *To live free of obstructing mists, problems of the morning should be solved in the morning and those of the evening should be solved by evening. Wisdom and knowledge should be applied like the sharpness of an axe to the blinding effect of the mists of obstruction. Then may the* kami *purify the world and free it of* tsumi.[7]

The *kami* of the high mountain rapids will carry the *tsumi* to the sea, where the whirlpool *kami* will swallow it and the wind *kami* will blow it to the netherworld, where *kami* of that place absorb and remove it.

> *After this has been completed, the heavenly* kami, *the earthly* kami *and the myriad of* kami *can recognise man as purified and everything can return to its original brightness, beauty and purity as before since all* tsumi *has wholly vanished from the world.*[8]

People may also be purified in a kind of spontaneous movement that washes over them, often in nature, bringing them into awareness of unity with the uni-

RELIGION IN PRACTICE

Purification by Waterfall

The cleansing power of waters, plentiful in natural Japan, is often used. One may take a ritual bath in the ocean, source of life. Or, in a lengthy ritual called **misogi**, a believer may stand beneath a waterfall, letting its force hit the shoulders and carry impurities and tensions away. Before even entering the waterfall, those seeking purification must undergo preliminary purification practices because the waterfall itself is *kami*. The women put on white kimonos and headbands, the men white loincloths and headbands.

The *misogi* ritual proceeds with shaking the soul by bouncing the hands up and down in front of the stomach, to help the person become aware of the soul's presence. Next comes a form of warm-up calisthenics called Bird Rowing. Following a leader, the participants then shout invocations that activate the soul, affirm the potential for realizing the infinite in one's own soul, and unify the people with the *kami* of earth, guidance, water, life, and the *ki* energy (which the Chinese know as *qi*).

Before entering the waterfall, the participants raise their metabolism and absorb as much *ki* as possible by practicing a form of deep breathing. They are sprinkled with purifying salt and are given *sake* to spray into the stream in three mouthfuls. The leader counts from one to nine, to symbolize the impurity of the mundane world and then cuts the air and shouts "Yei!" to dispel this impurity. With ritual claps and shouts the participants then enter the waterfall, continually chanting "*Harae-tamae-Kiyome-tamae-ro-kon-sho-jo!*" This phrase requests the kami to wash away all **tsumi** from the six elements that form the human being, from the senses, and from the mind. This part of the ritual has been scientifically proven to lower the blood pressure.

After this powerful practice, participants dry off, spend time in meditation to calm the soul, and share a ceremonial drink to unify themselves with the *kami* and with each other. The whole *misogi* ceremony is designed to restore one's natural purity and sense of mission in life. As Yukitaka Yamamoto explains:

> As imperfect beings, we often fail to recognize our mission. These failures come about because we have lost something of our natural purity. This is why purification, or misogi, is so central to Shinto. It enables man to cultivate spirituality and to restore his or her natural greatness.[9]

Misogi, *or ritual purification by standing beneath a waterfall.*

verse. Hitoshi Iwasaki, a young Shinto priest, says that he likes to look at the stars at night in the mountains where the air is clear:

> *When I am watching the thoroughly clear light of the stars, I get a pure feeling, like my mind being washed. I rejoice to think this is a spiritual* misogi *[purification ritual]. . . . Master Mirihei Ueshiba, the founder of Aikido, is said to have looked upon the stars one night, suddenly realized he was united with the universe, and burst into tears, covering his face with his hands. We human beings, not only human beings but everything existing in this world, are one of the cells which form this great universe.*[10]

In addition to these personal ways of cleansing, there are ritual forms of purification. One is **oharai**, a ceremony commonly performed by Shinto priests, which includes the waving of a piece of wood from a sacred tree, to which are attached white streamers (the Japanese version of the shaman's medicine fan of feathers or the Hindu yak-tail whisk, all used to sweep through the air and thus purify an area). This ceremony is today performed on cars and new buildings. A version used to soothe a *kami* that is upset by an impurity was called for in 1978 when there was a rash of suicides in a Tokyo housing complex by residents jumping off roofs.

Before people enter a Shinto shrine, they will splash water on their hands and face and rinse their mouth to purify themselves in order to approach the *kami*. Water is also used for purification in powerful ascetic practices, such as *misogi*, which involves standing under a waterfall (see box, opposite). Sprinkling salt on the ground or on ritual participants is also regarded as purifying.

Such ritual practices all have inner meaningfulness. At Tsubaki Grand Shrine in Japan, priests purify more than two hundred new cars every weekend, and the same practice is being adopted at Tsubaki Shrine in California. There, Tetsuji Ochiai explains to new car owners whose cars are being ritually purified that they themselves must also practice mental purification for the sake of traffic safety. Just as they attended the ceremony for their car with a calm mind, they should be calm as they drive. Thus, even though the ceremony is not guaranteed to protect them from accidents, it will help them to concentrate their energy on safe driving.

Festivals

In addition to elaborate regular ceremonies, Shinto is associated with numerous special festivals throughout the year and throughout a person's life. They begin four months before the birth of a baby, when the soul is thought to enter the fetus. Then, thirty-two or thirty-three days after the infant's birth, its parents take it to the family's temple for initiation by the deity. In a traditional family, many milestones—such as coming of age at thirteen, or first arranging one's hair as a woman at age sixteen, marriage, turning sixty-one, seventy-seven, or eighty-eight—are also celebrated with a certain spiritual awareness and ritualism.

The seasonal festivals are reminders to the people that they are descendants of the *kami*. They are exuberant affairs in which the people and the *kami* join in celebrating life. Many have an agricultural basis, ensuring good crops and then giving thanks for them. Often the local *kami* is carried about the streets in a portable shrine.

One of the biggest festivals is New Year's. It begins in December with ceremonial housecleaning, the placing of bamboo and pine "trees" at doorways of everything from homes to offices and bars to welcome the *kami*, and dressing in traditional kimonos. On December 31, there is a national day of purification. On

New Year's day, people watch the first sunrise of the year and will try to visit a shrine as well as friends and relatives.

Many ceremonies honor those reaching a certain age. For instance, on January 15, those who are twenty years old are recognized as full-fledged adults, and on November 15, children who are three, five, or seven years old (considered delicate ages) are taken to a shrine to ask for the protection of the *kami*. On February 3, the end of winter, people throw beans to toss out bad fortune and invite good, and at shrines the priests shoot arrows to break the power of misfortune. A month-long spring festival is held from March to April, with purification rites and prayers for a successful planting season. The month of June is devoted to rites to protect crops from insects, blights, and bad weather. Fall brings thanksgiving rites for the harvest, with the first fruits offered to the *kami* and then great celebrating in the streets.

Buddhist and Confucian influences

Over time, the ways of the *kami* that have been labeled "Shinto" have blended with other religions imported into Japan, particularly Buddhism, first introduced into Japan in the sixth century CE, and Confucianism, which has been part of Japanese culture since its earliest contact with China.

Buddhism is still practiced side-by-side with Shinto. The fact that their theologies differ so significantly has been accepted by the people as covering different kinds of situations. The Japanese often go to Shinto shrines for life-affirming events, such as conception, birth, and marriage, and to Buddhist temples for death rites. Buddhist monks of medieval times tried to convince the Japanese that the Shinto *kami* were actually Buddhist deities. The two religions were therefore closely interwoven in many ways throughout Japanese history, until the Meiji Government promoted its version of Shinto as part of its program of nationalistic revival in the nineteenth century, distinguishing it from Buddhism, which was denounced for its foreign origins. Parallel worship of the two paths continues. Some villages have stone monuments to the *kami* and statues of Nichiren placed next to each other.

Reverence toward the *kami* is mixed with Buddhist practices in traditions such as ritual ascent of sacred mountains in search of enlightenment. Mountain caves are considered to have special powers in Japan because of the spiritual power of the mountains plus that of the *kami* who are thought to spend the winters there. To reach the cave of Omine-san, a sacred mountain in Nara Prefecture, pilgrims and ascetics climb up a steep trail to the cave mouth while chanting the Buddhist Heart Sutra. Small shrines dedicated to various *kami* and also Buddhist figures are encountered on the mountainside. Crawling into the cave and then up a narrow shaft into an elevated upper chamber, pilgrims find themselves in a dark, wet, womb-like world with secretions dripping from the rocks. This sacred natural space in the deep recesses of the mountain is considered an excellent place for progressing toward full realization of the truth by Buddhist practices such as chanting of the Heart Sutra.

As for Confucianism, seventeenth-century Japanese Confucian scholars attempted to free themselves from Buddhism and to tie the Chinese beliefs they were importing to the ancient Japanese ways. One, for instance, likened *li* to the way of the *kami* as a means of social cohesion. Another stressed reverence as the common ground of the two paths and was himself revered as a living *kami*. The Neo-Confucianists' alliance with Shinto to throw off the yoke of Buddhism actually revived Shinto itself and made the ancient, somewhat formless tradition more self-conscious. Scholars began to study and interpret its teachings. The combination of Confucian emphasis on hierarchy and devotion to the *kami* helped pave the way for the establishment in 1868 of the powerful Meiji monarchy.

State Shinto

The Meiji regime took steps to promote Shinto as the spiritual basis for the government. The state cult, amplifying the Japanese traditions of ancestor veneration, had taught since the seventh century that the emperor was the offspring of Amaterasu, the Sun Goddess. *Naobi no Mitma* ("Divine Spirit of Rectification"), written in the eighteenth century, expressed this ideal:

> *This great imperial land, Japan, is the august country where the divine ancestral goddess Amaterasu Omikami was born, a superb country. ... Amaterasu deigned to entrust the country with the words, "So long as time endures, for ten thousand autumns, this land shall be ruled by my descendants."*
>
> *According to her divine pleasure, this land was decreed to be the country of the imperial descendants ... so that even now, without deviation from the divine age, the land might continue in tranquility and in accord with the will of the* kami, *a country ruled in peace.*[11]

It had been customary for the imperial family to visit the shrine to the Sun Goddess at Ise to consult the supreme *kami* on matters of importance. But Emperor Meiji carried this tradition much farther. He decreed that the way of the *kami* should govern the nation. This way was labeled State Shinto and was administered by government officials rather than Shinto priests, whose objections were silenced, and many of the ancient rituals were suppressed. State Shinto became the tool of militaristic nationalists as a way to enlist popular support for the throne and the expanding empire.

*On the nearest Sunday to November 15, boys of five and girls of three or seven years are dressed in traditional clothes and taken to a Shinto shrine by their parents to pray for health and good fortune. This father and daughter are celebrating this Seven-Five-Three (*Shichi-go-san*) festival in Narita, Japan.*

An illustration of the profound changes in Shinto ushered in by the Meiji "Restoration" occurs in pre- and post-Meiji versions of the Oracles of the Three Shrines. These are scrolls with sayings attributed to the *kami* of three major shrines. The versions popular before the Meiji Restoration emphasize virtues such as honesty, compassion, and purity. For instance:

If you plot and connive to deceive men, you may fool them for a while, and profit thereby, but you will without fail be visited by divine punishment. To be utterly honest may have the appearance of inflexibility and self-righteousness, but in the end, such a person will receive the blessings of sun and moon. Follow honesty without fail.[12]

A version prepared in the Meiji period taken from the eighth-century imperial cult asserts a direct link between the *kami* and the emperor:

Amaterasu Sumeomikami commanded her August Grandchild, saying: "This Reed-plain-1500-autumns-fair-rice-ear Land is the region which my descendants shall be lords of. Do thou, my August Grandchild, proceed thither and govern it. Go! and may prosperity attend thy dynasty, and may it, like Heaven and Earth endure for ever.[13]

After Japan's defeat in World War II, Emperor Hirohito, Meiji's grandson, also known as the Showa Emperor, became little more than a ceremonial figurehead. But he had previously been held up as a god, not to be seen or touched by ordinary people. At the end of the war he officially declared himself human.

During the social changes of the nineteenth and twentieth centuries, many new religious sects appeared that had their roots in Shinto beliefs and practices of communicating with the *kami*. These new sects were also labeled "Sect Shinto" by the Meiji regime. One of these new sects, Tenrikyo, will be considered separately in Chapter 13. Another, called Oomoto, developed from revelations given to Madame Nao Deguchi when she was reportedly possessed by the previously little-known *kami* Ushitora no Konjin in 1892. The revelations criticized the "beastly" state of humanity, with:

the stronger preying on the weaker. . . . If allowed to go on in this way, society will soon lose the last vestiges of harmony and order. Therefore, by a manifestation of Divine Power, the Greater World shall undergo reconstruction, and change into an entirely new creation. . . . The Greater World shall burst into bloom as plum blossoms at winter's end.[14]

As developed by Madame Deguchi's relatives and successors, the Oomoto movement survived persecution by the Meiji regime. It has denied that it is a Shinto sect and now has a universalist approach, recognizing founders of other religions as *kami*. Its leaders travel around the world encouraging self-examination, environmental restoration, and global religious cooperation.

Shinto today

In general, the ways of Shinto remain indigenous to Japan. Outside Japan, Shinto beliefs and practices are common only in Hawaii and Brazil, because many Japanese have settled there. Shinto does not seek to convert others. Most Japanese people who visit shrines and pray to the *kami* do not even think of themselves as Shinto adherents. This label is applied mostly by the priestly establishment.

Within Japan, reaction to the horrors of World War II, the elimination of the imperial mythology of State Shinto, and a desire for modernization threatened Shinto. After the war, the Japanese Teachers Association began teaching rejection of the imperial family, of Japanese history, and also of the beliefs and practices associated with Shinto. The Japanese national flag—a red circle on a white background—became a symbol of the past, although its symbolism transcends history. The red circle signifies the rising sun and the white background purity, righteousness, and national loyalty. As Hitoshi Iwasaki notes (see box, opposite), for a time it was difficult for young people to learn about Shinto. But the shrines remain and are visited by more than 80 million Japanese at New Year. People often visit more as tourists than as believers, but many say they experience a sense of spiritual renewal when they visit a shrine. Long-established households still have their *kami* shelf, often next to the Buddhist family altar, which combines tablets memorializing the dead with scrolls or statues dedicated to a manifestation of the Buddha. In Japan, Shinto also survives as the basis for the seasonal holidays.

Despite the fact that Japan is now one of the most technologically advanced countries in the world, with business its primary focus, there still seems to be a place for ritual—and in some cases, heartfelt—communion with the intangible *kami* that, in Shinto belief, permeate all of life. Before Japanese scientists launched their first satellite in 1970, the most senior scientists of the Space Development Agency went to the Chichibu Shinto shrine near Tokyo to request the shrine deity—the North Star—that their mission should be successful. When it was, they returned to the shrine to express their gratitude.

Modern life, instead of distancing Japanese from their ancient traditions, has ultimately encouraged renewed interest in Shinto beliefs. Rapid and extreme urbanization and industrialization in twentieth-century Japan brought extremes of pollution and disease. Minamata disease, for example, inflicted paralysis and painful suffering in an area of southern Japan where a chemical factory had been dumping mercury into the bay, contaminating the fish eaten by the residents. In another area of southern Japan, iron and steel factories had so polluted the air

AN INTERVIEW WITH HITOSHI IWASAKI

Living Shinto

Hitoshi Iwasaki is a young Shinto priest struggling to educate himself in the suppressed ancient ways of his people. He has officiated at the Shinto shrine in Stockton, California, and at its parent shrine in Japan, Tsubaki Grand Shrine in the Mie Prefecture, where a fine waterfall is used for *misogi*.

"We Japanese are very fortunate. We are grateful for every natural phenomenon and we worship the mountain, we worship the river, we worship the sea, we worship the big rocks, waterholes, winds.

"Unfortunately, after World War II, we were prohibited from teaching the Shinto religion in schools. We never learned about Shinto at school. Many young Japanese know the story of Jesus Christ, but nothing about Shinto. The government is not against Shinto. [The silence comes from] newspapers, the media, and the teachers' union, because they were established just after World War II. They have a very left-wing attitude [and associate Shinto with State Shinto]. Ordinary Japanese people don't link Shinto with politics nowadays, but the teachers' union and newspapers never give credence to religion, Shinto, or Japanese old customs.

"Against this kind of atmosphere, we learned in the school that everything in Japan was bad. Shinto and Japanese customs were bad. Many young people are losing Japanese customs. But I went to Ise Shrine University, where I learned that Shinto is not just State Shinto. Some young people like me study Japanese things and they become super-patriots. That's the problem. There is no middle, just super-left or super-right.

"I learned Shinto partly by learning aikido. The founder was a very spiritual person who studied in one of the Shinto churches. In Shinto we don't have services, we don't preach, we don't do anything for people who want to be saved. But I want to introduce the idea of Shinto to the people of the United States and young Japanese and I can do it through aikido. I think I learned the way of nature through aikido practice. We are born as a child of *kami*, which means we are part of the universe, like a tree. People practice aikido not to fight but to be a friend, to unite.

"In Japan some people are going to Shinto. They were all doing Zen before, but Zen is very difficult. In waterfall purification there is no choice, just standing under the waterfall.

"My friend, a Shinto priest, went to the Middle East, in complete desert. He says it was difficult to explain Shinto there. For them, nature is the enemy. They have to fight nature.

"In Japan we have water everywhere. Now the big rivers and streams are polluted. But people come to the shrines. People gather because this is a sacred place from ancient times where people have come to pray. And other people want to go where people are gathered, so some of the shrines become vacation places, surrounded by souvenir shops. Many come to Shinto shrines and pray Buddhist prayers. Why not? Buddha is one of the *kami*. Everything has *kami*."

---

that children developed severe respiratory diseases and the sky was never blue. However, citizens' groups—many of them led by concerned mothers—are intervening to protest the despoliation of the environment and of human health and to urge a new appreciation of the natural beauty of the islands. Such actions can perhaps be seen as practical applications of Shinto sentiments.

Some Shinto adherents now explain their path as a universal natural religion, rather than an exclusively Japanese phenomenon, and try to explain the way of harmony with the *kami* to interested non-Japanese, without striving for conversions. A Shinto shrine has been built in California, offering ritual ways of experiencing one's connection with nature and learning to see the divine in the midst of life.

Within Japan, there are new attempts to teach children the thousands-of-years-old rice cultivation ceremony, and with it, Shinto values such as co-existence and "co-prosperity" with the natural environment and with each other. The Association of Shinto Shrines feels that it can play a role in helping people to remember the natural world. The Association recently stated:

> [Traditionally] the Japanese viewed nature not as an adversary to be subdued, but rather as a sacred space overflowing with the blessings of the kami, and toward which they were to act with restraint. . . . While the Japanese have loathed environmental destruction, the advance of civilization centered on science and technology, and the rush toward economic prosperity has created a tidal wave of modernization that has frequently resulted in the loss of that traditional attitude handed down from ancestors. . . . By reconsidering the role of the sacred groves possessed by the some eighty thousand shrines in Japan, we hope to heighten Japanese consciousness, and expand the circle of active involvement in environmental preservation.[15]

Suggested reading

Bocking, Brian, *A Popular Dictionary of Shinto*, Richmond, Surrey: Curzon Press, 1996. Thorough discussions of ancient and contemporary facets of Shinto, including shrines, festivals, *kami*, new religious movements, historical events, and key figures.

Breen, John and Mark Teeuwen, eds., *Shinto in History: Ways of the Kami*, Honolulu: University of Hawaii Press, 2000. Scholarly essays distinguishing between unnamed shrine cults and establishment Shinto in historical context.

Hebert, Jean, *Shinto: At the Fountain-head of Japan*, New York: Stein and Day, 1967. A classic survey of the intricacies of Shinto practice.

Hori, Ichiro, *Folk Religion in Japan*, Chicago and London: University of Chicago Press, 1968. A lively study of Japanese folk traditions, such as shamanism and mountain worship, which contributed to Shinto.

Kitagawa, Joseph M., *On Understanding Japanese Religion*, Princeton, New Jersey and Guildford, Surrey: Princeton University Press, 1987. A scholarly history including Shinto and "new religions," making distinctions between shrine Shinto, folk Shinto, and sect Shinto.

Moore, Charles A., ed., *The Japanese Mind: Essentials of Japanese Philosophy and Culture*, Honolulu: University of Hawaii Press, 1967, 1971. A valuable collection of essays covering Shinto and Buddhism as well as secular aspects of Japanese lifeways.

Nelson, John K., *A Year in the Life of a Shinto Shrine*, University of Washington Press, 1995. Both an in-depth description of the ritual cycle at a major Shinto shrine and an accessible introduction to Shinto.

Picken, Stuart D. B., *Essentials of Shinto: An Analytical Guide to Principal Teachings*. Westport, Connecticut and London: Greenwood Press, 1994. A clear introduction by a minister of the Church of Scotland who is also a *misogi* practitioner.

Smith, Robert J., *Ancestor Worship in Contemporary Japan*, Stanford, California: Stanford University Press, 1974. A sociological study of the continuing tradition of venerating family ancestors in contemporary Japan, including historical chapters that are of help in understanding the roots of State Shinto.

Yamamoto, Yukitaka, *Way of the Kami*, Stockton, California: Tsubaki American Publications, 1987. A highly accessible introduction to Shinto, seen as a universal natural way.

Key terms

kami   The invisible sacred quality that evokes wonder and awe in us, the invisible spirits throughout nature that are born of this essence.
kannagara Harmony with the way of the *kami*.
oharai   Shinto purification ceremony.
misogi   The Shinto waterfall purification ritual.
tsumi   Impurity or misfortune, a quality that Shinto purification practices are designed to remove.

Study questions

1 Explain the Shinto involvement in nature and environmental concern. Discuss *kami*, mountains, stars, sexuality, and *kannagara*.
2 Describe the purpose of several Shinto rituals, such as for life cycles and seasons. Discuss aesthetic beauty, priests-priestesses, shrines, *torii*, mirrors, *oharai*, cars, and iconoclasm.
3 Explain the importance of purification in Shinto, both personal and collective. Discuss *misogi*, *tsumi*, and Mt. Fuji.
4 How has Shinto been related to Confucianism and Buddhism? Discuss meditation, death, social hierarchy, and social cohesion.
5 Explain the modern history of Shinto in relation to nationalism. Discuss patriotism, war, emperor deification, and post-World War II changes and renewals.

Refer to Pearson/Prentice Hall's **TIME Special Edition: World Religions** magazine for current articles on topics related to many of the world's religions.

Chapter 7 concludes the study of religions originating in China and Japan and focuses on Shinto. For further research in this area, use the tools available to you in Research Navigator:

As you investigate Shinto, consider this question: "What are the tensions that arise in viewing Shinto as a state religion?"

- **Ebsco's ContentSelect:** Search in the Philosophy, Political Science, Religion, and Sociology databases using terms such as "Shinto," "state religion," "Japanese religion."
- **Link Library:** Search in the Religion database under the category: "Religions of the Far East: Shinto."
- **The *New York Times* on the Web:** Search in the Religious Studies and all other databases for current articles on related topics.

ZOROASTRIANISM

A bridge between East and West

Zoroastrianism, a religion from ancient Iran, at present has perhaps only 130,000 remaining practitioners, but for more than 1,000 years it may have been the official religion of the vast Iranian Empire which extended from Iraq or Turkey to India. It is in some ways a bridge between Eastern and Western religions. Its origins are synchronous with, and similar to, Hinduism, it is thought to have influenced Buddhism, and it introduced beliefs that are similar to those later found in Jewish, Christian, and Muslim religions. Supplanting polytheism, it brought an early form of monotheism, which was subsequently central to those "Western" faiths, as well as to Sikhism, which was born on Indian soil.

However, the extent of Zoroastrianism's direct influence on later faiths is not clear. The theology of ancient Zoroastrianism itself is subject to debate, for over the centuries a large portion of its sacred scriptures was destroyed or forgotten and the meanings of the old language were lost.

In the early faith, people also worshipped a pantheon of gods representing the elements, aspects of nature, and abstract principles, such as justice and obedience. These gods often corresponded with those worshipped by the Vedic Indians and were similarly named *daevas*, like the Indian *devas*, meaning "Shining Ones," with the highest gods called *Ahuras* ("Lords"). The ritual worship conducted by the priests was designed, as in India, to maintain the natural order, truth, and righteousness of the universe by re-enacting the original sacrifice that led to its creation.

Zarathushtra's mission

Whereas the faith is known in Iran as Mazdayasna—"the worship of the Wise Lord, Ahura Mazda"—Western scholars refer to the tradition by the name of one of its great reformers, the prophet Zarathushtra (Greek: Zoroaster) who may have lived about 1100 to 550 BCE. The Greeks in the time of Plato mentioned him as an ancient prophet. German philosopher Karl Jaspers has referred him as one of the great figures of the "**Axial Age.**" During that period—which Jaspers dated as approximately sixth century BCE—a surprising number of great religious leaders and thinkers

appeared in many parts of the ancient world, including the sages who wrote the *Upanishads*, the Buddha, Mahavira, Confucius, Laozi, and Socrates, as well as Zarathushtra. Although the dating of some of these figures is still uncertain, their teachings ultimately had profoundly transformational impacts on the development of humanity which are still felt today.

It is thought that Zarathushtra was trained as a priest in the Indo-Iranian tradition. He was also apparently a mystical seeker who spent many years in spiritual retreat. At the age of thirty, he is said to have had a stunning vision of a great shining being, Vohu Manah, the embodiment of the loving mind. Vohu Manah led him into the presence of Ahura Mazda, the creator God. Ahura Mazda was surrounded by angelic presences manifesting six attributes of the divine. Scholars suggest that these attributes represent earlier Indo-Iranian deities, transformed by Zarathushtra to suit his monotheistic belief but still retaining their association with forces of nature—the earth, the arch of the sky, water, plants, cattle, and fire.

Zarathushtra said he experienced communion with Ahura Mazda and his attributes on many occasions. From these direct contacts with the divine, Zarathushtra reportedly determined that in contrast to the multiplicity of gods worshipped by the Indo-Iranians, Ahura Mazda was the Supreme Lord, from whom all good things flowed. Zarathushtra denounced all cruelty, selfishness, distortion, and hypocrisy in the name of religion. He insisted that Ahura Mazda creates only goodness and should be worshipped by good thoughts, words, and deeds. There is a cosmic battle between sustaining and destroying forces, and to assure the victory of good over evil, humans must dedicate themselves as spiritual warriors for goodness.

Zarathushtra poured forth his adoration for the Supreme in metric verses called **Gathas**. These hymns are the only words of the prophet that have been retained over centuries of vicissitudes. "Speak to me as friend to friend," he implores Ahura Mazda. "Grant us the support which friend would give to friend."[1] The Gathas are the major existing source of information about Zarathushtra's life and theology, but they are written in an ancient language whose meanings are now obscure. Scholars see close linguistic and thematic links between the Gathas and the earliest of the Rig Vedas.

Zarathushtra was long unable to convince anyone else to follow him in honoring Ahura Mazda above all other gods. At last he journeyed to another kingdom whose exact location is now unknown and convinced its king, Vishtapa, of the truth of his understanding. King Vishtapa adopted Zarathushtra's creed and proclaimed it the state religion. Zarathushtra is said to have preached for almost fifty years until his death by assassination at a fire temple at the age of seventy-seven.

Spread of Zoroastrian beliefs

It is very difficult to trace the later spread of Zarathushtra's teachings. The Magi—a tribe of priestly specialists in western Iran whose practices included magic and astrology—seem to have become involved with transmission of Zoroastrianism some time after Zarathushtra died, but they may have altered it significantly. They are mentioned in the book of Matthew in the Christian Bible, in which some Magi reportedly followed a star to present gifts to the infant Jesus, but it is thought that this may have been a legend written to interest the Magi of the gospel-writer's area in converting to Christianity.

Ahura Mazda was apparently revered by the Achaemenid kings of the great Persian Empire. The Persian Empire was the largest the world had known. It was built in the mid-sixth century BCE by King Cyrus, who seems to have been a follower of Ahura Mazda. However, he and the succeeding Achaemenid kings left no written mention of the prophet Zarathushtra. Cyrus's reign was noted for its religious tolerance as well as its power and wealth. The empire Cyrus created by far-reaching conquests stretched from the Indus Valley to what is now Greece. The Jews within this territory were allowed to practice their own religion but may have adopted certain Zoroastrian beliefs, such as the belief that there is an evil aspect in life, an immortal soul, reward or punishment in an afterlife, and final resurrection of the body at the apocalyptic end of the present age—for these beliefs were absent from earlier Judaic religion. From Judaism, they may have passed indirectly into Christianity and Islam.

The spiritual tradition of devotion to Ahura Mazda was severely threatened by the 331 BCE invasion of Alexander, known as "The Great" in the West but "The Accursed" in Iran. According to Zoroastrian belief, he ransacked the beautiful capital of Persepolis, destroying fire temples, burning the library containing the holy scriptures of Zarathushtra, and killing so many Zoroastrian priests that oral transmission of many scriptures was also lost. It is thought that the Gathas of Zarathushtra survived because many people knew them by heart, as they did the most commonly used ritual prayers.

Two centuries later, Zoroastrianism was re-established in a shrunken Iranian empire by the Parthians, who ruled for almost five hundred years to 224 CE. Under the Parthians the surviving revealed teachings of Zoroastrianism were reassembled as the **Avesta**, or "holy texts." Then under the Sassanids of the third to mid-seventh centuries CE, Zoroastrianism came to the fore as the state religion, serving the aristocracy of Iran, and was thus one of the major religions of the ancient world.

However, a major threat to Zoroastrianism came from the spread of Islam after the death of Muhammad in 632 CE. Arabic Muslims defeated the Zoroastrian Iranian forces, and when Mongols also invaded from the east, they were gradually converted to Islam rather than Zoroastrianism. A number of Persian Zoroastrians avoided conversion to Islam by migrating to western India, whose spiritual origins were similar to their own. In India they were called **Parsis** ("Persians"). The sacred fire they consecrated on reaching India is said to have been kept burning continuously ever since. Its temple in Upwada is a major pilgrimage spot for Parsis. Some also migrated to what is now Pakistan.

The numbers of Zoroastrians remaining in Iran dwindled over the centuries under Muslim dominance. Even when Zoroastrians had become a minority in Iran, detailed instructions about the rituals and customs of the faith were preserved in a vast new literature, the **Pahlavi** texts written or translated in Middle Persian from about the ninth century CE. A small community of believers still survives in Iran.

Today, India—particularly the Mumbai area—is the major center of Zoroastrian population, but whether it is also the repository of the purest surviving Zoroastrian teachings is a matter of debate. Zoroastrianism in India seems to have been affected by surrounding religious traditions—such as Hinduism, Buddhism, and Christianity—and from the nineteenth century onward, by modern spiritual movements such as Theosophy. In its Indian setting, it has nonetheless remained vibrant and meaningful.

Zoroastrian teachings

After Zarathushtra's death, his teachings seem to have been merged with earlier polytheistic trends. Today there is uncertainty about exactly what he taught, but enough is known that his theology can be sketched, along with its later transformations.

The primacy of Ahura Mazda

Zarathushtra is considered the first of the monotheists of the Western traditions, in the sense that he elevated one god above all others worshipped by the earlier Iranians. His mystical visions convinced him that there is only one divine being who creates and orders the universe. He refers to this God, Ahura Mazda, by the masculine gender. In the *Gathas* Zarathushtra makes impassioned pleas to Ahura Mazda to make him a more fit spiritual vehicle, so that he can "dedicate to Mazda the life-breath of his whole being."[2] He asks for Ahura Mazda's guidance in the mission of protecting "the poor in spirit, the meek and lowly of heart, who are Thine." He particularly emphasizes the need for clear thought in this mission:

> O Lord of Life, we long for Thy mighty Fire of
> Thought which is an enduring, blazing Flame
> bringing clear guidance and joy to the true believer,
> but as for the destruction-loving, this quickening
> Flame overcomes his evil in a flash.[3]

Although Zarathushtra perceived Ahura Mazda as the one Eternal Being, he also described six divine powers that radiate from the godhead: The Good Mind, Righteousness, Absolute Power, Devotion, Perfection, and Immortality. After the prophet's death, these six attributes were personified and worshipped as beings, and uttering their names was thought to bring great power. These Bountiful Immortals, the **Ameshta Spenta**, were described as luminous deities with shining eyes and beautiful forms, guardians of Ahura Mazda's creation who held celestial councils in the heavens and descended to earth on radiant paths. They are chief among the angels, who also include many of the deities worshipped by the earlier Iranians. One of these is the popular Mithra, guardian of the light, protector of the truth, and bestower of wealth. Mithra was worshipped in Hinduism, Manicheanism, and Mithraism, as well as in Zoroastrianism.

The choice between good and evil

Zarathushtra wrestled with the problem of the existence of evil. Many Western scholars describe Zarathushtra's theology as cosmic dualism, with Ahura Mazda opposed by a dark force of equal power. Others feel that this is a later development in Zoroastrianism and that the original teaching was that although there were two opposing forces in the universe, Ahura

Mazda was much the stronger. In any case, in Zoroastrian belief Ahura Mazda is a good creator who creates only perfection and purity.

Zarathushtra did speak of two opposing powers: *Spenta Mainyu*, the good spirit, and *Angra Mainyu*, the evil spirit. Spenta Mainyu is life, order, perfection, health, happiness, increase. Angra Mainyu is not-life, chaos, imperfection, disease, sorrow, destruction. The two principles will always actively oppose each other in humans and in creation as a whole until the good spirit is at last victorious. Evil, Zarathushtra asserts, is not all-powerful or eternal, but to assure the victory of good over evil, humans must dedicate themselves as spiritual warriors on the side of Spenta Mainyu. Human beings are given the free will and mental capacity to choose between the two powers. In their thoughts, words, and deeds, they can grow in love, devotion, and service, or they can contribute to evil.

Zarathushtra felt that non-loving acts in the name of religion aided the cause of evil. He railed against selfish ritualism and worship of the *daevas*, using the old word for the "shining deities" for what he considered dark forces and magic.

Heaven, hell, and resurrection

At death, Zoroastrians believe, each of us is judged according to the total goodness or evilness of our thoughts, words, and deeds. The greater the goodness, the wider the bridge to heaven, the Kingdom of Light where the souls of the righteous reside. The greater the accumulated evil, the narrower the bridge, until it is so narrow that souls cannot cross. They fall into hell, House of the Lie, a murky, woeful place. Tehmurasp Rustamji Sethna explains that this teaching pertains to this life as well as the next:

> When a man's actions are good he has self confidence
> and usually people say he has nothing to worry about,
> his road is clear. On the other hand, if a man's actions
> are bad, it is usually said he is following a precarious
> path and any moment he will fall.[4]

When the soul's evil actions are weighed against the good ones, it is not Ahura Mazda who judges and metes out reward or punishment. By natural law, good deeds bring their own reward and evil deeds their just punishment. This doctrine is similar to that of *karma* in Hinduism, Jainism, and Buddhism, but rather than shifting the effects of one's life to reincarnation to another life Zoroastrians feel that the effects of our actions will be felt in the present and in an afterlife.

There is no eternal hell in Zoroastrianism, for good is ultimately victorious. With the help of all individuals who choose goodness over evil, the world will gradually reach a state of perfection in which all souls, living or dead, are liberated forever from evil. This time is the *Frashokereti*, the "refreshment" of the world in which all of creation is resurrected into perfected immortality. Thenceforth the world will never grow old and never die. This refreshment of the world is not the work of a single savior; it requires the contributions of many people. Zoroastrianism therefore places great emphasis on the moral responsibility of each person, for the good of the whole.

Religious practices
Rituals are major elements of Zoroastrian practice. One that is particularly important is the act of tying the sacred cord (*kusti*) around one's mid-section, traditionally performed at least five times a day. Symbolically, the faithful are girding themselves as soldiers for Ahura Mazda, strengthening their resolve to follow the spiritual path. The *kusti* is worn by both males and females, in contrast with the male-only Hindu tradition of the sacred thread, for women and men are treated equally in many ways within Zoroastrianism. While tying the *kusti*, the faithful recite a prayer to keep evil at bay.

Zoroastrian rituals also emphasize purification. Water is venerated as a means or symbol of purification. The devout will often dip their fingers into water, apply it to their eyes and forehead, and raise their hands in prayer to Ahura Mazda. It is a great sin to pollute water or to place anything dead in it. Zoroastrians regard the natural world with profound reverence and are taught from childhood to avoid defiling it.

As of old, the other element emphasized in Zoroastrian rituals is fire, long used in Indo-Iranian tradition for its purifying, transformative power. Only Zoroastrians can enter a fire temple, and within the temple, certain areas are accessible only to priests in a highly elevated state of purity.

When the physical body dies, Zoroastrians carry it to a Tower of Silence, a special circular building open at the top so that vultures can alight on the corpse to pick the bones clean. This is done to avoid polluting the earth with decaying flesh, which the birds dispose of within an hour or two. The recent near-extinction of vultures in India, perhaps due to their eating the carcasses of animals who had been fed certain medicines, has posed a crisis for this tidy traditional way of disposing of the bodies of the dead.

The survivors continue to pray for the departed and continue to observe death anniversaries at which the *fravashi*, or eternal principle and guide, of the deceased

person is invoked. The *fravashi* is thought to continually evolve toward perfection and to help the living in their good works.

Zoroastrianism today
Few followers remain of this ancient way of combating evil with personal goodness. Conversion to the faith is not emphasized, partly because of a desire not to dilute the teachings or the identity as a distinct faith community. This issue is often debated, and there is some agreement that it is all right for outsiders to "accept" the Zoroastrian faith, if not to convert to it. In contemporary Iran, there is little incentive to convert, for Zoroastrians, like Jews and Christians, are tolerated but limited in their privileges under Muslim rule. Historically, however, many Muslims converted to Zoroastrianism during the last years of the Pahlavi dynasty. Some Zoroastrians in North America favor active conversion of non-Zoroastrians to the faith; others are opposed to proselytizing but favor the acceptance of those who are truly moved by personal religious experience to join the faith. In India, the high priests of the Mumbai Zoroastrian community declared in 2003 that anyone marrying outside the religion would be excommunicated, but this decision brought such an outcry that they clarified that their statement was only a "guideline" to assure the survival of the Parsi faith. It is the community that decides whether to accept converts.

Training is still available in Iran and India for the hereditary lineage of Zoroastrian priests, and there is now considerable interest in preserving and understanding the tradition. When the Parsis were influenced by Westernization and Protestant missionary activity, they became somewhat embarrassed about the mystical aspects of their faith. Some began reciting their prayers in English rather than the ancient Avestan language, and interpreting what they were doing as talking to God rather than uttering powerful sacred mantras. They tended to de-emphasize rituals and beliefs in an evil spirit and the end of the temporal world in favor of the more abstract philosophy and ethical standards of the Gathas.

The pendulum now seems to be swinging in the other direction. Religious historians, metaphysicians, and linguists have attempted to translate the ancient language, uncover the deep significance behind the rituals, and sift out the origins of the tradition from the thousands of years of later accretions. Such efforts have brought a renewed sense of pride and appreciation within Zoroastrianism.

JUDAISM

A covenant with God

Judaism, which has no single founder and no central leader or group making theological decisions, is the diverse tradition associated with the Jewish people, who may be defined either as a religious group or as an ethnic group.

In religious terms, Jews are those who experience their long and often difficult history as a continuing dialogue with God. In a religious sense, "Israel" refers to all those who answer the call of God and who acknowledge and strive to obey the one God, through the **Torah**, or "teaching," given to the patriarchs, Moses, and the prophets.

As a nation, "Israel" is an originally nomadic people who have been repeatedly dispersed and oppressed. After the horrors of the Holocaust in the twentieth century, some Jews founded a homeland in the land of Israel, the former center of their ancestors' faith. Other Jews live in communities around the world. Many who consider themselves Jews have been born into a Jewish ethnic identity but do not feel or practice a strong connection to Jewish religious traditions.

Given the persecution, dispersion, and even lack of religiosity among many Jews, how have they survived as anything more than fossils? Their survival has required constant accommodation to changing circumstances. Nonetheless, they have managed to sustain a remarkable degree of cohesiveness and similar practices and beliefs, though Jews have lived throughout the world under very different circumstances, and with little contact between far-flung communities.

In this chapter we will focus on Judaism as that which Mordecai Kaplan (1881–1983) called "an evolving religious civilization," first by taking an overview of the history of the Jewish people and then by examining the religious concepts and practices that generally characterize the followers of the Torah today.

A history of the Jewish people

The Jewish sense of history begins with the stories recounted in the Hebrew Bible or **Tanakh** (which Christians call "the Old Testament"). Biblical history begins with the creation of the world by a supreme deity, or God, and progresses through the patriarchs, matriarchs, and Moses who spoke with God and led the people according to God's commandments, and the prophets who heard God's warnings to those who strayed from the commandments. But Jewish history does not end where the stories of the Tanakh end, about the second century BCE. After the holy center of Judaism, the Temple of Jerusalem, was captured and destroyed by the Romans in 70 CE, Jewish history is that of a dispersed people, finding unity

TORAH	The Five Books of Moses		**NEVI'IM**	The Prophets
בראשית	GENESIS		יהושע	JOSHUA
שמות	EXODUS		שופטים	JUDGES
ויקרא	LEVITICUS		שמואל א	I SAMUEL
במדבר	NUMBERS		שמואל ב	II SAMUEL
דברים	DEUTERONOMY		מלכים א	I KINGS
			מלכים ב	II KINGS
			ישעיה	ISAIAH
			ירמיה	JEREMIAH
			יחזקאל	EZEKIEL
KETHUVIM	The Writings			
תהילים	PSALMS			The Twelve Minor Prophets
משלי	PROVERBS		הושע	HOSEA
איוב	JOB		יואל	JOEL
שיר השירים	THE SONG OF SONGS		עמוס	AMOS
רות	RUTH		עבדיה	OBADIAH
איכה	LAMENTATIONS		יונה	JONAH
קהלת	ECCLESIASTES		מיכה	MICAH
אסתר	ESTHER		נחום	NAHUM
דניאל	DANIEL		חבקוק	HABAKKUK
עזרא	EZRA		צפניה	ZEPHANIAH
נחמיה	NEHEMIAH		חגי	HAGGAI
דברי הימים א	I CHRONICLES		זכריה	ZECHARIAH
דברי הימים ב	II CHRONICLES		מלאכי	MALACHI

The Jewish scriptures consist of the Torah (or Pentateuch), the Prophets, and the Writings. These books date roughly from the 10th to 2nd century BCE, and were written mostly in classical Hebrew. They are often referred to as Tanakh, an acronym from the first syllables of each division—Torah, Nev'im, Kethuvim.

in their evolving teachings and traditional practices, which were eventually codified in the great compendium of Jewish law and lore, the **Talmud**.

Biblical stories

Although knowledge of the early history of the Children of Israel is based largely on the narratives of the Tanakh, scholars are uncertain of the historical accuracy of the accounts. Some of the people, events, and genealogies set forth cannot be verified by other evidence, such as archaeological findings or references to the Israelites in the writings of neighboring peoples. It may be that the Israelites were too small and loosely organized a group to be noted by historians of other cultures. No mention of Israel appears in other sources until about 1230 BCE, but biblical narratives and genealogies place Abraham, said to be the first patriarch of the Israelites, at about 1700 to 1900 BCE.

Jews hold the **Pentateuch**, the "five books of Moses" that appear at the beginning of the Tanakh, as the most sacred part of the scriptures. Traditionalists believe that these books were divinely revealed to Moses and written down by him as a single document. Some contemporary biblical researchers disagree. On the basis of clues, such as the use of variant names for God, they speculate that these books were oral traditions reworked and set down later by several different sources with

JUDAISM

BCE 1900	c.1900–1700 Abraham, the first patriarch
1500	
	c.13th or 12th century Moses leads the Israelites out of bondage in Egypt
1000	
	c.1010–970 David, king of Judah and Israel 961–931 King Solomon builds the first Temple in Jerusalem
600	586 First Temple destroyed; Jews exiled to Babylon
500	515 Second Temple built c.430 Torah read fo the public by Ezra the Scribe
100	
	30 BCE–10 CE Hillel the Elder
CE	
100	70 Jerusalem falls to the Romans c.90 Jewish Canon set
	c.200 Mishnah compiled
500	
600	c.600 Babylonian Talmud completed
1000	
	1095 Crusaders begin massacring Jews in Europe en route to the Holy Land 1135–1204 Life of Maimonides
	1480 The Inquisition begins 1492 Mass expulsion of Jews from Spain
1500	
	1555 onward: ghettos of Italy and Germany
1700	1700–1760 The Baal Shem Tov c.1720–1780 The Enlightenment in Europe 1881 Large-scale Jewish migrations to North America begin
1900	
	1935 Nüremberg Laws 1940–1945 The Holocaust 1947 Discovery of the Dead Sea Scrolls 1948 Israel declared an independent state 1967 The Six-Day War 1990 onward: Israeli–Palestinian conflicts and peace initiatives
2000	2003 Geneva Accords released 2003 Security wall under construction by Israel 2004 Hamas vows "100 retaliations" for assassination of its leader

the intent of interpreting the formation of Israel from a religious point of view, as the results of God's actions in human history. The Pentateuch seems to have assumed its final form in the days of Ezra the Scribe (fifth century BCE).

Some of the stories in the Pentateuch, such as the Creation, the Garden of Eden, the Great Flood, and the Tower of Babel, are similar to earlier Mesopotamian legends. In the narratives of the continuing history of the Israelites, only the last four books (I and II Samuel and I and II Kings) are thought to be edited directly from contemporary sources. Although the accuracy of many of the stories has not yet been independently documented, they are of great spiritual significance in Christianity and Islam as well as in Judaism. They are also politically important, for along with the Talmud they later gave a scattered people a special sense of group identity and of God's active role in Jewish history.

From creation to the God of Abraham   The Hebrew scriptures begin with a sweeping poetic account of the creation of heaven and earth by God in six days, from the time of "the earth being unformed and void, with darkness over the surface of the deep and a wind from (or: the spirit of) God sweeping over the water."[1] After creating the material universe, God created man and woman in the divine "image" or "likeness," placing them as masters of the earth, rulers of "the fish of the sea, the birds of the sky, and all the living things that creep on the earth."[2] In this account, God is portrayed as a transcendent Creator, without origins, gender, or form, a being utterly different from what has been created. Since Hebrew has no gender-neutral pronouns, God is generally—though not always—described in male singular terms. This creation story (in Genesis 1 and 2:1–4) is attributed by scholars to the "priestly source," thought to be editors writing immediately before or after the exile of the Jews to Babylon in 586 BCE.

A second, probably earlier, version of the creation story follows, beginning in Genesis 2:4. It is thought to be a contribution to the scriptures from the "Yahwist source," which used the word transliterated as "Yahweh" for the supreme male deity. Instead of presenting woman as the equal of man, it portrays her as an offshoot of Adam, the first man, formed to keep him company. This version has commonly been interpreted as blaming woman for the troubles of humanity, although this reading is not supported in the Hebrew manuscripts. According to the legend of Adam and Eve, originally God placed the first two humans in a garden paradise. The woman Eve ("mother of all the living") was promised wisdom by a serpent (later often interpreted as a symbol of Satan) to tempt her to taste the fruit of the tree of knowledge of good and evil, against God's command. She gave some to Adam as well. According to the legend, this ended their innocence. God cursed the serpent and the land, and banished Adam and Eve from their garden; their lives were no longer paradisical nor were they immortal, for they no longer had access to the "tree of life."

The theme of exile reappears continually in the Hebrew Bible, and in later Jewish history the people are rendered homeless again and again. The biblical narratives emphasize that the people risk God's displeasure every time they stray from God's commands. They are repeatedly exiled from their spiritual home and continually seek to return to it.

A more optimistic interpretation developed later, however. This was the feeling that the Jewish people were spread throughout the world by God's will, for a

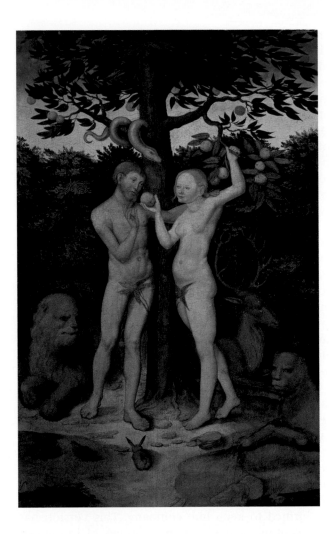

The Adam and Eve account in Genesis, as portrayed by Lucas Cranach the Elder (1472–1553).

sacred purpose: to be good citizens of whatever land they reside in, and to help raise the imperfect world back up to the condition of perfection in which God had created it. Israel would find its way home only when all of creation was lifted up. The rabbinic tradition, which began in the first century CE and has shaped Jewish theology into the modern period, emphasized that the way out of exile was through study and righteous living. Commandments have their origin in God and, if followed, will lead humanity back to a life in harmony with God.

Covenant A unique belief introduced into Jewish theology was the idea of a special covenantal relationship between the Jewish people and God. In this contract both are accountable. On the people's side, obedience to God is expected. On the divine side, God grants special favors and is also bound by his own ethical agreements to the people. The paradigm for this special relationship is the covenant between God and Abraham on behalf of the Jewish people. A more universal covenant with humanity as a whole is portrayed in the story of Noah, who was said to be the sole righteous man of his time.

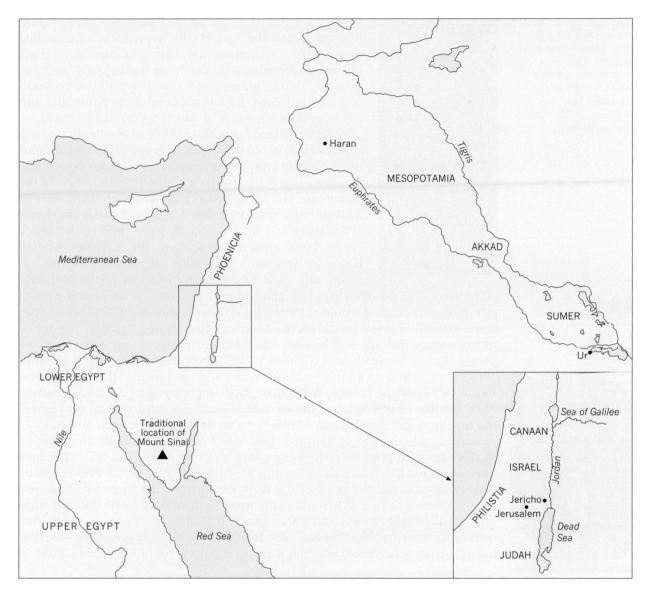

According to the biblical narrator, who attributes thoughts and emotions to God, God despairs of the general wickedness of humans, regrets having created them, and sends a great flood "to destroy all flesh under the sky."[3] The belief that a great flood did occur in Mesopotamia is now supported by non-biblical evidence from archaeology, geology, and legends of other peoples, grounding at least part of the narrative in historical fact. In the biblical story, God establishes a covenant with Noah and gives directions for the building of an ark, which saves Noah's family and two of each of God's creatures. God promises never again to destroy the created world or to interfere with the established natural order, with the rainbow as a sign of this covenant "between me and all flesh that is on earth."[4]

God does, however, continue to intervene in history, according to the narrators. Ten generations after the legend of Noah, the narrative focuses on Abraham,

The Israelites identified themselves as a people whose ancestors, Abraham and Sarah, moved from Ur and Haran in Mesopotamia to Canaan; Abraham's grandson, Jacob, called "Israel," resettled his large family in Egypt, where the Israelites were eventually treated as slaves.

Abraham's descendants are said to have given birth to the twelve tribes of Israel. They are symbolically depicted here as sitting in the patriach's lap. (Souvigny Bible, 12th century, France.)

Judaism:
Abraham

The settled agricultural peoples of Canaan paid homage to a high male god, called El, and an earlier Great Mother Goddess (Ishtar, disguised as his consort). The goddess (shown here), associated with vegetation, agricultural knowledge, and abundance, was worshipped as asherahs, sacred tree-symbol altar poles, which the Israelites destroyed.

Isaac, and Jacob (the "patriarchs"), and their wives, Sarah, Rebecca, Leah, and Rachel (the "matriarchs"). According to the biblical narratives, Abraham was born in Ur (now in Iraq), migrated to Haran (now in Turkey), and then was called by God to journey to Canaan. With his wife Sarah and his household, he left the land of his father and also the religion of his father, a worshipper of the old gods.

Abraham is held up as an example of obedience to God's commands. Without hesitation, he is said to undergo circumcision (cutting away of the foreskin of the penis) as an initiatory rite, a sign of the covenant in which God agrees to be the divine protector of Abraham and his descendants, with all males to be likewise circumcised on the eighth day after birth.

Abraham and his wife Sarah were childless for many years. Sarah offered her servant, the Egyptian woman Hagar, as Abraham's concubine. According to social tradition, any child who was born of this relationship was considered to be the offspring of Abraham and Sarah, and if Sarah herself were to give birth to a child, it would carry the inheritance rights of the first-born. After Hagar conceived a son by Abraham—Ishmael—God blessed Sarah at the age of ninety, saying that she will become the "mother of nations: the kings of many people shall spring from her" (Genesis 17:16). According to the biblical account, Sarah does indeed give birth to a son, Isaac, and then insists that Ishmael and Hagar be banished to the wilderness. God supports this demand, assuring Abraham that he will be father of two nations—one line through Isaac (to become the Israelites) and one through Ishmael (whom Arabs consider their ancestor).

According to the biblical narrative, God tested Abraham by demanding that he sacrifice his most precious possession, which was his beloved son Isaac. Thinkers have struggled to explain this demand, for human sacrifice was deemed to be very loathsome, but the point of the story seems to be the merit of Abraham's great obedience to God. When Abraham prepares to sacrifice Isaac, the Lord stops him, satisfied that "now I know that you fear God."[5] The Hebrew word *yirah*, usually translated as "fear" of God, also implies "awe of God's greatness," or what Rabbi Lawrence Kushner calls "trembling in the presence of ultimate holiness."[6]

Early monotheism   Scholars disagree on whether pure monotheism—the worship of a single God of the universe, exclusive of any other divine beings—was practiced by the early patriarchs. Many names for divinity are used in the early scriptures, and some researchers consider them names of separate gods. It is known that the religion of the Canaanites had some influence on that of the Israelites. The Canaanites were polytheistic, with highly developed mythology and ritual directed largely to agricultural fertility.

As is common in the growth of any new religion, elements of the older faiths of the area were incorporated into or adapted to the new one. However, the ultimate thrust of Judaism was the rejection of the gods of surrounding peoples. The Israelites came to see themselves as having been chosen by a single divine patron. In their patriarchal culture, this God was perceived as a ruler in a close relationship to the people, like a parent to children, or a sovereign to vassals. At first

Israel's God may have been perceived as a private tribal god, later known as the supreme and only deity of the universe.

Israel's birth in struggle   It is also unclear who the people of the biblical narratives were. Some scholars think the word "Hebrew" is derived from the generic term *habiru*, used for the low-class, landless people who lived as outlaws and were often hired as mercenaries. Others point to '*ibri* as the biblical word for Hebrew, meaning "children of Eber," an ethnic term. But because of frequent moving and intermarrying, the Israelites were actually of mixed ethnic stock, including Hebrew, Aramaean, and Canaanite. The word **Semite** is a modern linguistic term applied to Jews, Arabs, and others of eastern Mediterranean origin whose languages are classified as Semitic; it is often inaccurately used as an ethnic designation.

According to the genealogies set forth in the Pentateuch, the people who became known as Israelites were the offspring of Israel (first called Jacob), grandson of Abraham. Jacob received the new name after wrestling all night with a being who turned out to be an angel of God. "Israel" means "the one who struggled with God."

This story in which a human being struggles and finally is reborn at a higher level of spirituality has been taken as a metaphor for the spiritual evolution of the people of Israel. As a result of the struggle, Israel the patriarch receives not only a new name but also the promise that many nations will be born from him. The nation Israel—"the smallest of peoples"[7]—is perceived as the spiritual center for the world to grow toward God. This is its destiny, though Jews do not feel that it has yet been fulfilled.

Egypt: bondage and exodus   Jacob/Israel is said to have had one daughter and twelve sons by his two wives and their two maidservants. The twelve sons became the heads of the twelve tribes of Israel. The whole group left Canaan for Goshen in Egypt during a famine. Exodus, the second book of the Tanakh, opens about four centuries later with a statement that the descendants of Israel had become numerous. To keep them from becoming too powerful, the reigning pharaoh ordered that they be turned into slaves for massive construction projects. To further curb the population, the pharaoh ordered midwives to kill all boy babies born to the Israelite women.

One who escaped this fate was Moses, an Israelite of the tribe of Levi, who was raised in the palace by the pharaoh's own daughter. He is said to have fled the country after killing an Egyptian overseer who was beating an Israelite worker. While he lived in exile in Midian, the oppression of the Israelites in Egypt grew worse and worse.

According to the scriptural Book of Exodus, Moses was chosen by God to defy the pharaoh and lead the people out of bondage, out of Egypt. On a mountain, an angel of God appeared to him from within a bush blazing with fire but not consumed by it. God called to him out of the bush and yet cautioned, "Do not come closer.

God speaks to Moses from a burning bush, as depicted by Marc Chagall (1887–1985). (Stained-glass window, detail, Cathedral of St. Etienne, Metz, France.)

According to the legend of Exodus, God empowered Moses to hold back the waters of the Red Sea to let the children of Israel pass through, and then drown the pursuing Egyptians in the returning waters. (Hebrew MS 6 Haggadah.)

Judaism: Moses

Remove your sandals from your feet, for the place on which you stand is holy ground."[8] When God told Moses to go rescue "My people, the Israelites, from Egypt,"[9] Moses demurred, but God insisted:

> I will be with you ... Thus you shall say to the Israelites, "Ehyeh [I Am] sent me to you. ... The Lord, the God of your fathers, the God of Abraham, the God of Isaac, and the God of Jacob, has sent me to you."[10]

The word given in this biblical translation as "Lord" is considered too sacred to be pronounced. In the Hebrew scriptures it is rendered only in consonants as YHWH or YHVH; the pronunciation of the vowels is not known.

With his brother Aaron to act as spokesperson, Moses did indeed return to Egypt. Many chapters of Exodus recount miracles used to convince the pharaoh to let the people go into the wilderness to worship their God. These signs included a rod that turned into a serpent, plagues of locusts, flies, and frogs, animal diseases, a terrible storm, lasting darkness, and finally the killing by the Lord of all firstborn children and creatures. The Israelites were spared this fate, marking their doors with the blood of a slaughtered lamb so that the Lord would pass over them. (The holiday Passover commemorates this story.) At this, the pharaoh at last let the Israelites go. The redemption from bondage by the special protection of the Lord has served ever since as a central theme in Judaism.

According to the scriptural account, the Lord's presence led the Israelites, manifesting as a pillar of cloud by day and a pillar of fire by night. The armies of the deceitful pharaoh pursued them until the famous scene in which Moses stretched his staff toward the sea and God caused an east wind to blow all night, dividing the waters so that the Israelites could pass through safely on a dry seabed. As the Egyptians tried to follow, God told Moses again to hold out his arm over the sea, and the walls of water came crashing down on them, drowning every one.

Judaism:
Exodus

From the wilderness to Canaan   According to the Pentateuch, God told Moses that he would lead the people back to Canaan. First, however, it was necessary to travel to the holy Mount Sinai to re-establish the covenant between God and the people. The Lord is said to have descended to its summit in a terrifying show of lightning, thunder, fire, smoke, and trumpeting. God is said to have then given the people through Moses a set of rules for righteous living, later called the Torah. Among them were the Ten Commandments on stone tablets. God also gave a set of social norms, prescribed religious feasts, and detailed instructions for the construction of a portable tabernacle with a holy ark, the **Ark of the Covenant**, in which to keep the stone tablets on which God inscribed the commandments.

Judaism:
The Ten
Commandments

THE TEN COMMANDMENTS

"I am the Lord your God who brought you out of Egypt, out of the land of slavery. You shall have no other god to set against me.

You shall not make a carved image for yourself nor the likeness of anything in the heavens above, or on the earth below, or in the waters under the earth.

You shall not bow down to them or worship them; for I, the Lord your God, am a jealous god. I punish the children for the sins of the fathers to the third and fourth generations of those who hate me. But I keep faith with thousands, with those who love me and keep my commandments.

You shall not make wrong use of the name of the Lord your God; the Lord will not leave unpunished the man who misuses his name.

Remember to keep the sabbath day holy. You have six days to labor and do all your work. But the seventh day is a sabbath of the Lord your God; that day you shall not do any work, . . . for in six days the Lord made heaven and earth, the sea, and all that is in them, and on the seventh day he rested. Therefore the Lord blessed the sabbath day and declared it holy.

Honor your father and your mother, that you may live long in the land which the Lord your God is giving you.

You shall not commit murder.

You shall not commit adultery.

You shall not steal.

You shall not give false evidence against your neighbor.

You shall not covet your neighbor's house; you shall not covet your neighbor's wife, his slave, his slave-girl, his ox, his ass, or anything that belongs to him."

Exodus 20:2–17

God's presence abided with the Israelites, wandering or stationary, in the portable Ark of the Covenant, which was said to house the tablets of Moses. This third-century CE painting from the Dura Europos Synagogue shows the Ark leaving the land of the Philistines. They had captured the Ark but sent it back after being cursed by bubonic plague.

During the forty days that Moses was on the mountain receiving these instructions, the people who had just agreed to a holy covenant with God became disturbed and impatient. The biblical account says that under Aaron's reluctant supervision, they melted down their gold jewelry and cast it into the form of a golden calf, practicing what the authors of the biblical narratives considered idol-worship, which had been explicitly forbidden by God. Moses is said to have been so outraged by their idolatry that he smashed the stone tablets and destroyed the idol. He ordered the only people still siding with YHWH, the Levites, to slay 3,000 of those who had strayed.

After another forty-day meeting with God on the summit of Mount Sinai, Moses again returned with stone tablets on which God had inscribed the commandments. Moses' face was said to be so radiant from his encounter with God that he had to veil it. Aaron and his sons were invested as priests, the tabernacle was constructed as directed, and the people set off for the land of Canaan, with the Presence of the Lord filling the tabernacle.

Acceptance of the laws given to Moses at Mount Sinai brought a new dimension to the covenant between God and Israel. God had freed the Jews from slavery and extinction at the hands of the Egyptians, and now, the Jews freely agreed to accept the Torah. As Rabbi Irving Greenberg explains:

The teaching that guides the way of the Jews, the Torah, became the constitution of the ongoing relationship of God and the Jewish people. Israel promises to walk the way of the Lord. In faithfulness to that commitment, the people of Israel pledge to teach the way of justice and righteousness as best they can, to remain distinctive and unassimilated in the world and thus hold up the message for all people to see, to create a model community showing how the world can go about realizing the dream, and to work alongside others to move society toward the end goal of redemption. Thus, the Jewish covenantal mission will be a blessing for all families of the earth.

For its part, the Divine is pledged never to abandon Israel, to protect and safeguard the people, to help in the realization of the dream.[11]

Carrying the Ark representing this covenant, the Israelites had to wander for forty years through the desert before they could re-enter the promised land, fertile Canaan, which at that time belonged to other peoples. The long sojourn in the wilderness is a familiar metaphor in the spiritual search. Faith is continually tested by difficulties. But even in the wilderness, the Israelites' God did not forsake them. Every day they found their daily bread scattered on the ground, in the form of an unknown food, which they named manna.

A stone inscription, the Merneptah Stele, written for the Egyptian Pharaoh Merneptah, places the Hebrews as being in Canaan about 1207 BCE. Through what was described as the miraculous help of God, they fought many battles against the kings and tribes of Canaan. Archaeological evidence indicates that every Canaanite town was destroyed from one to four times between the thirteenth and eleventh centuries BCE, though the identity of the conquerors is not known. At Sinai, God had vowed to oust the inhabitants of the lands into which the Israelites advanced, warning them against adopting the local spiritual practices: "No, you must tear down their altars, smash their pillars, and cut down their sacred posts."[12] The editors of the scriptures clearly considered the Canaanite religion spiritually invalid and morally inferior to their own. But the Israelites' attention to their God was not absolute. According to the scriptures, whenever they turned away from YHWH, forgetting or worshipping other gods, surrounding peoples found them easy prey.

The first temple of Jerusalem   David, the second king of Israel, is remembered as Israel's greatest king. An obscure shepherd, David was chosen by the prophet Samuel to be anointed on the head with oil, for thus were future kings found and divinely acknowledged in those times. Composer and singer of psalms, David was summoned to the court of the first Israelite king, Saul, to play soothing music whenever an evil spirit seized the king. When Saul and his son were killed in battle, David was made king. By defeating or making allegiances with surrounding nations, David created the beginnings of a secure, prosperous Israelite empire. He made the captured city of Jerusalem its capital and brought the Ark of the Covenant there.

Judaism: Jerusalem

Under the reign of King Solomon (son of David), a great Temple was built in Jerusalem. It was to be a permanent home for the Ark of the Covenant, which was housed in the innermost sanctum, and a place for making the burned offerings of animals, grain, and oil to the divine. There already existed an ancient practice among pre-Israelite peoples of using high places for altars where sacrifices were made to the gods. After centuries of wandering worship, the Israelites now had a central, stationary place where God would be most present to them. God is

TEACHING STORY

From the Hebrew Bible—David and Goliath

David, the youngest son of Jesse of Bethlehem, was a bright-eyed, ruddy-cheeked shepherd, but from the time he was secretly anointed by the prophet Samuel as the future king of Israel, the power of the living God was with him.

One day Jesse asked David to carry some food to his three elder brothers who were doing battle with the Philistines in King Saul's Israelite army. When David arrived at the battlefield, he learned that every day, Goliath, the champion of the Philistines, came out of the Philistine encampment to challenge the Israelites to send one man to do battle with him. Goliath's challenge: If any Israelite could kill him in a fair one-to-one fight, the Philistines would surrender to the Israelites and become their slaves. If the Israelite lost, the Israelites would become slaves of the Philistines.

No Israelite had dared to take up this challenge, for Goliath was a giant of a man. He stood over nine feet tall, wore heavy bronze armor, and carried a massive spear. David alone was undismayed. When he presented himself to King Saul, Saul answered, according to the biblical account, "You cannot go and fight with this Philistine; you are only a lad, and he has been a fighting man all his life." David replied that he had often fought with lions or bears to defend his father's sheep. The giant Philistine would fare no better than they, for "he has defied the army of the living God. The Lord who saved me from the lion and the bear will save me from this Philistine."

"Go then," said Saul, "and the Lord will be with you." He put his own tunic on David, placed a bronze helmet on his head and gave him a coat of mail to wear; he then fastened his sword on David over his tunic. But David hesitated, because he had not tried them, and said to Saul, "I cannot go with these, because I have not tried them." So he took them off. Then he picked up his stick, chose five smooth stones from the brook and put them in a shepherd's bag which served as his pouch. He walked out to meet the Philistine with his sling in his hand.

The Philistine came on towards David, with his shield-bearer marching ahead; and he looked David up and down and had nothing but contempt for this handsome lad with his ruddy cheeks and bright eyes. He said to David, "Am I a dog that you come out against me with sticks?" And he swore at him in the name of his god. "Come on," he said, "and I will give your flesh to the birds and the beasts." David answered, "You have come against me with sword and spear and dagger, but I have come against you in the name of the Lord of Hosts, the God of the army of Israel which you have defied. The Lord will put you into my power this day; I will kill you and cut your head off and leave your carcass and the carcasses of the Philistines to the birds and the wild beasts; all the world shall know that there is a God in Israel. All those who are gathered here shall see that the Lord saves neither by sword nor spear; the battle is the Lord's, and he will put you all into our power."[13]

Indeed, according to the story, young David felled Goliath with a single stone from his slingshot, aimed at his forehead. Then David seized Goliath's sword and cut off his head, which he carried to Jerusalem as proof of the power of Israel's God.

said to have appeared to Solomon after the fourteen-day Temple dedication ceremony and pledged: "I consecrate this House which you have built and I set My name there forever. My eyes and My heart shall ever be there."[14]

The Temple became the central place for sacrifice in Judaism. But its builder, Solomon, also accumulated great personal wealth, at the expense of the people, and built altars to the gods of his wives, who came from other nations. This so angered the Lord, according to the scriptures, that he divided the kingdom after

Solomon's death. An internal revolt of the ten northern tribes established a new kingdom of Israel, which was independent of Jerusalem and the dynasty of David. The southern kingdom, continuing in its allegiance to the house of David and retaining Jerusalem as its capital, renamed itself Judah, after David's tribe.

Prophets such as Elijah warned the people against worshipping gods other than the Lord, and exhorted them to end their evil ways. Over the centuries, these prophets were men and women who had undergone transformational ordeals that made them instruments for the word of God. The "early prophets," such as Elijah, focused on the sin of idolatry; the "later prophets" warned that social injustice and moral corruption would be the ruin of the Jewish state.

By the reign of King Hoshea of Israel, the kingdom was so corrupt and idolatrous that, in the scriptural interpretation, God permitted the strong kingdom of Assyria to overtake what was left of the small country. To sustain the population needed for its empire-building and to keep Israel from rising again as a nation, Assyria carried off most of the Israelites to exile among the **Gentiles** (non-Jewish people). Most of the Israelites became dispersed within Assyria; these people who thenceforth lost a distinct ethnic identity are known as the "Ten Lost Tribes of Israel." This destruction of the northern kingdom took place in 722 BCE and is attested in Assyrian annals.

Judah maintained its independence, declining and continually warned of impending doom by its prophets. In graphic terms, the eighth-century BCE prophet Micah described the coming divine punishment of the chiefs of the House of Israel, "For you ought to know what is right, But you hate good and love evil" (Micah 3:7). Indeed, King Nebuchadnezzar of Babylonia (which by 605 BCE had taken over the Assyrian Empire) captured Jerusalem. In 586 BCE the great walls of Jerusalem were battered down and its buildings put to the torch by the Babylonians. The great Temple was emptied of its sacred treasures, the altar dismantled, and the building destroyed. Many Judaeans were taken to exile in Babylonia, where they were thenceforth known as "Jews," since they were from Judah. The psalmist describes the feeling of exile from Zion, God's chosen place:

> By the waters of Babylon there we sat, sat and wept, as we thought of Zion.
> There on the poplars we hung up our lyres,
> for our captors asked us there for songs, our tormenters, for amusement,
> "Sing us one of the songs of Zion."
> How can we sing a song of the Lord on alien soil?
>
> Psalms 137:1–4

The prophets interpreted these events as reasonable punishment by God for Judah's idolatry and misbehaviors. In exile among foreigners, the Jews nonetheless remained loyal to their God. They transformed the taunt of their captors into a spiritual challenge. This faithfulness in the midst of difficulties, without the security and support for community provided by territory, was an important development in the history of western religions. Remembering the terrestrial Zion, maintaining communities of Jews in the land of Israel, and turning in the direction of Zion three times a day in prayer helped preserve the Jews as a scattered people through what they experienced as their thousands of years of exile. It pushed the expectation of God's covenantal accountability into the future. Isaiah and a later anonymous prophet prophesied that God would soon usher in a new era of peace and justice among all peoples, from his holy Temple in Jerusalem.

> I never could forget you.
> See, I have engraved you
> On the palms of My hands . . .
>
> *Isaiah 49:15–16*

Return to Jerusalem

After fifty years of exile in Babylon, a small group of devoted Jews, probably fewer than 50,000, returned to their holy city. They were allowed to do so by the Persian king, Cyrus. But most of the Jews did not return to Jerusalem from Babylon, which was now their home. They were thenceforth said to be living in the **diaspora**, from the Greek word for "disperse." They always remembered Zion as a central part of their faith, but also learned to establish their creative lives in the diaspora.

King Cyrus authorized the rebuilding of the Temple in Jerusalem, which was completed in 515 BCE. The second Temple became the central symbol to a scattered Jewish nation. A new emphasis on Temple rites developed, with an hereditary priesthood tracing its ancestry to Aaron.

The priestly class, under the leadership of Ezra, a priest and a scribe, also undertook to revise, or redact, the stories of the people, editing the Pentateuch to reveal the hand of God. Some scholars think that it was these priestly editors who wrote the creation account in Genesis 1, glorifying the greatness and omnipotence of their God as creator of the universe.

The Torah was now established as the spiritual and secular foundation of the dispersed nation. In approximately 430 BCE, Ezra the scribe set the precedent of reading for hours from the Torah scrolls in a public square. These "five books of Moses" were accepted as a sacred covenant.

As the Jews lived under foreign rule—Persian, Greek, Parthian, and then Roman—Judaism became somewhat open to cross-cultural religious borrowings. Concepts of Satan, the hierarchy of angels, reward or punishment in an afterlife, and the final resurrection of the body on the Day of Judgment are thought by some scholars to have made their way into Jewish belief from the Zoroastrianism of the Persian Empire, for these beliefs were absent from earlier Judaic religion. However, they were not uniformly accepted. Greek lifestyle and thought were introduced into the Middle East by Alexander the Great in the fourth century BCE. The rationalistic, humanistic influences of Hellenism led many wealthy and intellectual Jews, including the priests in Jerusalem, to adopt a Hellenistic attitude of scepticism rather than unquestioning belief.

Tension between traditionalists and those embracing Greek ways came to a head during the reign of Antiochus IV Epiphanes, a Hellenistic ruler of Syria (175–164 BCE), the nation that then held political sovereignty over the land of Israel. Antiochus seems to have tried to achieve political unity by forcing a single Hellenistic culture on all his subjects, abolishing the Torah as the Jewish constitution, burning copies of the Torah, killing families who circumcised their sons, building an altar to Zeus in the Temple in Jerusalem, and sacrificing a hog on it (in defiance of the Mosaic law against eating or touching dead pigs as unclean). The Maccabean rebellion, a revolt led by the Hasmon family of priests, called in Hebrew the Maccabees ("Hammers"), won a degree of independence for Judaea in 164 BCE. The successful rebellion established a new and independent kingdom, once again called Israel, once again centered around Jerusalem, and ruled by the Hasmonean family. This kingdom lasted only until its conquest by the Roman general Pompey in 63 BCE, and was the last independent Jewish nation until the twentieth century.

Under the Hasmonean kings, three sects of Jews formed in Judaea. One was the **Sadducees**, priests and wealthy businesspeople, conservatives intent on preserving the letter of the law. The **Pharisees** were more liberal citizens from all classes who sought to study the applications of Torah to everyday life. A third group was uncompromising in their piety and their disgust with what they considered a corrupted priesthood. Some of them retreated to a fortified compound at Qumran, near the Dead Sea, where they joined or formed the **Essenes**. Their leader was the "Teacher of Righteousness," a priest, reformer, and mystic whose name was not uttered. The library of this Essene community, now known as the Dead Sea Scrolls, was discovered near Qumran at the northwest end of the Dead Sea in 1947. From these 2,000-year-old texts, we now know that the Essenes emphasized discipline, communal living, obedience, study, and spiritual preparation for the Day of Judgment they anticipated, the New Age when the "sons of light" would be victorious over the "sons of darkness."

Eventually the conflicts among the Hasmoneans erupted into civil war. The Roman general Pompey was called in from Syria in 63 BCE to choose between contenders to the Hasmonean throne, but he took over the country instead. There followed four centuries of oppressive Roman rule of Judaea.

Under Roman rule, belief grew among Jews about a messianic age in which the people would at last be rescued from their sufferings and Jews would return to their homeland. This belief had been voiced by earlier prophets who, combining the particular and universal orientations of Judaism, had prophesied a coming "End of Days" in which disaster would be followed by universal redemption, in which all nations, going up to the "mountain of the Lord, to the house of the God of Jacob" (Micah 4: 2), would recognize the one God. In the books of both Isaiah and Micah appears a famous passage about the coming reign of world peace:

Instruction shall come forth from Zion,
The word of the Lord from Jerusalem.
Thus He will judge among the many peoples,
And arbitrate for the multitude of nations,
However distant;
And they shall beat their swords into plowshares
And their spears into pruning hooks.
Nation shall not take up
Sword against nation;
They shall never again know war;
But every man shall sit
Under his grapevine or fig tree
With no one to disturb him.

Micah 4:2–4

The Essenes seem to have lived communally and ascetically, awaiting the final judgment in settlements such as this one excavated at Qumran, where ancient biblical scrolls were found hidden in caves.

Under oppressive Seleucid Greek rule of Palestine, **apocalyptic** literature became very popular. Such literature—which again became popular in recent western history, at the advent of the year 2000—sees the world in stark terms of good and evil, predicts the coming of God's victory over evil, asserts that God will then reward good people and punish evil people, and thus urges people to live righteous lives now in preparation for that time. Among some Jews, the belief grew that there would be a person, a **Messiah**, who would come to bring evil times to an end and establish the reign of peace. In the biblical book of Daniel, probably written while Jews were being persecuted by the Seleucid emperor Antiochus IV (who ruled from 175 until 164 BCE), the chief character Daniel describes a symbolic vision of "one like a human being" who would come on heavenly clouds, and on him the white-haired, fiery-throned "Ancient of Days" would confer "everlasting dominion" over all people, a kingship "that shall not be destroyed."[15] By the first century CE, expectations had developed that through this Messiah, God would gather the chosen people and not only free them from oppression but also reinstate Jewish political sovereignty in the land of Israel. Then all nations would recognize that Israel's God is the God of all the world. The messianic end of the age, or end of the world, would be heralded by a period of great oppression and wickedness. Many felt that this time was surely at hand. There were some who felt that Jesus was the long-awaited Messiah.

Spurred by anti-Roman militias called **Zealots**, the Jews rose up in armed rebellion against Rome in 66 CE. The rebellion was suppressed, and after heroic resistance, the Jewish defenders were slaughtered in the holy walled city of

Jerusalem in 70 CE. The Roman legions destroyed the Jewish Temple in Jerusalem, leaving only a course of foundation stones still standing. This Temple has never been rebuilt; the foundation stones, called the Western Wall, have been a place of Jewish pilgrimage and prayer for twenty centuries. The Essene movement was apparently annihilated in this uprising.

A second disastrous revolt followed in 132–135 CE. Ultimately, Jerusalem was reduced to ruins, along with all Judaean towns. Those remaining Jews who had not been executed were forbidden to read the Torah, observe the Sabbath, or circumcise their sons. None was allowed to enter Jerusalem when it was rebuilt as the Roman city Aelia Capitolina, except on the anniversary of the destruction of the Temple, when they could pay to lean against all that remained of it—the Western Wall—and lament the loss of their sacred home. Judaea was renamed Palestine after the ancient Philistines. Judaism no longer had a physical heart or a geographic center.

Rabbinic Judaism

Judaism could have died then, as its people scattered throughout the Mediterranean countries and western Asia. One of the groups who survived the destruction of Judaea were the **rabbis**, inheritors of the Pharisee tradition. They are the founders of rabbinic Judaism, which has defined the major forms of Jewish practice over the last two thousand years. Another was the messianic movement that had formed up around Jesus of Nazareth, later known as Christianity. Between them they have kept the teachings of the Tanakh vibrantly alive. Both Christianity and rabbinic Judaism used the Hebrew Bible as a foundation document, but from it they have developed in their own ways.

The rabbis were teachers, religious decision-makers, and creators of liturgical prayer. No longer were there priests or Temple for offering sacrifices. The substitute for animal sacrifice was liturgical prayer and ethical behavior. Without the Jerusalem Temple, the community itself gained new importance. The people met in **synagogues**, which simply means "meeting places," to read the Torah and to worship communally, praying simply and directly to God. Synagogue services did not involve animal sacrifices, but rather prayer, song, and readings from the Torah. A *minyan*—a quorum of ten adult males—had to be present for community worship.

Everyone was taught the basics of the Torah as a matter of course, but, from the age of five or six, many men also occupied themselves with deep study of the scriptures. Women were excluded or exempted from formal Torah study. Women's family responsibilities at home were considered primary for them; else-

A rabbi reading the Talmud.

where they were to be subordinate to men. Literacy was highly valued for men, and this characteristic persisted through the centuries even in the midst of largely illiterate societies. It is said that in the afterlife one can see the Jewish sages still bent over their books studying. This is Paradise.

The revealed scriptures were closed; what remained was to interpret them as indications of God's word and will in history. This process continues to the present, giving Judaism a continually evolving quality in tandem with unalterable roots in the ancient books of Moses. Centering the religion in books and teachings rather than in a geographical location or a politically vulnerable priesthood has enabled the dispersed community to retain a sense of unity across time and space, as well as a common heritage of law, language, and practice.

The rabbis set themselves the task of thoroughly interpreting the Hebrew scriptures. Their process of study, called **Midrash**, yielded two types of interpretation: legal decisions, called *halakhah* ("proper conduct"), and non-legal teachings, called *haggadah* (folklore, sociological and historical knowledge, theological arguments, ritual traditions, sermons, and mystical teachings).

In addition to delving into the meanings of the written Torah, the rabbis undertook to apply the biblical teachings to their contemporary lives, in very different cultural circumstances from those of the ancients, and to interpret scripture in ways acceptable to contemporary values. The model for this delicate task of living interpretation had been set by Hillel the Elder, who taught from about 30 BCE to 10 CE, probably overlapping with the life of Jesus. He was known as a humble and pious scholar, who stressed loving relationships, good deeds, and charity toward the less-advantaged. He also established a valuable set of rules for flexible interpretation of Torah.

What is hateful to you, do not do to your neighbor:
that is the entire Torah;
the rest is commentary;
go and learn it.

Hillel the Elder[16]

This process of Midrash yielded a vast body of legal and spiritual literature, known in Jewish tradition as the oral Torah. According to rabbinical tradition, God gave Moses two versions of the Torah at Sinai: the written Torah, which appears in the five books of Moses, and the oral Torah, a larger set of teachings, which was memorized and passed down through the generations all the way to the early rabbis. After the fixing of the Jewish canon—the scriptures admitted to the Tanakh in about 90 CE—the rabbinical schools set out to systematize all the commentaries and the oral tradition, which was continually evolving on the basis of expanded and updated understandings of the original oral Torah. In about 200 CE, Judah the Prince completed a terse edition of legal teachings of the oral Torah, which was thenceforth known as the **Mishnah**.

The Mishnah's method of deriving legal principles for social order is based on logical analysis of how things are and why they are so. It systematically sets up hierarchical classifications, such as levels of women's status and domestic responsibilities according to the number of slave girls they bring when married. If, for instance, she brings one slave girl, the wife does not have to grind flour, bake bread, or do laundry, but she must prepare the meals, feed her child, make the bed, and work in wool. This detailing of the woman's obligations to the household economy simultaneously makes clear her status within the family: She enjoys rights and protection from the capricious rule of her husband and benefits from the expectations that she be creative and a moral beacon.

Despite the subordination of women to men in traditional Jewish legal codes, there are also directives in the Mishnah regarding men's responsibility to women and, in general, the responsibility of rulers and privileged members of society to insure legal justice for people of all classes and to provide for the material well-being of the lower classes, widows, orphans, and resident aliens. Accordingly, Jews have often been prominent in movements for social justice.

The ultimate point in the hierarchy is God, but God's role is often implicit rather than explicit in the Mishnah. Professor Jacob Neusner explains:

> *The cases are particular, the principles universal. . . . God in the form, God in the order, God in the structure, God in the heights, God at the head of the great chain of hierarchical being. True, God is premise, scarcely mentioned. But it is because God's name does not have to be mentioned when the whole of the order of being says that name, and only that name, and always that name, the name unspoken because it is always in the echo, the silent, thin voice, the numinous in all phenomena.[17]*

The Mishnah became the basic study text for rabbinic academies in Judaea and Babylonia, and after several centuries, the Mishnah and the rabbis' commentaries on it were organized into the **Talmud**. This is a vast compendium of law, Midrash, and argument. It does not have a beginning, middle, and end in any traditional sense. It records disagreements among rabbis and sometimes leaves them standing. Drawing on "prooftexts" from the Torah, the rabbis came to different and often inventive conclusions.

There are actually two authorized Talmuds. The Jerusalem Talmud is the earlier one, written down about 400 CE. It emphasizes continual study of the Torah as a spiritual practice, a primary way of coming to know the will and ways of God. Studying the Torah is said to increase one's holiness and spiritual power. In the Jerusalem Talmud it is written, for instance, that a river parted at the word of a rabbi who was intent on studying the Torah:

> *Once Rabbi Phinehas was going to the house of study, and the river Ginai which he had to pass was so swollen that he could not cross it. He said, "O river, why do you prevent me from getting to the house of study?" Then it divided its waters, and he passed over. And his disciples said, "Can we too pass over?" He said, "He who knows that he has never insulted an Israelite can pass over unharmed."[18]*

The Babylonian Talmud grew out of the other major center of rabbinical study: Babylonia. Completed about 500 CE, it is more developed as an encyclopedia of the Torah, for Jewish life in Babylonia was less precarious. The Babylonian Talmud was also better preserved than the Jerusalem Talmud, and it has thus become the dominant version in Jewish theology and law. It, too, describes study of the Torah as essential to Israel's destiny as a nation upholding God's laws.

A father teaches his son the Talmud and Bible.

Midrash is still open-ended, for significant commentaries and commentaries on commentaries have continued to arise over the centuries. No single voice has dominated this continual study of the Torah and its interpretations. Rabbis have often disagreed in their interpretations, and these disagreements, sometimes between rabbis from different centuries, are presented together. This continual interweaving of historical commentaries, as if all Jewry were present at a single marathon Torah-study event, has been a significant unifying factor for the far-flung, often persecuted Jewish population of the world.

In the process of **exegesis**, the rabbis have actually introduced new ideas into Judaism, while claiming that they were merely revealing what already existed in the scriptures. Notions of the soul are not found in the Tanakh, but they do appear in the Talmud and Midrash. The ways in which God is referred to and perceived also change. In the early biblical narratives, the Lord appears to the patriarchs and Moses in dramatic forms, such as the burning bush and the smoking mountain. Later, the prophets are visited by angelic messengers, and they sometimes hear a divine inner voice speaking to them. In the rabbinical tradition, God is presented in even more transcendent, less anthropomorphic ways. God's presence in the world, in relationship to the people, is called the **Shekhinah**, a feminine noun that often represents the nurturing aspect of God.

According to Midrash, the Shekhinah came to the earth at creation, but as a result of human wickedness she withdrew to the heavens, to be brought down by human acts of faithfulness, charity, and loving-kindness. God spoke to Moses from a burning thorn-bush, rather than some more lofty object, to demonstrate that there is no place where the Shekhinah cannot dwell. Sometimes the loving protection of the Shekhinah is depicted as a radiant, winged presence.

At the same time that rabbinical Judaism was further developing beliefs expressed in earlier modes of Judaism, so was Christianity. Contemporary scholars think that Jesus, a Jew who can be seen within the context of the movements of his time, was influenced by the Essenes and may even have lived with them for a while, but that he was more closely related to the Pharisees and the school of Hillel. That is, he emphasized holiness in worldly life and, like the Jewish prophets, observance of the spirit and the full and often complex ethical implications of the law, not merely fulfilment of the letter of the Law. The early apostles of Jesus emphasized rabbinic traditions that with the arrival of the Messiah and the age of messianic redemption, observance of the ritual laws would be abrogated. The apostle Paul, who became the major missionary of the Christian sect, preached to both Jews and Gentiles in the diaspora that with the advent of Jesus, God would accept them without their practicing circumcision (which Greeks and Romans considered barbaric) and Mosaic laws governing many aspects of daily life and hygiene. Belief or disbelief in Jesus and the launching of the messianic age now had very practical implications as to whether they observed Jewish law in their daily lives. Both monotheistic and from common stock, Judaism and Christianity grew farther and farther apart.

The Throne of the Shekhinah, as depicted by contemporary artist Hannah Omer and cyber-architect Yitzhak Hayut-Man.

Judaism in the Middle Ages

In the early centuries of the Common Era, the Jewish population of the land of Israel declined though it never disappeared nor did the land of Israel ever lose its spiritual centrality in Jewish consciousness. Some Jews settled in other regions of the Roman Empire, and larger numbers established themselves beyond the boundaries of Rome among the Zoroastrian Persians in Mesopotamia. The city of Babylon, which already had a sizable Jewish population dating back to the biblical exile, became the major center of Jewish intellectual activity, a position it would hold well into the tenth century. The authoritative Babylonian Talmud received its final editing in the middle of the sixth century CE.

Even when the Talmud was complete, the rabbinic enterprise continued. The two great Babylonian rabbinic academies were often appealed to with difficult questions from far-flung Jewish communities. Their answers, which were considered binding on all Jews, and the questions themselves, became a new and enduring form of legal writing, *Responsa* literature, which continues to the present.

When Baghdad became the capital city of the great Abassid Empire in the eighth century, Jewish life concentrated around that city as well. Jews were treated relatively well under Islamic rule. Like Christians, they were recognized as a "People of the Book," and were allowed to maintain their religious traditions and run their communities autonomously as long as they paid a substantial head tax in acknowledgment of their subordinate status. In Baghdad, as throughout the Islamic Middle East, many Jews were prosperous merchants, professionals, and craftsmen. In the early Middle Ages, in fact, Jews tended to dominate international trade between Muslim and Christian realms because of their facility with languages and their ability to find supportive co-religionists in virtually any community.

Life under Islamic rule was also intellectually exciting for the Jewish community, which had rapidly adopted Arabic as its spoken language. During its early centuries, Islam was far advanced beyond Christian Europe in its explorations of science, medicine, philosophy, poetry, and the fine arts. Jews living in Muslim countries benefited from an atmosphere of cultural creativity and tolerance, and themselves developed Jewish religious philosophy and Hebrew secular poetry. Many Jews were well-known physicians. Muslim Spain, in particular, where some Jews rose to high political position in Muslim courts, is renowned for its outstanding Hebrew poets and major philosophical and scientific Jewish writers.

From time to time, however, Jews were threatened by intolerant Muslim rulers and were forced to flee to other territories. The great scholar and physician Maimonides (1135–1204) was forced to leave his ancestral home of Cordoba, Spain, in the mid-twelfth century; he and his family eventually settled in Egypt. Considered one of the greatest of all Jewish intellectuals, Maimonides is particularly famous for his synthesis between reason and faith. In writings such as *The Guide of the Perplexed* he spoke on behalf of the rationality that had characterized Judaism since the dawning of the rabbinic age:

> *What is man's singular function here on earth? It is, simply, to contemplate abstract intellectual matters and to discover truth ... And the highest intellectual contemplation that man can develop is the knowledge of God and his unity.*[19]

Jews who lived in Christian countries were less exposed to the vibrant intellectual energy of the Islamic world between the seventh and twelfth centuries. Christian Europe in those centuries was primarily a feudal agricultural society in which literacy mainly belonged to the Church. Jews, who were primarily merchants, were among the few town dwellers, and generally lived under charters of protection from the ruler of the area. In France and Germany, Jewish intellectual life flourished, but Christians assumed the financial functions. Jews became expendable, and throughout the later Middle Ages there was a steady pattern of expulsions of Jews from countries in which they had long lived.

Anti-semitism, or prejudice against Jews, had long been simmering among Christians. While Jews and Christians, like all humans, suffered from hatred and unwarranted attacks and often directed the vitriol against each other, Jews were hated all the more because Jesus was a Jew but many of his own people never accepted Christian claims that he was the Messiah. Jews were also blamed for his murder and for preventing his messianic successes ever after by refusing to believe in him.

Beginning in 1095, Jews became victims of mobs of Christian crusaders traveling through Europe with the intention to defend the Holy Land. They had been provoked by rumors that Christians were being harmed there by Muslims, with Jews as their accomplices. Believing in the holiness of their mission, crusaders and orders of knights also attacked Jews as non-conformists who did not agree with the doctrines of the Christian Church. They massacred so many Jews that many formerly prosperous Jewish communities in Germany were wiped out.

In the twelfth century, superstitious rumors were spread in England that Jews were engaged in ritual murders of Christians, and many were subsequently slaughtered. Then, in thirteenth-century Germany, Jews were accused of stealing the consecrated bread used by Christians for communion with Jesus, and then torturing it. Such strange rumors were never verified, but they spread rapidly, and with them, killings of Jews. They were suspected of knowing the truth about Jesus but hiding it, preferring to work with the forces of darkness to continue to harm Jesus and those who believed in him. In the fourteenth century, Jews were blamed for the Plague and thus were either killed or forced out of many countries. In 1492, tens of thousands of Jews were forced to leave Spain, where they had lived for over a thousand years. Some Jews fled to safety in Portugal or Italy, or the Muslim realms of North Africa and the Ottoman Empire of Turkey. Others chose to convert to Christianity rather than to leave their homeland even though staying in Spain as *conversos* (converted Jews) would expose them to the dreaded Inquisitions, which had been established in Spain in 1483. The Inquisition represented the Roman Catholic Church, and its mission was to discover perceived heretics within the Christian community. It had no power over Jews, but it did have jurisdiction over the large numbers of Jews who had converted to Christianity, whether voluntarily or by force, and who might be practicing their former religion in secret. The Inquisition, which had the power to torture the accused and to execute the convicted, continued to function in Spain and in Spanish territories well into the eighteenth century.

There was further deterioration of Jewish life in western Europe in the sixteenth and seventeenth centuries. After 1555, those Jews who remained in some cities of Italy and Germany were forced to live in **ghettos**, special Jewish-only

According to the Spanish inquisitors, the murder of hundreds of thousands of people—many of them marranos, *or secret Jews—was an* auto da fe, *an "act of faith" to rid the church of heretics.*

quarters, which were often walled in and locked at night and during Christian holy days, to limit mixing between Christians and Jews.

During the later Middle Ages, Poland had become a haven for the expelled Jews of western Europe. Jews were welcomed by Poland's feudal leaders who needed a middle class for the economic development of their agricultural country. Jews were allowed freedom of residence and occupation in Poland, and they rapidly grew in numbers, finding in their new home an enclave of peace and prosperity. By the sixteenth and early seventeenth centuries eastern Europe had become the major European center of Jewish life and scholarship. Jews lived an intensely religious life in villages and towns that were almost completely Jewish, speaking Yiddish, a distinctive Jewish language that was based on the medieval German they had spoken in western Europe. In 1648, the situation changed drastically with the revolt against Polish rule by the Cossack peasants of the Ukraine. Associating Jewry with their Roman Catholic Polish oppressors and being violently anti-semitic as well, Greek Orthodox people led terrible massacres against the Jews, which were followed by even more killing as Poland collapsed.

In this time of despair in both eastern and western Europe, Jews were heavily taxed and ill-treated. Their longing for deliverance from danger, poverty, and oppression fueled the old messianic dream. Among the "pseudo-Messiahs" who rose to the occasion, the most famous was Shabbatai Tzevi (1626–1676) of Smyrna, a Turkish port. A rather unstable personality, he became convinced that it was his calling to be the Messiah. A young man named Nathan, who became his enthusiastic prophet, sent letters to Jews throughout Europe, Asia, and Africa announcing that the Messiah had at last appeared in his master. Many believed him and prepared for their return to the Holy Land. However, when Tzevi entered the Ottoman Empire, he was arrested and put in jail. Given the choice of converting to Islam or being executed, he chose conversion and was given a government position. The shock to his supporters was terrible.

Enlightenment

In the late eighteenth and nineteenth centuries, the great majority of Jews lived in eastern European countries such as Poland and Russia, which were little affected by the eighteenth-century European movement called the Enlightenment. The Enlightenment, however, provided new opportunities and better conditions for the Jews in western Europe. It played down tradition and authority in favor of tolerance, reason, and material progress. In such a rational atmosphere, restrictions on Jews began to decrease. The French Revolution (1789–1792) brought equality for the masses, including Jews living in France, and in the course of the nineteenth century this trend slowly spread to other European nations. Ghettos were torn down, and some Jews even ascended to positions of prominence in western European society. The Rothschild family, for instance, became international financiers, benefactors, and patrons of the arts. Moses Mendelssohn (1729–1786), a German Jew, founded a movement known as the Jewish Enlightenment, whose goal was to integrate Jews more fully into European culture. Mendelssohn urged his fellow Jews to learn German and to dress and comport themselves as non-Jews, at the same time as he urged the governments of his time to separate Church and State, and to tolerate differences in beliefs among their citizens.

In the midst of such modernizing influences, some Jews began to revise Jewish worship to remove what were seen as antiquated and "oriental" practices. Hymns and sermons in the vernacular language instead of Hebrew began to replace the traditional liturgy, while references to a return to the land of Israel and the rebuilding of the Temple were removed from the service. Leaders of this new Reform Judaism saw their religion as continually evolving and harmonizing with the times; they believed that Jews could best accomplish "the mission of Israel" as loyal citizens of the countries in which they lived. Anti-semitism was still insidiously present throughout western and eastern Europe, however.

Kabbalah and Hasidism

Mystical yearning has always been a part of Jewish tradition. The fervent experience of and love for God is an undercurrent in several writings of the biblical prophets, and is incorporated into the Talmud as well. Some mystical writings are found outside the biblical canon, in the extra-biblical collections of texts known as the Apocrypha and the Pseudepigrapha. The apocryphal Book of Enoch describes the ascent to God as a journey through seven heavenly spheres to an audience with the King of the celestial court. The core mystical encounter with indescribable sanctity is based on the vision of the prophet Isaiah (Isaiah 6), and includes the chant of the heavenly court, "*Kadosh, Kadosh, Kadosh*" ("Holy, Holy, Holy"), which is included in all Jewish communal prayer.

In the Middle Ages, Jewish mystical traditions, known as **Kabbalah**, began to be put into writing. The most important of these books is the Zohar ("Way of Splendor"). The Zohar is a massive and complex offering of stories, explanations of the esoteric levels of the Torah, and descriptions of visionary practice and

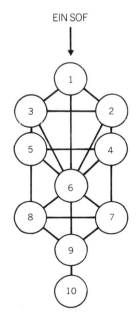

A central Kabbalistic image is the Tree of God, a representation of the emanation of the qualities of the infinite Ein Sof into revealed aspects, the sephiroth. *The topmost represents Will; the tenth represents the Shekhinah—the Presence of God.*

EIN SOF

In a Hasidic school, preservation of traditional ways is maintained in the teacher's dark dress, beard, and side curls.

experiences. It depicts the world we perceive with our senses as but a lower reflection of a splendid higher world. During the sixteenth century Kabbalah's most influential leader was Isaac Luria (1534–1572). He explained creation as the beaming of the divine light into ten special vessels, some of which were shattered by the impact because they contained lower forces that could not bear the intensity of the light. The breaking of the vessels spewed forth particles of evil as well as fragments of light into the world. Humans have a great responsibility to help end chaos and evil in the world by regathering the "sparks of holiness" in the unclean realms to repair the holy vessels. This concept of *tikkun olam* (repairing the world) has continued to be very important in Jewish thought, emphasizing the relationship between God and humans as a covenantal one with reciprocal responsibilities in which both are working together to uplift the world, and where every human act, both good and bad, has ultimate significance. To this end, Luria asked his followers to follow strict ascetic purification practices, prayer, and observance of the commandments of the Torah, and to chant sacred formulas. Once these practices release the Light, it will no longer be trapped in exile, the long-awaited Messiah or messianic period will appear, and chaos and evil will be replaced by redemption of the world.

Lurianic Kabbalism resurfaced in a very different form in the eighteenth century as **Hasidism**, the path of ecstatic piety. It developed in Ukraine and Poland, where Jews were subject to legal limitations, poverty-stricken, and fearful for their lives from riots and murders. The rabbis had little to offer them, retreating into academic debates about legal aspects of the Torah.

Into this grim setting came the Baal Shem Tov (1700–1760), a beloved healer and Hasidic teacher, who offered a joyful version of Jewish holiness. He believed that Torah study and obedience to the letter of the law were not superior to deep-felt, pure-hearted prayer; everyone is capable of the highest enlightenment. He asserted that the divine could be found everywhere, in the present, thereby de-emphasizing the perennial waiting for a future Messiah. "Leave sorrow and sadness," he cried; "man must live in joy and contentment, always rejoicing in his lot."[20] Followers of the Baal Shem Tov worshipped through joyous songs and ecstatic, swaying prayer, and found God in the midst of the ghetto.

God can be found everywhere, emphasized the Baal Shem Tov, but can be seen only by those who are not taken in by surface appearances and who really want to find him. God is here in the midst of even the most mundane everyday activities; if carried out in remembrance of God, even eating, drinking, and working become holy acts. It is through the ups and downs of everyday life that the soul advances toward God. The highest goal is *devekut*, "cleaving" to God, free of the egotism and vanity that separate humans from the Holy One.

> As the hand held before the eye conceals the greatest mountain, so the little earthly life hides from the glance the enormous lights and mysteries of which the world is full, and he who can draw it away from before his eyes, as one draws away a hand, beholds the great shining of the inner worlds.
>
> *Attributed to Reb Nachman of Bratzlav*

Soon an estimated half of all eastern European Jews were followers of the Hasidic path. Spread of the teachings is credited to Dov Ber, who emphasized the importance of the *tzaddik*, or enlightened saint and teacher, called *rebbe* (or Reb) when ordained as a Hasidic spiritual guide. Dov Ber urged Hasidim to take spiritual shelter with a *tzaddik*, whose prayers and wisdom would be more powerful than their own because of the *tzaddik*'s personal relationship with God. This idea stirred enormous opposition from non-Hasidic leaders, who believed that each Jew should be his or her own *tzaddik*. While the position of *tzaddik* became hereditary and was sometimes subject to exploitation by less-than-holy lineage carriers, such charismatic leadership remains a central element and perhaps one of the enduring attractions of modern Hasidism. The religious fervor associated with Hasidism clearly continues as an influence within Judaism, and many of the Hasidic movements themselves still thrive, despite the devastation of the Holocaust and the challenges of modernity.

American Judaism

Substantial Jewish immigration to the United States began in the mid-nineteenth century. By 1880, there were 250,000 Jews in the United States, mostly of German origin, and middle class in occupations and attitudes.

Between 1881 and the early 1920s, Jewish immigration to the United States totalled two million, mainly Jews from eastern Europe. This exodus was prompted by virulent anti-semitism in Czarist Russia and endemic Jewish poverty in both Russia and eastern provinces of Austria–Hungary. If these new immigrants were religious, they tended to be extremely Orthodox; if they were political, their politics were far to the left; socially, they tended to be craftsmen and laborers.

Today, the United States, with approximately six million Jews, has the largest Jewish population in the world. It continues to be a highly diverse population, consisting of both Jews who are religiously affiliated and those who are not.

The Holocaust

For many Jews the defining event of the twentieth century was the **Holocaust**, the murder of almost six million European Jews by the Nazi leadership of Germany during World War II. These Jews constituted over a third of the Jewish people in the world and half of all Jews in Europe. The Holocaust is the overwhelmingly tragic event of Jewish history, and an indelible marker for all time of the depths of twentieth-century inhumanity and evil.

Anti-semitism was part of Greco–Roman culture and had been present in Europe since the Roman Empire first adopted Christianity as its state religion in the fourth century CE. New and virulent strains of this disease appeared in western Europe at the end of the nineteenth century. Racist theories spread that those of "pure" Nordic blood were genetically ideal, while Jews were a dangerous "mongrel" race.

Reactionary anti-Jewish feelings also resurfaced late in the nineteenth century in Russia and in eastern Europe, where Jews formed a sizable minority of the population and where they were accumulating wealth and establishing a presence in higher educational circles. Jews were increasingly associated with left-wing movements pushing for social change, even though many Jewish socialists were non-observant Jews. Leon Trotsky, for example, was religiously indifferent but of Jewish ancestry. His leadership in the violent Bolshevik Revolution

A young Jewish man is forced to wear a Star of David armband for identification in Nazi Germany. The Star of David had begun to be widely used by Jews themselves as a symbol of Judaism in the 19th century.

and the Red Army brought terrible reprisals, called **pogroms**, against Jewish communities by the White Russians in the civil war. In a thousand separate incidents, up to 70,000 Jews were killed by unrestrained rioting mobs. Even after the Bolshevik Revolution, continuing social chaos in Russia led to massacres of an estimated quarter of a million Jews.

In the aftermath of Germany's defeat in World War I and the desperate economic conditions that followed, Adolf Hitler's Nazi Party bolstered its popular support by blaming the Jews for all of Germany's problems. Germany, the Nazis claimed, could not regain its health until all Jews were stripped of their positions in German life or driven out of the country. Demands to eliminate the Jews for the sake of "racial hygiene" were openly circulated. Seeing the writing on the wall, many Jews, including eminent professionals, managed to emigrate, leaving their homes, their livelihoods, and most of their possessions behind. Others stayed, hoping that the terrifying signs would be short-lived.

With Hitler's rise to power, acts of violence against Jews in Germany were instigated by his Nazi thugs. From the moment that he became Chancellor in 1933, laws were passed that separated Jews from the rest of the population and deprived them of their legal and economic rights. Most German Jews, full participants in German society and culture, could hardly be identified as different from their non-Jewish neighbors. The Nüremberg Laws of 1935 provided pseudo-biological definitions of who is a Jew by counting Jewish grandparents.

When Hitler annexed Austria in 1938, Austrian Jews fell under the same laws. Jewish businesses were forcibly taken over by "Aryans." Polish Jews living in Germany were rounded up into trucks and conveyed to the Polish border, where Polish officials refused to take them in.

By 1939, 300,000 of Germany's 500,000 Jews, together with another 150,000 from Austria, had fled. Few countries, however, would allow them to enter. Germany invaded Poland and then in rapid succession Denmark, Norway, Belgium, Holland, and France, thereby placing several million more Jews under Nazi control.

World War II began with the German invasion of Poland in 1939. Immediately, systematic oppression began, with orders to all Polish Jews to move into the towns, where walled ghettos were created to confine them. Jews were made to wear a yellow or white badge with the Star of David on it to reveal their stigmatized status, and since all other jobs were taken away from them, they could do only menial labor.

Along the Russian front, special "Action Groups" were assigned to slaughter Jews, gypsies, and commissars (heads of government departments) as the German troops advanced, and to incite the local militia to do the same. One cannot comprehend the numbers of men, women, and children killed in these mass murders—34,000 at Babi Yar, 26,000 at Odessa, 32,000 at Vilna—probably totalling hundreds of thousands.

By 1942, large-scale death camps had been set up by the Nazis to facilitate the "Final Solution"—the total extermination of all Jews in Europe, a population the Nazis estimated at 11 million. From the ghettos Jews were transported by cattle cars (in which many suffocated to death) from all over Europe to concentration camps. There they were starved, worked to death as slaves, tortured, "experimented" on, and/or shipped to extermination camps. Industrial-scale gas chambers were found to be the most efficient means of killing.

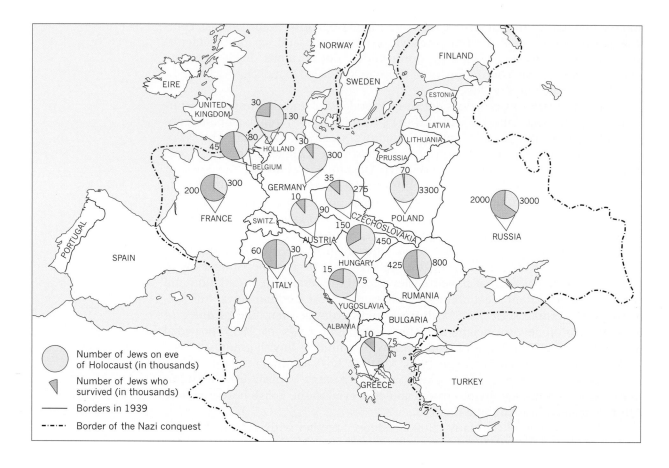

Hitler's Final Solution was to herd Jews into concentration camps throughout Nazi-occupied Europe and then ship the survivors east into extermination camps in Poland. The pie charts show the number of Jews in each country who were left after the Holocaust, relative to their previous populations.

Hitler was the architect and the motivating force behind the genocide, but he was not the only one responsible. There were tremendous numbers of people throughout western and eastern Europe whose active or passive participation was needed to carry out the killings.

The governments of some countries, to a greater or lesser extent, tried to protect their Jews; also some individuals, at great personal risk, in every part of Europe, hid Jews or tried to help them escape. For example, Chiune Sugihara, a Japanese diplomat stationed in Lithuania, and then Berlin and Prague, managed to issue Japanese transit visas to some 10,000 Jews, ignoring all risks to himself in order to help them quickly escape from danger. But there was little outcry against Hitler's genocidal actions from the outside world. In hindsight, many historians have concluded that Hitler's hideous policy could have been slowed by determined resistance from free Allied countries.

No modern Jewish thinker can ignore the challenge that the Holocaust poses to traditional Jewish beliefs of an omnipotent and caring God. Elie Wiesel (b. 1928), who as a boy survived a Nazi death camp in Poland, but lost all his other family members and was witness to and sufferer of great atrocities, had been a very religious child. But his experiences in the Holocaust so embittered him against God that he could not bring himself to utter the traditional prayers:

Why should I bless Him? In every fiber I rebelled. Because He had had thousands of children burned in His pits? Because He kept six crematoria working night and day, on Sundays and feast days? Because in His great might He had created Auschwitz, Birkenau, Buna, and so many factories of death? How could I say to Him: "Blessed art Thou, Eternal, Master of the Universe, Who chose us from among the races to be tortured day and night, to see our fathers, our mothers, our brothers, end in the crematory? Praised be Thy Holy Name, Thou Who has chosen us to be butchered on Thine altar?"[21]

Wiesel says that we cannot turn away from the questions about how it could happen, for genocidal actions are being undertaken against other minority groups in our times as well. As Wiesel points out:

According to Jewish tradition, the death of one innocent person tarnishes the cosmos. Other people's tragedies are our tragedies. We must study the past, the horrors of the past and the melancholy of the past, if we are to be sensitive in the present. [In this] there are eternities of distress—the terrifying power of evil over innocence—but also some strength in the resolve of the victim never to become a killer.[22]

In a relatively recent development, there have been some attempts in North America and Europe and on Internet websites to deny the extent of Jewish deaths from the Holocaust. The insinuation is that Jews use the "Auschwitz lie" to compel Western support for the State of Israel. Careful study of the historical evidence, however, still supports the chilling statistic that approximately six million Jews died in the Holocaust. Attempts to minimize recognition of this massive genocide seem to be motivated by persisting anti-semitism. As in the past, there is still suspicion that Jews are responsible for what happens in the world, by some global conspiracy effected through control of finances, media, or political influence over the policies of the United States and European governments.

Zionism

Zionism is the Jewish movement dedicated to the establishment of a politically viable, internationally recognized Jewish state in the biblical land of Israel. While political Zionism was a reaction to increasing anti-semitism in Europe in the late nineteenth century, it is a movement with deep roots in Judaism and Jewish culture. The desire to end the centuries-long exile from Zion (the site of the Jerusalem Temples) was a central theme in all Jewish prayer and in many religious customs. Jewish messianism is focused around a descendant of King David who will return his united people to the land of Israel, where Jewish sovereignty will be eternally re-established in an atmosphere of universal peace. Professor Aviezer Ravitzky describes the Zionist ideal:

It was a dream of utter perfection: the day would come when the entire Jewish people, the whole Congregation of Israel, would reassemble as one in an undivided Land of Israel, reconstituting its life there according to the Torah in all its aspects. The Jewish people would free itself completely from its subjugation to the great powers. It would then be a source of blessing for all nations, for its redemption would bring about the redemption of the world as a whole, "For the land shall be filled with devotion to the Lord as water covers the sea" (Isaiah 11:9).[23]

Zionism became an organized international political movement under the leadership of the Viennese journalist Theodor Herzl (1860–1904), who believed that the Jews could never defend themselves against anti-semitism until they had their own nation. Herzl worked to provide political guarantees for the Jewish settlement that existed in Palestine through the nearly two thousand years of exile and to offer institutional support to encourage Jews from around the world to immigrate to Palestine through the formation of various Zionist organizations. Simultaneously, pioneers, mainly secular Jews from eastern Europe, began increasing the Jewish presence on the land, which already had a significant Jewish population. The 1917 Balfour Declaration stated Britain's support for limited Jewish settlement in Palestine following World War I and the defeat of Turkey, when Britain expected to take over control of the region. While most Jews worldwide also applauded this Zionist victory, not all supported the movement. Most Reform Jews of that time believed the destiny of Jews was to be lived out among the Gentiles, where the Enlightenment had fueled hopes of a freer future and where Jews hoped they could be recognized as legitimate citizens of the countries in which they lived. Some support for Zionism came from traditional Orthodox Jews, but not all of the traditional community embraced the idea. Many felt it was God who had punished the people for their unfaithfulness by sending them away from the promised land and that only God would end the exile. They rejected active political initiative in favor of passive waiting for miraculous divine intervention, citing an oath from the Midrash and Talmud "not to force the End." Exile is not only a geographical matter; it is an internal absence of redemption, which will not be hastened by settling for partial, secular solutions.

Nonetheless, by a United Nations decision in 1947, Palestine was partitioned into two areas, one to be governed by Jews and the other by Arabs, with Jerusalem an international zone. The Jews, while disappointed by the territorial compromise of the partition plan, accepted it, and in 1948 declared Israel an inde-

Much of the Promised Land to which the Jews wanted to return was a desert. This group is celebrating the founding of Tel Aviv, now a modern city, on sand dunes in 1909.

pendent Jewish State with full rights for minorities. However, the Arabs did not accept the partition and as soon as British troops moved out, Israel was attacked by its Arab neighbors—Jordan, Iraq, Syria, Lebanon, and Egypt. Outnumbered, Israel nonetheless managed to control a larger area than was allotted to it in the partition plan, thus bringing many Arabs under its rule. Those Arabs who fled to avoid violence were not allowed into the surrounding countries; they were instead kept in refugee camps, in which for generations people have continued to live in distress and growing hatred for Israel. Egypt and Jordan kept sending guerrilla troops, known as *fedayeen*, to attack the Israelis, whose sovereignty they refused to recognize.

When an attack by Arab neighbors and Palestinians seemed imminent in 1967, with threats of capturing Israel and killing the Jews therein, Israel launched a stunningly successful pre-emptive strike—the "Six-Day War." Nevertheless, the Arab countries still refused to recognize Israel's nationhood and Palestinian resistance grew both within the expanded territories now occupied by Israel and in acts of terrorism against Jewish places elsewhere. In 1973, Egypt and Syria launched a surprise attack which the smaller but militarily superior Jewish forces managed to thwart. Despair over attaining any lasting peace with the surrounding Arabs brought hardliners to the fore in Israeli politics. They saw in expanded settlements a fulfilment of biblical prophecy and a defense against Palestinian terrorism.

From time to time, a negotiated peace has seemed almost possible, but it has not yet happened. Informal frameworks for Palestinian–Israeli settlement such as the Geneva Accords of 2003 have offered some hope of decreasing hostilities in the region by creating two independent states of Palestine and Israel, but they have not satisfactorily dealt with major sticking points. One of these is the "Right of Return" sought by Palestinian refugees from the 1948–49 war and their descendants. Countering this demand, which raises Israeli fears of rapid Palestinian repopulation of Israel and the loss of Jewish character to the State, some Jews point out that over 600,000 Jews likewise had to flee their homes in Arab countries where they were severely persecuted after the creation of Israel. There is also Palestinian concern that the new state of Palestine would consist only of isolated, dependent enclaves under Israeli control. Yet another problem is control of and access to sites which are holy to both Muslims and Jews such as the Temple Mount in Jerusalem, known to Muslims as the place from which the Prophet Muhammad began his Night Journey to the seven heavens. Extensive Israeli settlements in the West Bank and Gaza Strip make it difficult to establish Palestinian sovereignty there. The tragic cycle of violent attacks and counterattacks continues, with Palestinian militant groups such as Hamas increasingly turning to suicide bombings of civilians, contrary to Muslim tradition forbidding killing of non-combatants. In 2004, Hamas—which refuses to accept the existence of the state of Israel—vowed "100 retaliations" for the Israeli assassination of its leader, Abdel Aziz Rantisi, which had been preceded by Israeli assassination of its spiritual leader, Sheikh Ahmed Yassin, both of whom had publicly avowed that they had been involved with acts of terrorism against Jewish civilians.

The latest attempt of Jews to protect themselves from Palestinians is the building of massive security fences and walls up to twenty-five feet high that impede the mixing of the two communities. Critics claim that while the walls are supposedly built to stop the Palestinian suicide bombers, they are actually ways of

Palestinians and Israelis are now separated in many areas by a massive wall which Israelis have built to protect themselves from suicide bombers. Palestinians experience it as an "apartheid" wall.

appropriating more land and water resources. Palestinian communities are thus turned into isolated cages in which farmers are cut off from their own fertile land and water, and in some cases, even from the other side of their now-divided villages. Palestinians refer to the physical barriers as "the Apartheid Wall."

In a rather extraordinary decision, the Israeli Supreme Court has ruled against the government and in favor of Palestinians that the route of the fence must be adjusted to minimize the hardships to Palestinians, even if this reduces protection of Jews against terrorism. And many Israelis and Jews in other countries are actively seeking peace and reconciliation with Palestinians. Efforts persist to keep person-to-person contacts open between Israeli Jews and those who have been historically pitted as their opponents. For instance, an Israeli organization—the Interfaith Encounter Association—sponsors religious gatherings among Jews, Muslims, Christians, and other groups who live in the Holy Land, so that they may meet "the other." They study the teachings of their religious traditions on particular subjects, such as the humanity of people of different faiths, or the definition of a righteous person, or ways of dealing with death. They also offer prayers, ceremonies, and songs from their own traditions. Women's encounters have been particularly fruitful in developing interfaith friendships that transcend the political violence and separation.

Tensions also exist within the Jewish community in Israel. Jewish settlers have come to Israel from many divergent backgrounds. Those who are of eastern European origin—the Ashkenazi who founded the state—tend to regard themselves as superior to Jewish settlers from other areas. Ultra-Orthodox religious authorities insist on strict observance of religious rituals, assert considerable control over education and politics in the nation, and claim that converts consecrated by Reform and Conservative rabbis in the United States are not really Jews at all. The

Orthodox rabbis generally favor hardline political policies in Israel, and yet Orthodox Jews are exempted from military service. The Orthodox rabbis do not represent the majority of Israeli citizens in religious terms either, for only an estimated fifteen percent of Israelis claim to live completely according to religious laws. The majority are non-Orthodox or secular, not religiously observant at all. There is also internal dissension over relationships with the Palestinians. Some sympathize with the Palestinians' situation, while others believe that the land has been promised to them by God and should never be given into Arab hands. Thus the ancient Zionist vision remains unfulfilled, and the area is fraught with strife. Aviezer Ravitzky comments, "As the rabbis said, the End of Days continues to 'tarry.'"[24]

Torah

It is difficult to outline the tenets of the Jewish faith. As we have seen, Jewish spiritual understanding has changed repeatedly through history. Rationalists and mystics have often differed. Since the nineteenth century, there has been disagreement between liberal and traditional Jews, to be discussed later.

Nevertheless, there are certain major themes that can be extricated from the vast history and literature of Judaism. Jewish teachings are known as **Torah**. In its narrowest sense, Torah refers to the Five Books of Moses. On the next level, it means the entire Hebrew Bible and the Talmud, the written and the oral law. For

Judaism: Torah

A peach orchard in Kibbutz Sede Boquer, Israel, 1994. Kibbutzes, or collective farming communities of volunteers, were established with high social idealism and have developed successful methods of dry-land agriculture.

some, "Torah" can refer to all sacred Jewish literature and observance. At the highest level, Torah is God's will, God's wisdom.

The one God

The central Jewish belief is monotheism. It has been stated in different ways in response to different cultural settings (emphasizing the divine unity when Christians developed the concept of the Holy Trinity, for instance, and emphasizing that God is formless and ultimate holiness in opposition to the earthly local gods). But the central theme is that there is one Creator God, the "cause of all existent things."[25]

God is everywhere, even in the darkness, as David sings in Psalms:

Where can I escape from Your spirit?
Where can I flee from Your presence?
If I ascend to Heaven, You are there:
if I descend to Sheol [the underworld],
You are there too.

If I take wing with the dawn
to come to rest on the western horizon,
even there Your hand will be guiding me,
Your right hand will be holding me fast.
                                    Psalm 139:7–14

This metaphysical understanding of God's oneness is difficult to explain in linear language, which refers to the individual objects perceived by the senses. As the eleventh-century Spanish poet and mystical philosopher Ibn Gabirol put it, "None can penetrate . . . the mystery of Thy unfathomable unity."[26]

One of the most elegant attempts to "explain" God's oneness has been offered by the great twentieth-century thinker Abraham Joshua Heschel (1907–1972). He linked the idea of unity to eternity, explaining that in eternity, "past and future are not apart; here is everywhere, and now goes on forever." Time as we know it is only a fragment, "eternity broken in space." According to Heschel:

The craving for unity and coherence is the predominant feature of a mature mind. All science, all philosophy, all art are a search after it. But unity is a task, not a condition. The world lies in strife, in discord, in divergence. Unity is beyond, not within, reality. . . . The world is not *one with God, and this is why his power does not surge unhampered throughout all stages of being. Creature is detached from the Creator, and the universe is in a state of spiritual disorder. Yet God has not withdrawn entirely from this world. The spirit of this unity hovers over the face of all plurality, and the major trend of all our thinking and striving is its mighty intimation. The goal of all efforts is to bring about the restitution of the unity of God and world.*[27]

Plurality is incompatible with the sense of the ineffable. You cannot ask in regard to the divine: Which one? There is only one synonym for God: One.
                                          Abraham Joshua Heschel[28]

In traditional Judaism, God is often perceived as a loving Father who is nonetheless infinitely majestic, sometimes revealing divine power when the children need chastising.

Love for God

The essential commandment to humans is to love God. The central prayer in any Jewish religious service and the inscription on the *mezuza* at the doorpost of every traditional Jewish home is the *Shema Israel*:

Hear, O Israel! The Lord is our God, the Lord alone. You shall love the Lord your God with all your heart and with all your soul and with all your might. Take to heart these instructions with which I charge you this day. Impress them upon your children. Recite them when you stay at home and when you are away, when you lie down and when you get up. Bind them as a sign on your hand and let them serve as a symbol on your forehead; inscribe them on the doorposts of your house and on your gates.

Deuteronomy 6:4–9

Even Maimonides, the great proponent of reason and study, asserted the primacy of love for God. He emphasized that one should not love God from selfish or fearful motivations, such as receiving earthly blessings or avoiding problems in the life after death. One should study Torah and fulfill the commandments out of sheer love of God.

The sacredness of human life

Humans are the pinnacle of creation, created in the "image" of God, according to the account of Creation in Genesis 1. Jews do not take this passage to mean that God literally looks like a human. It is often interpreted in an ethical sense: that humans are so wonderfully endowed that they can mirror God's qualities, such as justice, wisdom, righteousness, and love.

All people are potentially equal; they are said to be common descendants of the first man and woman. But they are also potentially perfectible, and in raising themselves they uplift the world. God limited the divine power by giving humans free will, involving them in the responsibility for the world's condition, and their own. If we are suffering, according to the Talmud, we should examine our own deeds.

The German scholar Martin Buber (1878–1965) described the relationship between God and humans as reciprocal:

You know always in your heart that you need God more than everything; but do you not know too that God needs you—in the fulness of His eternity needs you? How would man exist, how would you exist, if God did not need him, did not need you? You need God, in order to be—and God needs you, for the very meaning of your life. ... There is divine meaning in the life of the world ... of human persons, of you and of me. ... We take part in creation, meet the Creator, reach out to him, helpers and companions.[29]

Jewish theology has been shaped by the most compelling thinkers of each era. In the 20th century, Martin Buber described the cherished human–divine encounter as an I–Thou relationship, in which the self experiences its wholeness.

Human life is sacred, rather than lowly and loathsome; Judaism celebrates the body. Sexuality within marriage is holy, and the body is honored as the instrument through which the soul is manifested on earth. Indeed, according to some thinkers, body and soul are an inseparable totality.

> *I praise You, for I am awesomely, wondrously made.*   Psalm 139:14

Law

Because of the great responsibility of humankind, traditional Jews give thanks that God has revealed in the written and oral Torah the laws by which they can be faithful to the divine will and fulfill the purposes of Creation by establishing a Kingdom of God here on earth, in which all creatures can live in peace and fellowship. In the words of the biblical prophet Isaiah, speaking for God,

> *The wolf and the lamb shall graze together,*
> *And the lion shall eat straw like the ox,*
> *And the serpent's food shall be earth.*
> *In all my sacred mount*
> *Nothing evil or vile shall be done.*[30]

To the extent that traditional Jews act according to the Torah, they feel they are upholding their part of the ancient covenant with God.

The Torah, as indicated through rabbinic literature, is said to contain 613 commandments, or **mitzvot** (singular: mitzvah). Jewish law does not differentiate between sacred and secular life, so these include general ethical guidelines such as the Ten Commandments and the famous saying in Leviticus 19:18—"Love your fellow as yourself"—plus detailed laws concerning all aspects of life, such as land ownership, civil and criminal procedure, family law, sacred observances, diet, and ritual slaughter. The biblical Book of Genesis also sets forth what is called the Noahide Code of seven universal principles for a moral and spiritual life: idolatry (worshipping many gods or images of God), blasphemy against God, murder, theft, sexual behaviors outside of marriage, and cruelty to animals are all prohibited, and the rule of law and justice in society is affirmed as a positive value.

From the time of its final editing in Babylonia in the mid-sixth century CE, the Talmud, together with its later commentaries, has served as a blueprint for Jewish social, communal, and religious life. Through the rabbinic tradition, law became the main category of Orthodox Jewish thought and practice, and learned study of God's commandments one of the central expressions of faith.

From a contemporary point of view, Ismar Schorsch notes that many of the ancient commandments are ecologically useful, for they restrain humanity's ways of using the natural environment. They are addressed to humans not as wise masters of the earth, as envisioned in the first account of Creation in Genesis, but as the Adam and Eve of the second Creation story, who are disobedient and must be saved from themselves lest they destroy the planet, "for as the Bible so often avers: the land ultimately belongs to its Creator and we mortals are but His tenants."[31]

A Sabbath prayer, *Ahavat Olam*, expresses Jews' profound gratitude for God's laws:

With everlasting love You have loved Your people Israel. You have taught us the Torah and its Mitzvot. *You have instructed us in its laws and judgments.*
    Therefore, O Lord our God, when we lie down and when we rise up we shall speak of Your commandments and rejoice in Your Torah and Mitzvot.
    For they are our life and the length of our days; on them we will meditate day and night.[32]

Suffering and faith

Jewish tradition depicts the universe as being governed by an all-powerful, personal God who intervenes in history to reward the righteous and punish the unjust. Within this context, Jews have had considerable difficulty in answering the eternal question: Why must the innocent suffer? This question has been particularly poignant since the Holocaust.

The Hebrew Bible itself brings up the issue with the challenging parable of Job, a blameless, God-fearing, and wealthy man. The story involves Satan, depicted as an angel beneath God, who, in a conversation with God, predicts that Job will surely drop his faith and blaspheme the Lord if he is stripped of all his possessions. With God's assent, Satan tests Job by destroying all that Job has, including his children and his health. On hearing the news of his children's deaths

Job arose, tore his robe, cut off his hair, and threw himself on the ground and worshipped. He said, "Naked came I out of my mother's womb, and naked shall I return there; the Lord has given, and the Lord has taken away, blessed be the name of the Lord."[33]

With an itchy inflammation covering him from head to foot, Job begins to curse his life and to question God's justice. In the end, Job acknowledges not only God's power to control the world but also his inscrutable wisdom, which is beyond human understanding. God then rewards him with long life and even greater riches than he had before the test.

Debate over the meanings of this ancient story has continued over the centuries. One rabbinical interpretation is that Satan was cooperating with God in helping Job grow from fear of God to love of God. Another is that faith in God will finally be rewarded in this life, no matter how severe the temporary trials. Another is that those who truly desire to grow toward God will be asked to suffer more, that their sins will be expiated in this life so that they can enjoy the divine bliss in the life to come. Such interpretations assume a personal, all-powerful, loving God doing what is best for the people, even when they cannot understand God's ways. In such belief, God is seen as always available, like a shepherd caring for his sheep, no matter how dark the outer circumstances.

Though I walk through a valley of deepest darkness,
I fear no harm, for You are with me;
Your rod and Your staff—they comfort me.

                                                            Psalm 23:4

On the other hand, oppression and then the Holocaust have led some Jews to complain to God in anguish. They, too, feel close to God, but in a way that allows them to scream at God, as it were. In questioning the justice of history, they hold God responsible for what is inexplicably monstrous. But even in the Holocaust, there were those who held fast to hope for better times. As they walked to their death in Nazi gas chambers, some were reciting the hymn *Ani maamin*: "I believe with complete faith in the coming of the Messiah, and even though he may delay, nevertheless I anticipate every day that he will come."[34]

Sacred practices

Since the rabbinic period began, a major Jewish spiritual practice has been daily scriptural study. Boys were traditionally taught how to read and write ancient Hebrew and how to interpret scripture through the process of exegesis, by means of the oral Torah. This required extensive knowledge of the scriptures and concentrated intellectual effort. This classical pattern continues today even in the Diaspora, where some children continue to be trained in special schools to carry on the study of the Torah, thus encouraging them not only to learn and obey the commandments but also through rational analysis to delve into deeper understanding of truth.

In addition to study, a Jew is urged to remember God in all aspects of life, through prayer and observance of the commandments. These commandments are not otherworldly. Many are rooted in the body, and spiritual practices often engage all the senses in awareness of God.

Boys are ritually circumcised when they are eight days old, to honor the seal of God's commandment to Abraham. Orthodox Jews consider women ritually unclean during their menstrual periods and for seven days afterwards, during which time they are not to have sexual intercourse with their husbands. At the end of this forbidden period Othodox Jewish women undertake complete immersion in a **mikva**, a special deep bath structure, symbolizing their altered state. Marital sex is sacred, with the **Sabbath** night the holiest time for making love. By contrast, adultery is strictly forbidden as one of the worst sins against God, for Jewish tradition is extremely concerned with maintaining pure lines of descent.

Judaism: Sabbath

What one eats is also of cosmic significance, for according to the Torah some foods are definitely unclean. For example, the only ritually acceptable, or **kosher**, meats, are those from warmblooded animals with cloven hoofs which chew their cuds, such as cows, goats, and sheep. Poultry is kosher, except for birds of prey, but shellfish is not. Meat is also kosher only if it has been butchered in the traditional way with an extremely sharp, smooth knife by an authorized Jewish slaughterer. Great pains are taken to avoid eating blood; meat must be soaked in water and then drained on a salted board before cooking. Meat and milk cannot be eaten together, and separate dishes are maintained for their preparation and serving.

These dietary instructions are laid out in the biblical Book of Leviticus, which quotes God as saying to Moses and Aaron, "For I the Lord am He who brought you up from the land of Egypt to be your God: you shall be holy, for I am holy."[35] The rules of diet, if strictly followed, give Jews a feeling of special sacred identity and link them to the eternal authority of the Torah.

Some contemporary Jews feel that consciousness about what they eat should be extended to environmental considerations. To them, the styrofoam box in which a cheeseburger is sold at fast-food places is as much a problem as the mixing of meat and milk. Nuclear power-generated electricity used for cooking might itself be non-kosher, as long as there is no safe provision for disposing of nuclear waste.

For traditional Jews, the morning begins with a prayer before they open their eyes to thank God for restoring the soul. The hands must then be washed before reciting blessings and, for all traditional male Jews, putting a special fringed rectangle of cloth around the neck. It is usually worn under the clothes as a reminder of the privilege of being given divine commandments. For weekday morning prayers men also put *t'fillin*, or phylacteries, small leather boxes containing biblical verses about the covenant with God, on the forehead and the upper arm, held against the heart, in fulfillment of the Shema commandment, as literally understood: "Bind them [the Shema's words about the primacy of love for God] as a sign on your hand and let them serve as a symbol on your forehead." Traditional Jewish men also wear a fringed prayer shawl, or **talit**, whose fringes act as reminders of God's commandments, and keep their heads covered at all times, if possible.

Traditionally, prayers are recited on waking and at bedtime. In addition, three prayer services are chanted daily in a synagogue by men if there is a *minyan* (quorum of ten). Women can say them also, but they are excused from rigid schedules partly because of their household responsibilities, and partly because of the belief that women have a more intuitive sense of spirituality.

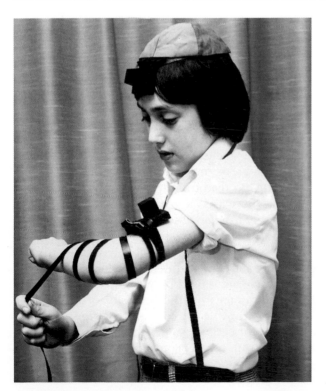

Before praying, traditional Jewish men bind t'fillin *to their arms and foreheads in remembrance of their covenant with God.*

Jews are also expected to give thanks continually. One should recite a hundred benedictions to God every day. To this end, there is a blessing to be said every time one takes a drink of water. There is even a blessing to be recited after using the toilet:

Blessed art thou, our God, Ruler of the universe, who hast formed (human) beings in wisdom, and created in them a system of ducts and tubes. It is well known before thy glorious throne that if but one of these be opened, or if one of those be closed, it would be impossible to exist in thy presence. Blessed art thou, O God, who healest all creatures and doest wonders.[36]

The Jewish Sabbath is observed as an eternal sign of the covenant between the Jews and God. The Sabbath runs from sunset Friday night to sunset Saturday night, because the Jewish "day" begins with nightfall. The Friday night service welcomes the Sabbath as a bride and is often considered an opportunity to drop away the cares of the previous week so as to be in a peaceful state for the day of rest. Just as God is said to have created the world in six days and then rested on the seventh, all work is to cease when the Sabbath begins. Ruth Gan Kagan describes the experience:

I am aware of a wave of peace flooding my heart and that transparent veils of tranquility are covering the World around me. A moment before I would probably be rushing around trying to finish all the preparations, . . . but all this tension and rush vanishes when the fixed moment arrives; not a second earlier nor a second later. The moment I light the Sabbath candles and usher in the Sabbath spirit everything undergoes a magical transformation.

The Queen has arrived. In Her presence there are not even talks of weekday matters. The mind quiets down leaving business, plans and worries behind as one quietly walks to the synagogue for services; the sky is aglow with the colours of sunset; the bird-song is suddenly more present; the people of the congregation gather to welcome in the Sabbath in song, prayer and silence.

Coming home, the stars are out; in a religious neighborhood, no travelling cars break the descended peace; children are holding their parents' hands, walking in the middle of the road without fear of death.[37]

The Saturday morning service incorporates public and private prayers, singing, and the reading of passages from the Pentateuch and Prophets sections of the Hebrew Bible. Torah scrolls are kept in a curtained ark on the wall facing Jerusalem. They are hand-lettered in Hebrew and are treated with great reverence. It is a great honor to be "called up" to read from the Torah.

More liberal congregations may place emphasis on an in-depth discussion of the passage read. Often it is examined not only from an abstract philosophical perspective but also from the point of its relevance to political events and everyday attempts to live a just and humane life. Torah study, and study of all Jewish literature, is highly valued as a form of prayer in itself, and synagogues usually have libraries for this purpose, sometimes in the same space that is used for worship.

In Hasidic congregations, the emphasis falls on the intensity of praying, or ***davening***, even in saying fixed prayers from the prayer book. Some sway their bodies to induce the self-forgetful state of ecstatic communion with the Loved One. Others quietly shift their attention from earthly concerns to "cleave to God." The rabbinical tradition states the ideal in prayer: "A person should always see himself as if the Shekhinah is confronting him."[38]

Living Judaism

Herman Taube is a poet, Professor Emeritus of Jewish Studies and Yiddish Literature, and volunteer chaplain to nursing home patients. He emigrated to the United States in 1947 from Poland with his wife, who had earlier been sent to a concentration camp where her younger sister and mother died. During World War II, Herman was a medic working side by side with Russian Orthodox and Muslim doctors in Uzbekhistan to aid people in a refugee camp. He says,

"If you do charitable work—if you help in clinics, if you help unfortunate children, if you go into the jails to help inmates—this is God's work. It is not the responsibility of the rich only to help the poor. Even the poorest man has to give charity. This is the law in Jewish religion.

"Maimonides says, and Jews are saying every morning in their prayers, that a human being has to believe every day in the coming of the Messiah. Messiah does not come with a long beard and a donkey. Messiah can be you. Messiah can be a man on the street who helps a fellow human being. In the Hebrew Bible, in the Talmud, there are quotations indicating that the Messiah will come in a generation which is full of innocence or full of guilt—one of the two. And he will spiritually lead the people away from evil. I think this will become a messianic era.

"Look at the fall of communism, the fall of fascism in our generation. Something is changing. You don't have to go far—look at Washington. You see good people living in the streets, with no roof over their head. They cannot make a meal. On the other side, you see those big parties where people spend millions. There is a need for a messianic age, a need for a better world.

"A reporter asked me, 'Can you believe in God after the Holocaust?' Belief is not something static. My wife and I sometimes ask, 'Where was God?' A million and a half Jewish children were killed. Little boys and girls who were just learning how to say, 'Mama,' and the grandmother said, 'How big is the baby?' and tried to pick up their hands. And this child was taken and thrown into a lamppost. So yes, there are questions. We have no answers.

"Why did Polish people, nuns and plain peasants risk their lives to save Jewish people, when they knew that for saving a Jew's life their house would be burned down? And their children were taken into forced labor. Why did the people of Assisi save sixty Jewish people under the noses of the Nazis? The Vatican wasn't too helpful, didn't speak up, but they, the simple people, risked their lives. So there is goodness in the world, too. There is goodness and Godness in the hearts of those people.

"The Talmud says God said, 'You don't believe in me? So you don't believe in me. But keep my commandments. Care for the poor and for the widows.' This is exactly what a lot of those Messiahs are doing.

"About chosenness: My grandfather was a really Orthodox Jew. He prayed three times a day, studied, studied the Bible, was always praying, always reciting Psalms, a really generous man. He found time to give charity. He did the same thing that I do now: He volunteered to go to the hospitals. Some of the people couldn't afford to go to the hospital, so he went to their homes, on the fifth floors in Poland, with no elevators, sitting with somebody sick all night. On the way home he would go to services. Then at home, something to eat—dry bread, a piece of herring, imitation coffee. This is the way he lived. This man, this chosen man, was one of the first Jews of the Lodz ghetto to be taken to the concentration camp. The Nazis used gas to kill them, and then disposed of them. If this is the chosenness that God wants us for—thank you, choose another people.

"My wife doesn't like to be interviewed. It's like pulling off a bandage from an open wound. Even after forty-five years, it comes to the holidays and she's missing her mother and her sister. That unbelievable guilt feeling: Why did we survive and they die?

"I believe in God. There is a Power above us that rules our life. We do not see it, we cannot comprehend it. But there is something. I do not deny Him—or Her; maybe it's a Her. And I don't deny my roots."

Celebration of the Sabbath meal at a kibbutz in Erez, Israel.

In addition to, or instead of, going to a service welcoming the Sabbath, observant families usually begin the Sabbath eve with a special Friday night dinner. The mother lights candles to bring in the Sabbath light; the father recites a blessing over the wine. Special braided bread, *challah*, is shared as a symbol of the double portions of manna in the desert. The rituals help to set a different tone for the day of rest, as do commandments against working, handling money, traveling except by foot, lighting a fire, cooking, and the like. The Sabbath day is set aside for public prayer, study, thought, friendship, and family closeness, with the hope that this renewed life of the spirit will then carry through the week to come.

It is customary to recognize coming of age, at thirteen, in Jewish boys by the **Bar Mitzvah** ("son of the commandment") ceremony. The boy has presumably undertaken some religious instruction, including learning to pronounce Hebrew, if not always to understand it. He is called up to read a portion from the Torah scroll and recite a passage from one of the books of the prophets, in Hebrew, and then perhaps to give a short teaching about a topic from the reading. Afterwards there may be a simple *kiddush*, a celebration with blessing of wine and sweet bread or cake, but a big party is more likely. This custom of welcoming the boy to adult responsibilities has been extended to girls in non-Orthodox congregations in the **Bat Mitzvah**. As in the Bar Mitzvah, this means "one obligated to observe the commandments."

Holy days

Judaism follows an ancient lunar calendar of annual holidays and memorials linked to special events in history. The spiritual year begins with the High Holy Days of Rosh Hashanah and Yom Kippur. Rosh Hashanah (New Year's Day), a time of spiritual renewal in remembrance of the original creation of the world, is celebrated on the first two days of the seventh month (around the fall equinox). For thirty days prior to Rosh Hashanah, each morning synagogue service brings the blowing of the *shofar* (a ram's horn that produces an eery, unearthly blast) to remind the people that they stand before God. At the service on the eve of Rosh Hashanah, a prayer is recited asking that all humanity will remember what God has done, that there will be honor and joy for God's people, and that righteousness will triumph while "all wickedness vanishes like smoke."[39]

The ten Days of Awe follow Rosh Hashanah. People are encouraged to change inwardly, by looking at their mistakes of the past year. It is said that during this period, God makes it easier for a person to be repentant and is also more likely to accept repentance. A biblical passage from the prophet Isaiah is cited: "Seek ye the Lord while He may be found, Call ye upon Him while He is near." [40]

Yom Kippur completes the High Holy Days, renewing the sacred covenant with God in a spirit of atonement and cleansing. Historically, this was the only time when the high priest entered the Holy of Holies in the Temple of Jerusalem, and the only time that he would pronounce the sacred name of the Lord, YHWH, in order to ask for forgiveness of the people's sins. Today, there is an attempt at personal inner cleansing, and individuals must ask pardon from everyone they may have wronged during the past year. If necessary, restitution for damages should be made. Congregations also confess their sins communally, ask that their negligence be forgiven, and pray for their reconciliation to God in a new year of divine pardon and grace.

Sukkot is a fall harvest festival. A simple outdoor booth (a *sukkah*) is built and decorated as a dwelling place of sorts for seven days. Usually this is done as a

Rosh Hashanah includes the blowing of the shofar *in three ways: a note of alarm, three wails, and nine sobbing blasts of contrition.*

ritual act, but seeking a deeper experience of the meaning of Sukkot, some contemporary Jews are actually attempting to live in the *sukkah* they construct. Michael Lerner relates:

> *The idea of moving out of my apartment or house to live in a* sukkah *always seemed impractical to me until I tried it. Living in a temporary shelter—particularly one with a water-permeable roof made of twigs, reeds, vines, tree branches, and other forms of vegetation arranged in such a way that one can see through them to the stars—has a special effect of reconnecting urban and suburban dwellers to the natural order, and to the transitory nature of our carefully constructed forms of material security.*[41]

The fragile home reminds the faithful that their real home is in God, who sheltered their ancestors on the way from Egypt to the promised land of Canaan. Some contemporary groups also pray for peace amid our vulnerability to nuclear war. Participants hold the *lulav* (a bundle made of a palm branch, myrtle twigs, and willow twigs) in one hand and the *etrog* (a citrus fruit) in the other and wave them together toward the four compass directions and to earth and sky, praising God and acknowledging him as the unmoving center of creation. Traditionally there was an offering of water, precious in the desert lands of the patriarchs, and great merrymaking. During the Second Temple days, the ecstatic celebration even included burning of the priests' old underclothes. The day after the seven-day Sukkot festival is Simhat Torah ("Joy in Torah"), ending the yearly cycle of Torah readings, from Creation to the death of Moses, and beginning again.

Near the winter solstice, the darkest time of the year, comes Hanukkah, the Feast of Dedication. Each night for eight nights, another candle is lit on a special candle holder. The amount of light gradually increases like the lengthening of sunlight. Historically, Hanukkah was a celebration of the victory of the Maccabean Rebellion against the attempt by Antiochus to force non-Jewish practices on the Jewish people. According to legend, when the Jews regained access to the Temple, they found only one jar of oil left undefiled, still sealed by the high priest. It was enough to stay alight for only one day, but by a miracle, the oil stayed burning for eight days. Many Jewish families also observe the time by nightly gift-giving. The children have their own special Hanukkah pastimes, such as "gambling" for nuts with the *dreidel*, a spinning top with four letters on its sides as an abbreviation of the sentence "A great miracle happened there."

Repentance and inner renewal are central themes of the High Holy Days. (Rothschild MS, c. 1470.)

As the winter rainy season begins to diminish in Israel, Jews everywhere celebrate the reawakening of nature on Tu B'shvat. Observances lavish appreciation on a variety of fruits and plants. In Israel, the time is now marked by the planting of trees to help restore life to the desert. On the full moon of the month before spring comes Purim. It theoretically commemorates the legend of Esther, queen of Persia, and Mordecai, who saved their fellow Jews from destruction

Simhat Torah is a joyous celebration of the Torah, with everyone joining in the dancing and singing. This one is taking place at the western "Wailing Wall," where for nearly two thousand years Jews have made pilgrimages to pray.

by the evil viceroy Haman. It has been linked to Mesopotamian mythology about the goddess Ishtar, whose spring return brings joy and fertility. Purim is a bawdy time of dressing in costumes and mocking life's seriousness, and the jokes frequently poke fun at sacred Jewish practices. As the story of Esther is read from an ornate scroll, the congregation responds with noisy stomping, rattles, horns, and whistles whenever Haman's name is read.

The next major festival is Pesach, or Passover, which celebrates the liberation from bondage in Egypt and the spring-time advent of new life. It was the tenth plague, death to all first-born sons of the Egyptians, that finally brought the pharaoh to relent. The Israelites were warned to slaughter a lamb for each family and mark their doors with its blood so that the angel of death would pass over them. They were to roast the lamb and eat it with unleavened bread and bitter herbs. So quickly did they depart that they didn't even have time to bake the bread, which is said to have baked in the sun as they carried it on their heads. The beginning of Pesach is still marked by a **Seder** dinner, with the eating of unleavened bread (*matzah*) to remember the urgency of the departure, and bitter herbs as a reminder of slavery, so that they would never impose it on other peoples. Also on the table are *charoset* (a sweet fruit and nut mixture, a reminder of the mortar that the enslaved Israelites molded into bricks) and salt water (a reminder of the tears of the slaves) into which parsley or some other plant (a reminder of spring life) is dipped and eaten. Children ask ritual questions about why these things are done, as basic religious instruction. A movement for contemporary **liturgical** renewal has yielded many new scripts for the Seder—such as special liturgies for feminists, for secular Zionists, and for co-celebration of Pesach with Muslims.

A new holy day may be celebrated in April or May: Holocaust Memorial Day. Observances often include the singing in Yiddish of a song from the Jewish Resistance Movement. In part:

Judaism: Passover

For children of all ages, the lighting of Hannukah candles is a special event in the darkness of winter.

*Never say that you are
going your last way,
though leaden skies
blot out the blue of day.
The hour for which we
long will certainly appear.*[42]

Early summer brings Shavuot, traditionally identified with the giving of the Torah to Moses at Mount Sinai and the people's hearing of the voice of God. It is likely that Shavuot was initially a summer harvest festival that later was linked with the revelation of the Torah. In Israeli kibbutzim, the old practice of bringing the first fruits to God has been revived. Elsewhere, the focus is on reading the Ten Commandments and on presenting the Torah as a marriage contract between God and Israel. In some congregations, Shavuot is a time to celebrate children's graduation from religious school.

Then come three weeks of mourning for the Temples, both of which were destroyed on the ninth day of the month of Av (July or August), Tisha Be-av. This is traditionally a time of fasting and avoidance of joyous activities. Some feel that there is no longer cause for mourning because even though the Temple has not been rebuilt, the old city of Jerusalem has been recaptured. Others feel that we are all still in exile from the state of perfection.

Contemporary Judaism

Within the extended family of Judaism, there are many groups, many different focuses, and many areas of disagreement. Currently disputed issues include the degree of adherence to the Torah and Talmud, requirements for conversion to Judaism, the extent of the use of Hebrew in prayer, and the full participation of women.

Major branches today

Judaism, like all modern religions, has struggled to meet the challenge of secularization: the idealization of science, rationalism, industrialization, and materialism. The response of the Orthodox has been to stand by the Hebrew Bible as the revealed word of God and the Talmud as the legitimate oral law. Orthodox Jews feel that they are bound by the traditional rabbinical *halakhah*, as a way of achieving closeness to God. But within this framework there are great individual differences, with no central authority figure or governing body. Orthodoxy includes mystics and rationalists, Zionists and anti-Zionists. The Orthodox also differ greatly in their tolerance for other Jewish groups and in their degree of accommodation of the surrounding secular environment. Thus, while some Hasidic groups practice complete withdrawal from the secular world and the rest of the Jewish community, others, such as the Lubavich Hasidim (originally from Lithuania, with strong communities in many countries), are devoted to extending their message to as many Jews as possible, using all the tools of modern technology for their sacred purpose. The Lubavich, who offer highly structured and nurturing communities in which male–female roles are strictly defined and an all-embracing piety and devotion to a charismatic leader are universally shared, have had considerable success in attracting young Jews to their way of life. They are seen as strong role models and present themselves as true Jews. This return to a structured practice of Judaism has surprised many observers. When the seventh Lubavich rabbi came to the United States, he was discouraged by other Jewish rabbis from trying to interest people in the Torah in a country where so many had abandoned their tradition and were living secular lives. To the contrary, the emphasis on the Torah proved to have great appeal and encouraged many to return to their Jewish roots.

The Reform movement, at the other end of the religious spectrum from Orthodoxy, began in nineteenth-century Germany as an attempt to help modern Jews appreciate their religion rather than regarding it as antiquated, meaningless, or even repugnant. In imitation of Christian churches, synagogues were redefined as places for spiritual elevation, with choirs added for effect, and the Sabbath service was shortened and translated into the vernacular. The liturgy was also changed to eliminate references to the hope of return to Zion and animal sacrifices in the Temple. Halakhic observances were re-evaluated for their relevance to modern needs, and Judaism was understood as an evolving, open-ended religion rather than one fixed forever by the revealed Torah. Reform congregations are numerous in North America, where they are continually engaged in a "creative confrontation with modernity." Rather than exclusivism, Reform rabbis cultivate a sense of the universalism of Jewish values. It is felt that only by making Judaism meaningful to modern tastes and modern minds can it survive.

Given this approach, it is not surprising that Reform Judaism, particularly in North America, has been at the forefront in the establishment of interfaith dialogue and civic cooperation with non-Jewish groups. Reform Judaism is not fully accepted in Israel, where the Israeli Rabbinate, which has considerable civil and political power, does not recognize the authority of non-Orthodox rabbis. For example, Israeli religious officials are reluctant to acknowledge Reform converts as true Jews who can be Israeli citizens.

The liberalization process has also given birth to other groups with intermediate positions. Conservative Judaism is the largest Jewish movement in the United States. While Conservative Jews feel they are totally dedicated to traditional rabbinical Judaism, at the same time they are restating and restructuring it in modern terms so that it is not perceived as a dead historical religion. To appeal to intelligent would-be believers, Conservative Judaism has sponsored critical studies of Jewish texts from all periods in history. They believe that Jews have always searched and added to their laws, liturgy, Midrash, and beliefs to keep them relevant and meaningful in changing times. Some of the recent changes introduced are acceptance of riding to a synagogue for Sabbath services and acceptance of women into rabbinical schools as candidates for ordination as rabbis.

Rabbi Mordecai Kaplan, a highly influential American thinker who died in 1983, branched off from Conservatism (which initially rejected his ideas as too radical), and founded a movement called Reconstructionism. Kaplan held that the Enlightenment had changed everything and that strong measures were needed to preserve Judaism in the face of rationalism. Kaplan asserted that "as long as Jews adhered to the traditional conception of the Torah as supernaturally revealed, they would not be amenable to any constructive adjustment of Judaism that was needed to render it viable in a non-Jewish environment."[43] He defined Judaism as an "evolving religious civilization," both cultural and spiritual, and asserted that the Jewish people are the heart of Judaism. The traditions exist for the people, and not vice versa, he said. Kaplan denied that the Jewish people were specially chosen by God, an exclusivist idea. Rather, they had chosen to try to become a people of God. Kaplan created a new prayer book, deleting traditional portions he and others found offensive, such as derogatory references to women and Gentiles, references to physical resurrection of the body, and passages describing God as rewarding or punishing Israel by manipulating natural phenomena such as rain. Women were accepted fully into synagogue participation.

In addition to those who affiliate with a religious movement, there are many Jews who identify themselves as secular Jews, affirming their Jewish origins and maintaining various Jewish cultural traditions while eschewing religious practice. There are also significant numbers of people of Jewish birth, particularly in North America and western Europe, whose Jewish identity is vestigial at best, and unlikely to survive in future generations. The possibilities for total assimilation into Western culture are evident in statistics indicating that over fifty percent of Western Jews marry non-Jews. In most cases, neither spouse in such a marriage converts, and research indicates that it is highly unlikely that their children will identify as Jews. Thus, one of the great ironies of the liberty offered to the Jewish people by democratic secular societies is the freedom to leave Judaism as well as to affirm it.

*Rabbi Pauline Bebe
with the Torah scroll.*

Jewish feminism

In contrast to the option of leaving Judaism, some feminists are coming back to religious observance, but not in the traditional mold, which they regard as patriarchal and sexist. Women have begun to take an active role in claiming their rights to full religious participation—to be counted as part of a *minyan*, for instance, to sit with the men rather than behind a curtain in the synagogue, or to be ordained as rabbis. They are also redefining Judaism from a feminist perspective. Part of this effort involves trying to reconstruct the history of significant Jewish women, for the Torah was written down by men who devoted far more space to the doings of men than of women. There are hints, for instance, that there were powerful prophetesses, such as Miriam and Huldah, but very little information is given about them.

Among those who champion the rights of women to participate equally with men in ritual and prayer, there are also some who are making an ongoing effort to revise liturgical language in gender-neutral and gender-inclusive ways, both in

Senator Joseph Lieberman

.Joseph Lieberman has long been active in American public life, including several terms as a U.S. Senator from Connecticut. In 2000, he almost became the Vice President of the United States as Albert Gore's running mate in an extraordinarily tight race. He maintains that despite scandals and abuses of power, public service deserves more positive attention if a democracy is to succeed. Senator Lieberman is himself an observant Jew, and Jewish observances and principles form the background for his public service. He explains:

I got into politics through the surprising portal of my faith because it has so much to do with the way I navigate each day, personally and professionally. It has provided a foundation, order, and purpose to my life.

I was raised in a religiously observant family, which gave me the clear answers of faith to life's most difficult questions. My parents and my rabbi, Joseph Ehrenkranz, taught me that our lives were a gift from God, the Creator, and with it came a covenantal obligation to serve God with gladness by living as best we could, according to the law and values that God gave Moses on Mount Sinai. The summary of our aspirations was in the Hebrew phrase tikkun olam, *which is translated "to improve the world," or "to repair the world," or, more boldly, "to complete the Creation which God began." In any translation, this concept of tikkun olam presumes the inherent but unfulfilled goodness of people and requires action for the benefit of the community. It accepts our imperfections and concludes that we, as individuals and as a society, are constantly in the process of improving and becoming complete. Each of us has the opportunity and responsibility to advance that process both within ourselves and the wider world around us. As Rabbi Tarfon says in the Talmud, "The day is short and there is much work to be done. You are not required to complete the work yourself, but you cannot withdraw from it either."*[44]

As is so often the case, Senator Lieberman credits his grandmother as being one of the major spiritual influences in his life. He relates:

Born and raised in Central Europe, widowed with five children while she was in her thirties, Baba was a deeply religious women and very resilient. ... [Before coming to America] she spent her life in a European village where Jews were not, to say the least, always treated kindly. To move from such a place to a small American city where, as she walked to synagogue on a Saturday, her Christian neighbors would pass and say respectfully, "Good Sabbath, Mrs. Manger!" was an endless source of delight and gratitude for her. ... She never took her freedom and opportunity here for granted, and she made sure I didn't either. Baba also set a standard for service in our family, as one of the founders of the Hebrew Ladies Educational League in Stamford, a classic immigrant, self-help, pre-welfare organization which raised money and gave it quietly to those who needed it for food or clothing or birth or burial.[45]

Though a committed Jew, Lieberman revels in the pluralism of American society. He cites his participation in Martin Luther King's 1963 March on Washington as a major formative experience in his life. The march, he relates,

culminated at the Lincoln Memorial in [King's] soaring "I Have a Dream" speech. For me, this was America at its best. ... Hundreds of thousands of us, of all religions, races, and nationalities, joined together peacefully but powerfully to petition our government to right the wrong of racial bigotry.[46]

Despite his deep commitment to public service, Senator Lieberman insists on setting aside time for the Sabbath except in cases of extreme emergency sessions of the Senate. He explains:

In the helter-skelter push and pull of Senate life, Hadassah [his wife] and I have found that our religious observances provide very welcome relief, particularly the Sabbath, that weekly sanctuary between sunset on Friday and sundown on Saturday. This is the time when the worldly concerns of the rest of the week are put on hold so that we can focus on appreciating all that God has given us. It is a day apart, when my family and I are able to reconnect with one another and with our spiritual selves, to pray, to talk, to read, to rest, or to just plain enjoy ourselves. It is a "time beyond time," as one rabbi called it. In fact, I usually don't wear a watch on the Sabbath. I treasure that time, twenty-four hours with no meetings, no telephone calls, no television, no radio, no traveling, no business of any sort.[47]

reference to worshippers, and in reference to God. The Hebrew scriptures describe God as both female and male, validating new translations from the Hebrew that use gender-neutral language. As an example of the shift from male-centered to gender-neutral language, the biblical passage: "And God created man in his own image, in the image of God created He them; male and female created He them"[48] has been re-translated thus: "Thus God created us in the divine image, creating us in the image of God, creating us male and female."[49]

Feminist Susannah Heschel explains that changing God-language has profound implications for one's spirituality:

Whereas God may be neither male nor female, our language for God is overwhelmingly and decidedly male. The consequences of that exclusivity are theological and practical. For instance, we might assume that if God were imaged as female, it might be difficult to justify women's relegation behind the mehitza *[partition separating men and women in a synagogue] as preventing men from being distracted during their prayers. . . . We might also speculate about the impact on our experience at prayer if God were imaged as Mother as well as Father. How would the experience of Yom Kippur be different if we asked forgiveness from "Our Mother, Our Queen," rather than "Our Father, Our King"?*[50]

There is also a feminist critique of women's position in the state of Israel. Women among the early Zionist settlers envisioned a society in which men and women would work side by side and each apply their full capabilities to the creation of a new society. Even though laws were created that supported gender equality, traditional sexual divisions of labor were perpetuated, especially once the Orthodox parties took a major role in the formation and governance of the state. Judith Plaskow links the discrimination against women in Israel to the disempowerment of other minorities, including Palestinians and non-Ashkenazi Jews. She argues passionately,

The recognition of diverse constituencies as parts of larger communities involves an obligation to redefine communal life as the sum of all pieces. When one part has been accustomed to speaking for the whole—male Ashkenazi Jewish Israelis for Israelis, elite male Jews for Jews, middle-class white feminists for women—this definition may mean dislodging long-fixed patterns of dominance with difficult and dramatic results.[51]

Jewish renewal

Both men and women from varied backgrounds are being attracted to newly revitalized expressions of Jewish spirituality. After the Holocaust, many Jews had retreated from religious observance to avoid being conspicuous. Now, not only are some Jews becoming comfortable with being openly religious, but also conversions to Judaism seem to be increasing.

Although anti-semitism continues to flare up here and there, many non-Jews are developing sensitivity against negative stereotyping of Jews. The Evangelical Lutheran Church in America has issued an historic public apology for the anti-Jewish writings of Martin Luther, the father of Protestant Christianity. In part, they declared:

As did many of Luther's own companions in the sixteenth century, we reject this
violent invective, and yet more do we express our deep and abiding sorrow over its
tragic effects on subsequent generations. In concert with the Lutheran World
Federation, we particularly deplore the appropriation of Luther's words by modern
anti-Semites for the teaching of hatred toward Judaism or toward the Jewish people
in our day. . . . We recognize in anti-Semitism a contradiction and an affront to the
Gospel, a violation of our hope and calling, and we pledge this church to oppose the
deadly working of such bigotry.[52]

In post-Soviet Russia, where under Stalin Jews had been so persecuted that
only a few rabbis remained in all of Russia, there are now Jewish seminaries and
universities, schools, and kindergartens. Rabbi Dovid Karpov, whose congregation
serves one hundred and fifty free hot meals a day in Moscow, says that Judaism
has begun to flourish again after years of secrecy and danger:

Now we can celebrate holidays such as Hanukkah openly. It is not yet a mass
movement, but there are more people than you can count on your fingers. We feel
that soon we will see the fruit of our work. Judaism survives despite all the
persecutions. The new world is coming very soon and it will have a very different
form. The Messiah is coming. The time will soon come when we will have the peace
that everyone is waiting for. It will happen sooner than anyone can imagine.[53]

Contemporary Jewish renewal is not just an absence of fear. It is an active search
for personal meaning in the ancient rituals and scriptures, and the creation of new
rituals for our times. There are now numerous small *havurot*, or communities of
Jews, who are not affiliated with any formal group but get together on a regular
basis to worship and celebrate the traditions. They favor a democratic organization
and personal experience, and are often engaged in trying to determine what parts
of the traditions to use and how. Some incorporate study groups, continuing the
ancient intellectual tradition of grappling with the ethical, philosophical, and spiritual meanings of the texts. Some are bringing fresh ideas to traditional celebrations,
so that they are actively transformational rather than simply matters of empty habit.

From highly conservative to highly liberal quarters, there are now attempts to
renew the ancient messianic ideal of Judaism, that by its practice the world might
be healed. Michael Lerner, whose magazine title, *Tikkun*, is a Hebrew word that
refers to the healing and transformation of the world, explains:

A new generation of teachers, rabbis, community activists, and thinkers has begun
to reclaim the central insights of Judaism. It is no wonder that after having faced
massive and staggering destruction and dislocations, many Jews feel spiritually and
emotionally dead. We sought refuge from pogroms and genocide in societies that
were themselves spiritually and emotionally dead, and we did our best to assimilate
our Judaism to these societies because we hoped that inconspicuousness would keep
us from becoming targets. It has taken many decades for Jews to feel secure enough
to begin to renew the spiritual tradition. We are witnessing today the miraculous
regeneration of the primary ideals of Judaism that have been part of our tradition
since Abraham and Moses. . . . In every historical period, there has been a recreation
of the tradition through commentary, Midrash, and creative reinterpretation. . . .

After reading the Torah on Shabbat morning, Jews return the Torah to its ark or
resting point, and in fervent devotion sing a moving prayer: "It is a tree of life

to those who hold fast to it, and its precepts are right. Its paths are paths of pleasantness, and all its paths are peace. Return us to thee, Lord, and we shall return."[54]

Suggested reading

Ariel, David S., *The Mystic Quest: An Introduction to Jewish Mysticism*, Northvale, New Jersey: Jason Aronson, 1988. An accessible introduction to mystical Jewish thinking.

Baskin, Judith R., ed., *Jewish Women in Historical Perspective*, Detroit: Wayne State University Press, second edition, 1998. Fifteen pioneering essays by modern scholars explore Jewish women and their activities in a variety of times and places.

Ben-Sasson, H. H., ed., *A History of the Jewish People*, Cambridge, Massachusetts: Harvard University Press, 1976. Leading scholars of the Hebrew University in Jerusalem offer a comprehensive, scholarly analysis of Jewish history, which assumes some knowledge of the tradition.

Berger, Alan L., ed., *Judaism in the Modern World*, New York: New York University Press, 1994. Articles by leading contemporary Jewish scholars on facets of the changing identities and paradoxes of modern Jewry.

Cohen, Arthur A. and Mendes-Flohr, Paul, eds., *Contemporary Jewish Religious Thought*, New York: Charles Scribner's Sons, 1987. Brief essays on all aspects of Jewish belief, from aesthetics to Zionism, by writers from all Jewish schools.

Encyclopedia Judaica, Jerusalem: Keter Publishing House Jerusalem Ltd., 1972. The authoritative, multi-volume reference on all aspects of Judaism, as seen from a broad spectrum of points of view.

Glatzer, Nahum N., ed., *The Judaic Tradition*, Boston: Beacon Press, 1969. A useful compilation of writings from all periods of Jewish history.

Grossman, Susan and Haut, Rivka, eds., *Daughters of the King: Women and the Synagogue*, Philadelphia: Jewish Publication Society, 1992. An excellent anthology of history, halakhah, and contemporary testimonies concerning women and synagogue participation.

Heschel, Abraham J., *Between God and Man: An Interpretation of Judaism*, ed., Fritz A. Rothschild, New York: The Free Press, 1959. An intimate exploration of the relevance of traditional Judaism for today's world, by a great twentieth-century theologian.

Holtz, Barry, *Back to the Sources*, New York: Schocken Books, 1984. Excellent introduction to classical Jewish religious texts. Each chapter takes the reader through a step-by-step approach on how to read representative selections of the Bible, Talmud, Midrash, the Zohar, liturgical texts, and others.

Jacobs, Louis, *Principles of the Jewish Faith*, Northvale, New Jersey: Jason Aronson, 1964, 1988. Many commentaries spanning the centuries are brought to bear on thirteen central principles of Judaism as set forth by Maimonides.

Johnson, Paul, *A History of the Jews*, New York: HarperCollins, 1987. Informative, balanced, and thoughtful presentation of the many facets of the great span of Jewish history.

Lerner, Michael, *Jewish Renewal: A Path to Healing and Transformation*, New York: Harper-Collins, 1994. Profound and moving analyses of why Jews left Judaism and the revitalization that is drawing them back to faith.

Levine, Hillel, *Economic Origins of Antisemitism: Poland and its Jews in the Early Modern Period*, New Haven: Yale University Press, 1991. Brilliant insights into the relationships between anti-semitic trends and failed modernization in Poland when it was home to half of the world's Jews, the great majority of whom were then killed in the Holocaust, and paradigmatic for relations between Jews and Christians elsewhere and in other periods.

Plaskow, Judith, *Standing Again at Sinai: Judaism from a Feminist Perspective*, San Francisco: Harper San Francisco, 1991. Studies of all aspects of Jewish feminism, including the reconstruction of women's history, women in Israel, gender-equal God-language, sexuality in feminist religious context, and women's role in the repair of the world.

Ravitzky, Aviezer, *Messianism, Zionism, and Jewish Religious Radicalism*, Chicago: University of Chicago Press, 1996. Extensive analysis of varying Orthodox religious responses to Jewish statehood in Israel.

Schachter-Shalomi, Zalman, with Donald Gropman, *The First Step: A Guide for the New Jewish Spirit*, New York: Bantam Books, 1983. A modern explanation of the essence of Judaism, of special interest to non-observant Jews who want to find their way back into the faith.

Scholem, Gershom G., *Major Trends in Jewish Mysticism*, New York: Schocken Books, 1974. The classic scholarly work on the development of mystical Judaism.

Seltzer, Robert, *Jewish People, Jewish Thought: The Jewish Experience in History*, New York: Macmillan, 1980. An excellent, comprehensive, one-volume history of the Jewish people, with a particular emphasis on philosophy, mysticism, and religious thought.

Tanakh: The Holy Scriptures, The New JPS Translation according to the Traditional Hebrew Text, Philadelphia: The Jewish Publication Society, 1988. The preferred translation of the Hebrew scriptures, in graceful and spiritually sensitive modern English.

Wiesel, Elie, *Night*, New York: Bantam, 1960. Short, searing memoir of a teenage boy's Holocaust experience.

Wouk, Herman, *This is my God*, Boston: Little, Brown, 1959, 1988. A very readable personal description of a lived faith.

Key terms

Torah	The Pentateuch; also, the whole body of Jewish teaching and law.
Pentateuch	The five books of Moses at the beginning of the Hebrew Bible.
Tanakh	The Jewish scriptures.
Talmud	Jewish law and lore, as finally compiled in the sixth century CE
Messiah	The "anointed", the expected king and deliverer of the Jews; a term later applied by Christians to Jesus.
minyan	The quorum of ten adult males required for Jewish communal worship.
Midrash	The literature of delving into the Jewish Torah.
Kabbalah	The Jewish mystical tradition.
Hasidism	Ecstatic Jewish piety, dating from eighteenth-century Poland.
mitzvah **(plural: *mitzvot*)**	In Judaism, a divine commandment or sacred deed in fulfillment of a commandment.
Zionism	Movement dedicated to the establishment of a politically viable internationally recognized Jewish state in the biblical land of Israel.

Study questions

1 What are the four major categories of the Jewish Tanakh? Name a book from each. Tell their major themes and some characters.
2 Tell the importance for Jewish history and religion of the years 1200–1300 BCE, 1000 BCE, 586 BCE, 515 BCE, 70 CE, 1492 CE, and 1940 CE.
3 Describe the two creation stories in Genesis, chapter 1 to 2:4 and 2:4 through chapter 3, and their major themes. What do the different sequences of plant and animal creation imply about how to interpret biblical texts?
4 Describe the major Jewish Holy Days and ritual practices, including those of the mystics.
5 Describe the evolving role of women in Judaism. Discuss Eve, Sarah, Mishnah, Shekhinah, minyan, Susannah Heschel, and Judith Plaskow.

Refer to Pearson/Prentice Hall's **TIME Special Edition: World Religions** magazine for these and other current articles on topics related to many of the world's religions:

* *The Religious Experience: The Legacy of Abraham*
* *Judaism: Pop Goes the Kabbalah; A Ritual for All Ages; Jerusalem at the time of Jesus*

Chapter 8 focuses on Judaism. For further research in this area, use the tools available to you in Research Navigator:

As you investigate Judaism, consider this question: "What is the significance of Judaism as both a sacred religion and a secular identity?"

* **Ebsco's ContentSelect:** Search in the History, Religion, and Sociology databases using terms such as "Judaism," "Jewish identity," "orthodox Judaism."
* **Link Library:** Search in the Religion database under the category: "Religions of Mediterranean and Middle Eastern Origins: Judaism."
* **The *New York Times* on the Web:** Search in the Religious Studies and all other databases for current articles on related topics.

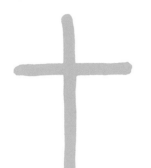

CHRISTIANITY

"Jesus Christ is Lord"

Christianity is a faith based on the life, teachings, death, and resurrection of Jesus. He was born as a Jew about two thousand years ago in Roman-occupied Palestine. He taught for fewer than three years and was executed by the Roman government on charges of sedition. Nothing was written about him at the time, although some years after his death, attempts were made to record what he had said and done. Yet his birth is now celebrated around the world and since the sixth century has been used as the major point from which public time is measured, even by non-Christians. The religion centered around him has more followers than any other.

In studying Christianity we will first examine what can be said about the life and teachings of Jesus, based on accounts in the Bible and on historians' knowledge of the period. We will then follow the evolution of the religion as it spread to all continents and became theologically and liturgically more complex. This process continues in the present, in which there are not one but many different versions of Christianity.

The Christian Bible

The Bibles used by various Christian churches consist of the Hebrew Bible (called the "Old Testament"), and in some cases non-canonical Jewish texts called the Apocrypha, and what Orthodox Christians call the Deuterocanonical books, plus the twenty-seven books of the "New Testament" written after Jesus's earthly mission.

Traditionally, the holy scriptures have been reverently regarded as the divinely inspired Word of God. Furthermore, in Eastern Orthodox Christianity, "the Gospel is not just Holy Scripture but also a symbol of Divine Wisdom and an image of Christ Himself."[1] Given the textual complexity of the Bible, some Christians have attempted to clarify what Jesus taught and how he lived, so that people might truly follow him.

The field of theological study that attempts to interpret scripture is called **hermeneutics**. In Jewish tradition, rabbis developed rules for interpretation. In the late second and early third centuries CE, Christian thinkers developed two highly different approaches to biblical hermeneutics. One of these stressed the literal meanings of the texts; the other looked for allegorical rather than literal meanings. Origen, an Egyptian theologian (c. 185–254 CE) who was a major proponent of the allegorical method, wrote:

Since there are certain passages of scripture which ... have no bodily [literal] sense at all, there are occasions when we must seek only for the soul and the spirit, as it were, of the passage. Who is so silly as to believe that God, after the manner of a farmer, "planted a paradise eastward in Eden," and set in it a visible and palpable "tree of life," of such a sort that anyone who tasted its fruit with his bodily teeth would gain life; and again that one could partake of "good and evil" by masticating the fruit taken from the tree of that name (Gen. 2: 8, 9)? And when God is said to "walk in the paradise in the cool of the day" and Adam to hide himself behind a tree, I do not think anyone will doubt that these are figurative expressions which indicate certain mysteries through a semblance of history and not through actual events (Gen. 3: 8).[2]

During medieval times, allowance was made for interpreting scriptural passages in at least four ways: literal, allegorical, moral (teaching ethical principles), and heavenly (divinely inspired and mystical, perhaps unintelligible to ordinary thinking). This fourfold approach was later followed by considerable debate on whether the Bible should be understood on the basis of its own internal evidence or whether it should be seen through the lens of Church tradition. During the eighteenth century, critical study of the Bible from a strictly historical point of view began in western Europe. This approach, now accepted by many Roman Catholics, Protestants, and some Orthodox, is based on the literary method of interpreting ancient writings in their historical context, with their intended audience and desired effect taken into account. In the nineteenth and twentieth centuries, emphasis shifted to questions about the process of hermeneutics, such as how to understand ancient texts that came from other cultures, how individual passages relate to the whole text, how the biblical message is conveyed through the medium of language, and how it is grasped by people in modern contexts.

There is very little historical proof of the life of Jesus outside of the Bible, but extensive scholarly research has turned up some shreds of evidence. The Jewish historian Josephus (born in approximately 37 CE), who was captured by the Romans and then defected to their side, wrote extensively about other details of Jewish history that have been confirmed by archaeological discoveries. He made two brief references to Jesus that may have been given a positive slant by Christian copyists, but are nonetheless now regarded as proof that Jesus did exist. In the *Baraitha* and *Tosefta*, supplements to the Jewish Mishnah, there are a few references to "Yeshu the Nazarene" who was said to practice "sorcery" (healings) and was "hanged."

What Christians believe about Jesus's life and teachings is based largely on biblical texts, particularly the first four books of the New Testament, which are called the **gospels** (good news). On the whole, they seem to have been originally written about forty to sixty years after Jesus's death. They are based on the oral transmission of the stories and discourses, which may have been influenced by the growing split between Christians and Jews. The documents, thought to be pseudonymous, are given the names of Jesus's followers Matthew and John, and of the apostle Paul's companions Mark and Luke. The gospels were first written down in Greek and perhaps Aramaic, the everyday language that Jesus spoke, and then copied and translated in many different ways over the centuries.

We do not know what Jesus, the founder of the world's largest religion, looked like. Rembrandt used a young European Jewish man as his model for this sensitive "portrait" of Jesus.

They offer a composite picture of Jesus as seen through the eyes of the Christian community.

Three of the gospels, Matthew, Mark, and Luke, are so similar that they are called the **synoptic** gospels, referring to the fact that they can be "seen together" as presenting rather similar views of Jesus's career, though they are organized somewhat differently. Most historians think that Matthew and Luke are largely based on Mark and another source called "Q." This hypothesized source would probably be a compilation of oral and written traditions. It is now thought that the author of Mark put together many fragments of oral tradition in order to develop a connected narrative about Jesus's life and ministry, for the sake of propagating the faith.

The other two synoptic gospels often parallel Mark quite closely but include additional material. The gospel according to Matthew (named after one of Jesus's original disciples, a tax collector) is sometimes called a Jewish Christian gospel. It represents Jesus as a second Moses as well as the Messiah ushering in the Kingdom of Heaven, with frequent references to the Old Testament. Matthew's stories emphasize that the Gentiles (non-Jews) accept Jesus, whereas the Jews reject him as savior.

Luke, to whom the third gospel is attributed, is traditionally thought to have been a physician who sometimes accompanied Paul the apostle. The gospel seems to have been written with a **Gentile** Christian audience in mind. Luke presents Jesus's mission in universal rather than exclusively Jewish terms and accentuates the importance of his ministry to the underprivileged and lower classes.

The Gospel of John, traditionally attributed to "the disciple Jesus loved," is of a very different nature from the other three. It concerns itself less with following the life of Jesus than with seeing Jesus as the eternal Son of God, the word of God made flesh. It is seen by many scholars as being later in origin than the synoptic gospels, perhaps having been written around the end of the first century CE. By this time, there was apparently a more critical conflict between Jews who believed in Jesus as the Messiah, and the majority of Jews, who did not recognize him as the Messiah they were awaiting. The Gospel of John seems to concentrate on confirming Jesus's Messiahship, and also to reflect Greek influences, such as a dualistic distinction between light and darkness. It is also more mystical and devotional in nature than the synoptic gospels.

> *The light shines on in the dark, and the darkness has never mastered it.*
> *The Gospel of John, 1: 5*

Other gospels circulating in the early Christian church were not included in the canon of the New Testament. They include magical stories of Jesus's infancy, such as an account of his making clay birds and then bringing them to life. The Gospel of Thomas, one of the long-hidden manuscripts discovered in 1945 by a peasant in a cave near Nag Hammadi, Egypt, is of particular interest. Some scholars feel that its core may have been written even earlier than the canonical gospels. It contains many sayings in common with the other gospels but places the accent on mystical concepts of Jesus:

*Jesus said: I am the Light that is above
them all. I am the All,
the All came forth from me and the All
attained to me. Cleave a (piece of) wood,
I am there; lift up the stone and you will
find Me there.[3]*

The life and teachings of Jesus

It is not possible to reconstruct from the gospels a single chronology of Jesus's life nor to account for much of what happened before he began his ministry. Nevertheless, the stories of the New Testament are important to Christians as the foundation of their faith. And after extensive analysis most scholars have concluded on grounds of linguistics and regional history that many of the sayings attributed to Jesus by the gospels may be authentic.

*Jesus is often pictured
as a divine child, born
in a humble stable,
and forced to flee on a
donkey with his parents.
(Monastère Bénédictin
de Keur Moussa,
Senegal, Fuite en
Egypte.)*

Birth

Most historians think Jesus was probably born a few years before the first year of what is now called the **Common Era**. When sixth-century Christian monks began figuring time in relationship to the life of Jesus, they may have miscalculated slightly. Traditionally, Christians have believed that Jesus was born in Bethlehem. This detail fulfills the rabbinic interpretation of the Old Testament

*"The Nativity," Jesus's
humble birth depicted
in a 14th-century fresco
by Giotto. (Scrovegni
Chapel, Padua, Italy.)*

*John the Baptist is said
to have baptized Jesus
only reluctantly, saying
that he was unworthy
even to fasten Jesus's
shoes. When he did so,
the Spirit allegedly
descended upon Jesus
as a dove. (Painting
by Esperanza Guevara,
Solentiname,
Nicaragua.)*

John the Baptist is said to have baptized Jesus only reluctantly, saying that he was unworthy even to fasten Jesus's shoes. When he did so, the Spirit allegedly descended upon Jesus as a dove. (Painting by Esperanza Guevara, Solentiname, Nicaragua.)

Christianity:
Jesus' Birth

prophecies that the Messiah would be born in Bethlehem, the home of David the great king, and in the lineage of David. The gospel of Matthew offers a genealogy tracing Jesus through David back to Abraham; the gospel of Luke traces his lineage all the way back to Adam, the son of God. Some scholars suggest that Jesus was actually born in or near Nazareth, his own home town in Galilee. This region, whose name meant "Ring of the Gentiles" (non-Jews), was not fully Jewish; it was also scorned as somewhat countrified by the rabbinic orthodoxy of Judaea. Both Judaea and Galilee were ruled by Rome at the time.

According to the gospels, Jesus's mother was Mary, who was a virgin when she conceived him by the Holy Spirit; her husband was Joseph, a carpenter from Bethlehem. Luke states that they had to go to Bethlehem to satisfy a Roman ruling that everyone should travel to their ancestral cities for a census. When they had made the difficult journey, there was no room for them in the inn, so the baby was born in a stable among the animals. He was named Jesus, which means "God saves." This well-loved birth legend exemplifies the humility that Jesus taught. According to Luke, those who came to pay their respects were poor shepherds to whom angels had appeared with the glad tidings that a Savior had been born to the people. Matthew tells instead of Magi, sages from "the east," who may have been Zoroastrians and who brought the Christ child symbolic gifts of gold and frankincense and myrrh, confirming his divine kingship and his adoration by Gentiles.

Preparation

No other stories are told about Jesus's childhood in Nazareth until he was twelve years old, when, according to the Gospel of Luke, he accompanied his parents on their yearly trip to Jerusalem for Passover. Left behind by mistake, he was said to have been discovered by his parents in the Temple discussing the Torah with the rabbis; "all who heard him were amazed at his understanding and his answers." When scolded, he reportedly replied, "Did you not know that I must be in my Father's house?"[4] This story is used to demonstrate his sense of mission even as a boy, his knowledge of Jewish tradition, and the close personal connection between Jesus and God. In later accounts of his prayers, he spoke to God as "Abba," a very familiar Aramaic and Hebrew word for father.

The New Testament is also silent about the years of Jesus's young manhood. What is described, however, is the ministry of John the Baptist, a prophet citing Isaiah's prophecies of the coming Kingdom of God. He was conducting baptism in the Jordan

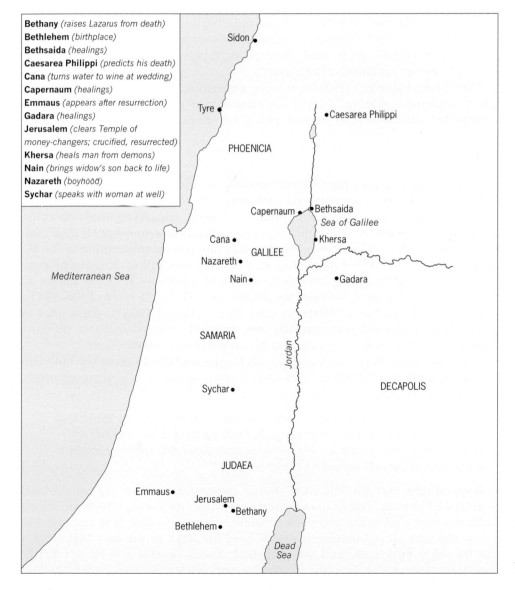

Bethany (raises Lazarus from death)
Bethlehem (birthplace)
Bethsaida (healings)
Caesarea Philippi (predicts his death)
Cana (turns water to wine at wedding)
Capernaum (healings)
Emmaus (appears after resurrection)
Gadara (healings)
Jerusalem (clears Temple of money-changers; crucified, resurrected)
Khersa (heals man from demons)
Nain (brings widow's son back to life)
Nazareth (boyhood)
Sychar (speaks with woman at well)

From north to south, the area covered by Jesus during his ministry was no more than 100 miles (161 km). Yet his mission is now worldwide, with more followers than any other religion.

River in preparation for the Kingdom of God. **Apocalyptic** expectations were running high at the time, with Israel chafing under Roman taxation and rule.

According to all four gospels, at the age of about thirty Jesus appeared before John to be baptized. John was calling people to repent of their sins and then be spiritually purified and sanctified by immersion in the river. He felt it improper to perform this ceremony for Jesus, whom Christians consider sinless, but Jesus insisted. How can this be interpreted? One explanation is that, for Jesus, this became a ceremony of his consecration to God as the Messiah. The gospel writer reports,

> *When he came up out of the water, immediately he saw the heavens opened and the Spirit descending upon him like a dove; and a voice came from heaven. "Thou art my beloved Son; with thee I am well pleased."*[5]

Another interpretation is that Jesus's baptism was the occasion for John's publicly announcing that the Messiah had arrived, beginning his ministry. A third interpretation is that by requesting baptism, Jesus identified himself with sinful humanity. Even though he had no need for repentance and purification, he accepted baptism on behalf of all humans.

After being baptized, Jesus reportedly undertook a forty-day retreat in the desert wilderness, fasting. During his retreat, the gospel writers say he was tempted by Satan to use his spiritual power for secular ends, but he refused.

Ministry

Christianity:
Jesus' Life and
Teachings

In John's gospel, Jesus's baptism and wilderness sojourn were followed by his gathering of the first disciples, the fisherman Simon (called Peter), Andrew (Peter's brother), James, and John (brother of James), who recognized him as the Messiah. Jesus warned his disciples that they would have to leave all their possessions and human attachments to follow him—to pay more attention to the life of the spirit than to physical comfort and wealth. This call to discipleship continues to be experienced by Christians today, and a person's response makes all the difference. The great German theologian Dietrich Bonhoeffer (1906–1945), who, opposing the Nazis, ultimately gave his life for his beliefs, wrote that to follow Jesus one must leave worldly ties and self-centered ways of thinking behind: "Only the man who is dead to his own will can follow Christ."[6]

Jesus said that it was extremely difficult for the wealthy to enter the kingdom of heaven. God, the Protector, takes care of physical needs, which are relatively unimportant anyway:

> *Is not life more than food, and the body more than clothing? Look at the birds of the air; they neither sow nor reap nor gather into barns, and yet your heavenly Father feeds them. Are you not of more value than they? And which of you by being anxious can add one cubit to his span of life?*[7]

Jesus taught that his followers should concentrate on laying up spiritual treasures in heaven, rather than material treasures on earth, which are short-lived. Because God is like a generous parent, those who love God and want to follow the path of righteousness should pray for help, in private: "Ask, and it will be given you; seek, and you will find; knock, and it will be opened to you."[8]

As Jesus traveled, speaking, he is said to have performed many miracles, such as turning water into wine, healing the sick, restoring the dead to life, walking on water, casting devils out of the possessed, and turning a few loaves and fish into enough food to feed a crowd of thousands, with copious leftovers. Jesus reportedly performed these miracles quietly and compassionately; the gospels interpreted them as signs of the coming Kingdom of God.

The stories of the miracles performed by Jesus have symbolic meanings taken from the entire Jewish and early Christian traditions. In the sharing of the loaves and fishes, for instance, it may have been more than physical bread that Luke was talking about when he said, "and all ate and were satisfied."[9] The people came to Jesus out of spiritual hunger, and he fed them all, profligate with his love. Bread often signified life-giving sustenance. Jesus was later to offer himself as "the bread of life."[10] On another level of interpretation, the story may prefigure the Last Supper of Jesus with his disciples, with both stories alluding to the Jewish tradition of the Great Banquet, the heavenly feast of God, as a symbol of the messianic age. The fish were a symbol of Christ to the early Christians; what he fed them was the indiscriminate gift of himself.

Theological interpretations of the biblical stories are based on the evidence of the Bible itself, but people also bring their own experiences to them. To William, a

Jesus is said to have brought Lazarus back to life four days after he died and was laid in a tomb. (Fresco by Giotto, Scrovegni Chapel, Padua, Italy.)

Living Christianity

Born into a devout small-town Southern Baptist family, David Vandiver is now the manager of a wilderness camp in the Appalachian Mountains near Washington, D.C., for inner-city African-American children whose backgrounds are very different from his own. Here he describes the evolution of his understanding and practice of Christianity.

"Becoming a Christian and a Baptist came as naturally as learning to walk and talk. The primary values as I grew up were ones of honesty, fairness, and caring for others. The great sins were the ones most affecting families—divorce, adultery, and irresponsible parenting. It was not until much later in my life that the vast scope of values held by Christians in differing places in the world came to my attention. I was not aware, for example, that there were Christians who believed God wanted them to influence politics for justice, work for equal rights for all people, protect the natural environment, or make peace with other nations and peoples of differing faiths. Our form of faith did a good job of supporting what was valuable in society, but did little to tear down what was destructive. We had no cause to practice tolerance because we were all so similar, except for the African-Americans in our town—about twenty per-cent of the population—who were already Christian and from whom we, as Anglo-Americans, wished to stay separated. I grew up with racism all around me.

"Nonetheless, as a high school youth in the early 1970s, I joined my friends in dragging my church into the foray of the U.S. Civil Rights Movement because I couldn't see Jesus as one who would keep any group of people powerless and poor. Christianity was a voice for the downtrodden and oppressed of the world, and if I was to follow Jesus, I would have to take up their cause for justice in some way.

"The most accessible way for me to take up this cause was to enter a path that would lead to a paid vocation as a Christian minister. It guided me to a Religion/Psychology major in college and later to a Masters of Divinity in Pastoral Counseling at a Baptist seminary. It was here that I began to consider the teachings of Jesus the Christ more deeply. What did it mean to 'love my neighbor as myself'? In practical terms, it came to mean that I could not simply spend the rest of my life pursuing a comfortable living while ignoring the fact that millions are living in poverty and oppression.

"Early in my seminary days, I was married to a wonderful woman, who lost her life in an automobile accident four months after our wedding. I found myself doubting the existence of a caring God. I was plunged into a dark night of the soul and feared I would never escape it. Slowly, as I re-emerged, it began to dawn on me that my plight was not mine alone; that millions had suffered and were suffering similar losses; that in fact, to love anyone was to risk such loss, and that the deeper the love the greater the loss. My understanding of God was transformed. It became clear to me that anything good and loving in life was a gift, sent as a precious favor.

"When I left seminary, on the one hand, I saw that following Jesus would take me out of the mainstream of the world in order to love it fully. On the other hand, I was painfully aware of the impossibility of loving others unconditionally. What as a child was an inherent identity that I learned as easily as learning to walk became a life-long journey that I would never fully complete.

"Vocationally and geographically, I have found a home as the manager of a wilderness camp for inner-city children from Washington. It is the perfect melding of my rural, small-town roots and the passion to serve the poor and oppressed. Many of the children who come to our camp have never been out of the city. As I watch and listen to them entering this environment that is foreign to them, they become my teachers, helping me to understand the fears with which they face the wilderness, and the fears they confront at home in the city. Each time I am with them, I am reminded of how I grew up, unaware of the larger world around me. I work to help them find the tools that will assist them in loving those they find difficult to love: their enemies, abusers, oppressors, and those who ignore them. The memories of all those who have given me those tools, and have held up the imperatives of Jesus to love the world, even those whom I find difficult to love, inspire me to carry on here in this wilderness of familiar and unfamiliar experiences and people."

twentieth-century Nicaraguan peasant, the miracle was not the multiplication of the loaves but the sharing: "The miracle was to persuade the owners of the bread to share it, that it was absurd for them to keep it all while the people were going hungry."[11]

Jesus preached and lived by truly radical ethics. In contrast to the prevailing patriarchal society and extensive proscriptions against impurity, he touched lepers and a bleeding woman to heal them; in his "table fellowship," he ate with people of all classes. In a culture in which the woman's role was strictly circumscribed, he welcomed women as his disciples. Mary Magdalene, Mary the mother of James the younger and Joses, Salome the mother of the disciples James and John, Mary of Bethany, Martha, Susanna, and Joanna are among those mentioned in the gospels. Some of them traveled with Jesus and even helped to support him and his disciples financially, a great departure from orthodox Jewish tradition. In addition, wives of some of Jesus's first male disciples who were married apparently accompanied them as they traveled with Jesus (1 Corinthians 9:5). His was a radically egalitarian vision.

He also extended the application of Jewish laws: "You have heard that it was said to the men of old," Jesus began, "You shall not kill; and whoever kills shall be liable to judgment. But I say to you that every one who is angry with his brother shall be liable to judgment."[12] Not only should a man not commit adultery; it is wrong even to look at a woman lustfully. Rather than taking revenge with an eye for an eye, a tooth for a tooth, respond with love. If a person strikes you on one cheek, turn the other cheek to be struck also. If anyone tries to rob you of your coat, give him your cloak as well. And not only should you love your neighbor, Jesus says:

> Love your enemies and pray for those who persecute you, so that you may be sons of your Father who is in heaven; for he makes his sun rise on the evil and on the good, and sends rain on the just and on the unjust.[13]

The extremely high ethical standards of the Sermon on the Mount (Matthew 5–7) may seem impossibly challenging. Who can fully follow them? And Jesus said these things to people who had been brought up with the understanding that to fulfill incompletely even one divine commandment is a violation of the Law. But when people recognize their helplessness to fulfill such commandments, they are ready to turn to the divine for help. Jesus pointed out, "With man this is impossible, but not with God; all things are possible with God."[14]

The main thing Jesus taught was love. He stated that to love God and to "love your neighbor as yourself"[15] were the two great commandments in Judaism, upon which everything else rested. To love God means placing God first in one's life, rather than concentrating on the things of the earth. To love one's neighbor means selfless service to everyone, even to those despised by the rest of society. Jesus often horrified the religious authorities by talking to prostitutes, tax-collectors, and the poorest and lowliest of people. He set an example of loving service by washing his disciples' feet. This kind of love, he said, should be the mark of his followers, and at the Last Judgment, when the Son of Man judges the people of all time, he will grant eternal life in the kingdom to the humble "sheep" who loved and served him in all:

> Then the righteous will answer him, "Lord, when did we see thee hungry and feed thee, or thirsty and give thee drink? And when did we see thee a stranger and

TEACHING STORY

The Good Samaritan

On one occasion a lawyer came forward to put this test question to Jesus: "Master, what must I do to inherit eternal life?" Jesus said, "What is written in the Law? What is your reading of it?" He replied, "Love the Lord your God with all your heart, with all your soul, with all your strength, and with all your mind; and your neighbor as yourself." "That is the right answer," said Jesus; "do that and you will live."

But he wanted to vindicate himself, so he said to Jesus, "And who is my neighbor?" Jesus replied, "A man was on his way from Jerusalem down to Jericho when he fell in with robbers, who stripped him, beat him, and went off leaving him half dead. It so happened that a priest was going down by the same road; but when he saw him, he went past on the other side. So too a Levite came to the place, and when he saw him went past on the other side. But a Samaritan [a person from a region against whom the Jews of Judaea had developed religious and racial prejudice] who was making the journey came upon him, and when he saw him was moved to pity. He went up and bandaged his wounds, bathing them with oil and wine. Then he lifted him on to his own beast, brought him to an inn, and looked after him there. Next day he produced two silver pieces and gave them to the innkeeper, and said, 'Look after him; and if you spend any more, I will repay you on my way back.' Which of these three do you think was neighbor to the man who fell into the hands of the robbers?" He answered, "The one who showed him kindness." Jesus said, "Go and do as he did."[16]

welcome thee, or naked and clothe thee? And when did we see thee sick or in prison and visit thee?" And the King will answer them, "Truly, I say to you, as you did it to one of the least of these my brethren, you did it to me."[17]

Jesus preached that God is forgiving to those who repent. He told a story likening God to the father who welcomed with gifts and celebration his "prodigal son" who had squandered his inheritance and then humbly returned home. He told story after story suggesting that those who considered themselves superior were more at odds with God than those who were aware of their sins. Those who sincerely repent—even if they are the hated toll-collectors, prostitutes, or ignorant common people—are more likely to receive God's forgiveness than are the learned and self-righteous. Indeed, Jesus said, it was only in childlikeness that people could enter the kingdom of heaven. In a famous series of statements about supreme happiness called the **Beatitudes**, Jesus is quoted as promising blessings for the "poor in spirit,"[18] the mourners, the meek, the seekers of righteousness, the pure in heart, the merciful, the peacemakers, and those who are persecuted for the sake of righteousness and of spreading the gospel.

Jesus's stories were typically presented as **parables**, in which earthly situations familiar to people of his time and place were used to make a spiritual point. He spoke of parents and children, of masters and servants, of sowing seeds, of fishing. For example,

The kingdom of heaven is like a dragnet cast into the sea that brings in a haul of all kinds. When it is full, the fishermen haul it ashore; then, sitting down, they

CHRISTIANITY

CE	c.4 BCE–30 CE Life of Jesus
50	c.50–60 St. Paul organizes early Christians c.70–95 Gospels written down
100	
	c.185–254 Life of Origen, who supports allegorical interpretation of Bible
300	
	306–337 Constantine emperor of Roman Empire 354–430 Life of St. Augustine, influential formulator of Christian doctrines 379–395 Christianity becomes state religion under rule of Emperor Theodosius 381–Nicene Creed adopted by Council of Constantinople
400 **500**	c.480–542 Life of St. Benedict and creation of his monastic rule
800	800–1300 Middle Ages in Europe; centralization of papal power
1000	
	1054 Split between Western and Eastern Orthodox Church 1095–1300 The Crusades
1100	
	1182–1226 Life of St. Francis of Assisi
1200	
	1232 The Inquisitions begin suppressing and punishing heretics
1300	1300s Proliferation of monastic orders
1400	
1500	
	1509–1564 Life of John Calvin 1517 Martin Luther posts 95 Theses 1534 Church of England separates from Rome 1545–1563 The Council of Trent; Roman Catholic Reformation
1700	1703–1791 Life of John Wesley, founder of Methodist Church c.1720–1780 The Enlightenment in Europe
1800	
	1859 Charles Darwin's *The Origin of Species* challenges beliefs in creation by God
1900	
	1945 Discovery of the Nag Hammadi manuscripts 1948 World Council of Churches formed 1962–1965 The Second Vatican Council 1988 Churches reopened in Russian Federation
2000	2000 Pope John Paul II asks forgiveness for sins of the Roman Catholic Church 2002 Boston's Roman Catholic Bishop resigns in growing scandal over sexual abuse by priests

collect the good ones in a basket and throw away those that are no use. This is how it will be at the end of time: the angels will appear and separate the wicked from the just to throw them into the blazing furnace where there will be weeping and grinding of teeth.[19]

As we have seen, messianic expectations were running very high among Jews of that time, oppressed as they were by Roman rule. They looked to a time when the people of Israel would be freed and the authority of Israel's God would be recognized throughout the world. Jesus reportedly spoke to them again and again about the fulfillment of these expectations: "The time is fulfilled, and the kingdom of God is at hand; repent, and believe in the gospel"[20]; "I must preach the good news of the kingdom of God ... for I was sent for this purpose."[21] He taught them to pray for the advent of this kingdom: "Thy kingdom come, Thy will be done on earth as it is in heaven."[22] However, in contrast to expectations of secular deliverance from the Romans, Jesus seems to refer to the kingdom as manifestation of God's full glory, the consummation of the world.

Every one who drinks of this water will thirst again, but whoever drinks of the water that I shall give him will never thirst; the water that I shall give him will become in him a spring of water welling up to eternal life.

Jesus, as quoted in the Gospel of John, 4:13–14

Jesus's references to the kingdom, as reported in the gospels, indicate two seemingly different emphases: one that the kingdom is expected in the future, and the other that the kingdom is already here. In his future references, as in the apocalyptic Jewish writings of the time, Jesus said that things would get much worse right before the end. He seemed to foretell the destruction of Jerusalem by the Romans that began in 70 CE. But:

then will appear the sign of the Son of man in heaven, and then all the tribes of the earth will mourn, and they will see the Son of man coming on the clouds of heaven with power and great glory; and he will send out his angels with a loud trumpet call, and they will gather his elect from the four winds, from one end of heaven to the other.[23]

It was his mission, he said, to gather together everyone who could be saved.

Challenges to the authorities

As Jesus traveled through Galilee, many people gathered around him to be healed. Herod Antipas, a Jew who had been appointed by the Romans as ruler of Galilee, had already executed John the Baptist and may have been concerned that Jesus might be a trouble-maker, perhaps one of the **Zealots** of Galilee who were stirring up support for a political uprising against the Romans. Jesus therefore moved outside Herod's jurisdiction for a while, to carry on his work in Tyre and Sidon (now in Lebanon).

According to the gospels, Jesus was also regarded with suspicion by prominent Jewish groups of his time—the emerging **Pharisees** (the shapers of rabbinic

Judaism), **Sadducees** (the temple priests and upper class), and the scribes (specially trained laymen who copied the written law and formulated the oral law of Judaism). Jesus seems not to have challenged Mosaic law, but rather, its interpretations in the evolving rabbinic traditions and the hypocrisy of some of those who claim to be living by the law. It is written in the Gospel of Matthew that the Pharisees and scribes challenged Jesus's disciples for not washing their hands before eating. Jesus responded:

> *Hypocrites! It was you Isaiah meant when he so rightly prophesied: "This people honors me only with lip service / while their hearts are far from me. / The worship they offer me is worthless; / the doctrines they teach are only human regulations."[24]*
>
> *He called the people to him and said, "Listen, and understand. What goes into the mouth does not make a man unclean; it is what comes out of the mouth that makes him unclean. . . . For things that come out of the mouth come from the heart, and it is these that make a man unclean. For from the heart come evil intentions. . . . But to eat with unwashed hands does not make a man unclean."[25] . . .*
>
> *"Alas for you, scribes and Pharisees, you hypocrites! You who are like whitewashed tombs that look handsome on the outside, but inside are full of dead men's bones and every kind of corruption. In the same way you appear to people from the outside like good honest men, but inside you are full of hypocrisy and lawlessness."[26]*

Many seemingly anti-Jewish statements in the New Testament are suspected by some modern scholars as additions or interpretations dating from the period after Jesus's death, when rabbinic Judaism and early Christianity were competing for followers. Nevertheless, more universal teachings are apparent in such stories attributed to Jesus. For instance, in all times and all religions there have been those who do not practice what they preach when claiming to speak with spiritual authority.

Jesus is said to have also confronted the commercial interests in the Temple of Jerusalem, those who were making a living by charging a profit when exchanging money for Temple currency and selling animals for sacrificial offerings:

> *So they reached Jerusalem and he went into the Temple and began driving out those who were selling and buying there; he upset the tables of the money changers and the chairs of those who were selling pigeons. Nor would he allow anyone to carry anything through the Temple. And he taught them and said, "Does not scripture say; 'My house will be called a house of prayer for all the peoples?'[27] But you have turned it into a robbers' den."[28] This came to the ears of the chief priests and the scribes, and they tried to find some way of doing away with him; they were afraid of him because the people were carried away by his teaching.[29]*

According to the gospel accounts, Jesus appropriated to himself the messianic prophecies of Second Isaiah. It is written that he privately asked his disciples, "Who do you say that I am?" Peter answered, "You are the Christ."[30] "Christ" is Greek for "anointed one," a translation of the Aramaic word *M'shekha* or **Messiah**, which also means "perfected" or "enlightened one." His disciples later spoke of him as the Messiah after he died and was resurrected. And his follower Martha, sister of Lazarus whom Jesus reportedly raised from the dead, is quoted as having said to Jesus, "I now believe that you are the Messiah, the Son of God who was to come

At the Last Supper, Jesus foretold his death and instructed his disciples to maintain mystic communion with him through a ceremony with bread and wine. (The Last Supper, attributed to Francisco Henriques, fl. 1500–18 [detail].)

into the world."[31] Some contemporary biblical scholars have concluded, however, that Jesus rejected the title of Messiah, for it might have been misunderstood.

According to the gospel tradition, a transcendental phenomenon, the "Transfiguration," was witnessed by three disciples. Jesus had climbed a mountain to pray, and as he did:

> *He was transfigured before them, and his face shone like the sun, and his garments became white as light. And behold, there appeared to them Moses and Elijah, talking with him. ... When lo, a bright cloud overshadowed them, and a voice from the cloud said, "This is my beloved Son, with whom I am well pleased; listen to him."[32]*

The presence of Moses and Elijah (who in Jewish apocalyptic tradition were expected to return at the end of the world) placed Jewish law and prophecy behind the claim that Jesus is the Christ. They were representatives of the old covenant with God; Jesus brought a new dispensation of grace.

Jesus claimed that John the Baptist was Elijah come again. The authorities had killed John the Baptist, and, Jesus prophesied, they would attack him, too, not recognizing who he was. John quotes Jesus as saying things like "My teaching is not mine, but his who sent me"; "I am the light of the world"; "You are from below, I am from above; you are of this world, I am not of this world"; and "Before Abraham was, I am."[33] Jesus characterized himself as a good shepherd who is willing to lay down his life for his sheep. Foreshadowing the Crucifixion, he said he would offer his own flesh and blood as a sacrifice for the sake of humanity. His coming death would mark a "new covenant" in which his blood would be "poured out for many for the forgiveness of sins."[34]

It is possible that such passages defining Jesus's role were later interpolations by the early Christians as they tried to explain the meaning of their Master's life and death in new terms during the decades when the New Testament was in the process of formation.

Crucifixion

The anti-institutional tenor of Jesus's teachings did not endear him to those in power. Jesus knew that to return to Jerusalem would be politically dangerous. But eventually he did so, at Passover. He entered the town in a humble way, riding on a donkey and accompanied by supporters who waved palm branches and announced him as the Messiah, crying,

> *"Hosanna! Blessed be he who comes in the name of the Lord! Blessed be the kingdom of our father David that is coming! Hosanna in the highest!"*[35]

However, Jesus warned his disciples that his end was near. At the Last Supper, a meal during the Passover season, he is said to have given them instructions for a ceremony with bread and wine to be performed thenceforth to maintain an ongoing communion with him. However, one of the disciples would betray him, he said. This one, Judas, had already done so, selling information leading to Jesus's arrest for thirty pieces of silver.

Jesus took three of his followers to a garden called Gethsemane, on the Mount of Olives, where he is said to have prayed intensely that the cup of suffering would pass away from him, if it be God's will, "yet not what I will, but what thou wilt."[36] The gospels often speak of Jesus's spending long periods in spontaneous prayer addressing God very personally as "Abba." It is possible to interpret Jesus's prayer at Gethsemane as a confirmation of his great faith in God's mercy and power. In the words of New Testament theologian Joachim Jeremias:

> *Jesus takes into account the possibility that God may rescind his own holy will . . . The Father of Jesus is not the immovable, unchangeable God who in the end can only be described in negations. He is not a God to whom it is pointless to pray. He is a gracious God, who hears prayers and intercessions, and is capable in his mercy of rescinding his own holy will.*[37]

Nevertheless, after this period of prayer Jesus said, according to Mark's gospel, "It is all over. The hour has come."[38] A crowd including Judas approached with swords and clubs; they led Jesus away to be questioned by the chief priest, elders, and scribes.

All four gospels include "passion narratives" describing Jesus's sufferings during his betrayal, trial, and execution by crucifixion. Matthew and Mark report a hearing before the high priest, Joseph Caiaphas. The high priest asked Jesus, "Are you the Christ?" Jesus answered:

> *You have said so. But I tell you, hereafter you will see the Son of man seated at the right hand of Power, and coming on the clouds of heaven.*[39]

Jesus's Crucifixion was interpreted by many later Christians as the sacrifice of an innocent lamb as atonement for the sins of humanity. Another interpretation was that God gave "himself or herself" in love, drawing the world into a loving relationship with the divine. (Rembrandt, The Three Crosses, *1653.)*

Caiaphas pronounced this statement blasphemy, punishable by death according to Jewish law. However, under Roman occupation the Sanhedrin (supreme Jewish court made up of chief priests, elders, and law teachers) was forbidden to pass the death sentence. Therefore Jesus was taken to Pontius Pilate, the Roman governor, for sentencing. To Pilate's leading question, "Are you King of the Jews?" Jesus is said to have replied, "You have said so."[40] According to the biblical accounts, Pilate seems to prefer to let Jesus off with a flogging, for he sees no reason to sentence him to death. Nevertheless, the crowd demands that he be killed on the grounds that he is a challenger to the earthly king, Caesar. The Gospel of John reports extraordinary dialogues between Pilate and Jesus as the crowd clamors for his execution. For instance, according to the Gospel of John, Pilate asks Jesus, "What have you done?" and Jesus reportedly replies:

> My kingdom does not belong to this world. My kingly authority comes from elsewhere." "You are a king then?" said Pilate. Jesus answered, "King is your word. My task is to bear witness to the truth. For this was I born; for this I came into the world, and all who are not deaf to truth listen to my voice." Pilate said, "What is truth?" and with those words went out again to the Jews.[41]

At last, unable to pacify Jesus's critics, Pilate turns him over to his military guard for execution by crucifixion, a form of death by torture widely used within the Roman Empire. In this method, the victim was typically tortured or beaten brutally with whips and then hung or nailed onto a wooden cross to die as a hideous example to intimidate the public. The guards put a crown made of thorns on Jesus's head and paraded him and his cross to the hill called Golgotha ("Place of the Skull"). It was probably used frequently for such executions. The accusation—"This is Jesus, King of the Jews"—was set over his head, and two robbers were crucified alongside him. The authorities, the people, and even the robbers mocked him for saying that he could save others when he could not even save himself.

Jesus hung there for hours until, according to the gospels, he cried out, "My God, my God, why hast thou forsaken me?"[42] This is the first line of Psalm 22, which is actually a great proclamation of the faith in God of one who is persecuted. Then Jesus died. This event is thought to have happened on a Friday some time between 27 and 33 CE. A wealthy Jewish disciple named Joseph of Arimathea asked Pilate for Jesus's body, which Joseph wrapped in a linen shroud and placed in his own tomb, with a large stone against the door. A guard was placed at the tomb to make sure that no followers would steal the body and claim that Jesus had risen from the dead.

Resurrection

That seemed to be the end of it. Jesus's disciples were terrified, so some of them hid, mourning and disheartened. The whole religious movement could have died out, as did other messianic cults. However, what is reported next in varying gospel accounts seemed to change everything. Some of the women who had been close to Jesus and had traveled with him from Galilee visited the tomb on Sunday to prepare the body for a proper burial, a rite that had been postponed because of the Sabbath. Instead, they found the tomb empty, with the stone rolled away. Angels then appeared and told them that Jesus had risen from death. The women ran and brought two of the male disciples, who witnessed the empty tomb with the shroud folded.

Christianity: Resurrection Story

Then followed numerous reports of appearances of the risen Christ to various disciples. He dispelled their doubts about his resurrection, having them touch his wounds and even eating a fish with them. He said to them, as recounted in the gospel of Matthew:

> All authority in heaven and on earth has been given to me. Go therefore and make disciples of all nations, baptizing them in the name of the Father and of the Son and of the Holy Spirit, teaching them to observe all that I have commanded you; and lo, I am with you always, to the close of the age.[43]

The details of the appearances of the resurrected Jesus differ considerably from gospel to gospel. However, some scholars think that to have women as the first witnesses to the empty tomb suggests that there must be some historical truth in the claims of Jesus's resurrection, for no one trying to build a case would have rested it on the testimony of women, who had little status in a patriarchal society. Feminist scholar Elisabeth Schüssler Fiorenza finds deep meaning in the presence of women disciples at the time of Jesus's death and resurrection. The gospels mention a woman who anoints Jesus, a sign that she recognizes him as the Messiah. (According to the gospel of John, this was Jesus's close follower, Mary of Bethany, sister of Lazarus.) The reports that it is women who faithfully visit the tomb suggest that, as Schüssler Fiorenza puts it,

Whereas according to Mark the leading male disciples do not understand this suffering messiahship of Jesus, reject it, and finally abandon him, the women disciples who have followed Jesus from Galilee to Jerusalem suddenly emerge as the true disciples in the passion narrative. They are Jesus' true followers who have understood that his ministry was not rule and kingly glory but diakonia, *"service" (Mark 15:41). Thus the women emerge as the true Christian ministers and witnesses. The unnamed woman who names Jesus with a prophetic sign-action in Mark's Gospel is the paradigm for the true disciple. While Peter had confessed, without truly understanding it, "you are the anointed one," the woman anointing Jesus recognizes clearly that Jesus' messiahship means suffering and death.*[44]

It was the resurrection that turned defeat into victory for Jesus, and discouragement into powerful action for his followers. As the impact of all they had seen set in, the followers came to believe that Jesus had been God present in a human life, walking among them.

The Early Church

Persecution became the lot of Jesus's followers. But by 380 CE, despite strong opposition, Christianity became the official religion of the vast Roman Empire. As it became the establishment, rather than a tiny, scattered band of dissidents within Judaism, Christianity continued to define and organize itself.

From persecution to empire

The earliest years of what became the mainstream of Christianity are described in the New Testament books that follow the gospel accounts of the life of Jesus. "The Acts of the Apostles" was presumably written by the same person who wrote the Gospel of Luke, for the style is the same, both books are addressed to the same person named Theophilus, and Acts refers back to the Gospel of Luke as an earlier part of a single history of the rise of Christianity. Acts is followed by letters to some of the early groups of Christians, most of them apparently written by Paul, a major organizer and apostle (missionary), in about 50 to 60 CE.

Like the gospel accounts, the stories in these biblical books are examined by many contemporary scholars as possibly romanticized, idealized documents, used to convert, to increase faith, to teach principles, and to establish Christian theology, rather than to accurately record historical facts.

According to Acts, an event called **Pentecost** galvanized the early Christians into action. At a meeting of the disciples, something that sounded like a great wind came down from the sky, and what looked like tongues of fire swirled around to touch each one's head. The narrative states that they all began speaking in different languages, so that all who listened could understand in their own language. Some mocked them, saying they were drunk, but Peter declared that they had been filled with the Spirit of God, as the Old Testament prophet Joel had prophesied would happen in the last days before the onset of the kingdom of God. He testified that the Jesus whom the people had crucified had been raised up by God, who had made him "both Lord and Christ."[45] Reportedly, 3,000 people were so convinced that they were baptized that day.

One of the persecutors of Christians was Saul. He was a Pharisee tentmaker who lived during the time of Jesus but never met him. Instead, after Jesus died, he helped to throw many of his followers into prison and sentence them to death. Acts relates that on the way to Damascus in search of more heretics, he saw a light brighter than the sun and heard the voice of Jesus asking why Saul was persecuting him. This resistance was useless, said the vision of Jesus, who then appointed him to do the opposite—to go to both Jews and Gentiles:

> *to open their eyes, that they may turn from darkness to light and from the power*
> *of Satan to God, that they may receive forgiveness of sins and a place among those*
> *who are sanctified by faith in me.*[46]

This meeting with the risen Christ, and through him, God, was an utterly transformational experience for Paul. He wrote about his previous life,

> *I count everything sheer loss, because all is so far outweighed by the gain of*
> *knowing Christ Jesus my Lord, for whose sake I did in fact lose everything. I count*
> *it so much garbage, for the sake of gaining Christ and finding myself incorporate in*
> *him, with no righteousness of my own, no legal rectitude, but the righteousness*
> *which comes from faith in Christ, given by God in response to faith. All I care for is*
> *to know Christ.*[47]

Saul was baptized and immediately began promoting the Christian message under his new name, Paul. His indefatigable work in traveling around the Mediterranean was of great importance in shaping and expanding the early Christian church. He was shipwrecked, stoned, imprisoned, and beaten, and probably died as a martyr in Rome, but nothing short of death deterred him from his new mission.

Paul tried to convince Jews that Jesus's birth, death, and resurrection had been predicted by the Old Testament prophets. This was the Messiah they had been waiting for, and now, risen from death, he presided as the cosmic Christ, offering God's forgiveness and grace to those who repented and trusted in God rather than in themselves. Some Jews were converted to this belief, and the Jewish authorities repeatedly accused Paul of leading people away from Jewish law and tradition. There was not only one Jewish tradition, however. The Pharisees, for instance, did not see God as belonging only to Israel, but rather as the parent watching over and taking care of every individual. They addressed God by new names, such as *Abinu she-Bashamayim* ("Our Father Who art in Heaven"), the same form of address by which Jesus reportedly taught his followers to pray to God (Matthew 6:9). However, a major difference remained between Jews and Christians over the central importance given to Jesus. It is possible that Jesus himself may not have claimed that he was the Messiah, and that it was Paul who developed this claim. To this day, Jews tend to feel that to put heavy emphasis on the person of Jesus takes attention away from Jesus's message and from God.

In Paul's time, those Jews who emphasized that Jews had been especially chosen by God were offended by interpretations of Jesus's life and teachings that saw Christianity as a universal mission of salvation for all peoples. These interpretations made the new sect, Christianity, seem irreconcilable with exclusive versions of Judaism, and the gap between the two became deep and bitter. The New Testament writings reflect the criticisms of the early Christians against the large Jewish majority who did not accept Jesus as their Messiah. These polemics have been echoed through the centuries as anti-semitism.

Paul also tried to sway Gentiles: worshippers of the old gods whose religion was in decline, supporters of the emperor as deity, ecstatic initiates of mystery cults, and followers of dualistic Greco-Roman philosophers who regarded matter as evil and tried to emancipate the soul from its corrupting influence. He taught them that God did not reside in any idol but yet was not far from them, "For in him we live and move and have our being."[48] For Gentiles embracing Christianity, Paul and others argued that the Jewish tradition of circumcision should not be required of them (as for example in Romans 2:29). As Paul interpreted the gospel, salvation came by repentant faith in the grace of Christ, rather than by observance of a traditional law. In Paul's letter to the church in Rome, he argues that even Abraham was **justified**, or accepted by God in spite of sin, because of his great faith in God rather than by his circumcision.

Christianity spread rapidly and soon became largely non-Jewish in membership. By 200 CE, it had spread throughout the Roman Empire and into Mesopotamia, despite fierce opposition. Many Christians were subjected to imprisonment, torture, and confiscation of property, because they rejected

Places visited by the apostle Paul during his far-reaching missionary journeys, 46–60 CE.

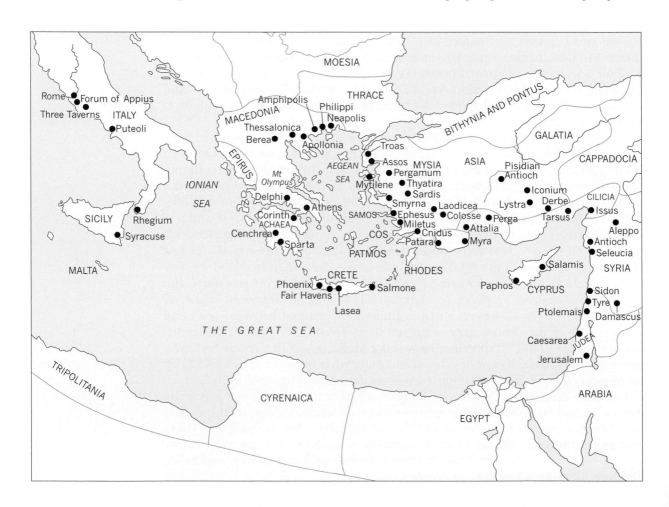

polytheistic beliefs, idols, and emperor worship in the Roman Empire. They were suspected of being revolutionaries, with their talk of a Messiah, and of strange cultic behaviors, such as their secret rituals of symbolically drinking Jesus's blood and eating his flesh. Persecution did not deter the most ardent of Christians; it united them intimately to the passion and death of Christ. In addition to martyrdom, many early Christians embraced a life of ascetic self-denial by fasting, wearing coarse clothes, renouncing sexuality, spending hours in prayer and contemplation, and serving others. They sought to be living sacrifices, giving up the pleasures of the material world for the sake of loving and serving God.

With the rise of Constantine to imperial rule early in the fourth century CE, opposition turned to the official embracing of Christianity. Constantine said that God showed him a vision of a cross to be used as a standard in battle. After he used it and won in 330 CE, he instituted tolerance of Christianity alongside the state cult, of which he was the chief priest. Just before his death, Constantine was baptized as a Christian.

By the end of the fourth century CE, people of other religions were stripped of all rights, and ordered into Christian churches to be baptized. Some paid outward service to Christianity but remained inwardly faithful to their old traditions. As Christianity became the favored religion, many converted for secular reasons.

By the end of the fifth century CE, Christianity was the faith claimed by the majority of people in the vast former Roman Empire. It also spread beyond the empire, from Ireland in the west to India and Ceylon (Sri Lanka) in the east.

Evolving organization and theology

During its phenomenal growth from persecuted sect to state religion throughout much of the ancient world, Christianity was developing organizationally and theologically. By the end of the first century CE, it had a bureaucracy that carried on the rites of the Church and attempted to define mainstream Christianity.

One form that was judged to be outside the mainstream was Gnostic Christianity, which appeared as a movement in the second century CE. **Gnosticism** means mystical perception of knowledge. The Nag Hammadi library found in Egypt presents Jesus as a great Gnostic teacher. His words are interpreted as the secret teachings given only to initiates. "He who is near to me is near to the fire," he says in the Gospel of Thomas.[49] The Gnostics held that only spiritually mature individuals could apprehend Jesus's real teaching: that the Kingdom of Heaven is a present reality experienced through personal realization of the Light.

When the New Testament canon of twenty-seven officially sanctioned texts was set and translated into Latin in the fourth century, the Gnostic gospels were not included. Instead, the Church treated possession of Gnostic texts as a crime against church law because the Christian faith community felt that Jesus had not taught an elitist view of salvation and had not discriminated against the material aspect of creation.

What became mainstream Christianity is based not only on the life and teachings of Jesus, as set forth in the gospels selected for the New Testament, but also on the ways that they have been interpreted over the centuries. One of the first and most important interpreters was Paul. His central contribution—which was

The Nag Hammadi manuscripts found in Egypt were buried about 400 CE. They contain copies and translations of early Christian texts condemned as heretical by the Church.

as influential as the four gospels in shaping Christianity—was his interpretation of Jesus's death and resurrection.

Paul spoke of *agape*—altruistic, self-giving love—as the center of Christian concern. He placed it above spiritual wisdom, asceticism, faith, and supernatural "gifts of the Spirit," such as the ability to heal, prophesy, or spontaneously speak in unknown tongues. Love was applied not only to one's neighbors but also to one's relationship with the divine. It was love plus gnosis—knowledge of God, permeated with love—that became the basis of contemplative Christianity, as it was shaped by the "Fathers" of the first centuries.

> *Let all that you do be done in love.*
>
> *1 Corinthians 16:14*

The cross, with or without an image of Jesus crucified on it, became a central symbol of Christianity. It marked the path of suffering service, rather than political domination, as the way of conquering evil and experiencing union with a compassionate God. To participate in Jesus's sacrifice, people could repent of their sins, be baptized, and be reborn to new life in Christ. In the early fifth century CE the bishop Augustine, one of the most influential theologians in the history of western Christianity, described this spiritual rebirth thus:

> *Where I was angry within myself in my chamber, where I was inwardly pricked, where I had sacrificed, slaying my old man and commencing the purpose of a new life, putting my trust in Thee—there hadst Thou begun to grow sweet unto me and "hadst put gladness in my heart."*[50]

Rowan Williams, the twenty-first-century theologian and Archbishop of the Anglican Church, explains this repentance and spiritual resurrection as:

the refusal to accept that lostness is the final human truth. Like a growing thing beneath the earth, we protest at the darkness and push blindly up in search of light, truth, home—the place, the relation where we are not lost, where we can live from deep roots in assurance. "Because I live, you will live also."[51]

The expectation of the coming of God's kingdom and final judgment of who would go to heaven and who to hell, so fervent in the earliest Christianity, began to wane as time went by and the anticipated events did not happen. The notion of the Kingdom of God began to shift to the indefinite future, with emphasis placed on a preliminary judgment at one's death. There was nevertheless the continuing expectation that Christ would return in glory to judge the living and the dead and bring to fulfillment the "new creation." This belief in the "Second Coming" of Christ is still an article of faith today for some Christians; others regard it as symbolizing pointing to the certainty of God's coming rule of love and peace.

Another early doctrinal development was the doctrine of the Holy **Trinity**. Christians believed that the transcendent, invisible God—the Father—had become immanent in the person of Jesus, God the Son. Furthermore, after his

The Holy Trinity, depicted in a famous Russian Orthodox icon by Rublev, is a distinctively Christian view of God. God is One as a communal plurality, an endless circle sharing the love intrinsic to the Godhead, inviting all to be healed and saved by this love.

physical death Jesus promised to send the Holy Spirit to his followers. This makes three "persons" within the one divine being: Father, Son, and Holy Spirit. The Father is envisioned as the almighty transcendent creator of heaven and earth. The Son is the incarnation of the Father, the divine in human form, who returned at the ascension to live with the Father in glory, though he remains fully present in and to his "mystical body" on earth—the community of believers. The Holy Spirit or Holy Ghost is the power and presence of God, actively guiding and sustaining the faithful.

Although Jesus had spoken in parables with several levels of meaning, the evolving Church found it necessary to articulate some of its beliefs more openly and systematically. A number of **creeds**, or professions of faith, were composed for use in religious instruction and baptism, to define who Jesus was and his relationship to God, and to provide clear stands in the face of various controversies. The Emperor Constantine was particularly concerned to bring doctrinal unity among the Christian churches which he had legalized and whose beliefs he was promoting throughout his widespread empire. One major controversy concerned the teachings of Arius, a leader of the congregation in Alexandria. The issue was the relationship between God and Jesus. The Christians worshipped Jesus, but at the same time came from monotheistic Jewish tradition, in which God alone is worshipped. Was Jesus therefore somehow the same as God? To Arius, the "Son of God" is a metaphor; it does not mean that Jesus has the same status as God, for Jesus was a human being. Opponents of this belief argued that Jesus is properly worshipped as the incarnation of God.

Constantine convened a general council of the elders of all area churches in Nicea in 325 CE to settle this critical issue. After decades of controversy, Arius's beliefs were ultimately rejected in the framing of the **Nicene Creed**, traditionally dated to another council held in Constantinople in 381 CE (and thus sometimes referred to as the Niceno-Constantinopolitan Creed). It is still the basic profession of faith for many Christian denominations in both East and West, including all Orthodox churches, and has been proposed as a basis for unifying all Christians:

We believe in one God, the Father, the almighty, maker of heaven and earth, of all that is, seen and unseen. We believe in one Lord, Jesus Christ, the only Son of God, eternally begotten of the Father, God from God, Light from Light, true God from true God, begotten not made, of one Being with the Father. Through him all things were made. For us men and for our salvation he came down from heaven; by the power of the Holy Spirit he became incarnate of the Virgin Mary, and was made man. For our sake he was crucified under Pontius Pilate; he suffered death and was buried. On the third day he rose again in accordance with the Scriptures; he ascended into heaven and is seated at the right hand of the Father. He will come again in glory to judge the living and the dead, and his kingdom will have no end. We believe in the Holy Spirit, the Lord, the giver of life, who proceeds from the Father (and from the Son). With the Father and the Son he is worshipped and glorified. He has spoken through the Prophets. We believe in one holy, catholic, and apostolic Church. We acknowledge one baptism for the forgiveness of sins. We look for the resurrection of the dead, and the life of the world to come. Amen.

As we will see later, the small phrase "and from the Son" was added to the creed by the Western part of the Church in the early Middle Ages and became a major point of disagreement between the Western Church and the Eastern Christian churches, which did not add it.

Christology—the attempt to define the nature of Jesus and his relationship to God—received further official clarification during the Council of Chalcedon in 451. This council issued a statement that allows considerable leeway in Christological interpretations by declaring that Jesus is of "two natures"—perfectly divine and also perfectly human. The Council of Chalcedon defined Jesus as:

> *perfect in divinity and humanity, truly God and truly human, consisting of a rational soul and a body, being of one substance with the Father in relation to his divinity, and being of one substance with us in relation to his humanity, and is like us in all things apart from sin (Hebrews 4:15). He was begotten of the Father before time in relation to his divinity, and in these recent days was born from the Virgin Mary, the Theotokos [Mother of God], for us and for our salvation.*

Early monasticism

Alongside the development of doctrine and the consolidation of church structure, another trend was developing. Some Christians were turning away from the world to live in solitary communion with God, as ascetics. There had been a certain amount of asceticism in Paul's writings. He himself was celibate, as he believed that avoiding family entanglements helped one to concentrate on the Lord.

By the fourth century CE, Christian monks were living simply in caves in the Egyptian desert with little regard for the things of the world. They had no central organization but tended to learn from the examples of sincere monks. Avoiding emphasis on the supernatural powers that often accompany the ascetic life, they told stories demonstrating the virtues they valued, such as humility, submission, and the sharing of food. For example, an earnest young man was said to have visited one of the desert fathers and asked how he was faring. The old man sighed and said, "Very badly, my child." Asked why, he said, "I have been here forty years doing nothing other than cursing my own self each day, inasmuch as in the prayers I offer, I say to God, 'Accursed are those who deviate from Your commandments.'"[52] The young seeker was moved by such humility and made it his model.

> *The carefree man, who has tested the sweetness of having no personal possessions, feels that even the cassock which he wears and the jug of water in his cell are a useless burden, because these things, too, sometimes distract his mind.*
>
> *A Desert Father*[53]

The desert monks were left to their own devices at first. In Christian humility, they avoided judging or trying to teach each other and attempted to be, at best, harmless. But by the fifth century CE, the monastic life shifted from solitary, unguided practice, to formal spiritual supervision. Group monasteries and structures for encouraging obedience to God through an abbot or abbess were set up, and rules devised to help monks persevere in their calling. The Rule of St. Benedict became a model for all later monastic orders in the West, with its

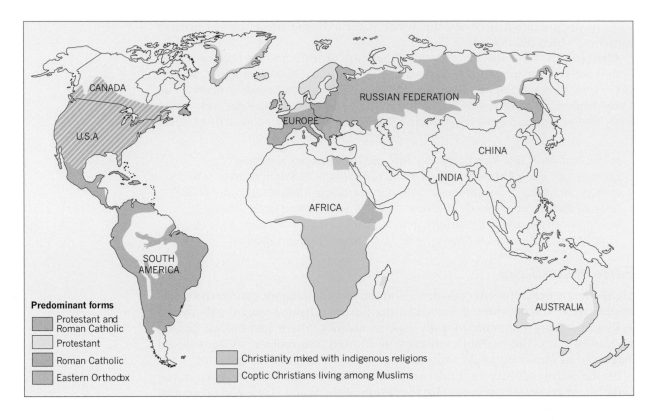

Map showing the approximate distribution of Christians in the world today.

Predominant forms
- Protestant and Roman Catholic
- Protestant
- Roman Catholic
- Eastern Orthodox
- Christianity mixed with indigenous religions
- Coptic Christians living among Muslims

emphasis on poverty, chastity, and obedience to the abbot, and its insistence that each monastery be economically self-sufficient through the labor of the monastics. The Benedictines have been famous over the centuries for their practice of hospitality to pilgrims and travelers, and are today active participants in inter-religious monastic dialogue.

The Eastern Orthodox Church

Christianity's history has been marked by internal feuds and divisions. One of the deepest schisms occurred in 1054, when the Roman Catholic Church, whose followers were largely in the West, and the Eastern Orthodox Church split apart.

The history of the Orthodox Church

Late in the third century CE, the Roman Empire had been divided into two: an eastern section and a western section. In the fourth century CE, Constantine established a second imperial seat in the east, in Constantinople (now Istanbul, Turkey). It was considered a "second Rome," especially after the sack of Rome by the Goths in 410. The two halves of the Christian world grew apart from each other, divided by language (Latin in the west, Greek in the east), culture, and religious differences.

In the western half, religious power was becoming more and more centralized in the Roman **pope** and other high officials. The Byzantine east was organized into a number of **sees**. The five major sees were those of Rome, Constantinople, Alexandria, Antioch, and Jerusalem. But this distinction was for organizational purposes; spiritually, all bishops, regardless of the status of the cities with which they are associated, are to today thought to be equal as successors to the original apostles, equally empowered to perform the sacraments and teach the faith. Rome was accorded a "primacy of honor" but not supreme jurisdiction.

The east did not recognize the Roman pope's claim to universal authority in the Church. By the early Middle Ages, there were also doctrinal disagreements. In its version of the Niceno-Constantinopolitan Creed, for example, the Western Church added the *filioque*, a formula professing that the Holy Spirit came from the Father *"and from the Son"*; the Eastern Church retained what is considered the more original text, professing that the Holy Spirit proceeds only from the Father.

In 1054, leaders of the eastern and western factions excommunicated each other over the disagreement about the Holy Spirit, and also over the papal claim, celibacy for priests (not required in the Eastern Church, which requires celibacy for bishops only), and whether the eucharistic bread should be leavened or unleavened. To the Eastern Church, the last straw was its treatment by crusaders.

From 1095 to about 1290, loosely organized waves of Christians poured out of Europe in what were presented as "Holy **crusades**" to recapture the holy land of Palestine from Muslims, to defend the Byzantine Empire against Muslim Turks, and in general to wipe out the enemies of Christianity. It was a tragic and bloody time. One of the many casualties was the already tenuous relationship between the Eastern and Western Churches. When crusaders entered Constantinople in 1204, they tried to intervene in local politics. Rebuffed, they were so furious that they ravaged the city. They destroyed the altar and sacred icons in Hagia Sophia, the awesome Church of the Holy Wisdom (later taken over as a Muslim mosque), and placed prostitutes on the throne reserved for the patriarch of the region. Horrified by such profanity, the Orthodox Church ended its dialogue with Rome and proceeded on its own path, claiming to be the true descendant of the apostolic Church. Despite periodic attempts at reconciliation the Eastern and Western Churches are still separate.

The Russian Orthodox Church

When the Muslim Ottoman Turks took Constantinople in the fifteenth century, Russia became more prominent in the Orthodox Church, calling itself the "third Rome." The Orthodox Church had spread throughout the Slavic and eastern Mediterranean countries.

Russian Orthodox Christianity was closely associated with Russian national history since its adoption by Vladimir I in 988. But it was severely repressed by the Soviet government during the twentieth century. Lenin saw institutionalized religion as a divisive, backward force in society, an apology for oppression, which should wither away in the socialist state. Following the 1917 Revolution, anti-Church propaganda was broadcast, and many intellectuals who sincerely wanted the good of society left the Church. Lenin proclaimed that all church property belonged to the State, and church properties were seized. Thousands of monasteries and churches were taken over during the Revolution, and in the early 1920s thousands of priests, nuns, and lay Christians were killed. During the 1930s more

RELIGION IN PRACTICE

Russian Orthodox Kenoticism

A great mystical spiritual tradition emerged on Russian soil. The **kenotic** pattern of loving and world-directed monastic work was set by the eleventh-century saint Theodosius, who attempted to imitate the poverty and self-sacrificing humility of Jesus. He ate nothing but dry bread and herbs, spent his nights in prayer and his days in work. He dressed in the rough clothes of a peasant, patiently bore insults, worked with his own hands—chopping wood, spinning thread, baking bread, comforting the sick—and refused to present himself as an authority, even though he became the revered leader of this monastic community.

It is recorded that once, after Theodosius had visited a distant prince, the prince sent his own coach to take the saint home in comfort. The coachman, seeing Theodosius's crude clothing, assumed he was a beggar, and asked him to mount the horse so that the coachman could sleep. The saint humbly did so and thus drove the coach all night, with the coachman sleeping inside. When St. Theodosius became too sleepy to drive, he dismounted and walked; when he became weary of walking, he rode again. As the morning sun rose, the noblemen of his area recognized him, dismounted, and bowed to him, whereupon the saint gently said to the coachman, "My child, it is light. Mount your horse." The coachman was amazed and terrified as he saw the great reverence paid to the saint as they proceeded. Rather than chastizing him, Theodosius led him by the hand to the refectory, ordered that he should be given all

the food and drink that he wanted, and paid him for the journey.

In the thirteenth century, Russia suffered from Mongolian invasions. Even though the Tartar Mongol khans nominally protected the Christians' freedom of religious practice when they themselves adopted Islam, spiritual and social life were in disarray. Monasticism shifted from urban settlements to the wilderness of the great forests of northern Russia. Hermit monks lived there in silence and solitary prayer until so many of the faithful gathered that thriving communities developed around them.

One of the most celebrated of the forest monks was St. Sergius. As a boy, Sergius retreated to the forest and built a small chapel for his intense devotions. Despite his noble lineage, he dressed like a peasant and did manual work. Even when he was abbot of the community that grew up around him, he was asked by one of his monks to build a cell, for which labor he was given a bit of moldy bread. In his contemplations, Sergius was said to be graced with visions of Mary, Mother of Christ, and of angels, fire, and light. He was nonetheless socially engaged with the national effort to resist foreign rule, and his blessing of the first victorious battle of Russians against the Tartars set the precedent for the future close links between Church and State in Russia. The relics of St. Sergius's body still lie undecayed in the huge and ornate Holy Trinity Lavra near Moscow in Zagorsk where once he had built his simple chapel. Among his followers were seventy famous saints of Russia.

monasteries and churches were closed, and great numbers of clergy were imprisoned. Bishops who refused to accept Soviet control issued what is called the Solovky Memorandum, which stated in part:

> *The Church recognizes spiritual principles of existence; communism rejects them. The Church believes in the living God, the Creator of the world, the leader of its life and destinies; communism denies his existence. Such a deep contradiction in the very basis of their Weltanschauungen [world views] precludes any intrinsic approximation or reconciliation between the Church and state, . . . because the very*

EASTERN ORTHODOX CHURCH

- Patriarchate of Constantinople
  (Turkey, Mt. Athos)
- Patriarchate of Alexandria
  (Egypt, Africa)
- Patriarchate of Antioch
  (Syria, Lebanon)
- Patriarchate of Jerusalem

- Self-governing local churches
  (Russia, Serbia, Rumania, Bulgaria,
  Georgia, Cyprus, Greece, Poland,
  Albania, Finland, Czech Republic)
- Plus archbishops or metropolitans
  in the Americas, Australia, India,
  and European countries

---

soul of the Church, the condition of her existence and the sense of her being, is that which is categorically denied by communism.[34]

The bishops were imprisoned in the Solovky labor camp; many were killed there. It is estimated that some 40,000 priests were killed from 1918 to 1940. Out of almost 80,000 churches and chapels in the Russian Empire in 1914, only a few hundred or a thousand remained by the beginning of World War II. Under Khrushchev, a new campaign against religion was unleashed, and perhaps two-thirds of the remaining Orthodox churches were closed.

Nevertheless, the Orthodox Church did not die, for it was deeply rooted in the minds and hearts of the people, and was closely linked to national identity. In the mid-1980s, the Russian Orthodox Church had an estimated 50 million members. Most of those who dared to worship publicly were the *babushkas*—the faithful old women who were apparently not regarded as politically dangerous.

After decades of severe oppression, the Russian Orthodox Church witnessed a great change in government policy in 1988, the celebration of its first millennium in Russia and Ukraine. Mikhail Gorbachev's government approached the Orthodox Church leaders, asking their help in Perestroika and returning some church buildings, which had been turned into museums or warehouses. Some 1,700 churches were reopened in 1988 and 1989, and each was immediately filled with worshippers again. Seminaries where new clergy are trained report a great increase in enrolment. Late in 1989, Soviet President Mikhail Gorbachev ended seven decades of suppression of religion, pronouncing the right of the Soviet faithful to "satisfy their spiritual needs."[55]

Nevertheless, many people are disillusioned with the contemporary Russian Orthodox Church because of its politics. As in all other institutions in the former Soviet Union, its staff included many KGB agents, and some of these people seem to have remained in their positions after the fall of the Soviet Union. Some church leaders felt that they had to make compromises in order to survive at all as a religion under Soviet rule. Now the Russian Orthodox Church has very powerful influence in government policy and is strongly supported by political leaders from all parties, including communists. Indeed, President Vladimir Putin, a former KGB officer, in 2000 praised the Orthodox Church's contribution to Russia's post-Soviet spiritual rebirth, and stated: "I believe that together (with the Church) we will achieve the spiritual revival of a strong, prospering Russia in the twenty-first century."[56] In the same year, the Orthodox Church declared the last Tsar a martyr and a saint because he was shot by a firing squad of Bolsheviks, described as enemies of the Church. The ceremony canonizing Tsar Nicholas and

A very visible symbol of the official recognition of the Russian Orthodox Church is the huge reconstructed Christ the Savior Temple, which now looms over the landscape of central Moscow.

his family was held in the huge new Christ the Savior Temple in Moscow, which had been torn down by Stalin and has been rebuilt on the same site.

Since the early days of the Soviet Union, there have also been Orthodox Christians who refused to collaborate or compromise with the government. At the risk of their jobs and lives, some Christian laypeople and priests began to worship secretly in what became known as catacomb churches, just as the early Christians had worshipped in underground catacombs to evade persecution. Father Alexey Vlasov, a catacomb priest, explains:

> *Members of this catacomb Church were risking their lives by worshipping. They tried to live by the Ten Commandments and live by love within society. It was not their intention to oppose the Orthodox Church but to bring Christ's love into society.*[57]

Even today, some Orthodox Christians continue to worship in secret rather than subject their congregations to the registration requirements of the state and disapproval of the official Church. Bishop Feodor, bishop of underground Christians in Moscow, Riga, and the Far East, objects to the assertive power of the Russian Orthodox Church:

> If the Church has pride, it has no holy power. We are all brothers in Adam and in Christ. We are all baptized by God. This is true for each Christian. If you cannot love your brother who is next to you, how can you love one you cannot see, such as Christ, who has not been with us for two thousand years?[58]

The Orthodox world today

There are now fifteen self-governing Orthodox Churches worldwide, each having its own leader, known as patriarch, metropolitan, or archbishop. The majority of Orthodox Christians now live in Russia, the Balkan states, and eastern Europe, in formerly communist countries where the teaching and propagation of Christianity had been severely restricted. Autocephalous (independent) churches there include the large Church of Russia, which is dominated by the Patriarchate of Moscow, plus the Churches of Serbia, Bulgaria, Romania, Albania, Poland, and the Czech Republic. The original and still central Patriarchate of Constantinople is based within Turkey, as a small minority within a Muslim country, which now has no Orthodox seminaries. This Patriarchate also includes islands in the Aegean and the precipitous Mount Athos peninsula. The latter was historically a great center of Orthodox monasticism, but its population

Contemporary Russian Orthodox worship in Sergeyev Posad before an elaborate iconostasis, where St. Sergius of Radonezh once built a small chapel in the forest to worship the Holy Trinity.

of monks declined considerably in the twentieth century when emigration of monks was prohibited by communist regimes. Now women are agitating to be allowed to enter Mount Athos, where even the presence of female animals is banned. Traditionalists maintain that Mount Athos is the only truly monastic community left in the world and should continue its antique ways unchanged and undistracted; women counter that the ban on women is degrading, a "sexist, anti-democratic decision taken by men, not by God."[59]

The Patriarchate of Alexandria is based in Egypt and includes all of Africa, where Orthodoxy arose independently in Uganda and has been embraced with considerable enthusiasm. The Patriarchate of Antioch consists mostly of Orthodox Christian Arabs in Syria and Lebanon. The Patriarchate of Jerusalem is charged with guarding the Holy Places of Christianity.

The Greek Orthodox Church dominates religious life in Greece and is assisting in the revival of interest in the classical books and arts of Orthodox spirituality. In the Church of Cyprus, the archbishop is also traditionally the political leader of the people. The Church of Sinai consists of only one monastery.

Extensive emigration, particularly from Russia during the first few years of communist rule, has also created large Orthodox populations in Western countries. Some retain direct ties to their home patriarchate, such as the New York-based Archdiocese of the Greek Orthodox Church in North and South America. Alongside that, the Orthodox Church in America was granted its independence in 1970, and now claims over four million members in a country where Protestantism and Roman Catholicism are the predominant forms of Christianity. Missionary activity by the Russian Orthodox Church also established Orthodoxy in China, Korea, Japan, and among the indigenous peoples in Alaska.

Most icon painters, such as this monk at Mt. Athos, Greece, use the ancient Byzantine style in creating sacred icons, which represent Christian stories and open windows to the divine.

Distinctive features of Orthodox spirituality

Over the centuries, the individual Orthodox Churches have probably changed less than have the many descendants of the early Western Church. There is a strong conservative tradition, attempting to preserve the pattern of early Christianity. Even though the religious leaders can make local adaptations suited to their region and people, they are united in doctrine and sacramental observances. Any change that will affect all churches is decided by a **synod**—a council of officials trying to reach common agreements, as did the early Church. Although women are important in local church affairs, they cannot be ordained as priests or serve in hierarchical capacities.

Christianity: Orthodox Easter

In addition to the Bible, Orthodox Christians honor the writings of the saints of the Church. Particularly important is a collection called the *Philokalia*. It consists of texts written by Orthodox masters between the fourth and fifteenth centuries. "Philokalia" means love of the exalted, excellent, and beautiful, in other words, the transcendent divine source of life and truth. The *Philokalia* is essentially a Christian guide to the contemplative life for monks, but it is also for laypeople. A central practice is called "unceasing prayer": the continual remembrance of Jesus or God, often through repetition of a verbal formula that gradually impresses itself on the heart. The most common petition is the "Jesus prayer": "Lord Jesus Christ, Son of God, have mercy on me, a sinner." The repetition of the name of Jesus brings purification of heart and singularity of desire. To call upon Jesus is to experience his presence in oneself and in all things.

The Orthodox Church has affirmed that humans can approach God directly. Some may even see the light of God and be utterly transformed by it:

He who participates in the divine energy, himself becomes, to some extent, light: he is united to the light, and by that light he sees in full awareness all that remains hidden to those who have not this grace; ... for the pure in heart see God ... who, being Light, dwells in them and reveals Himself to those who love Him, to His beloved.[60]

Another distinctive feature of Orthodox Christianity is its veneration of **icons**. These are stylized paintings of Jesus, his mother Mary, and the saints. They are created by artists who prepare for their work by prayer and ascetical training. There is no attempt at earthly realism, for icons are representations of the reality of the divine world. They are beloved as windows to the eternal. In addition to their devotional and instructional functions, some icons are reported to have great spiritual powers, heal illnesses, and transmit the holy presence. Believers enter into the grace of this power by kissing the icon reverently and praying before it.

Some of the major icons in an Orthodox church are placed on an iconostasis, a screen separating the floor area for the congregation from the Holy of Holies, the sanctuary that can be entered only by the clergy. On either side of the opening to the altar are icons of Jesus and the Virgin Mary ("Mother of God," often venerated as Protectress and Ruler of Russia).

Orthodox choirs sing the divine liturgy in many-part harmony, producing an ethereal and uplifting effect as the sounds echo and re-echo around each other. Everything strives toward that beauty to which the *Philokalia* refers. Archimandrite Nathaniel of the Russian Othodox Pskova-Pechorsky Monastery,

Christians light candles around a Christmas tree in Bucharest, Romania, December 25, 1989, as communism collapsed.

which has been a place of uninterrupted prayer for almost six hundred years despite eight hundred attacks on its walls and numerous sieges, speaks of the ideal of beauty in Orthodox Christianity:

> *The understanding of God is the understanding of beauty. Beauty is at the heart of our monastic life. The life of prayer is a constant well of beauty. We have the beauty of music in the Holy Liturgy. The great beauty of monastic life is communal life in Christ. Living together in love, living without enmity, as peaceful with each other as one dead body is peaceful with another dead body, we are dead to enmity.[61]*

Medieval Roman Catholicism

In the West, from the sixth to tenth centuries CE, the old Roman Empire gradually fell to non-Christian invaders. Islam also made spectacular advances in areas previously converted to Christianity. Arabs took Palestine, Syria, Mesopotamia, Egypt, North Africa, and part of Spain. However, the Angle and Saxon invaders of England were slowly converted to Christianity, with whole tribes joining the faith at the behest of their chiefs. By the fourteenth century, most of central and western Europe was claimed for Christianity, and missionaries spread the faith to isolated areas of Asia.

The Holy Roman Empire became politically decentralized into feudal kingdoms, with the Christian Church the major force uniting Europe. The chief factors sustaining Christianity through these chaotic centuries were its centralized organization under the Western pope and Eastern Orthodox Byzantine leaders and the periodic refreshing of its spiritual wellsprings through monasticism and mysticism.

Papal power

During the late first and early second centuries CE, some men and women had followed a charismatic Christian life, leaving home to preach, baptize, prophesy, and perhaps die as martyrs; others had moved toward an institutionalized patriarchal Church. By the beginning of the second century CE, a consolidation of spiritual power had begun with the designation of specific people to serve as clergy and bishops (superintendents) to administer the church affairs of each city or region. While some women served as deacons ministering to women, the clergy and bishops had to be male, with wife and children. The bishops of the chief cities of the Roman Empire had the greatest responsibilities and authority, with the greatest prestige being held by the Bishop of Rome, eventually known as the pope. By the fifth century CE, Pope Leo I argued that all popes were apostolic successors to Peter, the "rock" on which Jesus in Matthew's gospel said he would found his Church. The Roman emperor passed an edict that all Christians were to recognize the authority of the Bishop of Rome, the successor to Peter.

The young Catherine of Siena, "mother of thousands of souls," had a vision in which Christ, in the company of the Virgin Mary and other saints, gave her a wedding ring, the sign of the mystical marriage.

The strongest of church administrators during these early centuries was Gregory I ("the Great"), who died in 604 CE. Wealthy by birth but ascetic by choice, he devoted his personal fortune to founding monasteries and feeding the poor. Suffering from health problems and longing for the quiet life of a monk, he was reluctantly convinced to be pope at a time of pestilence, floods, and military invasions. Even in this setting, he managed to provide for the physical needs of the poor, promote the discipline of the clergy (including the Western ideal that priests should be celibate in order to concentrate on piety and ministry without family obligations and to avoid the economic loss of having to share church property with wives and children if priests and bishops were to marry), revamp the liturgy (Gregorian chanting is named after him), and to re-establish the Church as a decent, just institution carrying high spiritual values.

Pope Gregory also sent missionaries to convert England to Christianity. They were ultimately successful in gradually turning the people from worship of indigenous deities to worship of Jesus and the saints of the Church, partly because of the royal protection the missionaries and converts won and partly because rather than destroying the old religious shrines, Gregory instructed the missionaries to replace the old idols with relics of martyrs and saints—bits of bone, cloth, even dirt from their graves—which they carried to England. Worship of goddesses of the area was thus deflected to devotion to holy women from far away, whose deep spirituality was thought to be so strong that it was present in their relics.

The papacy began to wield tremendous secular power. Beginning in the eighth century, the approval of the papacy was sought as conferring divine sanction on feudal kings. In the ninth century the Church produced documents old and new believed to legitimate the hierarchical authority of the papacy over the Church, and the Church over society, as the proper means of transmitting inspiration from the divine to humanity. Those who disagreed could be threatened with **excommunication**. This exclusion from participation in the sacraments was a dread ban, cutting a person off from the redemption of the Church (blocking one's entrance to heaven in the afterlife), as well as from the benefits of the Church's secular power. Crusades were launched under the auspices of the Church, with war used ostensibly in defense of the faith, with no humane restraints on the treatment of the "infidel."

Late in the eleventh century, Pope Gregory VII set forth unprecedented claims for the papacy. The pope, he asserted, was divinely appointed and therefore could be ruled by no human. The pope had the right to depose emperors; the princes of the world should kiss his feet.

This centralization of power became a major unifying element in Europe of the Middle Ages. Kingdoms broke up between 800 and 1100 as Vikings invaded from the north and Magyars from the east. For the sake of military protection, peasants gave up their freedom to feudal lords. The feudal lords in turn began to war among themselves. In the midst of the ensuing chaos, people looked to the pope as an orderly wielder of power.

Church and states were at times locked in a mutual struggle for dominance, with popes alternately supporting, dominating, and being deposed by secular rulers. The power of the papacy was also somewhat limited by the requirement that the pope be elected by a council of cardinals. The position could not become

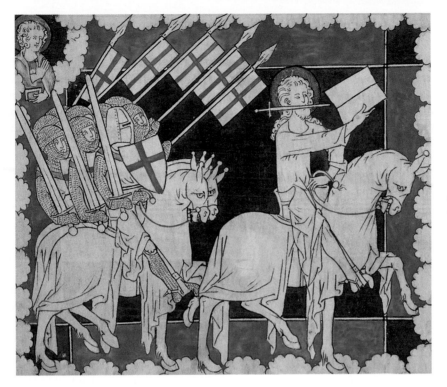

The Rider on the White Horse. After Jerusalem fell in 1077 to Turkish forces, who then denied Christian pilgrims access to the city, Western popes launched a series of Crusades to recover what Christians considered their Holy Land where Jesus had walked. The Crusaders' military expeditions were considered holy missions, carrying the cross and the Bible.

hereditary. But it was nonetheless open to intrigue, scandal, and power-mongering.

The thirteenth century saw the power of the papacy placed behind the **Inquisition**, an ecclesiastical court set up in 1229 to investigate and suppress heresy. This instrument of terror was based on Augustine's concept that heretics should be controlled for the sake of their own eternal salvation, out of love for their souls. But whereas Augustine saw fines and imprisonment as reasonable coercion to help people change their minds, in some cases the medieval Inquisitors had them tortured and burned to deter others from dangerous views. For example, in northern Italy and southern France a sect arose that was later called Cathari ("the pure"), for its members lived ascetically, emphasizing poverty and mutual aid. Though similar to Christianity in organization and worship, the movement denied that Jesus was the incarnation of God, and saw spirit as good but matter as bad. Such beliefs were proclaimed heretical by the papacy; the Cathari sect, attacked by the Inquisition, disappeared.

Though strong, the papacy was often embroiled in its own political strife. During the fourteenth century, the popes left their traditional seat in turbulent Rome for the more peaceful climate of Avignon, France. There they built up an elaborate administrative structure, increasingly involved in worldly affairs. After the papacy was persuaded to return to Rome, a would-be reformer, Pope Urban IV, turned to terror tactics to get his way. At one point he had five cardinals tortured and killed. Many people refused to follow him; for a while they followed an "anti-pope" they established in Avignon.

Intellectual revival and monasticism

Although the papacy was subject to abuses, mirrored on a lesser scale by the clergy, Christian spirituality was vigorously revived in other quarters of medieval society. During the twelfth and thirteenth centuries great universities developed in Europe, often from cathedral schools. Theology was considered the greatest of the sciences, with church ideals permeating the study of all areas of life. Soaring Gothic cathedrals were built to uplift the soul to heavenly heights, for God was perceived as being enthroned in the heavens, far above the workaday world.

The yearning for spiritual purity was particularly pronounced in monasticism. It was largely through monks and nuns that Christian spirituality survived and spread. Monasteries also became bulwarks of Western civilization. In Ireland, particularly, they were the centers of larger communities of laypeople and places of learning within illiterate warring societies.

During the twelfth century many new monastic orders appeared in the midst of a massive popular re-invigoration of spiritual activity. A major influence was a community in Cluny, France. Its monks specialized in liturgical elaborations and prayer, leaving agricultural work to serfs. An alternative direction was taken by the Cistercians, Gregorians, and Carthusians. They returned to St. Benedict's Rule of combining manual work and prayer; "to labor is to pray," said the monks. The Carthusians lived cloistered lives as hermits, meeting each other only for worship and business matters. Despite such austere practices, people of all classes flocked to monastic life as a pious refuge from decadent society.

> *It is not only prayer that gives God glory but work. . . . He is so great that all things give Him glory if you mean they should.*
>
> *Gerard Manley Hopkins*[62]

In contrast to monks and nuns living cloistered lives, mendicant friars, or brothers, worked among the people. In 1215, the Dominican Order was instituted primarily to teach the faith and refute heresies. A famous Dominican scholar, Thomas Aquinas, created a monumental work, *Summa Theologiae*, in which rational sciences and spiritual revelations were joined in an immense, consistent theological system. Aquinas was much influenced by the recovery of classical writings of Aristotle that had been preserved by Muslims and returned to Europe through Spain.

Franciscans, following the lead of the beloved St. Francis of Assisi (see below), wandered about without personal property or established buildings, telling people about God's love and accepting charity for their meager needs. The mendicant Dominicans and Franciscans, still noted as missionaries today, became one of the major features of medieval Christianity.

In addition to organized orders of nuns, there was a grassroots movement among thirteenth-century German and Flemish women to take private vows of chastity and simplicity. These women, who were called "beguines," lived frugally by their own work. Because they were not organized into a religious order, they chose their own lifestyles, intending simply to live "religiously." At times persecuted because it did not fit into any traditionally sanctioned pattern, the movement persisted, drawing tens of thousands of women. Eventually they built small convents for themselves; by the end of the fourteenth century, there were 169 beguine convents in Cologne, the heart of the movement.

Medieval mysticism

Mysticism also flowered during the Middle Ages, renewing the spiritual heart of the Church. Especially in cloistered settings, monks and nuns sat in contemplation of the meanings of the scriptures for the soul. Biblical stories of battles between heroes and their enemies were, for instance, interpreted as the struggle between the soul and one's baser desires. Beyond this rational thought, some engaged in quiet non-conceptual prayer, simply resting receptively in the presence of God.

In thirteenth-century Italy, there was the endearing figure of St. Francis of Assisi (1182–1226). The carefree, dashing son of a merchant, he underwent a radical spiritual transformation. He traded his fine clothes for simple garb and "left the world"[63] for a life of total poverty, caring for lepers and rebuilding dilapidated churches, since in a vision Jesus spoke to him from the cross, saying: "Repair my Church." Eventually Francis understood that his real mission was to rebuild the Church by re-emphasizing the gospel and its commands of love and poverty. A band of brothers and then of sisters, led by the saintly Clare, gathered around him. The friars preached, worked, begged, tended lepers, and lived a simple life of penance and prayer while wandering from town to town. This ascetic life was permeated with mystical joy, one of St. Francis's hallmarks. He was also known for his rapport with wild animals and is often pictured with birds resting lovingly on his shoulders. Two years before his death, Francis received the "stigmata," replicas on his own body of the crucifixion wounds of Jesus. This miracle was interpreted as a sign of the saint's union with Christ by suffering, prayer, holiness, and love.

The flowering of English mysticism during the fourteenth century was exemplified by Julian of Norwich (1342–c. 1416). As a girl, she had prayed that when she reached the age of thirty (the age at which Jesus began his public mission) she would have an illness that would bring her an understanding of his Passion (the sufferings of his final days). As requested, she did indeed become so ill when she was thirty that she almost died. During this crisis, she had visions and conversations with Christ, which revealed the boundless love with which he continually offers himself for humanity. Her writings delve into the perennial problem of reconciling the existence of evil with the experience of a loving God, whom she sometimes referred to as "God our Mother."

An anonymous fourteenth-century English writer contributed a volume entitled *The Cloud of Unknowing*. Christianity then and now largely follows what is called the affirmative way, with art, liturgy, scriptures, and imagery to aid devotion. But the author of *The Cloud* spoke to those who were prepared to undertake the negative way of abiding in sheer love for God, with no thoughts. God cannot be known through ideas or physical images; "a naked intent toward God, a desire for him alone, is enough."[64] In the silence of wordless prayer, the light of God may pierce the cloud of human unknowing that obscures the divine from the seeker.

Statues of St. Francis often show birds perched on him, representing his kinship with the natural world.

Fourteenth-century Italy witnessed a period of unprecedented degradation among the clergy, while the papacy occupied itself with organizational matters in Avignon. In this spiritual vacuum, laypeople gathered around saintly individuals to imbibe their atmosphere of genuine devotion. One of the most celebrated of these was the young Catherine of Siena. In her persistent efforts to restore spiritual purity and religious discipline to the Church, she gained the ear of Pope Gregory XI, helping to convince him to return to Rome. She was called "mother of thousands of souls," and people were said to be converted just by seeing her face.

The Protestant Reformation

Despite the genuine piety of individuals within the Catholic Church, some who clashed with its authority claimed that those in power seemed often to have lost touch with their own spiritual tradition. With the rise of literacy and printing in the late fifteenth century, many Christians were rediscovering early Christianity and comparing it unfavorably with what the Roman Catholic Church had made of it. Roman Catholic fund-raising or church-building financial activities were particularly criticized. These included **indulgences** (remission of the punishment for sin by the clergy in return for services or payments), the sale of relics, purchases of masses for the dead, spiritual pilgrimages, and the earning of spiritual "merit" by donating to the Church.

Salient among the reformists was Martin Luther (1483–1546). Luther was a monk, priest, and Professor of Biblical Studies at the University of Wittenberg. He struggled personally with the question of how one's sins could ever be totally atoned for by one's own actions. The Roman Catholic Church's position was that to be forgiven of post-baptismal sins, people should repent and then confess their sins to a priest and be pardoned. In addition, the punishment after death due to sins could be remitted either for the performance of prescribed penances or through the granting of an indulgence. Indulgences could even be purchased to make sure that the souls of those who had died repentant were freed from **Purgatory** (the intermediate place of purifying suffering for those who died in a state of repentance and grace but who were not yet sufficiently stainless to enter

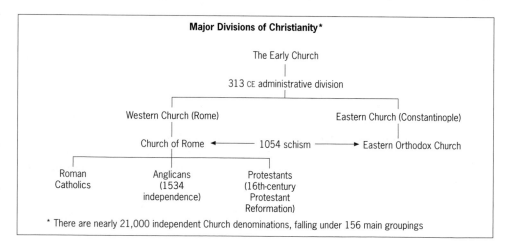

Major Divisions of Christianity*

The Early Church
|
313 CE administrative division

Western Church (Rome)   Eastern Church (Constantinople)

Church of Rome ◄──── 1054 schism ────► Eastern Orthodox Church

Roman   Anglicans   Protestants
Catholics   (1534   (16th-century
               independence)   Protestant
                                  Reformation)

* There are nearly 21,000 independent Church denominations, falling under 156 main groupings

heaven). The Castle Church at Wittenberg housed an immense collection of relics, including what were believed to be hairs from the Virgin Mary and a thorn from the "crown" of thorns placed on Jesus's head before he was crucified. This relic collection was deemed so powerful that those who viewed them on the proper day and contributed sufficiently to the Church could receive indulgences from the pope freeing themselves or their loved ones from almost two million years in Purgatory.

By intense study of the Bible, Luther began to emphasize a different approach. Both Paul and Augustine could be interpreted as saying that God, through Jesus, offered salvation to sinners in spite of their sins. This salvation was offered by God's grace alone and received solely by repentant faith. The good works and created graces prescribed by Catholics to earn merit in heaven were not part of original Christianity, Luther argued. Salvation from sin comes from faith in God, which itself comes from God, by grace. This gift of faith brings justification (being found righteous in God's sight) and then flowers as unselfish good works, which characterize the true Christian:

> *From faith flows love and joy in the Lord, and from love a joyful, willing and free mind that serves one's neighbor willingly and takes no account of gratitude or ingratitude, of praise or blame, of gain or loss. ... As our heavenly father has in Christ freely come to our help, we also ought freely to help our neighbor through our body and its works, and each should become as it were a Christ to the other.*[65]

In 1517 Luther invited the university community to debate this issue with him, by the established custom of nailing his theses to the door of the church. He apparently had no intention of splitting with the Church. But a papal bull (decree) of June 15, 1520 excommunicated him.

Cut off from Rome, Luther sought support from the secular princes of Germany. For reasons sometimes more political than spiritual, many came over to his side and helped to enforce his ideas. Although there were some attempts at compromise by followers of both Luther and Rome, conciliatory efforts collapsed.

Luther's evolving theology took him farther and farther from the institutions of the Roman Catholic Church. He did not think that the Bible supported the Roman Catholic tradition that pope, bishops, priests, and monks should have spiritual authority over laypeople; instead, he asserted that there is "a priesthood of all believers." He also felt that the sacred rites, or **sacraments**, of the Church were ways of nourishing faith instituted by Jesus and that they included only **baptism** and the **eucharist** (also known as the Lord's Supper, Holy Communion, or mass).

Another major reformer who eventually broke with Rome was the Swiss priest Ulrich Zwingli (1484–1531). He rejected practices not mentioned in the Bible, such as abstaining from meat during Lent, veneration of relics and saints, religious pilgrimages, and celibacy for monks and priests. Zwingli asserted that the Lord's Supper should be celebrated only as a memorial of Jesus's sacrifice; he did not believe in the myserious presence of Jesus's blood and body in the consecrated wine and bread. He even questioned the spiritual efficacy of rituals such as masses for the dead and confession of one's sins to a priest:

> *It is God alone who remits sins and puts the heart at rest, so to Him alone ought we to ascribe the healing of our wounds, to Him alone display them to be healed.*[66]

Martin Luther's political influence and prolific writings led to a deep split in the Western Church, severing Protestant reformers from the Roman Catholic Church. (Lucas Cranach the Elder, Martin Luther, *1533.)*

The ideals of these reformists were adopted by many Christians. The freedom of scriptural interpretation opened numerous options. Protestantism, as the new branch of Christianity came to be called, was never as monolithic as the Roman Catholic Church had been. Reform movements branched out in many directions, leading over time to a great proliferation of Protestant **denominations** (organized groups of congregations).

A major seat of Protestantism developed in Geneva, under John Calvin (1509–1564). He shared the reform principles of salvation by faith alone, the exclusive authority of the Bible, and "the priesthood of all believers." But Calvin carried the doctrine of salvation by faith to a new conclusion. To him, the appropriate response to God is a zealous piety and awe-struck reverence in which one "dreads to offend him more than to die."[67] Human actions are of no eternal significance because God has already decided the destiny of each person. By grace, some are to be saved; for God's own reasons, others are predestined to be damned eternally. Although there was therefore nothing that people could do about it, their behavior would reveal which fate awaited them.

Although only God absolutely knew who was saved, there are three signs which humans could recognize: profession of faith, an upright life, and participation in the sacraments. Calvin felt that the Church has the right to chastise and, in some extreme situations, excommunicate those who seemed to violate the sanctity of the Church. Calvin envisioned a holy commonwealth in which the Church, government, and citizens all cooperate to create a society dedicated to the glory and mission of God.

Calvin's version of Christianity made its followers feel that they should fear no one except God. Convinced that they were predestined to do God's will, they

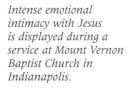

Intense emotional intimacy with Jesus is displayed during a service at Mount Vernon Baptist Church in Indianapolis.

were impervious to worldly obstacles to the spread of their faith. Calvinism became the state religion of Scotland and also had a following in England.

Concurrently, the Church of England separated from the Church of Rome when Henry VIII declared the English Church's independence from the Church of Rome. His daughter Elizabeth I finalized the breach with Rome in the Elizabethan Settlement of 1559. Now called Anglicanism, this form of Christianity is in communion with Old Catholics and also shares some similarities with the Protestant churches. The Anglican Church retains many of the Roman Catholic rituals but rejects the authority of the Roman Catholic pope (referring instead to its Archbishop of Canterbury as its spiritual leader) and allows priests to marry. One of its thirty-seven autonomous Churches is the Protestant Episcopal Church in the United States, a name referring to its being a Church with bishops. Another offshoot of the Church of England is Methodism. It originated with the evangelist John Wesley (1703–1791), who emphasized personal holiness and methodical devotions. He travelled an average of 8,000 miles (12,874 km) a year by horseback to promote "vital practical religion and by the grace of the life of God to beget, preserve, and increase the life of God in the souls of men."[68]

Martin Luther's reformation of the German Church led directly to present-day Lutheranism. It maintains a strong emphasis on liturgy and sacraments and is currently practiced mostly in Germany, Scandinavia, the Baltics, and the northeastern United States. As the Protestant Reformation progressed, political entities in Europe chose specific forms of Christianity as their official religions. Spain, France, and Italy remained largely Roman Catholic. Northern Germany was largely Lutheran. Ireland split between Catholicism and Protestantism, leading to wars that continue today. The two major Reformed Churches that sprung from Calvinism were the Scottish movement called Presbyterianism (in which the congregation is governed by **presbyters**, who rank second below bishops, ministers, and elders) and Congregationalism (which emphasizes the independence of each local church and the "priesthood" of all members). Some Polish and Hungarian communities adopted a form of Unitarianism, which rejected original sin, the Trinity, and Jesus's divinity in favor of a simple theism and imitation of Jesus.

Some Protestant groups that were outlawed by the Church of England emigrated to new colonies in North America. One of the largest of these groups is the Baptists, a denomination in which people are baptized as conscious adult believers rather than as infants. Quakers (formally known as the Religious Society of Friends) date from the seventeenth-century followers of George Fox. They traditionally worshipped without any liturgy or minister, in the hope that as they sat in worshipful silence, God would speak through any one of their members.

During the nineteenth and twentieth centuries, yet more Protestant churches sprang up in the United States, including evangelical churches—those emphasizing salvation by personal faith in Jesus, personal conversion, the importance of the Bible, and preaching instead of ritual. Seventh Day Adventists believe that the Second Coming of Christ will soon occur, and they regard the Bible as an absolute guide to faith and spiritual practice in anticipation of the return of Jesus. Jehovah's Witnesses criticize other Christian Churches as having developed false doctrines from the second century onward, and they urge people to leave these "false religions" and prepare for a coming time when all who do not hold true belief will be destroyed.

A Quaker ("Society of Friends") meeting, in York, England, in which worshippers sit silently, awaiting direct experience of the inner light of God.

Protestant missionary societies and evangelists were also active in carrying the gospel to Asia and Africa, where many independent denominations have evolved, and to South America, where Protestant groups are gaining strongholds in areas that had formerly been largely Roman Catholic since the Spanish conquests of these countries. This multi-culturalism and contemporary evangelism will be examined in detail at the end of this chapter.

Despite the great diversity among Protestant denominations, most share several characteristics that distinguish them somewhat from Orthodoxy and Roman Catholicism, though the Catholic Church's positions are now much closer to those of Protestants as a result of the profound changes introduced in 1962 by the Second Vatican Council. Both take the Bible as their foundation, but differ on how it is to be interpreted. Protestants tend to follow Martin Luther in believing that the individual's conscience and reason are the ultimate guides to understanding the scripture. This is in contrast to Roman Catholics who assert the authority of church tradition and the infallibility of the Vatican's pronouncements about essentials of the faith, and Orthodox, who regard the Bible as a "verbal icon" of Christ and thus tend to focus more on venerating it than on interpreting it. A second point that has divided Protestants and Roman Catholics is the Protestant belief that we can achieve salvation only by God's grace, through repentance and faith; Roman Catholics support the doctrine of salvation by both faith and good works. A third divisive issue is that of spiritual authority. Protestantism asserts the "priesthood of all believers" and the individual's direct relationship to God and Jesus, in contrast to Roman Catholicism, which stands on mediation of God's grace through the officials of the Church. The officials themselves differ in many respects, such as the provision that Protestant ministers can be married, unlike Catholic priests, who are expected to remain celibate in the belief that restraint of physical desires enhances spirituality. Fourth, Protestants have radically redefined the Roman Catholic and Orthodox concept of sacraments; Luther and Zwingli insisted that the only holy sacraments are those instituted by Jesus and regarded even those as instructive or commemorative rather than as mystical vehicles for God's grace. The sacraments and their meanings for Protestants, Roman Catholics, and Orthodox believers will be examined in depth later in this chapter.

The Roman Catholic Reformation

As the Protestant reformers were defining their positions, so was the Roman Catholic Church. Because reform pressures were underway in Catholicism before Luther, Catholics refer to the movement as the Catholic Reformation, rather than the "Counter-Reformation," as Protestants call it. However, the Protestant phenomena provoked the Roman Catholic Church to clarify its own position through councils of bishops, especially the Council of Trent (1545–1563). It attempted to legislate moral reform among the clergy, to tighten the church administration, and to recognize officially the absolute authority of the pope as the earthly vicar of God and Jesus Christ. The Council also took historic stands on a number of issues, emphasizing that its positions were **dogmas**, or authoritative truths. For example, one of the fundamental doctrines of the Roman Catholic Church is the dogma of **original sin**. All humans are said to be morally defective, or "fallen," having inherited a sinful nature from the first human ancestors. They can be saved from this condition only by the grace of God, as mediated through the death and resurrection of Jesus.

The Council of Trent reiterated that salvation requires "good works" as well as faith. These works include acts of mercy, veneration of the saints, relics, and sacred images, and participation in the sacraments. In the sacrament of the eucharist, the Council reiterated the doctrine of **transubstantiation**: what appear to be ordinary bread and wine are mysteriously transformed into the body and blood of Christ.

In addition to the actions of the Council of Trent, the Roman Catholic Church gradually chose more virtuous popes than some in the past, and several new monastic orders grew out of the desires for reform. The Jesuits offered themselves as an army for God at the service of the pope. The Society of Jesus, as the order was formally called, was begun by Ignatius Loyola (1491–1556) in the sixteenth century. His *Spiritual Exercises* is still regarded as an excellent guide to meditation and spiritual discernment. However, it was as activists and educators in the everyday world that Jesuits were highly influential in the Reformation, and they were among the first to carry Roman Catholicism to Asia.

Roman Catholicism was also carried to the western hemisphere and the Philippines by Spanish *conquistadores*. At home, Spain was host to a number of outstanding mystics during the sixteenth and seventeenth centuries. St. Teresa of Avila (1515–1582), a Carmelite nun, became at mid-life a dynamo of spiritual activity, in an order of ascetic Reformed (or Discalced, which means "barefooted") Carmelite nuns and monks. Discalced Carmelites usually pray much, and eat and sleep little. Despite her organizational activity, St. Teresa was able to maintain a calm sense of deep inner communion with God. In her masterpiece entitled *The Interior Castle*, she described the state of "spiritual marriage":

> *Here it is like rain falling from the heavens into a river or a spring; there is nothing but water there and it is impossible to divide or separate the water belonging to the river from that which fell from the heavens.*[69]

St. Teresa's great influence fell onto a young friend, now known as St. John of the Cross. He became a member of one of the Carmelite houses for men; when imprisoned by other Carmelites who opposed the reforms, he experienced visions and wrote profound spiritual poetry. For John, the most important step for the soul longing to be filled with God is to surrender all vestiges of the self. This state he called the "dark night of the soul," a relinquishing of human reasoning into a state of not-knowing into which the pure light of God may enter without resistance. He is still considered one of the great masters of the spiritual life.

The impact of the Enlightenment

Major potential threats to Christianity arose during the eighteenth-century Enlightenment in Europe. Intellectual circles exalted human reason and on this basis rejected faith in biblical miracles and revelations. Some people felt that nineteenth-century scientific advances undermined the biblical story of the creation of the world. However, many nineteenth-century scientists were devout Christians who viewed the truth of science as supporting the truth of faith. There emerged two opposing trends: a liberal one, trying to join faith with modern knowledge, and a conservative one, emphasizing the conflict between faith and science. Both views spread rapidly, dividing between them much of Christendom, especially Protestantism. In 1911, "fundamentalists" in the United States published as their uncompromising tenets the total inerrancy of the Bible, and Christ's literal virgin birth, substitutionary atonement, bodily resurrection, and anticipated second coming. Meanwhile, "modernist" theologians were interpreting such concepts in symbolic terms, with an aversion to dogmatism. Individuals were encouraged to judge religious beliefs by their own experience.

Undaunted, and in some cases invigorated, by these challenges to traditional faith, Protestantism developed a strong missionary spirit, joining Roman Catholic efforts to spread Christianity to every country, along with colonialism. As John Wesley, the founder of Methodism, had explained:

> *I looked upon all the world as my parish; ... that in whatever part of it I am, I judge it meet, right, and my bounden duty to declare unto all that are willing to hear, the glad tidings of salvation.*[70]

The "social gospel" movement brought Protestant churches to the forefront of efforts at social and moral reform. Women, long excluded from important positions in the Church, played major roles in Church-related missionary and reform efforts, such as the abolition of slavery; they cited certain biblical passages as supporting equality of the sexes. When Sarah Grimke (1792–1873) and other women were criticized by their Congregational church for speaking publicly against slavery, Grimke asserted, "All I ask of my brethren is that they will take their feet from off our necks and permit us to stand upright on that ground which God has designed us to occupy."[71]

Liberal trends in Protestant theology led to efforts to analyze the Bible as literature. What, for instance, were the earliest texts? Who wrote them? How did they relate to each other? Such questions, unthinkable in earlier generations, continue to enliven Christian theological debate.

The Second Vatican Council

In the meantime, the Roman Catholic and Eastern Orthodox Churches had continued to defend tradition against the changes of modern life. A general council of the Roman Catholic hierarchs was held in 1869–1870. It found itself embroiled chiefly in the question of papal infallibility, a doctrine it ultimately upheld. The pope, proclaimed the bishops of the council, can never err when he speaks from the seat of his authority (*ex cathedra*), on matters of faith and morals.

In 1962, Pope John XXIII, known for his holiness and friendliness, convened the Second Vatican Council for the express purposes of updating and energizing the Church and making it serve the people better as a living force in the modern world rather than being an old, embattled citadel. When questioned about his intentions, he demonstrated by opening a window to let in fresh air. With progressives and traditionalists often at odds, the majority nevertheless voted for major shifts in the Church's mission.

Many of the changes involved the liturgy of the mass, or the eucharist. Rather than celebrate it in Latin, which most people did not understand, the liturgy was to be translated into the local languages. Rites were to be simplified. Greater use of sacred music was encouraged, and not just formal, traditional organ and choir offerings.

For the first time the laity were to be invited to participate actively. After Vatican II thus unleashed creativity and simplicity in public worship, entirely new forms appeared, such as informal folk masses—with spiritual folk songs sung to guitar accompaniment.

Another major change was the new emphasis on **ecumenism**, in the sense of rapprochement among all branches of Christianity. The Roman Catholic Church acknowledged that the Holy Spirit is active in all Christian churches, including Protestant denominations and the Eastern Orthodox churches. It pressed for a restoration of unity among all Christians, proclaiming that each could preserve its traditions intact. It also extended the concept of revelation, increasing the hope of dialogue with Jews, with whom Christians share "spiritual patrimony"[72] and with Muslims, upon whom the Church "looks with esteem," for they "adore one God" and honor Jesus as a prophet. Appreciative mention was also made of other world religions as ways of approaching the same One whom Christians call God. Specifically described were Hinduism ("through which men contemplate the divine mystery") and Buddhism ("which acknowledges the radical insufficiency of this shifting world").[73]

Vatican II clearly marked major new directions in Catholicism. Its relatively liberal, pacificistic characteristics are still meeting with some opposition within the Church decades later. In the late twentieth century, conservative elements in

the Vatican began to reverse the direction taken by Vatican II to some extent, to the dismay of liberal Catholics. In the final section of this chapter, concerning current trends in Christianity, we will note several ways in which the renewed conservatism in the Vatican is being expressed.

Central beliefs in contemporary Christianity

Christianity: Mother Teresa and Sister Emmanuel

The history of Christianity is characterized more by divisions than by uniformity among Christian groups. The Church is vast and culturally diverse, and Christian theologies are complex and intricate. Nevertheless, there are a few basic motifs on which the majority of faithful Christians would probably agree today.

A central belief is the divine Sonship of Jesus—the assertion that Jesus is the incarnation of God. According to the Gospel of John, before Jesus's death he told his disciples that he would be going to "my Father's house . . . to prepare a place for you." When they asked how they would find the way to that place, Jesus reportedly said:

> *I am the way, I am the truth and I am life. No one comes to the Father except by me. . . . Anyone who has seen me has seen the Father. . . . It is the Father who dwells in me doing his own work.*[74]

Throughout most of Christian history, there has been the belief that Jesus was the only incarnation of God. Interestingly, Thomas Aquinas argued that although

God could become incarnate in multiple incarnations (as in Hindu belief), in fact he chose to do so only once, in Christ. Theologian Paul Knitter is one of the contemporary voices calling for a less exclusive approach that still honors the unique contribution of Jesus:

> *What Christians do know, on the basis of their praxis of following Jesus, is that his message* is *a sure means for bringing about liberation from injustice and oppression, that it* is *an effective, hope-filled, universally meaningful way of realizing* Soteria *[human welfare and liberation of the poor and oppressed] and promoting God's kingdom. . . . Not those who proclaim "only Lord, only Lord," but those who* do *the will of the Father will enter the kingdom (Matthew 7:21–23).*[75]

For Christians, Jesus is the Savior of the world, the one whom God sent to redeem people from their sins and reconcile them with God. Matthew reports that Jesus said he "did not come to be served, but to serve, and to give up his life as a ransom for many."[76] His own suffering and death are regarded as a substitute sacrifice on behalf of all those who follow and place their faith in him. According to the Gospel of John,

> *God loved the world so much that he gave his only Son, that everyone who has faith in him may not die but have eternal life. It was not to judge the world that God sent his Son into the world, but that through him the world might be saved.*[77]

According to one strand of Christian belief, humanity has a sinful character, illustrated metaphorically in the Old Testament by the fall of Adam and Eve. We have lost our original purity. Given free will by God, we have chosen disobedience rather than surrender to the will of God. We cannot save ourselves from our fallen condition; we can only be forgiven by the compassion of a loving God. However, some Christians such as Methodists and Quakers are more optimistic about human nature.

Through fully surrendered faith in Jesus, Christians hope to be washed of their egotistical sinfulness, regenerated, made righteous, adopted by God, sanctified, and glorified in the life to come. These are the blessings of salvation, which Christians feel Jesus won for them by his sacrifice.

Although Christians worship Jesus as Savior, as the incarnation of a merciful God, they also see him as a human being showing fellow human beings the way to God. His own life is seen as the perfect model for human behavior. Archbishop Desmond Tutu of South Africa emphasizes Jesus's identification with the human condition:

> *God does not occupy an Olympian fastness, remote from us. He has this deep, deep solidarity with us. God became a human being, a baby. God was hungry. God was tired, God suffered and died. God is there with us.*[78]

This is the central mystery of Christianity: that God became human in order to lead people back to God.

The human virtue most often associated with Jesus is love. Many Christians say they experience Jesus's love even though he is no longer walking the earth in human form. And in turn, they have deep love for Jesus. Those who are experiencing problems are comforted to feel that Jesus is a living presence in their lives, supporting them spiritually, loving them even in the darkest of times.

Reverend Larry Howard, the African–American pastor of Hopps Memorial Christian Methodist Episcopal Church in Syracuse, New York, declares:

> We found a Jesus. A Jesus who came in the midnight hour. A Jesus that was able to rock babies to sleep. A Jesus that stood in the midst and walked the miles when the freedom train rode through the South all the way through Syracuse. Jesus brought us through the mighty trials and tribulations. Why did Jesus do that? Jesus loved us and through that love and because of that love we stand here today. Not because the world has been so good to us. Not because we have been treated fair. Not because we have been able to realize the dream that God has given every man, woman, and child. But we stand here because we love Jesus. We love him more and more and more each day.[79]

The basic thrust of Jesus's message is to invite us into divine union, which is the sole remedy for the human predicament.

Father Thomas Keating[80]

In addition to being the paragon of love, Jesus also provides a model of sinlessness. To become like God, humans must constantly be purified of their lower tendencies. This belief has led some Christians to extremes of penance, such as the monks who flogged themselves and wore hairshirts so that their conscience might always be pricked. In a milder form, confession of one's sinfulness is a significant part of Christian tradition. There is an emphasis on self-discipline to guard against temptations, on examination of one's own faults, and on rituals, such as baptism, that help to remove the contamination that is innate in humanity. Although one must make these efforts at purification, most Christians believe that it is only through the grace of God—as mediated by the saving sacrifice of Jesus—that one can be delivered from sin and rise above ordinary human nature toward a divine state of sinlessness.

Sacred practices

Imitation of the model set by Jesus in his own life is the primary practice of Christians. In the widely read fourteenth-century book, *The Imitation of Christ*, people are encouraged to aspire to Jesus's own example as well as his teachings:

> O how powerful is the pure love of Jesus, which is mixed with no self-interest, nor self-love! ... Where shall one be found who is willing to serve God for naught?[81]

In addition to the inner attempt to become more and more like Jesus, Christians have developed a variety of spiritual practices. Although forms and understandings of the practices vary among the branches of Christendom, they may include public worship services with sermons and offering of the sacraments, celebrations of the liturgical year, private contemplation and prayer, and devotions to Mary and the saints.

Mother Teresa's Missionaries of Charity

The love of which Christ spoke is not an intellectual abstraction. According to the diminutive nun who was known around the world as Mother Teresa, love must be put into action.

Mother Teresa (1910–1997) was born in Albania, to a wealthy family that lost all its money when her father died. She entered a convent of the Loreto Sisters when she was eighteen, but she felt called to India, where she initially taught at a girls' school in Calcutta. Then came an even more difficult inner calling "to be God's love in action to the poorest of the poor." At a time when India was in turmoil after the shooting of Gandhi and the separation into Hindu and Muslim states, Calcutta was crowded with refugees. With no resources, Mother Teresa simply walked through the streets, with only loving care to give to those who had been abandoned by society, beggars, lepers, the dying. She wanted to live and serve the poor like Jesus, claiming nothing for herself, not even the security of knowing where she would sleep. She says, "There is but one person in the poor—Jesus. To be able to love him with undivided love we take a vow of poverty which frees us from all material possessions. We bind ourselves to be one of [the poor], to depend solely on divine providence, to have nothing, yet possess all things in possessing Christ."[83]

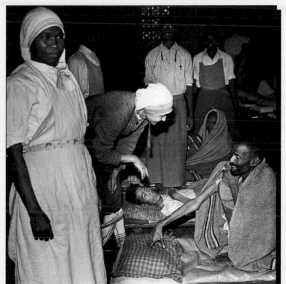

To assist in this work, Mother Teresa eventually received permission to found a new order, the Missionaries of Charity. The sisters wore simple white saris with blue stripes, the colors of the Virgin Mary and the garment of Indian women; they lived in poverty, without possessions or grand institutions, to help them understand the poor. In training them to work without the assurance of financial backing or physical safety, Mother Teresa emphasized that the most important thing is to pray and pray and pray; divine providence will always give what is needed.

As her work expanded around the globe to 230 houses on all continents, the results of her faith have been demonstrated again and again. There is no plan, no fundraising organization (although the Missionaries of Charity do accept individual donations). Wherever the sisters go, they try to help the poorest of the poor in whatever ways are needed. In each person they care for, they see the face of Jesus. In Calcutta, the Missionaries have picked up tens of thousands of sick, starving, and dying people from the streets and given them tender personal care, hand-feeding them a special formula made from soybeans. In New York City, they feed the homeless, shop and clean for the elderly poor, and care for those with AIDS.

During a period of intense mortar-bombing between Christian and Muslim militia in Beirut, Mother Teresa learned that a home for sixty spastic children had been stranded without caretakers on the Muslim side of the battle lines. When she insisted on crossing the lines to get them, the local clergy assured her that it was impossible. With utter faith, she said that she had asked the Virgin to arrange a ceasefire, which did indeed happen the next day, giving her time to rescue the terrified, helpless children. Within a day, the children were smiling. Mother Teresa said: "The Missionaries do small things with great love. It is not how much we do, but how much love we put into doing it. To God there is nothing small. The moment we have given it to God, it becomes infinite."

Worship services and sacraments

Christian worship typically takes place in a church building, which may be revered as a sacred space. The late nineteenth-century Russian Orthodox saint Ioann Kronshtadtsky (d. 1908) explained:

> Entering the church you enter some special realm which is not like the visible one. In the world you hear and see everything earthly, transient, fragile, liable to decay, sinful. In the church you see and hear the heavenly, the non-transient, the eternal, the holy. A temple is the threshold of heaven. It is like the heaven itself, because here is God's throne, the service of angels, the frequent descent of the Holy Spirit. ... Here everything from icons to censer and the priests' robes fills you with veneration and prayer; everything tells you that you are in God's shrine, face to face with God himself.[83]

The word sacrament can be translated as "mystery." In Roman Catholicism and Orthodoxy, the sacraments are the sacred rites that are thought capable of transmitting the mystery of Christ to worshippers. Roman Catholic and Eastern Orthodox Churches observe seven sacraments: baptism (initiation and symbolic purification from sin by water), confirmation (of membership in the Church), eucharist (the ritual meal described below), penance (confession and absolution of sins), extreme unction (anointing of the sick with oil, especially before death), holy orders (consecration as a deacon, priest, or bishop), and matrimony. In general, Protestant Churches recognize only baptism and the eucharist as sacraments and have a somewhat less mystical understanding of their significance.

The ritual of public worship, or liturgy, usually follows a set pattern, though in some Churches the actions of the Holy Spirit are thought to inspire spontaneous expressions of faith.

Christianity:
Eucharist

In most forms of Christianity, the central sacrament is the Holy Eucharist (also called Holy Communion, mass, or Lord's Supper). It is a mystery through which the invisible Christ is thought to grant communion with himself. Believers are given a bit of bread to eat, which is received as the body of Christ, and a sip of wine or grape juice, understood as his blood. The priest or minister may consecrate the bread and wine in ritual fashion and share them among the people. In Roman Catholic or Orthodox masses, the cup of wine and the bread are thought to be mystically transformed by the Holy Spirit into the blood and body of Christ. They are treated with profound reverence. In sharing the communion "meal" together, the people are united with each other as well as with Christ. The traditional ideal was to take communion every day and certainly every Sunday (the day set aside as the Sabbath).

Jesus is pictured in the Bible as having set the pattern for this sacrament at what is called the Last Supper, the meal he shared with his inner circle before his capture by the authorities in Jerusalem. The body and blood of Christ are seen as the spiritual nourishment of the faithful, that which gives them eternal life in the midst of earthly life.

Mother Julia Gatta, an Anglican priest in Connecticut, describes this sacred experience from the point of view of the clergy who preside at the liturgy:

> To be the celebrant of Eucharist is, I think, the most wonderful experience on earth. In a sense, you experience the energy flowing both ways. ... One experiences the

The sacrament of the eucharist, celebrated here in the Philippines, engages believers in a communal mystical encounter with the presence of Christ.

Spirit in them offering their prayer through Christ to the Father. But at the same time, you experience God's love flowing back into them. When I give communion to people, I am aware that I am caught in that circle of love.[84]

The partaking of sacred bread and wine is the climax of a longer liturgy of Holy Communion. The communion service, often called a mass in Catholicism, begins with liturgical prayers, praise, and confession of sinfulness. A group confession chanted by some Protestant congregations enumerates these flaws:

Most merciful God, we have sinned against you in thought, word, and deed, by what we have done and by what we have left undone. We have not loved you with our whole heart; we have not loved our neighbors as ourselves.[85]

Catholics were traditionally encouraged to confess their sins privately to a priest before taking communion, in the sacrament of **penance**, or "reconciliation." After hearing the confession, the priest pronounces forgiveness and blessing over the penitent, or perhaps prescribes a penance. Orthodox Christians were also traditionally expected to spend several days in contrition and fasting before receiving communion. The reason for the emphasis on purification is that during the service the church itself is perceived as the Kingdom of God, in which everything is holy. In Orthodox services, the clergy walk around the church, swinging an incense censer to set apart the area as a sacred space and to lift the prayers of the congregants to God.

In all Christian churches, passages from the Old and New Testaments may be read and the congregation may sing several hymns, songs of praise or thanks-giving to God. The congregation may be asked to recite a credal statement of Christian beliefs, and to make money offerings. There may be an address by the priest or minister (called a sermon or a homily) on the readings for the day. These parts of the liturgy constitute the Liturgy of the Word, in which Christ is thought to be present as the living Word, addressing the people through scripture and preaching. In Protestant churches, the Liturgy of the Word is often offered by itself, without the communion service.

In both Protestantism and Roman Catholicism, there are now attempts at updating the liturgy to make it more meaningful and personally relevant for contemporary Christians. One innovation that seems to have taken hold everywhere is the "sharing of the peace." Partway through the worship service, congregants turn to everyone around them to hug or shake hands and say, "The Peace of Christ be with you"—"and also with you."

In addition to regular liturgies and the sacrament of the mass or communion, there are special events treated in sacred ways. The first to be administered is the sacrament of baptism. Externally, it involves either immersing the person in water or, more commonly, pouring sanctified water (representing purification) on the candidate's head, while invoking the Holy Trinity. In a recent ecumenical document, the World Council of Churches defined the general meaning of the practice:

Christianity:
Baptism

> *By baptism, Christians are immersed in the liberating death of Christ where their sins are buried, where the "old Adam" is crucified with Christ, and where the power of sin is broken ... They are raised here and now to a new life in the power of the resurrection of Jesus Christ.*[86]

Aside from adult converts to Christianity, the rite is usually performed on infants, with parents taking vows on their behalf. There are arguments that infant baptism has little basis in the Bible and that a baby cannot make the conscious repentance of sin and "conversion of heart" implied in the ceremony. Baptists and several other Protestant groups therefore reserve baptism for adults.

A second ceremony—**confirmation**—is often offered in early adolescence in Roman Catholicism and Protestantism. After a period of religious instruction, a group of young people are allowed to make a conscious and personal commitment to the Christian life.

Some Christians observe special days of fasting. Russian Orthodox Old Believer priest Father Appolinari explains fasting as a way of *soprichiastna*, of becoming part of something very large, the spiritual aura of the Lord. He says,

> *More and more ordinary people are seeking a comfortable life. More and more we leave spirituality. We try to fill this vacuum with material things. I told my students that there was a fast coming up. They groaned, "Why?" I said that we fast for spiritual reasons. The rule is that you should fast not with a spirit of suffering but with such elevated spirit that your soul sings.*

When we limit our physicality, as in limiting our food intake, then we grow in our spirituality. I advise my students to notice whether their brain works better when their stomach is full or when it is almost empty. Monks refuse physical things in order to get spiritual benefits. We look at them and see their lives as dark, but for them, it is light.[87]

The liturgical year

Just as Christians repeatedly enact their union with Christ through participation in the eucharist sacrament, Christian churches celebrate a yearly cycle of festivals, leading the worshipper through the life of Jesus and the gift of the Spirit. As the faithful repeat this cycle year after year, they hope to enter more deeply into the mystery of God in Christ, and the whole body of believers in Christ theoretically grows toward the kingdom of God.

Christmas and Epiphany There are three major events in the church calendar, each associated with a series of preparatory celebrations. The first is the season of light: Christmas and **Epiphany**. Christmas is the celebration of Jesus's birth on earth. Epiphany means "manifestation" or "showing forth." It celebrates the recognition of Jesus's spiritual kingship by the three Magi (in the Western Church), his acknowledgement as the Messiah and the beloved Son of God when he is baptized by John the Baptist, and his first recognized miracle, the turning of water into wine at the wedding in Cana.

Young children re-enact the Christmas story, adoring Jesus as a baby.

In early Christianity, Epiphany was more important than the celebration of Jesus's birth. The actual birth date is unknown, but the setting of the date near the winter solstice allowed Christianity to take over the older "pagan" rites celebrating the return of longer periods of daylight at the darkest time of year. In the Gospel of John, Jesus is "the true light that enlightens every man,"[88] the light of the divine appearing amid the darkness of human ignorance.

Advent, the month preceding Christmas, is supposed to be a time of joyous anticipation. But in industrialized countries, it is more likely a time of frenzied marketing and buying of gifts, symbolizing God's gift of Jesus to the world.

In some countries churches stage pageants re-enacting the birth story, with people taking the parts of Mary, Joseph, the innkeeper who has no room, the shepherds, and the three Magi. Since the nineteenth century, it has been traditional to cut or buy an evergreen tree (a symbol of eternal life, perhaps borrowed from indigenous ceremonies) and erect it in one's house, decorated with lights and ornaments. On Christmas Eve some Christians gather for a candlelit "watch-night" service, welcoming the turn from midnight to a new day in which Christ has come into the world. On Christmas Day, Catholic and Protestant children are sometimes told that presents have been magically brought by St. Nicholas, a fourth-century bishop noted for his great generosity. The exchange of gifts may be followed by a great feast.

Easter In terms of religious significance, the most important event of the Christian liturgical year is Easter. This is the commemoration of Jesus's death (on "Good Friday") and resurrection (on Easter Sunday, which falls in the spring but is celebrated at different times by the Eastern and Western Churches). Like Christmas, Easter is a continuation of earlier rites—those associated with the vernal (spring) equinox, celebrating the regeneration of plant life and the return of warm weather after the cold death of winter. It is also related to Pesach, the Hebrew Passover, the Jewish spring feast of deliverance.

Liturgically, Easter is preceded by a forty-day period of repentance and fasting, called Lent. Many Christians perform acts of asceticism, prayer, and charity, to join in Jesus's greater sacrifice. In the Orthodox Church, the last Sunday before Lent is dedicated to asking forgiveness. People request forgiveness from each other, bowing deeply. In the West, Lent begins with Ash Wednesday, when many Christians have ash smudges placed on their foreheads by a priest who says, "Remember, man, thou art dust and unto dust thou shalt return." On the Sunday before Easter, Jesus's triumphal entry into Jerusalem is honored by the waving of palm or willow branches in churches and the proclaiming of Hosannas. His death is mourned on "Good Friday." The mourning is jubilantly ended on Easter Sunday, with shouts of "Christ is risen!"

In Russia, the Great Vigil welcoming Easter morning lasts from midnight until dawn, with the people standing the entire time. Jim Forest describes such a service in a church in Kiev, with 2,000 people crowding into the building and as many more standing outside:

The dean went out the royal doors into the congregation and sang out, "Christos Voskresye!" [Christ is risen!] Everyone responded in one voice, "Veyeastino voskresye!" [Truly he is risen!] It is impossible to put on paper how this sounds in the dead of night in a church overheated by crowds of people and hundreds of candles. It is like a shudder in the earth, the cracking open of the tomb. Then there was an explosion of ringing bells.[89]

Pentecost Fifty days after the Jewish Passover (which Jesus is thought to have been celebrating at the Last Supper with his disciples) comes the Jewish celebration Shavuot (which commemorates the giving of the Torah to Moses, as well as the first fruits of the harvest). Jews nicknamed it Pentecost, which is Greek for "fiftieth." Christians took over the holiday but gave it an entirely different meaning.

In Christianity, Pentecost commemorates the occasion described in Acts when the Holy Spirit descended upon the disciples after Jesus's death and resurrection, filling them with the Spirit's own life and power and enabling them to speak in foreign tongues they had not known. In early Christianity, Pentecost was an occasion for baptisms of those who had been preparing for admission to the Church.

The Transfiguration and Assumption Some Christian Churches also emphasize two other special feast days. On August 6, people honor the Transfiguration of Jesus on the mountain, revealing his supernatural radiance. On August 15, they celebrate the Assumption of Mary, known as "The Falling Asleep of the Mother of God." These feasts are prominent in the Eastern Church, which generally places more emphasis on the ability of humanity to break out of its earthly bonds and rise into the light, than on the heaviness and darkness of sin.

Contemplative prayer

The contemplative tradition within Christianity is beginning to re-emerge. The hectic pace and rapid change of modern life make periods of quietness essential, if only for stress relief. Many Christians, not aware of a contemplative way within their own Church, have turned to Eastern religions for instruction in meditation.

One of the most influential twentieth-century Christian contemplatives was the late Thomas Merton (1915–1968). He was a Trappist monk who received a special dispensation to live as a hermit in the woods near his abbey in Kentucky. Merton lived simply in nature, finding joy in the commonplace, experienced attentively in silence. He studied and tried to practice the great contemplative traditions of earlier Christianity and reintroduced them to a contemporary audience through his writings. In meditative "prayer of the heart," or "contemplative prayer," he wrote:

We seek first of all the deepest ground of our identity in God. We do not reason about dogmas of faith, or "the mysteries." We seek rather to gain a direct existential grasp, a personal experience of the deepest truths of life and faith, finding ourselves in God's truths. … Prayer then means yearning for the simple presence of God, for a personal understanding of his word, for knowledge of his will and for capacity to hear and obey him.[90]

The Christian monk Thomas Merton and the Tibetan Buddhist Dalai Lama, two great ecumenical figures of the 20th century, met shortly before Merton died in 1968 during his trip to visit the monks of the Eastern traditions.

Before he became a Christian monk, Merton had studied Eastern mysticism, assuming that Christianity had no mystical tradition. He became friends with a Hindu monk who advised him to read St. Augustine's *Confessions* and *The Imitation of Christ*. These classic works led Merton toward a deep appreciation of the potential of the Christian inner life, aligned with a continuing openness to learn from Eastern monasticism. He died in an accident while in Asia visiting Buddhist and Hindu monastics.

Spiritual renewal through inner silence has become an important part of some Christians' practice of their faith. Syrian Orthodox Bishop Paulos Mar Gregorios of India, past-President of the World Council of Churches, concluded from the Bible evidence that Jesus himself was a contemplative:

> *Christ spent seventy percent of his whole life in meditation. He would sleep rarely. All day he gave himself to healing the sick. At night he would pray, sometimes all night. He was not seeking his own self-realization. His meditation and prayer were not for himself but for the world—for every human being. He held the world in his consciousness through prayer, not with attachment but with compassion. He groaned and he suffered with humanity. To follow Jesus in the way of the cross means to say, "I lay aside all personal ambition and dedicate myself to God: 'Here I am, God. I belong to you. I have no idea where to go. It matters not what I am, so long as You lead me.'"*[91]

A form of Christian meditation instituted by the Franciscans and still practiced in many Catholic and Anglican churches is the Stations of the Cross. These are fourteen plaques or paintings placed on the walls of the church depicting scenes from the death of Jesus. As one sees him taking up the cross, falling three times under its weight, being stripped of his clothes and being nailed to the cross, one becomes painfully and humbly aware of the suffering that God's Son experienced in manifesting as a human redeemer.

Contemplation of the humanness of Jesus is used to help believers identify with him and thence to aspire to his divine model. Theology professor and spiritual director Kathleen Dugan says that when she teaches devotions on the deep humanity of Jesus:

> my students have difficulty assimilating it. "You mean to say that he felt sorrow like I do?" "Yes." "That he cried?" "Yes." "That he felt joy?" "Yes." The Gospel examples show that he wept before Lazarus's tomb. He wept at the sorrow of Martha and Mary over their brother. He rejoiced with the couple that were being married at the wedding of Cana. He felt terrible isolation; so many things in the Gospels speak of that. He said on the cross, "My God, my God, why have you forsaken me?" There is no human emotion that he did not experience. He did suffer. Crucifixion was a long, lingering death, with great agony. Jesus is our brother, our spouse, our son. When students think about these things, it is often transforming.
>
> Here is a living, breathing image of what it means to be God. We are called to imitate the saints, but primarily we are called to imitate Jesus.[92]

In Orthodoxy, the central contemplative practice is repetition of the Jesus Prayer: "Lord Jesus Christ, have mercy on me" (and some add, "a sinner"). Eventually its meaning imbeds itself in the heart and one lives in a state of unceasing prayer. An unknown nineteenth-century Russian peasant who lived with continual repetition of the Jesus Prayer described its results:

> The sweetness of the heart, warmth and light, unspeakable rapture, joy, ease, profound peace, blessedness, and love of life are all the result of prayer of the heart.[93]

Devotion to Mary

Thus far in this chapter, little has been said about Mary, the mother of Jesus, for she has not been in the forefront of historical theological disputes. Veneration of Mary has come as much from the grassroots as from the top. Drawings of her were found in the catacombs in which the early Christians met; explicit devotion to her was well developed by the third or fourth century CE. Despite the absence of detailed historical information, she serves as a potent and much-loved spiritual symbol. She is particularly venerated by Roman Catholics, Eastern Orthodoxy, and Anglicans.

Some researchers feel that devotion to Mary is derived from earlier worship of the Mother Goddess. They see her as representing the feminine aspect of the Godhead. She is associated with the crescent moon, representing the receptive willingness to be filled with the Spirit. In the story of the **Annunciation**—the appearance of an angel who told her she would have a child conceived by the Holy Spirit—her reported response was "Behold, I am the handmaid of the Lord; let it be to me according to your word."[94] This receptivity is not seen as utter powerlessness, however. Mary, like Christ, embodies the basic Christian paradox: that power is found in "weakness."

The Virgin of Guadalupe, who reportedly appeared in the 16th century to an indigenous convert to Catholicism, speaking the native language Nahuatl, has been embraced as patron saint of the Americas.

Whether or not devotion to Mary is linked to earlier Mother Goddess worship, oral Christian traditions have given her new symbolic roles. One links her with Israel, which is referred to as the daughter of Zion or daughter of Jerusalem in Old Testament passages. God comes to her as the overshadowing of the Holy Spirit, and from this love between YHWH and Israel, Jesus is born to save the people of Israel.

Mary is also called the New Eve. The legendary first Eve disobeyed God and was cast out of the Garden of Eden; Mary's willing submission to God allows birth of the new creation, in which Christ is in all.

In the Orthodox and Catholic traditions, she is referred to as the Mother of God. In Russia, she is also revered as the protectress of all humanity, and especially of the Russian people. Before he died on the cross, Jesus is said to have told John, the beloved disciple, that thenceforth Mary was to be his Mother. The story is interpreted as meaning that thenceforth all humanity was adopted by Mary.

Another symbolic role ascribed to Mary is that of the immaculate virgin. According to the gospels of Matthew and Luke, she conceived Jesus by heavenly intervention rather than human biology. Roman Catholicism asserts that at the Immaculate Conception, she herself was conceived without any of the "original sin" exhibited by the rest of humanity. Even in giving birth to Jesus, she remained a virgin. Orthodoxy does not insist on these doctrines, nor on the Catholic dogma that Mary ascended bodily to heaven after her physical death. The emphasis on virginity is a spiritual sign of being dedicated to God alone, rather than to any temporal attachments.

According to the faithful, Mary is not just a symbol but a living presence, like Christ. She is appealed to in prayer and is honored in countless paintings, statues, shrines, and churches dedicated to her name. Catholics are enjoined to repeat the "Hail Mary" prayer:

Hail, Mary, full of grace, the Lord is with thee. Blessed art thou among women, and blessed is the fruit of thy womb, Jesus. Holy Mary, Mother of God, pray for us sinners, now and at the hour of our death.

Theologians point out that veneration of Mary is really directed toward God; Mary is not worshipped in herself but as the mother of Christ, reflecting his glory. If this were not so, Christians could be accused of idolatry.

Be this as it may, Mary has been said to appear to believers in many places around the world. At Lourdes, in France, it is claimed that she appeared repeatedly to a young peasant girl named Bernadette in the nineteenth century. A spring found where she indicated has been the source of hundreds of medically authenticated healings from seemingly incurable diseases. In 1531, in Guadalupe (within what is now Mexico City), Mary appeared to a converted Aztec, Juan Diego. She asked him to have the bishop build a church on the spot. To convince the sceptical bishop, Juan filled his cloak with the out-of-season roses to which she directed him. When he opened the cloak before the bishop, the petals fell away to reveal a large and vivid image of Mary, with Indian features. The picture is now enshrined in a large new church with moving walkways to handle the crowds who come to see it, and the Virgin of Guadalupe has been declared Celestial Patroness of the New World.

Sightings of Mary continue around the world. What are perceived as her ethereal images have drawn crowds to worship before a large office window in Florida, before a closed church in eastern Europe, and at a site where she reportedly appeared two decades ago in Vietnam. In Mexico, her image is said to be seen frequently, miraculously manifesting in everything from dented car fenders and stovetops to garlic and fruits. In 1997, crowds worshipping what appeared to be the apparition of Mary on the floor of a Mexico City metro station became so thick that the authorities had to remove that section of the floor and place it outside in a shrine. Surrounded by blue tiles, the image—which sceptical officials refer to as a stain from a leaking pipe beneath the floor—was ceremonially blessed by a priest and draws queues of people who reverently touch and pray before it. Such is the perennial appeal of the holy mother.

Veneration of saints and angels

Roman Catholics and Orthodox Christians honor their spiritual heroes as saints. These are men and women who are recognized as so holy that the divine life of Christ is particularly evident in them. After their death, they are carefully judged by the Church for proofs of exalted Christian virtue, such as tolerance under extreme provocation, and of miraculous power. Those who are canonized by this process are subject to great veneration.

> *Each saint is a unique event, a victory over the force of evil. So many blessings can pour from God into the world through one life.*
>
> *Father Germann, Vladimir, Russia*[95]

Orthodox Christians are given the name of a saint when they are baptized. Each keeps an icon of this patron saint in his or her room and prays to the saint daily. Icons of many saints fill an Orthodox church, helping to make them familiar presences rather than names in history books. Saints are often known as having special areas of concern and power. For instance, St. Anthony of Padua is invoked for help in finding lost things. **Relics**, usually parts of the body or clothes of saints, are felt to radiate the holiness of the saints' communion with God. They are treasured and displayed for veneration in Catholic and Orthodox churches. It is said that saints' physical bodies were so transformed by divine light that they do not decay after death, and continue to emit a sweet fragrance.

Roman Catholics and Orthodox Christians also pray to the **angels** for protection. Angels are understood as spiritual beings who serve as messengers from and adoring servants of God. They are usually pictured as humans with wings. In popular piety, each person is thought to have a guardian angel for individual protection and spiritual help.

The lives of saints are considered inspiring models of devotion. Here Carmelite nuns in California view the relics of the beloved young nineteenth-century French nun, St. Therese of Lisieux ("The Little Flower"), which were taken on a worldwide tour.

Contemporary trends

The year 2000 was the subject of major celebrations around the world, as the beginning of the third millennium since the birth of Jesus. At this time, Christianity is gaining membership and enthusiastic participation in some quarters and losing ground in others.

The fall of communism in the former Soviet Union and its satellites has brought reopening and renovation of many churches and a renewed interest in spirituality throughout that large area. Orthodox Christianity has also received a boost from the activist approach of Ecumenical Patriarch Bartholomew, Archbishop of Constantinople, whose position makes him the leading voice in Orthodoxy. He is known as the "Green Patriarch" for his environmental activism, and has also taken an active role in improving Orthodox relations with Roman Catholics and Protestants, and in conflict resolution in areas where people of different religions are at war with each other.

In Egypt, Orthodox Coptic Christians, heirs to the ancient tradition of the Desert Fathers, have long been submerged under Muslim rule, but the monasteries have begun to flourish again. The 16 million Coptic Christians have their own pope.

Roman Catholicism is experiencing divisions between conservatives and liberals. After the liberal tendencies of Vatican II, Pope John Paul II reaffirmed certain traditional stands and strengthened the position of the right wing of the Church. In a 1995 encyclical, he emphatically insisted upon what he called the fundamental right to human life as opposed to the "culture of death," condemning abortion and euthanasia as "crimes which no human law can claim to legitimize" and condemning the death penalty.[96] In 2000, Cardinal Joseph Ratzinger, head of the Vatican's highly conservative Congregation for the Doctrine of the Faith (the successor to the Inquisition), delivered *"Dominus Jesu,"* a thirty-six-page document proclaiming, "There exists a single Church of Christ, which subsists in the Catholic Church," which has been entrusted with "the fullness of grace and truth." Other Christian communities "are not churches in the proper sense" and non-Christians are in a "gravely deficient situation" with regard to salvation.[97]

Despite his conservative stances, Pope John Paul II uses the latest technologies, including a major Internet website, to spread his messages. He also travels extensively, urging a return to traditional family values. In 1998 the world was stunned to see his tremendous welcome in Cuba, which had been officially atheist for two decades and then neutrally secular since 1991. The Young Communist League encouraged its half a million members to see the pope in Havana, in order to "hear the message of a man of great talent and culture who is concerned about the most pressing problems of modern humanity."[98]

On a special "Day of Forgiveness" held during the Lenten season in the millennial year of 2000, Pope John Paul II delivered a statement asking forgiveness for the past sins of the Roman Catholic Church, including its treatment of Jews, other Christians, other religions, women, ethnic groups, indigenous peoples, and heretics. "For the role that each of us has had, with his behaviour, in these evils, contributing to a disfigurement of the face of the Church, we humbly ask forgiveness," he said. Pope John Paul II also took a strong public stance opposing the American-led attack on Iraq in 2003 and expressing solidarity with the people of Iraq.

In spite of the public attention paid to the pope as a person, the priesthood is dwindling considerably in most Western countries, partly because of the requirement that Catholic priests be celibate. In recent years, revelations of sexual abuses by some priests of their parishioners—often innocent children—have rocked people's confidence in the priesthood. By early 2003, some 1,200 priests in the United States had been accused of sexual abuse, and the actual number may be greater. In the process of these revelations, the cardinal in Boston who allowed known sex offenders to continue as priests, merely transferring them to different parishes, had to resign his position in 2002. American bishops are trying to repair the damage by declaring "zero tolerance" for such behaviors, but at the same time, they have refused to deny the Catholic tradition of expecting priests to be celibate males. Catholic theologian Father Joe Mannath explains the potential for good or bad in the institutionalized celibacy of Catholic priests, monks, and nuns:

The Catholic Church has the largest body of full-time, life-long celibates, a veritable force for doing good, if love is the fuel behind our celibate commitment. Our structures, rules and routine can be used in the service of love, if we are men and women of inner freedom, who have found meaning and joy, who radiate enthusiasm and transparent goodness. In the hands of unloving or power-hungry (or sexually frustrated) men and women, these same structures and rules can become instruments of oppression. Celibates can be the most loving of people or the most cruel. History carries examples of both. If not "maintained" (like a good road) as a channel of God's love, celibacy degenerates to a barren state of being merely

Televised evangelism on America's Memorial Day, from the Crystal Cathedral, California.

unmarried. Then, our unhealthy drives will easily take over, undeterred by the balancing elements of family love and care of children. Power, jealousy, pleasure and superficiality can take the place of what love was meant to fill.[99]

There is increased interest in participation by women (who are not allowed by the Vatican to be priests), and widespread disregard of papal prohibitions on effective birth control, abortion, test-tube conception, surrogate motherhood, genetic experimentation, divorce, and homosexuality.

While cautioning against a recreational view of sexuality, Sean McDonagh SSC emphasizes that the environmental and social consequences of unlimited population growth require a rethinking of the traditional Catholic ban on birth control:

The pro-life argument needs to be seen within the widest context of the fragility of the living world. Is it really pro-life to ignore the warnings of demographers and ecologists who predict that unbridled population growth will lead to severe hardship and an increase in the infant mortality rate for succeeding generations? Is it pro-life to allow the extinction of hundreds of thousands of living species which will ultimately affect the well-being of all future generations on the planet?[100]

The Vatican has responded to these trends by insisting on the value of tradition and authority. But many American Catholic leaders are concerned that, in the words of Father Frank McNulty of Newark, New Jersey, "people often do not perceive the church as proclaiming integral truth and divine mercy, but rather as sounding harsh, demanding."[101] Acting as a group, Roman Catholic bishops in the

United States have issued statements deploring sexism as a "sin" (recommending that spiritual positions of responsibility and authority be opened to women and that non-sexist language be used in liturgy), supporting peace efforts, and insisting on the morality of economic social justice.

In Protestantism, traditional denominations in Europe and the United States are declining in membership. According to a Gallup poll, only a minority of the "unchurched" actually disagree with their denomination's teachings. They are more likely to drop away because of apathy, a lack of services, or a lack of welcome on the part of the minister. In the Anglican Church, the new Archbishop of Canterbury, Rowan Williams, is waking people out of apathy by his controversial actions, such as his support for the appointment of a homosexual bishop in New Hampshire. Opposition to this move has been so strong in Africa and other non-Western parts of the Anglican Church that some fear that it may divide the global Anglican Communion, which encompasses 79 million people.

Although many traditional Christian churches are losing members, other groups and trends are taking vigorous root. These include evangelical and charismatic groups, non-Western Christian churches, liberation theology, feminist theology, creation-centered Christianity, and the ecumenical movement.

Evangelicalism

To evangelize is to preach the Christian gospel and convert people to Christianity. Evangelical theology, with its emphasis on experiencing the grace of God, has been important throughout the history of American Protestantism. The current evangelical movement has its roots in the fundamentalist–modernist controversy of the early twentieth century.

The fundamentalists were reacting against the liberal or modern movement in Christianity that sought to reconcile science and religion and to use historical and archaeological data to understand the Bible. This movement had an optimistic view of human nature and stressed reason, free will, and self-determination. In response, a group of Christians called for a return to the "fundamentals" which they identified as (1) the inspiration and authority of scripture (and sometimes its inerrancy); (2) an emphasis on the virgin birth of Christ and other miracles; (3) the deity of Christ and the bodily resurrection as a literal historical event; (4) Christ's atoning and substitutionary death; and (5) an emphasis on the literal and imminent second coming of Christ. The controversy between these two groups received its most famous public expression in the Scopes trial in 1925 when John Thomas Scopes, a high school teacher in Tennessee, challenged a state law forbidding the teaching of Darwin's theory of evolution in schools.

Beginning in the 1930s and with waves of enthusiasm in the 1950s and late twentieth century, heirs of this movement, who can broadly be called "evangelicals," have become a vigorous movement in many Protestant denominations. Evangelicals study the Bible together and value being "born again" in Christ. They vary from conservative to liberal on other theological and ethical issues (such as the literal interpretation of the Bible and involvement in social issues such as peace movements and the alleviation of poverty).

Evangelicals' messages now enjoy widespread visibility through international electronic media. Television programs relayed around the world by communication satellites and Internet websites offer enthusiastic preaching, videotapes, audiotapes, CDs, and books, prayers for those in need, and the inevitable appeals for financial contributions to support these huge organizations, each centered on a charismatic speaker.

On the ground, evangelicalism is also making great strides in South America, in areas that were largely Roman Catholic as a result of colonization by Spain centuries ago. In the early 1990s, an average of five evangelical churches were being established each week in Rio de Janeiro, most of them in the slum areas, offering food, job training, day care, and perhaps conversion to the very poor.

Charismatics

The Pentecostalist-charismatic movement has brought spontaneous spiritual expressiveness into previously restrained cultures, such as this congregation in Kent, England.

Overlapping somewhat with the evangelical surge, there is a rising emphasis on charismatic experience—that is, divinely inspired powers—among Christians of all classes and nations. While Christian fundamentalists stress the historical Jesus, charismatics feel they have also been touched by the "third person" of the Trinity, the Holy Spirit. These include members of Protestant Pentecostal churches but also Roman Catholics, members of mainline Protestant denominations, and Orthodox churches who are caught up in a widespread contemporary spiritual renewal that harkens back to the biblical descent of the Holy Spirit upon the disciples of Jesus, firing them with spiritual powers and faith.

Mainstream Christian churches, which have often rejected emotional spiritual experience in favor of a more orderly piety, are gradually becoming more tolerant of it. Among Roman Catholics the movement is often called "Charismatic Renewal," for it claims to bring true life in the Spirit back to Christianity. By broad definition, up to one-fourth of all Christians today could be considered members of this Pentecostal-charismatic movement.[102]

Under the alleged influence of the Spirit, Pentecostalist-charismatics stand and gesture as they lovingly sing praises of Jesus and God, speak in tongues, pray and utter praises, spontaneously heal by the laying on of hands and prayer, and bear witness to spiritual miracles. Spontaneous spiritual gestures are especially prevalent at large renewal sites. A reporter witnessing the gathering of 5,300 people at the Toronto Airport Christian Fellowship described the following scene:

The ballroom carpets were littered with fallen bodies, bodies of seemingly straightlaced men and women who felt themselves moved by the phenomenon they say is the Holy Spirit. So moved, they howled with joy or the release of some buried pain. They collapsed, some rigid as corpses, some convulsed in hysterical laughter. From room to room come barnyard cries, calls heard only in the wild, grunts so deep women recalled the sounds of childbirth, while some men and women adopted the very position of childbirth. Men did chicken walks. Women jabbed their fingers as if afflicted with nervous disorders. And around these scenes of bedlam, were loving arms to catch the falling, smiling faces, whispered prayers of encouragement, instructions to release, to let go.[103]

Speaking of the descent of the Holy Spirit, Roman Bilas, Moscow head of the Union of Pentecostal Christians of Evangelical Faith, says passionately,

This moment when you really feel God's power in yourself brings so much peace and joy within you. It transforms you and society. There comes a sense of total forgiveness for your sins, and the ability in you to forgive others. At that moment, you start to speak in different languages, maybe such that no one can understand.

We may also receive the gift of prophecy. . . . We check to see if the message is consistent with the Bible. If it is, then we will listen. Otherwise, the person is told not to speak publicly because he would create confusion in the Church.

The main thing is that the person should be filled with God's Power. A nice-looking car will not move unless it is fueled. God's Power will only fill those who are pure. That is why in the early Church people went into the wilderness to fast and repent. Then God could fill them with His Power. Each sermon should have this Power of God; then the people will really listen and repent of their sins.[104]

Cultural broadening

Although contemporary Christianity was largely shaped in Europe and its North American colonies, the largest percentage of the Christian Church now lies outside these areas. It has great numerical strength and vigor in Africa, Latin America, and parts of Asia and its strength in these areas may change the face of Christianity. Some signs of the times: instead of the old pattern in which the West sent missionaries to spread Christianity to Asia, Africa, and South America, congregations in those areas are now being asked to send volunteers to the West to help spread the gospel in new missionary efforts there. Catholic prayer requests are now being "outsourced" through the Vatican to India from the United States, Canada, and Europe, where there are not enough clergy to handle the requests. Churches in Europe are becoming empty of worshippers as the people become more and more secular in their approach to life.

Christianity remains relatively vigorous in the United States, primarily because of the growth of evangelical and charismatic churches and a linking of fundamentalist Christianity with right-wing political claims to patriotism and a defense of traditional American values. By contrast, some of the most active remnants of Christianity in Europe are involved in peace and reconciliation movements and, like many other Christian denominations in the United States, tried to oppose the US-led attack on Iraq. Not only in the United States but around the globe, many fundamentalists feel they are fighting a cultural war against liberalism, secularism, and materialism—within as well as beyond Christianity. Spiritually diverse, Christianity is also politically and culturally diverse.

When Western missionaries spread Christianity to other regions, they often assumed that European ways were culturally superior to the indigenous ways and peoples. But some of these newer Christians have come to different conclusions. Theologians of the African Independent Churches, for instance, reject the historical missionary efforts to divorce them from their traditions of honoring their ancestors. This effort tore apart their social structure, they feel, with no scriptural justification:

> *As we became more acquainted with the Bible, we began to realise that there was nothing at all in the Bible about the European customs and Western traditions that we had been taught. What, then was so holy and sacred about this culture and this so-called civilisation that had been imposed upon us and was now destroying us? Why could we not maintain our African customs and be perfectly good Christians at the same time? . . .*
>
> *We have learnt to make a very clear distinction between culture and religion. . . . [For instance], the natural customs of any particular nation or race must never be confused with the grace of Jesus Christ our Saviour, Redeemer and Liberator.*[105]

Contemporary perceptions of Jesus have been deeply enriched by those from the inhabitants of poor Third World countries who have brought personal understanding of Jesus's ministry to the outcasts and downtrodden. In Asia, where Christians are usually in the minority, there is an emphasis on a Christ who is present in the whole cosmos and who calls all people to sit at a common table to partake of his generous love. In Latin America, Jesus is viewed as the liberator of the people from political and social oppression, from dehumanization, and from sin. In Africa, the African Independent Churches have brought indigenous traditions of drumming, dancing, and singing into community worship of a Jesus who is seen as the greatest of ancestors—a mediator carrying prayers and offerings between humans and the divine, and watchful caretaker of the people.

Liberation theology

Although many Christians make a distinction between the sacred and the secular, some have involved themselves deeply with social issues as an expression of their Christian faith. For instance, the Baptist preacher, Martin Luther King, Jr. (1929–1968), became a great civil rights leader, declaring: "It was Jesus of Nazareth that stirred the Negroes to protest with the creative weapon of love."[106] This trend is now called **liberation theology**, a faith that stresses the need for

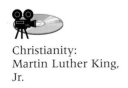

Christianity:
Martin Luther King,
Jr.

Roman Catholic procession of the eucharist, including veneration of Mary, mother of Jesus, in a Kunama village, Eritrea, Africa.

concrete political action to help the poor. Beginning in the 1960s with Vatican II and the conference of Latin American bishops in Colombia in 1968, Roman Catholic priests and nuns in Latin America began to make conscious, voluntary efforts to understand and side with the poor in their struggles for social justice. A biblical basis for this approach is found in the Acts of the Apostles:

> *The group of believers was one in mind and heart. No one said that any of his belongings was his own, but they all shared with one another everything they had. ... There was no one in the group who was in need. Those who owned fields or houses would sell them, bring the money received from the sale and turn it over to the apostles; and the money was distributed to each one according to his need.*[107]

The Peruvian theologian Gustavo Gutierrez (b. 1928), who coined the expression "theology of liberation," explains the choice of voluntary poverty as:

> *a commitment of solidarity with the poor, with those who suffer misery and injustice. ... It is not a question of idealizing poverty, but rather of taking it on as it is—an evil—to protest against it and to struggle to abolish it.*[108]

For their sympathetic siding with those who are oppressed, Catholic clergy have been murdered by political authorities in countries such as Guatemala. They have also been strongly criticized by conservatives within the Vatican. Cardinal Ratzinger, who heads the Congregation for the Doctrine of the Faith, has decried liberation theology. He says that it inappropriately emphasizes liberation from material poverty rather than liberation from sin. The movement has nevertheless spread to all areas where there is social injustice. Bakole Wa Ilunga, Archbishop of Kananga, the Democratic Republic of Congo (formerly Zaire), reminds Christians that Jesus warned the rich and powerful that it would be very difficult for them to enter the kingdom of heaven. By contrast, writes Ilunga:

For liberation theologians, the message of the gospel often entails down-to-earth physical help to the poor. Maryknoll lay sisters Norma Jejia, Julia Mamani, and Delia Gamboa are here lending a hand to the families of a Peruvian barrio.

Jesus liberates the poor from the feeling that they are somehow less than fully human; he makes them aware of their dignity and gives them motives for struggling against their lot and for taking control of their own lives.[109]

Taking control is not easy for those who are oppressed minorities. In the United States, the church offers the large African-American community of Christians a way of developing an alternative reality in the midst of poverty, urban violence, and discrimination. As theologian Dwight Hopkins observes,

The black community has a long tradition of practicing faith as a total way of life. ... Within worship, especially, the church is noted for its uplifting preaching, singing, shouting, dancing, and recognition of individual achievements and pain. ... The rituals of individual healing and celebration serve to recharge the worshipers' energy to deal with the rigors and racism of a 'cruel, cruel world' from Monday through Saturday. ... In addition, the church has functioned as the practical organizing center of all major aspects of group life. ... Truly, black faith is public talk about God and the human struggle for a holistic salvation, liberation, and the practice of freedom.[110]

The practical activities of the Black Church range from building shelters and arranging jobs to treatment for addiction, campaigns against police brutality, voter registration drives, and leadership training. Even without social empowerment, people often feel inwardly empowered and cherished by the presence of Jesus in their lives.

Despite the vibrancy of the liberation theology movement, racism has not been eradicated in Christianity. Pioneering Black theologian James H. Cone proclaims that it is time to end the silence over this issue. Rather, he claims, "The challenge for Black theology in the twenty-first century is to develop an enduring race critique that is so comprehensively woven into Christian understanding that no one will be able to forget the horrible crimes of white supremacy in the modern world."[111]

RELIGION IN PUBLIC LIFE

Archbishop Desmond M. Tutu

During the years of struggle against apartheid in South Africa, one voice that refused to be silenced was that of the Anglican Archbishop of Cape Town, Desmond Mpilo Tutu (b. 1931). Afterward, he served his country as Chairperson of the Truth and Reconciliation Commission, "looking a beast in the eye" to investigate abuses from all sides that were perpetrated during the apartheid era. In this capacity, he still refused to mute his criticisms of those wielding power, no matter what their race and stature. In 1995 he proclaimed,

The so-called ordinary people, God's favourites, are sick and tired of corruption, repression, injustice, poverty, disease and the violation of their human rights. They are crying out "enough is enough!" It is exhilarating when you are able to say to dictators everywhere: You have had it! You have had it! This is God's world and you will bite the dust! They think it will not happen but it does, and they bite the dust comprehensively and ignominiously.

'We will want to continue to be the voice of the voiceless. It is the role of the church to be the conscience of society.[112]

The "Arch's" fearless stance on behalf of truth and justice for the oppressed earned him the Nobel Peace Prize in 1984. He confronted not only those in power but also those who sought change through violence and those in the Church who witnessed the horrors of apartheid but kept silent. He explains, "Our task is to be agents of the Kingdom of God, and this sometimes requires us to say unpopular things."[113]

The former archbishop feels that faith requires one to be actively engaged in politics because government affects the people, but at the same time to remain independent of political factionalism in order to freely stand for truth. He says of the link between religion and politics:

Faith is a highly political thing. At the centre of all that we believe as Christians is the incarnation— the participation of God in the affairs of this world.

As followers of that God we too must be politically engaged. We need inner resources, however, in order to face the political demands of our time.[114]

How has Archbishop Tutu developed his inner resources? Through meditation, prayer, and fasting. He observes the traditional daily devotions of the Anglican Church, always starts meetings with prayer, and annually takes a long spiritual retreat. He regularly prays for others, and many are also praying for him; he asserts that intercessory prayer has practical effects. His spiritual confessor, Francis Cull, describes Archbishop Tutu's inner life as rooted in the Benedictine monastic discipline that underlies Anglican spirituality. He explains:

As I ponder on the prayer life of Desmond Tutu I see the three fundamental Benedictine demands that there shall be: rest, prayer, and work and in that order. It is a remarkable fact, and it is one reason at least why he has been able to sustain the burdens he has carried, that he has within him a stillness and a need for quiet solitude. . . . The "rest" of which St. Benedict speaks is not a mere switching off; it is a positive attempt to fulfill the age-old command to rest in God. . . . The pattern of Jesus which he follows here: "Come apart and rest awhile," is an urgent need for all those who are caught up in the busyness of church and world.[115]

Desmond Tutu himself insists that spiritual practice is essential in order to know and follow the will of God:

God's will has to do with what is right, just, decent and healing of the wounds of society. To know what this means we need to cleanse ourselves of ourselves—of our fears, greed, ambitions and personal desires. . . . We must be vigilant in ensuring that the good that is within all people triumphs over the evil that is also there. . . . We must commit ourselves to tell the truth. We must identify evil wherever we see it.[116]

Feminist theology

The issue of taking control of one's life and defining one's identity has also been taken up by feminists within the Christian Church. The Church institution has historically been dominated by men, although there is strong evidence that Jesus had active women disciples and that there were women leaders in the early churches. Reconstructing their history in the early Christian movement and the effects of patriarchical domination is a task being addressed by considerable in-depth scholarship at present. The effect of the apostle Paul in shaping attitudes toward women as he guided the developing Christian communities is one area of particular concern. Some of the statements attributed to him in the biblical Epistles seem oppressive to women; some seem egalitarian. He argues, for example, that men should pray or prophesy with their head uncovered but that women should either wear a veil or have their hair cut off:

> *For a man ought not to have his head veiled, since he is the image and reflection of God; but woman is the reflection of man. Indeed, man was not made from woman, but woman from man. Neither was man created for the sake of woman, but woman for the sake of man. . . . Nevertheless, in the Lord woman is not independent of man or man independent of woman. For just as woman came from man, so man comes through woman; but all things come from God.*[117]

Many contemporary scholars are trying to sort out the cultural and historical as well as the theological contexts of such statements. Elisabeth Schüssler Fiorenza, for example, explains:

In Bristol, England, newly ordained priest Reverend Susan Shipp blesses the sacramental offerings of bread and wine during her first service.

I argue that women were not marginal in the earliest beginnings of Christianity;
rather, biblical texts and historical sources produce the marginality of women.
Hence texts must be interrogated not only as to what they say *about women but*
also how they construct what they say *or do not say.*[118]

Another area of feminist theological scholarship is the role models for women offered by the Bible. A central female figure in the New Testament is Mary, mother of Jesus. Ivone Gebara and Maria Clara Bingemer of Brazil look at Mary from the perspective of "the great masses of Latin America, the overwhelming majority of whom are poor, enjoy no adequate quality of life, and lack respect, bread, love, and justice." While acknowledging that the dogmas developed by the Catholic Church about Mary may be inflated, they nonetheless reveal a well-spring of hope for women and other oppressed humans:

The exaltation that understandably comes out in dogma cannot ... hide what is
essential in God's salvation, that is, making God's glory shine on what is regarded as
insignificant, degrading or marginal. ... In exalting her they exalt precisely her poverty,
her dispossession, and her simplicity. This is the only key for understanding the mystery
of God's incarnation in human history, of which Jesus and Mary are the protagonists.
This is, moreover, the only key for understanding the mystery of the church as a
community of salvation, holy and sinful, striving amid the most diverse kinds of
limitations and problems to be a sign of the Kingdom in the midst of the world.[119]

A third major area of Christian feminist theology is the concept of God. The Divine is commonly referred to as "He" or "Father," but scholarship reveals that this patriarchal usage is not absolute; there also existed other models of God as Mother, as Divine Wisdom, as Justice, as Friend, as Lover. Sally McFague points out that to envision God as Mother, for instance, totally changes our understanding of our relationship to the Divine:

What the father-God gives us is redemption from sins; what the mother-God
gives is life itself, ... not primarily judging individuals but calling us back,
wanting to be more fully united with us. ... All of us, female and male, have
the womb as our first home, all of us are born from the bodies of our mothers,
all of us are fed by our mothers. What better imagery could there be for
expressing the most basic reality of existence: that we live and move and have
our being in God?[120]

Creation-centered Christianity

Another current trend in Christianity is an attempt to develop and deepen its respect for nature. In the Judeo-Christian tradition, humans are thought to have been given dominion over all the things of the earth. Sometimes this "dominion" was interpreted as the right to exploit, rather than the duty to care for, the earth. This view contrasts with indigenous beliefs that the divine resides everywhere, that everything is sacred, and that humans are only part of the great circle of life. Some Christians now feel that the notion of having a God-given right to control has allowed humans to nearly destroy the planet. In some cases, they are turning to indigenous spiritual leaders for help in extricating the planet from ecological destruction. Historian and passionate earth-advocate Father Thomas Berry feels that "we need to put the Bible on the shelf for twenty years until we learn to read the scripture of life."[121]

A Christianity that would accord greater honor to the created world would also tend to emphasize the miracle that is creation, thus helping to unite science and religion. Creation-centered Christians—such as the late Jesuit priest and paleontologist Teilhard de Chardin—see the mind of God in the perfect, intricate balances of chemistry, biology, and physics that allow life as we know it to exist.

Creation-centered Christianity is being passionately espoused by Matthew Fox, whose views as a Dominican theologian were not accepted by the Vatican. He now heads the University of Creation Spirituality in California. He opposes what he regards as the Roman Catholic tendency to focus on the sufferings of Jesus and thus encourage a perpetual sense of guilt, rather than Jesus's love of all life and his compassion for the sufferings of the weak, exploited, and oppressed.

Ecumenical movement

Christianity: The Living Cathedral—St. John the Divine

The restoration of religious freedom to multitudes of Christians in formerly communist countries has increased the great diversity of Christian ways of worshipping. Another contemporary trend is the attempt to unify all Christians around some point of agreement or at least fellowship with each other.

Vatican II asserted that the Roman Catholic Church is the one Church of Christ, but opened the way to dialogue with other branches of Christianity by declaring that the Holy Spirit was active in them as well. The Orthodox Church likewise believes that it is the "one, holy, Catholic, and Apostolic Church." Although it desires reunion of all Christians and denies any greed for organizational power, it insists on uniformity in matters of faith. Orthodox and Roman Catholic Churches therefore do not share Holy Communion with those outside their respective disciplines. Some Protestant denominations have branches that also refuse to acknowledge each other's validity.

In the attempt to restore some bonds among all Christian Churches, there are dozens of official ecumenical dialogues going on. The World Council of Churches, centered in Geneva, was founded in 1948 as an organizational body allowing Christian Churches to cooperate on service projects even in the midst of their theological disagreements. Its Faith and Order Commission links three hundred culturally, linguistically, and politically, not to mention theologically, different Christian Churches in working out the problems of Christian unity. However, the Orthodox Church representatives are always in the minority within the Council and therefore typically lose when decisions call for a majority vote. The consensus model for decision-making has been proposed as being closer to the original spirit of Christianity. As Father Denis G. Pereira explains:

> This model may be more difficult and involve more time. But it is inspired by a spirit of love, respect and generosity rather than suspicion and competition. The method supposes that the Church must be always open to the Spirit of God, and that the Spirit often speaks through the least and the last, at times even through a minority of one.[122]

As Christians around the world struggled to find an appropriate Christian response to the September 11, 2001 terrorist attacks on the United States, the World Council of Churches announced a "Decade to Overcome Violence." They proposed that the members would be using this decade as:

- *an opportunity to discover afresh the meaning of sharing a common humanity, to confirm our commitment to the unity of all God's people and to the ministry of reconciliation*
- *a call to repent for our own complicity in violence, and explore, from within our faith traditions, ways to overcome the spirit, logic and practice of violence*
- *a forum in which to work together for a world of peace with local communities, secular movements, and people of other faiths*
- *a time to analyse and expose different forms of violence and their interconnection, and to act in solidarity with those who struggle for justice and the integrity of creation.*[123]

Suggested reading

Abbott, Walter M., ed., *The Documents of Vatican II*, New York: The America Press, 1966. Landmark conclusions of the Council Fathers, with special emphasis on the poor, religious unity, and social justice.

Achtmeier, Paul, J., general editor, *The HarperCollins Bible Dictionary*, 1966, New York: HarperCollins, 1996. Extensive contemporary scholarship on the Bible, with its historical contexts and modern interpretations.

Borg, Marcus, J., *Meeting Jesus Again for the First Time: The Historical Jesus and the Heart of Contemporary Faith*, San Francisco: HarperSanFrancisco, 1994. An accessible and appreciative discussion of the Jesus of history, as opposed to the Jesus of faith, by a leading figure in the Jesus Seminar.

Bainton, Roland Herbert, *Christianity*, New York: Houghton Mifflin, 2000. A contemporary survey of Christian history.

Braybrooke, Marcus, *The Explorer's Guide to Christianity*, London: Hodder & Stoughton, 1998. With the sensitivity of a global interfaith leader, Rev. Braybrooke offers a succinct introduction to Christianity for people of every faith and country.

Dawes, Gregory W., ed., *The Historical Jesus Quest: A Foundational Anthology*, Westminster John Knox Press, 2000. A collection of scholarly investigations into the life of Jesus.

Dillenberger, John and Welch, Claude, *Protestant Christianity Interpreted through its Development*, New York: Charles Scribner's Sons, 1954. The classic history and interpretation of Protestantism.

Fosdick, Harry Emerson, ed., *Great Voices of the Reformation*, New York: Random House, 1952. Extensive quotations, with commentary, from major early Protestant leaders.

Hopkins, Dwight N., ed., *Black Faith and Public Talk*, Maryknoll, New York: Orbis Books, 1999. Taking off from James H. Cone's influential *Black Theology and Black Power*, these essays probe how people of color relate Christian understanding to economic, social, and religious situations and ideals in today's world.

Irvin, Dale T. and Scott W. Sunquist, *History of the World Christian Movement, vol. 1: Earliest Christianity to 1453*. Maryknoll, New York: Orbis Books, 2001. An inclusive view of early Christian history extending to inputs from and influences on the cultures and people of Asia, Africa, and West Asia.

King, Ursula, ed., *Feminist Theology from the Third World: A Reader*, Maryknoll, New York: Orbis Books, 1994. Excellent compendium of the voices of marginalized peoples, which give a special poignance and depth of meaning to efforts to give women a voice in shaping and interpreting Christianity.

Pope-Levison, Priscilla and Levison, John R., *Jesus in Global Contexts*, Louisville, Kentucky: Westminster/John Knox Press, 1992. Examinations of the question "Who is Jesus?" from poor cultures and feminist perspectives.

Price, James L., *Interpreting the New Testament*, second edition, New York: Holt, Rinehart and Winston, 1971. An excellent survey of the literature and interpretation of the New Testament.

Robinson, James M., ed., *The Nag Hammadi Library*, San Francisco: Harper & Row, 1977. A fascinating collection of early scriptures that are not included in the Christian canon.

Schüssler Fiorenza, Elisabeth, *In Memory of Her: A Feminist Theological Reconstruction of Christian Origins*, New York: Crossroad, 1983, 1994. Extensive scholarship about the role of women in early Christianity.

Theissen, Gerd, *The Religion of the Earliest Churches: Creating a Symbolic World*, Minneapolis, Minnesota: Fortress Press, 1999. An excellent survey of the emergence of Christian religion that emphasizes the development and diversity of early Christian myth, ethics, and ritual in their socio-historical contexts.

Tugwell, Simon, *Ways of Imperfection*, London: Darton, Longman and Todd, 1984, and Springfield, Illinois: Templegate Publishers, 1985. Spirituality as a whole vision of life, as seen by a series of great Christian practitioners.

Walker, Williston, Norris, Richard A., Lotz, David W., and Handy, Robert T., *A History of the Christian Church*, fourth edition, New York: Charles Scribner's Sons, 1985, and Edinburgh: T&T Clark, 1986. A classic history of Christianity.

Ware, Timothy, *The Orthodox Church*, Middlesex, England and Baltimore, Maryland: Penguin Books, 1984, 1993. An excellent overview of the history, beliefs, and practices of the Eastern Church.

Wilson, Ian, *Jesus: The Evidence*, Washington, D.C.: Regnery Publishing, 2000. Neutral survey of historical evidence of the life of Jesus.

Key terms

gospel	The "good news" that God has raised Jesus from the dead and in so doing has begun the transformation of the world.
Common Era	Years after the traditional date used for the birth of Jesus, previously referred to in exclusively Christian terms as AD and now abbreviated to CE as opposed to BCE ("before Common Era").
Messiah	In Christianity, the "anonted one", Jesus Christ.
Trinity	The Christian doctrine that in the One God are three divine persons: the Father, the Son, and the Holy Spirit.
baptism	A Christian sacrament by which God cleanses all sin and makes one a sharer in the divine life, and a member of Christ's body, the Church.
Eucharist	The Christian sacrament by which believers are renewed in the mystical body of Christ by partaking of bread and wine, understood as his body and blood.
confirmation	A Christian sacrament by which awareness of the Holy Spirit is enhanced.
original sin	A Christian belief that all human beings are bound together in prideful egocentricity. Described mythically in the Bible as an act of disobedience on the part of Adam and Eve.

Study questions

1 What are the major categories of the Christian Bible? Name one book in each category. Explain the major types of biblical hermeneutics.
2 Why were Jesus's teachings radical? Explain five specific examples.
3 What was the importance in the early Church of the following: Paul, Constantine, gnosticism, the Trinity, the Nicene Creed, Christology, monasticism.
4 Describe the history, geography, and main principles of the Eastern Orthodox Church. Discuss Byzantium, 1054 CE, *filioque*, the pope, Crusades, Russia, synod, Philokalia, icons.
5 Describe the history, geography, and main principles of the Roman Catholic Church. Discuss the Pope, Gregory I, the Middle Ages, Aquinas, Francis, mystics, Trent, celibacy, Vatican II, Mother Teresa, sacraments, Merton, Mary, liberation theology, creation-centered theology.
6 Describe the history, geography, and main principles of the Protestant Church. Discuss Luther, Zwingli, Calvin, Anglicans, Methodists, holidays, charismatics, Tutu, fundamentalists, evangelicals, liberals, feminist theology, the ecumenical movement.

Refer to Pearson/Prentice Hall's **TIME Special Edition: World Religions** magazine for these and other current articles on topics related to many of the world's religions:

- *The Religious Experience: The Legacy of Abraham*
- *Christianity: Missionaries Under Cover; The Lord's Business*

Chapter 9 continues the study of religions originating in the Middle East and focuses on Christianity. For further research in this area, use the tools available to you in Research Navigator:

As you investigate Christianity, consider this question: "What ecumenical movements are having an impact on the development of Christianity in the world today?"

- **Ebsco's ContentSelect:** Search in the Religion and Sociology databases using terms such as "ecumenical," "world Christianity," "Catholic Protestant."
- **Link Library:** Search in the Religion database under the category: "Religions of Mediterranean and Middle Eastern Origins: Rise of Christianity; Catholicism; Roman Catholic Church; Vatican." Also search under the category of "Western Christianity: Protestantism; Episcopalians; Lutheranism."
- **The *New York Times* on the Web:** Search in the Religious Studies and all other databases for current articles on related topics.

ISLAM

"There is no god but God"

In about 570 CE, a new prophet was born. This man, Muhammad, is considered by Muslims to be the last of a continuing chain of prophets who have come to restore the true religion. They regard the way revealed to him, Islam, not as a new religion but as the original path of monotheism, which also developed into Judaism and Christianity.

After carrying the torch of civilization in the West while Europe was in its Dark Ages, in the twentieth century Islam began a great resurgence. It is now the religion of nearly one-fifth of the world's people. Its monotheistic creed is simple: "There is no god but God, and Muhammad is his Messenger." Its requirements of the faithful are straightforward, if demanding. But beneath them lie profundities and subtleties of which non-Muslims are largely unaware. In fact, ignorance about Islam and perceived targeting of Muslims in general by the U.S.-led "war on terrorism" have exacerbated a dangerous and growing divide between Muslims and non-Muslims in the contemporary world. Therefore it is extremely important to carefully study the origins, teachings, and modern history of this major world religion.

The Prophet Muhammad

Islam, like Christianity and Judaism, traces its ancestry to the patriarch Abraham. Isma'il (Ishmael) was said to be the son of Abraham and an Egyptian slave, Hagar. When Abraham's wife, Sarah, also bore him a son (Isaac), Abraham took Isma'il and Hagar to the desert valley of Becca (Mecca) in Arabia to spare them Sarah's jealousy.

The sacred book of Islam, the Holy Qur'an, received as a series of revelations to Muhammad, relates that Abraham and Ishmael together built the holiest sanctuary in Islam, the Ka'bah. It was thought to be the site of Adam's original place of worship; part of the cubic stone building is a venerated black meteorite. According to the Qur'an, God told Abraham that the Ka'bah should be a place of pilgrimage. It was regarded as a holy place by the Arabian tribes.

According to Islamic tradition, the region sank into historical oblivion as it turned away from Abraham's monotheism. For many centuries, the events of the rest of the world passed it by, aside from contact through trading caravans. Then into a poor clan of the most powerful of the tribes in the area was born a child named Muhammad ("the praised one"). His father died before he was born, and after the death of his mother and then his grandfather, Muhammad became the ward of his uncle, who put him to work as a shepherd.

The Ka'bah in Mecca is Islam's holiest place of worship.

Muhammad allegedly undertook spiritual retreats in this cave on Mount Hira outside Mecca. It was here that he received the first revelations of the Qur'an.

ISLAM

CE	
500	c.570 Birth of Prophet Muhammad
600	c.610 Revelation of the Qur'an to Prophet Muhammad begins
	622 The *hijrah* (migration) from Mecca to Medina
	630 Prophet Muhammad's triumphant return to Mecca
	632 Death of Prophet Muhammad; election of Abu Bakr as first caliph
	650 Written text of the Qur'an established
	661–750 Umayyad dynasty
700	680 Karbala massacre of Husayn, grandson of the Prophet, and his relatives
	732 European advance of Islam stopped at Battle of Tours
	750–1258 Islam reaches its cultural peak under Abbasid caliphs
800	
900	922 al-Hallaj killed
1000	
	1058–111 Life of al-Ghazali
1100	
	1187 Salah-al-Din recaptures Jerusalem from Crusaders
1200	
1300	
1400	
	1453 Turks conquer Constantinople, renaming it Istanbul
	1478–1834 Spanish Inquisition
	1492 Surrender of Granada, last foothold of Islam in Spain
1500	
	1556 Akbar becomes Mogul emperor in India
1600	
1700	
1800	1800s–1900s Muslim areas fall under European domination
1900	
	1947 Partition of Muslim Pakistan from Hindu India
	1970s Oil-rich Muslim states join OPEC and Muslim resurgence begins
2000	2001 Muslim terrorists fly aircraft into US buildings
	2003 U.S. attacks Iraq in "war on terrorism"

Allah (God) is *the* focus in Islam, the sole authority, not Muhammad. But Muhammad's life story is important to Muslims, for his character is considered a model of the teachings in the Qur'an. The stories of Muhammad's life and his sayings are preserved in a vast, not fully authenticated literature called the **Hadith**, which reports on the Prophet's **Sunnah** (sayings and actions). When he was a teenager, on a trip to Syria with his uncle, Muhammad was noticed by a Christian monk who identified marks on his body indicating his status as a prophet. As a young man, Muhammad managed caravans for a beautiful, intelligent, and wealthy woman named Khadijah. When she was forty and Muhammad was twenty-five, she offered to marry him. Khadijah became Muhammad's strongest supporter during the difficult and discouraging years of his early mission.

With Khadijah's understanding of his spiritual propensities, Muhammad began to spend periods of time in solitary retreat. These retreats were not uncommon in his lineage. They were opportunities for contemplation, away from the world.

When Muhammad was forty years old, he made a spiritual retreat during the month called Ramadan. An angel in human-like form, Gabriel, reportedly came to him and insisted that he recite. Three times Muhammad demurred that he could not, for he was unlettered, and three times the angel forcefully commanded him. In desperation, Muhammad at last cried out, "What shall I recite?" and the angel began dictating the first words of what became the Qur'an:

Proclaim! (or Recite!)
In the name
Of thy Lord and Cherisher,
Who created—
Created man, out of
A (mere) clot
Of congealed blood:
Proclaim! And thy Lord
Is Most Bountiful,—
He Who taught
(The use of) the Pen,—
Taught man that
Which he knew not.[1]

Muhammad returned home, deeply shaken. Khadijah comforted him and encouraged him to overcome his fear of the responsibilities and ridicule of prophethood. The revelations continued intermittently, asserting the theme that it was the One God who spoke and who called people to Islam (which means complete, trusting surrender to God). According to tradition, Muhammad described the form of these revelations thus:

Revelation sometimes comes like the sound of a bell; that is the most painful way. When it ceases I have remembered what was said. Sometimes it is an angel who talks to me like a human, and I remember what he says.[2]

The Prophet shared these revelations with the few people who believed him: his wife, Khadijah; his young cousin, 'Ali; his friend, the trader Abu Bakr; and the freed slave, Zayd.

Islam:
Mecca

After three years, Muhammad was instructed by the revelations to preach publicly. He was ridiculed and stoned by the Qurayshites, the aristocrats of his tribe who operated the Ka'bah as a pilgrimage center and organized profitable trading caravans through Mecca. While Muhammad was somewhat protected by the influence of his uncle, his followers were subject to persecution. A dark-skinned Abyssinian slave named Bilal, who was among the first converts, was imprisoned and brought out daily under the hot sun, pinned to the ground with a heavy stone on his chest, and ordered to deny the Prophet and worship the old gods. He staunchly refused, saying, "One, one." Once bought by the Prophet's friend Abu Bakr, Bilal became the first **muezzin** (one who calls the people to prayer from a high place), illustrating the Prophet's discarding of racial and social class distinctions. Finally, according to some accounts, Muhammad and his followers were banished for three years to a desolate place where they struggled to survive by eating wild foods such as tree leaves.

The band of Muslims was asked to return to Mecca, but the persecution by the Qurayshites continued. Muhammad's fiftieth year, the "Year of Sorrows," was the worst of all: he lost his beloved wife Khadijah and his protective uncle. With his strongest backers gone, persecution of the Prophet increased.

According to tradition, at the height of his trials, Muhammad experienced the Night of Ascension. He is said to have ascended through the seven heavens to the far limits of the cosmos, and thence into the Divine Proximity. There he met former prophets and teachers from Adam to Jesus, saw paradise and hell, and received the great blessings of the Divine Presence.

Pilgrims to Mecca from Yathrib, an oasis to the north, recognized Muhammad as a prophet. They invited him to come to their city to help solve its social and political problems. Still despised in Mecca as a potential threat by the Qurayshites,

Faithful Muslims pray five times a day, no matter where they are. The prayer rug provides a sacred precinct from which one can turn toward Mecca, the center of the faith.

Although representations of humans, including himself, were forbidden by the Prophet to avoid idolatry, Persian artists later gave imaginative expression to Muslim stories, such as the Miraj, *or Ascension, of the Prophet. (*Ascent of the Prophet Muhammad to Heaven, *by Aqa Mirak, 16th century, Persia.)*

Muhammad and his followers left Mecca secretly. Their move to Yathrib, later called al-Medina ("The City [of the Prophet]"), was not easy. The Prophet left last, accompanied (according to some traditions) by his old friend Abu Bakr. To hide from the pursuing Meccans, it is said that they took refuge in a cave, where the Prophet taught his friend the secret practice of the silent remembrance of God.

This **hijrah** (migration) of Muslims from Mecca to Medina took place in 622 CE. The Muslim era is calculated from the beginning of the year in which this event took place, for it marked the change from persecution to appreciation of the Prophet's message.

In Medina, Muhammad drew up a constitution for the city of Yathrib/Medina that later served as a model for Islamic social administration. The departure of Muslims from Mecca was viewed with hostility and suspicion by the leaders of Mecca. Their assumption was that Medina had become a rallying point for enemies of the Meccans who, under Muhammad's leadership, would eventually attack and destroy Mecca. To forestall this, Mecca declared war on Medina, and a period of open conflict between the two cities followed.

Muhammad himself directed the first raid against a Meccan caravan on its return journey. The battle between Muslim emigrants and Meccans took place at Badr near Medina; the small group of Muslims was victorious.

According to the Qur'anic revelations, God had sent thousands of angels to help Muhammad. Furthermore, Muhammad threw a handful of pebbles at the Meccans and this turned the tide, for it was God who threw, and "He will surely weaken the designs of the unbelievers."[3] Enraged by the Islamic victory, Mecca made a surprise attack against Medina and routed the Muslims, injuring Muhammad and scattering the Islamic forces. Within two years, Mecca had mounted a much larger force, including cavalry and numerous archers, for a siege intended to subdue Medina permanently. Warned by spies, the Muslims defended Medina with a large trench encircling the city. Unable to press their attack, the Meccans were forced to retreat. Rather than continue hostilities, Muhammad negotiated a truce between the two warring cities.

The Qur'anic revelations to Muhammad emphasize the basic religious unity of Jews, Christians, and Muslims, members of the same monotheistic tradition of Abraham. But most of the Jews of Medina refused to accept Islam, because it recognized Jesus and claimed to complete the Torah. In addition, they were politically allied to those who opposed the Prophet. Eventually, their farms were appropriated by increasing numbers of Muslim converts, and some Jews were killed as political opponents. The Qur'an taught that the Jews and Christians had distorted the pure monotheism of Abraham; Muhammad had been sent to restore and supplement the teachings of the apostles and prophets. He was instructed to have the people face Mecca rather than Jerusalem during their prayers.

In 630 CE the Prophet returned triumphant to Mecca with such a large band of followers that the Meccans did not resist. Reportedly, only thirty people were killed in the historic conquest of Mecca. The Ka'bah was purged of its idols, and from that time it has been the center of Muslim piety. Acquiescing to Muhammad's political power and the Qur'anic warnings about the dire fate of those who tried to thwart God's prophets, many Meccans converted to Islam. Muhammad declared a general amnesty. Contrary to tribal customs of revenge, the Prophet showed his unusual gentleness by forgiving those who had been his opponents.

The Prophet then returned to Medina, which he kept as the spiritual and political center of Islam. From there, campaigns were undertaken to spread the faith. In addition to northern Africa, the Persian states of Yemen, Oman, and Bahrain came into the fold. As the multi-cultural, multi-racial embrace of Islam evolved, the Prophet declared that the community of the faithful was more important than the older tribal identities that had divided people. The new ideal was a global family, under God. In his "Farewell Sermon," Muhammad stated, "You must know that a Muslim is the brother of a Muslim and the Muslims are one brotherhood."[4]

In the eleventh year of the Muslim era, Muhammad made a final pilgrimage to the Ka'bah to demonstrate the rites that were to be followed thenceforth. After his return to Medina, he became very ill. As he recognized that the end was near, he gave final instructions to his followers, promising to meet them at "the Fountain" in Paradise. Muhammad died in 632 CE. He left no clear instructions as

Islam:
Night Journey

TEACHING STORY

The Humility of the Prophet

The Prophet Muhammad's followers had such reverence for him that they caught the very water dripping from his arms when he did his ablutions, in order to rub it on themselves as a blessing. But he himself was so humble that he asked for God's forgiveness at least seventy times a day.

Once the Prophet asked his companions to prepare goat's meat for the group as they were traveling. One said he would kill the goat; another said he would skin it; another volunteered to cook it. The Prophet said he would gather the wood for the fire. His companions immediately protested: "You are God's Messenger. We will do everything." "I know you would," said the Prophet, "but that would be discrimination. God does not want His servants to behave as if they were superior to their companions."

When the Prophet was the recognized head of Medina, he borrowed some money from Zaid ibn Sana'a. Several days before the repayment of the loan, Zaid came to the Prophet, grabbed his clothes, and roughly demanded his money, saying, "Your relatives are always late in paying their debts." Umar, the Prophet's supporter, voiced his outrage and prepared to manhandle the moneylender. The Prophet merely said to Zaid, "Three days remain for the fulfillment of my obligation." He reserved his strong words for Umar: "You should have treated us both better. You should have told me to be better at repaying my debts, and you should have told him to be better at demanding payment. Pay him the amount due and give him 40 kilograms extra of dates as compensation for the alarm that you have caused him."

to who should succeed him. In the circumstances that followed Muhammad's death, his steadfast friend Abu Bakr was elected the first **caliph** (successor to the Prophet). Another possible successor was the trustworthy and courageous 'Ali, the Prophet's cousin and husband of his favorite daughter, Fatima. Tradition has it that the Prophet Muhammad actually transferred his spiritual light to Fatima before his death, but that in the midst of funeral arrangements, neither she nor 'Ali participated in the selection of the first caliph. The Shi'ite faction would later claim 'Ali as the legitimate heir.

Muhammad's own life has continued to be very precious to Muslims, and it is his qualities that a good Muslim tries to emulate. He always denied having any superhuman powers, and the Qur'an called him "a human being like you," just "a servant to whom revelation has come," and "a warner."[5] The only miracle he ever claimed was that, though unlettered, he had received the Qur'anic revelations in extraordinarily eloquent and pure Arabic. He did not even claim to be a teacher—"God guides those whom He will,"[6] he was instructed to say—although Muslims consider the Prophet the greatest of teachers.

Nevertheless, all who saw the Prophet remarked on his touching physical beauty, his nobility of character, the fragrance of his presence, his humility, and his kindness. Many stories are told of his affectionate compassion toward animals, children, women, widows, and orphans, contrary to prevailing customs. When asked the short cut to heaven, he reportedly said that Paradise lies under the feet of the mother. In his devotion to God, he quietly endured poverty so extreme that he tied a stone over his stomach to suppress the pangs of hunger. He explained, "I eat as a slave eats, and sit as a slave sits, for I am a slave (of God)." Although the Qur'an says that the Prophet is the perfect model for humanity, the purest vehicle for God's message, he himself perpetually prayed for God's forgiveness. When he was asked how best to practice Islam, he said, "The best Islam is that you feed the hungry and spread peace among people you know and those you do not know."[7]

Muhammad's mystical experiences of the divine had not led him to forsake the world as a contemplative. Rather, according to the Qur'an, the mission of Islam is to reform society, to actively combat oppression and corruption, "inviting to all that is good, enjoining what is right, and forbidding all that is wrong."[8] The Prophet's task—which Muslims feel was also undertaken by such earlier prophets as Moses and Abraham—is not only to call people back to faith but also to create a just moral order in the world as the embodiment of God's commandments.

The Qur'an

Islam:
Qur'an

The heart of Islam is not the Prophet but the revelations he received. Collectively they are called the Qur'an ("reading" or "reciting"). He received the messages over a period of twenty-three years, with some later messages replacing earlier ones. At first they were striking affirmations of the unity of God and the woe of those who did not heed God's message. Later messages also addressed the organizational needs and social lives of the Muslim community.

Reading the Qur'an in Java.

After the *hijrah*, Muhammad heard the revelations and dictated them to a scribe; many of his companions then memorized them. They are said to have been carefully safeguarded against changes and omissions. Recited, the passages have a lyrical beauty and power that Muslims believe to be unsurpassed; these qualities cannot be translated. The recitation is to be rendered in what is sometimes described as a sad, subdued tone, because the messages concern God's sadness at the waywardness of the people. Muhammad said, "Weep, therefore, when you recite it."[9]

Recitation of the Qur'an is thought to have a healing, soothing effect, but can also bring protection, guidance, and knowledge, according to Islamic tradition. It is critical that one recite the Qur'an only in a purified state, for the words are so powerful that the one who recites it takes on a great responsibility. Ideally, one learns the Qur'an as a child, when memorization is easiest and when the power of the words will help to shape one's life.

During the life of the Prophet, his followers attempted to preserve the oral tradition in writing as an additional way of safeguarding it from loss. The early caliphs continued this effort until a council was convened by the third caliph around 650 CE to establish a single authoritative written text. This is the one still used. It is divided into 114 **suras** (chapters). The first is the **Fatiha**, the opening sura, which reveals the essence of the Qur'an:

In the name of God, Most Gracious, Most Merciful.
Praise be to God,
The Lord of the Worlds;
Most Gracious, Most Merciful;
Master of the Day of Judgment.
Thee do we worship,
And Thine aid we seek.
Show us the straight way,
The way of those on whom
Thou has bestowed Thy Grace
Those whose portion
Is not wrath,
And, who go not astray.

The verses of the Qur'an are terse, but are thought to have multiple levels of meaning. Translator and commentator Abdullah Yusuf Ali notes that in the mystical early passages there are often three layers: (1) a reference to a particular person or situation; (2) a spiritual lesson; and (3) a deeper mystical significance. He offers interpretation of these three levels in the first two verses of Sura 74 ("O thou wrapped up / [In a mantle]! / Arise and deliver thy warning!"):

As to 1, the Prophet was now past the stage of personal contemplation, lying down or sitting in his mantle; he was now to go forth boldly to deliver his Message and publicly proclaim the Lord ... As to 2, similar stages arise in a minor degree in the life of every good man, for which the Prophet's life is to be a universal pattern. As to 3, the Sufis understand, by the mantle and outward wrappings, the circumstances of our phenomenal existence, which are necessary to our physical comfort up to a certain stage; but we soon outgrow them, and our inner nature should then boldly proclaim itself.[10]

The Qur'an makes frequent mention of figures and stories from Jewish and Christian sacred history, all of which is considered part of the fabric of Islam by Muslims. Islam is the original religion, according to the Qur'an. Submission has existed as long as there have been humans willing to submit. Adam was the first prophet. Abraham was not exclusively a Jew nor a Christian; he was a mono-theistic, upright person who had surrendered to Allah. Jesus was a very great prophet.

Muslims believe that the Jewish prophets and Jesus all brought the same mess-ages from God. However, the Qur'an teaches that God's original messages have been added to and distorted by humans. For instance, Muslims do not accept the idea developed historically in Christianity that Jesus has the authority to pardon or atone for our sins. The belief that this power lies with anyone except God is considered a blasphemous human interpolation into what Muslims understand as the basic and true teachings of all prophets of the Judeo-Christian-Islamic tra-dition: belief in one God and in our personal moral accountability before God on the Day of Judgment. In the Muslim view, the Qur'an was sent as a final correc-tive in the continuing monotheistic tradition. Muslims, citing John 14:16, 26 from the Christian New Testament, believe that Jesus prophesied the coming of Muhammad when he promised that the **Paraclete** (advocate) would come to assist humanity after him.

The Qur'an revealed to Muhammad is understood as a final and complete reminder of the prophets' teachings, which all refer to the same God. For example, in Sura 42, Muhammad is told:

> Say: "I believe in whatever Book Allah has sent down; and I am commanded to judge justly between you. Allah is our Lord and your Lord! For us is the responsibility for our deeds, and for you for your deeds. There is no contention between us and you. Allah will bring us together, and to Him is our final goal."[11]

The central teachings

On the surface, Islam is a very straightforward religion. Its teachings can be summed up very simply, as in this statement by the Islamic Society of North America:

> Islam is an Arabic word which means peace, purity, acceptance and commitment. As a religion, Islam calls for complete acceptance of the teachings and guidance of God.
>
> A Muslim is one who freely and willingly accepts the supreme power of God and strives to organize his life in total accord with the teachings of God. He also works for building social institutions which reflect the guidance of God.[12]

This brief statement can be broken down into a number of articles of faith.

The Oneness of God and of humanity

The first sentence chanted in the ear of a traditional Muslim infant is the **Shahadah**—"*La ilaha ill-Allah Muhammad-un Rasulu-llah*" ("There is no god but God, and Muhammad is the Messenger of God"). Exoterically, the Shahadah sup-ports absolute monotheism. As the Qur'an reveals in Sura 2:163,

Your God is One God:
There is no god but He,
Most Gracious, Most Merciful.

Esoterically, the Shahadah means that ultimately there is only one Absolute Reality; the underlying essence of life is eternal unity rather than the apparent separateness of things in the physical world. Muslims think that the Oneness of God is the primordial religion taught by all prophets of all faiths. Muhammad merely reminded people of it.

It has been estimated that over ninety percent of Muslim theology deals with the implications of Unity. God, while One, is referred to by ninety-nine names. These are each considered attributes of the One Being, such as *al-Ali* ("The Most High") and *ar-Raqib* ("The Watchful"). Allah is the name of God that encompasses all the attributes. Each of the names refers to the totality, the One Being.

Unity applies not only to the conceptualization of Allah, but also to every aspect of life. In the life of the individual, every thought and action should spring from a heart and mind intimately integrated with the divine. Islam theoretically rejects any divisions within itself; all Muslims around the globe are supposed to embrace as one family. All humans, for that matter, are a global family; there is no one "chosen people," for all are invited into a direct relationship with God. Science, art, and politics are not separate from religion in Islam. Individuals should never forget Allah; the Oneness should permeate their thoughts and actions. Abu Hashim Madani, an Indian Sufi sage, is said to have taught: "There is only one thing to be gained in life, and that is to remember God with each breath; and there is only one loss in life, and that is the breath drawn without the remembrance of God."[13]

Muslims express their belief in the Oneness of the divine by saying the Shahadah ("There is no god but God, and Muhammad is the Messenger of God"), the sentence emblazoned on this Turkish plaque.

> "The 'remembrance of God' is like breathing deeply in the solitude of high mountains: here the morning air, filled with purity of the eternal snows, dilates the breast; it becomes space and heaven enters our heart."
>
> *Frithjof Schuon*[14]

Prophethood and the compass of Islam

Devout Muslims feel that Islam encompasses all religions. Islam honors all prophets as messengers from the one God:

Say ye: We believe
In God, and the revelation
Given to us, and to Abraham,
Isma'il, Isaac, Jacob,
And the Tribes, and that given
To Moses and Jesus, and that given
To (all) Prophets from their Lord:
We make no difference
Between one and another of them:
And we bow to God in surrender.[15]

Farid Esack

Although Farid Esack is known as one of the world's most brilliant young Muslim scholars, his life has not been spent only in poring through books and speaking to intellectuals. On the contrary, he grew up as a victim of apartheid in South Africa and was active in the resistance that has led to the liberation of South Africa's oppressed peoples. Farid remembers running to school in bare feet to avoid frostbite, for often he had no shoes. His family was so poor that they had to beg for food and search through gutters for bits of food. Farid observes:

> When you live in poverty and isolation, one of the things you hold on to is religion for your sanity, to keep you going. When you hear people crying in suffering and pain, instead of asking, "Where is God?", this is God crying out to you, "Why are you allowing this?"[16]

Thus it was not only poverty that drove Farid to risk his life again and again to build resistance to apartheid policies. It was also his deep commitment to Islam. He understands his religion as a mandate for struggling against injustice in society. He explains:

> I was strangely and deeply religious as a child, with a deep concern for the suffering which I experienced and witnessed all around me. I dealt with these two impulses by holding on to an indomitable belief that for God to be God, God had to be just and on the side of the marginalized. More curious was a logic, based on a text in the Qur'an, "If you assist Allah then He will assist you and make your feet firm" (47:7). For me this meant that I had to participate in a struggle for freedom and justice and, if I wanted God's help in this, then I had to assist Him.[17]

Muslims constituted only 1.32 percent of the population of South Africa, and yet in 1984 Farid and three friends founded the Call of Islam as an affiliate of the United Democratic Front, the major liberation movement. The Call of Islam was very active in organizing resistance to apartheid, gender inequality, environmental destruction, and tensions between religions. At last, after years fraught with danger, Farid found himself in a queue of the rural poor, armed with a ballot and a pencil to cast his vote for a freely elected government. He mused:

> I thought of the pain our country had endured in its long march to freedom, the loneliness of exile, of detention without trial, the political murders, the dispossession, the sighs of the tired and the exploited factory and farm workers, the months of living on the run like a fugitive, the attacks by police dogs, the clandestine pamphleteering . . . all for a single mark with a cheap little lead pencil![18]

Earlier, he had said at public meetings,

> "Can you imagine that we are the generation responsible for the death of apartheid; that we are going to slay the monster of racial arrogance; that we are going to be the first South Africans in 350 years who are going to live in a non-racial, non-sexist and democratic homeland?" Difficult as it was to sustain this belief at times, we did it.[19]

Farid embodies and wrestles with the tensions between having full faith in one's own religion and keeping one's heart open to people of other faiths. During the freedom struggle and later in other struggles against "the madness of humankind in our day and age,"[20] Farid has often found himself working side by side with people of different religions. He is trying to show through intense Muslim scholarship that if a person of another religion is righteous, just, and God-fearing, he or she should be accepted by Muslims as a *mu'min* (believer), not a *kafir* (non-believer). In this context, he cites the Qur'anic Sura 8:2–4:

> Indeed, the mu'minun [believers] are those whose hearts tremble with awe whenever God is mentioned; and whose iman [faith, belief] is strengthened whenever His ayat [signs] are conveyed unto them; and who place their trust in their Sustainer. Those who are constant in prayer and spend on others out of what We provide for them as sustenance. It is they who are truly the mu'minun.

Having served as a member of South Africa's Gender Equality Commission, Farid concludes:

> In the Last Judgment, I will not be asked whether I succeeded or not. It is not our task to solve the problems of the world. We will only be asked what we did with the gifts He gave us. In Islam and in the Christian Gospels, it is said that God will ask you on the Day of Judgment, "When I was hungry, why did you not feed Me?"[21]

Muslims believe that the original religion was monotheism, but that God sent prophets from time to time as religions decayed into polytheism. Each prophet came to renew the message, in a way specifically designed for his culture and time. Muhammad, however, received messages meant for all people, all times. The Qur'anic revelations declared him to be the "Seal of the Prophets," the last and ultimate authority in the continuing prophetic tradition. The prophets are mere humans; none of them is divine, for there is only one Divinity.

Islam is thought to be the universal religion in its pure form. All scriptures of all traditions are also honored, but only the Qur'an is considered fully authentic, because it is the direct, unchanged, untranslated word of God. Whatever exists in other religions that agrees with the Qur'an is divine truth.

Human relationship to the divine

> We are nearer to [a person] than his jugular vein.
>
> The Holy Qur'an, Sura 50:16

In Muslim belief, God is all-knowing and has intelligently created everything for a divine purpose, governed by fixed laws that assure the harmonious and wondrous working of all creation. Humans will find peace only if they know these laws and live by them. They have been revealed by the prophets, but the people often have not believed. To believe is to surrender totally to Allah. As the Qur'an states,

> None believes in Our revelations save those who, when reminded of them, prostrate themselves in adoration and give glory to their Lord in all humility; who forsake their beds to pray to their Lord in fear and hope; who give in charity of that which We have bestowed on them. No mortal knows what bliss is in store for these as a reward for their labors.[22]

The Qur'an indicates that human history provides many "signs" of the hand of God at work bestowing mercy and protection on believers. Signs such as the great flood, which was thought to have occurred at the time of Noah, illustrate that non-believers and evil-doers ultimately experience great misfortune in this life or the afterlife. None is punished without first being warned by a messenger of God to mend his or her ways. Creation itself is a sign of God's compassion, as well as of God's omnipotent will.

According to Islam, the two major human sins involve one's relationship to God. One is **shirk** (associating anything else with divinity except the one God). The Qur'an instructs,

> Say: "Oh People of the book!
> Come to common terms as between us and you:
> That we worship none but Allah;
> That we associate no partners with Him;
> That we erect not from among ourselves
> Lords and patrons other than Allah."[23]

In other words, in Islam's pure monotheism one is enjoined not to worship anything but God—not natural forces, or mountains, or stones, or incarnations of

God, or lesser deities, or human rulers. Idol-worship is vigorously denounced, as is worship of natural phenomena: "Adore not the sun nor the moon, but adore Allah Who created them."[24]

The other major sin is *kufr* (ungratefulness to God, unbelief, atheism). Furthermore, a major human problem is forgetfulness of God. God has mercifully sent us revelations as reminders. The veils that separate us from God come from us, not from God; Muslims feel that it is ours to remove the veils by seeking God and acknowledging the omnipresence, omniscience, and omnipotence of the Divine. For the orthodox, the appropriate stance is a combination of love and fear of God. Aware that God knows everything and is all-powerful, one wants to do everything one can to please God, out of both love and fear. This paradox was given dramatic expression by the Caliph 'Umar ibn al-Khattab:

> *If God declared on the Day of Judgment that all people would go to paradise except one unfortunate person, out of His fear I would think that I am that person. And if God declared that all people would go to hell except one fortunate person, out of my hope in His Mercy I would think that I am that fortunate person.*[25]

The unseen life

Muslims believe that our senses do not reveal all of reality. In particular, they believe in the angels of God. These are non-physical beings of light who serve and praise God day and night. They are numerous, and each has a specific responsibility. For instance, certain angels are always with each of us, recording our good and bad deeds. The Qur'an also mentions archangels, including Gabriel, highest of the angelic beings, whose main responsibility is to bring revelations to the prophets from God. But neither he nor any other angel is to be worshiped, according to strict monotheistic interpretation of Islam, for the angels are simply utterly submissive servants of God. By contrast, according to Islamic belief, there is a non-submissive being called Satan. He was originally one of the *jinn*— immaterial beings of fire, whose nature is between that of humans and angels. He proudly refused to bow before Adam and was therefore cursed to live by tempting Adam's descendants—all of humanity, in other words—to follow him rather than God. According to the Qur'an, those who fall prey to Satan's devices will ultimately go to hell.

Popular Muslim piety also developed a cult of saints. The tombs of mystics known to have had special spiritual powers have become places of pilgrimage. Many people visit them out of devotion and desire for the blessings of the spirit, which is thought to remain in the area. This practice is frowned upon by some reformers, who assert that Muslim tradition clearly forbids worship of any being other than God.

The Last Judgment

In the polytheistic religion practiced by Arabs before Muhammad, the afterlife was only a shadow, without rewards or punishments. People had little religious incentive to be morally accountable. By contrast, the Qur'an emphasizes that after a period of repose in the grave, all humans will be bodily resurrected and

According to Muslim belief, angels are everywhere; they come to our help in every thought and action. A group of angels is here shown helping the 8th-century Sufi ascetic, Ibrahim ibn Adham.

assembled for a final accounting of their deeds. At that unknown time of the Final Judgment, the world will end cataclysmically: "The earth will shake and the mountains crumble into heaps of shifting sand" (Sura 73:14). Then comes the terrible confrontation with one's own life:

> *The works of each person We have bound about his neck. On the Day of Resurrection, We shall confront him with a book spread wide open, saying, "Read your book."* [26]

Hell is the grievous destiny of unrepentant non-believers—those who have rejected faith in and obedience to Allah and His Messenger, who are unjust and who do not forbid evil. Hell also awaits the hypocrites who even after making a covenant with Allah have turned away from their promise to give in charity and to pray regularly:

> *It is a flaming Fire. It drags them down by their scalps; and it shall call him who turned his back and amassed riches and covetously hoarded them.* [27]

Muslim piety is ever informed by this belief in God's impartial judgment of one's actions, and of one's responsibility to remind others of the fate that may await them.

Basically, Islam says that what we experience in the afterlife is a revealing of our tendencies in this life. Our thoughts, actions, and moral qualities are turned into our outer reality. We awaken to our true nature, for it is displayed before us. For the just and merciful, the state after death is a Garden of Bliss. Those who say, "Our Lord is God ... shall have all that your souls shall desire. ... A hospitable gift from One Oft-Forgiving, Most Merciful!" (Sura 41:30–32). The desire of the purified souls will be for closeness to God, and their spirits will live in different levels of this closeness. For them, there will be castles, couches, fruits, sweetmeats, honey, houris (beautiful virgin women), and immortal youths serving from goblets and golden platters. Such delights promised by the Qur'an are interpreted metaphorically to mean that human nature will be transformed in the next life to such an extent that the disturbing factors of this physical existence will no longer have any effect.

> *People are asleep, but when they die, they wake up.*
>
> *Hadith of the Prophet Muhammad*

By contrast, sinners and non-believers will experience the torments of hell, fire fueled by humans, boiling water, pus, chains, searing winds, food that chokes, and so forth. It is they who condemn themselves; their very bodies turn against them "on the Day when their tongues, their hands, and their feet will bear witness against them as to their actions" (Sura 24:24). The great medieval mystic al-Ghazali speaks of spiritual torments of the soul as well: the agony of being separated from worldly desires, burning shame at seeing one's life projected, and terrible regret at being barred from the vision of God. Muslims do not believe that hell can last forever for any believer, though. Only the non-believers will be left there; the others will eventually be lifted to paradise, for God is far more merciful than wrathful.

The Sunni–Shi'a split

The preceding pages describe beliefs of all Muslims, although varying interpretations of these beliefs have always existed. Groups within Islam differ somewhat on other issues. After Muhammad's death, resentments over the issue of his succession began to divide the unity of the Muslim community into factions. The two main opposing groups have come to be known as the **Sunni**, who now comprise about eighty percent of all Muslims worldwide, and the **Shi'a** (adj. Shi'ite).

As discussed earlier, a caliph was elected to lead the Muslim community after Muhammad's death. The office of caliph became a lifetime appointment. The first three caliphs, Abu Bakr, Umar, and Uthman, were elected from among the Prophet's closest companions. The fourth caliph was 'Ali, the Prophet's cousin and son-in-law. He was reportedly known for his holy and chivalrous qualities, but the dynasty of Umayyads never accepted him as their leader, and he was assassinated by a fanatic who was a former member of his own party. 'Ali's son Husayn, grandson of the Prophet, challenged the legitimacy of the fifth caliph, the Umayyad Mu'awiyya. When Mu'awiyya designated his son Yazid as his successor, Husayn rebelled and was massacred in 680 by Yazid's troops in the desert of Karbala along with many of his relatives, who were also members of the Prophet's own family. This martyrdom unified Shi'ite opposition to the elected successors and they broke away, claiming their own legitimate line of succession through the direct descendants of the Prophet, beginning with 'Ali. The two groups are still separate.

Sunni Muslims today form the majority of the population in Saudi Arabia, Egypt, Turkey, northern African countries, Pakistan, Afghanistan, Central Asian countries of the former Soviet Union, and Indonesia. Syria and Iraq have more mixed populations of Sunnis and Shi'as. The major Shi'a majority country is Iran.

Sunnis

Those who follow the elected caliphs are "the people of the Sunnah" (the sayings and practices of the Prophet, as collected under the Sunni caliphs). They consider themselves traditionalists, and they emphasize the authority of the Qur'an and the Hadith and Sunnah. They believe that Muhammad died without appointing a successor and left the matter of successors to the **ummah**, the Muslim community. They look to the time of the first four "rightly guided caliphs" (Abu Bakr, Umar, Uthman, and 'Ali) as the golden age of Islam. They regard the caliph as the leader of worship and the administrator of the **Shari'ah**, the sacred law of Islam. Sunnis regard not only the life of the Prophet but also the lives of the rightly guided caliphs—who had heard the revelations of the Prophet firsthand and been inspired by his personal example—and a few other close companions of the Prophet as the models for the ideal Muslim.

The Shari'ah is based chiefly on the Qur'an and Sunnah of Muhammad, who was the first to apply the generalizations of the Qur'an to specific life situations. Religion is not a thing apart; all of life is to be integrated into the spiritual unity that is the central principle of Islam. The Shari'ah specifies patterns for worship (known as the Five Pillars of Islam) as well as detailed prescriptions for social conduct, to bring remembrance of God into every aspect of daily life and practical ethics into the fabric of society. These prescriptions include injunctions against drinking intoxicating beverages, eating certain meats (including pork, rodents, predatory animals, certain birds, and improperly slaughtered animals), gambling and vain sports, sexual relations outside of marriage, and sexually provocative dress, talk, or actions. They also include positive measures, commanding justice, kindness, and charity. Women are given many legal rights, including the right to own property, to divorce (according to certain schools of law), to inherit, and to make a will. These rights divinely decreed during the time of the Prophet, fourteen hundred years ago, were not available to women in the West until the nineteenth century. Polygyny is allowed for men who have the means to support several wives, to bring all women under the protection of a husband. Women are allowed to inherit only half as much as men because men have the obligation to support women financially. The faithful are enjoined to exercise justice and honesty in their relationships and business interactions, to manage their wealth carefully, and to avoid arrogance.

The Shari'ah is said to have had a transformative effect on Muhammad's community. Before Muhammad, the people's highest loyalty was to their tribe. Tribes made war on each other with no restraints. Women were possessions like animals. Children were often killed at birth either because of poverty or because they were females in a male-dominated culture. People differed widely in wealth. Drunkenness and gambling were commonplace. Within a short time, Islam made great inroads into these traditions, shaping tribes into a spiritual and political unity with a high sense of ethics.

In the second century of Islam, the Abbasid dynasty replaced the Umayyads, who had placed more emphasis on empire-building and administration than on spirituality. At this point, there was a great concern for purifying and regulating social and political life in accord with Islamic spiritual tradition. Mechanisms for establishing the Shari'ah were developed. Since then, Sunnis have felt that as life circumstances change, laws in the Qur'an, Hadith, and Sunnah should be continually interpreted by a consensus of opinion and the wisdom of learned men and jurists. For example, a contemporary Muslim faces new ethical questions not specifically addressed in the Qur'an and Hadith, such as whether or not test-tube fertilization is acceptable. Divorce has always been addressed by the Shari'ah, but the conditions under which a wife may petition for divorce have been closely examined in recent years.

Careful study of the Qur'an and Sunnah as the basis for legal opinions is undertaken by the **ulama**, scholars who devote their lifetimes to developing this knowledge. The most renowned school for the training of the *ulama* is al-Azhar in Cairo. Founded in the tenth century, it is the world's oldest university. A **fatwa**, or legal opinion, from the scholars of al-Azhar is considered authoritative by Sunni Muslims around the world.

Shi'a

The Shi'a feel that 'Ali was the rightful original successor to the Prophet Muhammad. Several weeks before the death of the Prophet Muhammad, the Prophet reportedly took 'Ali's hand and said, "Whoever I protect, 'Ali is also his protector. O God, be a friend to whoever is his friend and an enemy to whoever is his enemy." This is construed by the Shi'a as a veiled way of designating 'Ali as his successor. They feel that spiritual power was passed on to 'Ali, and that the caliphate is based on this spiritual as well as temporal authority. They are ardently devoted to the memory of Muhammad's close relatives: 'Ali, Fatima (the Prophet's beloved daughter), and their sons Hasan and Husayn. The martyrdom of Husayn at Karbala in his protest against the alleged tyranny, oppression, and injustice of the Umayyad caliphs is held up as a symbol of the struggle against human oppression. It is commemorated yearly as 'Ashura, a memorial on the tenth day of the month of Muharram. Participants in mourning processions cry and beat their chests or, in some areas, offer cooling drinks to the populace in memory of the martyred Husayn. Shi'ite piety places great emphasis on the touching stories told of 'Ali and Husayn's dedication to truth and integrity, even if it leads to personal suffering, in contrast to the selfish power politics ascribed to their opponents.

Rather than recognize the Sunni caliphs, the Shi'a pay allegiance to a succession of seven or twelve **Imams** (leaders, guides). The first three were 'Ali, Hasan, and Husayn. According to a saying of the Prophet acknowledged by both Sunni and Shi'a:

> I leave two great and precious things among you: the Book of Allah and my
> Household. If you keep hold of both of them, you will never go astray after me.[28]

"Twelver" Shi'a believe that there were a total of twelve Imams, legitimate hereditary successors to Muhammad. The twelfth Imam, they believe, was commanded by God to go into an occult hidden state to continue to guide the people and return publicly at the Day of Resurrection as the Mahdi. A minority of the Shi'a, the Isma'ilis and "Seveners," recognize a different person as the seventh and last Imam, and believe that it is he who is hidden and still living. There must always be an Imam.

Unlike the Sunni caliph, the Imam combines political leadership (if possible) with continuing the transmission of Divine Guidance. This esoteric religious knowledge was given by God to Muhammad, from him to 'Ali, and thence from each Imam to the successor he designated from 'Ali's lineage. It includes both the outer and inner meanings of the Qur'an. The Shari'ah is therefore interpreted for each generation by the Imam, for he is closest to the divine knowledge.

The Five Pillars and Jihad

Aside from the issue of succession to Muhammad, Sunnis and Shi'a are in general agreement on most issues of faith. The Shi'a follow the same essential practices as Sunnis, but add several that express their ardent commitment to re-establishing what they see as the true spirit of Islam in a corrupt, unjust world. The general practices they share are known as the Five Pillars of Islam. A Muslim must do his or her best to fulfill the Five Pillars because they are considered God's commandments.

Belief and witness

The first pillar of Islam (the Shahadah) is believing and professing the unity of God and the messengership of Muhammad: "There is no god but God, and Muhammad is the Messenger of God." The Qur'an requires the faithful to tell others of Islam, so that they will have the information they need to make an intelligent choice. However, it rules out the use of coercion in spreading the message:

> Let there be [or: There is] no compulsion
> In religion: Truth stands out
> Clear from Error: whoever
> Rejects Evil and believes
> In God hath grasped
> The most trustworthy
> Hand-hold, that never breaks.[29]

The Qur'an insists on respect for all prophets and all revealed scriptures.

Daily prayers

The second pillar is the performance of a continual round of prayers. Five times a day, the faithful are to perform ritual ablutions with water (or sand or dirt if necessary), face Mecca, and recite a series of prayers and passages from the Qur'an, bowing and kneeling. Around the world, this joint facing of Mecca for prayer unites all Muslims into a single world family. When the prayers are recited by a

For one and a half weeks every year, a huge event is held in the Hadhramaut area of Yemen to praise the Prophethood.

At a Muslim mosque, there are no social distinctions, as all worshippers line up shoulder to shoulder to pray together.

Islam:
Istanbul-style
Mosques

congregation, all stand and bow shoulder to shoulder, with no social distinctions. In a mosque, women and men usually pray separately, with the women in rows behind the men, to avoid sexually distracting the men. There may be an **imam**, or prayer-leader, but no priest stands between the worshipper and Allah. On Friday noon, there is usually a special prayer service in the mosque, but Muslims observe no Sabbath day. Remembrance of God is an everyday obligation; invoking the Name of Allah continually polishes the rust from the heart.

Repeating the prayers is thought to strengthen one's belief in God's existence and goodness and to carry this belief into the depths of the heart and every aspect of external life. Praying thus is also expected to purify the heart, develop the mind and the conscience, comfort the soul, encourage the good and suppress the evil in the person, and awaken the innate sense of higher morality and higher aspirations. The words of praise and the bowing express continual gratefulness and submission to the One. At the end, one turns to the two guardian angels on one's shoulders to say the traditional Muslim greeting—"*Assalamu Alaykum*" ("Peace be on you")—and another phrase adding the blessing, "and mercy of God."

While mouthing the words and performing the outer actions, one should be concentrating on the inner prayer of the heart. The Prophet reportedly said, "Prayer without the Presence of the Lord in the heart is not prayer at all."[30]

Zakat

The third pillar is **zakat**, or spiritual tithing and almsgiving. At the end of the year, all Muslims must donate at least two and a half percent of their accumulated wealth to needy Muslims. This provision is designed to help decrease inequalities in wealth and to prevent personal greed. Its literal meaning is "purity," for it purifies the distribution of money, helping to keep it in healthy circulation.

Saudi Arabia devotes fifteen percent of its kingdom's GDP to development and relief projects throughout the world. The Islamic Relief Organization that it funds makes a point of helping people of all religions, without discrimination, where there is great need following disasters. Many stories from the life of the Prophet Muhammad teach that one should help others whether or not they are Muslims. For example, the Prophet's neighbor was Jewish. The Prophet reportedly gave him a gift every day, even though the neighbor daily left garbage at his door. Once the neighbor was sick, and the Prophet visited him. The neighbor asked, "Who are you to help me?" The Prophet replied, "You are my brother. I must help you."

In addition to *zakat*, the Shi'a are obligated to give one-fifth of their disposable income to the Imam. Because the Imam is now hidden, half of this now goes to his deputy to be used however he thinks appropriate; the other half goes to descendants of the Prophet to spare them the humiliation of poverty.

Fasting

The fourth pillar is fasting. Frequent fasts are recommended to Muslims, but the only one that is obligatory is the fast during Ramadan, commemorating the first revelations of the Qur'an to Muhammad. For all who are beyond puberty, but not infirm or sick or menstruating or nursing children, a dawn-to-sunset abstention from food, drink, sexual intercourse, and smoking is required for the whole month of Ramadan.

Because Muslims use a lunar calendar of 354 days, the month of Ramadan gradually moves through all the seasons. When it falls in the summer, the period of fasting is much longer than in the shortest days of winter. The hardship of abstaining even from drinking water during these long and hot days is an unselfish surrender to God's commandment and an assertion of control over the lower desires. The knowledge that Muslims all over the world are making these sacrifices at the same time builds a special bond between haves and have-nots, helping the haves to experience what it is to be hungry, to share in the condition of the poor. Those who have are encouraged to be especially generous in their almsgiving during Ramadan.

Fasting is expected to allow the body to burn up impurities and provide one with "a Transparent Soul to transcend, a Clear Mind to think and a Light Body to move and act."[31] Many people feel that they are spiritually more sensitive and physically more healthy during Ramadan fasting, and they look forward eagerly to this period each year. Fasting liberates a person's body from the heaviness of food and it is also a lesson for the soul, teaching it not to allow anything into the mind and heart that would distract one from God. It is believed that control of the body's desires also builds the mastery needed to control the lower emotions, such as anger and jealousy.

Hajj

The fifth pillar is **hajj**, the pilgrimage to Mecca. All Muslims who can possibly do so are expected to make the pilgrimage at least once in their lifetime. It involves

The Prophet's Mosque in Medina has been enlarged to allow room for over one million praying pilgrims.

a series of symbolic rituals designed to bring the faithful as close as possible to God. Male pilgrims wrap themselves in a special garment of unsewn cloths, rendering them all alike, with no class distinctions. The garment is like a burial shroud, for by dying to their earthly life they can devote all their attention to God. It is a time for *dhikr*, the constant repetition of the Shahadah, the remembrance that there is no god but God.

Pilgrims walk around the ancient Ka'bah seven times, like the continual rotation around the One by the angels and all of creation, to the seventh heaven. Their hearts should be filled only with remembrance of Allah.

Another sacred site on the pilgrimage is the field of Arafat. It is said to be the place where Adam and Eve were taught that humans are created solely for the worship of God. Here pilgrims pray from noon to sunset to be forgiven of anything that has separated them from the Beloved. In addition, pilgrims carry out other symbolic gestures, such as sacrificing an animal and throwing stones at the devil, represented by pillars. The animal sacrifice reminds the *hajjis* of Abraham's willingness to surrender to God that which was most dear to him, his own son, even though in God's mercy he was allowed to substitute a ram for the sacrifice. Most of the meat is distributed to the needy, a service for which Saudi Arabia has had to develop huge preservation and distribution facilities. *Hajjis* also perform

Pilgrims to Mecca circumambulate the Ka'bah, like angels rotating around the One.

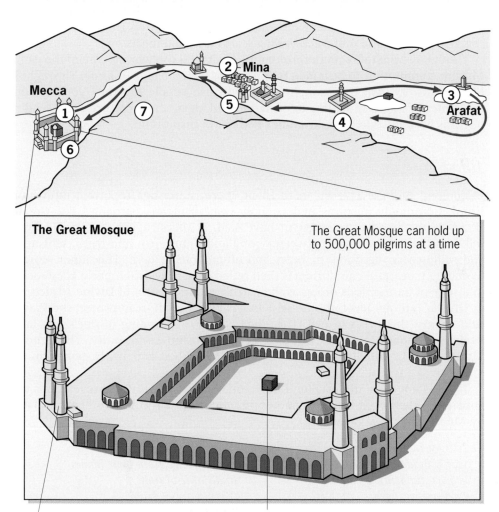

1. Pilgrimage begins at the Great Mosque, with seven circumambulations of the Ka'bah

2. Pilgrims stop at Mina

3. They pray from noon to evening in the Arafat valley. The prophet Muhammad gave his last talk here

4. Pilgrims gather 49 stones

5. They throw their stones at three pillars which represent the devil. Three days of ritual sacrifice begin

6. They return to the Great Mosque and again circle the Ka'bah seven times

7. Pilgrims walk seven times between hills near the Great Mosque and then drink from the sacred spring Zum-Zum

Mecca

Mina

Arafat

The Great Mosque

The Great Mosque can hold up to 500,000 pilgrims at a time

Seven minarets, 90 meters tall

The Ka'bah is a black stone 15 meters high, draped in black silk, engraved with the sacred names of Allah. Pilgrims walk around it seven times until they reach the center and touch the Ka'bah itself

The pilgrimage to Mecca.

symbolic acts at the holy well of Zam-Zam, the spring that God is said to have provided for Hagar when she and Ishmael were left alone in the desert.

Hajj draws together Muslims from all corners of the earth for this intense spiritual experience. Because Islam is practiced on every continent, it is truly an international gathering. The crowds are enormous. During the month of the pilgrimage, over two million pilgrims converge upon Mecca. To help handle the crowds, the Saudi government has built the immense King Abdul Aziz International Airport near Jedda. The journey was once so hazardous that many people and camels died trying to cross the desert in fulfillment of their sacred obligation.

Now there are new dangers from the presence of such masses of pilgrims. The Saudi government has tried to organize the sites to avoid tragedies, but still in recent years hundreds of *hajjis* have died in stampedes and fires. To lessen the danger of cooking fires, the government has made arrangements for 10,000 fireproof air-conditioned tents and 600 trucks selling sealed fast-food meals.

Though considerably modernized now, *hajj* is still the vibrant core of the global Muslim community. To be a *hajji* is as much as ever a badge of pride. Throughout Muslim history, *hajj* has brought widely diverse people together, consolidating the center of Islam, spreading information and ideas across cultures, and sending pilgrims back into their communities with fresh inspiration.

Jihad

In addition to these Five Pillars of Islam, there is another important injunction: **jihad**. Commonly mistranslated as "holy war," it means "striving." The Greater Jihad, Muhammad is reported to have said, is the struggle against the lower self. It is the internal fight between wrong and right, error and truth, selfishness and selflessness, hardness of heart and all-embracing love. This inner struggle to maintain peaceful equilibrium is then reflected in outer attempts to keep society in a state of harmonious order, as the earthly manifestation of Divine Justice.

On the external level, the Lesser Jihad is exerting effort to protect the Way of God against the forces of evil. This jihad is the safeguarding of one's life, faith, livelihood, honor, and the integrity of the Muslim community. The Prophet Muhammad reportedly said that "the preferred jihad is a truth spoken in the presence of a tyrant."[32]

Jihad is not to be undertaken for personal gain. The Qur'anic revelations that apparently date from the Medina period when the faithful were being attacked by Meccans make it clear that

To those against whom　　　　　　*(They are) those who have*
War is made, permission　　　　　*Been expelled from their homes*
Is given (to fight), because　　　 *In defiance of right,*
They are wronged;—and verily,　　 *(For no cause) except*
God is Most Powerful　　　　　　　*That they say, "Our Lord*
For their aid;　　　　　　　　　　*Is God."*[33]

The Qur'an gives permission to fight back under such circumstances, but also gives detailed limitations on the conduct of war and the treatment of captives, to prevent atrocities.

Forbidden to indulge in pictorial representation, Muslim artists lavished great devotion on elaborate calligraphy and decoration for the word of God, revealed in the Holy Qur'an. The illuminations express the luminous flowing outward from the Sacred Word.

Muḥammad is the prototype of the true ***mujahid***, or fighter in the Path of God, one who values the Path of God more than life, wealth, or family. He is thought to have had no desire for worldly power, wealth, or prestige. By fasting and prayer, he continually exerted himself toward the One, in the Greater Jihad. In defending the Medina community of the faithful against the attacking Meccans, he was acting from the purest of motives. It is believed that a true *mujahid* who dies in defense of the faith goes straight to paradise, for he has already fought the Greater Jihad, killing his ego.

The absolute conviction that characterizes jihad derives from the recognition of the vast disparity between evil and the spiritual ideal, both in oneself and in society. Continual exertion is thought necessary in order to maintain a peaceful equilibrium in the midst of changing circumstances. Traditionalists and radicals have differed in how this exertion should be exercised in society.

In terms of the Lesser Jihad, support can be found in the Qur'an both for a pacifist approach and for active opposition to unbelievers. The Qur'an asserts that believers have the responsibility to defend their own faith as well as to remind unbelievers of the truth of God and of the necessity of moral behavior. In some passages, Muslims are enjoined simply to stand firm against aggression. For example, "Fight for the sake of Allah those that fight against you, but do not be aggressive. Allah does not love the aggressors."[34] In other passages, Qur'an suggests active opposition to people who do not believe in the supremacy of the one God:

> *Tumult and oppression are worse than slaughter.*
> *Nor will they cease fighting you*
> *Until they turn you back from your faith*
> *If they can. . . .*
> *Fight them on*
> *Until there is no more tumult or oppression*
> *And there prevail justice and faith in God.*[35]

The ultimate goal and meaning of Islam, and of jihad, is peace through devoted surrender to God. A peaceful society is like paradise. Sri Lankan Sufi Shaykh M. R. Bawa Muhaiyaddeen observes:

> *If one knows the true meaning of Islam, there will be no wars. All that will be heard are the sounds of prayer and the greetings of peace. Only the resonance of God will be heard. That is the ocean of Islam. That is unity. That is our wealth and our true weapon. Not the sword in your hand.*[36]

Sufism

In addition to the two orthodox traditions within Islam—Sunni and Shi'a—there is also an esoteric tradition, which is said to date back to the time of the Prophet. He himself was at once a political leader and a contemplative with a deep prayer life. He reportedly said that every verse of the Qur'an has both an outside and an inside. Around him were gathered a group of about seventy people. They lived in his Medina mosque in voluntary poverty, detached from worldly concerns, praying night and day. After the time of the first four caliphs, Muslims of this deep faith and piety, both Sunni and Shi'a, were distressed by the increasingly secular, dynastic, wealth-oriented characteristics of Muhammad's Umayyad successors. The mystical inner tradition of Islam, called **Sufism** (Arabic: *tasawwuf*), also involved resistance to the legalistic, intellectual trends within Islam in its early development.

Sufis have typically understood their way as a corrective supplement to orthodoxy. For their part, some orthodox Sunnis do not consider Sufis to be Muslims. Sufis consider their way a path to God that is motivated by longing for the One. In addition to studying the Qur'an, Sufis feel that the world is a book filled with "signs"—divine symbols and elements of beauty that speak to those who understand. The intense personal journeys of Sufis and the insights that have resulted from their truth-seeking have periodically refreshed Islam from within. Much of the allegorical interpretation of the Qur'an and devotional literature of Islam is derived from Sufism.

The early Sufis turned to asceticism as a way of deepening their piety. The Prophet had said: "If ye had trust in God as ye ought He would feed you even as He feeds the birds."[37] Muhammad himself had lived in poverty, reportedly gladly so. Complete trust in and surrender to God became an essential step in the journey. **Dervishes** (poor mendicant mystics) with no possessions, no attachments in the world, were considered holy people like Hindu *sannyasins*. But Sufi asceticism is based more on inner detachment than on withdrawal from the world; the ideal is to live with feet on the ground, head in the heavens.

To this early asceticism was added fervent, selfless love. Its greatest exponent was Rabi'a (c. 713–801). A famous mystic of Iraq, she scorned a rich man's offer of marriage, saying that she did not want to be distracted for a moment from God. All her attention was placed on her Beloved, which became a favorite Sufi name for God. Rabi'a emphasized disinterested love, with no selfish motives of hope for paradise or fear of hell. "I have served Him only for the love of Him and desire for Him."[38] Any other motivation is a veil between lover and Beloved. When no veils of self exist, the mystic dissolves into the One she loves.

Sufi dervishes enter a state of ecstatic unity with the divine by repeating the Shahadah.

Islam:
Sufis

> *The Beloved is all, the lover just a veil.*
> *The Beloved is living, the lover a dead thing.*
>
> *Julal al-Din Rumi*[39]

In absolute devotion, the lover desires *fana*, total annihilation in the Beloved. This Sufi ideal was articulated in the ninth century CE by the Persian Abu Yazid al-Bistami. He is said to have fainted while saying the Muslim call to prayer. When he awoke, he observed that it is a wonder that some people do not die when saying it, overwhelmed by pronouncing the name Allah with the awe that is due to the One. In his desire to be annihilated in God, al-Bistami so lost himself that he is said to have uttered pronouncements such as "Under my garment there is nothing but God,"[40] and "Glory be to Me! How great is My Majesty!"

Hajji Waris Ali Shah (1819–1905) of Deva Sharif near Lucknow, India, was a great shaykh *revered by people of all religions. Understanding Islam as ideally encompassing every religion, he said, "All are equals in my eyes."*

The authorities were understandably disturbed by such potentially blasphemous statements. Sufis themselves knew the dangers of egotistical delusions inherent in the mystical path. There was strict insistence on testing and training by a sufficiently trained, tested, and illumined **murshid** (teacher) or **shaykh** (spiritual master). Advanced practices were taught only to higher initiates. It was through the *shaykh* that the **barakah** (blessing, sacred power) was passed down, from the *shaykh* of the *shaykh*, and so on, in a chain reaching back to Muhammad, who is said to have transmitted the barakah to 'Ali.

A number of **tariqas** (esoteric orders) evolved, most of which traced their spiritual lineage back to Junayd of Baghdad (who died in 910 CE). He taught the need for constant purification, a continual serious examination of one's motives and actions. He also knew that it was dangerous to speak openly of one's mystical understandings; the exoteric-minded might find them blasphemous, and those who had not had such experiences would only interpret them literally and thus mistakenly. He counseled veiled speech, and much Sufi literature after his time is couched in metaphors accessible only to mystics.

Despite such warnings, the God-intoxicated cared little for their physical safety and exposed themselves and Sufism to opposition. The most famous case is that of Mansur al-Hallaj (c. 858–922). After undergoing severe ascetic practices, he is said to have visited Junayd. When the master asked, "Who is there?", his disciple answered, *"ana'l-Haqq"* ("I am the Absolute Truth," i.e., "I am God"). After Junayd denounced him, al-Hallaj traveled to India and throughout the Middle East, trying to open hearts to God. He wrote of the greatness of the Prophet Muhammad, and introduced into the poetry of divine love the simile of the moth that flies ecstatic into the flame and, as it is burned up, realizes Reality.

Political maneuverings made a possible spiritual revival a threat to authorities back home, and they imprisoned and finally killed al-Hallaj for his *"ana'l-Haqq."* Now, however, al-Hallaj is considered by many to be one of the greatest Muslim saints, for it is understood that he was not speaking in his limited person. Like the Prophet, who had reportedly said, "Die before ye die,"[41] al-Hallaj had already died to himself so that nothing remained but the One.

What's in your head—toss it away! What's in your hand—give it up! Whatever happens—don't turn away from it. . . . Sufism is the heart standing with God, with nothing in between.

Abu Sa'id Abu al-Khayr[42]

A more moderate Sufism began to make its way into Sunni orthodoxy through Abu Hamid al-Ghazali (1058–1111). He had been a prominent theologian but felt compelled to leave his prestigious position for a life of spiritual devotion. Turning within, he discovered mystical truths, which saved him from his growing scepticism about the validity of religion. Like mystics of all religions, he urged awareness of the certainty of death as an antidote to entanglements in worldly concerns:

> *You do not normally sell two things for one; how can you give up an endless life for a limited number of days? ... Suppose that death is near and say to yourself, "I shall endure the hardship today; perhaps I shall die tonight," ... for death does not come upon us at a specified time or in a specified way or at a specified age; but come upon us he does, and so preparation for death is better than preparation for this world. You know that you remain here for only a brief space—perhaps there remains but a single day in your allotted span, perhaps but a single breath. Imagine this in your heart every day and impose upon yourself patience in obeying God daily.*[43]

Al-Ghazali's persuasive writings combined accepted Muslim theology with the assertion that Sufism is needed to keep the mystical heart alive within the tradition. By the fourteenth century, three sciences of religion were generally accepted by the orthodoxy: jurisprudence, theology, and mysticism.

Over the centuries, other elements have been added to Sufism. Some Sufis have embraced teachings from various religions, emphasizing that the Qur'an clearly states that the same Voice has spoken through all prophets. Shihabuddin Suhrawardi (1153–1191), for instance, combined many currents of Islam with spiritual ideas from the Zoroastrians of ancient Iran and the Hermetic tradition from ancient Egypt. His writings are full of references to the divine light and hierarchies of angels. We humans have descended from the angels and realms of light, he wrote; we are in exile here on earth, longing for our true home, searching for that radiant purity, dimly remembered, in this dark world of matter.

Pilgrimage to the tombs of the Sufi saints is a popular form of piety. Women are not allowed to enter this tomb of a Chisti Sufi saint in Delhi, so they tie bits of fabric with their prayers to the grillework outside.

Although Sufi teachings and practices have been somewhat systematized over time, they resist doctrinal, linear specification. They come from the heart of mystical experiences which defy ordinary logic. Paradox, metaphor, the world of creative imagination, of an expanded sense of reality—these characteristics of Sufi thought are better expressed through poetry and stories. A favorite character in Sufi teaching tales is Mulla Nasrudin, the wise fool. An example, as told by Idries Shah:

> *One day Nasrudin entered a teahouse and declaimed, "The moon is more useful than the sun." Someone asked him why. "Because at night we need the light more."*[44]

These "jokes" boggle the mind, revealing the limitations of ordinary thinking at the same time that they offer flashes of metaphysical illumination for those who ponder their deeper significances.

Poetry has been used by Sufis as a vehicle for expressing the profundities and perplexities of relationship with the divine. The Turkish dervish Jalal al-Din Rumi (c. 1207–1273), by whose inspiration was founded the Mevlevi Dervish Order in Turkey (famous for its "Whirling Dervishes" whose dances lead to transcendent rapture), was a master of mystical poetry. He tells the story of a devotee whose cries of "O Allah!" were finally answered by God:

> *Was it not I that summoned thee to service?*
> *Did not I make thee busy with My name?*
> *Thy calling "Allah!" was My "Here am I,"*
> *Thy yearning pain My messenger to thee.*
> *Of all those tears and cries and supplications*
> *I was the magnet, and I gave them wings.*[45]

The aim of Sufism is to become so purified of self that one is a perfect mirror for the divine attributes. The central practice is called *dhikr*, or "remembrance." It consists of stirring the heart and piercing the solar plexus, seat of the ego, by movements of the head, while continually repeating "*la ilaha illa Allah*," which Sufis understand in its esoteric sense: "There is nothing except God." Nothing in this ephemeral world is real except the Creator; nothing else will last. As the seventy thousand veils of self—illusion, expectation, attachment, resentment, egocentrism, discontent, arrogance—drop away over the years, this becomes one's truth, and only God is left to experience it.

The spread of Islam

In the time of Muhammad, Islam combined spiritual and secular power under one ruler. This tradition, which helped to unify the warring tribes of the area, was continued under his successors. Islam expanded phenomenally during the centuries after the Prophet's death, contributing to the rise of many great civilizations. The ummah became a community that spread from Africa to Indonesia. Non-Muslims have the impression that it was spread by the sword, but this was not typically the case. The Qur'an forbids coercion in religion, recommending instead that Muslims invite others to the Way by their wisdom, beautiful teaching, and personal example. Islam spread mostly by personal contacts: trade, attraction to charismatic Sufi saints, appeals to Muslims from those feeling oppressed by Byzantine and Persian rule, unforced conversions. There were some military battles conducted by Muslims over the centuries, but they were not necessarily for the purpose of spreading Islam, and many Muslims feel that wars of aggression violate Muslim principles. Non-Muslim citizens of newly entered territories were asked to pay a poll tax entitling them to Muslim defense against enemies and exempting them from military service.

Muhammad's non-violent takeover of Mecca occurred only two years before he died. It was under his successors that Islam spread through West Asia and far beyond. Only a year after Muhammad died, a newly converted Qurayshite, Khalid ibn al-Walid (d. 642), commanded a series of campaigns that within seven years had claimed the entire Arabian peninsula and Syria for Islam. Newly Islamic Arab armies quickly swept through the elegant Sassanian Persian Empire, which

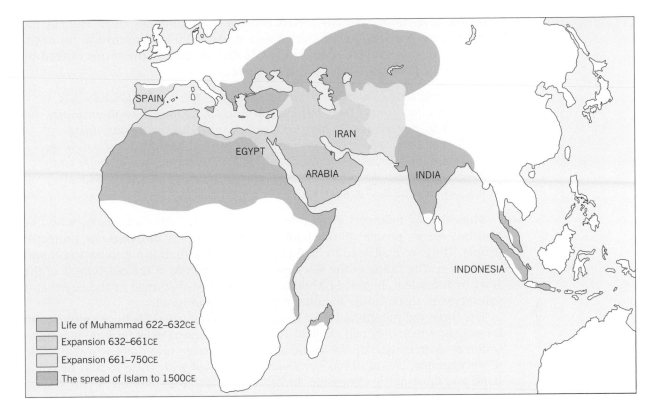

Life of Muhammad 622–632CE
Expansion 632–661CE
Expansion 661–750CE
The spread of Islam to 1500CE

had stood for twelve centuries. Defeated in battle in 637 CE, the Persian emperor fled, leaving the capital in Arab hands. Within ten years of the Prophet's death, a mere 4,000 horsemen commanded by Amr ibn al-As took the major cities of Egypt, centers of the brilliant Byzantine Empire. Another wave of Islamization soon penetrated into Turkey and Central Asia, North Africa, and north through Spain, to be stopped in 732 CE in France at the battle of Tours. At this point, only a hundred years after Muhammad died, the Muslim *ummah* under the Umayyad caliphs was larger than the Roman Empire had ever been.

Muslims cite the power of the divine will to establish a peaceful, God-conscious society as the reason why this happened. By contrast with their strong convictions, the populations they approached were often demoralized by border fighting among themselves and by grievances against their rulers. Many welcomed them without a fight. For example, the Christians of Damascus expected Muslim rule to be more bearable than Byzantine rule, so they opened the city gates to the Muslim armies. Jerusalem and Egypt accepted the Muslims in similar fashion. Syrian Christians at Shayzar under Byzantine rule reportedly went out to meet the Muslim commander and accompanied him to their city, singing and playing tambourines. In Spain, Visigoth rule and taxation had been oppressive; the persecuted Jews were especially glad to help Islam take over. Both Christians and Jews often converted to Islam.

Some historians cite economic factors as an underlying motive for Arabs' expansion beyond their original territory. Although Islamic civilization did become quite opulent, the central leadership did not always support the far-

Only one hundred years after Muhammad's death, Islam had spread around the Mediterranean. Its diffusion continued for centuries and the numbers of converts are still increasing, making Islam the fastest growing religion today. Of areas previously converted to Islam, all remain Muslim except Spain, Greece, and the Mediterranean islands.

reaching adventures. The conquered peoples were generally dealt with in the humane ways specified in the Qur'an and modeled by Muhammad in his negotiations with tribes newly subjected to Muslim authority. The terms offered by Khalid to the besieged Damascans were these:

> *In the name of God, the merciful, the compassionate. This is what Khalid would grant the inhabitants of Damascus when he enters it. He shall grant them security for their lives, properties and churches. Their city wall shall not be demolished, neither shall any Moslem be quartered in their homes. Thereunto we give them the pact of God and the protection* (dhimmah) *of His Messenger, upon whom be God's blessing and peace, the caliphs and the Believers. So long as they pay poll-tax nothing but good shall befall them.*[46]

Monotheistic followers of revealed traditions, Christians and Jews, who like Muslims were "people of the book," were treated as **dhimmis**, or protected people. They were allowed to maintain their own faith, but not to try to convert others to it. The Dome of the Rock was built on the site of the old Temple of the Jews in Jerusalem, honoring Abraham as well as Muhammad in the city that is still sacred to three faiths: Judaism, Christianity, and Islam.

The Umayyad caliphs had their hands full administering this huge *ummah* from Damascus, which they had made its capital. They tended to focus more on organizational matters than on the spiritual life. Some were also quite worldly; Walid II, for example, is said to have enjoyed a pool filled with wine so that he could swim and drink at the same time. In 747 CE a rival to the caliphate is said to have invited eighty of the princes of the line to a banquet, where he had them all killed. Three years after "the bloodshedder," a new series of caliphs took over: the Abbasids. They held power until 1258 CE.

Islamic culture

Under the Abbasids, who took over the caliphate in 750 CE, Muslim rule became more Persian and cosmopolitan and Islamic civilization reached its peak. The capital was moved to the new city of Baghdad. No more territories were brought under centralized rule, and merchants, scholars, and artists became the cultural heroes. A great House of Wisdom was built, with an observatory, a famous library, and an educational institution where Greek and Syriac manuscripts on subjects such as medicine, astronomy, logic, mathematics, and philosophy were translated into Arabic. In Cairo, Muslims built in 972 CE the great university and mosque, Al-Azhar, which is still important in Muslim scholarship and legal decisions.

In its great cities, Islam went through a period of intense intellectual and artistic activity, absorbing, transmitting, and expanding upon the highest traditions of other cultures. For instance, from Persia, which was to become a Shi'ite stronghold, it adopted a thousand-year-old tradition of exquisite art and poetry. To these avid cultural borrowings Islam added its own innovations. The new system of nine Arabic numerals and the zero derived from Indian numbers revolutionized mathematics by liberating it from the clumsiness of Roman numerals. A love of geometry and a spiritual understanding of numbers, from the One to infinite divisions, provided the basis for beautifully elaborated art and architectural

Whereas non-Muslims tend to think of Islam as a religion carried by the sword, Muslims believe their faith spread by its innate appeal and its reputation for humane, just government. The inhabitants of a besieged city are depicted welcoming the Muslim conquerors.

forms. Muslim philosophers were highly interested in Aristotelian and Neo-Platonic thought, but in their unique synthesis these intellectual ways were harmonized with revealed religion. Muslim scholars' research into geography, history, astronomy, literature, and medicine lifted these disciplines to unprecedented heights.

The pivotal institution of Islamic society was the *ulama*, whose primacy and influence was unchallenged. The *ulama* were not only guardians of the faith but were also the pervasive force holding together Islamic society. They were *qadis* (judges), *muftis* (jurisconsultants), guides and pastors of the artisans' guilds, spiritual leaders, mosque *imams*, the sole teachers of the civil and military schools, state scribes, and market inspectors. The major sources of their economic power and their independence from the state were religious endowments and private endowments, run and controlled by the *ulama*.

Although Baghdad was the capital of the Abbasids, independent caliphates were declared in Spain and Egypt. Muslim Spain was led by successors to the Umayyads and became a great cultural center. Cordoba, the capital, had seven hundred mosques, seventy libraries, three hundred public baths, and paved streets. Europe, by contrast, was in its Dark Ages; Paris and London were only mazes of muddy

AN INTERVIEW WITH KHALED ALY KHALED

Living Islam

Trained as a doctor of pharmacy, Khaled aly Khaled of Egypt did not appreciate his Muslim heritage when he was a child. He explains that his faith grew slowly as he became aware of the scientific accuracy and literary genius of the Qur'an.

"For a very long time in Egypt, we had the idea that it is better for you not to stick to a religion. If you stuck to a religion, people looked at you as just a fool. They thought there is a correlation between the success in the real life and the religion. If you have success in the real world, you didn't have to do these things that were religious. If you pray and fast and talk about Qur'an, the people start to think that you are not having any success.

"Ten years ago I could not even read Qur'an. So I started from the very end, very far from religion, but I am getting back to it. For me, maybe the most important thing is scientific interpretation of the Qur'an. I can just believe what I can see, what I can feel, and just try to make interpretation of what I can collect from data. I started to read about the planets and their movement, from the scientific point of view. It is hard to believe these kind of things come just from blind nature. But a Big Mind behind this system? I could not believe that. That's against the science. But it cannot come as an accident. If you change one part out of one hundred million parts, the whole universe will collapse. So you cannot be accurate unless you have some mind or some knowledge to control the whole thing.

"Now I'm sure that someone is behind the universe, is creating it, is creating me. You cannot feel the miracle of the universe unless you work in science. The human body cannot come from a primary cell reacting to another primary cell to create a creature from two cells and construct the body. It is beyond probability. Some supreme power created everything.

"Some of the statements in the Qur'an had no scientific verification at that time, fourteen hundred years ago, but now they have meaning. For example, 'We have created this universe and we have made it expanding.' 'We have made the earth look like an egg.' Such statements cannot come from just an average person living fourteen hundred years ago. Among ancient Egyptians, ancient Syrians, we cannot find this information. I started to believe that someone was giving the knowledge to Muhammad. I'm not a very good believer—don't ask me to believe just because there is a book. But this information cannot come from any source except One Source.

"As for the language of the Qur'an, scholars who speak Arabic have tried to write just one statement similar to this book in beauty. They could not. One computer scientist did a computer analysis of the Qur'an. He found that the number of chapters, the number of statements, and the number of times each letter is used are all multiples of nineteen (which is the number of angels in the Hellfire). Then he tried to see if he could write a book about any subject, using multiple numbers of any figure. No one could do it. The beauty of the Qur'an is pure, supreme.

"If you compare the speech of Muhammad to the Qur'an, there is a big difference in beauty. He himself cannot make even one statement like that. He cannot write, he doesn't have knowledge, he just was taking care for the sheep. From this, I started to believe that there is a God."

alleys. Spanish Muslim scientists developed a prototype of a flying machine, mechanical clocks, and highly accurate astronomical clocks, many centuries before such inventions were introduced into Europe through translations of Arabic manuscripts.

Tunisia and Egypt comprised a third center of Islamic power: the Shi'ite Fatimid imamate (so named because they claimed to be descendants of Muhammad's daughter Fatima). Under the deranged Fatimid caliph, al-Hakim (985–c. 1021), the Fatimids broke with Islamic tradition and persecuted *dhimmis*; they also destroyed the Church of the Holy Sepulcher in Jerusalem, provoking European Christian crusades to try to recapture the Holy Lands.

Crusading Christians fought their way to Jerusalem, which

Dome in the Alhambra, Granada, an exquisite example of the heights to which architecture evolved in Muslim Spain.

they placed under a month-long siege in 1099. When the small Fatimid garrison surrendered, the crusaders slaughtered the inhabitants of the holy city. Eyewitnesses recount the beheading of seventy thousand captives at the el-Aqsa mosque, near the altar site of the ancient Jewish temple. Severed hands and feet were piled everywhere. Anti-crusading Muslims led by the famous Salah-al-Din (known in the West as Saladin) retook Jerusalem in 1187 and treated its Christian population with the generous leniency of Islam's highest ideals for the conduct of war. But widespread destruction remained in the wake of the crusaders, and a reservoir of ill-will against Christians lingered, to be exacerbated centuries later by European colonialism in Muslim lands.

The Islamic period in Spain was known for its tolerance of Judaism. But during the thirteenth century, Christians took Spain and later instituted the dread Inquisition against those not practicing Christianity. By the beginning of the sixteenth century, an estimated three million Spanish Muslims had either been killed or had left the country.

Eastward expansion

Its westward advance stopped at Europe, Islam carried its vitality to the north, east, and south. Although Mongol invasions from Central Asia threatened, the Mongols were converted to Islam; so were the Turks. While Uzbek Khan, Mongol leader from 1313 to 1340, zealously desired to spread Islam throughout Russia, he nonetheless maintained tolerance toward the Christians in the conquered lands. He granted a charter to the Orthodox Metropolitan concerning the treatment of Christians: "Their laws, their Churches; their monasteries and chapels shall be respected; whoever condemns or blames this religion, shall not be allowed to excuse himself under any pretext but shall be punished with death."[47]

Similar tolerance toward other religions was practiced by the Muslim Turks, but in 1453 the Turks conquered Constantinople, the heart of the old Byzantine Empire, and renamed it Istanbul; Hagia Sophia was turned into a mosque even though it did not face Mecca. At its height, the Turkish Ottoman Empire dominated the eastern Mediterranean as well as the area around the Black Sea.

Farther east, Islam was carried into northern India, where Muslims destroyed many Hindu idols and temples but allowed the Hindu majority a protected *dhimmi* status. The Chishti Sufi saints drew people to Islam by their great love for God. "The heart of a mystic is a blazing furnace of love which burns and destroys everything that comes into it because no fire is stronger than the fire of love," declared Khwaja Muinuddin Chishti.[48]

Under the Muslim Moguls, the arts and learning flourished in India. In the ecumenical spiritual curiosity of the Emperor Akbar, who rose to the Mogul throne in 1556, representatives from many traditions—Hindu, Zoroastrian, Jain, Christian—were invited to the world's first interfaith dialogues. Eventually Akbar devised a new religion that was a synthesis of Islam and all these other religions, with himself as its supposedly enlightened head, but it died with him, and Muslim orthodoxy returned.

Under British colonization of India, tensions between Hindus and Muslims were inflamed, partly to help Britain divide and rule. India gained its independence under the influence of Mahatma Gandhi, who was unable to end the enmity

Islam:
Taj Mahal

Southern arch of the Taj Mahal, Agra, India, surrounded by verses from the Qur'an in fine marble inlay. From 1632 to 1654, the finest masons and twenty thousand laborers worked under the Mogul emperor Shah Jahan to create this mausoleum for his beloved wife, Mumtaz Mahal.

between the two faiths. In 1947, West and East Pakistan (now the independent nation of Bangladesh) were partitioned off to be Muslim-ruled and predominantly populated by Muslims, while India was to be run by Hindus. The creation of Pakistan was one of the major contemporary attempts to create a model nation based on the principles of Islam. Mohammed Ali Jinnah, the London-educated lawyer who is regarded as the founder of Pakistan, conceived of Pakistan as a modern and democratic state in which women, minorities, and human rights would be respected, according to Islam's true tenets of tolerance, compassion, and justice. However, the entrenched powers and ethnic and cultural divisions within the country have prevented realization of his dream. At its inception, the partition of India into Muslim majority and Hindu majority nations turned into a violent and chaotic nightmare. Millions lost their lives trying to cross the borders. The strife between the two faiths continues despite recurrent attempts to renew peaceful relationships between the peoples of Pakistan and India, who though divided into different religions, actually share one culture. In India, Hindus and Muslims long lived side by side in relative harmony, but in December 1992, militant Hindus set off renewed communal violence by destroying a mosque in Ayodhya, India, in the belief that it had been built by the Moguls on the site of an ancient temple to Lord Rama. Another terrible wave of Hindu violence against Muslims occurred in the state of Gujarat in 2002, in retaliation for the burning of a train illegally carrying Hindu volunteers to build a new Ram temple on the disputed Ayodhya site.

The greatest concentration of Muslims developed even farther east, in Indonesia, where Muslim traders and missionaries may have first landed as early as the tenth century CE. Nearly 90 percent of the people are now Sunni Muslims, but despite recent violence between Muslims, Hindus, and Christians, the government has attempted to preserve a secular, pluralistic society rather than establish Islam as the state religion. In 1989, then-President Suharto stated: "We want each and all religions existing and developing in our country to achieve progress in an atmosphere of unity and mutual respect."[49]

China and the former Soviet Union encompass tens of millions of Muslims. To the south, Islam spread into Africa along lines of trade. In competition with Christianity, Islam sought the hearts of Africans and eventually won in many areas. Many converted to Islam; many others maintained some of their indigenous ways in combination with Islam. The prosperous Mali Empire was headed by a Muslim, who made an awe-inspiring pilgrimage to Mecca with a gold-laden retinue of 8,000 in 1324. As the spread of Islam encompassed an increasing diversity of cultures, *hajj* became important not only for individuals but also for the religion as a whole, holding its center in Mecca in the midst of worldwide variations.

Relationships with the West

Although Islam honors the prophets of all traditions, its own religion and prophet were denounced by medieval Christian Europe. Some people fear that the medieval "clash of civilizations" may be replayed in our times if ignorance, distrust, and fear lead to exclusivist, simplistic, and violent responses to the rapid changes in the modern globalized world. Christianity had considered itself the ultimate religion and had launched its efforts to bring the whole world under its wings. Islam felt the same way about its own mission. In the struggle for souls, the Church depicted Muhammad as an idol-worshipper, an anti-Christ, the Prince of Darkness. Islam was falsely portrayed as a religion of many deities, in which Muhammad himself was worshipped as a god (thus the inaccurate label "Muhammadanism"). Europeans watched in horror as the Holy Lands became Muslim and the "infidel" advanced into Spain. Even though Muslim scholars and artists preserved, shared, and advanced the classic civilizations while Europe was benighted, the wealth of Arabic culture was interpreted in a negative light.

By the nineteenth century, Western scholars began to study the Arabic classics, but the ingrained fear and loathing of Muhammad and Muslims remained. The ignorance about, and negative stereotyping of, Muslims continues today. Annemarie Schimmel, Professor of Indo-Muslim Culture, Harvard University, explains:

> The idea that the Muslims conquered everything with fire and sword was unfortunately deeply ingrained in the medieval mind. All these misconceptions about Islam as a religion and the legends and lies that were told about it are really unbelievable. I have often the feeling that this medieval image of Islam as it was perpetuated in ever so many books and even scholarly works is part of our subconscious. When someone comes and says, "But real Islam is something completely different," people just will not believe it because they have been indoctrinated for almost fourteen hundred years with the image of Islam as something fierce and something immoral. Unfortunately, some of the events of our century have revived this medieval concept of Islam.[50]

> Borrow the Beloved's eyes. Look through them and you'll see the Beloved's
>   face everywhere. . . .
> Let that happen, and things you have hated will become helpers.
>
> Jalal al-Din Rumi[51]

Although it had enjoyed great heights of culture and political power, the Muslim world fell into decline. It seems that the Mongol invasions were at least partly responsible, for they eradicated irrigation systems and libraries and killed scholars and scientists, erasing much of the civilization that had been built up over five hundred years. Some Muslims today feel that spiritual laxness was the primary reason that some of the previously glorious civilizations became impoverished Third World countries. Another theory is that Muslim culture was no longer dynamic. As it rigidified and stagnated, it was overwhelmed by cultures both less civilized than itself (the Mongols) and more civilized (the Europeans, who were becoming major world powers on the strength of their industrialization and colonizing navies).

During the late eighteenth and early nineteenth centuries, many Muslim populations fell under European domination. From the mid-twentieth century onward, most gained their independence as states that had adopted certain Western ideals and practices. In many cases, they had let go of some aspects of their Muslim heritage, considering it a relic that prevented them from success in the modern world. Arabic was treated as an unimportant language; Western codes of law had replaced the Shari'ah in social organization. But yet they were not totally Westernized, and they resumed local rule with little training for self-government and participation in a world economy dominated by industrial nations.

Societies that had been structured along traditional lines fragmented from the mid-nineteenth century onward, as wide-ranging programs of reforms and modernization were unleashed throughout the Muslim world. The local autonomy of the traditional Islamic society was swept away and replaced by centralized regulations of Western origin. Traditional schools, markets, guilds, and courts into which the societies had been organized lost much of their reason for being.

Before the colonial forces moved out, foreign powers led by Britain helped to introduce a Jewish state in the midst of the Middle East. After long and terrible persecution in many countries, Jewish Zionists sought resettlement in what they considered their ancient homeland. But some historians allege that the chief motive of the countries supporting this claim was to protect European interests. Lord Palmerston of Britain suggested that a wealthy Jewish population transplanted to Palestine, and highly motivated to protect itself, would prop up the decaying Ottoman Empire so that it could serve as a bulwark against Russian imperialism; the new Jewish presence in Palestine would also serve as a check against the attempts of Egypt to create a pan-Islamic state encompassing Egypt, Syria, and the Arabian peninsula.

Dome of the Rock, Jerusalem. In an area held sacred by Jews, Christians, and Muslims, the dome was completed in 692 as the first major Muslim monument. The rock had been associated with Abraham's sacrifice of his son. Muslim tradition identified it as the place of the Prophet Muhammad's ascension to heaven during his night journey.

Islam in the United States

Even as Muslims were feeling humiliated by foreign domination elsewhere, they were growing in numbers and self-pride within the United States. Islam is the fastest growing religion in the United States, and may now be the second largest religion in the country. Two-thirds of American Muslims are immigrants; one-third of American Muslims are converts, most of them African–Americans.

Conversion to Islam by African–Americans was encouraged early in the twentieth century as a form of separatism from white oppression. The Christianity espoused by the dominant white population was interpreted as part of the pattern

Malcolm X visiting Egypt's Al-Azhar University in 1964

Islam:
United States and
Islam

of oppression, and awareness grew that many of the slaves who had been brought from West Africa had been of Muslim faith. A number of movements developed to bring the former slaves back to their suppressed ancestral faith. For instance, in 1913 Noble Drew Ali (1886–1929) began a movement, eventually called the Moorish Science Temple of America, that was designed to begin teaching the elements of the faith to African–Americans and thus give them a strong sense of their own identity. Members were encouraged to adopt Noble Drew Ali's understanding of Muslim lifestyles, with modest dress, gender separation, traditional family structure, and community solidarity. The Holy Prophet Noble Drew Ali declared that it was his "Divine Mission" to "uplift fallen humanity."

Some other early Muslim communities in the United States were based on missionary efforts, such as that of the Ahmadiyyah Movement from India, which was active in publishing tracts and English translations of the Qur'an and in helping African–American converts learn Arabic. By the end of the twentieth century, the Ahmadiyyah Movement had established branches in thirty-eight cities in the United States as part of its global family of ten million members, complete with social service programs.

Other movements had a strong nation-building character. In particular, under the leadership of Elijah Muhammad, who proclaimed himself a messenger of Allah, tens of thousands of African–Americans became "Black Muslims," calling themselves the Nation of Islam. However, faith in Elijah Muhammad himself was shaken by allegations about his sexual relationships with his secretaries. Some followers—especially the influential leader Malcolm X and Warith Deen Muhammad, son of Elijah Muhammad—developed contacts with mainstream Muslims in other countries and came to the conclusion that Elijah Muhammad's version of Islam was far removed from Muslim orthodoxy. They steered converts toward what they perceived as the true traditions of Islam and alliance with the world Muslim community.

Others of African–American heritage, especially Minister Louis Farrakhan, current leader of the Nation of Islam, maintain Elijah Muhammad's more political focus on unifying against white oppression, despite Islam's strong tradition of non-racism. However, politicization of Islamic identity is probably not the main aspect of the growth of Islam. Many American Muslims embrace their religion as a bulwark of discipline and faith against the degradations of materialism. The Nation of Islam has played a strong role in combating violence and drug abuse in some inner cities, and members are encouraged to observe a disciplined "December Fast" in contrast to the commercial frenzy of the Christmas season.

The homes of African–American Muslims become places of refuge from the surrounding culture, with Qur'anic inscriptions, provisions for prayer spaces, cleanliness and lack of clutter, and windows covered as privacy screens. Soon after birth, children are placed with their mothers on their prayer rugs and gradually learn to recite portions of the Qur'an. They are carefully trained in politeness to elders, modest dress, and proper behavior. The environment these children encounter in public schools is a great contrast to this traditional upbringing. Young Muslim girls are taunted about their head scarves, and sex education classes, which begin at an early age, are offensive to Muslim parents who do not accept dating and extramarital sexuality for their children. Some African–American Muslim parents thus attempt to home-school their children.

Muslim resurgence

Islam:
Muslim Resurgence in
Tatarstan

The Muslim world had lost its own traditional structure and was also generally helpless against manipulations by foreign nations until it found its power in oil. In the 1970s, oil-rich nations found that by banding together they could control the price and availability of oil. OPEC (the Organization of Petroleum Exporting Countries) brought greatly increased revenues into previously impoverished countries and strengthened their self-image as well as their importance in the global balance of power. Most of the oil-rich nations are predominantly Muslim.

As the wealth suddenly poured in, it further disrupted established living patterns. Analysts feel that some people may have turned back to a more conservative version of Islam in an effort to restore a personal sense of familiarity and stability amid the chaos of changing modern life; the increase in literacy, urbanization, and communications helped to spread revived interest in Islam. There was also the hope that Islam would provide the blueprint for enlightened rule, bringing spiritual values into community and politics as Muhammad had done in Medina. It is thought that the Prophet had intentionally tried to create a united community in which each Muslim is responsible for his fellow human beings, in which no one should be hungry or unfairly treated, and in which the leader of the community is a just and religious person. This ideal has perhaps never been fully realized, but it continues to inspire committed Muslims today as the best defense against social decadence and, perhaps, the salvation of the world.

Traditionally, Muslims have seen the world as divided into *dar al-Islam*, "the abode of Islam" (those places where Muslims are a majority and Shari'ah governs worldly life), *dar al-sulh*, "the abode of peace" (where Muslims are a minority but can live in peace and freely practice Islam), and *dar al-harb*, "the abode of conflict" (where Muslims are in the minority, struggling to practice Islam).

As overt colonialism wanes, the world has become divided into autonomous nation-states with strong central governments. In this process, forty-three primarily Islamic nation-states have been created. They differ greatly in culture and in the degree to which each society is ruled by Islamic ethics. But all are now being reconsidered as possible frameworks for *dar al-Islam*, within which the Muslim dream of religion-based social transformation might be accomplished. Those who seek to establish Islamic states in which the sovereignty of God is supreme are often now referred to as **Islamists**.

In the past few centuries, modern industrial societies separated religion from politics. Social, political, and economic issues have been treated without any reference to a higher authority or to the values taught by the prophets; religion has been considered a largely private matter, even within some Muslim majority states such as Turkey. By contrast, a re-emerging ideal among contemporary Muslim social reformers is that, as Professor Muhammad Mashuq ibn Ally explains:

The human being, the servant, is the trustee of creation under the sovereignty of God, capable of transforming it within the framework of the divine will. Humankind's obedience to, and fulfillment of, the divine command results in happiness and thus unites worldly and cosmic justice. This visionary paradigm in the unity of religious and cultural consciousness enables the assembly of a formidable force to spearhead a new world order, where the consensus is salam—*peace.*[52]

Tradition and modern life

The resurgence of Islam takes several forms. One is a call for a return to Shari'ah rather than secular law derived from European codes. The feeling of the ortho-dox is that the world must conform to the divine law, rather than diluting the law to accommodate it to the material world. In Iran, for instance, an attempt has been made to shape every aspect of life according to Shari'ah. Fasting during Ramadan is strictly enforced in Saudi Arabia and Iran, and restaurants in many Muslim countries close during the fasting hours. In Muslim-dominated northern Nigeria, a 1999 Shari'ah ruling barred men and women from traveling in the same public vehicles, in an effort to combat immorality and crime.

Private behaviors are also becoming more traditional. In particular, to honor the Qur'anic encouragement of physical modesty to protect women from being molested, many Muslim women have begun covering their bodies except for hands, face, and feet, as they have not done for decades. In Saudi Arabia, where women have been ordered to be "properly covered" outside their homes, some wear not only head-to-toe black cloaks but also full veils over their faces without even slits for their eyes. Some Muslim women assert that they like dressing more modestly so that men will view them as persons, not stare at them as sex objects. Others feel that men are simply treating women as slaves.

In some largely Muslim countries, such as Egypt, it is the possibility of employ-ment that motivates women to adopt **hijab** (veiling for the sake of modesty). Women are allowed to join the work force only if they are veiled. In Iran, the replacement of more Westernized customs with Muslim moral codes, including veiling of women, has allowed women from conservative backgrounds to leave their homes and enter public life without antagonizing their families. Now that a great number of Iranian Muslim women have been educated and have entered the

In November 2001, when Taliban forces were defeated, an Afghan woman bared her face in public for the first time since five years of Taliban law requiring women to wear head-to-toe burqas.

workforce and politics, they are a formidable part of reformist efforts to challenge the control of the male clerical elite over social life.

Women's rights to divorce and to choose their own marriage partners are among the hotly debated issues in contemporary attempts to define Shari'ah. Shari'ah has been locally adapted to various societies over the centuries; to attempt to restore its original form designed for Muhammad's time or any other form from another period is to deny the usefulness of its flexibility. Some customs thought to be Muslim are actually cultural practices not specified in the basic sources; they are the result of Islamic civilization's assimilation of many cultures in many places. Muhammad worked side-by-side with women, and the Qur'an encourages equal participation of women in religion and in society. Veiling and seclusion were practices absorbed from conquered Persian and Byzantine cultures, particularly the upper classes; peasant women could not carry out their physical work under encumbering veils or in seclusion from public view.

Muslim women scholars are now carefully re-examining the Qur'an and Hadith to determine the historical realities and principles of women's issues that have long been hidden behind an exclusively male interpretation of the traditions. Qur'anic scholar Amina Wadud, for instance, asserts that the Qur'an is potentially a "world-altering force" that offers universal moral guidance for all believers, be they male or female:

Islam:
Women and Islam

> *The more research I did into the Qur'an, unfettered by centuries of historical androcentric reading and Arabo-Islamic cultural predilections, the more affirmed I was that in Islam a female person was intended to be primordially, cosmologically, eschatogologically, spiritually, and morally a full human being, equal to all who accepted Allah as Lord, Muhammad as Prophet, and Islam as* din *[religious way]. . . . In the area of gender, conservative thinkers read explicit Qur'anic reforms of existing historical and cultural practices as the literal and definitive statement on these practices for all times and places. What I am calling for is a reading that regards those reforms as establishing precedent for continual development toward a just social order. A comprehensive just social order not only emphasizes fair treatment of women, but also includes women as agents, responsible for contributing to all matters of relevance to human society.*[53]

Another problem with applying Shari'ah as civil law is that some ethical issues that arise today either did not exist in their present form at the time of Muhammad or were not specifically addressed by the Qur'an or Hadith. Artificial birth control methods, for example, were not available then. However, infanticide and abortion were mentioned by the Qur'an: "Do not kill your children for fear of poverty. We will provide for them and for you." Does this mean that all forms of population control should be considered forbidden by Islam, or should the overpopulation of the earth be a major contemporary consideration? According to Islamic legal reasoning, the accepted method for determining such ambiguous issues is to weigh all the benefits and disadvantages that might result from a course of action and then discourage it if the likely disadvantages outweigh the advantages. For those Muslim intellectuals who want to retain their faith within the context of modern life, the process of **ijtihad** (reasoned interpretation, independent judgment by a qualified scholar) is critical.

The global family of Islam is not a political unit; its unity under Arab rule broke up long ago. There is as yet no consensus among Muslim majority states about how to establish a peaceful, just, modern society based on basic Muslim principles. But there is widespread recognition that there are problems associated with modern Western civilization that should be avoided, such as crime, drug abuse, corruption of values, and unstable family life.

> *Today everyone cries for peace but peace is never achieved, precisely because it is metaphysically absurd to expect a civilization that has forgotten God to possess peace.*
>
> Seyyed Hossein Nasr[54]

Outreach and education

Another sign of Muslim resurgence is the increase in outreach, as Muslims become more confident of the value of their faith. Islam is the fastest growing of all world religions, with approximately 1,300 million followers. New mosques are going up everywhere, including one thousand new mosques each year in Turkey alone. Muslims who constitute a minority in their countries are trying to assert their rights to practice their religion by praying five times a day, leaving work to attend Friday congregational prayer at noon, and wearing traditional head-coverings. Special Islamic satellite channels offer alternatives to Western-oriented programming that Muslims find offensive, and also act as a force for international Muslim unity. The channel Iqra, for instance, is financed by a Saudi Arabian millionaire, offering free broadcasting of what it describes as "entertaining programmes that are devoid of decadence and impropriety and are appropriate for viewing by Muslim families."[55]

A third sign of Muslim resurgence is the increasing attention being given to developing educational systems modeled on Islamic thought. Islam is not anti-scientific or anti-intellectual; on the contrary, it has historically bridged reason and faith and placed a high value on developing both in order to tap into the fullness of human potential. Western education has omitted the spiritual aspects of life, so Muslims consider it incomplete and imbalanced.

While there are many excellent Muslim educational institutions, the numerous *madrasas*, traditional religious schools, typically teach a narrow version of Islam, ignoring its sophisticated cultural and scientific heritage and nuanced philosophy. Because some of these schools have proved to be breeding grounds for militants, fanning hatred of the West, particularly among the poor rural students, they are now coming under closer scrutiny. The Sustainable Development Policy Institute in Islamabad released a report in 2003 which identified a number of troubling features of textbooks and curricula in Pakistan:

- inaccuracies and omissions of facts that lead to distorted interpretations of national history
- insensitivity to the diversity of religions in the country
- glorification of violence
- encouragement of prejudices toward women, religious minorities, and other countries
- omission of material and perspectives for developing critical thinking
- outdated teaching practices that fail to stimulate interest and insight.[56]

Similarly, Saudi Arabia, the homeland of 15 of the 19 airplane hijackers of September 11, has come under criticism for giving distorted religious messages through its schools, and says it is now revising its curricula and textbooks to promote peace and harmony. At the same time, necessary efforts are being made in some countries to increase the accuracy and sensitivity of portrayals of Islam in the education of non-Muslims. Western textbooks have tended to present history as the progress of Western civilization, from which perspective Islam is described mainly as an adversary rather than a high civilization in its own right which has made great contributions to science and culture, not to mention philosophy.

Islam in politics

At present, the facet of Islam that is of greatest concern around the world to both Muslims and non-Muslims is its association with politics. Many governments are becoming Islamicized. There are more frequent references to Islam and Qur'anic statements by political leaders. Some use this approach to support the status quo and glorify Islam's past heights. In Arabic countries, others have used Muslim idealism to rally opposition to ruling elites who are perceived as being corrupt or tied to the West. Some charismatic leaders have used their own interpretations of Islam to ignite violent political expressions of frustration and hatred against Western global domination. These include suicidal terrorist attacks against civilian targets by those who have been assured that their self-sacrifice for the cause will earn them entry to Paradise. Behind this contemporary violence are varying historical, cultural, and political circumstances in each country. There is as yet no political unity among Muslim states, but growing antagonism toward the West is tending to create a certain political unity in opposition to Western use of its military power against Muslim countries in the "war against terror." Many Muslim countries are now sharing feelings of helplessness, humiliation, and fear vis-à-vis American militarism and pre-emptive use of power. They feel that Islam itself is under siege.

Tracing the previous history of these rather recent developments, one of the leading voices that emerged in the twentieth century was that of the Egyptian scholar and activist Sayyib Qutb (1906–1966). After World War II, he saw most Muslim countries being controlled either by corrupt monarchies or by cruel military dictatorships. He had also visited the United States, but was disgusted by its culture. Devoutly religious, he saw the sex, violence, and selfish greed in Western culture as the headwaters of evil that was spreading around the world. His writings during years of imprisonment by the Egyptian government before they eventually executed him have been pivotal in the thinking of all later Islamists. Qutb had earlier thought that Islam could be compatible with parliamentary democracy, but at last he gave up hoping that secular governments would conduct themselves according to religious principles. Compared to the ideal example of the life of the Prophet Muhammad, he described Westernization thus:

> *Humanity today is living in a large brothel! One has only to glance at its press, films, fashion shows, beauty contests, ballrooms, wine bars, and broadcasting stations! Or observe its mad lust for naked flesh, provocative postures, and sick-suggestive statements in literature, the arts and the mass media! And add to all this, the system of usury which fuels man's voracity for money and engenders vile*

methods for its accumulation and investment, in addition to fraud, trickery, and blackmail dressed up in the garb of law.[57]

Similar thinking later came to the fore in Iran, one of the first Muslim majority countries in which violence was used in recent times as a political tool to advance the cause of Islam. In predominantly Shi'ite Iran, the Pahlavi Shahs had tried to rapidly modernize their country, turning it into a major military and industrial power. In the process, they eroded the authority of the *ulama*, the clerics and expounders of the Shari'ah. A revolutionary leader emerged from this disempowered group, the Ayatollah Khomeini (c. 1900–1989), and swept the Shah from power in 1979. Once in power, however, the *ulama* had no clear program for reorganizing society according to Muslim principles. Shari'ah has never specified a single political or economic system as best. Khomeini insisted that social transformation should be linked with spiritual reformation, but made some drastic changes in interpretation of Islam in order to justify violent revolutionary behavior.

He also attempted to export his revolution to other Muslim countries with Shi'ite populations that could carry on the work. He conducted a war against "atheist" Iraq (where the fifty percent of citizens who are Shi'a were ruled by the forty-five percent who were Sunni), denounced predominantly Sunni Saudi Arabia for its ties to the West, and inspired some Lebanese Shi'a to see their political struggle

Appreciative posters of the mystic and political reformer Ayatollah Khomeini continued to be displayed in Iran after his death in 1989.

Being involved in conflicts around the world, many Muslims are mourning the loss of their loved ones, becoming refugees, or being attacked or killed. This scene of grief occurred in Falluja, Iraq.

against Christians and Jews as part of a great world battle between Islam and the satanic forces of Western imperialism and Zionism. He issued a **fatwa** that Indian-born British author Salman Rushdie could be sentenced to death under Islamic law, because his novel, *The Satanic Verses*, seemed to defame the Prophet and his wives. Many people died in resultant riots over the still-controversial book.

Khomeini's call for governmental change was not heeded, so radicals resorted to sabotage and terrorism as their most powerful weapons. Their surprise attacks on civilians tended to turn world opinion against Islam, rather than promoting its ideals. More moderate leadership is now in power in Iran. Islamist reformers propose that the government should be founded on Islamic law, but that this law should be interpreted in ways that allow a considerable degree of individual freedom and free expression rather than authoritarianism.

Iraq is another Muslim nation that has used Islam as a rallying point for political power. When Saddam Hussein of Iraq tried to re-annex Kuwait, from which Iraq and Saudi Arabia had been separated in 1922 by a "divide and rule" decision of the occupying British forces, Islam was cast as a political football by both sides in the Gulf War. Hussein, an Arab nationalist, resorted to Islam as a means of mass mobilization against what he saw as Western intrusion in the Gulf. Even after the Gulf War, years of economic sanctions by the United Nations against Iraq over continuing suspicion of its military intentions created such hardships for the populace that Iraqis referred to the sanctions as a means of genocide.

Then the United States launched massive bombings of Iraq in 2003 in a campaign it said would "shock and awe" the Iraqi regime and liberate the people from the tyrannical rule of Saddam Hussein, as well as saving the world from what it claimed were Iraq's massive stockpiles of weapons of mass destruction. By contrast, many Muslims around the world perceived the American-led attacks and occupation of the country as an unprovoked attack on innocent Muslim civilians as well as an attempt to control its oil resources. No such weapons of mass destruction were found, and the population has shown considerable resistance to the occupying forces. Terrorist activity has already increased in Iraq and elsewhere in protest of the American-led invasion.

In Afghanistan during the 1980s, the United States supported armed Muslim militants—including Osama bin Laden, the Saudi leader of Al Qaeda who ran terrorist-training camps in rural Afghanistan—to help them drive out the Soviet Union. When the Russian troops left, Afghanistan collapsed into factional fighting and chaos, from which emerged oppressive control by the Taliban from 1996 to 2001. Theirs was an extreme and exclusivist view of the ideal Muslim state. Originally Islamists trained in a particular school in Kandahar, the ardent Taliban discarded all secular laws and replaced them with their interpretation of Shari'ah. To deter crime, for instance, they organized public spectacles in which the hands of thieves were amputated and adulterers were whipped. While they succeeded in bringing a certain orderliness to the poor, war-ravaged country, they did so in ways that outraged the outside world and contradicted the Prophet's insistence on compassion and tolerance. They bombed the huge ancient cliff-hewn statues of Buddha at Bamiyan with the understanding that they were idolatrous, and severely restricted women, keeping them out of the workplace, denying them education, and insisting that they wear head-to-toe *burqas*. The tenacious Revolutionary Association of the Women of Afghanistan resisted the anti-women regimes of both the Taliban and other ruling factions in Afghanistan, documenting the raping, killing, and kidnapping of women by militia members as an instrument of social repression. During the Taliban regime, law professor Azizah Y. al-Hibri analyzed the issue of how they were interpreting and using the Shari'ah:

> *While there is no central interpretive authority in Islam, an acceptable interpretation must satisfy a minimum number of requirements. For example, the interpretation must be based on the Qur'an and* Sunnah. *It must be based on knowledge and motivated by Piety. It must also serve (rather than harm)* maslaha, *the public interest of Muslims in particular and humanity in general. . . . The Taliban seems to have no such concerns. This is consistent with their rejection of other basic Islamic principles, such as* shura *(consultation with other Muslims) and* bay-ah *(a system of elective non-authoritarian governance). It is also consistent with their rejection of the Islamic injunction that the pursuit of education is the duty of every Muslim, male and female. Finally, it is consistent with their rejection of the overarching Islamic model of harmonious gender, racial, religious, and general human relations.*[58]

Under heavy military attack by the United States, the Taliban's political power in Afghanistan was broken. Hundreds of women in the capital city of Kabul shed their *burqas* publicly, demanding the right to work, education for their daughters, and a voice in politics. While a coalition backed by the United States tries to maintain order in faction-torn Afghanistan, based on a constitution that attempts to combine the teachings of the Qur'an with democracy, extremists still attack girls' schools under a rigid interpretation of Islam.

Since 1932, Saudi Arabia has been under the absolute monarchical control of the huge al-Sa'ud family. Friendly to the West and using its oil wealth lavishly, the regime is often criticized for exposing the populace to the corrupting influence of Western culture by allowing Western troops on its soil. Despite the plush modern lifestyles and technologies of the elite, the country is religiously conservative, harkening to the ideas of the eighteenth-century reformer Muhammad ibn 'abd al-Wahhab, who urged discarding of all practices that are not specifically approved by the Qur'an and Sunnah. He portrayed Western civilization as the enemy of Islam and America as Satan, trying to lure humankind from the righteous path. Thus Wahhabi morality squads actively enforce the obligatory prayers, and women are not allowed to drive cars or leave home unless they are accompanied by a close male relative. They cannot work outside their homes except as teachers or nurses.

An exiled member of the Saudi aristocracy, Osama bin Laden, was among those who had established training camps in Afghanistan where recruits from many Muslim countries were taught to mix religion with politics. Bin Laden's militant organization, Al Qaeda, is reportedly responsible for many acts of terrorism around the globe, including the devastating September 11, 2001 attacks on the World Trade Center and Pentagon in the United States which set in motion a sea-change in relationships between Muslims and non-Muslims everywhere. Al Qaeda's agenda is to strike back at the United States for its support for Israel and its intrusive presence in the Arabian peninsula, which bin Laden and others interpret as non-Muslim control over Muslim lands. Contrary to United States government predictions, elimination of particular Al Qaeda leaders has not ended the movement, and its highly motivated operatives in many countries seem to be willing to risk their lives to continue the struggle against Western cultural and political domination.

Similarly, the 2004 Israeli assassination of Sheikh Ahmed Yassin, leader of the anti-Israeli grassroots Palestinian welfare organization Hamas, led to his replacement by a greater hardliner. When he, too, was assassinated less than a month later, the leadership went underground but violence further increased nonetheless, with Palestinian militants pledging "100 retaliations" for his death.[59] Before his assassination, Yassin had said, "The Palestinian people do not have Apache helicopters or F-16s (fighter-bombers) or tanks or missiles. The only thing they can have is themselves to die as martyrs."[60]

At present, despite some attempts at encouraging dialogue, the major trend is an increase in tensions between Muslims and non-Muslims. Terrorist activities that have killed civilians have brought a backlash of anti-Muslim sentiments, with growing perception of Islam as a religion encouraging violence and fanaticism. As the United States increases its military bases around the world, its "war on terrorism" has brought an increase in acts of terrorism and made it more difficult for moderate Muslim leaders to hold their ground against critics within their countries. As Islamophobia grows among non-Muslims, many leading Muslims are trying to explain to them that Islam does not equal violence. Anwar Ibrahim, for instance, former deputy prime minister of Malaysia, asserts:

One wonders how, in the 21st century, the Muslim world could have produced a bin Laden. In the centuries when Islam created civilizations, men of wealth created pious foundations supporting universities and hospitals. Princes competed with one another to patronize scientists, philosophers and men of letters. . . . But bin Laden uses his personal fortune to sponsor terror and murder, not learning or creativity, and to wreak destruction rather than promote creation. Osama bin Laden and his protégés are the children of desperation; they come from countries where political struggle through peaceful means is futile. . . .

Muslim intellectuals and elites carry the enormous moral responsibility of stamping out terrorism in their midst, unless they want Islam to be demonized everywhere because of the outrageous acts of a small band of misguided faithfuls.[61]

While the Qur'an speaks of *jihad,* or "striving," it permits the *jihad* of violence only under very specific conditions. To fight, people must have been deprived of their right to live and support themselves. The action must be undertaken not by individuals but by the collective wisdom of the Muslim community. *Jihadis* are never allowed to harm women, children, or unarmed civilians. They cannot wilfully destroy property. The tactics of terrorists are therefore not permitted by the Qur'an. In general, relations with people of other religions are to be as tolerant as possible. It is written in the Qur'an:

Do not argue with the followers of the earlier revelations otherwise than in a most kindly manner—unless it be such of them as are bent on evil-doing—and say: We believe in that which has been bestowed from on high upon us, as well as that which has been bestowed upon you; for our God and your God is one and the same, and it is unto Him that we all surrender ourselves. (Holy Qur'an 29:46)

Nevertheless, after a long history of foreign domination which is being repeated in our times by the spread of Western culture and military might, many young Muslims have become so distressed that they are willing to offer their lives as suicide bombers in the hopes that the world will pay attention to their grievances.

Particularly after September 11, there have been hate crimes against Muslims as a result of a renewed idea among non-Muslims that Islam breeds violence and fanaticism. But, alongside this reaction, there are also attempts at deeper understanding of the complex factors that support terrorism. John Esposito, American Professor of Religion and International Affairs and Director of the Center for Muslim–Christian Understanding, writes:

If we are to understand and respond to the challenge of political Islam, its diverse manifestations must be seen within the multiplicity of intellectual and political contexts in which it occurs. While the threats of extremism and violence must be countered forcefully and effectively, the long-term relations of the West with the Muslim world— like the legitimacy of governments within the Muslim world—will hinge on its response to the emergence of new social and political forces and its respect for their legitimate aspirations for greater political participation, social justice, and human rights.[62]

Islam for the future

While media attention is centered on sensational manifestations of Islamism in present-day societies, a deeper current of thought is forward-looking, exploring how Islam can help to shape a new social order in the world. Professor Asaf

Hussain of the University of Leicester, England, points out that the goal of a just society inspires but still eludes Muslim resistance movements:

> Today many Islamic fundamentalist movements have declared war on their own people and are trying to transform their states on the model of the First Islamic state. But the conditions of the seventh century do not obtain today. A new model of the Islamic state has to be devised. The dominating civilization of the present day is Western and its models control the Third World, including the Muslim world. Islamic movements have revolted against this but their strategies have not been well thought out. They do not have to dominate Western civilization but create a parallel which excels it. This will be a long, arduous task but the struggle has just begun.[63]

Mahmoon-al-Rasheed, Founder of the Comprehensive Rural Educational, Social, Cultural and Economic Center in Bangladesh, maintains that there is violence within and between nations because people have not developed a sense of duty toward each other and have not recognized how inseparably all people of the earth are related to each other. He proposes that Islamic values are not aimed at creating a political state but rather a harmoniously integrated world society, for:

> We cannot begin to realize our full potential until we have achieved a community which knows no limit but that of human society and renders all obedience to a Law common to all.[64]

Dr. Ahmad Kamal Abu'l Majd, an ex-Minister of Culture in Egypt, looks toward the future:

> I'm glad and proud I'm a Muslim. I carry on my shoulders a scale of values, a code of ethics that I genuinely believe is good for everybody. ... I even venture sometimes to say that Islam was not meant to serve the early days of Islam when life was primitive and when social institutions were still stable and working. It was meant to be put in a freezer and to be taken out when it will be really needed. And I believe that time has come. But the challenge is great because not all Muslims are aware of this fact: That the mission of Islam lies not in the past but in the future.[65]

Suggested reading

Ahmed, Akbar, S., *Islam Under Siege*, Cambridge: Polity Press, 2003. Careful explanation of Islamic ideals and concerns in the context of contemporary violence in the name of Islam.

Ahmed, Akbar S., *Discovering Islam: Making Sense of Muslim History and Society*, London and New York: Routledge, revised edition, 2002. A well-known Pakistani diplomat and scholar teaching in the United States offers keen insights into the spirituality and history of modern Muslim cultures.

Ali, Maulana Muhammad, *The Religion of Islam*, sixth edition, Columbus, Ohio: Ahmadiyya Anjuman Isha'at Islam, 1994. A classic reference explaining all aspects of Muslim belief and practice, with extensive scriptural quotations.

Armstrong, Karen, *The Battle for God*, New York: Alfred A. Knopf, 2000. A monumental study of the development of fundamentalism in the United States, Israel, and Egypt in response to modernity.

Dessouki, Ali E. Hillal, ed., *Islamic Resurgence in the Arab World*, New York: Praeger Publishers, 1982. A scholarly study of the contemporary Islamic resurgence in specific Arab nations.

Esack, Farid, *Qur'an, Liberation and Pluralism: An Islamic Perspective of Interreligious Solidarity against Oppression*, Oxford: Oneworld Publications, 1997. A first-person account of the struggle for justice in South Africa from the point of view of a Muslim scholar and activist, exploring Qur'anic principles that lead to inter-religious fraternity.

Esposito, John L., *The Islamic Threat: Myth or Reality?*, third edition, New York: Oxford University Press, 1999. An insighful survey of militant Islamic movements around the world.

Esposito, John L., *Islam: The Straight Path*, New York, Oxford: Oxford University Press, 1988. A scholarly, clear introduction to historical and contemporary Islam.

Hefner, Robert W. and Patricia Horvatich, eds., *Islam in an Era of Nation-states: Politics and Religious Renewal in Muslim Southeast Asia*, Honolulu: University of Hawaii Press, 1997. Detailed analyses of Muslim reformist movements in Southeast Asia with reference to modern governmental structures.

The Holy Qur'an. Although the Qur'an is considered untranslatable, numerous translations from the Arabic have been attempted. Many Muslims' favorite English translation is by Abdullah Yusuf Ali (Durban, South Africa: Islamic Propagation Center International, 1946). The King Fahd Holy Qur'an Printing Complex in Medina has published a very helpful revision based on Yusuf Ali's translation, with extensive thematic index. Thomas Ballantine Irving (Al-Hajj Ta'lim'Ali) has prepared "The First American Version" of the Qur'an (translation and commentary, Brattleboro, Vermont: Amana Books, © 1985).

Lings, Martin, *Muhammad*, London: George Allen & Unwin, and Islamic Text Society, 1983. A highly regarded biography of the Prophet.

McCloud, Aminah Beverly, *African American Islam*, New York and London: Routledge, 1995. An accessible inside view of contemporary African–American Muslim communities and issues they face in a contrasting cultural context.

Nasr, Seyyed Hossein, *Ideals and Realities of Islam*, second edition, London: Unwin Hyman Ltd., 1985. Thoughtful presentation of both esoteric and exoteric features of Islam.

Nasr, Seyyed Hossein, ed., *Islamic Spirituality I: Foundations*, New York: Crossroad Publishing Company, 1987 and London: SCM Press, 1989. Excellent chapters on key features of Muslim spirituality, from fasting to angels, with sections on Sunnism, Shi'ism, and Sufism.

Nasr, Seyyed Hossein, *Traditional Islam in the Modern World*, London and New York: Kegan Paul International, 1990. Religiously sensitive discussions of varied topics in attempts to bring forth traditional Muslim values within contemporary social settings.

Nasr, Seyyed Hossein, Dabashi, Hamid, and Nasr, Seyyed Vali Reza, *Shi'ism: Doctrines, Thought, and Spirituality*, Albany, New York: State University of New York Press, 1988. To balance the predominant media attention to Shi'ite politics, a set of thoughtful essays on aspects of Shi'ite spirituality.

Paige, Glenn D., Satha-Anand, Chaiwats, and Gilliatt, Sarah, *Islam and Nonviolence*, Honolulu: University of Hawaii, Center for Global Nonviolence Planning Project, 1993. Strong essays on theories and practice of non-violence stemming from Muslim values.

Pinault, David, *The Shiites: Ritual and Popular Piety in a Muslim Community*, New York: St. Martin's Press, 1992. Sensitive discussions of Shi'ite interpretations of Muslim history and how these inform communal life and action.

Rashid, Ahmed, *Taliban: Militant Islam, Oil and Fundamentalism in Central Asia*, New Haven: Yale University Press, 2000. A Pakistani journalist chronicles the Taliban's rise to power, including global politics and economics as well as religion.

Schimmel, Annemarie, *And Muhammad is His Messenger: The Veneration of the Prophet in Islamic Piety*, Chapel Hill, North Carolina: University of North Carolina Press, 1985. Extensive exploration of Muslims' love for the Prophet.

Schimmel, Annemarie, *Mystical Dimensions of Islam*, Chapel Hill, North Carolina: University of North Carolina Press, 1975. A classic survey of Sufi history, teachings, and saints.

Schuon, Frithjof, *Understanding Islam*, London: George Allen & Unwin, 1963. Profound and lyrical observations about the way of Islam.

Stowasser, Barbara Freyer, *The Islamic Impulse*, Washington, D.C.: Center for Contemporary Arab Studies, Georgetown University, 1987. Sensitive articles exploring the meanings of Islamist movements.

Wadud, Amina, *Qur'an and Woman*, New York/Oxford: Oxford University Press, 1999. Probing hermeneutic analysis of the Qur'an, revealing its principles of social justice, including gender equality.

Webb, Gisela, *Windows of Faith: Muslim Women Scholar-Activists in North America*, Syracuse, New York: Syracuse University Press, 2000. Articles revealing the depth of feminist scholarship within Islam, particularly with reference to the ideal of social justice as seen from the point of view of women of faith.

Key terms

Allah   The one God, in Islam.
muezzin   In Islam, one who calls the people to prayer from a high place.
Sunni   A follower of the majority branch of Islam which tells that successors to Muhammad are to be chosen by the Muslim community.
Shi'a   The minority branch of Islam which tells that Muhammad's legitimate successors were 'Ali and a series of Imams; a follower of this branch.
Shari'ah   The divine law in Islam.
Sufism   The mystical path in Islam.
hajj   The holy pilgrimage to Mecca for Muslims.
jihad   The Muslim's struggle against the inner forces that prevent God-realization and the outer barriers to establishment of the order.

Study questions

1 Tell Muhammad's life story, including dates, places, religious experiences, wars, his character and education.
2 Explain the Five Pillars of Islam, the ways they are practiced, and the purpose of each.

3 What are the most important religious themes and people common to Islam, Judaism, and Christianity?
4 What is the Muslim view of life after death?
5 Discuss the role of women in Islam today, its rationales pro and con, and its varieties in various countries.
6 What are the major historical, religious, and political roots of the current conflicts between Muslim and Western countries? Write a neutral essay, fair to each side. What solutions do you propose for both sides?

Refer to Pearson/Prentice Hall's **TIME Special Edition: World Religions** magazine for these and other current articles on topics related to many of the world's religions.

- *The Religious Experience: The Legacy of Abraham*
- *Islam: The Women of Islam; A Jihadi's Tale; As American As . . .; Voices of Islam*
- *The Impact of Religion: In the Heart of Hate*

Chapter 10 continues the study of religions originating in the Middle East and focuses on Islam. For further research in this area, use the tools available to you in Research Navigator.

As you investigate Islam, consider this question: "How have leaders of Islamic religious communities responded to the increased interest and scrutiny of Islam in the aftermath of September 11, 2001?"

- **Ebsco's ContentSelect:** Search in the History, Philosophy, Political Science, Religion, and Sociology databases using terms such as "Islamic leader," "September 11 or 9/11," "Islamic fundamentalism."
- **Link Library:** Search in the Religion database under the category: "Religions of Mediterranean and Middle Eastern Origins: Islam; Qur'an/Koran; Women & Islam."
- **The *New York Times* on the Web:** Search in the Religious Studies and all other databases for current articles on related topics.

CHAPTER 11
SIKHISM

"By the Guru's grace shalt thou worship Him"

Another great teacher made his appearance in northern India in the fifteenth century CE: Guru Nanak. His followers were called Sikhs, meaning "disciples, students, seekers of truth." In time, he was succeeded by a further nine enlightened Gurus, ending with Guru Gobind Singh (1666–1708). Despite the power of these Gurus, the spiritual essence of Sikhism is little known outside India and its **diaspora** (dispersed communities), even though Sikhism is the fifth largest of all world religions. Many Sikhs understand their path not as another sectarian religion but as a statement of the universal truth within, and transcending, all religions. Their beliefs have been interpreted as a synthesis of the Hindu and Muslim traditions of northern India, but Sikhism has its own unique quality, independent revelation, and history. As awareness of Sikh spirituality spreads, Sikhism is becoming a global religion, although it does not actively seek converts. Instead, it emphasizes the universality of spirituality and the relevance of spirituality in everyday life.

The *sant* tradition

Before Guru Nanak, Hinduism and Islam had already begun to draw closer to each other in northern India. One of the foremost philosophers in this trend was the Hindu saint Ramananda, who held theological discussions with teachers from both religions. But a deeper marriage occurred in the hearts of **sants**, or "holy people," particularly Sufi mystics, such as Shaikh Farid, and Hindu *bhaktas*, such as Sri Caitanya. They shared a common cause in emphasizing devotion to the Beloved above all else. Many of them were from lower castes, but their spiritual realization was of great heights. They were basically non-sectarian monotheists who did not accept ritualism or casteism.

The most famous of the bridges between Hindu and Muslim is the fifteenth-century weaver Kabir (1440–1518). He was the son of Muslim parents and the disciple of the Hindu guru Ramananda. Rather than taking the ascetic path, he remained at work at his loom, composing songs about union with the divine that are at once earthly and sublime. He could easily transcend theological differences between religions, for he was opposed to outward forms, preferring ecstatic personal intimacy with God. Speaking for the One, he wrote:

O human, where dost thou seek Me?
Lo! I am beside thee.

I am neither in temple nor in mosque:
  I am neither in Kaaba nor in Kailash:
Neither am I in rites and ceremonies; nor in yoga and renunciation.
If thou art a true seeker, thou shalt at once see Me: thou shalt meet Me in a moment
  of time.
Kabir says, "O Sadhu! God is the breath of all breath."[1]

Guru Nanak

Sikhism:
Amritsar, Guru Nanak

When Guru Nanak (1469–c. 1539) was born, the area of northern India called the Punjab was half-Muslim, half-Hindu, and ruled by a weak Afghan dynasty. For centuries, the Punjab had been the lane through which outer powers had fought their way into India. In 1398, the Mongolian leader Tamerlane had slaughtered and sacked Punjabis on his way both to and from Delhi. Toward the end of Nanak's life, it was the Mogul emperor Babur who invaded and claimed the Punjab. This casting of the Punjab as a perpetual battleground later became a crucial aspect of Sikhism.

Nanak was reportedly little concerned with worldly things. As a child he was of a contemplative nature, resisting the formalities of his Hindu religion. Even after he was married, it is said that he roamed about in nature and gave away any money he had to the poor. At length he took a job as an accountant, but his heart was not in material gain.

When Nanak was thirty, his life was transformed after immersion in a river, from which it is said he did not emerge for three days. Some people now think he was meditating on the opposite side, but at the time he could not be found until he suddenly appeared in town, radiant. According to one account, he had been taken into the presence of God, who gave him a bowl of milk to drink, saying that it was actually nectar (*amrit*) which would give him "power of prayer, love of worship, truth and contentment."[2] The Almighty sent him back into the world to redeem it from Kali Yuga (the darkest of ages). Later Nanak sang:

Me, the worthless bard, the Lord has blest with Service.
Be it night or day, many a time He gives His call,
And calls me verily into His presence.
And there I praise Him and receive the robe,
And the Nectar-Name [of God] becomes my everlasting food.[3]

After his disappearance in the river in 1499, Nanak began traveling through India, the Himalayas, Afghanistan, Sri Lanka, and Arabia, teaching in his own surprising way. When people asked him whether he would follow the Hindu or Muslim path, he replied, "There is neither Hindu nor Mussulman [Muslim], so whose path shall I follow? I shall follow God's path. God is neither Hindu nor Mussulman."[4] Nanak mocked the Hindu tradition of throwing sacred river water east toward the rising sun in worship of their ancestors—he threw water to the west. If Hindus could throw water far enough to reach their ancestors thousands of miles away in heaven, he explained, he could certainly water his parched land several hundred miles distant in Lahore by throwing water in its direction. Another tradition has it that he set his feet toward the Ka'bah when sleeping as a pilgrim in Mecca. Questioned about this rude conduct, he is said to have remarked, "Then kindly turn my feet toward some direction where God is not."

Again and again, Guru Nanak emphasized three central teachings as the straight path to God: working hard in society to earn one's own honest living (rather than withdrawing into asceticism and begging); sharing from one's earnings with those who are needy; and remembering God at all times as the only Doer, the only Giver. Encouraging people to stay in the world and to help others rather than live a life of detachment in search of spiritual fulfilment, at the end of his travels Guru Nanak himself settled with his family as a farmer. The multitudes

Guru Nanak holding spiritual dialogue with Hindu ascetics. (Illustration from Biography of Guru Nanak *by Kartar Singh.)*

of *sikhs* who came to him contributed foods or labor to a free community kitchen in which there were no caste distinctions. The Guru encouraged them to live a disciplined life of rising early in the morning to praise God and working hard to support themselves and share with those in need. To a society that stressed distinctions of caste, class, gender, and religions, Guru Nanak introduced the idea of a social order based on equality, justice, and service to all, in devotion to the One God whom Guru Nanak perceived as formless, pervading everywhere.

Nanak's commitment to practical faith, as opposed to external adherence to religious formalities, won him followers from both Hinduism and Islam. Before he died, they argued over who would dispose of his body. He reportedly told Muslims to place flowers on one side of his body, Hindus on the other; the side whose flowers remained fresh the next day could bury or cremate him. The next day they raised the sheet that had covered his body and reportedly found nothing beneath it; all the flowers were still fresh, leaving only the fragrance of his being.

Oh my mind, love God as a fish loves water:
The more the water, the happier is the fish,
  the more peaceful his mind and body.
He cannot live without water even for a moment.
God knows the inner pain of that being without water.

Guru Nanak[5]

The succession of Gurus

There were eventually a total of ten Sikh Gurus, all of whom were thought to be transmitting the spiritual light of Nanak. Before he passed on, Guru Nanak passed his spiritual authority to Lehna, a devotee of the goddess Durga. Lehna had become so dedicated to Guru Nanak's mission that the Guru gave him the name Angad— a part of his body (*ang*). Although the spiritual transmission from Guru Nanak reportedly made him so powerful that he became famous for healing incurable diseases such as leprosy, Guru Angad (1504–1552) was a model of humility and service to the poor and needy. He continued the tradition of *langar* and served the people with his own hands. One of the many stories told of his humility concerns an ascetic who was jealous of the Guru's popularity. The monsoon rains which were essential for the crops had not come, so the ascetic used the opportunity to turn the poor farmers against Guru Angad. He taunted them that if the Guru was so powerful, he should call for rain. The desperate villagers begged Guru Angad to do so, but he peacefully replied that one should not interfere with God's ways; rain would come only when God so willed. The ascetic persisted in turning the people against Guru Angad, telling them that he himself would magically bring the rains if they would get rid of the Guru. Thus the simple people drove Guru Angad away. Agreeably, he left the village. Refused shelter anywhere nearby, he settled in a forest. Thereafter the ascetic fasted and tried all his mantras, but the rains did not come. At last, Amar Das, who later became the third of the Sikh Gurus, learned of the situation and reproached the villagers for forsaking the sun for the light of a small lamp. Recognizing their mistake, the villagers begged Guru Angad to forgive them and return to the village. He did so, amid great rejoicing, and the rains came.

The Third and Fourth Gurus, Amar Das and Ram Das, developed organizational structures for the growing Sikh **Panth** (community) while also setting personal examples of humility. Ram Das founded the holy city of Amritsar, within which the Fifth Guru, Guru Arjun Dev (1536–1606), built the religion's most sacred shrine, the Golden Temple. The Fifth Guru also compiled the sacred scriptures of the Sikhs, the **Adi Granth** (original holy book, now known as the **Guru Granth Sahib**), from devotional hymns composed by Guru Nanak, the other Gurus, and Hindu and Muslim saints, including many spiritual figures from low social castes. Among the latter are holy people like Bhagat Ravi Das, a low-caste Hindu shoemaker who achieved the heights of spiritual realization. His powerful poetry incorporated into the Guru Granth Sahib includes this song:

When I was, You were not.
When You are, I am not.
As huge waves are raised in the wind in the vast ocean,
But are only water in water,
O Lord of Wealth, what should I say about this delusion?
What we deem a thing to be,
It is not, in reality.
It is like a king falling asleep on his throne
And dreaming that he is a beggar.
His kingdom is intact,
But separating from it, he suffers. . . .
Says Ravi Das, the Lord is nearer to us than our hands and feet.[6]

When a copy of the Adi Granth was sent to Emperor Akbar on his demand, he was so pleased with its universalism that he offered a gift of gold to the book. But the Fifth Guru was tortured and executed by Akbar's son and successor, Jehangir, in 1606, apparently because of suspicions that the Guru supported a rival successor to his throne. It is said that Guru Arjun Dev remained calmly meditating on God as he was tortured by heat, with his love and faith undismayed. His devotional hymns include words such as these:

Merciful, merciful is the Lord.
Merciful is my master.
He blesses all beings with His bounties.
Why waverest thou, Oh mortal? The Creator Himself shall protect you.
He who has created you takes care of you. . . .
Oh mortal, meditate on the Lord as long as there is breath in your body.[7]

To protect Sikhism and to defend the weak of all religions against tyranny, the Sixth Guru, Hargobind (1595–1644), established a Sikh army, carried two swords (one symbolizing temporal power, the other, spiritual power), and taught the people to defend their religion. The tender-hearted Seventh Guru, Har Rai (1630–1661), was a pacifist who never used his troops against the Moguls. He taught his Sikhs not only to feed anyone who came to their door, but also to:

do service in such a way that the poor guest may not feel he is partaking of some
charity but as if he had come to the Guru's house which belonged to all in equal

measure. He who has more should consider it as God's trust and share it in the same spirit. Man is only an instrument of service: the giver of goods is God, the Guru of us all.[8]

The Eighth Guru, Har Krishan (1656–1664), became successor to Guru Nanak's seat when he was only five years old and died at the age of eight. When taunted by Hindu *pandits* (learned men) the "Child Guru" reportedly touched a lowly deaf and dumb Sikh watercarrier with his cane, whereupon the watercarrier expounded brilliantly on the subtleties of the Hindu scripture, *Bhagavad-Gita*.

The ninth master, Guru Teg Bahadur (c. 1621–1675), was martyred. According to Sikh tradition, he was approached by Hindu *pandits* who were facing forced conversion to Islam by the Mogul emperor, Aurangzeb. The emperor viewed

TEACHING STORY

Guru Arjun Dev's Devotion

Throughout his life, Guru Arjun Dev, the Fifth Sikh Guru, responded with calm faith in God to jealous plots against him.

The Mogul emperor Jehangir claimed that the Adi Granth—the sacred scripture that Guru Arjun Dev had compiled—was negative toward Hindus and Muslims, even though both were becoming followers of the gentle Guru. Jehangir ordered that all references to Hinduism and Islam be deleted from the holy book and that the Guru be fined 200,000 rupees. The Guru reportedly replied that the hymns of the Sikh Gurus and Muslim and Hindu saints were inspired praises of God and that no one could change them. Furthermore, monies were not his own property but rather belonged to the Sikh community, to be used for the welfare of those in need. Even though his Sikhs started collecting money to pay the fine, the Guru stopped them, saying that he had not done anything wrong and that compromising with wrong is irreligious.

Ostensibly for his refusal to follow the emperor's orders—but more likely to end his popular influence—the Guru was subjected to torture by heat, during the already terrible heat of summer. He was made to sit on a hot iron sheet. Hot sand was dumped onto his body and he was placed into boiling water.

As these tortures were being inflicted, Mian Mir, an established saint of Islam who reportedly laid the foundation stone of the Holy Temple at Amritsar, pleaded with the Guru to let him use his mystical power against the persecutors. Guru Arjun Dev refused, telling Mian Mir to patiently accept the reality that everything is under God's control; every leaf that moves does so by God's will.

The daughter-in-law of Chandu, the rich man of Lahore who had turned the emperor against the Guru, tried to offer sherbet to the Guru to ease his agony. But just as he had refused attempts to wed his son to Chandu's daughter, saying that a rich man's daughter would not be happy in the home of a dervish, he refused her food, saying that he would accept nothing. Nonetheless, he blessed her for her devotion.

Through five days of torture, Guru Arjun Dev persisted in calm faith in God. His torturers then forced him to bathe in the river alongside the Mogul fort. His followers wept to see the blisters covering his body. As he walked on blistered feet, he repeated again and again, "Your will is sweet, Oh God; I only seek the gift of Your Name." Calmly, he walked into the water and breathed his last.

Hinduism as a totally corrupt, idolatrous religion, which did not lead people to God; he had ordered the destruction of Hindu temples and mass conversion of Hindus throughout the land, beginning in the north with Kashmir. Reportedly, one of the Kashmiri *pandits* dreamed that only the Ninth Guru, the savior in Kali Yuga, could save the Hindus. With the firm approval of his young son, Guru Teg Bahadur told the Hindu *pandits* to inform their oppressors that they would convert to Islam if the Sikh Guru could be persuaded to do so. Imprisoned and forced to witness the torture and murder of his aides, the Ninth Guru staunchly maintained the right of all people to religious freedom. Aurangzeb beheaded him before a crowd of thousands. But as his son later wrote, "He has given his head, but not his determination."[9]

The martyred Ninth Guru was succeeded by his young son, who became the tenth master, Guru Gobind Singh (1666–1708). It was he who turned the intimidated Sikhs into saint-soldiers. In 1699 he reportedly told a specially convened assembly of Sikhs that the times were so dangerous that he had developed a new plan to give the community strength and unity. Total surrender to the master would be necessary, he said, asking for volunteers who would offer their heads for the cause of protecting religious ideals. One at a time, five stepped forward. Each was escorted into the Guru's tent, from which the Tenth Guru emerged alone with a bloody sword. According to the story, after this scene was repeated five times, the Guru brought all the men out of the tent, alive. Some say the blood was that of a goat, in a test of the people's loyalty; others say that Guru Gobind Singh had killed the men and then resurrected them. At any rate, their willingness to sacrifice themselves was dramatically proven, and the Five Beloved Ones became models for Sikhs. It is noteworthy that those who became the Five Beloved Ones came from the lowest classes.

Guru Gobind Singh instituted a special initiation rite using **amrit**: water, which was stirred with a double-edged sword to turn his followers into heroes and mixed with sugar symbolizing that they would also be compassionate. After initiating the Five Beloved Ones, he established a unique Guru–Sikh relationship by asking that they initiate him—thus underscoring the principle of equality among all Sikhs. The initiated men were given the surname *Singh* ("lion"); the women were all given the name *Kaur* ("princess") and treated as equals. Together, they formed the **Khalsa** (Pure Ones), a community pledged to a special code of personal discipline. They were sworn to wear five distinctive symbols of their dedication: long unshorn hair bound under a turban or a veil, a comb to keep it tidy, a steel bracelet as a personal reminder that

Guru Gobind Singh writing Jaap Sahib, *a hymn praising the attributes of God, "without form, beyond religion." (Painting by Mehar Singh.)*

one is a servant of God, short underbreeches for modesty, and a sword for dignity and the willingness to fight for justice and protection of the weak.

These "5 Ks" (so called because all the words begin with a "K" in Punjabi) clearly distinguished Sikhs from Muslims and Hindus, supporting the assertion that they constituted a third path with its own right to spiritual sovereignty. All of these innovations were designed to turn the meek into warriors capable of shaking off Mogul oppression and protecting freedom of religion; the distinctive dress made it impossible for the Khalsa to hide from their duty by blending with the general populace. In Sikh history, their bravery was proven again and again. For example, it is reported that the Tenth Guru's own teenage sons were killed as they single-handedly engaged several thousand Mogul soldiers in battle.

In addition to transforming the Sikh faithful into a courageous, unified community, Guru Gobind Singh ended the line of bodily succession to Guruship. As he was dying in 1708, he transferred his authority to the Adi Granth rather than to a human successor. Thenceforth, it was called the Guru Granth Sahib—the living presence of the Guru embodied in the sacred scripture, to be consulted by the congregation for spiritual guidance and decision-making.

As the Mogul Empire began to disintegrate and Afghans invaded India, the Sikhs fought for their own identity and sovereignty. At the end of the eighteenth century and beginning of the nineteenth century under Maharaja Ranjit Singh, they formed the Sikh Empire, a non-sectarian government noted for its generous tolerance toward Muslims, despite the earlier history of oppression by the Muslim rulers. Maharaja Ranjit Singh is said to have been unusually kind to his subjects and to have humbly accepted chastisement by the Sikh religious authorities for his rather immoral private life. The Sikh Empire attempted to create a pluralistic society, with social equality and full freedom of religion. It also blocked the Khyber Pass against invaders. The empire lasted only half a century, for the British subdued it in 1849.

Resistance to oppression became a hallmark of Sikhism, for the times were grim for India's people. Despite heavy losses, Guru Gobind Singh's outnumbered Sikhs began the protection of the country from foreign rule, a process that continued into the twentieth century. During the Indian struggle against British rule, despite their military abilities Sikhs set heroic examples of nonviolent resistance to oppression. One famous story concerns Guru ka Bagh, a garden and shrine that had been used by Sikhs for cutting wood for the community free kitchen. After tearing up that agreement, the British police began arresting and then beating and even killing Sikhs who went to the garden to collect firewood. Every day a new wave of one hundred Sikhs would come voluntarily to suffer fierce beatings and perhaps even be killed, without a murmur except for the Name of God on their lips, to resist injustice.

An English missionary and educator, C. F. Andrews, wrote in a press report that he witnessed "hundreds of Christs being crucified":

It was a sight which I never wish to see again, a sight incredible to an Englishman. There were four Akali Sikhs with black turbans facing a band of about a dozen policemen, including two English officers. . . . [The Sikhs] were perfectly still and did not move further forward. Their hands were placed together in prayer and it was clear that they were praying. Then, without the slightest provocation on their part, an Englishman lunged forward the head of his lathi which was bound with brass. He lunged it forward in such a way that his fist which held the staff struck the Akali

Sikh, who was praying, just at the collar bone with great force. . . . The blow which I saw was sufficient to fell the Akali Sikh and send him to the ground. He rolled over and slowly got up once more, and faced the same punishment over again. Time after time one of the four who had gone forward was laid prostrate by repeated blows, now from the English officer and now from the police who were under his control. . . . When one of the Akali Sikhs had been hurled to the ground and was lying prostrate, a police sepoy stamped with his foot upon him, using his full weight. . . . The vow they had made to God was kept. I saw no act, no look, of defiance. It was true martyrdom for them as they went forward, a true act of faith, a true deed of devotion to God.[10]

At one point, Sikh political prisoners arrested at Guru ka Bagh were being shifted by train. The Sikh community in Hasanavdal asked the stationmaster there to stop the train so they could offer food to the prisoners. He refused, saying that it was a special train and would not stop at Hasanavdal. Determined to care for the prisoners, three leading Sikhs told the *sangat* (congregation) to bring food and then courageously lay down on the tracks to force the train to stop. It ran over them, crushing their bodies, and then stopped. As the *sangat* tried to help the dying martyrs, one of them ordered, "Don't care for us. Feed the prisoners." Thus the *langar* (community meal) was served to the prisoners on the train, and the Sikhs who had laid their bodies on the track died.

High praise for Guru Gobind Singh's military effect has been offered by Dr. S. Radhakrishnan, the respected second President of India:

For one thousand years, after the defeat of Raja Jaipal, India had lain prostrate. The raiders and invaders descended on India and took away the people, to be sold as slaves. . . . Guru Gobind Singh raised the Khalsa to defy religious intolerance, religious persecution and political inequality. It was a miracle that heroes appeared out of straws and common clay. Those who grovelled in the dust rose proud, defiant and invincible in the form of the Khalsa. They bore all sufferings and unnamable tortures cheerfully and unflinchingly. . . . India is at long last free. This freedom is the crown and climax and a logical corollary to the Sikh Guru's and Khalsa's terrific sacrifices and heroic exploits.[11]

In addition to the bravery evident in Sikh history, stories of the Gurus are full of miracles that reportedly happened around them, such as the Eighth Guru's empowering a lowly watercarrier to give a profound explanation of the *Bhagavad-Gita*. Neither age, nor caste, nor gender is thought to have any relevance in Sikh spirituality. In contrast to the restricted position of women in Indian society, the Sikh Gurus accorded full respect and freedom of participation to women.

God is like sugar scattered in the sand. An elephant cannot pick it up. Says Kabir, the Guru has given me this sublime secret:
  "Become thou an ant and partake of it."

Kabir, Guru Granth Sahib p. 1377

Although the Sikh Gurus gave their followers no mandate to convert others, their message was spread in a nonsectarian way by the **Udasis**, renunciates who

Baba Siri Chand, elder son of Guru Nanak, combined the power of intense meditation with the power of hard work.

do not withdraw from the world but rather practice strict discipline and meditation while at the same time trying to serve humanity. Their missionary work began under Baba Siri Chand, the ascetic elder son of Guru Nanak. He had a close relationship with the Sikh Gurus and was highly respected by people of all castes and creeds because of his spiritual power, wisdom, and principles. During the reign of the Mogul emperor Shah Jahan, a census showed that Baba Siri Chand had the largest following of any holy person in India. Nevertheless, he directed all attention and pr aise to his father, and never claimed to be a Guru himself. Udasi communities and educational institutions are still maintained in the subcontinent, and old Udasi inscriptions have been discovered in Baku, Azerbaijan.

Central beliefs

Sikhism's major focus is loving devotion to one God, whom Sikhs recognize as the same One who is worshipped by many different names around the world. God is formless, beyond time and space, the only truth, the only reality. This boundless concept was initially set forth in Guru Nanak's *Mul Mantra* (basic sacred chant), which prefaces the Guru Granth Sahib, and **Jap Ji**, the first morning prayer of Sikhs:

> *There is One God*
> *Whose Name is Truth,*
> *The Creator,*
> *Without fear, without hate,*
> *Eternal Being,*
> *Beyond birth and death,*
> *Self-existent,*
> *Realized by the Guru's grace.*[12]

Following Guru Nanak's lead, Sikhs often refer to God as *Sat* ("truth") or as *Ik Onkar*, the One Supreme Being. God is pure being, without form.

Guru Gobind Singh, a great custodian of scholars who kept many poets in his court, offered a litany of praises of this boundless, formless One. His inspired composition, *Jaap Sahib*, includes 199 verses such as these:

> *Immortal*
> *Omnipotent*
> *Beyond Time*
> *And Space*

Invisible
Beyond name, caste, or creed
Beyond form or figure
The ruthless destroyer
Of all pride and evil
The Salvation of all beings . . .
The Eternal Light
The Sweetest Breeze
The Wondrous Figure
The Most Splendid.[13]

The light of God is thought to shine fully through the Guru, the perfect master. In Sikh belief, the light of God is also present in the Guru Granth Sahib, the Holy Word of God, and in all of creation, in which **Nam**, the Holy Name of God dwells. God is not separate from this world. God pervades the cosmos and thus can be found within everything. As the Ninth Guru wrote:

Why do you go to the forest to find God? He lives in all and yet remains distinctly detached. He dwells in you as well, as fragrance resides in a flower or the reflection in a mirror. God abides in everything. See him, therefore, in your heart.[14]

Sikhism does not claim to have the only path to God, nor does it try to convert others to its way. It has beliefs in common with Hinduism (such as *karma* and reincarnation) and also with Islam (such as monotheism). It is said that the respected Muslim mystic, Mian Mir, was invited to lay the cornerstone of the Golden Temple in Amritsar. It was constructed with four doors, inviting people from all traditions to come in to worship. When Guru Gobind Singh created an army to resist tyranny, he admonished Sikhs not to feel enmity toward Islam or Hinduism. The enemy, he emphasized, was oppression and corruption.

Sikh soldier-saints are pledged to protect the freedom of all religions. Sikhism is, however, opposed to empty ritualism, and Guru Nanak and his successors sharply challenged hypocritical religious practices. "It is very difficult to be called a Muslim," said Guru Nanak. "A Muslim's heart is as soft as wax, very compassionate, and he washes away the inner dirt of egotism."[15] By contrast, said Guru Nanak, "The Qazis [Muslim legal authorities] who sit in the courts to minister justice, rosary in hand and the name of *Khuda* (God) on their lips, commit injustice if their palm is not greased. And if someone challenges them, lo, they quote the scriptures!"[16]

According to the Sikh ideal, the purpose of life is to realize God within the world, through the everyday practices of work, worship, and charity, of sacrificing love. All people are to be treated equally, for God's light dwells in all and ego is a major hindrance to God-realization. From Guru Nanak's time on, Sikhism has refused to acknowledge the traditional Indian caste system. In their social services, such as hospitals, leprosariums, and free kitchens, Sikhs observe a tradition of serving everyone, regardless of caste or creed. A special group of Sikhs, known as Seva Panthis, place great emphasis on this aspect of Sikhism, refusing to accept any offerings to support their services to the needy. They are inspired by the example of Bhai Kanahia, who in the time of Guru Gobind Singh was found offering water to the fallen opponents as well as to Guru Gobind Singh's wounded soldiers. The Guru's people complained about his behavior to

the Guru, who questioned Bhai Kanahia about what he was doing. Bhai Kanahia reportedly said that he was obeying the Sikh Gurus' teaching that one should look upon all with the same eye, whether friend or foe. Guru Gobind Singh praised him and gave him ointment, with the instruction not only to give water but also to soothe the wounds of soldiers from both armies.

In contrast to the low status of women in Indian society, the Gurus accorded considerable respect to women. Guru Nanak asked: "Why denounce her, who even gives birth to kings?"[17] Many women are respectfully remembered in Sikh history. Among them are Guru Nanak's sister Bibi Nanaki, who first recognized her brother's great spiritual power and became his first devotee. A group of Guru Gobind Singh's soldiers deserted him in the face of seemingly impossible odds when his citadel at Anandpur was being besieged, but their women refused to allow them to return to their homes. The women threatened to dress in the men's clothes and return to fight for the Guru, to expunge the shame of the men's cowardice. One woman—Mai Bhago—did so and helped to lead forty of the deserters back to battle on the Guru's side against Muslim attackers. The men all died on the battlefield, asking the Guru to forgive them, but Mai Bhago survived and remained in the Guru's personal security guard, dressed as a man, with his permission. When *amrit* was first prepared for Khalsa initiation, it was Guru Gobind Singh's wife who added sugar crystals to make the initiates sweet-tempered as well as brave. In Brahmanic Hindu tradition, such an action by a woman would have been considered a defilement. During the fifteenth century, women were active as missionaries carrying Guru Gobind Singh's program. During the terrible Mogul persecutions of the eighteenth century, Sikh women were noted for their courage and steadfast faith.

A preference for sons nonetheless persisted, in part because of the heavy dowry burden traditionally expected of females in India. To counter this trend, Guru Gobind Singh reportedly forbade female infanticide, and in 2001, the chief Sikh authorities issued an order that anyone practicing female foeticide would be excommunicated from the faith.

In developing the military capabilities of his followers in order to protect religious freedom, Guru Gobind Singh set forth very strict standards for battle. He established five stringent conditions for "righteous war": (1) Military means are a last resort to be used only if all other methods have failed; (2) Battle should be undertaken without any enmity or feeling of revenge; (3) No territory should be taken or captured property retained; (4) Troops should be committed to the cause, not mercenaries fighting for pay, and soldiers should be strictly disciplined, forswearing smoking, drinking, and abuse of opponents' women; and (5) Minimal force should be used and hostilities should end when the objective is attained.

Like Hinduism, Sikhism conceives a series of lives, with *karma* (the effects of past actions on one's present life) governing transmigration of the soul into new bodies, be they human or animal. The ultimate goal of life is mystical union with the divine, reflected in one's way of living.

Surrounded by a sacred pool, the central structure in the Golden Temple at Amritsar houses the Guru Granth Sahib. It has a door on each of its four sides, symbolizing its openness to people of all faiths.

> *I was separated from God for many births, dry as a withered plant,*
> *But by the grace of the Guru, I have become green.*
>
> Guru Arjun, the Fifth Guru[18]

Sacred practices

To be a true Sikh is to live a very disciplined life of surrender and devotion to God, with hours of daily prayer, continual inner repetition of the Name of God (Nam), and detachment from negative, worldly mind-states. Nam carries intense spiritual power, making a person fearless, steady, inwardly calm and strong in the face of any adversity, willing to serve without any reward, and extending love in all directions without any effort. Why is it so powerful? It comes from the Guru as a transmission of spiritual blessing that automatically transforms people and links them with God. Some feel that Nam is the essence of creation, the sound and vibration of which the cosmos is a material manifestation. The mystics and Gurus whose writings are included in the Guru Granth Sahib refer to many Names of God, such as *Sohang* (What You are, I am), *Narain* (the One present in water), *Allah*, and *Ram*. Some Sikhs recite *"Wahe Guru,"* (God wondrous beyond words), some say *"Ik Onkar Sat nam Siri Wahe Guru"* (God is One, the Truth Itself, Most Respectful, Wondrous beyond words), some recite the whole Mul Mantra.

In the Sikh path, at the same time that one's mind and heart are joined with God, one is to be working hard in the world, earning an honest living, and helping those in need. Of this path, the Third Sikh Guru observed:

> *The way of devotees is unique; they walk a difficult path.*
> *They leave behind attachments, greed, ego, and desires, and do not speak much.*
> *The path they walk is sharper than the edge of a sword and thinner than a hair.*
> *Those who shed their false self by the grace of the Guru are filled with the fragrance*
>   *of God.[19]*

The standards set by Guru Gobind Singh for the Khalsa are so high that few people can really meet them. In addition to outer disciplines, such as abstaining from drugs, alcohol, and tobacco, the person who is Khalsa, said the Guru, will always recite the Name of God:

> *The Name of God is light, the Light which never extinguishes, day or night. Khalsa*
> *recognizes none but the One. I live in Khalsa; it is my body, my treasure store.[20]*

The one who is Khalsa renounces anger and does not criticize anybody. He fights on the front line against injustice and vanquishes the five evils (lust, anger, greed, attachment, and ego) in himself. He burns his *karmas* and thus becomes egoless. Not only does he not take another person's spouse, he doesn't even look at the things that belong to others. Perpetually reciting Nam is his joy, and he falls in love with the words of the Gurus. He faces difficulties squarely, always attacks evil, and always helps the poor. He joins other people with the Nam, but he is not bound within the forts of narrow-mindedness.[21]

Sikhism:
Meals for All

The Sikh Gurus formed several institutions to help create a new social order with no caste distinctions. One is *langar*, the community meal, which is freely offered to all who come, regardless of caste. This typically takes place at a **gurdwara**, the building where the Guru Granth Sahib is enshrined and public worship takes place. The congregation is called the *sangat*, in which all are equal; there is no priestly class nor servant class. During community worship as well as langar, all strata of people sit together, though men and women may sit separately, as in the Indian custom. People of all ethnic origins, ideologies, and castes,

His Holiness Baba Virsa Singh

For decades, His Holiness Baba Virsa Singh (born c. 1934) has been developing farms and communities in India in which people are trying to live by the teachings of the Sikh Gurus. Not only Sikhs but also Hindus, Muslims, and Christians, literate and illiterate, live and work side by side as brothers and sisters there. Baba Virsa Singh himself is illiterate, the son of a village farmer. From childhood he had an intense yearning for communion with God. He relates,

His Holiness Baba Virsa Singh

> From childhood, I kept questioning God, "In order to love Jesus, must one become a Christian or just love?" He told me, "It is not necessary to become a Christian. It is necessary to love him."
> I asked, "To believe in Moses, does one have to observe any special discipline, or just love?" The divine command came: "Only love." I asked, "Does one have to become a Muslim in order to please Muhammad, or only love?" He said, "One must love." "To believe in Buddha, must one become a monk or a Buddhist?" He replied, "No. To believe in Buddha is to love." God said, "I created human beings. Afterward, human beings created sectarian religions. But I created only human beings, not religions."[22]

Intense spirituality is the base of Baba Virsa Singh's communities, which are known collectively as Gobind Sadan ("The House of God"). Volunteers work hard to raise record crops on previously barren land. The harvests are shared communally and also provide the basis for Gobind Sadan's continual free kitchens (*langar*) for people of all classes, free medical services, and celebrations of the holy days of all religions. Devotions are carried on around the clock, with everyone from gardeners and pot washers to governors and professors helping to clean the holy areas and maintain perpetual reading of the Sikh scriptures. Everyone is encouraged to do useful work, including small children, elderly men and women, mentally disturbed people, and people with physical handicaps. Thus under Baba Virsa Singh's guidance, there is a living example of the power of Guru Nanak's straightforward, nonsectarian spiritual program: Work hard to earn your own honest living, share with others, and wake early to meditate upon and remember God in your everyday life.

Another social effect of the work of Baba Virsa Singh is an easing of the tensions that have arisen between people of different religions. Even the most rigid proponents of their own religions come to Babaji and are

gently convinced to open their eyes toward the validity of other faiths. He teaches Sikhs that their own scripture repeatedly praises and invokes the "Hindu" gods and goddesses. He teaches Hindu extremists that there is no one tradition that can be called "Hinduism" and that to take the name of Ram is to invoke the heights of moral character and selfless service to humanity. He likewise encourages Muslims to appreciate the spiritual depths of their religion.

To religious leaders, he highly recommends the method he uses at Gobind Sadan—celebrating the holy days of all prophets with great enthusiasm—as a way to combat religious intolerance. The blame, he feels, lies with religious leaders:

> When religious leaders speak, the issue is not whether they have read books. The question is whether or not they themselves have awakened spiritually. Dharma is very powerful. It transforms people's minds, transforms their lives, and transforms their inner habits. It is only spirituality that changes people.
> If priests, pujaris, or granthis are sitting in temples, mosques, churches, or gurdwaras, it does not necessarily mean that they have realized God. They are managers. Religious leaders will know whether they themselves are spiritual or not. Do we have the forgiveness of Jesus, who from the cross prayed, 'Forgive them, for they know not what they do'? When the prophets were here, they had no gold-covered buildings. They built a beautiful inner temple where peace prevailed. If we are spiritual, we will be contemplating all prophets, loving their messages, loving their commandments, loving their ethical codes.
> Throughout the world, religion has become a great fort made of hatred. All the prophets have taught us otherwise. All prophets, messiahs, and nabis have come in love, and all have in common the same thing: Love.[23]

Another area in which Baba Virsa Singh is influencing public life in India and other countries is his effect on government officials. He urges them to attend to the practical needs of the people and to uphold order and justice in society.

Baba Virsa Singh also gives people spiritual hope for a new world order. To editors of a Russian magazine, he explained,

> Truth is always tested. Who tests it? Evil—evil attacks the truth. But truth never stops shining, and evil keeps falling back. Truth's journey is very powerful, with a very strong base. It never wavers. It is definitely a long journey, full of travails, but evil can never suppress the truth.[24]

including untouchables, may bathe in the tank of water at Sikh holy places. Baptism into the Khalsa does away with one's former caste and makes a lowly person a chief. At least one-tenth of one's income is to be contributed toward the welfare of the community. In addition, the Sikh Gurus glorified the lowliest forms of manual labor, such as sweeping the floor and cleaning shoes and dirty pots, especially when these are done as voluntary service to God.

The morning and evening prayers take about two hours a day, starting in the very early morning hours. The first morning prayer is Guru Nanak's *Jap Ji. Jap,* meaning "recitation," refers to the use of sound, especially the Name of God (Nam), as the best way of approaching the divine. Like combing the hair, hearing and reciting the sacred word combs all negative thoughts out of the mind. Much of the *Jap Ji* is devoted to the blessings of Nam. For example,

> *The devotees are forever in bliss, for by hearing the Nam their suffering and*
> *sins are destroyed.*
> *Hearkening to the Nam bestows Truth, divine wisdom, contentment.*
> *By hearing the Nam, the blind find the path of Truth and*
> *realize the Unfathomable.*[25]

"The Lord is stitched into my heart and never goes out of it even for a moment."
Fifth Guru, Jaitsri

The second morning prayer is Guru Gobind Singh's universal Jaap Sahib. It names no prophet, nor creates any religion. It is sheer homage to God. The Guru addresses God as having no form, no country, and no religion but yet as the seed of seeds, song of songs, sun of suns, the life force pervading everywhere, ever merciful, ever giving, indestructible. Complex in its poetry and profound in its content, *Jaap Sahib* asserts that God is the cause of conflict as well as of peace, of destruction as well as of creation; God pervades in darkness as well as in light. In verse after verse, devotees learn that there is nothing outside of God's presence, nothing outside of God's control.

In addition to recitation of prayers, passages from the Guru Granth Sahib are chanted or sung as melodies, often with musical accompaniment. This devotional tradition of **kirtan** was initiated by Guru Nanak. But great discipline is required to attend the pre-dawn songs and recitations every day, and in contrast to the self-respect developed by Guru Gobind Singh in the Khalsa, worshippers humble themselves before the sacred scriptures. The Guru Granth Sahib is placed on a platform, with a devotee waving a whisk over the sacred book to denote the royalty of the scripture. Worshippers bow to it, bring offerings, and then sit reverently on the floor before it. Every morning and evening, the spirit of God reveals its guidance to the people as an officiant opens the scripture at random, intuitively guided, and reads a passage that is to be a special spiritual focus for the day. For many occasions, teams of people carry out Akhand Path, reading the entire Guru Granth Sahib from start to finish within forty-eight hours, taking turns of two hours each.

Some *gurdwaras*, including the Golden Temple in Amritsar, have previously allowed only men to read publicly from the Guru Granth Sahib, to preach, to offi-

Sikhism:
The *Gurdwara*

ciate at ceremonies, or to sing sacred songs. This has been a cultural custom, however, for nothing in the Sikh scriptures or the Code of Conduct bars women from such privileges. Indeed, Guru Gobind Singh initiated women as well as men into the Khalsa and allowed women to fight on the battlefield. In 1996, the central body setting policies for Sikh *gurdwaras* ruled that women should be allowed to perform sacred services.

Langar, *a free meal, is provided daily at some* gurdwaras *and all visitors are expected to partake. Rich and poor must sit side-by-side, with no distinction.*

In addition to group chanting, singing, and listening to collective guidance from the Guru Granth Sahib, devout Sikhs are encouraged to begin the day with private meditations on the name of God. As one advances in this practice and abides in egoless love for God, one is said to receive guidance from the inner Guru, the living word of God within each person.

Sikhism today

Sikhism is spreading around the world, largely by emigration from India, but the center of Sikhism remains the Punjab. The area of this territory, which is under Indian rule, was dramatically shrunk by the partition of India in 1947, for two-thirds of the Punjab was in the area thenceforth called Pakistan. The two million Sikhs living in that part were forced to migrate under conditions of extreme hardship. Some managed to migrate to other countries and parts of India other than the Punjab. Emigration continued, and there are now large Sikh communities in Britain, Canada, the United States, Malaysia, and Singapore. The global Sikh community reconverged in the Punjab in 1999, when a massive celebration of the 300th anniversary of the birth of the Khalsa was held in Anandpur Sahib. The event turned out to be the largest human gathering in history without any accident of any sort. Such an atmosphere of peace and joy prevailed that witnesses attributed the peacefulness to the blessings of Guru Gobind Singh himself.

In India, Sikhs and Hindus have lived side by side in mutual tolerance until recent years, when violent clashes occurred between Hindus and Sikhs. Sikh separatists want to establish an independent Sikh state, called Khalistan, with a commitment to strong religious observances. Another purpose of Khalistan would be to protect Sikhs from oppression and exploitation by the much larger Hindu community. In 1984, Prime Minister Indira Gandhi chose to attack the Golden Temple, Sikhism's holiest shrine, for Sikh separatists were thought to be using it as a shelter for their weapons. The attack seemed an outrageous desecration of the holy place, and counter-violence increased. The Prime Minister herself was killed later in 1984 by her Sikh bodyguards. In retribution, terrible killings of Sikhs followed. At least 8,000 Sikhs were murdered by mobs in Delhi alone.

Many Sikhs have "disappeared" in the Punjab, allegedly at the hands of both separatists and police terrorists. Sikhs in India generally are going on with their lives now that violence has abated, but tensions are kept alive by Sikhs living outside India who persist in demanding the formation of Khalistan. Many Internet websites have been set up devoted to this purpose and to promoting a militant, rigid version of the religion.

The Punjab at the end of the reign of the Mogul (Mughal) emperor, Akbar. The 1947 partition of India left two-thirds of the Punjab, including many of its Sikh temples, inside Pakistan, a Muslim state.

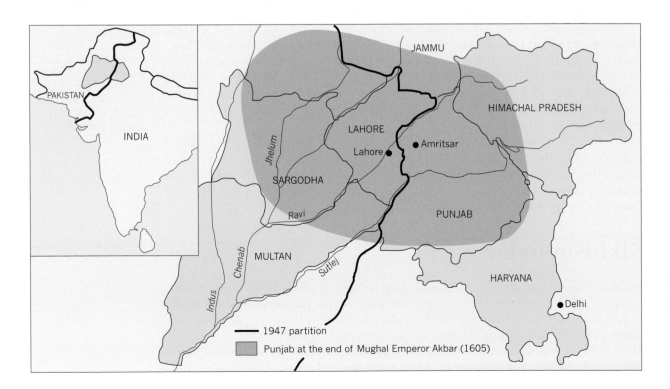

1947 partition

Punjab at the end of Mughal Emperor Akbar (1605)

AN INTERVIEW WITH G. S. JAUHAL

Living Sikhism

G. S. Jauhal is a Punjabi Sikh, a commandant in the Indian military service and a member of Gobind Sadan established by Baba Virsa Singh. His words illustrate the humility which characterizes those who truly live the teachings of the Sikh Gurus:

"I am not an authority. I'm just a student in the very beginning stage. I want to learn so much. I've been a Sikh since birth and I'm forty-seven now. But I think one needs many births and then the Guru's grace— then only can he learn Sikhism. It is so deep, so vast.

"We can only get something if first of all Guru's grace is there. Then we keep on endeavoring sincerely, from the core of our heart, and keep on learning. Again and again reading, reciting Guru Granth Sahib, trying to understand what it means. I myself feel that I am one of those who, without understanding ourselves, we try to teach others. This is a pity. Whatever the Guru has given in the Granth Sahib, we are supposed to practice so that everyone knows that what we say, we do. Otherwise people will not take us as true persons. This is the teaching of Guru Granth Sahib—whatever you do outwardly, the same thing should be in your heart. I do try to recite and follow Gurbani, but I am far, far away from the goal which is desired by the Guru.

"There are five things which we should not have —lust, anger, greed, attachment to worldly things, ego. These things take us toward the worldly side and away from the true path. The difficult path is chosen by the Gurus. Once man is trying from his inner being to follow that path, and he prays to his Gurus to help him to achieve that path, the Guru always helps this small being, and there is nothing difficult in the world. As the Guru described, to perfect ourself is a very thin path the Sikh is supposed to walk.

"When I was young, I learned from my mother. She was totally uneducated. She knew some hymns from Guru Granth Sahib which she learned verbally from her brother. She used to recite when I was just a small child; she used to put me on her lap and recite the Name. Still I remember today some of the words recited by my mother, so it has gone deep into my mind.

"I think Sikhism is a unique religion, and the latest. All the good things of all the religions have been combined in one. It is meant to be spread all over the world. We should understand other religions also; there are so many good things in other religions. But I find that the work toward spreading our religion in other parts of the world has not been done as much as it should have been. That could have been possible if the message of the Gurus had been printed in all the languages and then taken to the doorsteps of the other people. People will not come to you to learn your religion in your language. So it was our duty to make it convenient, to translate our Guru Granth Sahib and Guru's teachings into simple speaking language and take it to the people in their own languages. It is a world religion, and we should not have kept it in our closed doors."

Historical tensions have also arisen within Sikhism, as it became institutional-ized and used by some factions for their own ends, such as acquiring the land-holdings of the *gurdwaras*. Leadership of *gurdwaras* is democratic, by elected committees, but this provision has not stopped fractiousness within the organiz-ations. In 1998, factions of a Canadian *gurdwara* had to be separated by police in their fight over the issue of using chairs and tables in the *langar* rather than the tradition of sitting in rows on the ground.

The Guru Granth Sahib arrived in state atop an elephant for the three hundredth anniversary of the Khalsa at Anandpur Sahib, which drew Sikhs from around the world.

A tradition has developed in which the *jathedars* (leaders) of five large historic *gurdwaras* issue directives for all Sikhs. Of these, the *jathedar* of the Golden Temple's Akal Takht ("Eternal Throne") has assumed the most power. However, this assumption of power is presently being challenged as contrary to the spirit of Sikhism by those who feel that it has the revolutionary quality of rejecting clergy and rigid authoritarianism in favor of the direct relationship between the devotee, the Guru, and God.

There are also tensions between those Sikhs who favor a more spiritual and universal understanding of their religion and those who interpret it more rigidly and exclusively. During the years when Sikhs were asserting their distinct identity, lest they be subsumed under Hinduism, the ecumenical nature of Sikhism was not generally emphasized. There were no forcible attempts to convert anyone else to Sikhism, but Sikhs became proud of their heroic history and tended to turn inward.

In the diaspora, Sikhs attempted to resist assimilation to the surrounding cultures and to raise their children according to their Indian traditions. Whenever communities of Sikhs have collected in the diaspora, they have tried to build a *gurdwara* for their own worship services. In the wake of the September 11, 2001 attacks in the United States, many Sikhs in the diaspora who had kept their traditional dress and long hair with beards and turbans found themselves the mistaken victims of hate crimes, since they were confused with Muslims. Over three hundred cases of hate crimes and discrimination were suffered by Sikhs in the United States in the period following September 11. The Sikh community found it necessary to explain their religion publicly, and inevitably stressed its universality, democratic nature, and spirit of religious tolerance.

Without going so far as to deny the uniqueness or continuing tradition of Sikhism, many contemporary Sikh and non-Sikh scholars are appreciating the message of the Sikh Gurus as supporting the underlying unity of people of all religions. There is a growing consciousness of Sikhism as a world religion that can establish itself in any soil. Thus Sikhs are now engaged in self-criticism about their insularity and their disinclination to actively try to convert others to their path. Nonetheless, even though the missionary spirit is largely missing, the way of Guru Nanak is in fact universal in nature. His Holiness Baba Virsa Singh (see box, p. 431) expresses this point of view:

> *That which we call dharma, that which we call Sikhism, that which we call the religion of Guru Nanak, that which we call the command of Guru Gobind Singh is this: That we should not forget God even for one breath.*
>
> *Guru Nanak prepared a lovely ship, in which all the seats were to be given to those who were doing both manual work and spiritual practice.*
>
> *The religion of Guru Gobind Singh, of Guru Nanak was not given to those of one organization, one village, one country. Their enlightened vision was for the whole cosmos. Guru Granth Sahib is not for some handful of people. It is for everyone.*[26]

In the words of Guru Gobind Singh:

> *Same are the temple and the mosque*
> *And same are the forms of worship therein.*
> *All human beings are one though apparently many,*
> *Realize, therefore, the essential unity of mankind.*[27]

Suggested reading

Cole, W. Owen, and Sambhi, Piara Singh, *The Sikhs: Their Religious Beliefs and Practices*, second edition, Sussex, England: Academic Press, 1995. A clearly written survey of the Sikh tradition.

Duggal, K. S., *Secular Perceptions in Sikh Faith*, New Delhi: National Book Trust, revised edition, 1999. Clear and touching presentation of aspects of Sikh history and belief promoting universalist thought.

Macauliffe, Max Arthur, *The Sikh Religion: Its Gurus, Sacred Writings, and Authors*, Oxford: Oxford University Press, reprinted in Delhi: S. Chand and Company, 1963. The most respected general account of Sikhism in English, even though its author was not Sikh.

McLeod, W. H., trans. and ed., *Textual Sources for the Study of Sikhism*, Totowa, New Jersey: Barnes and Noble Books, 1984 and Manchester: Manchester University Press, 1984. Interesting compilation of Sikh literature, from selections from the Adi Granth to rules for the Khalsa initiation ceremony, all with explanatory comments.

Singh, Dharam, *Sikhism: Norm and Form*, New Delhi: Vision and Venture, 1997. Convincing discussion of Sikhism as a vision of a new social order: a classless and casteless brotherhood of enlightened humans.

Singh, Guru Gobind, *Jaap Sahib*, English translation by Surendra Nath, New Delhi: Gobind Sadan Publications, 1997. Powerful praises of the formless, ultimately unknowable God, without reference to any particular religion.

Singh, Dr. Gopal, *A History of the Sikh People 1469–1978*, New Delhi: World Sikh University Press, 1979. Thorough and scholarly history of the Sikhs to modern times.

Singh, Harbans, ed., *The Encyclopedia of Sikhism*, Patiala: Punjabi University, 1992–1999. Four volumes on all aspects of Sikhism prepared by leading scholars.

Singh, Khushwant, trans., *Hymns of Guru Nanak*, New Delhi: Orient Longmans Ltd., 1969. Stories about Guru Nanak's life and selections from his sacred songs.

Singh, Manmohan, trans., *Sri Guru Granth Sahib*, eight vols., Amritsar: Shromani Gurdwara Parbandhak Committee, 1962. A good English translation of the Sikh sacred scripture.

Singh, Nikky-Guninder Kaur, *The Name of My Beloved: Devotional Poetry from the Guru Granth and the Dasam Granth*, San Francisco: HarperSanFrancisco, 1995. Daily devotional hymns in contemporary English translation.

Singh, Trilochan, Singh, Jodh, Singh, Kapur, Singh, Bawa Harkishen, and Singh, Khushwant, trans., *The Sacred Writings of the Sikhs*, New York: Samuel Weiser, 1973. Selections from the Adi Granth and hymns by Guru Gobind Singh in English translation.

Key terms

Guru Granth Sahib (Adi Granth)	The sacred scripture compiled by the Sikh Gurus.
Panth	The religious community in Sikhism.
Khalsa	The body of the pure, as inspired by the Sikh Guru Gobind Singh.
Udasi	An ascetic Sikh order.
Jap Ji	The first morning prayer of Sikhs, written by Guru Nanak.
Nam	The holy name of God reverberating throughout all of Creation, as repeated by Sikhs.
gurdwara	A Sikh temple.
sangat	A Sikh congregation, in which all are ideally considered equal.

Study questions

1 Describe the life and thoughts of Guru Nanak (1469–1539 CE). Discuss Punjab, river, amrit, relations to Islam and Hinduism, three central teachings, kitchen, caste, class, and gender.
2 Explain the lives and ideas of the Gurus who succeeded Guru Nanak, between 1539 and 1708 CE. Discuss rain, Panth, Amritsar, Golden Temple, Adi Granth, Guru Granth Sahib, Emperor Akbar, swords, food, Mogal Aurangzeb, martyrdom, five beloved ones, Singh, Kaur, Khalsa, the five symbols, and warriors.
3 What role did the following play in Sikh history? Sikh Empire, non-violent resistance, train, Bibi Nanaki, Mai Bhago, and Udasis.
4 Describe the central beliefs of Sikhs. Discuss God, *karma*, reincarnation, monotheism, freedom of religions, ritualism, sincerity, purpose of life, infanticide, five conditions for righteous war, various names of God, self-disciplines, *langar*, *gurdwara*, *sangat*, baptism, and labor.

5 Explain major examples of contemporary Sikh faith. Discuss Baba Virsa Singh, Gobind Sadan, Jaap Sahib, Kirtan, 9/11/2001, leadership, and exclusivism.

Refer to Pearson/Prentice Hall's **TIME Special Edition: World Religions** magazine for these and other current articles on topics related to many of the world's religions:

- *As American As. . . .*

Chapter 11 concludes the study of religions originating in India and focuses on Sikhism. For further research in this area, use the tools available to you in Research Navigator.

As you investigate Sikhism, consider this question: "Why do Sikhs place high value on community meals in their gurdwaras?"

- **Ebsco's ContentSelect:** Search in the Religion database using terms such as "Sikhism," "gurdwara," "guru," "Guru Nanak."
- **Link Library:** Search in the Religion database under the category "Religions from India: Sikhism."
- **The** *New York Times* **on the Web:** Search in the Religious Studies and all other databases for current articles on related topics.

CHAPTER 12

NEW RELIGIOUS MOVEMENTS

"That yielding of the human mind to the divine"

The history of religions is one of continual change. Each religion changes over time, new religions appear, and some older traditions disappear. Times of rapid social change are particularly likely to spawn new religious movements, for people seek the security of the spiritual amidst worldly chaos. In the period since World War II, thousands of new religious groups have sprung up around the world. In sub-Saharan Africa, there are now over 7,000 different religions; every Nigerian town of several thousand people now has up to fifty or sixty different kinds of religion.[1] In Japan, an estimated thirty percent of the population belongs to one of hundreds of new religious movements. Imported versions of Eastern traditions, such as Hinduism and Buddhism, have made many new converts in areas such as North America, Europe, and Russia, where they are seen as "new religions." Internet websites now offer global opportunities for new religious movements to explain themselves and attract new followers.

To move into a new religious movement may be a fleeting experience or it may signal a deep change in one's life. In religion, as in other life commitments such as marriage, there are potential benefits in dedication and obedience. Many religions, including the largest world religions, teach self-denial and surrender as cardinal virtues, which help to vanquish the ego and allow one to approach ultimate reality. The question for a spiritual person is where to place one's faith.

Social context of new religious movements

New religious movements are often popularly referred to as **cults** or **sects**. These words have specific, neutral meanings: a cult represents a distinct break from other traditions, while a sect is a splinter group or a subgroup associated with a larger tradition. Both words have sometimes been used imprecisely and pejoratively to distinguish new religions from older ones, each of which already claims to be the best or only way. The word cult has often been used to signify a group temporarily gathered around a charismatic leader whose influence may be dangerous to his or her followers.

The label "new religious movement" seems more neutral at this time and is becoming widely used, particularly in academic circles, to avoid such negative connotations. However, the word "new" is itself imprecise, for many of these groups have a rather lengthy history and have survived long after the death of the original founder.

Professors Rodney Stark and William Sims Bainbridge have attempted to classify new religious movements on the basis of their relationship to their social environment as well as to previous traditions. A mainstream religious tradition typically accepts and accommodates itself to the society in which it operates. A sect, by contrast, rejects its social environment as "worldly" and "unbelieving," i.e., opposed to its beliefs. Sects usually have previous ties to a religious organization but have broken off from it, often in the attempt to return to what they perceive as its pristine original form. Cults are independent religious traditions. But they may also be in conflict with the surrounding society because they are perceived as new and different. They may refer back to some ancient tradition but over a long gap in time, rather than being a direct split from that tradition.

According to Stark and Bainbridge's typology, cults can be further defined by the degree to which they influence their followers' relationship to society. What they call "audience cults" do not require conversion, and allow their followers great flexibility. They may sample many religious movements and attend workshops here and there, making their own choices about what to believe and do. New Age groups tend to fall in this category. California-based Dr. Deepak Chopra, for instance, has such a large following that approximately 10 million copies of his books have been sold in English and his seven-day workshops sell out even at the price of $2,900. However, those who practice his teachings about healing of mind and body based on ancient Indian ayurvedic principles plus psychological "self-knowledge" do not become members of a distinct religious group.

"Client cults" offer some kind of service, usually some kind of therapy. Involvement with the organization may become deeper and more socially defining over time. Scientology, which is based on the writings of L. Ron Hubbard (1911–1986), is considered such a group. The initial agenda is therapeutic: "auditing" in order to clear the mind of the negative effects of past experiences. But once this process begins, the client learns of more complex levels of involvement, and other members may become their primary social group. Auditing to clear the mind often leads to membership in the Church of Scientology, which worships the greater spirit that observes and directs the mind.

What Stark and Bainbridge call a "cult movement" is a full-fledged organization that requires conversion and does not allow dual allegiances to other organizations. Some offer a total way of life, with community-based lodging and work as well as group worship. Commitment to this way of life ranges from partial, with people still involved with family and friends outside the movement, to total, in which they are largely cut off from the larger social environment.

In this chapter we will survey some representative examples of the new religious movements that developed in the nineteenth to twenty-first centuries. All have some link with previous traditions but are sufficiently different to be studied independently. Previous chapters included groups that are modern and perhaps exported versions of older ways, such as the Hare Krishna movement, which is clearly allied with the sixteenth-century Hindu *bhakti* tradition of Sri Caitanya. The pages that follow provide a sampling of more distinct manifestations of the current burgeoning of spiritual vitality. The headings do not delineate separate categories, but rather common aspects of the new religious movements.

Apocalyptic and millennial expectations

As the twenty-first century began, according to Christian dating, speculations abounded that some major change was about to occur in the world. Some people expected better times ahead; some prophesied forthcoming planetary disaster. The disastrous weather patterns in 1997 and 1998 linked with the worst El Niño in history, unstable political and economic conditions around the world, the sudden collapse of the Asian "tiger" economies, and epidemic exposures of government scandals gave many people the impression that we were experiencing a global crisis of supernatural dimensions. After 2000 came and went without any world-shaking events, the 2001 terrorist attacks on the United States and subsequent bombing of Afghanistan reawakened fears of worldwide calamity.

The expectation of major world changes appears in many established religions, including Hinduism, Zoroastrianism, Judaism, Christianity, Islam, and some indigenous religions. Hindus, for instance, anticipate that the current depraved age of Kali Yuga will be followed by the return of Sat Yuga (when *dharma* will again prevail). This anticipation leads periodically to the formation of movements which preach that the time of great changes is imminent. In Christianity, the last book in the Bible, Revelation, predicts an **apocalypse**, or dramatic end of the present world. Revelation foretells a titanic war at Armageddon between the forces of Satan and the forces of God, with great destruction, followed by the **millennium**, a thousand-year period of special holiness in which Christ rules the earth. Some nineteenth-century Christians developed the idea of the **rapture**, using Paul's letter to the Thessalonians (1 Thess. 4:17) to say that Christians would be caught up in clouds to meet Jesus when he returned to earth.

In a general sense, millennial movements are those which anticipate the imminent coming of an age in which the faithful will be rewarded on earth. Professor Catherine Wessinger makes a distinction between "catastrophic millennialism," which takes the pessimistic view that humans are so corrupted that the world must be destroyed before the millennium can begin, and "progressive millennialism," which takes the optimistic view that humans working in cooperation with the divine can transform the world.

When members of a new religious movement anticipate that the end times or new world order are coming soon, they tend to be regarded as eccentrics by the rest of their society. To maintain their faith, they may isolate themselves from mainstream society and try to prepare for the coming changes. This was the strategy of the Branch Davidians, whose devotional community in Waco, Texas, was attacked in 1993 by federal officials on weapons charges (even though Texas has twice as many guns per capita as was apparently the case within the community), with the result that over eighty of the members died in a fire. Alternatively, those who anticipate the end of the present world may accept social scorn and try to share their prophecies with others in order to save them from the anticipated coming destruction or prepare them for the new world order.

Catastrophic millennialism

People in some catastrophic millennial movements have managed to lead relatively normal lives despite their expectations of disaster. These include Jehovah's Witnesses. Others have taken a path leading to violence against themselves or others.

Jehovah's Witnesses   Those who call themselves Jehovah's Witnesses foresee a new world in which people of all races (including many raised from the dead) will join hands in peace. They believe that this will happen only after the majority of humanity is destroyed for not obeying the Bible. In the understanding of Jehovah's Witnesses, God will not let anyone, including "false Christians," ruin the earth. Those who are of the true religion will be saved from the general destruction, reunited with their dead loved ones in a paradise on earth (except for 144,000 who will live with God in heaven). According to the teachings, in the earthly paradise there will be no pain, no food shortages, no sickness, no death.

The founder of Jehovah's Witnesses, Charles Taze Russell (1852–1916), supported a prediction that 1873 or 1874 would be the date of this apocalypse. When that period passed uneventfully, the date for the "harvest of believers" was changed to 1878, and then 1914, 1925, and 1975. As the dates came and went without any apparent end of the world, Russell developed the idea that Christ had arrived, but was invisibly present. Only the faithful "Jehovah's Witnesses" would recognize his presence. Their mission is to warn the rest of the populace about what is in store.

A Jehovah's Witness shares Bible study lessons.

They thus go from door to door, encouraging people to follow their program of studying the Bible as an announcement of the millennium and to leave politics and "false religions." The latter include mainstream Christian Churches, which, the Witnesses feel, began to deviate from Jesus's message in the second and third centuries by developing untrue doctrines: that God is a Trinity, that the soul is resurrected after death, and that the unrepentant wicked endure eternal torment (rather than utter annihilation that the Witnesses predict for them).

During the 1930s and 1940s in the United States, many Jehovah's Witnesses were persecuted and arrested for their refusal to engage in military activities. Their trials became tests of the preservation of freedom of speech, press, assembly, and worship, and ultimately they won forty-three Supreme Court cases. They have been similarly successful in high courts of other countries. The movement continues to grow, with over 90,000 congregations in 235 countries. Despite their apocalyptic expectations, their website shows them as ordinary people concerned about the state of the world who go door-to-door to deliver their message:

> *In most ways Jehovah's Witnesses are like everyone else. They have their problems—economic, physical, emotional. They make mistakes at times, for they are not perfect, inspired, or infallible. But they try to learn from their experiences and diligently study the Bible to make needed corrections. They have made their dedication to God to do his will, and they apply themselves to fulfil this dedication. In all their activities they seek guidance from God's Word and his holy spirit. ... They understand that many of the prophecies of the Bible have been fulfilled, others are in the course of fulfilment, and still others await fulfilment.*[2]

Violence in apocalyptic movements   In contrast with the non-violent persistence of Jehovah's Witnesses, there have been a number of tragic instances of catastrophic millennialism in recent times. The Branch Davidians were anticipating the millennium and trying to obey what they understood as God's will preparing for the end of the world, as interpreted for them by their messiah, David Koresh. Expecting Armageddon, they had armed themselves to defend their community. About eighty members died when fire engulfed their compound in Waco, Texas, in 1993. The blaze broke out as FBI agents moved into the compound to end a 51-day siege.

In 1994 and 1995, seventy-four members of the Order of the Solar Temple committed suicide, or were killed by the others, in Switzerland, France, and Quebec. The group had claimed to be descendants of the medieval Knights Templars and to be receiving communications from super-human "Masters of the Temple" through their founder, Joseph di Mambro. When his health worsened, membership declined, and French and Canadian authorities challenged the group, its leaders apparently decided that the apocalypse they awaited was near and that ritual death would transport them safely to another planet.

In 1995, members of the Japanese new religious movement Aum Shinrikyo killed twelve people and injured thousands by releasing sarin gas in the Tokyo subway system. The movement had begun with secret meditation training more or less based on Buddhism but with long night rituals that reportedly include drinking pots of sea water and then vomiting, for purification. Perhaps due to declining membership and attacks in the media, the founder, Shoko Asahara, began propagating apocalyptic teachings that justified murder as beneficial to the *karma* of the victims.

Members of Aum Shinrikyo are watched by riot police as they walk through the Aum's complex in Kamikuishiki village in 1995 after the movement was accused of poison gas attacks on the Tokyo subway.

In 2000, over 1,000 members of the Movement for the Restoration of the Ten Commandments of God died in a fire in their headquarters in Uganda or were found in mass graves elsewhere in the country. It appears that they were expecting the apocalypse and hoped that the Virgin Mary would come to conduct them to heaven. As in the case of the Order of the Solar Temple, it seems that many were "helped" to die by the core members, perhaps as traitors.

As indicated in Chapter 1, there are both potential dangers and potential benefits associated with giving power over one's life to any religion, new or old. After members of the Aum Shinrikyo movement were accused of launching a poison gas attack on the Tokyo subway and its leader of murdering a lawyer and his wife and child, Japanese people asked themselves how their intelligent countrymen could have been drawn to the movement. Previously associated with secret meditation training, after the subway attack the movement was described in the media as a doomsday cult making chemical weapons. Author Reiko Hatsumi, wondering how this could happen, concluded that modern Japanese society creates the tendency to obedience:

> *I think most of my countrymen are honest and hardworking, yet also gullible, with a childlike naivete and a disinclination to think on their own. Japanese education has always encouraged this. Students are taught to absorb knowledge but not to judge or rationalize. . . .*
>
> *By being childlike, we also demand emotional security, a guiding hand. Unfortunately, we no longer have a family system. Fathers have abdicated their position as head of the family. They are too busy working late and commuting. The mothers spur their children to get into good schools. . . . The children don't have*

much to look forward to, except a struggle to get ahead in a crowded, competitive society.

So when someone such as Asahara [leader of Aum Shinrikyo] comes along and takes time to listen and to give advice that seems to resolve dilemmas and solve problems, the young hand over their hearts and follow.[3]

Law enforcement agencies are now trying to understand and anticipate what makes some religious movements turn violent and thus pose a threat to themselves or others. One theory is that members are brainwashed by an evil guru. Another theory is that some leaders are simply mad, as are those who follow them. According to another line of thinking, conversion to a new religious movement is a sign of psychopathology—but this argument could be made about commitment to any religion. Another theory is "deviance amplification," as in the case of the Branch Davidians killed at Waco, Texas; there is a widespread feeling that the tragedy might have been avoided if law enforcement agencies had not been so provocative.

As we will see in the last chapter, religion-related violence is not limited to new religious movements; religious extremists who claim to be followers of major established religions are resorting to violence in many parts of the globe. Are new religious movements' followers different? Not only in Japan, but also in Europe and North America, research indicates that recruits to new religious movements tend to come from the mainstream of society. As sociology professor Lorne Dawson summarizes the research, people usually enter new religious movements by learning about them from their friends and relatives. They are often attracted by the joy, vibrancy, and enthusiastic outlook of other members and are drawn more into the movement the more they interact with them. Though each movement differs in the kind of people it attracts, members of new religious movements tend to be middle or upper-middle-class and to be well educated. Primarily young adults who do not have family commitments when they join, they may be actively seeking answers to their profound questions about the meaning of life. They are no more psychologically imbalanced than other young people in their society. In the new movement, they may find affectionate relationships, a sense of community, increased self-esteem, prestige, career opportunities, and material help, as well as spiritual experiences they had been seeking.

How, then, do such apparently reasonable people turn violent? One explanation that applies to some groups is that when, in sincere expectation of world changes, they have isolated themselves to prepare for the end, they distance themselves from other points of view. In isolation and group solidarity, seemingly irrational beliefs—such as the apocalyptic scenario of the biblical book of Revelation—seem to make perfect sense. In 1997, 39 members of a group called Heaven's Gate committed ritual suicide in anticipation of being transported in UFOs to the Kingdom of Heaven. They had been living monastically in seclusion under the tutelage of Marshall Herff Applewhite, son of a Presbyterian minister, and, until her death, Bonnie Lu Truesdale Nettles, a Baptist who had studied astrology, Spiritualism, and Theosophy (new religious movements to be discussed later). These leaders taught a complex millennial philosophy in which the spiritual goal was release from the cycle of births and deaths into the Kingdom of Heaven, an aspiration which was being thwarted by Luciferians, evil space aliens.

Furthermore, humans had become so depraved that they were like soulless plants. The world was overgrown with such weeds, and according to Heaven's Gate beliefs, the elect few who could still be saved were about to be lifted up to "The Level Above Human" (TELAH), after which the earth would be "spaded under." As one member wrote,

> There is no life here in the human world. This planet has become the planet of the living dead. The human plants walk, talk, take careers, procreate, and so forth, but there is no life in them. It is all just a counterfeit illusion crafted by the forces in opposition to the Next Level.[4]

Thus when the Hale-Bopp comet was sighted, with rumors that it was being followed by a UFO, the Heaven's Gate followers concluded that Nettles was returning in a mothership to carry them to TELAH. They committed suicide in order to leave the earth before its destruction and assist their evolution to the Next Level. Such an act was logically consistent with their catastrophic millennial beliefs.

In addition to isolation and group support in their beliefs, religious movements may turn violent in response to hostility from the surrounding culture. This response is called "deviance amplification" in the literature. New Religious Movements specialists Massimo Introvigne and Jean-Francois Mayer have observed that when some groups perceive threats from the outside, they encourage their members to feel that they are not of this world. When under attack from the outside and also perhaps shaken by defections from within, they may conclude that suicide is their only good option. People enter the group of their own free will, but when the trend toward suicide or violence becomes apparent they may find it difficult to leave if the leader is extremely charismatic or even coercive, as was the case with Aum Shinrikyo.

Progressive millennial movements

In contrast to the violence that sometimes occurs in catastrophic millennial movements, progressive millennial movements tend to adopt a no less zealous but nonetheless peaceful approach, focusing on ushering in the anticipated new age. Here we will examine two examples: Rastafari and the Unification Movement.

Rastafari   In Jamaica, progressive millennial expectations have been expressed as Rastafari. In 1895, Alexander Bedward of the Baptist Free Church in Jamaica prophesied a coming holocaust in which all the white people would be killed, leaving the Blacks, "the true people," to celebrate the new world. He sat in his special robes as the predicted date came and went; eventually he was placed in an asylum for the insane. A more generalized hopeful vision was spread by Marcus Garvey (1887–1940), who saw a fundamental change in society that would be led by Blacks. Garvey linked these dreams to the return of Blacks to Africa, from which their ancestors had been taken as slaves; there they would rebuild a great civilization. A prophecy attributed to Garvey—"Look to Africa when a black king shall be crowned, for the day of deliverance is near"[5]—was thought to have been realized when Ras (Prince) Tafari of Ethiopia was crowned as Haile Selassie, Emperor of Ethiopia. An elaborate mystique was built up

Rastafari male musicians carry the message of reasserting black spiritual and social rights.

around Haile Selassie as the living God (though neither Selassie nor Garvey shared this view). Hopeful lore was based on interpretations of Selassie's statements and passages from the Old Testament and the New Testament Book of Revelation. Poor Jamaicans (who likened themselves to the Jews in captivity in Babylon) repeatedly prepared to be given free passage back to Africa.

Haile Selassie's reign (until his death in 1974) did nothing to liberate Jamaican Africans, but Blacks in Jamaica nevertheless developed a new religious movement around these ideals. They intend to revive the "Way of the Ancients," their concept of the lost civilization of pre-colonial Africa, and to free people of African extraction from subservience. "Babylon," the oppressor, is the United States, Britain (the former colonial power in Jamaica), the state of Jamaica, and the Christian Church. In protest against Babylon, Rastafarians wear their hair in long uncombed curls, called "dreadlocks," a lion-like mane symbolizing the natural non-industrial life. Some give use of marijuana (ganja) religious significance as a sacrament. A distinctive music, reggae, has evolved as an expression of Black pride, social protest, and Rastafarian millenarian ideals with the legendary Bob Marley as its musical prophet. In many areas the movement has developed mostly through men; they consider women incapable of experiencing Rasta awareness except through their husbands.

The Rastafari movement has spread beyond Jamaica to Blacks and a few whites elsewhere in the Caribbean, North America, Europe, Southern Africa, Australia, and New Zealand. It is a very localized and diverse movement. Rastas insist that the truths they espouse are not just for people of African descent. According to a Rasta website, until a "secret hour known only to a devout few," when "Babylon" will fall and they will return to Ethiopia, "As Rastas they could now await with dignity the Judgment Day, when the last shall be first and the first shall be last."[6]

Unification movement   Another millennial movement that has gone through many manifestations but is increasingly announcing itself as a harbinger of a renewed earth is called the Unification Movement. Its founder, Sun Myung Moon, has proclaimed himself and his second wife, Hak Ja Han, to be jointly the Messiah. He was born in 1920 in what is now North Korea into a family of farmers. Christians met underground, hiding first from the Japanese occupation authorities and then from the communists, who began to suppress religion in North Korea in 1945. Many of the Christian Churches had strong messianic expectations. Moon's parents converted to Christianity, and the young Moon became a Sunday school teacher. He says that in Easter 1935, while he was praying in the mountains, Jesus appeared to him in a vision. Jesus reportedly told him that it had not been God's desire that he be crucified, for his mission on earth was left unfinished. By Moon's account, Jesus asked him to complete the task of establishing God's kingdom on earth.

To this end, Moon developed the "Unification Principle," according to which God created the universe in order to manifest true love. The family is considered the primary institution for the growth of love. Based on spiritual and moral education in the family, people are to live for the sake of others in all situations. However, concludes Moon, humans do not live according to God's design; selfishness prevails in human relationships and in relationships between ethnic groups and nations.

Moon traces this situation to the story of the fall of Adam and Eve. In Moon's unique interpretation, Eve lost her purity through an illicit relationship with Satan, symbolized as a serpent, and she in turn seduced Adam. Their son Cain murdered his brother Abel because he inherited a false and selfish kind of love from his parents. According to Moon's theology, false love has thence been passed down from generation to generation, infecting the whole human race.

Moon says that God directed him to teach publicly in North Korea, where communist leaders were seeking to quash religious activity. He was arrested and tortured, and his apparently lifeless body was thrown into a snowdrift. After followers found him and nursed him back to health, he continued preaching in public, was arrested again, and sentenced to five years of hard labor in a concentration camp. Moon was liberated when American forces bombed the prison.

In the 1970s, the Unification Church staged a series of well-publicized rallies in the United States and saw a rapid growth in membership. Middle-class youths put aside their careers, gave up their worldly possessions, broke off from their girlfriends and boyfriends, and devoted themselves to the religious path. They saw their sacrificial and ascetic way of life as a rejection of the materialistic and hedonistic American lifestyle. However, alarmed parents accused the church of brainwashing their adult children. The church was viewed with suspicion by the established Christian Churches and vilified by the political left because of its anti-communist activities. In 1982, Rev. Moon was subjected to criminal prosecution over a purported tax liability of $7,300, but the ruling was criticized by the National Council of Churches as a "miscarriage of justice" and a denial of religious liberty, and it was overturned by the Supreme Court.

Dodging controversy and mockery, the Unification Movement began engaging in large-scale international activities reportedly designed to transform the world. For instance, the Unification-sponsored Inter-Religious Federation for World Peace

Living New Religions

Ursula is German and was matched by the Unification Movement to David McLackland from England; they have three children and live in Bahrain, where Ursula is a Regional Director for the Unification Movement. She explains why Unification appeals to her:

"I was raised in a Protestant church, but I was not interested in religion. I just learned whatever prayers by heart, but I had never any experience. When I was fifteen I followed my elder sister and left the church. I went to the government and officially said, 'I am not a Christian any more.' When I was a student I joined the communist movement at the university. But I soon became disappointed in the difference between theory and practice of the communists.

"Maybe the most motivating experience was when I was in a project trying to help drug addicts overcome their internal spiritual addiction to drugs. I was confronted with them with the question 'What is the purpose of life?' They said, 'I don't care if I die in two years or twenty years, so why?' So then I felt if I want to help drug addicts, I must give them the purpose of life—why they could have hope. I felt if I want to help them, I have to invest the same sincerity as they do. A friend had by that time introduced me to a yoga group. I felt the love among the people, the sacred singing, the meditation was what really drew and completely changed my life. Through the moral principles and starting a disciplined lifestyle, many questions in my life were answered, and I felt my mind got cleared up.

"When I met the Unification Movement, that is the point which really attracted me, because they had a very clear logical explanation about the relationship between man and woman, and they were teaching about the ideal of the family. I could see in their own members that even though they were married, now as a family they were sacrificing for society and for the world, not just an individual living for the sake of the world.

"David and I were matched and then engaged for one and a half years. We got to know each other through writing letters. When I met him after one and a half years, I felt tremendous love from God for my husband. This feeling was really immense. I felt this love is not me for him; it is God's love coming through us.

"[In contrast to criticisms that the 'Moonies' are being exploited as cheap labor by the higher-ups in the movement] I see that the higher people are in the hierarchy, the more loving, the more sacrificial they are. I couldn't live like Reverend Kwak (Reverend Moon's direct assistant) or Reverend Moon. Literally, they sleep just a few hours a day, and all day they are active and busy. They are always loving, they are always there for you, they are always supporting you. I want to become like them because they really show me what is a parent's heart, what is a father's or mother's love.

"For us, of course it's true that we are not looking for job security in that sense of money or savings. I think our members come because all of them are very idealistic, that we look for internal satisfaction. Maybe what is most commonly accused is that our members start with sales to support our projects. But some of my most beautiful and wonderful experiences are doing these sales. When I go out and work hard all day to sell, I can really feel God's love, because I do this to do some good work. This money is not for me, it is to help others. I have such beautiful experiences where I can just feel actually it is God who is selling it. It is not me. Actually I could not sell by myself. I think that is for all of our members who have these experiences: We have the most beautiful and wonderful experiences with God doing this.

"We feel that through this type of experience, for example going door to door, you meet all kinds of people in all levels of society. Normally we would meet maybe people from our background—that's it. As a laborer, you wouldn't meet a manager. As a manager you wouldn't get involved with laborers or academics. But through this we meet all kinds of people, and that is really Reverend Moon's internal motivation: To give members broad experience and to train them to get to know all kinds of people and relate to them and love them and understand them.

"When I met the movement, I felt, 'Wow—here are people who are more sincere than I am, people who are more sacrificial, who are more sincere to live for others.' I felt I want to become like them. I think that is really the motive of our members—we don't want to live for ourselves, we really want to live for others."

Reverend and Mrs. Sun Myung Moon conclude a Blessing Ceremony in Seoul for 30,000 couples from around the world.

and the Religious Youth Service have created international inter-religious dialogues among scholars of religion and political leaders, and service projects in many countries. Such expensive projects, including air travel and hotel accommodations for participants in elite conferences, are financially supported by members' door-to-door sales and their establishment of business companies such as industrial-scale fishing ventures. The Unification Church has become extremely financially successful and even wields some political power as, for instance, the owner of a major Washington, D.C. newspaper.

A unique aspect of the Movement's work is massive wedding ceremonies in which couples matched by the movement or already-wed couples wanting to dedicate themselves to "live for the sake of others" and "create an ideal family which contributes to world peace" are simultaneously "blessed" by Reverend and Mrs. Moon, tens of thousands in a large stadium and many more by satellite links. Over 300 million couples are said to have been thus "blessed," although some who are counted may have been administered Holy Wine and Holy Water or given "holy candy" in public places without knowing the meaning the Unification Movement placed on these acts. With Reverend Moon announcing himself as the "Second Adam," Unificationists view these mass weddings as a movement to create one human family, with couples of all races and nationalities being "engrafted" onto "God's lineage of true love."

Reverend and Mrs. Moon also undertake global speaking tours, giving the same prepared speeches in many countries to announce that they are the True Parents of all humankind, come to establish the reign of true love. They are now developing a huge territory in the center of South America as the "New Hope East Garden." Comprising some 7.5 million acres (3 million ha) of land they have bought, some of it deforested, some pristine, it is being promoted as "the zero point for the Kingdom of Heaven on Earth." Agricultural and reclamation projects are beginning there, with an emphasis on sustainable development. Families who have been "blessed" are requested to attend a forty-day workshop there as one of the requirements for "registration for Heaven." As we shall see in the next section, there is also a strong spiritualist component to Reverend Moon's attempts to bring about a new world.

Supernatural powers and revelations

Numerous new religious movements operate in the realm of the supernatural—that is, beyond the experiences of the senses and therefore mysterious to most people. Those who are interested in penetrating these mysteries may do so to attain personal power, or they may seek to use their presumed contacts with invisible realities to bring healing to those who are suffering and insights for those who want to understand what they cannot see.

Many founders of these new religions are women with shamanistic gifts. Miki Nakayama, founder of the Tenrikyo movement in 1838, was acting as a trance medium for the healing of her son when she was reportedly possessed by ten *kami* (spirits), including the chief God the Parent. They proclaimed through her, "Miki's mind and body will be accepted by us as a divine shrine, and we desire to save this three-thousand-world through this divine body."[7] It is said that she later spontaneously composed 1711 poems under divine inspiration, and that these became the sacred scriptures of a new religion. One of these begins with this revelation:

> *Looking all over the world and through all ages, I find no one who has understood My heart. No wonder that you know nothing, for so far I have taught nothing to you. This time I, God, revealing Myself to the fore, teach you all the truth in detail.*[8]

Tenrikyo has continued to be popular since Miki's death, and she is revered as the still-living representative of the divine will.

The Mahikari movement was founded in Japan in 1959 by Sukui Nushi Sama, who believes he is the successor to the Buddha and Christ as God's representative on earth. The path he taught has become popular in the Caribbean. Although it does not claim to be a religion in itself, but rather to bring all religions together, it involves certain distinctive practices centering on spiritual "light." Mahikarians are taught to heal by radiating light out of their hands, to send light to disturbed ancestral spirits to help them find peace, and to spread the divine civilization through the world by transmitting light. Inverting the conventional opinion of such practices, Mahikarians are taught that the spiritual realm is the only reality; science and medicine are ignorant superstitions.

Communication with spirits of the dead has surfaced within a Christian context in the United States as Spiritualism. The National Spiritualist Association of Churches defines Spiritualism as "the science, philosophy, and religion of continuous life." Its services resemble Christian worship services, with a sermon and hymns, but without the focus on Jesus or sinfulness. They include periods of spiritual healing in which trained "healing vehicles" are believed to serve as channels for God's healing power, which is transmitted through their hands to a seated person. Equally important are messages transmitted by a medium who delivers them to members of the congregation from deceased relatives "on the other side." Spiritualist medium Sandra Pfortmiller explains:

> The gift and faculty of mediumship is to prove that life continues, that our loved ones are only a prayer away, that we do have help, guidance, communication and inspiration from another Plane of existence. It shows that we should not fear death but rather understand that the personality continues, always growing.[9]

The Unification Movement has developed a strongly spiritualist component, especially in its South Korean headquarters. It is said that Mrs. Moon's deceased mother and Reverend and Mrs. Moon's son, who died in a car crash, are assisting Unificationists from the spirit world, through the help of a medium. Hundreds of thousands of members have participated in workshops designed to free them from evil spirits, who are then said to be given training in the Unification Principle and duly "blessed." People cite miraculous physical healings and visions of spirits leaving their bodies. There are also liberation ceremonies for ancestors and even historical "infamous personages," such as Hitler, Lenin, and Stalin. A Unification spokesman reports that they have been "blessed as the representatives of all wicked people, thereby opening the gate for the 'liberation of Hell.' "[10]

Throughout human history, certain people have felt that they are receiving revelations from unseen spiritual powers. Some of them, such as the Prophet Muhammad, have become the founders of major religions as others became convinced of the truth of their revelations. This process continues today with great numbers of people around the world feeling that they are serving as "channels" for divine wisdom.

Offshoots of older religions

In previous chapters we have looked at contemporary versions of ancient religions, such as Hare Krishna in Hinduism and Soka Gakkai in Buddhism. Since newer offshoots of older religions are often sufficiently different from the parent religion that they are considered new religious movements—whether they regard themselves as such or not—we will examine two contemporary examples below: the Mormon Church and Radhasoami.

Mormon Church

The chief feature of the Mormon Church, more formally known as the Church of Jesus Christ of Latter-Day Saints, that distinguishes it from the many variations of mainstream Christianity is that Mormons believe not only in the Bible but also in another scripture, *The Book of Mormon*. It is said that in 1822, under angelic guidance, Joseph Smith found the book in New York State, engraved on golden plates. The plates are no longer to be seen, but in the Book of Mormon the names of eleven people are given as witnesses who claim that they were shown the plates. In essence, *The Book of Mormon* purports to be the account of several of the lost tribes of Israel, who crossed the ocean to become the ancestors of the American Indians, and the appearance of Jesus to them in the Americas after his death and resurrection. Mormon is one of the faithful who is believed to have survived tribal conflict and managed to write down the teachings about Jesus in the Americas for posterity. In 3 Nephi of *The Book of Mormon*, for instance, it is written that after "tempests, earthquakes, fires, whirlwinds, and physical upheavals attest the crucifixion of Christ—Many people are destroyed—Darkness covers the land for three days," Jesus appeared to the Nephites as "a Man descending out of heaven; and he was clothed in a white robe; and he came down and stood in the midst of them, . . . saying, 'Behold, I am Jesus Christ, whom the prophets testified shall come into the world.'" Jesus reportedly gave them teachings very similar to the Sermon on the Mount from the New Testament, and urged them to practice baptism by immersion and not to quarrel over doctrine, for "he that hath the spirit of contention is not of me, but is of the devil."[11]

Convinced of the authenticity of *The Book of Mormon*, followers of Joseph Smith moved from one place to another to escape persecution and try to build a "New Jerusalem," "the land of Zion." With great effort, they built a great city in Illinois which they called Nauvoo, Hebrew for "beautiful place," and began to develop some political power. Conversions increased but then Joseph Smith was assassinated by angry area residents. In the struggle for succession, several separate groups of Latter-Day Saints developed, the largest of which was led by Brigham Young (1801–1877) to Salt Lake City, Utah to build "Zion in the Wilderness" and

Mormons have become politically powerful and well established, and the Mormon Tabernacle Choir in Salt Lake City, Utah, is world-famous.

restore what the Mormons consider true Christianity, as opposed to the **apostasy** (abandonment of principles) which they feel characterizes the Christian Churches.

By now, the Mormon Church numbers 13 million followers worldwide and is one of the fastest-growing of all religions. Its members control great material wealth and also exercise considerable political influence in the United States, especially in Utah. The Mormon Church's success is perhaps due partly to the efforts of its 65,000 volunteer missionaries, and partly due to the appeal of its emphasis on clean living and strong family values in contrast to the prevailing Western culture. Despite an extensive lay leadership structure in the Church, all men are ordained to the priesthood, and authority resides in fathers as the heads of the family households. Bishop Thomas Thorkelson from California explains:

> *The father at the head of his household holds the priesthood of God. That father can baptize his child when the child reaches the age of accountability. When the child gets sick, the father can heal it. When the children go off to school, the father gives them a blessing just like Abraham blessed his sons. He is the patriarch of his family and lays his hands upon their heads and gives them a blessing.*
>
> *The Church also teaches that a father should periodically interview each of his children. As holder of the priesthood, the father calls his children in and they kneel down in prayer, and he asks for discernment as he talks with his kids. He talks with them about everything in their lives. If they are old enough, they talk about dating, about their relationships with the opposite sex. They talk about honesty. Or what happens if there is a child in school who is not accepted by the other members of the class. We try to teach them that you need to go out and make a special inclusionary effort. We talk about what happens if somebody wants to copy your term paper, what happens if somebody wants to cheat on a test. How do you maintain what you know is right and honest, and still maintain your status as a welcome person within the community?[12]*

Following the revelations given to Joseph Smith, Mormons typically eschew alcohol, tobacco, coffee, and tea, and eat meat only sparingly, thus focusing on a healthy diet of vegetables, fruits, and grains. They have developed a strong social welfare system to help families in need but also make them self-sufficient. Using volunteer labor alone, they have developed large-scale farms, ranches, peanut product factories, coal mines, and the like, using the symbol of the hive, in which honey bees cooperate in order to meet the needs of all the members. Children are trained in preaching from a young age, as part of the system of shared responsibility. Sexual conduct outside marriage is strongly discouraged, and only virgins can be missionaries.

Mormon theology is still evolving, due to its theology of continuing revelation, by which all believers may receive revelations directly from God. The head of the Church is specially empowered to receive divine guidance on contemporary issues that are not clearly addressed in the Bible and *The Book of Mormon*. Theological beliefs are also subject to change, the most controversial of which—from the point of view of other Christians—may be the nature of God. For some time, Mormons believed that the "Heavenly Father" was originally a man but had risen to exaltation, and that humans can likewise become like gods. This belief still exists, but the current prophet, President Gordon Hinckley, has not stressed the controversial first part of this doctrine, and has restated the second half: "We believe in the progression of the human soul. We believe in the eternity and the infinity of the human soul, and its great possibilities."[13]

Radhasoami

The Radhasoami movement is an outgrowth of Sikhism in India. Its leaders often have Sikh backgrounds, but while orthodox Sikhs believe in a succession of masters that stopped with the Tenth Guru and was transferred to the holy scripture, Radhasoamis believe in a continuing succession of living masters. The first of the Radhasoami gurus was Shiv Dayal Singh. In 1861, he offered to serve as a spiritual savior, carrying devotees into "Radhasoami," the ineffable Godhead. Some 10,000 took initiation under him. After his death, the movement eventually split into what are now over thirty branches, each with its own living master, although there is theoretically only one of these at a time on the earth. The Punjabi branches are known collectively as Sant Mat, or Path of the Masters.

Radhasoami is primarily an esoteric path, without exoteric ceremonies. Initiates are taught a secret yoga practice of concentrating on the third eye with attention to the inner sound and inner light in order to commune with the all-pervading power of God, the "Word" or Nam. The faithful are told that the experience must be both initiated and guided by a perfected being. Sant Mat masters teach respect for all earlier Perfect Masters for they feel they are of the same continuing lineage that includes Buddha, Mahavira, Jesus, Muhammad, Kabir, and the Sikh saints.

The Radhasoami movement now claims an estimated 1.7 million initiates. Those in the Agra area of India have created whole spiritual suburbs who live and work as well as worship together. Outside of India, devotees gather in *satsangs* (spiritual congregations), who are supposed to support each other in the path. They are required to be vegetarians, to meditate every day, to forego alcohol and, if possible, tobacco, and to be employed.

Sant Rajinder Singh, the contemporary "god–man" in one Sant Mat lineage which is now called the Science of Spirituality, emphasizes universal harmony among people of different religions and different countries. He says his aim is to "take the mystery out of mysticism, to help people put mysticism into action in their own lives. By doing so, they will help themselves as well as those around them attain bliss and universal love."[14]

Combinations of older religions

Mixtures of more than one religion have historically arisen in many places. As we have seen, Buddhism, Confucianism, and Daoism have long intermingled in China, to the extent that it is difficult to sort out the threads as distinct traditions. When this process produces what seems to be a new religion of sorts as a combination of normally differing beliefs, it is referred to as **syncretism**. Contemporary examples which could be considered new religious movements in themselves are occurring with the mixture of Christian and African beliefs both in the Americas and in Africa.

In the Caribbean and Latin America, many mixtures of African and Catholic traditions have evolved, with a prevailing interest in contacting and cooperating with spirits. **Santeria**, which literally means "the way of the saints," blends some

In the Radhasoami tradition, the living master is seen as one's beloved and essential guide to the divine. Master Sant Darshan Singh died in 1989; his position was filled by his son Rajinder Singh, who is standing in the left background in this photograph.

of the deities and beliefs of slaves from Dahome, baKonga, and Yoruban cultures with images of Catholic saints. Since the slaves were prevented from openly practicing their ancestral faiths, they continued to do so in symbolic ways, such as hanging a white cloth from a doorway or tying bananas with red string, and also by worship of the African *orisa* in the form of Catholic saints. For instance, the female *orisa* Oshun is worshipped in Nigeria as the patron of love, marriage, and fertility, and is associated with river water. In Cuba and in areas of the United States with large Cuban populations, devotions to Oshun have merged into reverence of the Virgin Mary as Our Lady of Charity, the patron saint of Cuba. She is said to have appeared to three shipwrecked fishermen at sea.

Santeria specialists have techniques for "magical" intervention in people's lives to help solve problems that cannot be fixed by ordinary means. The *santeros*, for example, say they are able to clear away negative spiritual influences around people, help them get jobs, heal sickness, attract mates, block their enemies, and get ahead financially. The Yoruba see the world as a mesh of interconnections among all beings, linked by the energy known as *ashe*. Human efforts are required to keep the ashe flowing properly through creation and to nourish the *orisa*. Then, by knowing how to feed and communicate with the *orisa* and understanding the principles of energy, practitioners are thought to be able to wield some control over the environment.

In the syncretism of Santeria, the Yoruba river goddess Oshun is merged with the Christian Our Lady of La Caridad del Cobre, patron saint of Cuba.

Where remnants of slave populations have coalesced, the renewed practice of African traditions has given the people a link with their cultural heritage, a sense of inner integrity, and a means of sheer survival. But these African traditions have been viewed with some suspicion by the dominant societies. For instance, traditional African methods of communicating with the spirits include divination and the consecrated slaughter of animals, in the context of a community meal. The latter practice was outlawed in Hialeah, Florida, as "animal sacrifice," but in a landmark judgment in 1993, the United States Supreme Court overruled the ban as an unconstitutional barrier to religious freedom. According to a majority of the Supreme Court Justices: "Religious beliefs need not be acceptable, logical, consistent, or comprehensible to others in order to merit First Amendment protection."[15] Santeria has become so popular in Latin America and the United States that it has an estimated 100 million practitioners, as well as Internet websites, and there are pilgrimages to Nigeria for people seeking to explore the roots of their religion.

Syncretism has also developed in Africa itself. For example, a number of "new" religions in West Africa combine ritual elements of indigenous and Christian traditions which had been brought by missionaries. The missionaries regarded worship of ancestors as religiously invalid, but communications with ancestors and spirits had been a major aspect of the indigenous religions. The syncretistic new religions take seriously problems with the spirit world, such as retaliations from spirits who have not been treated respectfully, and mix Christian prayers and incense with fetishes, talismans, divining, chanting, and drumming. This syncretistic mixture gives a sense of power against evil spirits and is also applied to contemporary, this-worldly problems. These groups are most popular in urban areas, where they offer a refuge from unpleasant aspects of city life. Those such as the Brotherhood of the Cross and Star are deeply committed to serving the people in areas where the governments have failed them. They therefore operate their own schools, food shops, industries, health care centers, and transportation services. Those who say they once felt like nobodies, alienated within modern impersonal culture, now feel recognized as important individuals within a loving group. The movements revive the traditional African community spirit as a stable support network within a changing society. They may also build a sense of African pride and spiritual destiny. Rev. William Kingsley Opoku of Ghana, International Coordinator of the African Council of Spiritual Churches and member of the Brotherhood of the Cross and Star asserts:

> African Scriptures confirm that the world peace process will finally be founded in Africa, and the whole world will come and help build it, to signify the unity of mankind under the Government of God on earth.[16]

Nature spirituality

If religion is defined in the broadest sense as that which ties us back to the sacred, one of the strongest trends in our time is that of the religion of nature. Many who are experiencing a reconnection with the natural world do not think of this path as a religion, for it has no clear structure. It is growing spontaneously, from within. Its power as a global "religion" was illustrated by the 1992 UN Earth Summit in Rio de Janeiro, Brazil, to which tens of thousands of people from all religions and all countries flocked to voice and coordinate their mutual concerns for the ways in which we humans are destroying our planetary home. The effects of unchecked industrialization are gruesome. The unique ecosystem of Russia's huge Lake Baikal, for instance, has been highly contaminated by the production of cellulose on its shores and by the discharge into the lake of millions of tons of waste water from industrial and agricultural projects. Some heavily industrialized areas are nearly dead ecologically, with high rates of birth defects and disease among their human inhabitants.

Revival of old models

Some who seek to practice a nature-oriented spirituality look to the past for models. This trend is sometimes called Neo-Paganism, with reference to pre-Christian spiritual ways that are thought to have been practiced in Europe. Some, particularly women, are interested in evidence that the divine was once worshipped as a female power. They feel that by worshipping the Goddess they are reviving an ancient tradition, rejecting what they see as the negative aspects of patriarchal religions. Some call their way Witchcraft, despite the negative connotations associated with this label. As Starhawk, minister of the Covenant of the Goddess, explains:

> Modern Witches are thought to be members of a kooky cult, . . . lacking the depth, the dignity and seriousness of purpose of a true religion. But Witchcraft is a religion, perhaps the oldest religion extant in the West . . . and it is very different from all the so-called great religions. The Old Religion, as we call it, is closer in spirit to Native American traditions or to the shamanism of the Arctic. It is not

based on dogma or a set of beliefs, nor on scriptures or a sacred book revealed by a great man. Witchcraft takes its teachings from nature, and reads inspiration in the movements of the sun, moon, and stars, the flight of birds, the slow growth of trees, and the cycles of the seasons.[17]

Some Neo-Pagans honor pantheons such as the Egyptian gods and goddesses, balancing "masculine" and "feminine" qualities. Some try to reproduce some of the sacred ways of earlier European peoples, such as the Celts in the British Isles or the ancient Scandinavians. Reconstructing these ways is difficult, for they were largely oral rather than written traditions. After religions such as Christianity were firmly established, the remaining practitioners of the old ways were often tortured and killed as witches and blamed for social ills such as the plague. They were said to be in league with the devil against God, but the pagan pantheons had no devil—he was introduced by the Jewish-Christian-Muslim traditions.

The popular way known as **Wicca** can be partly traced to the writings of Gerald Gardner in England in the 1940s. He claimed to have been initiated into a secret coven of witches who allowed him to write about some of their practices as well as their historical persecutions by Christians, and added other rituals and "magickal" practices from various sources to replace those which had been lost because of the isolation and secrecy of the few remaining covens.

Yet other Neo-Pagans are members of new religions known collectively as **ethnic religions**. These have emerged since the fall of communism as revivals of pre-Christian ethnic traditions in countries such as Russia and Eastern Europe. In Estonia, pagan rituals are now celebrated in a rather happy, mocking fashion as a form of entertainment. In other places such as the Udmurt Republic in Russia, faith in prayer and ceremony had been maintained at least up to communist times, only partially replaced by Christian worship. Special groves were reserved for communal prayers to the Progenitress in summer and late autumn. Now that freedom of religion is permitted, people are returning to the traditional agrarian rites for the earth's fertility and human links with the cosmic rhythms and energies. Though newly revived on the basis of folk lore, mythology, and ethnic pride and given the label "ethnofuturism," the antecedents of these ways may be very ancient. Images of animal guardians have been found in peatbogs that date back as far as the eighth millennium BCE.

Teachers from earth-affirming religions that were never totally destroyed, such as certain Native American sacred ways, are highly valued as guides to worship for the natural world. From them, contemporary seekers have learned to use traditions, such as vision quests, sweat lodges, and medicine wheels. But the traditions are complex, requiring life-long training, and are interwoven with ways of life that have passed; Neo-Pagans from non-native backgrounds usually cannot experience them in their original fullness. What remains is the intent: to honor and cooperate with the natural forces, to celebrate the circle of life rather than destroy it, as "civilization" has done.

In the absence of sure knowledge of ancient traditions, Neo-Pagans often develop new forms of group ritual. Usually they are held outside, with the trees and rocks and waters, the sun, moon, and stars as the altars of the sacred. Speakers may invoke the pantheistic Spirit within all life or the invisible spirits of the place. At ceremonies dedicated to a phase of the moon or the change of the seasons, worshippers may be reminded of how their lives are interwoven with

Fountain International members invoke the Earth spirit at the Merry Maidens stone circle, Land's End, Cornwall, England.

and affected by the natural rhythms. Prayers and ritual may be offered for the healing of the earth, the creatures, or the people.

Certain spots have traditionally been known as places of high energy, as indicated in Chapter 2, and these are often used for ceremonies and less structured sacred experiences. Ancient ceremonial sites in the British Isles, such as Stonehenge and Glastonbury Tor, draw a new breed of tour groups wanting to experience the atmosphere of the places.

Neo-Pagan festivals—some sixty each year in the United States alone—are popular gatherings where participants shed their usual identities and perhaps their clothes, create temporary "kinship groups," and enjoy activities such as ritual fires, storytelling, dancing, drumming, and workshops on subjects ranging from astrology to old methods of herbal healing.

Deep ecology

In addition to groups that are looking to replicate or re-invent past ways of earth-centered worship, many people in non-traditional societies are now feeling their way toward new ways of connecting themselves with the cosmos. What is called deep ecology is the experience of oneness with the natural world. By contrast, most Western religions have cast humans as controllers of the natural world, of a different order of being than bears and flowers, mountains and rivers. Australian deep ecologist John Seed refers to this attitude as **anthropocentrism**—"human chauvinism, the idea that humans are the crown of creation, the source of all value, the measure of all things."[18]

What is man without the beasts? If all the beasts were gone, men would die from a great loneliness of spirit. For whatever happens to the beasts soon happens to the man. ... The earth does not belong to man; man belongs to the earth. This we know. All things are connected like the blood which unites one family.

Attributed to Chief Seattle[19]

During the twentieth century, many people came to a new awareness of our planetary home when they first saw it photographed from space. Rather than a globe divided by natural political boundaries, it appeared as a beautiful being, its surface mostly covered by oceans, wreathed in clouds, floating in the darkness of space. Some scientists have taken up this metaphor of the earth as a being and are finding evidence of its scientific plausibility. Biogeochemist James Lovelock (b. 1919) proposed in 1969 that the biosphere ("the entire range of living matter on Earth, from whales to viruses, and from oaks to algae") plus the earth's atmosphere, oceans, and soil can be viewed as "a single living entity, capable of manipulating the Earth's atmosphere to suit its overall needs and endowed with faculties and powers far beyond those of its constituent parts."[20] Lovelock named this complex, self-adjusting entity Gaia, after the Greek name for the Earth Goddess. In more recent elaborations of his Gaia theory, Lovelock emphasizes the "feminine" and divine characteristics of this being:

> Any living organism a quarter as old as the Universe itself and still full of vigour is as near immortal as we ever need to know. She is of this Universe and, conceivably, a part of God. On Earth she is the source of life everlasting and is alive now; she gave birth to humankind and we are part of her.[21]

A corollary to the Gaia hypothesis is the concept that humans are becoming the global brain of the planet, its mode of conscious evolution. In the "body" of Gaia, the tropical rainforests function as the liver and/or lungs, the oceans as the circulatory system, and so on. As the evolving brain of the planet, we are becoming conscious of the dangers our activities pose to these other parts of "our body." Peter Russell, author of *The Global Brain*, warns that we have little time to become fully conscious of our potential destructiveness, our connectedness to everything else, and to take appropriate action to forestall environmental disaster:

> As a species we are facing our final examination; ... it is in fact an intelligence test—a test of our true intelligence as a species. In essence we are being asked to let go of our self-centred thinking and egocentric behaviour. We are being asked to become psychologically mature, to free ourselves from the clutches of this limited identity, and express our creativity in ways which benefit us all.[22]

Those who perceive a oneness of all life may be inspired to take political action to protect other members of the earth's body. Many support "Green" political agendas on behalf of the environment. In Australia and the northwest coast of the United States, people have chained themselves to giant trees to try to keep loggers from cutting them down. Julia Butterfly Hill spent 736 days living high in a thousand-year-old redwood tree to protect it from loggers. She braved winter storms with 90-mile-per-hour (145-kph) winds and harassment by helicopter, refusing to come down until an agreement was negotiated with the logging company to protect the tree and the surrounding 2.9 acres (1.2 ha) of virgin forest. She was sustained by spirituality. As she wrote,

> One day, through my prayers, an overwhelming amount of love started flowing into me, filling up the dark hole that threatened to consume me. I suddenly realized that what I was feeling was the love of the Earth, the love of Creation. Every day we, as a species, do so much to destroy Creation's ability to give us life. But that Creation continues to do everything in its power to give us life anyway. And that's true love.[23]

Similarly, in 1974, the women and children of Reni, a Himalayan village, wrapped themselves around trees to protect them from woodcutters seeking wood for the cities. They knew that the trees' roots were like hands that kept the hillside from washing away, that they shaded the plants they used for medicine and homes for the animals and birds. They said, "The trees are our brothers and sisters."[24] Although some view such actions as romantically naive and hopeless, the "Tree Hugging" movement grew to such proportions in northern India that the government banned commercial wood-cutting in Uttar Pradesh.

Universalist religions

At the same time that an amorphous new religious movement toward "Green" spirituality is bringing humans into connection with nature, efforts are being made to harmonize the world's religions. To cite some examples, the Theosophical Society encourages the study of all religions and maintains interfaith libraries. Their books are made available to all who are interested in world religions. Many Protestant ministers are trained at interfaith theological seminaries in the United States. A number of temples are being built to honor all religions. In addition, several groups have religious unity as their major focus.

Theosophical Society

One of the pioneering universalist religious movements began in Russia during the nineteenth century, the Theosophical Society. "Theosophy" means "divine wisdom," as revealed to Madame Helena Blavatsky (1831–1891) by unseen Ascended Masters. Born into a noble Russian family, she was a fierce character with notable psychic powers. She traveled around the globe studying with masters of esoteric schools and said she had undergone initiations with Tibetan masters. She founded the Theosophical Society with the motto, "There is no religion higher than truth." It was an attempt, she said, "to reconcile all religions, sects and nations under a common system of ethics, based on eternal verities."[25]

The Theosophical Society introduced ancient Eastern ideas to Western seekers, especially Hindu beliefs such as *karma*, reincarnation, and subtle energies. Madame Blavatsky was particularly interested in the secret esoteric teachings of each religion, which collectively she called the "Wisdom Religion" or the "secret doctrine." Madame Blavatsky insisted that:

> *Theosophy is not a Religion. Theosophy is Religion itself. A Religion in the true and only correct sense, is a bond uniting men together—not a particular set of dogmas and beliefs. Now Religion, per se, in its widest meaning is that which binds not only all MEN, but also all BEINGS and all things in the entire Universe into one grand whole. ... Theosophy is RELIGION, and the Society its one Universal Church; the temple of Solomon's wisdom,—in building which "there was neither hammer, nor axe, nor any tool of iron heard in the house while it was building" (1 Kings, vi.); for this "temple" is made by no human hand, nor built in any locality on earth—but, verily, is raised only in the inner sanctuary of man's heart wherein reigns alone the awakened soul.*[26]

H. P. BLAVATSKY

Madame Blavatsky, mystic and founder of the Theosophical Society.

The Theosophical Society now has members in seventy countries. The movement has splintered into several factions, which use the same name, and has also spawned other groups, such as the Roerich Society. Nicholas Roerich (1874–1947), a Russian painter, philosopher, and humanitarian, traveled in the Himalayas with his wife, Helena. He painted the spiritual light he perceived in those mountains and placed in his paintings holy figures from many religious traditions. After his death, Helena encouraged students to revere unseen Masters from India as well as Jesus. Now a steady stream of Russian pilgrims visit Roerich's mountain home in Kulu, India, seeking to establish the same connection with Indian spirituality which they see in his paintings.

Baha'i

A major new religion has been developed that attempts to unite all of humanity in the belief that there is only one God, the foundation of all religions. This is the Baha'i faith. It was foreshadowed in Persia in 1844 when a young man called the Bab ("Gate") announced that a new messenger of God to all the peoples of the world would soon appear. Because he proclaimed this message in a Muslim state, where Muhammad was considered the Seal of the Prophets, he was arrested and executed in 1850. Some 22,000 of his followers were reportedly massacred as well. One of his imprisoned followers was Baha'u'llah (1817–1892), a member of an aristocratic Persian family. He was stripped of his worldly goods, tortured, banished to Baghdad, and finally imprisoned for life in Palestine by the Turks. From prison, he revealed himself as the messenger proclaimed by the Bab. He wrote letters to the rulers of all nations, asserting that humanity was becoming unified and that a single global civilization was emerging.

Despite vigorous initial persecution, this new faith has by now spread to over 5 million followers in 233 countries and territories around the world, involving people from a wide variety of racial and ethnic groups. They have no priesthood but they do have their own sacred scriptures, revealed to Baha'u'llah. Baha'is compare this new messenger to previous great prophets, such as Abraham, Moses, Jesus, Muhammad, Krishna, and the Buddha. In fact, they see Baha'u'llah as the fulfillment of the prophecies of all religions. He did not declare himself to be the ultimate messenger, however. Rather, he prophesied that another would follow in a thousand years.

The heart of Baha'u'llah's message appears in the *Kitab-i-Iqan* ("The Book of Certitude"). God, Baha'u'llah says, is unknowable. Mere humans cannot understand God's infinite nature with their limited minds. However, God has become known through divine messengers, the founders of the great world religions. All

In Pearl of Searching, *the Russian painter Nicholas Roerich depicted a spiritual seeker and his guru in the Himalayas, a magnet for spiritual aspiration.*

are manifestations of God, pure channels for helping humanity to understand God's will. The spiritual education of humans has been a process of "progressive revelation," said Baha'u'llah. Humanity has been maturing, like a child growing in the ability to grasp complex ideas as it grows in years and passes through grade school and college. Each time a divine messenger appeared, the message was given at levels appropriate to humanity's degree of maturity. Baha'u'llah proclaimed his own message as the most advanced and the one appropriate for this time. It contains the same eternal truths as the earlier revelations, but with some new features, which humanity is now ready to grasp, such as the oneness of all peoples, prophets, and religions, and a program for universal governance for the sake of world peace and social justice. Contemporary Baha'is are active in trying to develop a just order in the world, creating projects such as schools promoting global awareness, the European Business Forum encouraging business ethics, environmental awareness campaigns, and rural development projects.

Baha'i Houses of Worship, which are open to all, have nine doors and a central dome symbolizing the diversity and oneness of humanity. Devotional services include readings from the scriptures of all religions, meditations, unaccompanied singing, and prayers by the Bab, Baha'u'llah, and his successor 'Abdu'l-Baha, his oldest son. 'Abdu'l-Baha describes the unified world that Baha'is envision:

> *The world will become the mirror of the Heavenly Kingdom. . . . All nations will become one, all religions will be unified . . . the superstitions caused by races, countries, individuals, languages and politics will disappear; and all men will attain to life eternal under the shadow of the Lord of Hosts. . . . The relations*

RELIGION IN PRACTICE

The Baha'i Model for Governance of the World

One of the most unusual features of the Baha'i faith is its own organization, which it sees as a good model for democratic governance of the whole world. Everywhere that people have converted to Baha'i faith, there is a highly organized framework designed not only to propagate the faith but also to democratize its leadership. Campaigning, electioneering, and nominations are prohibited, thus avoiding the empty promises to voters, corruption, and negative campaigning that tarnish elections in contemporary worldly democracies.

In the Baha'i "administrative order," each local group yearly elects nine or more people to a local Spiritual Assembly. Each local member is asked to pray and meditate and then write down the names of nine adults from the local Baha'i community who seem best qualified to lead the community. The necessary qualities are those of "unquestioned loyalty, of selfless devotion, of a well-trained mind, of recognized ability and mature experience."[27] By this simple and unusual process, Baha'is feel they choose leaders who are mature and humble rather than politically bold and egotistical. By the same process, the Local Spiritual Assemblies elect the National Spiritual Assemblies, and by the same process, the National Spiritual Assemblies choose the nine members of the Universal House of Justice, seated in Haifa. Baha'is feel that this

framework allows both grassroots access to decision-making and a superstructure for efficient international coordination of activities. However, women are not seated at the Universal House of Justice, and this omission is currently the subject of intense debate.

Within these elected groups—and also within business, school, and family settings—Baha'is attempt to reach decisions by a non-adversarial process of "consultation." The point of the process is to investigate truth in depth and to build consensus rather than struggle for power. Participants are enjoined to gather information from as many sources as possible and to be at once truthful and courteous to each other. Any idea once proposed is thereafter considered group property; it does not belong to one person or group to cling to, but rather is investigated impartially. As Svetlana Dorzhieva, formerly Executive Secretary of the National Spiritual Assembly of Baha'is of Russia, Georgia, and Armenia, explains: "What is wonderful is that when a person says his opinion, he just forgets that it belonged to him. It is offered and then it is discussed."[28] Attempts are made to reach unanimous consensus, but failing that, a majority vote may be taken. The success of this process is demonstrated in the fact that people from very diverse backgrounds manage to work and worship together.

between the countries, the mingling, union and friendship of the people ... will reach to such a degree that the human race will be like one family. ... The light of heavenly love will shine, and the darkness of enmity and hatred will be dispelled from the world.[29]

If the religions are true it is because each time it is God who has spoken, and if they are different it is because God has spoken in different "languages" in conformity with the diversity of the receptacles. Finally, if they are absolute and exclusive, it is because in each of them God has said "I."

Frithjof Schuon[30]

Islam opposes Baha'i as theological heresy, for Baha'i denies that Muhammad is the final prophet. Baha'i also finds theological legitimacy in religions such as Hinduism and Buddhism, which Islam does not consider acceptable God-worshipping traditions of revealed scriptures. Baha'is in Iran have been subjected to persecution since the 1979 Revolution, and one hundred and seventy were reportedly killed in the first five years after the revolution.

Baha'is' attempts to unite the earth in faith extend into the political sphere, where they actively support the United Nations' efforts to unify the planet. Their goal is a unified, peaceful global society built on these principles:

1 The end of prejudice in all forms.
2 Equality for women.
3 Acceptance of the relativity and unity of spiritual truth.
4 Just distribution of wealth.
5 Universal education.
6 The individual responsibility to seek truth.
7 Development of a world federation.
8 Harmony of science and true religion.[31]

Baha'is' efforts are partly devotional and partly worldly, such as the sponsorship of a radio station in Ecuador. Its programs range from information about vaccination of livestock to revitalization of traditional Quechua music.

New Age spirituality

A great variety of spiritual movements developed in the West in the 1970s and 1980s that drew on many characteristics of other older movements mentioned already—progressive millennialism, interest in the supernatural and "channeled" revelations from invisible beings such as "Ascended Masters," reverence for nature, and universalism. In addition, they are often characterized by a quest for self-improvement but in highly individualistic, anti-institutional formats. Collectively, these ways, rather than being called "religions," are therefore often called "New Age spiritual movements."

Many believers in planetary consciousness feel that there is some mechanism by which the consciousnesses of all members of our species are interlinked, and if enough of us change our way of thinking, the rest of us will spontaneously change as well. Such thinking is a hallmark of New Age spirituality. Promoted in books and workshops, this amorphous but widespread movement anticipates that a network of personally transformed individuals will eventually lead to the transformation of the planet. Author Marianne Williamson voices this hope:

> A mass movement is afoot in the world today, spiritual in nature and radical in its implications. After decades of declining influence on the affairs of the world, there is once again a widespread consideration of spiritual principles as an antidote to the pain of our times. Like flowers growing up through pieces of broken cement, signs of hope and faith appear everywhere. These signs reflect the light of a transcendent force at the center of things, present in our lives in a corrective and even miraculous manner, a light we can reach personally through internal work of a devotional nature. We are experiencing now an alteration of collective consciousness, centered not in government or science or religion per se. It is centered nowhere because it is present, at least potentially, everywhere. It is the rising up of our true divine nature, a reassertion of God in the consciousness of modern man.[32]

The roots of New Age spiritual movements are many, including Western esotericism, Spiritualism, Theosophy, astrology, and introduction of the Eastern religions to the West. Another antecedent is found in discoveries about the power of the mind, as propagated by Phineas Parkhurst Quimby (1802–1866) and then developed into a full-fledged religious movement by Mary Baker Eddy (1821–1910) as Christian Science. In her *Science and Health with Key to the Scriptures*, Eddy proposed that negative inner states such as hatred, fear, selfishness, and envy obscure one's relationship with God's love. When they are surrendered, healing occurs naturally as one's true spiritual being emerges. Only God is real; the physical body, with its ailments, is not. Christian Scientists usually refuse medical treatment, turning instead to prayerful affirmations.

Another related trend utilizing the power of the mind is New Thought, which spread widely due to the efforts of Emma Curtis Hopkins (1849–1925). At first these groups were quite open to female leadership, but during the twentieth century, some tended to revert to patriarchal male structures, with women only in supporting roles. Some are based on the teachings of a single charismatic leader, with organizations that support dissemination of their teachings without church buildings, a priesthood, or other features of organized religions.

One of the offshoots of New Thought that has proved relatively long-lived is the Unity School of Christianity, which dates back to 1886. Its inspirational publication *The Daily Word* is now distributed in twelve languages. Like many other new religious movements, the Unity School makes extensive use of the Internet for sharing its teachings and practices. One Unity website includes an "Affirmation Machine" in which a person can choose a topic and instantly receive a brief message supporting positive spiritual thinking, such as "I am a beacon of light for others" or "I let my loving light encompass the world."[33]

New Age spirituality is often mystical, favoring direct communion with the unseen. The Findhorn community is a striking example. One of the leaders of the community, Dorothy Maclean, studied with Sufi masters, learning how to receive "inner guidance," before joining with Eileen and Peter Caddy in developing Findhorn, a transformation of desolate dunes on the coast of Scotland into a lush farming community. Dorothy's role was to receive communications from the energies that she called the plant *devas*, after the Hindu term for the invisible "shining ones." Dorothy developed a cooperative relationship with the *devas*, asking for their "advice" on matters such as what nutrients the plants needed. Findhorn now hosts many workshops in such meditation practices and their practical application to gardening in cooperation with nature.

The main thrust of the 1970s and 1980s New Age movement was the belief that a new era was arising in which poverty, war, racism, and despair would give way to a new feeling of global human community, with peace, harmony, and happiness prevailing. Since this was not to be accomplished through any religious or political organization, the idea developed that groups of people could act as receivers for positive cosmic energies so that their effects would create a "planetary consciousness" that would spread to the rest of the world. This belief was strengthened by widespread distribution of a book, *The Hundredth Monkey*, which described what later turned out to be a false report that monkeys on a Japanese island were affected by behavioural changes of monkeys on another island. Many New Age groups thus gathered to receive the cosmic energies and try to create enough critical mass to change the world. The most successful global event of this kind was the "Harmonic Convergence," August 16 and 17, 1987, seemingly predicted by the Mayan calendars as a time of major transition in the consciousness of humanity toward less anthropocentric thinking, drew hundreds of thousands of people to gatherings and sacred power spots around the earth. They were attempting to raise their own awareness above self-centeredness to planetary and even cosmic conciousness, in the hope that this mental/spiritual energy would have an impact on the whole globe.

The longed-for era of peace and harmony did not emerge, and talk of a "New Age" gradually faded away. However, the many professionals who were making a living as workshop leaders, holistic health practitioners, publishers of New Age literature, and the like were still on the scene. Collectively they shifted to emphasizing transformation in individual consciousness, perhaps coupled with the longer-term goal of global transformation.

While part of the New Age movement lost its millennial nature and focused instead on personal growth and the search for mystical communion through techniques such as meditation, a different millennial thrust has developed in some circles: the idea that gradually "higher consciousness" will spread among enough humans that others will be drawn into the same enlightened world view and thus the whole world will "ascend." This idea has been popularized by the bestselling book by James Redfield, *The Celestine Prophecy*, a tantalizing story which claims to be true and presents "nine key insights into life itself—insights each human being is predicted to grasp sequentially, one insight then another, as we move toward a completely spiritual culture on earth." The Ninth Insight is this:

> *As we humans continue to increase our vibration, an amazing thing will begin to happen. Whole groups of people, once they reach a certain level, will suddenly become invisible to those who are still vibrating at a lower level. ... It will signal that we are crossing the barrier between this life and the other world from which we came and to which we go after death. This conscious crossing is the path shown by the Christ. ... At some point everyone will vibrate highly enough so that we can walk into heaven, in our same form.*[34]

A series of sequels to the novel followed yearly, including *The Tenth Insight*, in which spiritually evolved people jointly create a new spiritual culture in the world.

Sociologists note that many people who participate in nature rituals and New Age movements are nomads, dabbling here and there without any deep commitment to what Stark and Bainbridge called "audience cults." In countries allowing freedom of religious choice, they may wander through a growing supermarket of spiritual offerings, taking a bit here and there according to their needs of the moment. Sandra Duarte de Souza describes "spiritual nomadism" in contemporary Brazil, where most people remain nominally Christian but many are also attracted to nature-oriented New Age groups. As opposed to a "radical change of life, marking the biography of the converted forever and demanding his faithfulness, ... the idea of 'religious transit' admits the 'walk through' several religions, does not demand intestinal changes in the way of life of the 'transilient,' and exempts or attenuates the commitment."[35] Of course, the same can be said of established religions—that many people belong to them in a superficial way, without deeply transformational inner commitment.

Opposition to new religious movements

Throughout history, new religious movements have met with opposition from previously organized religions, which perceive them as threats to their own strength or brand them as heresies. In Russia, various foreign-based new religious movements are fighting for freedom of worship against a 1997 law passed at the behest of the Russian Orthodox Church and restricting the activities of groups that were newly introduced to Russia. Lawyers defending these groups have had some success in court cases with reference to Jehovah's Witnesses and organizations sponsored by the Unification Movement.

With or without prompting by established religions, nations may attempt to suppress new religious movements. China has taken strong measures to stamp out Falun Gong, one of many movements based on traditional Daoist Qigong energy practices. Falun Gong has a living charismatic teacher, Li Hongzhi, who

now lives in exile in New York City, from where he has spread Falun Gong to thirty countries. He claims that the simple exercises are of no value and may even be destructive unless they are practiced in combination with Zhen-Shan-Ren, the Daoist, Confucian, and Buddhist virtues of truthfulness, benevolence, and forbearance. Falun Gong members assert that Falun Gong is not a religion in itself, but rather a set of exercises for self-cultivation which may be practiced by people of any religion. However, in 1999, the Chinese government declared Falun Gong an "evil cult" that has cheated and brainwashed its followers, leading to 1,500 deaths by suicide or failure to seek medical care due to faith in the teachings. Not agreeing with this assessment, 10,000 Falun Gong followers staged a silent protest in Tiananmen Square. The government remained staunchly opposed to the movement, perhaps because it has such an extensive following in China and also abroad, thus posing a perceived political threat. Protestors were jailed and beaten, followed by wave upon wave of peaceful protests by daring members who met the same fate. Some are said to have died from torture while in police custody. Nonetheless, members refuse to give up their new religion. Practitioners claim that Falun Gong has brought them physical healing, inner peace, and answers to the central questions of life.

In addition to negative reactions from governments and previously organized religions, new religious movements usually meet with opposition from family members of those who join. There is also concern that new religious movements may cause psychological damage, especially to vulnerable young people. In the United States, the "anti-cult" movement employed special agents who captured and "deprogrammed"

Falun Gong members doing their meditation practices.

followers of new religions, at the request of their parents. However, the claim that members of new religious movements had been "brainwashed" has been largely discredited. As Professor Catherine Wessinger notes, mainstream social and religious institutions all practice some kind of indoctrination in which people's thinking is molded. This process is also used by parents in socializing their children. According to the research on new religious movements, Wessinger writes:

> Usually the processes utilized by members of NRMs to attract and socialize converts are not different from those used in mainstream families and institutions. Belief in brainwashing offers a simplistic explanation for why people adopt unconventional beliefs. It obscures the fact that people adopt alternative beliefs because those beliefs make sense to them, and that people join groups because those groups offer them benefits. [The new religious movements that she examined] all regarded people in mainstream society as being brainwashed by television, the media, educational institutions, and by the values of materialistic society. They believed that their respective groups taught the truth as opposed to the delusions of the brainwashed people in external society. In most cases, the members willingly undertook the discipline and lifestyle of their unconventional religion, which they believed would lead to achieving salvation, their ultimate concern.[36]

In addition to the discrediting of the brainwashing theory of why people join new religious movements, the coercive deprogramming techniques of the anti-cult movement have been deemed illegal in themselves. The Cult Awareness Network went bankrupt in 1996 after one of its deprogramming victims won a multi-million dollar damage suit against it. Nevertheless, what are now called "counter-cult" activities continue in the hands of other organizations, such as the American Family Foundation. The effort to eliminate or control new religious movements is also active in Europe, where governments are struggling with issues of religious freedom versus public safety. France is home to hundreds of new religious groups, including several that have committed mass suicide. There is concern that some are using a religious front to carry on illegal businesses or extort money from gullible followers. Some are neo-fascist groups in the guise of medieval cults whose intentions seem to involve the propagation of white supremacy ideas and hatred of immigrants.

The French government is currently enacting secularizing legislation that inhibits the practice of many mainstream religions, in addition to counter-cult legislation and police scrutiny of groups such as Mormons, Jehovah's Witnesses, and Scientology, as well as evangelical and charismatic Christian groups. In Italy, by contrast, the Supreme Court in 1997 overruled a lower court judgement that had defined "religion" only as Judaism or Christianity; non-profit recognition and tax exemption was extended to Scientology by the court ruling. Germany grants this status only to a few long-established religions, excluding not only new religious movements but also Islam, Hinduism, and Buddhism.

Will new religious movements last?

All of the major religions we have examined were once new and were once resisted by more entrenched institutions. Will any of today's new religious movements last more than a few generations? Those who study the sociology of religion are researching the secular factors that seem to predispose a new religious movement to become widespread and longlasting. One of these is a balance between similarities to existing beliefs (making it attractive and nonthreatening to potential converts) and differences compelling enough for people to convert. A second factor is organization, personal commitment, and bonds between members that will survive the death of the prophet and the original followers. Third is the social setting: Times of great social change, places that allow freedom of choice in matters of religion, and societies with fragmented relationships between people are most conducive to the recruitment of new members. Fourth is the status of prevailing religions; if they have become merely institutional with little spiritual life, they are susceptible to being supplanted by more vibrant new faiths. Fifth is the younger generations: Children must be continually born or recruited into the faith, taught its values, and given responsible parts to play in keeping the faith alive.

The spiritual aspects of new religions are also of major importance but they cannot easily be quantified. Among these are the genuine spirituality of the founder or spreader of the message, and the ability of the new teachings and their presentation to capture people's hearts, change their lives, motivate them to act collectively, and give them the courage to face social opposition. Finally, there is the necessity of divine assistance, in the parlance of theistic religions, or alliance with absolute truth, from the point of view of nontheistic religions.

Suggested reading

Barker, Eileen, *New Religious Movements: A Practical Introduction*, London: Her Majesty's Stationery Office, 1989. A sociological study on the effects of new religious movements on people's lives.

Blavatsky, H. P., *The Key to Theosophy*, Los Angeles: The United Lodge of Theosophists, 1920. A wide-ranging survey of esoterica from many of the world's religions.

Bromley, David G. and Hammond, Phillip E., eds., *The Future of New Religious Movements*, Macon, Georgia: Mercer University Press, 1987. Interesting sociological analyses of the likelihood of longrun success of some contemporary movements.

Bryant, M. Darrol and Dayton, Donald W., *The Coming Kingdom*, Essays in American Millennialism and Eschatology, Barrytown, New York: International Religious Foundation, 1983. Studies of Christianity-based movements, such as Jehovah's Witnesses and Mormons, which foretell a dramatic coming of the Kingdom of God on earth.

Dawson, Lorne L., *Comprehending Cults: The Sociology of New Religious Movements*, Oxford: Oxford University Press, 1998. Sociological study of the emergence and members of new religious movements, and predictors of violent tendencies.

Ellwood, Robert S. and Partin, Harry B., *Religious and Spiritual Groups in Modern America*, Englewood Cliffs, New Jersey: Prentice Hall, 1988. Useful source of information and appreciation of new religions that have flourished in the United States.

Gaver, Jessyca Russell, *The Baha'i Faith: Dawn of a New Day*, New York: Hawthorn Books, Inc., 1967. The history and beliefs of Baha'is, in appreciative detail.

Hall, John R., Sylvaine Trinh, Philip Schuyler, eds., *Apocalypse Observed: Religious Movements, Social Order and Violence in North America, Europe, and Japan*, Routledge, 2000.

Articles analyzing situations within which violent new religious movements have developed.

Melton, J. Gordon, *Encyclopedic Handbook of Cults in America*, New York: Garland Publications, 1992. History and criticism of new religious movements that are considered controversial in North America.

Miller, Timothy, ed., *When Prophets Die: The Postcharismatic Fate of New Religious Movements*, Albany, New York: State University of New York Press, 1991. Contemporary case studies of how the followers of strong founders have or have not succeeded in keeping the faith alive.

Miller, Timothy, *America's Alternative Religions*, Albany: State University of New York Press, 1995. A lengthy survey of the major alternative traditions in America, with chapters written by scholars specializing in specific groups.

Seed, John, Macy, Joanna, Fleming, Pat, Naess, Arne, *Thinking Like a Mountain: Towards a Council of All Beings*, Philadelphia: New Society Publishers, 1988. Some of the leaders of the deep ecology movement offer a collection of thoughts and exercises leading one into the experience of kinship with all life.

Starhawk, *The Spiral Dance: A Rebirth of the Ancient Religion of the Great Goddess*, San Francisco and London: Harper and Row, 1979. A lyrical, experimental introduction to the interweaving of the God and Goddess principles.

Stark, Rodney and William Sims Bainbridge, *The Future of Religion: Secularization, Revival, and Cult Formation*, University of California Press, 1985. Includes a sociological classification of religous groups in relation to their broader environment.

Wessinger, Catherine, *How the Millennium Comes Violently: From Jonestown to Heaven's Gate*, Seven Bridges Press, 2000. Develops the theory that violence is catalyzed by certain types of interactions.

Key terms

cult	Any religion that focuses on worship of a particular person or deity.
sect	A sub-group within a larger tradition.
millennium	One thousand years, a term used in Christianity and certain newer religions for a hoped-for period of a thousand years of holiness and happiness, with Christ ruling the earth, as prophesied in the Book of Revelation.
rapture	Nineteenth-century belief amongst some Christians, using Paul's letter to the Thessalonians, to say that Christians would be caught up in clouds to meet Jesus when he returned to earth.
apostasy	The accusation of abandonment of religious principles.
syncretism	A form of religion in which otherwise differing traditions are blended.
Santeria	The combination of African and Christian practices which developed in Cuba.
Wicca	Neo-Pagan sect of secret coven of witches traced to the writings of Gerald Gardner in England in the 1940s.
ethnic religions	New religions which emerged since the fall of communism as revivals of pre-Christian ethnic traditions in Eastern Europe and Russia.

Study questions

1 Define and give an example for each of the following: a new religion, a sect, a cult, an audience cult, a client cult, and a cult movement.
2 What are apocalyptic and millennial beliefs? Distinguish between catastrophic and progressive apocalyptic religions and give two examples of each type.
3 Which category of new religions is Caribbean Santeria? Explain its formation and practices.
4 What are the common themes and the differences among Nature Spirituality, Deep Ecology, and New Age Spirituality? Give examples of each.
5 Describe the arguments between those opposed to tolerating new religions and those who favor religious toleration for them. Which is stronger now?

Refer to Pearson/Prentice Hall's **TIME Special Edition: World Religions** magazine for these and other current articles on topics related to many of the world's religions:

• *The Impact of Religion: Cult Shock; Relaxing in a Labyrinth; Will Politicians Matter?; Essay   God Is Not On My Side. Or Yours.*

Chapter 12 begins the study of some of the more widespread new religious movements in the world today. For further research in this area, use the tools available to you in Research Navigator.

As you investigate New Religious Movements, consider this question: "Why do new religions emerge as some older religions disappear?"

• **Ebsco's ContentSelect:** Search in the Religion database using terms such as "New Age," "Jehovah Witness," "Unification."
• **Link Library:** Search in the Religion database under the category: "New Age," or "New Religious Movements."
• **The *New York Times* on the Web:** Search in the Religious Studies and all other databases for current articles on related topics.

CHAPTER 13

RELIGION IN THE TWENTY-FIRST CENTURY

As the twenty-first century begins, the global landscape is a patchwork of faiths. Religious expressions are heading in various directions at the same time, and political conflicts involving religions are assuming great importance on the world scene. Therefore, as we conclude this survey of religions as living, changing movements, an overview of religion is necessary to gain a sense of how religion is affecting human life now and what impact it may have in the future.

Religious pluralism

A major feature of religious geography is that no single religion dominates the world. Although authorities from many faiths have historically asserted that theirs is the best and only way, in actuality new religions and new versions of older religions continue to spring up and then divide, subdivide, and provoke

This chart shows current followers of the world's religions. Percentages of the world's population following each religion or none, and approximate numbers of followers are based on statistics in the Encyclopaedia Britannica *1998. [Chinese Religions include Confucianism, Daoism, ancestor veneration, worship of local deities, etc. in China and Korea.]*

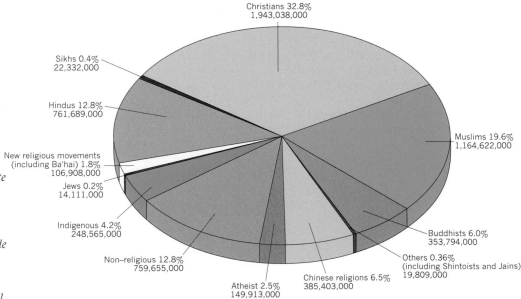

Christians 32.8%
1,943,038,000

Sikhs 0.4%
22,332,000

Hindus 12.8%
761,689,000

New religious movements
(including Ba'hai) 1.8%
106,908,000

Jews 0.2%
14,111,000

Indigenous 4.2%
248,565,000

Non–religious 12.8%
759,655,000

Atheist 2.5%
149,913,000

Chinese religions 6.5%
385,403,000

Others 0.36%
(including Shintoists and Jains)
19,809,000

Buddhists 6.0%
353,794,000

Muslims 19.6%
1,164,622,000

reform movements. Christianity claims the most members of any global religion, but Christianity is not a monolithic faith. Thousands of forms of Christianity are now being professed.

With migration, missionary activities, and refugee movements, religions have shifted from their country of origin. It is no longer so easy to show a world map in which each country is assigned to a particular religion. In Russia there are not only Russian Orthodox Christians but also Muslims, Catholics, Protestants, Jews, Buddhists, Hindus, shamanists, and members of new religions. At the same time, there are now sizable Russian Orthodox congregations in the United States. Buddhism arose in India but now is most pervasive in East Asia and popular in France, England, and the United States. Islam arose in what is now Saudi Arabia, but there are more Muslims in Indonesia than in any other country. There are large Muslim populations in Central Asia, and growing Muslim populations in the United States, with over fifty mosques in the city of Chicago alone.

Professor Diana Eck, Chairman of the Pluralism Project at Harvard University, describes what she terms the new "geo-religious reality":

> Our religious traditions are not boxes of goods passed intact from generation to generation, but rather rivers of faith—alive, dynamic, ever-changing, diverging, converging, drying up here, and watering new lands there.
>
> We are all neighbors somewhere, minorities somewhere, majorities somewhere. This is our new geo-religious reality. There are mosques in the Bible Belt in Houston, just as there are Christian churches in Muslim Pakistan. There are Cambodian Buddhists in Boston, Hindus in Moscow, Sikhs in London.[1]

Hardening of religious boundaries

As religions proliferate and interpenetrate geographically, one common response has been the attempt to deny the validity of other religions. In many countries there is tension between the religion that has been most closely linked with national history and identity and other religions that are practiced or have been introduced into the country. Protestant congregations are rushing to offer Bibles

Religions are now practiced far from the countries where they originated. This Tibetan Buddhist nun is practicing on the Holy Island of Lindisfarne in the United Kingdom.

and religious tracts to citizens of formerly atheistic communist countries, with the idea that they are introducing Christianity there. But Orthodox Christianity, established more than a thousand years ago in Russia, had continued to exist there despite communist rule, sometimes by collaboration with the oppressive authorities, and sometimes by sheer devotion in the midst of hardship, even though the Church structures were limited and controlled by the State. People from the more established religions seek to find a balance between freedom of religion for all and the threat they perceive to their traditional values, customs, and sense of national identity.

The issue arises of which religions will receive state funding. In Ontario, Canada, for instance, the government has given funding to Roman Catholic schools for a hundred years, yet such funds have been denied to Jewish, Muslim, and Protestant Christian schools. In some countries, there is resistance to offering such public funds to new groups that are organized and well financed from abroad. For example, it was not until 1997 that the British government recognized Islamic schools on a par with the long-established Christian and Jewish academic institutions.

Registration requirements are another means used to help control or at least track the introduction of religions into countries where they did not originate. Another is outright banning of new or minority religions. In 1997, the Russian parliament passed a law prohibiting religions that had not been officially existing in Russia longer than fifteen years from distributing religious materials or newspapers or running schools. The law protects the traditional status of the Russian Orthodox Church and Islam, Buddhism, and Judaism with some concessions to Protestant and Roman Catholic Christianity.

Religious symbols have become the focus for the French government's attempts to keep religion within bounds. In 2004, a controversial law was passed forbidding wearing of religious symbols including Muslim veils, Jewish yarmulkes, and large Christian crosses in French public schools and colleges. The government has also tried to restrict the activities of new religious movements, as well as charismatic and evangelical Christian groups, even though its constitution states "France shall respect all beliefs."

In some previously communist countries, old animosities between people of different ethnic groups resurfaced with great violence once totalitarian regimes toppled. These intense ethnic and political struggles often pit people of different faiths against each other, as in former Yugoslavia. Where there had been a seemingly peaceful society, horrifying atrocities arose among largely Orthodox Christian Serbs, Roman Catholic Croats, and the Muslims living mainly in Bosnia and Hercegovina. Gyorgy Bulanyi, founder of the Hungarian Bokor Movement, charged that religious leaders were instigators of rather than dissuaders from violence:

> Neither the cardinal in Zagreb nor the Patriarch of Belgrade nor the Great Mufti of Sarajevo preaches to his people that Serbians—or Croats or Muslims—are also created by God, and that it is therefore a cardinal sin to kill them. This is not the line we hear from them, but rather another one: "It is a human right and duty to defend one's family and nation against attack."[2]

The twentieth-century rush for materialism and secular values also fanned a reactionary increase in "fundamentalism." Along with the salient features of

modernity—complex technologies, globalization, urbanization, bureaucratiza-
tion, and rationality—have come the values known as "**Modernism.**" They
include individualism, a preference for change rather than continuity, quantity
rather than quality, efficiency rather than traditional skills and aesthetics, and
pragmatism and profiteering rather than eternal truths and values. Modernism is
perceived by some as threatening the very existence of traditional religious
values; to them, contemporary secular culture seems crude, sacrilegious, and
socially dangerous. Jerry Falwell, who founded the "Moral Majority" in the
1970s in the United States, describes what he sees as signs that America is "losing
its soul":

> *During the past 35 years or so, we have expelled prayer from our schools and
> legalized abortion on demand. Our divorce rate has soared to 50%. There are one
> million teen pregnancies each year. We have a drug epidemic. We are considering
> legalizing same sex marriages and trying hard to normalize the gay and lesbian
> lifestyle. School violence has burst upon the scene, Our culture is collapsing.
> Hollywood, television, video games, internet pornography and other influences are
> destroying our children and our values. America is in serious jeopardy of self-
> destroying.*[3]

Fundamentalists have responded to such perceptions in various ways. Some
have tried to withdraw socially from the secular culture even while surrounded
by it. Others have actively tried to change the culture, using political power to
shape social laws or lobbying for banning of textbooks that they feel do not
include their religious point of view. As described by the Project on Religion and
Human Rights:

> *Fundamentalists' basic goal is to fight back—culturally, ideologically, and
> socially—against the assumptions and patterns of life that are taken for granted in
> contemporary secular society and culture, refusing to celebrate them or to embrace
> them fully. They keep their distance and refuse to endorse the legitimacy of any
> culture that opposes what they perceive as fundamental truths. Secular culture, in
> their eyes, is base, barbarous, crude, and essentially profane. It produces a society
> that respects no sacred order and ignores the possibility of redemption.*[4]

Although fundamentalism may be based on religious motives, it often turns to
political means to accomplish its objectives. At the same time, political leaders
have found the religious loyalty and absolutism of some fundamentalists an expe-
dient way to mobilize political loyalties. Thus, Hindu extremists in India have
been encouraged to demolish Muslim mosques built on the foundation of older
Hindu temples and to rebuild Hindu temples in their place. The United States,
which had prided itself on being a "melting pot" for all cultures, with full freedom
of religion and no right of government to promote any specific religion, has witnessed attempts by Christian fundamentalists—the "Religious Right"—to control
education and politics, and a simultaneous rise in violence against ethnic and religious minorities. Buddhism, long associated with nonviolence, became involved
in the violent suppression of the Hindu minority in Sri Lanka. Christians and
Muslims are clashing in Indonesia, Nigeria, India, and elsewhere. Violence among
different branches of the same religion also rages—Roman Catholic churches in
Northern Ireland have been burned by Protestants, and Sunni and Shi'ite Muslims

have taken up arms against each other in neighboring Arabic countries. The Internet reveals the sentiments and activities of a troubling number of hate groups promoting intolerance, bigotry, hatred, and violence against specific others in the name of religion.

The stunning attacks by terrorists on United States targets in 2001 brought instant polarization along religious and ethnic lines. Hundreds of hate crimes were committed in the United States against Muslims and foreign immigrants who were mistaken for Muslims and were suddenly seen as "outsiders" as some Americans responded in fear and rage. With the subsequent bombing of Afghanistan and Iraq, the perpetrators of terrorism such as Osama bin Laden incited Muslims to see the world in terms of Muslims versus the infidels, and to join together to drive the United States out of its strategic positions in Muslim lands. Both sides claimed that God was on their side and their cause a holy one.

While the Christian Identity movement promoted ideas of Christian supremacy in the United States, leaders of Al Qaeda selectively cited passages from the Holy Qur'an to give the appearance of spiritual legitimacy to their militant teachings. Osama bin Laden proclaimed in a videotaped address in October 2001:

> These events have divided the world into two camps, the camp of the faithful and the camp of infidels. . . . Every Muslim must rise to defend his religion. The wind of faith is blowing and the wind of change is blowing to remove evil from the Peninsula of Muhammad, peace be upon him. . . . God is the greatest and glory be to Islam.[5]

Once groups have taken such oppositional standpoints, violence seems inevitable. Feelings have been inflamed to the point that people are even ready to sacrifice their lives as suicide bombers, kill innocent people in terrorist attacks, conduct assassinations, or drop bombs on populated areas, for the sake of what they consider to be a holy cause. When suicide attacks became common, observers at first reported that those giving their lives were primarily uneducated and poor. As this trend has increased, more careful study of suicide bombers in organizations such as Al Qaeda and Hamas in Palestine shows that the suicide attackers tend to be well-educated and to come from relatively well-off families. Theirs is not the easily exploited despair of poverty and ignorance; it is the conviction of ideology. Pilots dropping bombs on Iraq and soldiers treating prisoners brutally may similarly be motivated by the conviction that they are doing the right thing and attacking evil by "countering terrorism."

These convictions do not represent the heart of religious teachings. Whether state-sponsored or incited by militant extremists, violence finds no support in any religion. Thus there has been a strong outcry against fundamentalist violence by the mainstream religions from which militants have drawn their faith. Muslims are trying to point out that *jihad* must not be confused with terrorism, for *jihad* (spiritual struggle, particularly against one's own inner flaws) is the holy duty of every Muslim, whereas terrorist killing of innocent people is forbidden by the Holy Qur'an. Likewise, many Christian organizations have come out strongly against violence of any sort, including state terrorism. Roman Catholic theologian Vimal Tirimanna explains:

Terrorism is an evil that needs to be eradicated if we sincerely wish to make this world a place suitable for all human beings. Besides, ordinary human experience shows that terrorism can never be a moral good, because of the horrendous evils it causes to human lives and to property. Let us not forget here that terrorism also damages the very existence of the terrorist himself/herself as a human being with others; it is demeaning of his/her own basic human dignity. Terrorism is an evil also because it is always a deliberately planned act to hurt, to damage, to injure other human lives, and also to devastate God's creation. Moreover it is intimidation which seeks to eliminate the basic human freedom of the would-be victims and which tends to impose the will of the terrorists forcefully on those who are at the receiving end. Terrorism, no matter whatever form it takes, no matter who are its perpetrators, and no matter what "noble" goals it seeks to promote, can never be justified by a conscientious person.That is why the official Church, using her cherished moral principal, the end does not justify the means, *has not hesitated to condemn terrorism as morally evil.*[6]

Interfaith movement

What can be done to end the increasing political deadlock and hatreds between followers of various religions? There is already an existing counter-current growing in the world. At the same time that boundaries between religions are hardening in many areas, there has been a rapid acceleration of **interfaith dialogue**—the willingness of people of all religions to meet, explore their differences, and appreciate and find enrichment in each other's ways to the divine. This approach has been historically difficult, for many religions have made exclusive claims to being the best or only way. Professor Ewert Cousins, editor of an extensive series of books on the spiritual aspects of major religions, comments: "I think all the religions are overwhelmed by the particular revelation they have been given and are thus blinded to other traditions' riches."[7]

Religions are quite different in their external practices and culturally-influenced behaviors. There are doctrinal differences on basic issues, such as the cause of and remedy for evil and suffering in the world, or the question of whether the divine is singular, plural, or nontheistic. And some religions make apparent claims to superiority which are difficult to reconcile with other religions' claims. The Qur'an, for instance, while acknowledging the validity of earlier prophets as messengers of God, refers to the Prophet Muhammad as the "Seal of the Prophets" (Sura 33:40). This description has been interpreted to mean that prophecy was completed with the Prophet Muhammad. If he is believed to be the last prophet, no spiritual figures after he passed away in c. 632—including the Sikh Gurus and Baha'u'llah of the Baha'is—could be considered prophets, though they might be seen as teachers. Similarly, Christians read in John 14:6 that Jesus said, "I am the way, the truth, and the life; no one comes to the Father but by me." But some Christian scholars now feel that it is inappropriate to take this line out of its context (in which Jesus's disciples were asking how to find their way to him after they died) and to interpret it to mean that the ways of Hindus and Buddhists are invalid. Relationships with other faiths was not the question being answered.

Control of the Mind

The necessity of controlling our mind is one of the common themes that can be found in all religions.

Hinduism: Arjuna said: "The mind is restless, turbulent, obstinate and very strong, O Krishna, and to subdue it, I think, is more difficult than controlling the wind." Lord Shri Krishna said: "It is undoubtedly very difficult to curb the restless mind, but it is possible by suitable practice and by detachment."

Bhagavad-Gita 6:34

Jainism: "Fight with yourself; why fight with external foes?
He who conquers himself through himself will obtain happiness."

Uttaradhyayana Sutra 9:34–36

Buddhism: "Check your mind, be on your guard. Pull yourself out, as an elephant from mud."

The Dhammapada

Taoism: "One who overcomes others has physical might;
One who overcomes the self is strong."

Tao te Ching 33

Judaism: "Better to govern one's temper than capture a city."

Proverbs 16:32

Christianity: "Do not set yourself against the person who wrongs you.
If someone slaps you on the right cheek, turn and offer him the left.
Love your enemies and pray for your persecutors."

Matthew 5:39, 44

Islam: "The greatest *jihad* [striving] is that against the *nafs*, the base instincts."

Hadith of the Prophet Muhammad

Sikhism: "He who conquers his mind conquers the world."

Jap Ji 28

Many people of broad vision have noted that many of the same principles reappear in all traditions. All religions teach the importance of setting one's own selfish interests aside, loving others, harkening to the divine, and exercising control over the mind (see box). What is called the "Golden Rule," expressed by Confucius as "Do not do unto others what you do not want others to do unto you," and by the Prophet Muhammad as "None of you truly have faith if you do not desire for your brother that which you desire for yourself," is found in every religion.

The absolute authority of scriptures is being questioned by contemporary scholars who are interpreting them in their historical and cultural context and thus casting some doubt upon their exclusive claims to truth. Some liberal scholars are also proposing that there is an underlying experiential unity among religions. Wilfred Cantwell Smith, for instance, concluded that the revelations of all religions have come from the same divine source. Christian theologian John Hick suggests that religions are culturally different responses to one and the same reality. The Muslim scholar Frithjof Schuon feels that there is a common mystical base underlying all religions, but that only the enlightened will experience and understand it, whereas others will see the superficial differences.

Responses to other faiths

With these contrasting views, there are several different ways in which people of different religions may relate to each other. Diana Eck, Professor of Comparative Religion and Indian Studies of Harvard Divinity School and Chair of the World Council of Churches committee on interfaith dialogue, observes that there are three responses to contact between religions. One is **exclusivism**: "Ours is the only true way." Eck and others have noted that such a point of view has some value, for deep personal commitment to one's faith is a foundation of religious life and also the first essential step in interfaith dialogue.

Eck sees the second response to interfaith contact as **inclusivism**. This may take the form of trying to create a single world religion, such as Baha'i. Or it may appear as the belief that our religion is spacious enough to encompass all the others, that it supersedes all previous religions, as Islam said it was the culmination of all monotheistic traditions. In this approach, the inclusivists do not see other ways as a threat. Some Sikhs, for instance, understand their religion as

Guidelines for Inter-religious Understanding

1 The world religions bear witness to the experience of the Ultimate Reality to which they give various names: Brahman, the Absolute, God, Allah, Great Spirit, the Transcendent.

2 The Ultimate Reality surpasses any name or concept that can be given to it.

3 The Ultimate Reality is the source (ground of being) of all existence.

4 Faith is opening, surrendering, and responding to the Ultimate Reality. This relationship precedes every belief system.

5 The potential for human wholeness—or in other frames of reference, liberation, self-transcendence, enlightenment, salvation, transforming union, *moksha*, nirvana, *fana*— is present in every human person.

6 The Ultimate Reality may be experienced not only through religious practices but also through nature, art, human relationships, and service to others.

7 The differences among belief systems should be presented as facts that distinguish them, not as points of superiority.

8 In the light of the globalization of life and culture now in process, the personal and social ethical principles proposed by the world religions in the past need to be re-thought and re-expressed. For example:

a In view of the increasing danger of global destruction, the world religions should emphasize the corresponding moral obligation of nations and ethnic groups to make use of nonviolent methods for the resolution of conflicts.

b The world religions should encourage civil governments to respect every religion without patronizing one in particular.

c The world religions should work for the practical acceptance of the dignity of the human person; a more equitable distribution of material goods and of opportunities for human development; the cause of human rights, especially the right to choose and practice one's own religion or no religion; the solidarity and harmony of the human family; the stewardship of the earth and its resources; the renewal of their respective spiritual traditions; and inter-religious understanding through dialogue.[8]

Father Thomas Keating

actively promoting interfaith appreciation and thus propose that their holy scripture, the *Guru Granth Sahib*, can serve as a roadmap to harmony among people of all religions, without denying the right of each religion to exist as a respected tradition.

The third way Eck discerns is **pluralism**: to hold one's own faith and at the same time ask people of other faiths about their path, about how they want to be understood. Uniformity and agreement are not the goals—the goal is to collaborate, to combine our differing strengths for the common good. From this point of view, for effective pluralistic dialogue, people must have an openness to the possibility of discovering sacred truth in other religions. Raimundo Panikkar, a Catholic-Hindu-Buddhist doctor of science, philosophy, and theology, has written extensively on this subject. He speaks of "concordant discord":

> We realize that, by my pushing in one direction and your pushing in the opposite, world order is maintained and given the impulse of its proper dynamism. ... One animus does not mean one single theory, one single opinion, but one aspiration (in the literal sense of one breath) and one inspiration (as one spirit). Consensus ultimately means to walk in the same direction, not to have just one rational view. ... To reach agreement suggests to be agreeable, to be pleasant, to find pleasure in being together. Concord is to put our hearts together.[9]

Interfaith initiatives

People of all faiths have begun to put their hearts together. Initially, ecumenical conferences involved pairs of related religions that were trying to agree to disagree, such as Judaism and Christianity. Now a large number of interfaith organizations and meetings draw people from all religions in a spirit of mutual appreciation. In 1986, Pope John Paul II invited one hundred and sixty representatives of all religions to Assisi in honor of the humble St. Francis, to pray together for world

Leaders of many religions gather in Westminster Cathedral, London, in 1996 on the tenth anniversary of the Assisi interfaith gathering.

peace. "If the world is going to continue, and men and women are to survive in it, it cannot do without prayer. This is the permanent lesson of Assisi," declared the pope.[10]

Two years later, the Assisi idea was extended to include governmental leaders, scientists, artists, business leaders, and media specialists as well as spiritual leaders. Some two hundred of them from around the globe met in Oxford, England, in 1988 at the Global Forum of Spiritual and Parliamentary Leaders on Human Survival. They held their plenary sessions beneath an enormous banner with the image of the earth as seen from space. Statements of concern for the environment brought participants to the conclusion that the ecological dangers now threatening the entire human race may be the key that draws us together. But it was spiritual camaraderie rather than shared fear that brought the participants together. Dr. Wangari Maathai, leader of the Green Belt movement in Kenya, observed:

All religions meditate on the Source. And yet, strangely, religion is one of our greatest divides. If the Source be the same, as indeed it must be, all of us and all religions meditate on the same Source.[11]

In 1990, a great assembly of spiritual leaders of all faiths with scientists and parliamentarians took place in what, until a few years before, would have been the most unlikely place in the world for such a gathering—Moscow, capital of the previously officially atheistic Soviet Union. The final speaker was Mikhail Gorbachev, who called for a merging of scientific and spiritual values in the effort to save the planet.

Throughout 1993, special interfaith meetings were held around the world to celebrate the one hundredth anniversary of the Parliament of the World's Religions in Chicago. In 1893, the figure who most captured world attention was Swami Vivekananda (1863–1902), a disciple of Sri Ramakrishna. He brought appreciation of Eastern religions to the West, and made these concluding remarks:

If the Parliament of Religions has shown anything to the world it is this: It has proved to the world that holiness, purity, and charity are not the exclusive possessions of any church in the world, and that every system has produced men and women of the most exalted character. In the face of this evidence, if anybody dreams of the exclusive survival of his own religion and the destruction of others, I pity him from the bottom of my heart.[12]

The largest 1993 centenary celebration of the Parliament of the World's Religions was again held in Chicago. It gathered hundreds of well-known teachers from all faiths and thousands of participants to consider the critical issues facing humanity. It included an attempt to define and then use as a global standard for behavior the central ethical principles common to all religions. The provisional conference document signed by many of the leaders, "The Declaration Toward a Global Ethic," included agreement on what has been called the Golden Rule:

There is a principle which is found and has persisted in many religious and ethical traditions of humankind for thousands of years: What you do not wish done to yourself, do not do to others. Or in positive terms: What you wish done to yourself, do to others! This should be the irrevocable, unconditional norm for all areas of life, for families and communities, for races, nations, and religions.[13]

Baba Virsa Singh prays to the Light some perceive as shining through all the prophets and pervading all Creation.

The global gathering model has been replicated in various locations such as Barcelona in 2004, drawing participants from around the world to deliberate how religions can collectively help to solve the world's problems. Many people have also had the vision that the United Nations could be home to representatives or leaders from all faiths, jointly advising the United Nations on international policy from a religious perspective.

Questions arise in such an effort, in addition to the necessity for substantial funding. Which religions should be represented? As we have seen, most major religions have many offshoots and branches that do not fully recognize each other's authority. And which, if any, of the myriad new religious movements should be included? Should indigenous religions be included? If so, could one representative speak for all the varied traditions? Would such an organization reflect the bureaucratical patriarchal structures of existing religions, or would it include women, the poor, and enlightened people rather than managers? If the members of the body were not elected by their respective organizations, but were rather simply interested individuals, what authority would they have?

The Internet carries the efforts of many organizations to provide accurate information about a variety of religions to help overcome ignorance and intolerance. The Ontario Consultants on Religious Practice, for instance, sponsor www.religioustolerance.org, a rich offering of articles and resources on a long list of religions plus essays on interfaith themes. Non-governmental organizations, such as the Council for Global Education in Washington, D.C., are attempting to develop curricula for teaching children about the world's religions in classrooms.

In addition to global projects, there are many local interfaith initiatives. A common response in the United States to the September 2001 terrorist attacks was interfaith prayer meetings, from local communities to the National Cathedral. Many leaders broadcast appeals against confusing Islam with terrorism. To help prevent hate attacks on their Muslim sisters, non-Muslim women in the United States, Britain, and Australia donned head scarves in the "Scarves for Solidarity" campaign. They explained:

> *To protect Muslim women who have been afraid to leave their houses because of ignorant hatred, we will dress piously. The hijab is worn outwardly to show the inner hijab of compassion, honesty, and love, which is carried in the hearts and souls of Islamic men and women alike. It is not meant to be a political symbol in any way, just a symbol of love.*[14]

Inter-religious groups and projects are quite active in Britain, with its increasingly multi-cultural population. The Leicester Council of Faiths, for instance, includes representatives from Christianity, Hinduism, Islam, Sikhism, Judaism, Jainism, Buddhism, and the Baha'i faith. Their efforts include developing a multi-

TEACHING STORY

The Frog in the Well

A frog lived in a well. It had lived there a long time. One day another frog, which lived in the sea, came and fell into the well. "Where are you from?" the first frog asked. "I am from the sea," the second one said. "The sea! What is it like? Is it as big as my well?" The second tried to describe how impossibly big was the sea and leapt to the other side of the well and said to the other frogs, "What nonsense this frog is speaking to compare the sea with your well." But the frog in the well retorted, "Nothing can be bigger than my well. There can be nothing bigger than this. This fellow is a liar, so turn him out."

As told by Swami Vivekananda to the 1893 Parliament of the World's Religions, Chicago

faith Welcome Centre, ensuring that there is balanced representation of all faiths at civic events, providing multi-faith counseling and a multi-faith chaplaincy service in some healthcare institutions, informing the various faiths about political matters that affect them, and working with the National Health Service on care that is sensitive to people's specific faiths.

> *"Spirituality is not merely tolerance. . . . It is the absolute recognition of the other's faith in God as one's own."*
>
> Sri Chinmoy

In some places, interfaith efforts are being applied directly to difficult real-life situations, such as the fighting between Protestants and Catholics in Northern Ireland. In Mayfair, a neighborhood of Washington, D.C., people lived in fear of drug dealers armed with semi-automatic weapons. A group of African–American Muslims went into the area and chased out the drug dealers, making Mayfair a safe place to live. Then, rather than consolidating their own power, they invited African–American Baptist ministers to come in and help teach the people of Mayfair about the spiritual life. In Israel, the Interfaith Encounter Association brings Muslims, Christians, and Jews together for intimate sharing of cultural and spiritual experiences from each other's traditions. There are even groups bringing together the families and friends of those from all sides who have been killed in conflicts.

In India, where communal violence between people of varying religions is daily news, the Sikh-based interfaith work of Gobind Sadan is bringing together volunteers of all religions in practical farm work on behalf of the poor, and in celebrations of the holy days of all religions. Baba Virsa Singh, the spiritual inspiration of Gobind Sadan, continually quotes from the words of all the prophets and says:

All the Prophets have come from the same Light; they all give the same basic messages. None have come to change the older revealed scriptures; they have come

*to remind people of the earlier Prophets' messages which the people have forgotten.
We have made separate religions as walled forts, each claiming one of the Prophets
as its own. But the Light of God cannot be confined within any manmade
structures. It radiates throughout all of Creation. How can we possess it?[15]*

Where people have seen their relatives tortured and killed by fanatics of
another faith, reconciliation is very difficult but necessary if the cycle of violence
and counter-violent reactions is to be halted. Andreas D'Souza and Diane
D'Souza, who are working to heal hatreds among Muslim victims of violence in
India, point out that we tend mentally to divide society into opposing camps:

*In our world today, particularly in Western countries, we are tending to demonize
the other. It is "us," the sane and balanced, against "them," the demented, violent,
and inhuman. We must resist this attempt to polarize "the good" and "the bad,"
for it leads to complacency at best, and to the rationalization of violence, death,
and destruction at worst.[16]*

However, embedded within religions themselves is the basis for harmony, for all
teach messages of love and self-control rather than murderous passions.

Religion and social issues

Within every religion, there are contemporary attempts to bring religious perspectives to bear on the critical issues facing humanity. Today we are facing new
issues that were not directly addressed by older teachings, such as the ethics of
genetic engineering. And some issues have reached critical proportions in our
times, such as terrorism, the gap between rich and poor, and the deterioration of
the natural environment. Many religious groups, including indigenous spiritual
traditions, sent representatives to the huge 1992 Earth Summit in Rio de Janeiro,
lobbying for careful environmental stewardship. At the 1994 Cairo Conference
on Population and Development, Christian and Muslim delegations took strong
stands on behalf of just economic development and education and health care for
women rather than forced population control or abortion as means of stabilizing
population. Buddhists are spearheading efforts to ban landmines. Hindus and
Muslims are trying to stop the spread of immoral, violent, and cynical mass media
communications, to help protect the minds of the young. Racism and violence are
challenging people of all faiths to deepen their spiritual understanding and to
ponder appropriate responses to these scourges. Poverty and injustice in societies
are being addressed by many religious groups. South Africa, long known for
oppression and injustice, has become an example of peace and forgiveness under
its new leadership, with an overtly spiritual basis. The Catholic liberation theologian Gustavo Gutierrez asserts:

*In the last analysis, poverty means an unjust and early death. Now everything is
subordinated to market economies, without taking into consideration the social
consequences for the weakest. People say, for example, that in business there are
no friends. Solidarity is out of fashion. We need to build a culture of love, through
respect of the human being, of the whole of creation. We must practice a justice
inspired by love. Justice is the basis of true peace. We must, sisters and brothers,*

Jimmy Carter

When Jimmy Carter left the White House after being the President of the United States from 1977 to 1981, he did not retire from public service. He went on to found the Habitat for Humanity, which helps to build houses for the poor, and the Carter Center, which works on many fronts to help governments solve conflict through peace talks rather than violence. The Carter Center also promotes development, health, and human rights in many countries. Jimmy Carter explains the philosophy that underlies all these efforts:

Bringing deaths and injuries, massive destruction of property, and the interruption of normal law and order, war is the greatest violation of basic human rights that one people can inflict upon another. Starvation, exposure, and disease caused by war often produce more casualties than the fighting itself. War touches not only soldiers in battle and leaders in government but ordinary citizens—men, women, and children—as well.

Because of numerous bloody struggles [in our times, many of them in poor countries], millions of people have lost their homes, livelihoods, and opportunities for medical care and education. Children in particular suffer—many do not know when to expect their next meal, whether they will ever attend school again, or where their parents might be.

It is one thing to say that we each have the right not to be killed. It is another to say that we each have the right to live comfortably, with adequate food, health care, shelter, education, and opportunities for employment. It is even more powerful to say that we each have the right to worship as we choose, to say what we choose, and to be governed by leaders we choose. And perhaps the most powerful statement of all is to say that we each hold these rights equally—that no one person is more entitled to any of these rights than the next, regardless of his or her sex, race, or station in life.[17]

Ex-President Carter is a highly respected and effective statesman whose personal intervention and reconciliation efforts during his presidency brought the Camp David peace accords between the leaders of Egypt and Israel. Nevertheless, he has not always been successful in accomplishing his high ideals. For instance, he thought his public life was humiliatingly finished when he was defeated in his first race for the governorship of Georgia by "an avowed segregationist, whose symbol was a pick handle that he used to drive potential black customers from the door of his restaurant in Atlanta."[18] But Jimmy Carter is a deeply religious person, a committed Christian who has been teaching Bible study classes since he was a young adult. He brings a strong grounding in faith to the inevitable trials and setbacks in life. He asserts:

Faith is the gift of God, and it is more precious than gold; to face life, we should put on the shield of faith, the breastplate of faith and love. ... Without a central core of beliefs or standards by which to live, we may never experience the challenge and excitement of seeking a greater life. We will have ceased to grow, like Jesus, "strong in spirit, filled with wisdom; and the grace of God upon him" (Luke 2:4).[19]

In the midst of difficulties, Jimmy Carter is comforted by a personal sense of the presence of God. He reflects:

In addition to the intellectual realization of a supreme being, we have a purely subjective need to meet a personal yearning. We have an innate desire to relate to the all-knowing, the all-powerful, and the ever-present—to some entity that transcends ourselves. I am grateful and happy when I feel the presence of God within me, as a tangible influence on my thoughts and on the ultimate standards of my life. It is reassuring to me to know that God will always be with me and cares for me. I think of the words of Isaiah: "When you pass through the waters, I will be with you; and through the rivers, they shall not overwhelm you; when you walk through fire you shall not be burned, and the flame shall not consume you; For I am the Lord your God. ... You are precious in my sight, and honoured, and I love you" (Isaiah 42: 2–4).

Our Sunday school class often becomes involved in a discussion about how to achieve this closeness to God. Except in moments of crisis, when we reach desperately for some sustaining force, the relationship requires some effort on our part, some reaching out.[20]

Jimmy Carter recommends that this reaching out to God should include some introspection about what we are making of our lifetime, no matter how old or young we may be—how we interact with others, whether we are happy with our decisions, whether our life is "meaningful, or at least interesting and gratifying." He cites a sermon delivered at the funeral for the mother of Reverend Martin Luther King:

Rev. Otis Moss from Cleveland, Ohio, preached a brief but remarkable sermon about "the little dash in between." He said there would be a marker on Mrs. King's grave, with her name and a couple of dates—when she was born and when she died—and a little dash in between. He said he didn't want to talk about when she was born, or when she died, but about that little dash. He described Mrs. King's great life and then shifted his attention to the audience. He said that everybody has what might be considered just a tiny dash but that to us, with God, it is everything. The question is, What do we do with that little dash in between, which represents our life on earth?

After we satisfy all our personal needs and desires, then what? It is not through gratifying physical needs that we find our purpose in life. We shouldn't carry around what we are in a closed jar and use a medicine dropper to expend it. The "little dash" can be a glorious experience.[21]

avoid being sorry for or comforting the poor. We must wish to be friends of the poor in the world.[22]

In 1994 and 1995, Buddhists of the Nipponzan Myohoji order sponsored an Interfaith Pilgrimage for Peace and Life, in which approximately one hundred people from many countries and many faiths walked from Auschwitz in Poland to Hiroshima and Nagasaki in Japan to commemorate the fiftieth anniversary of the end of World War II, with personal witness to the need for non-violence and respect for all of life. The group walked and chanted through many areas of conflict, including former Yugoslavia, Israel, Iraq, and Cambodia, with considerable impact both on the participants and those they met along the way. Martha Penzer, a Quaker from Boston who made the pilgrimage, reflects:

What united us in this was our hunger, our yearning, our searching to find a better way, our acknowledgement that in the fifty years since that war humanity had to face itself and make reckoning with the demonic forces in us. . . . We should never forget that there are people struggling for reconciliation. The supreme grace of it is when we don't run away and get stuck in our own enmities, when we allow God to enter into those enmities and transform them. I think that is the task of religious people—not that we are perfected, by any means, but that we are willing to say to God, "I am just a work in progress and I need Your help."[23]

The terrorist attacks on the United States in 2001 brought a sea change in ways of thinking in that country and have shaken people around the world into re-examining the underlying motives of their governments, as well as their own assumptions. It may be that the kind of truthfulness and altruism that can ultimately lead to greater harmony is beginning to sprout.

Marcus Braybrooke, patron of the Interfaith Centre, reports:

On September 11, a young Muslim from Pakistan was evacuated from the World Trade Center where he worked. He saw a dark cloud coming towards him. Trying to escape, he fell. A Hasidic Jew held out his hand, saying, "Brother, there's a cloud of glass coming at us, grab my hand, let's get the hell out of here."

People of all faiths have held hands to support and comfort each other and to join together in prayer. Can we continue to hold hands as we shape a world society in which all people share to the full the precious gift of life? . . .

As Anne Frank wrote in her diary at the age of fourteen, "How wonderful it is that nobody need wait a single moment before beginning to improve the world."[24]

Religion and materialism

All religions teach that one should not hurt others, should not lie, should not steal, should not usurp others' rights, should not be greedy, but rather should be unselfish, considerate, and helpful to others, and humble before the Unseen. These universal spiritual principles were swamped by the expansion of capitalism in the twentieth century, as the profit motive triumphed as the most important value in economies around the world.

Many people live by material greed alone, with no further meaning to their lives. As Vaclav Havel, President of the Czech Republic, wrote to his wife Olga when he was imprisoned for his courageous human rights work:

The person who has completely lost all sense of the meaning of life is merely vegetating and doesn't mind it; he lives like a parasite and doesn't mind it; he is entirely absorbed in the problem of his own metabolism and essentially nothing beyond that interests him: other people, society, the world, Being—for him they are all simply things to be either consumed or avoided or turned into a comfortable place to make his bed. Everything meaningful in life, though it may assume the most dramatic form of questioning and doubting, is distinguished by a certain transcendence of individual human existence. Only by looking outward ... does one really become a person, a creator of the "order of the spirit," a being capable of a miracle: the re-creation of the world.[25]

By the end of the twentieth century, many individuals and corporations stepped back to consider how to reconcile spiritual motives with earning a living. Books on voluntary simplicity have proliferated on the bestseller lists. Typically, they encourage the relatively wealthy to cut back on their breakneck work pace for the sake of their own spiritual peace, and to cut back on unnecessary individual expenditures for the sake of sharing with others. Many people are also taking a second look at the effect of economic systems. Liberal capitalism, for example, is being reinterpreted not as a means of allowing industrious people to climb out of poverty, but as a potentially amoral system. In free market capitalism, as Pope Paul VI commented: "The right to the means of production is absolute. It has no limits. It has no social obligation."[26]

A new social consciousness, which reflects religious values, is beginning to enter some workplaces. Professor Syed Anwar Kabir, a faithful Muslim on the faculty of the Management Development Institute in New Delhi, India, teaches his managerial students to do mind-stilling meditation daily in order to listen to their own conscience and make ethical choices from a base of inner tranquility. He observes:

Businessmen themselves say that the uninhibited, reckless way in which you accumulate wealth will not give you a good name. For a company to survive in a highly competitive world in the long term means creating an image in the mind of the public, creating good will, creating its own impact and niche in the market. ... If you treat human beings not as means but also as ends, naturally it is reflected in your products and services and creates an impact in the world of consumers so that they also come to respect the company's principles and strategies.[27]

However, at the beginning of the twenty-first century, power-mongering, self interest, and corruption are at the forefront of political activities; honesty, altruism, service, harmony, justice, and the public good are not the primary motivating forces in most government actions.

Religion and the future of humanity

The new century has dawned with flagrant materialistic greed, crime, amorality, ethnic hatreds, violence, and family crises, together with ignorant demonizing,

Drawing inspiration from the past in order to greet the future, contemporary Russians gather in a Moscow park to celebrate the Spring Equinox according to ancient Slavic rites.

power-mongering, and moneymaking in religions themselves. But being sick, perhaps the world is ready to be cured. There is indeed a global increase in interest in religion, particularly in new forms of traditional religions as well as new religious movements.

The negative signs of our times are interpreted by some as the darkness before the dawn, chaos from which will emerge a new and greater order. As Yasuhiro Nakasone, former Prime Minister of Japan, optimistically states: "Perhaps we are undergoing a trial—a test that will facilitate the rebirth of the human race."[28]

Baba Virsa Singh confidently asserts that sweeping change in the hearts and actions of humanity is not difficult at all for the One who has created the entire cosmos. He reminds people of the value of practicing the eternal spiritual teachings and advises them to ignore religious leaders who do not practice what they preach and who have led people away from the truth because they themselves are not connected to it. He says that truth and love are ultimately very powerful:

Anticipate that day when God transforms the world, and the Truth, which is now hidden, comes out and starts working among the people again. That day is upon us.[29]

At the beginning of the twenty-first century, the world stage is ready for a true moral and spiritual revolution, in which people of every faith truly begin to practice in their own lives what their prophets have taught. The words of the late French sage Teilhard de Chardin are often quoted in these apocalyptic days:

Some day, after mastering the winds, the waves, the tides, and gravity, we shall harness for God the energies of love. And then, for the second time in the history of the world, man will have discovered fire.

Suggested reading

Barney, Gerald O. and others, *Threshold 2000: Critical Issues and Spiritual Values for a Global Age*, Ada, Michigan: CoNexus Press, 2000. Projections of environmental and social crises in the twenty-first century, with multi-faith spiritual perspectives that may offer solutions.

Beversluis, Joel V., ed., *A Sourcebook for Earth's Community of Religions*, second edition, Grand Rapids, Michigan: 1995. Essays on contemporary issues, reflections on how religious people might come together in harmony, and resources guides for religious education, first prepared for the 1993 Chicago Parliament of the World's Religions.

Braybrooke, Marcus, *Faith and Interfaith in a Global Age*, Grand Rapids, Michigan: CoNexus Press and Oxford: Braybrooke Press, 1998. One of the world's central interfaith coordinators surveys the interfaith movement at the turn of the century.

Cenkner, William, *Evil and the Response of World Religion*, St. Paul, Minnesota: Paragon House, 1997. Leading scholars from many religions explore the diversity of religious beliefs about a major spiritual issue: Why is there evil and suffering in the world?

Fisher, Mary Pat and Bailey, Lee W., *An Anthology of Living Religions*, Upper Saddle River, New Jersey: Prentice Hall, 2000. Readings from the various religions, following the outline of this book, to deepen understanding of the material herein.

Forward, Martin, *Ultimate Visions: Reflections on the Religions we Choose*, Oxford: Oneworld Publications, 1995. Interesting personal essays by scholars and leaders of many religions, reflecting upon why they like their religion and how it can contribute to a future of harmony among all religions.

Kelsay, John and Sumner, B. Twiss, eds., *Religion and Human Rights*, New York: The Project on Religion and Human Rights, 1994. A sensitive introduction to conflicts caused by religious "fundamentalism," with positive suggestions as to the potential of religions for insuring human rights.

Khan, Hazrat Inayat, *The Unity of Religious Ideals*, New Lebanon, New York: Sufi Order Publications, 1927, 1979. A master of Sufi mysticism explores the underlying themes in the religious quest that are common to all religions.

Swidler, Leonard, ed., *Toward a Universal Theology of Religion*, Maryknoll, New York: Orbis Books, 1988. Leaders in the evolving interfaith dialogue grapple with the issues of transcending differences.

Tobias, Michael, Morrison, Jane, and Gray, Bettina, eds., *A Parliament of Souls: In Search of Global Spirituality*, Ada, Michigan: CoNexus Press, 1994. Interviews with twenty-eight spiritual leaders from the 1993 Parliament of the World's Religions, plus supplementary material.

World Scripture: A Comparative Anthology of Sacred Texts, New York: Paragon House/International Religious Foundation, 1991. A thematic compendium of appealing excerpts from the scriptures and oral traditions of many religions, in excellent translations selected by major scholars.

Key terms

modernism	Twentieth-century values including individualism, preference for change rather than continuity, quantity rather than quality, efficiency, pragmatism, and profiteering, all seen by some as threatening the existence of traditional religious values.
interfaith dialogue	Appreciative communication between people of different religions.

exclusivism   The idea that one's own religion is the only valid way.
inclusivism   The idea that all religions can be accommodated within one religion.
pluralism   An appreciation of the diversity of religions.

Study questions

1 Describe the current conflict between the expansion of religious pluralism in various nations and the efforts to harden religious boundaries, such as restricting minority religions, ethnic wars, and fundamentalism.
2 Explain five major themes in interfaith movement. Discuss the nature of the divine, the mind, prophets, common elements, and scriptural authority.
3 What initiatives are being undertaken to strengthen interfaith dialogue? First distinguish between exclusivism, inclusivism, and pluralism. Discuss Pannikar, Keating, Assisi, Oxford, Moscow, Vivekananda, fair representation, scarves, Britain, Mayfair, Israel, and India.
4 Explain this chapter's discussion about what major social issues religions are confronting today. Discuss biology, violence, ecology, weapons, media, Gutierrez, Auschwitz, Carter, and Braybrooke.
5 What do the spiritual leaders mentioned in this chapter say about materialism and future solutions?

Refer to Pearson/Prentice Hall's **TIME Special Edition: World Religions** magazine for current articles on topics related to many of the world's religions:

• *The Impact of Religion: Cult Shock; Relaxing in a Labyrinth; Will Politicians Matter?; Essay—God Is Not On My Side. Or Yours.*

Chapter 13 discusses not only emerging religions, and the blending of traditional religions, but also an overview of religion and its importance to human experience. For further research in this area, use the tools available to you in Research Navigator:

As you investigate New Religious Movements, consider this question: "Why do humans seem to need religion?"

• **Ebsco's ContentSelect:** Search in the Religion database using terms such as "Pluralism," "Social Issues."
• **Link Library:** Search in the Religion database under the category: "Interfaith Relations."
• **The *New York Times* on the Web:** Search in the Religious Studies and all other databases for current articles on related topics.

NOTES

CHAPTER ONE
RELIGIOUS RESPONSES

1 Martin Luther, as quoted in Gordon Rupp, "Luther and the Reformation," in Joel Hurstfield, ed., *The Reformation Crisis*, New York: Harper & Row, 1966, p. 23.

2 William James, *The Varieties of Religious Experience*, New York: New American Library, 1958, p. 298.

3 AE (George William Russell), *The Candle of Vision*, Wheaton, Illinois: The Theosophical Publishing House, 1974, pp. 8–9.

4 John White, "An Interview with Nona Coxhead: The Science of Mysticism—Transcendental Bliss in Everyday Life," *Science of Mind*, September 1986, pp. 14, 70.

5 Abu Yazid, as quoted in R. C. Zaehner, *Hindu and Muslim Mysticism*, London: University of London, The Athalone Press, 1960, p. 105.

6 Rudolf Otto, *The Idea of the Holy*, translated by John W. Harvey, New York: Oxford University Press, 1958, p. 1.

7 Sallie McFague, *Models of God: Theology for an Ecological, Nuclear Age*, Philadelphia: Fortress Press, 1987, p. 133.

8 *Marx and Engels on Religion*, Introduction by Reinhold Niebuhr, New York: Schocken Books, 1964, pp. viii–ix.

9 As quoted by Huston Smith, "The Future of God in Human Experience," *Dialogue and Alliance*, vol. 5, no. 2, Summer 1991, p. 11.

10 Maimonides, "Guide for the Perplexed," 1, 59, as quoted in Louis Jacobs, *Jewish Ethics, Philosophy, and Mysticism*, New York: Behrman House, 1969, p. 80.

11 Guru Gobind Singh, *Jaap Sahib*, English translation by Surendra Nath, New Delhi: Gobind Sadan, 1992, verses 7, 29–31.

12 Bede Griffiths, *Return to the Center*, Springfield, Illinois: Templegate, 1977, p. 71.

13 Antony Fernando, "Outlining the Characteristics of the Ideal Individual," paper for the Inter-Religious Federation for World Peace conference, Seoul, Korea, August 20–27, 1995, p. 9.

14 Pir Vilayat Inayat Khan, "The Significance of Religion to Human Issues in the Light of the Universal Norms of Mystical Experience," *The World Religions Speak on the Relevance of Religion in the Modern World*, Finley P. Ounne, Jr., ed., The Hague: Junk, 1970, p. 145.

15 Akka Mahadevi, in A. K. Ramanujan, *Speaking of Shiva*, London: Penguin, 1973: vol. 17, p.116, quoted in Vijaya Ramaswamy, *Walking Naked: Women, Society, Spirituality in South India*, Shimla, India: Indian Institute of Advanced Study, 1997, p. 33.

16 Lame Deer, "How the Sioux Came to Be," in Richard Erdoes and Alfonso Ortiz, *American Indian Myths and Legends*, New York: Pantheon Books, 1984, pp. 93–95.

17 Joseph Campbell, *The Hero with a Thousand Faces*; second edition, Princeton, New Jersey: Princeton University Press, 1972, p. 29.

18 Rev. Valson Thampu, "Religious Fundamentalisms in India Today," *Indian Currents*, November 2, 1995, p. 3.

19 Karl Marx, from "Contribution to the Critique of Hegel's Philosophy of Right," 1884, *Karl Marx, Early Writings*, translated and edited by T. B. Bottomore, London: C. A. Watts and Co., 1963, pp. 43–44; Capital, vol. 1, 1867, translated by Samuel Moore and Edward Aveling, F. Engels, ed., London: Lawrence & Wishart, 1961, p. 79; "The Communism of the Paper 'Rheinischer Beobachter'," *On Religion*, London: Lawrence & Wishart, undated, pp. 83–84.

20 Karl Marx, "Religion as the Opium of the People," in Karl Marx and Friedrich Engels, *On Religions*, Moscow: Foreign Language Publishing House, 1955, p. 42.

21 Quoted in John Gliedman, "Mind and Matter," *Science Digest*, March 1983, p. 72.

22 Ilya Prigogine, abstract for "The Quest for Certainty," Conference on a New Space for Culture and Society, New Ideas in Science and Art, November 19–23, 1996.

23 Murray Gell-Mann, in Kitty Ferguson, Stephen Hawking: *Quest for a Theory of Everything*, London: Bantam Press, 1992, p. 30.

24 Albert Einstein, *The World As I See It*, New York: Wisdom Library, 1979; *Ideas and Opinions*, translated by Sonja Bargmann, New York: Crown Publishers, 1954.

25 Kenneth R. Miller, "Finding Darwin's God: The New Battle over Evolution," Keynote Address at Science Teaching and the Search for Origins, April 14–15, 2000, The University of Kansas, p. 10 on www.aaas.org/spp/dser/evolution/science/kennethmiller.

26 Francis Collins, in "Science and God: A Warming Trend?" *Science*, vol. 277, August 15, 1997, p. 892.

27 Fred Hoyle, quoted in Patrick Glynn, *God, the Evidence*, Rocklin, California: Prima Publishing, 1997.

28 Stephen Hawking, *A Brief History of Time: From the Big Bang to Black Holes*, London: Bantam Press, 1988.

29 Quoted in Merlin Stone, *When God was a Woman*, San Diego, California: Harcourt Brace Jovanovich, 1976, p. x.

30 Rosemary Radford Ruether, *Woman-Church: Theology and Practice of Feminist Liturgical Communities*, San Francisco: Harper & Row, 1985, p. 3.

31 Randolph C. Byrd, "Positive Therapeutic Effects of Intercessory Prayer in a Coronary Care Unit Population," *Southern Medical Journal* 81–7, July 1988, pp. 826–29.

32 Tenzin Gyatso, "The Monk in the Lab," New York Times, April 26, 2003, p. A29.

33 Mata Amritanandamayi, *Awaken Children!* vol. IV, Amritapuri, Kerala, India: Mata Amritanandamayi Mission Trust, 1992, pp. 103–104.

34 Jiddu Krishnamurti, *The Awakening of Intelligence*, New York: Harper & Row, 1973, p. 90

35 Buddha, *The Dhammapada*, translated by P. Lal, 162/92 Lake Gardens, Calcutta, 700045 India. (Originally published by Farrar, Straus & Giroux, 1967, p. 97.) Reprinted by permission of P. Lal.

36 Mahatma Gandhi, quoted in Eknath Easwaran, *Gandhi the Man*, Petaluma, California: Nilgiri Press, 1978, p. 121.

37 *The Bhagavad-Gita*, portions of Chapter 2, translated by Eknath Easwaran, quoted in *Easwaran*, op. cit., pp. 121–122.

38 Excerpted from Agnes Collard, in "The Face of God," *Life*, December 1990, p. 49

39 Philippians 4:7, *The Holy Bible*, King James Version.

40 *Brihadaranyaka Upanishad*, Fourth Adhyaya, Fourth Brahmana, 20, 13, translated by F. Max Müller, *Sacred Books of the East*, vol. 15, Oxford: Oxford University Press, 1884, pp. 178–179.

41 William James, op. cit., p.49.

42 From *The Kabir Book* by Robert Bly, copyright 1971, 1977 by Robert Bly, copyright 1977 by Seventies Press. Reprinted by permission of Beacon Press.

43 William Wordsworth, "Ode on Intimations of Immortality from Recollections of Early Childhood."

44 John Welwood, "Principles of Inner Work: Psychological and Spiritual," *The Journal of Transpersonal Psychology*, 1984, vol. 16, no. 1, pp. 64–65.

45 Dr. Syed Z. Abedin, "Let There be Light," *Saudi Gazette*, Jeddah, June 1992, reprinted in *Council for a Parliament of the World's Religions Newsletter*, vol. 4, no. 2, August 1992, p. 2.

CHAPTER TWO
INDIGENOUS SACRED WAYS

1 Vine Deloria, Jr., *God is Red*, New York: Grosset & Dunlap, 1973, p. 267.

2 Lorraine Mafi Williams, personal communication, September 16, 1988.

3 Gerhardus Cornelius Oosthuizen, "The Place of Traditional Religion in Contemporary South Africa," in Jacob K. Olupona, *African Traditional Religions in Contemporary Society*, New York: Paragon House, 1991, p. 36.

4 Quoted by Bob Masla, "The Healing Art of the Huichol Indians," Many Hands: Resources for Personal and Social Transformation," Fall 1988, p. 30.

5 George Tinker, *Missionary Conquest: The Gospel and Native American Genocide*, Minneapolis: Fortress Press, 1993, p. 122.

6 Wilmer Stampede Mesteth (Oglala Lakota), Darrell Standing Elk (Sicangu Lakota), and Phyllis Swift Hawk (Kul Wicasa Lakota), "Declaration of War Against Exploiters of Lakota Spirituality," undated handbill reproduced on http://puffin.creighton,edu/lakota/war.html, April 19, 2001.

7 John (Fire) Lame Deer and Richard Erdoes, *Lame Deer: Seeker of Visions*, New York: Pocket Books, 1972, p. 100.

8 Knud Rasmussen, *Across Arctic America*, New York: G. P. Putnam's Sons, 1927, p. 386.

9 Interview with Rev. William Kingsley Opoku, August 1992.

10 Clyde Ford, *The Hero with an African Face: Mythical Wisdom of Traditional Africa*, New York: Bantam Books, 2000, p. 146.

11 Adapted from a Yoruba story told by Deidre L. Badejo. Deidre L. Badejo, "Osun Seegesi: The Deified Power of African Women and the Social Ideal," paper presented at the Inter-Religious Federation for World Peace Conference, Seoul, Korea, August 20–27, 1995.

12 Josiah U. Young III, "Out of Africa: African Traditional Religion and African Theology," in *World Religions and Human Liberation*, Dan Cohn-Sherbok, ed., Maryknoll, New York: Orbis Books, 1992, p. 93.

13 Jo Agguisho/Oren R. Lyons, spokesman for the Traditional Elders Circle, Wolf Clan, Onondaga Nation, Haudenosaunee, Six Nations Iroquois Confederacy, from the speech to the Fourth World Wilderness Conference, September 11, 1987, p. 2.

14 Quoted in Keith Basso, *Wisdom Sits in Places: Landscape and Language among the Western Apache*, Albuquerque: University of New Mexico Press, 1996, p. 127.

15 Audrey Shenandoah, "A Tradition of Thanksgiving," in Steven C. Rockefeller and John E. Elder, *Spirit and Nature: Why the Environment is a Religious Issue*, Boston: Beacon Press, 1992, p. 20.

16 Bill Neidjie, *Speaking for the Earth: Nature's Law and the Aboriginal Way*, Washington: Center for Respect of Life and Environment, 1991, pp. 40–41. Reprinted from *Kakadu Man* by Big Bill Neidjie, Stephen Davis, and Allan Fox, Northryde, New South Wales, Australia: Angus and Robertson.

17 Jaime de Angulo, "Indians in Overalls," *Hudson Review*, II, 1950, p. 372.

18 Kahu Kawai'i, interviewed by Mark Bochrach in *The Source*, as quoted in Hinduism Today, December 1988, p. 18.

19 Quoted in Matthew Fox, "Native teachings: Spirituality with power," *Creation*, January/February 1987, vol. 2, no. 6.

20 John (Fire) Lame Deer and Richard Erdoes, op. cit., p. 116.

21 Tlakaelel, talk at Interface, Watertown, Massachusetts, April 15, 1988.

22 As quoted in Georges Niangoran-Bouah, "The Talking Drum: A Traditional African Instrument of Liturgy and of Meditation with the Sacred," in Jacob K. Olupona, ed., *African Traditional Religions in Contemporary Society*, New York: Paragon House, 1991, pp. 86–87.

23 Leonard Crow Dog and Richard Erdoes, *The Eye of the Heart*, unpublished manuscript, quoted by Joan Halifax, *Shamanic Voices: A Survey of Visionary Narratives*, New York: E. P. Dutton, 1979, p. 77.

24 Quoted in John Neihardt, *Black Elk Speaks 1932*, Lincoln, Nebraska: University of Nebraska Press, 1961, pp. 208–209.

25 Mado (Patrice) Somé, interviewed September. 14, 1989.

26 John (Fire) Lame Deer with Richard Erdoes, op. cit., pp. 145–146.

27 From an interview conducted for this book by Tatiana Kuznetsova.

28 Igjugarjuk, in Knud Rasmussen, *Intellectual Culture of the Hudson Bay Eskimos*, report of the Fifth Thule Expedition, 1921–1924, translated by W. E. Calvert, vol. 7, Copenhagen: Gyldendal, 1930, p. 52.

29 Tsering, in Ian Baker, "Shaman's Quest," *Hinduism Today*, November 1997, p. 23.

30 Ruth M. Underhill, *Papago Woman*, New York: Holt, Rinehart and Winston, 1979, p. 9.

31 Dhyani Ywahoo, personal communication, May 31, 1988.

32 In Mark St. Pierre and Tilda Long Soldier, *Walking in the Sacred Manner*, New York: Simon and Schuster, 1995, pp. 69–70.

33 Dhyani Ywahoo, *Voices of our Ancestors*, Boston: Shambhala Publications, 1987, p. 89.

34 Leonard Crow Dog and Richard Erdoes, in Joan Halifax, *Shamanic Voices*, op. cit., p. 77.

35 Interview with Wande Abimbola, August 6, 1992.

36 In Jean-Guy Goulet, *Ways of Knowing: Experience, Knowledge, and Power among the Dene Tha*, Lincon, University of Nebraska Press, 1998, p. 73.

37 Tlakaelel, op. cit.

38 Quoted by Black Elk in Joseph Epes Brown, *The Sacred Pipe*, op. cit., p. 71.

39 In James Treat, ed., *Native and Christian: Indigenous Voices on Religious Identity in the United States and Canada*, New York: Routledge, 1996, p. 52.

40 "Aborigine aiming to be first native woman MP," AFP, *Asian Age*, September 30, 1998, p. 5.

41 In Lee Romney and James F. Smith, "Crowds hail Zapatistas' Arrival in Mexico City," *Los Angeles Times*, March 13, 2001.

42 Jameson Kurasha, "Plato and the Tortoise: A Case for the death of ideas in favour of peace and life?", paper presented at Assembly of the World's Religions, Seoul, Korea, August 1992, pp. 4–5.

43 Jace Weaver, Jace Weaver, ed., *Native American Religious Identity: Unforgotten Gods*, Maryknoll, New York: Orbis Books, 1998.

44 Winona LaDuke, *Last Standing Woman*, Stillwater, Minnesota: Voyageur Press, 1997, p. 17.

45 Winona LaDuke, as quoted by Jamie Marks, "A campaign-less campaign," *Becker County Record*, September 8, 1996, p. 1A.

46 Winona LaDuke, as quoted by Willmar Thorkelson, "Indians ask for help in regaining land," *Post-Bulletin*, Rochester, Minnesota.

47 Winona LaDuke, *Last Standing Woman*, op. cit., p. 299.

48 Richard Allen, as quoted by Carol Morello, "Native American Roots, Once Hidden, Now Embraced," Washington Post, April 7, 2001, page A01.

49 "The Hopi Message to the United Nations General Assembly," submitted by Thomas Banyacya, Kykyotsmovi, Arizona, December 10, 1992, reprinted on http://www.alphacdc.com/banyacya/un92.html

50 Rigoberta Menchú, quoted in Art Davidson, *Endangered Peoples*, San Francisco: Sierra Club Books, 1994, p. ix.

CHAPTER THREE
HINDUISM

1 Sukta-yajur-veda XXVI, 3, as explained by Sai Baba in *Vision of the Divine* by Eruch B. Fanibunda, Bombay: E. B. Fanibunda, 1976.

2 *The Upanishads*, translated by Swami Prabhavananda and Frederick Manchester, The Vedanta Society of Southern California, New York: Mentor Books, 1957.

3 *Chandogya Upanishad*, ibid., p. 46.

4 *Brihadaranyaka Upanishad*, ibid.

5 *The Patanjala Yogasutra with Vyasa Commentary*, translated from Sanskrit into English by Bengali Baba, second edition, Poona, India: N. R. Bargawa, 1949, pp. 96–97.

6 Swami Sivananda, *Dhyana Yoga*, fourth edition, Shivanandanagar, India: The Divine Life Society, 1981, p. 67.

7 Ramana Maharshi, *The Spiritual Teaching of Ramana Maharshi*, Boston: Shambhala, 1972, pp. 4, 6.

8 Swami Vivekananda, *Karma-Yoga and Bhakti-Yoga*, New York: Ramakrishna-Vivekananda Center, 1982, p. 32.

9 *Bhagavad-Gita as It Is*, op. cit., Chapter 2:49 (p. 36), Chapter 5:8, p. 12.

10 Bhakta Nam Dev, as included in Sri Guru Granth Sahib, p. 693, adapted from the translation by Manmohan Singh, Amritsar, India: Shiromani Gurdwara Parbandhak Committee, 1989.

11 Bhakta Ravi Das, as included in Sri Guru Granth Sahib, p. 694, op. cit.

12 Mirabai, *Mira Bai and Her Padas*, English translation by Krishna P. Bahadur, Delhi: Munshiram Manoharlal Publishers Pvt. Ltd., 1998, no. 46, pp. 76–77.

13 Ramakrishna, quoted in Carl Jung's introduction to *The Spiritual Teaching of Ramana Maharshi*, op. cit., p. viii.

14 Leela Arjunwadkar, "Ecological Awareness in Indian Tradition (Specially as Reflected in Sanskrit Literature)," paper presented at Assembly of the World's Religions, Seoul, Korea, August 24–31, 1992, p. 4.

15 *The Thousand Names of the Divine Mother: Sri Lalita Sahasranama*, with commentary by T. V. Narayana Menon, English translation by Dr. M. N. Namboodiri, Amritapuri, Kerala, India: Mata Amritanandamayi Math, 1996, verses 1–2, 8, 158–161, 220–224, pp. 5–6, 11, 82–3, 106–107.

16 Swami Sivasiva Palani, personal communication, October 26, 1989.

17 Appar, as quoted in R. de Smet and J. Neuner, eds., *Religious Hinduism*, fourth edition, Bangalore, India: St. Paul's Society, 1996, p. 321.

18 T. M. P. Mahadevan, *Outlines of Hinduism*, second edition, Bombay: Chetana Ltd., 1960, p. 24.

19 A condensation by Heinrich Zimmer of the *Vishnu Purana*, Book IV, Chapter 24, translated by H. H. Wilson, London, 1840, in *Zimmer's Myths and Symbols in Indian Art and Civilization*, New York: Pantheon Books, 1946, p. 15.

20 Uttara Kandam, *Ramayana*, third edition, as told by Swami Chidbhavananda, Tiriuuparaitturai, India: Tapovanam Printing School, 1978, pp. 198–199.

21 Chapter III:30, p. 57. All quotes from the *Bhagavad-Gita* are from *Bhagavad-Gita as It Is*, translated by A. C. Bhaktivedanta Swami Prabhupada, New York: Copyright 1972, The Bhaktivedanta Book Trust. Reproduced with permission of The Bhaktivedanta Book Trust International.

22 Ibid., III:30, p. 57.

23 Ibid., IV:3, p. 64.

24 Ibid., IV:7–8, pp. 68–69.

25 Ibid., VII:7–8, 12, pp. 126, 128.

26 Ibid., IX:26, p. 157.

27 Srimad-Bhagavatam, second canto, "The Cosmic Manifestation," part one, chapter 6:3 and 1:39, translated by A. C. Bhaktivedanta Swami Prabhupada, New York: Bhaktivedanta Book Trust, 1972, pp. 59 and 275–276.

28 Swami Vivekananda, *The Complete Works of Swami Vivekananda*, vol. III, Mayavati, India: Advaita Ashrama, 1948, p. 259.

29 Swami Palani, op. cit.

30 The Code of Manu, IV.43, as quoted in Roderick Hindery, *Comparative Ethics in Hindu and Buddhist Traditions*, second edition, Delhi: Motilal Banarsidass Publishers, 1996, p. 85.

31 *Thus Spake Sri Ramakrishna*, fifth edition, Madras: Sri Ramakrishna Math, 1980, p. 54.

32 Swami Prajnananda, introduction to *Light on the Path*, Swami Muktananda, South Fallsburg, New York: SYDA Foundation, 1981, p. x.

33 William F. Fisher, "Sacred Rivers, Sacred Dams: Competing Visions of Social Justice and Sustainable Development along the Narmada," in Christopher Key Chapple, and Mary Evelyn Tucker, eds., *Hinduism and Ecology*, Boston: Harvard University Press, 2000, p. 413.

34 Ibid., p.410.

35 Aditi Sengupta De, "The 'holy' mess," c/o editor@ip.eth.net, July 31, 2000.

36 "Kumbha Mela," *Hinduism Today*, September 1998, p. 32.

37 Robert N. Minor, "Sarvepalli Radhakrishnan and 'Hinduism': Defined and Defended," in Robert D. Baird, ed., *Religion in Modern India*, New Delhi: Manohar Publications, 1981, p. 306.

38 Condensed Gospel of Sri Ramakrishna, Mylapore, Madras: Sri Ramakrishna Math, 1911, p. 252.

39 Ramakrishna, as quoted in Swami Vivekananda, *Ramakrishna and His Message*, Howra, India: Swami Abhayananda, Sri Ramakrishna Math, 1971, p. 25.

40 Lectures delivered by Shastriji Pandurang Vaijnath Athavale at the Second World Religious Congress held at Shimizu City, Japan in October 1954.

41 Shri Pandurang Vaijnath Athavale Shastri, *Nivedanam*, third edition, Bombay, 1973, p. 6.

42 Shri Pandurang Shastri Athavale, discourse on January 10, 1988, Bombay, on the occasion of Diamond Jubilee Celebration of Shrimad Bhagvad Geeta Pathshala by Sagar-Putras of the Fishing Community, p. 5.

43 Shahid Faridi, "RSS is teaching distorted history in its schools," *Asian Age*, August 28, 2000, p. 3.

44 VHP tells all missionaries to leave India immediately," *Asian Age*, November 12, 1999, p. 2.

45 Aziz Haniffa, "Southern Baptists apologise for anti-Hindu book," *Asian Age*, November 5, 1999, p. 3.

46 All quotations are from an interview with Dr. Karan Singh, November 17, 1998.

47 Mahatma Gandhi, Young India, 6-12-1928, as quoted in Supreme Court of India Judgement 12 September, 2002, in the matter of The National Curriculum Framework for School Education, 2000, New Delhi: national Council of Educational Research and Training, 2002, p.72.

48 Abbreviation of Indian Supreme Court definition of Hinduism, as itemized in "The DNA of Dharma," *Hinduism Today*, December 1996, p. 33.

49 Karan Singh, *Essays on Hinduism*, second edition, New Delhi: Ratna Sagar, 1990, p. 43.

CHAPTER FOUR
JAINISM

1 *Akaranga Sutra*, translated by Padmanabh S. Jaini in *The Jaina Path of Purification*, Berkeley: University of California Press, 1979, p. 26.

2 Akaranga Sutra, Fourth Lecture, First Lesson, in *Sacred Books of the East*, F. Max Müller, ed., vol. XXII, Jaina Sutras part 1, Oxford: Clarendon Press, 1884, p. 36.

3 R. P. Jain, personal communication.

4 Acharya Tulsi, as quoted in *Anuvibha Reporter*, vol. 3, no. 1, October–December 1997, p. 54.

5 Acharya Tulsi, "World Peace through Self-Restraint," in *Anuvibha Reporter*, Vo. 1, No. 4 and 5, July–December 2003, inside front cover.

6 Samani Sanmati Pragya, interviewed December 11, 1993, Rishikesh, India.

7 Avasyaka Sutra, as quoted in Padmanabh S. Jaini, *Collected Papers on Jaina Studies*, Delhi: Motilal Banarsidass Publishers, 2000, p. 223.

8 Amitagati's Dvatrimsika, 1, as quoted in Padmanabh S. Jaini, ibid., p. 224.

9 Address to the North American Assisi Interfaith Meeting in Wichita, Kansas, October 31, 1988.

10 Gurudev Shree Chitrabhanu, *Twelve Facets of Reality: The Jain Path to Freedom*, New York: Dodd Mead and Company, 1980, p. 93.

11 Lala Sulekh Chand, in "A Rare Renunciation," *The Hindustan Times*, New Delhi, February 17, 1992, p. 5.

12 Muni Amit Sagar, in "A Rare Renunciation," ibid.

13 Padma Agrawal, "Jainism: Mahavira as Man-God," *Dialogue and Alliance*, p. 13.

14 Acharya Kund Kund, *Barasa Anuvekkha (Twelve Contemplations)*, M. K. Dhara Raja, ed., New Delhi: Kund Kund Bharati, 1990, p. 32.

15 Ibid., p. 11.

16 Acharya Tulsi, in S. L. Ghandi, "Acharya Tulsi's Legacy," *Anuvibha Reporter*, vol. 3, no. 1, October–December 1997, p. 2.

17 Acharya Shri Sushil Kumar, personal communication, October 30, 1989.

18 Acharya Mahapragya, as quoted in Prof. R. P. Bhatnagar, "Acharya Mahapragya: A Living Legend," in *Anuvibha Reporter*, January–March 1995, p. 8.

CHAPTER FIVE
BUDDHISM

1 Majjhima-Nikaya I.80.

2 Muhaparinibbana Sutta, Digha Nikaya, 2.99f, 155–156, quoted in *Sources of Indian Tradition*, William Theodore de Bary, ed., New York: Columbia University Press, 1958, pp. 110–111.

3 "A message from Buddhists to the Parliament of the World's Religions," Chicago, September 1993, as quoted in *World Faiths Encounter* no. 7, February 1994, p. 53.

4 Majjhima-Nikaya, "The Lesser Matunkyaputta Sermon," Sutta 63, translated by P. Lal in the introduction to *The Dhammapada*, op. cit., p. 19.

5 Walpola Sri Rahula, *What the Buddha Taught*, revised edition, New York: Grove Press, 1974, p. 17.

6 Ajahn Sumedho, "Now is the Knowing," undated booklet, pp. 21–22.

7 Ajahn Sumedho, cited in Satnacitto Bhikku, ed., *Buddha-nature, World Wide Fund for Nature*, London, 1989.

8 Sigalovada Sutta, Dighanikaya III, pp. 180–193, quoted in H. Saddhatissa, *The Buddha's Way*, New York: George Braziller, 1971, p. 101.

9 *The Dhammapada*, translated by P. Lal, op. cit., p. 152.

10 Ibid., p. 49.

11 Achaan Chah in *A Still Forest Pool*, Jack Kornfield and Paul Breiter, eds., Wheaton, Illinois: Theosophical Publishing House, 1985.

12 Lankavatara Sutra, as quoted in Christopher Key Chapple, "Animals and Environment in the Buddhist Birth Stories," in Mary Evelyn Tucker and Duncan Ryuken Williams, eds., *Buddhism and Ecology*, Cambridge: Harvard University Press, 1997, p. 143.

13 *The Mahavagga* 1.

14 *Suttanipatta* 1093–4.

15 *Majjhima-Nikaya* 1:161–4.

16 *The Dhammapada*, translated by P. Lal, op. cit., pp. 71–72.

17 Samyutta Nikaya, quoted in the introduction to *The Dhammapada*, translated by P. Lal, op. cit., p. 17.

18 Chatsumarn Kabilsingh, *Thai Women in Buddhism*, Berkeley, California: Parallax Press, 1991, p. 25.

19 Joko Beck, as quoted in Lenore Friedman, *Meetings with Remarkable Women*, Boston: Shambhala, 1987, p. 119.

20 *Mahaparinibbana Sutta* ii.142
21 His Holiness the Fourteenth Dalai Lama, speaking on February 15, 1992, in New Delhi, India, Ninth Dharma Celebration of Tushita Meditation Centre.
22 As quoted in Lenore Friedman, *Meetings with Remarkable Women*, op. cit., p. 75.
23 Ruben Habito, *Introducing Buddhism: Varieties of Buddhist Experience*, Maryknoll, New York: Orbis Books, 2005.
24 David W. Chappell, personal communication, July 26, 1995.
25 Lama Drom Tonpa, as quoted in "Gems of Wisdom from the Seventh Dalai Lama," *Snow Lion Newsletter*, vol. 14, no. 4, Fall 1999, p. 14.
26 "Gems of Wisdom from the Seventh Dalai Lama," op. cit., p. 14.
27 Stories and Songs from the Oral Tradition of Jetsun Milarepa, translated by Lama Kunga Rimpoche and Brian Cutillo in *Drinking the Mountain Stream*, New York: Lotsawa, 1978, pp. 56–57.
28 His Holiness the fourteenth Dalai Lama, *My Land and my People*, New York: McGraw-Hill, 1962; Indian edition, New Delhi: Srishti Publishers, 1997, p. 50.
29 His Holiness the fourteenth Dalai Lama, evening address after receiving the Nobel Peace Prize, 1989, in Sidney Piburn, ed., *The Dalai Lama: A Policy of Kindness*, second edition, Ithaca, New York: Snow Lion Publications, 1993, p. 114.
30 Platform Scripture of the Sixth Patriarch, Hui-neng, quoted in *World of the Buddha*, Lucien Stryk, ed., New York: Doubleday Anchor Books, 1969, p. 340.
31 From "Hsin hsin ming" by Sengtsan, third Zen patriarch, translated by Richard B. Clarke.
32 Poems by Chinese Zen master Kuon, translated into English by Urs. App, 1996, www.iijnet.or.jp
33 Roshi Philip Kapleau, *The Three Pillars of Zen*, New York: Anchor Books, 1980, p. 70.
34 Bunan, quoted in *World of the Buddha*, Stryk, op. cit., p. 343.
35 Genshin, The Essentials of Salvation, quoted in William de Bary, ed., *The Buddhist Tradition in India, China, and Japan*, New York: Modern Library, 1969, p. 326.
36 The Most Venerable Nichidatsu Fujii, quoted in a booklet commemorating the dedication for the Peace Pagoda in Leverett, Massachusetts, October 5, 1985.
37 The Most Venerable Nichidatsu Fujii, ibid.
38 "Rissho Kosei-kai, Practical Buddhism and Interreligious Cooperation," brochure from Rissho Kosei-kai, Tokyo.
39 Thich Nhat Hanh, *Being Peace*, Indian edition, Delhi: Full Circle, 1997, pp. 53–54.
40 Richard B. Clarke, personal communication, October 2, 1981
41 Alan Wallace in Brian Hodel, "Tibetan Buddhism in the West: Is it working? An interview with Alan Wallace," *Snow Lion*, vol. 15, no. 4, Fall 2000, p. 17.
42 Stephen Batchelor, *Buddhism without Beliefs: A Contemporary Guide to Awakening*, New York: Riverhead Books, 1997.
43 Walpola Rahula, "The Social Teachings of the Buddha," in *The Path of Compassion*, Fred Eppsteiner, ed., Berkeley, California: Parallax Press, 1988, pp. 103–104.
44 Metta Sutta, as translated by Maha Ghosananda, in "Invocation: A Cambodian Prayer," *The Path of Compassion*, op. cit., p. xix.
45 Maha Ghosananda, Step by Step, quoted in "Letter from Cambodia," Coalition for Peace and Reconciliation, January 2001.
46 Sulak Sivaraksa, "Buddhism in a World of Change," in *The Path of Compassion*, op. cit., p. 16.

CHAPTER SIX
DAOISM AND CONFUCIANISM

1 Tu Weiming, "The Continuity of Being: Chinese Visions of Nature," in Mary Evelyn Tucker and John Berthrong, *Confucianism and Ecology*, Cambridge, Massachusetts: Harvard University Press, 1998, pp. 106–108.
2 *The I Ching*, translated by Richard Wilhelm (German)/ Cary F. Baynes (English), Princeton, New Jersey: Princeton University Press, 1967, pp. 620–621.
3 Excerpt from verse 1 in *Tao-te Ching*, translated by Stephen Mitchell. Translation copyright 1988 by Stephen Mitchell. Reprinted by permission of Harper & Row, Publishers, Inc.
4 *Tao-te Ching*, translated by Lin Yutang, New York: Modern Library, 1948, verse 1, p. 41.
5 Lao-tzu, *Tao-te Ching*, translated by D. C. Lau, London: Penguin Books, 1963, verse 25, p. 82.
6 Lao-tzu, op. cit., p. 82.
7 Chang Chung-yuan, *Creativity and Taoism*, New York: Harper Colophon, 1963, p. 5.
8 Chuang-tzu, *Basic Writings*, translated by Burton Watson, op. cit., p. 40.
9 Chuang-tzu, *Basic Writings*, translated by Burton Watson, New York: Columbia University Press, 1964, p. 36.
10 *The Way to Life: At the Heart of the Tao-te Ching*, non-literal translation by Benjamin Hoff, New York/Tokyo: Weatherhill, 1981, p. 52, chapter 78.
11 *The Way to Life*, translated by Benjamin Hoff, op. cit., p. 33, chapter 35.
12 Guanzi, "Inward Training," as quoted in Harold D. Roth, "The Inner Cultivation Tradition of Early Daoism," in Donald S. Lopez, Jr., ed., *Religions of China in Practice*, Princeton, New Jersey: Princeton University Press, 1996, pp. 133–134.
13 *Tao-te Ching*, translated by Stephen Mitchell, op. cit., Chapter 15.
14 *The Secret of the Golden Flower*, translated by Richard Wilhelm/Cary Baynes, New York: Harcourt Brace Jovanovich, 1962, p. 21.
15 Chuang-tzu, op. cit., p. 59.
16 Excerpted from Huai-Chin Han, translated by Wen Kuan Chu, *Tao and Longevity: Mind–Body Transformation*, York Beach, Maine: Samuel Weiser, 1984, pp. 4–5.
17 Sun Bu-er, in *Immortal Sisters: Secrets of Taoist Women*, translated by Thomas Cleary, Boston: Shambhala Publications, 1989, p. 50.
18 Quoted in *T'ai-chi, Cheng Man-ch'ing and Robert W. Smith*, Rutland, Vermont: Charles E. Tuttle, 1967, p. 106.
19 Ibid., p. 109.
20 Excerpted from Al Chung-liang Huang, *Embrace Tiger, Return to Mountain*, Moab, Utah: Real People Press, 1973, pp. 12, 185.
21 "Brooms, Gourds, and the Old Ways, An Interview with Daoist Master An," *Heaven Earth: The Chinese Art of Living*, vol. 1, no. 1, May 1991, p. 2.
22 Yu Yingshi, "A Difference in Starting Points," *Heaven Earth*, ibid., p. 1.
23 The Analects, VII: 1, in *Sources of Chinese Tradition*, vol. 1, William Theodore de Bary, Wing-tsit Chan, and Burton Watson, eds. , New York: Columbia University Press, 2000, p. 23.

24 Ibid. XIII: 6, p. 32, and Analects II: 1, as translated by Ch'u Chai and Winberg Chai in *Confucianism*, Woodbury, New York: Barron's Educational Series, 1973, p. 52.
25 Confucius, *The Analects*, translated by D. C. Lau, London: Penguin Books, 1979, VIII:19, p. 94.
26 *The Texts of Confucianism, Sacred Books of the East*, Max Müller, ed., Oxford: Oxford University Press, 1891, vol. 27, pp. 450–451.
27 The Analects, XI:11, in Ch'u Chai and Winberg Chai, *The Sacred Books of Confucius and Other Confucian Classics*, New Hyde Park, New York: University Books, 1965, p. 46.
28 Ibid., X:25.
29 Ibid., X:103.
30 Mencius, in De Bary, op. cit., p. 91.
31 Ibid., p. 89.
32 From the Hsun Tzu, Chapter 17, in de Bary, op. cit., p. 101.
33 Chang Tsai's Western Inscription, in William Theodore de Bary et al., *Sources of Chinese Tradition*, op. cit.
34 A prayer offered by the Ming dynasty emperor in 1538, in James Legge, *The Religions of China*, London, 1880, pp. 43–44.
35 Mao Zedong, "Overthrowing the Clan Authority of the Ancestral Temples and Clan Elders, the Religious Authority of Town and Village Gods, and the Masculine Authority of Husbands," 1927, as quoted in Deborah Sommer, ed., *Chinese Religion: An Anthology of Sources*, New York and Oxford: Oxford University Press, 1995, p. 305.
36 Quotations from Chairman Mao tse-Tung, second edition, Peking: Foreign Language Press, 1967, pp. 172–173.
37 *China Daily*, January 30, 1989, p. 1.
38 Xinzhong Yao, "Confucianism and the Twenty-first Century: Confucian Moral, Educational and Spiritual Heritages Revisited," First International Conference on Traditional Culture and Moral Education, Beijing, August 1998, p. 4.
39 Tu Wei-ming, "Confucianism," in Arvind Sharma, ed., *Our Religions*, New York: HarperCollins Publishers, 1993, pp. 221–222.
40 Korean Overseas Information Service, Religions in Korea, Seoul, 1986, pp. 55–57.
41 Mary Evelyn Tucker, in Tu Weiming and Mary Evelyn Tucker, *Confucian Spirituality*, New York: Crossroad Publishing Company, 2003, p. 1.

CHAPTER SEVEN
SHINTO

1 Yukitaka Yamamoto, *Way of the Kami*, Stockton, California: Tsubaki America Publications, 1987, p. 75.
2 Adapted from the *Nihon Shoki (Chronicles of Japan)*, I:3, in Stuart D. B. Picken, *Shinto: Japan's Spiritual Roots*, Tokyo: Kodansha International, 1980, p. 10.
3 Sakamiki Shunzo, "Shinto: Japanese Ethnocentrism," in Charles A. Moore, ed., *The Japanese Mind*, Hawaii: University of Hawaii Press, p. 25.
4 Kishimoto Hideo, "Some Japanese Cultural Traits and Religions," in Charles A. Moore, ed., *The Japanese Mind*, op. cit., pp. 113–114.
5 Ise-Teijo, Gunshin-Mondo, Onchisosho, vol. x., quoted in *Genchi Kato*, p. 185.
6 Yamamoto, op. cit., pp. 73–75.
7 Unidentified quotation, Stuart D. B. Picken, ed., *A Handbook of Shinto*, Stockton, California: The Tsubaki Grand Shrine of America, 1987, p. 14.
8 Ibid.
9 Yamamoto, op. cit., p. 97.
10 Hitoshi Iwasaki, "Wisdom from the night sky," *Tsubaki Newsletter*, June 1, 1988, p. 2.
11 Motoori Norinaga (1730–1801), Naobi no Mitma, quoted in *Tsubaki Newsletter*, November 1, 1988, p. 3.
12 Tensho Kotaijingu oracle, English translation by Norman Havens based on Japanese translation by Kamata Jun'ichi, as reproduced in Brian Bocking, "Changing images of Shinto: Sanja takusen or the three oracles," in John Breen and Mark Teeuwen, eds., *Shinto in History: Ways of the Kami*, Honolulu: University of Hawaii Press, 2000, p. 169.
13 In W. G. Aston, Nihongi, Rutland, Vermont and Tokyo: Tuttle, 1972, p. 77.
14 Ofudesaki, as quoted in *Aizen Newsletter of the Universal Love and Brotherhood Association*, no. 17, September–October 1997, p. 2.
15 Jinja-Honcho (The Association of Shinto Shrines), "The Shinto View of Nature and a Proposal Regarding Environmental Problems," Tokyo, 1997.

ZOROASTRIANISM

1 *The Hymns of Zarathushtra*, translated by Jacques Duchesne-Guillemin/Mrs. M. Henning, London: John Murray Publishers, 1952, p. 7.
2 Yasna 33: 14, *Songs of Zarathushtra*, The Gathas translated by Dastur Framroze Ardeshir Bode and Piloo Nanavutty, London: George Allen and Unwin, 1952, p. 66
3 Yasna 34: 5,4, ibid., p. 67
4 T. R. Sethna, *Book of Instructions on Zoroastrian Religion*, Karachi, Pakistan: Informal Religious Meetings Trust Fund, 1980, p. 87.

CHAPTER EIGHT
JUDAISM

1 Genesis 1:1. *Tanakh—The Holy Scriptures: The New JPS Translation According to the Traditional Hebrew Text*, Philadelphia: The Jewish Publication Society, 1985. This translation is used throughout this chapter.
2 Genesis 1:28.
3 Genesis 6:17.
4 Genesis 9:17.
5 Genesis 22:12.
6 Personal communication, March 24, 1989.
7 Deuteronomy 7:7.
8 Exodus 3:5.
9 Exodus 3:10.
10 Exodus 3:12, 14–15.
11 Irving Greenberg, "History, Holocaust, and Covenant," in Alan L. Berger, *Judaism in the Modern World*, New York and London: New York University Press, 1994, p. 129.
12 Exodus 34:13.
13 I Samuel 17:32–54, and the Ten Commandments on p. 224, Exodus 20:2–17, *New English Bible*, © Oxford University Press and Cambridge University Press, 1961, 1970.
14 I Kings 9:3.
15 Daniel 7:13–14.
16 From the Talmud and Midrash, quoted in *The Judaic Tradition*, Nahum N. Glatzer, ed., Boston: Beacon Press, 1969, p. 197.

17 Jacob Neusner, *Recovering Judaism*, Minneapolis: Fortress Press, 2001, p. 25.

18 Jerusalem Talmud, Demai 22a, in C. G. Montefiore and H. Lowe, eds., *A Rabbinic Anthology*, New York: Schocken Books, 1974.

19 Maimonides, *The Guide of the Perplexed*.

20 Quoted in S. A. Horodezky, *Leaders of Hasidism*, London: Ha-Sefer Agency for Literature, 1928, p. 11.

21 Elie Wiesel, *Night*, New York: Bantam Books, 1960, 1982, p. 64.

22 Elie Wiesel, speech for the UConn Convocation, September 7, 1988, University of Connecticut, Storrs, Connecticut.

23 Aviezer Ravitzky, *Messianism, Zionism, and Jewish Religious Radicalism*, Chicago: The University of Chicago Press, 1993, p. 1.

24 Ravitzky, op. cit.

25 Maimonides' "First Principles of Faith," as quoted in Louis Jacobs, *Principles of Jewish Faith*, Northvale, New Jersey: Jason Aronson, 1988, p. 33.

26 Ibn Gabirol, Keter Malkhut, quoted in Abraham J. Heschel, "One God," in *Between God and Man: An Interpretation of Judaism, from the Writings of Abraham J. Heschel*, Fritz A. Rothschild, ed., New York: Free Press, 1959, p. 106.

27 Abraham Joshua Heschel, *Man is not Alone*, New York: Farrar, Straus & Giroux, 1951, 1976, p. 112.

28 Abraham J. Heschel, "One God," op. cit., p. 104.

29 Martin Buber, in *The Way of Response: Martin Buber – Selections from His Writings*, Nahum N. Glatzer, ed., New York: Schocken Books, 1968, p. 53.

30 Isaiah 65:25, JPS Tanakh.

31 Ismar Schorsch, "Learning to Live with Less: A Jewish Perspective," in Steven C. Rockefeller and John E. Elder, *Spirit and Nature: Why the Environment is a Religious Issue*, Boston: Beacon Press, 1992, p. 35.

32 Translated from the Hebrew by Rabbi Sidney Greenberg, *Likrat Shabbat*, Bridgeport, Connecticut: Media Judaica/The Prayer Book Press, 1981, p. 61.

33 Job 1:20–21.

34 The Jewish Prayer Book, as quoted by Jocelyn Hellig, "A South African Jewish Perspective," in Martin Forward, ed., *Ultimate Visions*, Oxford: Oneworld Publications, 1995, p. 136.

35 Leviticus 11:45.

36 Talmud Berakhoth 11a, in *Ha-Suddur Ha-Shalem*, translated by Philip Birnbaum, New York: Hebrew Publishing Company, 1977, p. 14.

37 Excerpted from Ruth Gan Kagan, "The Sabbath: Judaism's Discipline for Inner Peace," paper presented at the Assembly of the World's Religions, Seoul, Korea, August 24–31, 1992, pp. 3, 7.

38 Sanhedrin 22a, quoted in *The Second Jewish Catalog*, Sharon Strassfeld and Michael Strassfeld, eds., Philadelphia: The Jewish Publication Society, 1976.

39 Rabbi Yochanan ben Nuri, Rosh Hashanah prayer quoted by Arthur Waskow, *Seasons of Our Joy*, New York: Bantam Books, 1982, p. 11.

40 Isaiah 55:6–7.

41 Michael Lerner, *Jewish Renewal: A Path to Healing and Transformation*, New York: HarperCollins, 1994, p. 365.

42 Prayer quoted by Arthur Waskow, op. cit., p. 175.

43 Mordecai M. Kaplan, "The Way I Have Come," in *Mordecai M. Kaplan: An Evaluation*, I. Eisenstein and E. Kohn, eds., New York: Jewish Reconstructionist Foundation, 1952, p. 293.

44 Joseph I. Lieberman with Michael D'Orso, *In Praise of Public Life: The Honor and Purpose of Political Service*, New York: Simon & Schuster/Touchstone, 2000, pp. 24–25.

45 Ibid., pp. 26–27.

46 Ibid., p. 34

47 Ibid., pp.100–101

48 Genesis 1:26 from The Torah, Philadelphia: The Jewish Publication Society, 1962.

49 The Gates of Repentance, New York: Central Conference of American Rabbis, p. 197.

50 Susannah Heschel, "The Feminist Confrontation with Judaism," in Alan L. Berger, ed., *Judaism in the Modern World*, New York: New York University Press, 1994, p. 276.

51 Judith Plaskow, *Standing Again at Sinai*, San Francisco: HarperCollins, 1991, p. 120.

52 "Declaration of the ELCA to the Jewish Community," as quoted in Joel Beversluis, *A Sourcebook for Earth's Community of Religions*, revised edition, Grand Rapids, Michigan: CoNexus Press-Sourcebook Project, 1995, p. 170.

53 Rabbi Dovid Karpov, interviewed October 24, 1994.

54 Michael Lerner, op. cit., pp. xvii, xxviii.

CHAPTER NINE
CHRISTIANITY

1 Publishing Department of Moscow Patriarchate, The Russian Orthodox Church, Moscow, 1980, p. 239 in English translation by Doris Bradbury, Moscow: Progress Publishers, 1982.

2 "Origen on First Principles," in Hugh T. Kerr, ed., *Readings in Christian Thought*, Nashville, TN: Abingdon Press, 1966, p. 46.

3 *The Gospel According to Thomas*, Coptic text established and translated by Guilloaumont et al., Leiden: E. J. Brill; New York: Harper & Row, 1959, verse 77.

4 Luke 2:47, 49. Most biblical quotations in this chapter are from the *Revised Standard Version of the Bible*, copyright 1946, 1952, 1971 by The Division of Christian Education of the National Council of the Churches of Christ in the USA. Used by permission.

5 Mark 1:10–11.

6 Dietrich Bonhoeffer, *The Cost of Discipleship*, New York: Simon & Schuster, 1959, 1995, p. 90.

7 Matthew 6:25–27.

8 Matthew 7:7.

9 Luke 9:17.

10 John 6:48.

11 William, quoted in *The Gospel in Art by the Peasants of Solentiname*, Philip and Sally Scharper, eds., Maryknoll, New York: Orbis Books, 1984, p. 42.

12 Matthew 5:21–22.

13 Matthew 5:44–45.

14 Mark 10:27.

15 Matthew 22:39.

16 Luke 10:25–37, *The New English Bible*.

17 Matthew 25:37–40.

18 Matthew 5:3.

19 Matthew 13:47–50, *The New English Bible*, Cambridge, England: Cambridge University Press, corrected impression, 1972.

20 Mark 1:15.

21 Luke 4:43.

22 Matthew 6:10.

23 Matthew 24:29–31.

24 Isaiah 29:13, *The New English Bible.*

25 Matthew 15:1–20, *The New English Bible.*

26 Matthew 23:1–3, 27–28, *The New English Bible.*

27 Isaiah 56:7.

28 Jeremiah 7:11.

29 Mark 11:15–18, *The New English Bible.*

30 Mark 8:29–30.

31 John 11:27.

32 Matthew 17:2–5.

33 John 7:16, 8:12, 23, 58.

34 Matthew 26:28.

35 Mark 11:10.

36 Mark 14:36.

37 Joachim Jeremias, *New Testament Theology: The Proclamation of Jesus*, translated by John Bowden, New York: Charles Scribner's Sons, 1971, p. 40.

38 Mark 14:41.

39 Matthew 26:64.

40 Matthew 27:11.

41 John 18:35–38.

42 Matthew 27:46.

43 Matthew 28:18–20.

44 Elisabeth Schüssler Fiorenza, *In Memory of Her*, New York: Crossroad, 1983, 1994, p. xliv.

45 Acts 2:36.

46 Acts 26:18.

47 Philippians 3:8–10.

48 Acts 17:28.

49 The Gospel According to Thomas, op. cit., 82.

50 Confessions of St. Augustine, translated by Edward Bouverie Pusey, Chicago: Encyclopedia Britannica, vol. 18 of *Great Books of the Western World*, 1952, p. 64.

51 Rowan Williams, *Resurrection*, New York: The Pilgrim Press, 1984, p. 46 with quotations from John 14:19.

52 Archimandrite Chrysostomos, *The Ancient Fathers of the Desert*, Brookline, Massachusetts: Hellenic College Press, 1980, p. 78.

53 Ibid., p. 80.

54 The Solovky Memorandum, as quoted in Barbara von der Heydt, *Candles Behind the Wall*, Grand Rapids, Michigan: William B. Eerdmans Publishing Company, 1993, p. 46.

55 Mikhail S. Gorbachev, quoted in Michael Dobbs, "Soviets, Vatican to Establish Ties," *The Hartford Courant*, December 2, 1989, p. 1.

56 Vladimir Putin, quoted in Elizabeth Piper, "Putin backs Orthodox 'spiritual revival,'" *Asian Age*, May 1, 2000, p. 5.

57 Father Alexey Vlasov, interviewed October 26, 1994.

58 Father Feodor, interviewed October 29, 1994.

59 Fotini Pipili, in Iina Kyriakidou, "Greek women poised to take on all-male monastic community," *Asian Age*, October 14, 1997, p. 7.

60 St. Gregory Palamas, "Homily on the Presentation of the Holy Virgin in the Temple," in Sophocles, 22 Homilies of St. Gr. Palamas, Athens, 1861, pp. 175–177, quoted in Vladimir Lossky, *The Mystical Theology of the Eastern Church*, New York: St. Vladimir's Seminary Press, 1976, p. 224.

61 Jim Forest, *Pilgrim to the Russian Church*, New York: Crossroad Publishing Company, 1988, p. 50.

62 From A Hopkins Reader, John Pick, ed., New York: Oxford University Press, 1953, quoted in D. M. Dooling,

ed., *A Way of Working*, New York: Anchor Press/ Doubleday, 1979, p. 6.

63 St. Francis, Testament, April 1226, p. 3, quoted in Jean Leclerc, Francois Vandenbroucke, and Louis Bouyer, eds., The Spirituality of the Middle Ages, vol. 2 of *A History of Christian Spirituality*, New York: Seabury Press, 1982, p. 289.

64 *The Cloud of Unknowing and The Book of Privy Counseling*, Garden City, New York: Image Books, 1973 edition, p. 56.

65 Martin Luther, A Treatise on Christian Liberty, quoted in John Oillenberger and Claude Welch, *Protestant Christianity*, New York: Charles Scribner's Sons, 1954, p. 36.

66 Ulrich Zwingli, "On True and False Religion," quoted in Harry Emerson Fosdick, ed., *Great Voices of the Reformation*, New York: Random House, 1952, p. 169.

67 John Calvin, "Instruction in Faith," quoted in Fosdick, op. cit., p. 216.

68 John Wesley, as quoted in F. L. Cross and E. A. Livingstone, eds., *The Oxford Dictionary of the Christian Church*, Oxford: Oxford University Press, 1983, p. 1467.

69 St. Teresa of Avila, *The Interior Castle*, translated by E. Allison Peers from the critical edition of P. Silverior de Santa Teresa, *Garden City*, New York: Image Books, 1961, p. 214.

70 John Wesley, as quoted in John Dillenberger and Claude Welch, *Protestant Christianity*, New York: Charles Scribner's Sons, 1954, p. 134.

71 Sarah Grimke, "Letters on the Equality of the Sexes and the Condition of Women" (1836–37), in *Feminism: The Essential Historical Writings*, M. Schneir, ed., New York: Vintage, 1972, p. 38.

72 *The Documents of Vatican II*, Walter M. Abbott, ed., New York: Guild Press, 1966, p. 665.

73 Ibid., pp. 661–662.

74 John 14:2–10, *The New English Bible.*

75 Paul Knitter, in John Hick and Paul F. Knitter, eds., *The Myth of Christian Uniqueness: Toward a Pluralistic Theology of Religions*, Maryknoll, New York: Orbis Books, 1987, pp. 192–193.

76 Matthew 20:28.

77 John 3:16–17, *The New English Bible.*

78 Archbishop Desmond Tutu, "The Face of God," *Life*, December 1990, pp. 49–50.

79 Rev. Larry Howard, interfaith service, Syracuse, New York, October 25, 1992.

80 Thomas Keating, *The Mystery of Christ: The Liturgy as Spiritual Experience*, Amity, New York: Amity House, 1987, p. 5.

81 (Thomas a Kempis), *The Imitation of Christ*, p. 139.

82 From Mother Teresa, as quoted in Malcolm Muggeridge, *A Gift for God*, London: Collins, 1975, pp. 37–38.

83 F. Ioann Kronshtadtsky, as quoted in F. Veniamin Fedchenkov, *Heaven on Earth*, Moscow: Palmnik, 1994, p. 70.

84 Julia Gatta, personal communication, July 22, 1987.

85 "Brief Order for Confession and Forgiveness," Lutheran Book of Worship, prepared by the churches participating in the Inter-Lutheran Commission on Worship, Minneapolis, Minnesota: Augsburg Publishing House, 1978, p. 56.

86 World Council of Churches, Baptism, Eucharist and Ministry, Faith and Order Paper No. 111, Geneva, 1982, p. 2.

87 Father Appolinari, interviewed October 28, 1994.

88 John 1:9.

89 Jim Forest, Pilgrim to the Russian Church, op. cit., p. 72.

90 Thomas Merton, *Contemplative Prayer*, Garden City, New York: Image Books, 1969, p. 67.

91 Bishop Paulos Mar Gregorios, World Congress of Spiritual Concord, Rishikesh, India, December 11, 1993.

92 Interview with Professor Kathleen Dugan, February 4, 1993.

93 *The Way of a Pilgrim and The Pilgrim Continues His Way*, translated by Helen Bacovcin, New York/London: Doubleday, 1978, 1992, p. 160.

94 Luke 1:38.

95 Quoted in Jim Forest, *Pilgrim to the Russian Church*, New York: Crossroad Publishing Company, 1988, p. 63.

96 New York Times, as reprinted in "The Gospel of Life," *Indian Currents*, April 8, 1995, p. 1.

97 Associated Press, Vatican City: "Only Catholicism 'proper': Vatican," *The Globe and Mail*, September 6, 2000, A14; Philip Pullella (Reuters), "Vatican says no religion equals Roman Catholicism," Asian Age, September 6, 2000, p. 5.

98 Young Communist League, as quoted by Gerardo Tena, "Catholic imagery for papal visit transforms Havana," *Asian Age*, January 20, 1998, p. 6.

99 Joe Mannath SDB, "Sexuality, Cwelibacy and the Religious Quest," *Vidyajyoti Journal of Theological Reflection*, vol. 67, no. 1, January 2003, p. 54.

100 Sean McDonagh, *The Greening of the Church*, Maryknoll, New York: Orbis Books, p. 65.

101 Quoted in Don A. Schanche and Russell Chandler, Los Angeles Times, "Tensions confront pope in U.S.," *The Hartford Courant*, September 11, 1987, p. 1.

102 Harvey Cox, *Fire from Heaven: The Rise of Pentecostal Spirituality and the Reshaping of Religion in the Twenty-first Century*, Reading, Massachusetts: Addison-Wesley, 1995.

103 Leslie Scrivener, in *Toronto Star*, October 8, 1995, as quoted in Margaret M. Poloma, "Mysticism and Identity Formation in Social Context: The Case of the Pentecostal-Charismatic Movement," The Seventh International Congress of Professors World Peace Academy, Washington, D.C., November 1997, p. 5.

104 Roman I. Bilas, interviewed October 25, 1994.

105 Members of African Independent Churches Report on their Pilot Study of the History and Theology of their Churches, "Speaking for Ourselves," Braamfontein, South Africa: Institute for Contextural Theology, 1985, pp. 23–24.

106 Martin Luther King, Jr., "An Experiment in Love," in *A Testament of Hope: The Essential Writings of Martin Luther King, Jr.*, James Melvin Washington, ed., San Francisco: Harper & Row, 1986, p. 16.

107 Acts 4:32–35.

108 Gustavo Gutierrez, quoted in Phillip Berryman, *Liberation Theology*, New York: Pantheon Books, 1987, p. 33.

109 Bakole Wa Ilunga, *Paths of Liberation: A Third World Spirituality*, Maryknoll, New York: Orbis Books, 1984, p. 92.

110 Dwight N. Hopkins, ed., *Black Faith and Public Talk*, Maryknoll, New York: Orbis Books, 1999, pp. 1–2.

111 James H. Cone, "Looking Back, Going Forward," in Hopkins, op. cit., p. 257.

112 Desmond Tutu, quoted in Charles Vila-Vicencio, "Tough and Compassionate: Desmond Mpilo Tutu," in Leonard Hulley, Louise Kretzschmar, and Luke Lungile Pato, eds.,

Archbishop Tutu: Prophetic Witness in South Africa, Cape Town: Human and Rousseau, 1996, pp. 41–42.

113 Ibid., p. 37.

114 Ibid., p. 38.

115 Francis Cull, "Desmond Tutu: Man of Prayer," in Hulley et al., op. cit., pp. 31–32.

116 Desmond Tutu, in Vila-Vicencio, op. cit., pp. 44–45.

117 1 Corinthians 11:7–12.

118 Fiorenza, op. cit., p. xx.

119 Ivone Gebara and Maria Clara Bingemer, *Mary, Mother of God, Mother of the Poor*, Maryknoll, New York: Orbis Books, 1989, as excerpted in Ursula King, ed., *Feminist Theology from the Third World*, Maryknoll, New York, Orbis Books, 1994, pp. 277, 280–281.

120 Sally McFague, *Models of God: Theology for an Ecological, Nuclear Age*, Philadelphia: Fortress Press, 1987, pp. 101, 106.

121 Thomas Berry, remarks at "Seeking the True Meaning of Peace" conference in San Jose, Costa Rica, June 27, 1989.

122 Father Denis G. Pereira, "A New Model for India's Pastoral Clergy," *Vidyajyoti Journal*, vol. 67, no. 1, January 2003, p. 67.

123 "Decade to Overcome Violence," World Council of Church website, www.wcc-coe.org, October 1, 2001.

CHAPTER TEN
ISLAM

1 *The Holy Qur'an*, XCVI:1–5, English translation by Abdullah Yusuf Ali, Durban, R.S.A.: Islamic Propagation Center International, 1946. This translation is used throughout this chapter, by permission. Note that despite the layout of this translation, the Qur'an is not a work of poetry.

2 Abu Abdallah Muhammad Bukhari, Kitab jami as-sahih, translated by M. M. Khan as Sahih al-Bukhari, Lahore: Ashraf, 1978–80, quoted in Annemarie Schimmel, *And Muhammad is His Messenger*, Chapel Hill, North Carolina: University of North Carolina Press, 1985, p. 11.

3 Sura 8:18.

4 Maulana M. Ubaidul Akbar, *The Orations of Muhammad*, Lahore: M. Ashraf, 1954, p. 78.

5 Sura 41:6.

6 Sura 28:56.

7 Hadith quoted by Annemarie Schimmel, *And Muhammad is His Messenger*, Chapel Hill, North Carolina: University of North Carolina Press, 1985, pp. 48 and 55.

8 *The Holy Qur'an*, III:104.

9 Quoted by Mahmoud Ayoub, *The Qur'an and its Interpreters*, Albany: State University of New York Press, 1984, vol. 1, p. 14.

10 Footnote 5778, Sura 74:1, p. 1640.

11 Sura 42:15.

12 Islamic Society of North America, "Islam at a Glance," Plainfield, Indiana: Islamic Teaching Center.

13 Abu Hashim Madani, quoted in Samuel L. Lewis, *In the Garden*, New York: Harmony Books/Lama Foundation, 1975, p. 136.

14 Frithjof Schuon, *Understanding Islam*, translated by D. M. Matheson, London: George Allen & Unwin, 1963, p. 59.

15 Sura 2:136.

16 Farid Esack, personal communication, March 29, 1998.

17 Farid Esack, *Qur'an, Liberation and Pluralism: An Islamic Perspective of Interreligious Solidarity against Oppression*, Oxford: Oneworld Publications, 1997, p. 4.

18 Ibid., p. 223.
19 Ibid., p. 222.
20 Ibid., p. 259.
21 Farid Esack, personal communication, March 29, 1998.
22 *Sura* 32:16–17.
23 *Sura* 3:63.
24 *Sura* 41:37.
25 Quoted by Abdur-Rahman Ibrahim Doi, *"Sunnism," Islamic Spirituality: Foundations*, Seyyed Hossein Nasr, ed., New York: Crossroad, 1987, p. 158.
26 Sura 17:13–14.
27 Sura 70:16–18.
28 Quoted by Muhammad Rida al-Muzaffar, *The Faith of Shi'a Islam*, London: The Muhammadi Trust, 1982, p. 35.
29 Sura 2:256.
30 Hadith quoted by Syed Ali Ashraf, "The Inner Meaning of the Islamic Rites: Prayer, Pilgrimage, Fasting, Jihad," in *Islamic Spirituality: Foundations*, op. cit., p. 114.
31 Hammudah Abdalati, *Islam in Focus*, Indianapolis, Indiana: American Trust Publications, 1975, p. 88.
32 Hadith of the Prophet, as quoted in *Fakhr al-Din Al-Razi, Tafsir al-Fakhr al-Razi*, 21 vols., Mecca: al-Kaktabah al-Tijariyyah, 1990, vol. 7, p. 232.
33 *Sura* 22:39–40.
34 *Sura* 2:190.
35 *Sura* 2:217, 192.
36 M. R. Bawa Muhaiyaddeen, "Islam's Hidden Beauty: The Sufi Teachings of M. R. Bawa Muhaiyaddeen," tape from New Dimensions Foundation, San Francisco, 1989, side 1.
37 Hadith #535 cited in Badi'uz-Zaman Furuzanfar, Ahadith-i Mathnawi, Tehran, 1334 sh./1955, in Persian, quoted in Annemarie Schimmel, *Mystical Dimensions of Islam*, Chapel Hill: University of North Carolina Press, 1975, p. 118.
38 Rabi'a al-'Adawiyya al-Qaysiyya, quoted in Abu Talib, Qut al-Qulub, II, Cairo, A. H. 1310, p. 57, as quoted in Margaret Smith, *Rabi'a the Mystic and her Fellow-Saints in Islam*, Cambridge: Cambridge University Press, 1928, 1984, p. 102.
39 Jalal al-Din Rumi, opening lines of the *Mathnawi*, as translated by Edmund Helminski, *The Ruins of the Heart: Selected Lyric Poetry of Jelaluddin Rumi, Putney*, Vermont: Threshold Books, 1981, p. 20.
40 Jalal al-Din Rumi, *Mathnawi-i ma'nawi*, ed. and translated by Reynold A. Nicholson, London, 1925–40, vol. 4, line 2102.
41 Hadith of the Prophet, #352 in *Zaman Furuzanfar*, Ahadith-i Mathnawi, op. cit.
42 Quoted in Javad Nurbakhsh, *Sufism: Meaning, Knowledge, and Unity*, New York: Khaniqahi-Nimatullahi Publications, 1981, pp. 19, 21.
43 Al-Ghazali, in *The Faith and Practice of Al-Ghazali*, translated by William Montgomery Watt, Oxford: Oneworld Publications, 1953, 1994, pp. 77, 130.
44 Idries Shah, *The Sufis*, London: Jonathan Cape, 1964, p. 76.
45 Jalal al-Din Rumi, *Mathnawi, VI, 3220–3246*, as translated by Coleman Barks in Rumi: We Are Three, Athens, Georgia: Maypop Books, 1987, pp. 54–55.
46 Treaty cited in Philip K. Hitti, *Islam and the West*, Princeton, New Jersey: D. Van Nostrand, 1962, p. 112.
47 Uzbek Khan, 1313 charter granted to Metropolitan Peter, as quoted in *Al Risala*, June 1994, p. 12.
48 Dalil-ul-Arifin, p. 37, as quoted in W. D. Begg, *The Holy Biography of Hazrat Khwaja Muinuddin Chishti*, Botswana, Africa: G. N. Khan, 1979, p. 41.
49 Indonesian President Suharto, quoted in *Hinduism Today*, July 1989, p. 20.
50 Annemarie Schimmel, speaking in "Islam's Hidden Beauty," tape from New Dimensions Foundation, San Francisco, 1989, side 1.
51 Jalal al-Din Rumi, Mathnawi, IV, in Rumi: We Are Three: op. cit., Barks, p. 52.
52 Muhammad Mashuq ibn Ally, "Theology of Islamic Liberation," in Dan Cohn-Sherbok, ed., *World Religions and Human Liberation*, Maryknoll, New York: Orbis Books, 1992, p. 47.
53 Amina Wadud, *Qur'an and Woman*, New York: Oxford University Press, 1999, pp. ix–x, xiii, xx (italics added); Amina Wadud, "Alternative Qur'anic Interpretation and the Statues of Muslim Women," in Gisela Webb, ed., *Windows of Faith: Muslim Women Scholar-Activists in North America*, Syracuse: Syracuse University Press, 2000, p. 11.
54 Seyyed Hossein Nasr, "The Pertinence of Islam to the Modern World," *The World Religions Speak on the Relevance of Religion in the Modern World*, Finley P. Dunne Jr., ed., The Hague: Junk, 1970, p. 133.
55 "Islamic TV channel to counter the West," *Asian Age*, October 20, 1998, p. 1.
56 Ardeshir Cowasjee, "As Pak mocks education," *Dawn*, in *Asian Age*, 8january 2004, p. 16.
57 Quoted in Karen Armstrong, *The Battle for God: Fundamentalism in Judaism, Christianity and Islam*, London: HarperCollins, 2000, p. 240.
58 Azizah Y. al-Hibri, "The Taliban and Islamic Teaching," in *Sightings*, an e-mail journal published by the Martin Marty Center at the University of Chicago Divinity School, March 14, 2001.
59 Nical Al-Mughrabi, "Israelis kill five more in Gaza, " *Asian Age*, 22 April, 2004, p.8.
60 Reuters, "Invalid cleric was 'marked for death,' *Asian Age*, 23 March 2004, p.8.
61 Anwar Ibrahim, "Democracy is missing in terror and tyranny," *International Herald Tribune*, reprinted in Asian Age, October 15, 2001, p. 12.
62 John L. Esposito, *The Islamic Threat: Myth or Reality?*, New York: Oxford University Press, 1993, pp. ix–x.
63 Asaf Hussain, "Fundamentalism—An Islamic Perspective," *International Interfaith Center News*, December 2000, p. 7.
64 Mahmoon-al-Rasheed, "Islam, Nonviolence, and Social Transformation," Glenn D. Paige, Chaiwat Satha-Anand, and Sarah Gilliatt, eds., Honolulu: University of Hawaii, Center for Global Nonviolence Planning Project, 1993, p. 70.
65 Dr. A. K. Abu'l Majd, quoted in the video "Islam," Smithsonian World series, Smithsonian Institution and WETA, Washington, D.C., originally broadcast July 22, 1987, transcript pp. 6, 17.

CHAPTER ELEVEN
SIKHISM

1 *Songs of Kabir*, translated by Rabindranath Tagore, New York: Samuel Weiser, 1977, p. 45.
2 Puratan, quoted in Khushwant Singh, *Hymns of Guru Nanak*, New Delhi: Orient Longmans Ltd., 1969, p. 10.
3 Guru Nanak, Guru Granth Sahib, p. 150 (as translated by Dr. Gopal Singh, New Delhi: World Book Centre, 1997).

4   Guru Nanak, as quoted in W. Owen Cole and Piara Singh Sambhi, *The Sikhs: Their Religious Beliefs and Practices*, London: Routledge & Kegan Paul, 1978, p. 39.

5   Sri Rag, p. 59, quoted in Trilochan Singh, Jodh Singh, Kapur Singh, Bawa Harkishen Singh, and Kushwant Singh, trans., *The Sacred Writings of the Sikhs*, reproduced by kind permission of Unwin Hyman Ltd., 1973, p. 72.

6   Bhagat Ravi Das, Rag Sorath, Guru Granth Sahib, p. 657.

7   Guru Granth Sahib, p. 724.

8   Guru Har Rai, as quoted in Dr. Gopal Singh, *A History of the Sikh People*, New Delhi: World Sikh University Press, 1979, p. 257.

9   Guru Gobind Singh, *Bachittar Natak*, autobiography.

10 C. F. Andrews, press report of events witnessed on 12 September, 1922, quoted in Harbans Singh, Editor-in-Chief, *The Encyclopedia of Sikhism*, vol. 2, Patiala, India: Punjabi University, 1996, pp. 206–206.

11 From Dr. S. Radhakrishnan, letter in the Baisakhi edition of "The Spokesman," 1956, reprinted as introduction to Giani Ishar Singh Nara, Safarnama and Zafarnama, New Delhi: Nara Publications, 1985, pp. iv–v.

12 Mul Mantra, quoted in *Hymns of Guru Nanak*, op. cit., p. 25.

13 *Jaap Sahib*, verses 84, 159, English translation by Harjett Singh Gill, New Delhi: Gobind Sadan Institute for Advanced Studies in Comparative Religion.

14 *Adi Granth* 684, quoted in Cole and Sambhi, op. cit., p. 74.

15 Guru Nanak, Guru Granth Sahib, p. 141.

16 Ibid.

17 Ibid., p. 473.

18 Guru Arjun, Rag Majh, p. 102, quoted in Singh et al., *Sacred Writings of the Sikhs*, op. cit., p. 180.

19 *Anand Sahib*, verse 14.

20 Excerpt from Guru Gobind Singh, *Rahitnamas*, as translated by Gurden Singh.

21 Excerpted from *Rahitnamas*, op. cit.

22 Baba Virsa Singh, quoted by Juliet Hollister in *News from Gobind Sadan*, August 1997, p. 1.

23 Baba Virsa Singh, "Challenge to Religious Leaders," *Gobind Sadan Times*, August 2000, p. 1.

24 Baba Virsa Singh, in *News from Gobind Sadan*, April 1997, p. 3.

25 Jap Ji verses 9–10.

26 Baba Virsa Singh, in *News from Gobind Sadan*, May 1994, p. 4.

27 Guru Gobind Singh, *Dasam Granth*.

CHAPTER TWELVE
NEW RELIGIOUS MOVEMENTS

1   Friday M. Mbon, "The Social Impact of Nigeria's New Religious Movements," in James A. Beckford, ed., *New Religious Movements and Rapid Social Change*, Paris and London: Unesco/Sage Publications, 1986, p. 177.

2   www.watchtower.org

3   Reiko Hatsumi, "In a spiritual vacuum anything can flourish, even destruction," *Asian Age*, May 28, 1995, p.9.

4   "Glnody," as quoted in Catherine Wessinger, *How the Millennium Comes Violently: From Jonestown to Heaven's Gate*, New York: Seven Bridges Press, 2000, p. 245.

5   Quoted in Ernest Cashmore, *Rastaman*, London: Unwin Paperbacks, 1983, p.22.

6   www.bobmarley.com/life/rastafari/beliefs/html

7   Tenri kyoso den ("Life of the Founder of the Tenri-kyo Sect") compiled by the Tenri-kyo doshi-kai, Tenri, 1913,

quoted in Ichiro Hori, Folk *Religion in Japan*, Chicago: University of Chicago Press, 1968, p. 237.

8   Miki Nakayama, *Ofudesaki: The Tip of the Divine Writing Brush*, Tenri City, Japan: The Headquarters of the Tenrikyo Church, 1971, verses 1–3.

9   Sandra Pfortmiller, "Messages," The National Spiritualist Summit, January 1989, p. 31.

10 Andrew Wilson, "Visions of the Spirit World: Sang Hun Lee's 'Life in the Spirit World and on Earth' Compared with Other Spiritualist Accounts," *Journal of Unification Studies* 2, 1998, p. 123.

11 Nephi, introduction to Chapter 8, and Chapter 11:8–10, 29, *The Book of Mormon: Another Testament of Jesus Christ*, Salt Lake City, Utah: The Church of Jesus Christ of Latter-Day Saints, 1981, pp. 422, 428, 429.

12 Thomas Thorkelson, interviewed February 21, 2004.

13 Gordon B. Hinkley, PBS interview broadcast on July 18, 1997.

14 "A Brief Biography of Rajinder Singh," Delhi: Sawan Kirpal Publications Spiritual Society, p.11.

15 Justice Anthony M. Kennedy, United States Supreme Court majority opinion summation in The Church of the Lucumi vs. The City of Hialeah, June 11, 1993.

16 Rev. William Kingsley Opoku, personal communication, February 6, 1993

17 Starhawk, *The Spiral Dance: A Rebirth of the Ancient Religion of the Great Goddess*, San Francisco: Harper & Row, 1979, pp. 2–3.

18 John Seed, "Anthropocentrism," *Awakening in the Nuclear Age*, Issue #14 (Summer/Fall 1986), p. 11.

19 Chief Seattle, "Chief Seattle's Message," quoted in *Thinking Like a Mountain: Toward a Council of All Beings*, John Seed, Joanna Macy, Pat Fleming, and Arne Naess, eds., Santa Cruz, California: New Society Publishers, 1988, p. 71.

20 J. E. Lovelock, *Gaia: A new look at life on Earth*, Oxford: Oxford University Press, pp. 9, 11.

21 James Lovelock, *The Ages of Gaia*, New York: Bantam Books, 1990, p. 206.

22 Peter Russell, "Endangered Earth: Psychological roots of the environmental crisis," *Link Up*, Issue #38 (Spring 1989), pp. 7–8.

23 Julia Butterfly Hill, circleoflifefoundation.org./review4.html

24 David Albert, "A Children's Story: Gaura Devi Saves the Trees," *Awakening in the Nuclear Age*, op. cit., p. 15.

25 H. P. Blavatsky, *The Key to Theosophy*, Los Angeles: The United Lodge of Theosophists, 1920, p. 3.

26 H. P. Blavatsky, "Is Theosophy a Religion," [to follow].

27 "The Baha'is: A Profile of the Baha'i Faith and its Worldwide Community," Leicestershire, UK: Baha'i Publishing Trust, p. 42.

28 Svetlana Dorzhieva, interviewed October 26, 1994.

29 'Abdu'l-Baha', as quoted in "One World, One Faith," New Delhi: *National Spiritual Assemblies of the Baha'is of India*, 1979, p. 3.

30 Frithjof Schuon, *Understanding Islam*, London: George Allen & Unwin Ltd., translated from French, 1963, p. 41.

31 Adapted from "The Baha'i Faith," New York: Baha'i International Community (unpaginated).

32 Marianne Williamson, *Illuminata*, New York: Riverhead Books, 1994, p. xvii.

33 Uniticsonline/inspiration/affirm/html

34 James Redfield, *The Celestine Prophecy*, London/New York: Bantam Books, 1994, cover and pp.276–77.

35 Sandra Duarte de Souza, "Religious Transit and Ecological Spirituality in Brazil," paper presented at "The Spiritual

Supermarket: Religious Pluralism in the 21st Century," April 19–22, 2001, London School of Economics, sponsored by the Center for Studies on New Religions, Italy, p. 4.

36 Catherine Wessinger, *How the Millennium Comes Violently*, New York: Seven Bridges Press, 2000, p. 6.

CHAPTER THIRTEEN
RELIGION IN THE TWENTY-FIRST CENTURY

1 Diana Eck, "A New Geo-Religious Reality," paper presented at the World Conference on Religion and Peace Sixth World Assembly, Riva del Garda, Italy, November 1994, p. 1.

2 Gyorgy Bulanyi, "Church and Peace: Vision and Reality," address at Overcoming Violence, a Church and Peace Conference in Pecel, Hungary, April 1995, as printed in Church and Peace, Spring 1995, p. 4.

3 Jerry Falwell, http://www.falwell.com/?a=meet_falwell, July 9, 2004

4 Charles Strozier et al., "Religious Militancy or 'Fundamentalism,'" *Religion and Human Rights*, New York: The Project on Religion and Human Rights, 1994, p. 19.

5 Osama bin Laden, videotaped address, October 7, 2001, reprinted in Bruce Lincoln, *Holy Terrors*: Thinking about Religion after September 11, Chicago: University of Chicago Press, 2003, p.103.

6 Vimal Tirimanna, "Can the War against Terrorism be Won?", *Vidyajyoti Journal of Theological Reflection*, July 2004, vol. 68, no. 7, pp. 529–530.

7 Ewert Cousins, Speech at North American Interfaith Conference, Buffalo, New York, May 1991.

8 By Father Thomas Keating, as reprinted in Susan Walker, ed., *Speaking of Silence: Christians and Buddhists on the Contemplative Way*, Boulder, Colorado: Naropa Institute, 1987. Used by permission of Paulist Press.

9 Raimundo Panikkar, "The Invisible Harmony: A Universal Theory of Religion or a Cosmic Confidence in Reality?", *Toward a Universal Theology of Religion*, Leonard Swidler, ed., Maryknoll, New York: Orbis Books, 1987, p. 147.

10 Pope John Paul II, quoted in Richard N. Ostling, "A Summit for Peace in Assisi," *Time*, November 10, 1986, p. 78.

11 Wangari Maathai, speaking at the Oxford Global Survival Conference, quoted in *The Temple of Understanding Newsletter*, Fall 1988, p. 2.

12 Swami Vivekananda, speech for the Parliament of the World's Religions, Chicago, 1893.

13 "Towards a Global Ethic," Assembly of Religious and Spiritual Leaders, at the Parliament of World Religions, Chicago, 1993.

14 www.religioustolerance.org/news-01oct.html

15 Baba Virsa Singh, in Mary Pat Fisher, ed., *Loving God: The Practical Teachings of Baba Virsa Singh*, New Delhi: Gobind Sadan Institute for Advanced Studies inComparative Religion, pp. 7–8.

16 D'Souza and Diane D'Souza, "Reconciliation: A New Paradigm for Missions," Hyderabad, India: Henry Martyn Institute of Islamic Studies, p. 5.

17 Jimmy Carter, *Talking Peace*, New York: Penguin Books, 1995, pp. xi–xii, 21.

18 Jimmy Carter, *Living Faith*, New York: Random House, 1998, p. 202.

19 Ibid., pp. 5, 13.

20 Ibid., p. 32.

21 Ibid., pp. 236–238.

22 Gustavo Gutierrez, address to the World Conference on Religion and Peace, Riva del Garda, Italy, November 1994.

23 Martha Penzer, interviewed March 31, 1995, in New Delhi.

24 Marcus Braybrooke, *International Interfaith Centre newsletter* no. 16, December 2001, p. 1.

25 Vaclav Havel, *Letters to Olga*, translated by Paul Wilson, London and Boston: Faber & Faber, 1988 edition of 1983 original, pp. 236–237.

26 Pope Paul VI, *Populorum Progressio Encyclical*, 1967.

27 Professor Syed Anwar Kabir, interviewed April 12, 1995.

28 Yasuhiro Nakasone, speech at the Sixth World Conference on Religion and Peace, Riva del Garda, Italy, November 4, 1994, p. 3.

29 Baba Virsa Singh, *Loving God*, New Delhi: Gobind Sadan Institute for Advanced Studies in Comparative Religion, second edition, 1995, p. 60.

GLOSSARY

In the glossary, most words are accompanied by a guide to pronunciation. This guide gives an accepted pronunciation as simply as possible. Syllables are separated by a space and those that are stressed are underlined. Letters are pronounced in the usual manner for English unless they are clarified in the following list.

a *as in*	flat	ow	now
aa	father	u	but
aw	saw	ă, ĕ, ŏ, ŭ,	about (unaccented vowels represented by "ə" in some phonetic alphabets)
ay	pay		
ai	there	er, ur, ir	fern, fur, fir
ee	see		
e	let	ch	church
i	pity	j	jet
ī	high	ng	sing
o	not	sh	shine
ŏŏ	book	wh	where
oo	food	y	yes
oy	boy	kh	guttural aspiration (ch in Welsh and German)
ō	no		

absolutist Someone who holds rigid, literal, exclusive belief in the doctrines of their religion.

Advaita Vedanta (ad vī ee ta ve dan ta) Non-dualistic Hindu philosophy, in which the goal is the realization that the self is Brahman.

Adi Granth (Guru Granth Sahib) Sacred scriptures of the Sikhs.

Agni (aag nee) The god of fire in Hinduism.

agnosticism (ag nos ti siz ĕm) The belief that if there is anything beyond this life, it is impossible for humans to know it.

ahimsa (ă him să) Non-violence, a central Jain principle.

Allah (aa lă) The one God, in Islam.

allegories Narratives that use concrete symbols to convey abstract ideas.

Ameshta Spenta In Zoroastrianism, six divine powers (The Good Mind, Righteousness, Absolute Power, Devotion, Perfection, and Immortality), personified and worshipped as deities with shining eyes and beautiful forms after Zarathustra's death.

Amida (ă mee dă) (Sanskrit: Amitabha) The Buddha of infinite light, the personification of compassion whom the Pure Land Buddhists revere as the intermediary between humanity and Supreme Reality; esoterically, the Higher Self.

amrit (am ret) The water, sweetened with sugar, used in Sikh baptismal ceremonies.

anekantwad (ă nay kant wăd) The Jain principle of relativity or open-mindedness.

angel In the Zoroastrian, Jewish, Christian, and Islamic traditions, an invisible servant of God.

Annunciation (aˇ nun see ay shun) In Christianity, the appearance of an angel to the Virgin Mary to tell her that she would bear Jesus, conceived by the Holy Spirit.

anthropocentrism (an thro po sen triz ĕm) The assumption that the whole universe revolves around the human species.

anti-semitism Prejudice against Jews.

aparigraha (ă paa ree gră hă) The Jain principle of non-acquisitiveness.

apocalypse (ă paw kă lips) In Judaism and Christianity, the dramatic end of the present age.

apostasy Accusation of abandonment of religious principles

arhant (aar hănt) (Pali: *arhat* or *arahat*) A "Worthy One" who has followed the Buddha's Eightfold Path to liberation, broken the fetters that bind us to the suffering of the Wheel of Birth and Death, and arrived at nirvana; the Theravadan ideal.

Ark of the Covenant In Judaism, the shrine containing God's commandments to Moses.

Aryan Invasion Theory Speculation originally advanced by Western scholars that the Vedas were written by people invading India rather than by people already there.

Aryans (ayr ee ăns) The Indo-European pastoral invaders of many European and Middle Eastern agricultural cultures during the second millennium BCE.

asana (<u>aa</u> să nă) A yogic posture.

ashram (<u>ash</u> ram) In Indian tradition, a usually ascetic spiritual community of those who have gathered around a guru.

atheism (<u>ay</u> thee is em) Belief that there is no deity.

atman (<u>aat</u> man) In Hinduism, the soul.

avatar In Hinduism, the earthly incarnation of a deity.

Avesta Holy text of Zoroastrian teaching and liturgy, only fragments of which have survived.

Axial Age Period dating approximately sixth century BCE during which a large number of great religious leaders and thinkers appeared in many parts of the ancient world, including the authors of the Upanishads, the Buddha, Mahavir, Confucius, Laozi, Socrates, and Zarathushtra.

baptism A Christian sacrament by which God cleanses all sin and makes one a sharer in the divine life, and a member of Christ's body, the Church.

barakah (ba˘ <u>raa</u> ka) In Islamic mysticism, the spiritual wisdom and blessing transmitted from master to pupil.

Bar Mitzvah (baar <u>mitz</u> vă) The coming-of-age ceremony for a Jewish boy.

Bat Mitzvah (bat <u>mitz</u> vă) The coming-of-age ceremony for a Jewish girl in some modern congregations.

Beatitudes (bee <u>at</u> ĕ toods) Short statements by Jesus about those who are most blessed.

Bhagavad-Gita (<u>ba</u> gă văd <u>gee</u> tă) A portion of the Hindu epic *Mahabharata* in which Lord Krishna specifies ways of spiritual progress.

bhakta (<u>bak</u> taa) Devotee of a deity, in Hinduism.

bhakti (<u>bak</u> tee) In Hinduism, intense devotion to a personal aspect of the deity.

bhakti yoga In Hinduism, the path of devotion.

bhikshu (bi kshoo) (Pali: *bhikkhu*; feminine: *bhikshuni* or *bhikkhuni*). A Buddhist monk or nun who renounces worldliness for the sake of following the path of liberation and whose simple physical needs are met by lay supporters.

Bodhisattva (<u>boo</u> dee <u>sat</u> vă) In Mahayana Buddhism, one who has attained enlightenment but renounces nirvana for the sake of helping all sentient beings in their journey to liberation from suffering.

Brahman (<u>braa</u> măn) The impersonal Ultimate Principle in Hinduism.

Brahmanas (braa mă năs) The portion of the Hindu Vedas concerning rituals.

brahmin (<u>braa</u> min) (brahman) A priest or member of the priestly caste in Hinduism.

Buddha-nature A fully awakened consciousness.

caliph (<u>kay</u> lif) In Sunni Islam, the successor to the Prophet.

canon Authoritative collection of writings, works, etc., applying to a particular religion or author.

caste (kast) Social class distinction on the basis of heredity or occupation.

catholic Universal, all-inclusive. Christian churches referring to themselves as Catholic claim to be the representatives of the ancient undivided Christian church.

chakra (<u>chuk</u> ră) An energy center in the subtle body, recognized in *kundalini yoga*.

charisma (kă <u>riz</u> mă) A rare personal magnetism, often ascribed to a founder of a religion.

Christology The attempt to define the nature of Jesus and his relationship to God.

Common Era Years after the traditional date used for the birth of Jesus, previously referred to in exclusively Christian terms as AD and now abbreviated to CE as opposed to BCE ("before Common Era").

communion *see* Eucharist.

comparative religion Scholarly discipline attempting to understand and compare religious patterns from around the world.

confirmation A Christian sacrament by which awareness of the Holy Spirit is enhanced.

cosmogony (kos <u>mog</u> ŏn ee) A model of the evolution of the universe.

creed A formal statement of the beliefs of a particular religion.

crusades Military expeditions undertaken by the Christians of Europe in the 11th–13th centuries to recover the Holy Land from the Muslims; any war carried on under Papal sanction.

cult Any religion that focuses on worship of a particular person or deity.

Dao (dow) (also Tao) The way or path, in Far Eastern traditions. The term is also used as a name for the Nameless.

darsan (<u>daar</u> shan) Visual contact with the divine through encounters with Hindu images or gurus.

davening (<u>daa</u> věn ing) In Hasidic Judaism, prayer.

deity yoga (<u>dee</u> i tee <u>yō</u> gă) In Tibetan Buddhism, the practice of meditative concentration on a specific deity.

denomination (di nom ĕ <u>nay</u> shun) One of the Protestant branches of Christianity.

dervish (<u>der</u> vish) A Sufi ascetic, in the Muslim tradition.

deva (<u>day</u> vă) In Hinduism, a deity.

Dhammapada (<u>dam</u> ă pă dă) A collection of short sayings attributed to Buddha.

dharma (<u>daar</u> mă) (Pali: *dhamma*) In Hinduism, moral order, righteousness, religion. In Buddhism, the doctrine or law, as revealed by the Buddha; also the correct conduct for each person according to his or her level of awareness.

dhimmi (dĕ <u>hem</u> ee) A person of a non-Muslim religion whose right to practice that religion is protected within an Islamic society.

diaspora (dī <u>ass</u> po ra) Collectively, the practitioners of a faith living beyond their traditional homeland. When spelled with a capital "D", the dispersal of the Jews after the Babylonian exile.

Digambara (di <u>gŭm</u> bă ră) A highly ascetic order of Jain monks who wear no clothes.

dogma (<u>dog</u> mă) A system of beliefs declared to be true by a religion.

Dreaming (Dream Time) The timeless time of Creation, according to Australian Aboriginal belief.

dualistic Believing in the separation of reality into two categories, particularly the concept that spirit and matter are in separate realms.

dukkha (<u>dŏŏ</u> kă) According to the Buddha, a central fact of human life, variously translated as discomfort, suffering, frustration, or lack of harmony with the environment.

Durga (<u>dŏŏr</u> ga) The Great Goddess as destroyer of evil, and sometimes as *sakti* of Siva.

ecumenism (ek <u>yoo</u> mĕ niz ĕm) Rapprochement between branches of Christianity or among all faiths.

epic A long historic narrative.

Epiphany (ee <u>pi</u> făni) "Manifestation"; in Christianity the recognition of Jesus's spiritual kingship by the three Magi.

eschatology (es kă <u>tol</u> ŏ ji) Beliefs about the end of the world and of humanity.

Essenes (<u>es</u> eenz) Monastic Jews who were living communally, apart from the world, about the time of Jesus.

ethnic religions New religions which emerged since the fall of communism as revivals of pre-Christian ethnic traditions in Eastern Europe and Russia.

Eucharist (<u>yoo</u> kă rist) The Christian sacrament by which believers are renewed in the mystical body of Christ by partaking of bread and wine, understood as his body and blood.

evangelism (i <u>van</u> jĕ liz ĕm) Ardent preaching of the Christian gospel.

exclusivism The idea that one's own religion is the only valid way.

excommunication Exclusion from participation in the Christian sacraments (applied particularly to Roman Catholicism), which is a bar to gaining access to heaven.

exegesis (ex a <u>gee</u> sis) Critical examination of a religious text.

Falun Gong/Falun Dafa A form of Qigong mixing Buddhism with Daoist energy practices, and emphasizing ethics—the development of truthfulness, benevolence, and forbearance.

Fatiha (fat <u>haa</u>) The first *sura* of the Qur'an.

fatwa In Islam, a legal opinion issued by an authority according to a particular school of law.

feng shui (fĕng <u>shwee</u>)The Taoist practice of determining the most harmonious position for a building according to the natural flows of energy.

fundamentalism (fun dă <u>men</u> tăl iz ĕm) Insistence on what people perceive as the historical form of their religion, in contrast to more contemporary influences. This ideal sometimes takes extreme, rigidly exclusive, or violent forms.

Gathas In Zoroastrianism, metric verses or hymns which were the words of the prophet Zarathushtra.

Gayatrimantra (gī a <u>tree</u> man tră) The daily Vedic prayer of upper-caste Hindus.

Gentile (<u>jen</u> tīl) Any person who is not of Jewish faith or origin.

Geonim In Judaism, the administrators of the two great rabbinic academies in medieval Babylon.

ghetto An urban area occupied by those rejected by a society, such as quarters for Jews in some European cities.

gnosis (nō sis) Intuitive knowledge of spiritual realities.

Gnosticism (<u>nos</u> ti siz ĕm) Mystical perception of spiritual knowledge.

gospel In Christianity, the "good news" that God has raised Jesus from the dead and in so doing has begun the transformation of the world.

gurdwara (gŏŏr <u>dwa</u> ră) A Sikh temple.

guru (<u>gŏŏ</u> roo) In Hinduism, an enlightened spiritual teacher.

Guru Granth Sahib (goo roo granth <u>sa</u> heeb) The sacred scripture compiled by the Sikh Gurus.

Hadith (<u>haad</u> ith) In Islam, a traditional report about a reputed saying or action of the Prophet Muhammad.

haggadah (hă <u>gaa</u> dă) The non-legal part of the Talmud and Midrash.

hajj (haaj) The holy pilgrimage to Mecca, for Muslims.

halakhah (haa laa <u>khaa</u>) Jewish legal decision and the parts of the Talmud dealing with laws.

Hasidism (<u>has</u> īd iz ĕm) Ecstatic Jewish piety, dating from eighteenth-century Poland.

hatha yoga (<u>ha</u> thǎ <u>yo</u>gǎ) Body postures, diet, and breathing exercises to help build a suitable physical vehicle for spiritual development.

havan In Hunduism, a sacred fireplace around which ritual fire ceremonies are conducted.

heretic (<u>hair</u> i tik) A member of an established religion whose views are unacceptable to the orthodoxy.

Hermeneutics The field of theological study that attempts to interpret scripture.

heyoka (hay <u>yo</u> kǎ) "Contrary" wisdom or a person who embodies it, in some Native American spiritual traditions.

hijab (<u>hay</u> jab) The veiling of women for the sake of modesty in Islam.

hijrah (<u>hij</u> rǎ) Muhammad's migration from Mecca to Medina.

Hinayana (<u>hee</u> nǎ <u>ya</u> nǎ) In Mahayana Buddhist terminology, the label "lesser vehicle," given to the orthodox southern tradition now represented by Theravada; in Tibetan terminology, one of the three vehicles for salvation taught by the Buddha.

Holocaust (<u>haw</u> lō cawst) The genocidal killing of six million Jews by the Nazis during World War II.

icon (<u>ī</u> kon) A sacred image, a term used especially for the paintings of Jesus, Mary, and the saints of the Eastern Orthodox Christian Church.

ijtihad (ij ti <u>haad</u>)In Islam, reasoned interpretation of sacred law by a qualified scholar.

Imam (i <u>maam</u>) In Shi'ism, the title for the person carrying the initiatic tradition of the Prophetic Light.

imam (i <u>maam</u>) A leader of Muslim prayer.

immanent Present in Creation.

incarnation Physical embodiment of the divine.

inclusivism The idea that all religions can be accommodated within one religion.

indigenous (in <u>dij</u> ĕ nĕs) Native to an area.

Indra (<u>in</u> drǎ) The old Vedic thunder god in the Hindu tradition.

indulgence In Roman Catholic Christianity, granting of a remission of sins.

infidel (<u>in</u> fid ĕl) The Muslim and Christian term for "nonbeliever," which each tradition often applies to the other.

Inquisition (in kwi <u>zi</u> shun) The use of force and terror to eliminate heresies and nonbelievers in the Christian Church starting in the thirteenth century.

interfaith dialogue Appreciative communication between people of different religions.

Islamist A person seeking to establish Islamic states in which the rule of God is supreme.

Jap Ji (<u>jap</u> jee) The first morning prayer of Sikhs, written by Guru Nanak.

jen (yen) Humanity, benevolence—the central Confucian virtue.

jihad (<u>ji</u> had) The Muslim's struggle against the inner forces that prevent God-realization and the outer barriers to establishment of the divine order.

Jina (<u>jī</u> nǎ) In Jainism, one who has realized the highest, omniscient aspect of his or her being and is therefore perfect.

jinn (jin) In Islam, an invisible being of fire.

jiva (<u>jee</u> vǎ) The soul in Jainism.

jnana yoga (ya na <u>yo</u> gǎ) The use of intellectual effort as a yogic technique.

Juchiao (jee tzǔ yow) The Chinese term for the teachings based on Confucius.

justified In Christianity, having been absolved of sin in the eyes of God.

Kabbalah (kǎ <u>baa</u> lǎ) The Jewish mystical tradition.

Kali (<u>kaa</u> lee) Destroying and transforming Mother of the World, in Hinduism.

Kali Yuga (<u>kaa</u> lee <u>yoo</u>gǎ) In Hindu world cycles, an age of chaos and selfishness, including the one in which we are now living.

kami (<u>kaa</u> mee) The Shinto word for that invisible sacred quality that evokes wonder and awe in us, and also for the invisible spirits throughout nature that are born of this essence.

kannagara (kǎ nǎ gǎ rǎ) Harmony with the way of the *kami* in Shinto.

karma (<u>kaar</u> mā) (Pali: *kamma*) In Hinduism and Buddhism, our actions and their effects on this life and lives to come. In Jainism, subtle particles that accumulate on the soul as a result of one's thoughts and actions.

karma yoga (<u>kaar</u> mǎ <u>yo</u> gǎ) The path of unselfish service in Hinduism.

kenotic (ki <u>not</u> ik) In Russian Orthodox Christianity, belief in the monastic pattern of ascetic poverty combined with service in the world.

kensho (ken shō) Sudden enlightenment, in Zen Buddhism.

kevala (<u>kay</u> vǎ lǎ) The supremely perfected state in Jainism.

Khalsa (<u>kal</u> sǎ) The body of the pure, as inspired by the Sikh Guru Gobind Singh.

kirtan (<u>keer</u> tan) Devotional singing of hymns from the Guru Granth Sahib in Sikhism.

koan (<u>kō</u> aan) In Zen Buddhism, a paradoxical puzzle to be solved without ordinary thinking.

kosher (<u>kō</u> sher) Ritually acceptable, applied to foods in Jewish Orthodoxy.

kshatriya (<u>ksha</u> tree ă) A member of the warrior or ruling caste in traditional Hinduism, Jainism, and Buddhism.

kufr (<u>kŏŏ</u> fer) In Islam, the sin of atheism, of ingratitude to God.

kundalini (koon dă <u>lee</u> nee) In Hindu yogic thought, the life-force that can be awakened from the base of the spine and raised to illuminate the spiritual center at the top of the head.

Lakshmi In Hinduism, the consort of Vishnu.

lama (<u>laa</u> mă) A Tibetan Buddhist monk, particularly one of the highest in the hierarchy.

langar (<u>lan</u> găr) In Sikh tradition, a free communal meal without caste distinctions

li (lee) Ceremonies, rituals, and rules of proper conduct, in the Confucian tradition.

liberal Flexible in approach to religious tradition; inclined to see tradition as metaphorical rather than literal truth.

liberation theology Christianity expressed as solidarity with the poor.

lingam (<u>ling</u> ăm) A cylindrical stone or other similarly shaped natural or sculpted form, representing for Saivite Hindus the unmanifest aspect of Siva.

liturgy (<u>lit</u> ĕr jee) In Christianity and Judaism, the rites of public worship.

Mahabharata (mă haa <u>baa</u> ră tă) A long Hindu epic that includes the *Bhagavad-Gita*.

Mahayana (maa hă <u>ya</u> nă) The "greater vehicle" in Buddhism, the more liberal and mystical Northern School, which stressed the virtue of altruistic compassion rather than intellectual efforts at individual salvation.

mandala (man <u>daa</u> lă) A symmetrical image, with shapes emerging from a center, used as a meditational focus.

mantra (<u>man</u> tră) A sound or phrase chanted to evoke the sound vibration of one aspect of creation or to praise a deity.

mass The Roman Catholic term for the Christian eucharist.

materialism The tendency to consider material possessions and comforts more important than spiritual matters, or the philosophical position that nothing exists except matter and that there are no supernatural dimensions to life.

maya (<u>mī</u> yă) In Indian thought, the attractive but illusory physical world.

medicine Spiritual power, in some indigenous traditions.

Messiah The "anointed," the expected king and deliverer of the Jews; a term later applied by Christians to Jesus.

metta (<u>met</u> ă) In Buddhist terminology, loving-kindness.

Midrash (<u>mid</u> rash) The literature of delving into the Jewish Torah.

mikva (<u>mik</u> vă) A deep bath for ritual cleansing in Judaism.

millennium One thousand years, a term used in Christianity and certain newer religions for a hoped-for period of a thousand years of holiness and happiness, with Christ ruling the earth, as prophesied in the Book of Revelation.

minyan (<u>min</u> yăn) The quorum of ten adult males required for Jewish communal worship.

Mishnah In Judaism, the systematic summation of the legal teachings of the oral tradition of the Torah.

misogi (mee <u>sō</u> gee) The Shinto waterfall purification ritual.

mitzvah (<u>mitz</u> vă) (plural: *mitzvot*) In Judaism, a divine commandment or sacred deed in fulfillment of a commandment.

Modernism Twentieth-century values including individualism, preference for change rather than continuity, quantity rather than quality, efficiency, pragmatism, and profiteering, all seen by some as threatening the existence of traditional religious values.

moksha (<u>mōk</u> shă) In Hinduism, liberation of the soul from illusion and suffering.

monistic (<u>mon</u> iz tik) Believing in the concept of life as a unified whole, without a separate "spiritual" realm.

monotheistic (mon ō <u>thee</u> iz tik) Believing in a single God.

muezzin (moo <u>ez</u> in) In Islam, one who calls the people to prayer from a high place.

mujahid (<u>moo</u> jă hid) In Islam, a selfless fighter in the path of Allah.

muni (<u>moo</u> nee) A Jain monk.

murshid (<u>moor</u> shid) A spiritual teacher, in esoteric Islam.

mystic One who values inner spiritual experience in preference to external authorities and scriptures.

mysticism The intuitive perception of spiritual truths beyond the limits of reason.

myth A symbolic story expressing ideas about reality or spiritual history.

naga (<u>naa</u> gă) A snake, worshipped in Hinduism.

Nam (naam) The Holy Name of God reverberating throughout all of Creation, as repeated by Sikhs.

Neo-Confucianism Confucianism stressing the importance of meditation and dedication to becoming a "noble person" established during the Chinese Han and Sung dynasties.

Nicene Creed Basic profession of faith for many Christian denominations in East and West, including all Orthodox churches, framed in a council held in Constantinople in 381 CE, and proposed as a basis for unifying all Christians.

nirvana (ner <u>va</u> nă) (Pali: *nibbana*) In Buddhism, the ultimate egoless state of bliss.

nontheistic Perceiving spiritual reality without a personal deity or deities.

occult Involving the mysterious, unseen, supernatural.

oharai Shinto purification ceremony.

OM (ōm) In Hinduism, the primordial sound.

original sin The Christian belief that all human beings are bound together in prideful egocentricity. In the Bible, this is described mythically as an act of disobedience on the part of Adam and Eve.

orisa The Yoruba term for a deity, often used in speaking of West African religions in general.

orthodox Adhering to the established tradition of a religion.

Pali (<u>paa</u> lee) The Indian dialect first used for writing down the teachings of the Buddha, which were initially held in memory, and still used today in the Pali Canon of scriptures recognized by the Theravadins.

Pahlavi Texts written or translated in Middle Persian from about the ninth century CE with detailed instructions about the rituals and customs of the Zoroastrians in Iran.

Panth In Sikhism, the religious community.

parable (<u>par</u> ă bŭl) An allegorical story.

Paraclete (<u>par</u> ă kleet) The entity that Jesus said would come after his death to help the people.

Parsis Persian Zoroastrians who avoided conversion to Islam by migrating to western India.

Parvati (<u>paar</u> vă tee) Siva's spouse, sweet daughter of the Himalayas.

penance An act of self-punishment to atone for wrongdoings.

Pentateuch (<u>pen</u> tă took) The five books of Moses at the beginning of the Hebrew Bible.

Pentecost (<u>pen</u> tĕ kost) The occasion when the Holy Spirit descended upon the disciples of Jesus after his death.

Pharisees (<u>fair</u> ĕ seez) In Roman-ruled Judaea, liberals who tried to practice Torah in their lives.

phenomenology An approach to the study of religions that involves appreciative investigation of religious phenomena to comprehend their meaning for their practitioners.

pluralism An appreciation of the diversity of religions.

pogrom An attack against Jews.

polytheistic (<u>pol</u> ĕ thee iz ĕm) Believing in many deities.

pope The Bishop of Rome and head of the Roman Catholic Church.

Prakriti (<u>praak</u> ri tee) In Samkhya Hindu philosophy, the cosmic substance.

prana (<u>praa</u> nă) In Indian thought, the invisible life-force.

pranayama (<u>praa</u> nă ya mă) Yogic breathing exercises.

prasad (pră <u>saad</u>) In Indian traditions, blessed food.

presbyter A governor of the Christian Reformed Church that sprung from Calvinism.

profane Worldly, secular, as opposed to sacred.

puja (<u>poo</u> jă) Hindu ritual worship.

Puranas (po͝o <u>raa</u> năs) Hindu scriptures written to popularize the abstract truths of the Vedas through stories about historical and legendary figures.

Pure Land A Buddhist sect in China and Japan that centers on faith in Amida Buddha, who promised to welcome believers to the paradise of the Pure Land, a metaphor for enlightenment.

Purgatory (<u>pur</u> gă tor ee) In some branches of Christianity, an intermediate after-death state in which souls are purified from sin.

Purusha (poo <u>roo</u> shă) The Cosmic Spirit, soul of the universe in Hinduism; in Samkhya philosophy, the eternal Self.

qi (ki) (also *ch'i*) (chee) The vital energy in the universe and in our bodies, according to Far Eastern esoteric traditions.

Qiqong (also ch'i-kung) (chee kung) A Daoist system of harnessing inner energies for spiritual realization.

rabbi (<u>rab</u> ī) Historically, a Jewish teacher; at present, the ordained spiritual leader of a Jewish congregation.

raja yoga Mental concentration yoga (ancient technique for spiritual realization).

rapture Nineteenth-century belief amongst some Christians, using Paul's letter to the Thessalonians (I Thess. 4:17) to say that Christians would be caught up in clouds to meet Jesus when he returned to earth.

Ramayana (raa <u>maa</u> yă nă) The Hindu epic about Prince Rama, defender of good.

redaction Editing, organizing

reincarnation The transmigration of the soul into a new body after death of the old body.

relic In some forms of Christianity, part of the body or clothing of a saint.

Rig Veda (rig <u>vay</u> dă) Possibly the world's oldest scripture, the foundation of Hinduism.

rishi (<u>rish</u> ee) A Hindu sage.

ritual A repeated, patterned religious act.

Sabbath (<u>sab</u> ăth) The day of the week set aside for rest and worship in Judaism and Christianity.

sacrament Outward and visible signs of inward and spiritual grace in Christianity. Almost all churches recognize baptism and the eucharist as sacraments; some churches recognize five others as well.

sacred The realm of the extraordinary, beyond everyday perceptions, the supernatural, holy

sacred thread In Hinduism, a cord worn over one shoulder by men who have been initiated into adult upper-caste society.

Sadducees (<u>saj</u> ŭ seez) In Roman-ruled Judaea, wealthy and priestly Jews.

sadhana (<u>saad</u> hă nă) In Hinduism, especially yoga, a spiritual practice.

sadhu (<u>sad</u> oo) An ascetic holy man, in Hinduism.

Saivite (<u>sīv</u> īt) A Hindu worshipper of the divine as Siva.

Sakta (<u>sak</u> ta) A Hindu worshipper of the female aspect of deity.

sakti (<u>sak</u> tee) The creative, active female aspect of Deity in Hinduism.

samadhi (sa <u>maa</u> dee) In yogic practice, the blissful state of superconscious union with the Absolute.

Samkhya (<u>saam</u> khyă) One of the major Hindu philosophical systems, in which human suffering is characterized as stemming from the confusion of Prakriti with Purusha.

samsara (săm <u>saa</u> ră) The continual round of birth, death, and rebirth in Hinduism, Jainism, and Buddhism.

Sanatana Dharma (să <u>na</u> tă nă <u>daar</u> mă) The "eternal religion" of Hinduism.

sangat A Sikh congregation, in which all are ideally considered equal.

sangha (<u>sung</u> ă) In Theravada Buddhism, the monastic community; in Mahayana, the spiritual community of followers of the *dharma*.

sannyasin (sun <u>yaa</u> sin) In Hinduism and Buddhism, a renunciate spiritual seeker.

Sanskrit (<u>san</u> skrit) The literary language of classic Hindu scriptures.

sant A Sikh holy person.

Santeria The combination of African and Christian practices which developed in Cuba.

satori (să <u>taw</u> ree) Enlightenment, realization of ultimate truth, in Zen Buddhism.

scientific materialism School of thought which developed during the nineteenth and twentieth centuries claiming that the supernatural is imaginary; only the material world exists, and from this point of view religions have been invented by humans.

sect A sub-group within a larger tradition.

secularism Government policy of not favoring any one religion.

Seder Ceremonial Jewish meal in remembrance of the Passover.

see An area under the authority of a Christian bishop or archbishop.

Semite (<u>sem</u> ite) A Jew, Arab, or other, of eastern Mediterranean origin.

shabd (<u>shaabd</u>) The Sikh term for a Name of God that is recited or a hymn from the Guru Granth Sahib, considered the Word of God.

Shahadah (shă <u>haa</u> dă) The central Muslim expression of faith: "There is no god but God," and Muhammad is the messenger of God.

shaktipat (<u>shaak</u> tă păt) In the Siddha tradition of Hinduism, the powerful, elevating glance or touch of the guru.

shaman (<u>shaa</u> măn) A "medicine person," a man or woman who has undergone spiritual ordeals and can communicate with the spirit world to help the people in indigenous traditions.

Shangdi (also Shang Ti) In ancient China, a deity (or perhaps deities) with overarching powers.

Shari'ah (shă <u>ree</u> ă) The divine law, in Islam.

shaykh (shaik) A spiritual master, in the esoteric Muslim tradition.

Shekhinah (she <u>kī</u> nă) God's presence in the world, in Judaism.

Shi'a, (shee īt) (adj. Shi'ite) The minority branch of Islam, which feels that Muhammad's legitimate successors were 'Ali and a series of Imams; a follower of this branch.

shirk (shirk) The sin of believing in any divinity except the one God, in Islam.

shudra (<u>shoo</u> dră) A member of the manual laborer caste in traditional Hinduism.

Sikh (seek) "Student," especially one who practices the teachings of the ten Sikh Gurus.

Siva (<u>shee</u> vă) In Hinduism, the Supreme as lord of yogis, absolute consciousness, creator, preserver, and destroyer of the world; or the destroying aspect of the Supreme.

soma (sō ma) An intoxicating drink used by early Hindu worshippers.

stupa (stoo pă) A rounded monument containing Buddhist relics or commemorative materials.

Sufism (soo fis ĕm) The mystical path in Islam.

Sunnah (soo nă) The behavior of the Prophet Muhammad, used as a model in Islamic law.

Sunni (soo nee) A follower of the majority branch of Islam, which feels that successors to Muhammad are to be chosen by the Muslim community.

sunyata (soon yă tă) Voidness, the transcendental ultimate reality in Buddhism.

sura (sŏŏ ră) A chapter of the Qur'an.

sutra (sŏŏ tră) (Pali: *suta*) Literally, a thread on which are strung jewels—the discourses of the teacher; in yoga, *sutras* are terse sayings.

Svetambara (swe taam bă ră) Jain order of monks who are less ascetic than the Digambara.

symbol Visible representation of an invisible reality or concept.

synagogue (sin ă gog) A meeting place for Jewish study and worship.

syncretism (sing kri tis ĕm) A form of religion in which otherwise differing traditions are blended.

synod In Christianity, a council of church officials called to reach agreement on doctrines and administration.

synoptic (sin op tik) Referring to three similar books of the Christian Bible: Matthew, Mark, and Luke.

Taiji quan (also T'ai-chi chu'an) (tī chee hwaan) An ancient Chinese system of physical exercises, which uses slow movements to help one become part of the universal flow of energy.

talit (ta lit) A shawl traditionally worn by Jewish men during prayers.

Talmud (tal mŏod) Jewish law and lore, as finally compiled in the sixth century CE.

Tanakh (ta nakh) The Jewish scriptures.

Tantras (tan trăs) The ancient Indian texts based on esoteric worship of the divine as feminine.

Tantrayana (tăn tră ya nă) *see* Vajrayana.

tariqa (ta ree ka) In Islam, an esoteric Sufi order.

t'fillin (tĕ fil in) A small leather box with verses about God's covenant with the Jewish people, bound to the forehead and arm.

thangka (tang ka) In Tibetan Buddhism, an elaborate image of a spiritual figure used as a focus for meditation.

theistic (thee is tik) Believing in a God or gods.

Theravada (ter ă vă dă) The remaining orthodox school of Buddhism, which adheres closely to the earliest scriptures and emphasizes individual efforts to liberate the mind from suffering.

Tipitaka (ti pi ta ka) (Sanskrit: *Tripitaka*) the foundational "Three Baskets" of Buddha's teachings.

Tirthankaras (tir tăn kăr ăs) The great enlightened teachers in Jainism, of whom Mahavira was the last in the present cosmic cycle.

Torah (tō raa) The Pentateuch; also, the whole body of Jewish teaching and law.

transcendent Existing outside the material universe.

transpersonal Referring to an eternal, infinite reality, in contrast to the finite material world.

transubstantiation (tran sŭb stan shee ay shun) In some branches of Christianity, the idea that wine and bread are mystically transformed into the blood and body of Christ during the eucharist sacrament.

Trinity The Christian doctrine that in the One God are three divine persons: the Father, the Son, and the Holy Spirit.

Triple Gem ("Three Refuges") The three jewels of Buddhism: Buddha, *dharma*, *sangha*.

tsumi (tzoo mee) Impurity or misfortune, a quality that Shinto purification practices are designed to remove.

tzaddik (tzaa dik) An enlightened Jewish mystic.

Udasi (oo daa see) An ascetic Sikh order.

ulama (oo lă maa) The influential leaders in traditional Muslim society, including spiritual leaders, *imams*, teachers, state scribes, market inspectors, and judges.

ummah (o maa) The Muslim community.

untouchable The lowest caste in Brahmanic Hindu society.

Upanishads (oo pan i shăds) The philosophical part of the Vedas in Hinduism, intended only for serious seekers.

Vaishnavite (vīsh nă vīt) (or Vaishnava) A Hindu devotee of Vishnu, particularly in his incarnation as Krishna.

vaishya (vīsh yă) A member of the merchant and farmer caste in traditional Hinduism.

Vajrayana (văj ră yaa nă) (or Tantrayana) The ultimate vehicle used in Mahayana, mainly Tibetan, Buddhism, consisting of esoteric tantric practices and concentration on deities.

Vedas Ancient scriptures revered by Hindus.

vipassana (vi pas ă nă) In Buddhism, meditation based on watching one's own thoughts, emotions, and actions.

Vishnu (vish noo) In Hinduism, the preserving aspect of the Supreme or the Supreme Itself, incarnating again and again to save the world.

vision quest In indigenous traditions, a solitary ordeal undertaken to seek spiritual guidance about one's mission in life.

Vodou (voo doo) Latin American and Caribbean ways of working with the spirit world, a blend of West African and Catholic Christian teachings.

Wicca Neo-Pagan sect of secret coven of witches traced to the writings of Gerald Gardner in England in the 1940s.

wu-wei (woo way) In Taoism, "not doing," in the sense of taking no action contrary to the natural flow.

yang In Chinese philosophy, the bright, assertive, "male" energy in the universe.

yantra (yan trǎ) In Hinduism, a linear cosmic symbol used as an aid to spiritual concentration.

yi (yee) Righteous conduct (as opposed to conduct motivated by desire for personal profit), a Confucian virtue stressed by Mencius.

yin (yin) In Chinese philosophy, the dark, receptive, "female" energy in the universe.

Yoga (yō gǎ) A systematic approach to spiritual realization, one of the major Hindu philosophical systems.

yoga (yō gǎ) Ancient techniques for spiritual realization, found in several Eastern religions.

yoni (yō nee) Abstract Hindu representation of the female vulva, cosmic matrix of life.

yuga (yoo gǎ) One of four recurring world cycles in Hinduism.

zakat (zak at) Spiritual tithing in Islam.

zazen (zaa zen) Zen Buddhist sitting meditation.

Zealots Jewish resistance fighters who fought the Romans and were defeated in the siege of Jerusalem.

Zen (zen) (Chinese: Ch'an) A Chinese and Japanese Buddhist school emphasizing that all things have Buddha-nature, which can only be grasped when one escapes from the intellectual mind.

zendo (zen dō) A Zen meditation hall.

	2000 BCE	1500	1000	500	0 CE
INDIGENOUS	←				
HINDUISM	← Vedas heard	Vedas first written down c.1500 BCE		*Ramayana* and *Mahabharata* in present form after 400 BCE Patanjali systematizes Yoga Sutras by 200 BCE	Code of Manu compiled before 100 CE
JAINISM	Series of 23 Tirthankaras before c.777 BCE →			Life of Mahavira 599–527 BCE Digambaras and Svetambaras diverge from 3rd century BCE	
BUDDHISM			Life of Gautama Buddha c.563–483 BC	King Asoka spreads Buddhism c.258 BCE Theravada Buddhism develops 200 BCE–200 CE	Mahayana Buddhism develops 1st century CE
DAOISM AND CONFUCIANISM				Life of Laozi between c.600–300 Life of Confucius c.551–479 Life of Zhuangzi c.365–290	Educational system based on Confucian Classics from 205 BCE
SHINTO	Shinto begins in pre-history as local nature- and ancestor-based traditions				
JUDAISM	Life of Abraham c.1900–1700 BCE	Moses leads Israelites out of Egypt c.13th or 12th century BCE	David, King of Judah and Israel c.1010–970 BCE	First Temple destroyed; Jews exiled 586 BCE	Jerusalem falls to Romans 70 CE
CHRISTIANITY					Life of Jesus c.4 BCE–30 CE Paul organizes early Christians c.50–60 CE Gospels written down c.70–95 CE
ISLAM					
SIKHISM					
INTERFAITH					

300	600	900	1200	1500	1800	2000 CE

Ancient ways passed down and adapted over millennia ⟶

Tantras written down c.300   Bhakti movement 600–1800 ⟶   Life of Ramakrishna 1836–1886

Jain monks establish Jain centers outside India 1970s–1980s

Life of Songstan (c.609–650) who declares Buddhism national religion of Tibet   Persecution of Buddhism begins in China 845   Ch'an Buddhism to Japan as Zen 13th century   Buddhism spreads in the West 20th century

Full ordination of nuns from 23 countries 1998

Japan imports Confucianism to unite tribes into empire   Sung dynasty revives ritualistic Confucianism ("neo-Confucianism")   Cultural Revolution attacks religions 1966–1976

Confucian revival in China; International Association of Confucianism established; Daoist sects and temples re-established 1990–2000

Shinto name adopted 6th century CE   State Shinto established 1868

Rabbinical tradition develops 1st to 4th centuries   Life of Maimonides 1135–1204   Expulsion of Jews from Spain 1492   The Baal Shem Tov 1700–1760   Israeli wall for separation from Palestinians 2003

The Holocaust 1940–1945

Independent state of Israel 1948

Centralization of papal power after 800   Split between Western and Eastern Orthodox Churches 1054   Spanish Inquisition established 1478   Second Vatican Council 1962–65

Churches reopened in USSR 1989

Monastic orders proliferate 1300s   Protestantism established 1521

Life of Muhammad c.570–632

Spread of Islam begins 633

Sunni–Shi'a split c.682

Islam's cultural peak 750–1258   Akbar becomes Mogul emperor in India 1556   European dominance 1800s–1900s   Terrorism and counterterrorism increase 2001

Muslim resurgence and OPEC 1970s

Life of Guru Nanak 1469–1504   At death of Guru Gobind Singh (1708), living presence of the guru is embodied in Guru Granth Sahib (scriptures)   300th anniversary of Khalsa 2003

Mogul emperor Akbar initiates interfaith dialogues 1556–1605   First International Human Unity Conference 1974

Parliament of the World's Religions centenary celebrations 1993

INDEX